RED GRANGE

RED GRANGE

The Life and Legacy of the NFL's First Superstar

Chris Willis

ROWMAN & LITTLEFIELD
Lanham • Boulder • New York • London

Published by Rowman & Littlefield
An imprint of The Rowman & Littlefield Publishing Group, Inc.
4501 Forbes Boulevard, Suite 200, Lanham, Maryland 20706
www.rowman.com

6 Tinworth Street, London, SE11 5AL, United Kingdom

British Library Cataloguing in Publication Information Available

Library of Congress Cataloging-in-Publication Data

Names: Willis, Chris, 1970– author.
Title: Red Grange : the life and legacy of the NFL's first superstar / Chris Willis.
Description: Lanham : Rowman & Littlefield, [2019] | Includes bibliographical
    references and index.
Identifiers: LCCN 2019001926 (print) | LCCN 2019004901 (ebook) | ISBN
    9781538101957 (Electronic) | ISBN 9781538101940 (cloth : alk. paper)
Subjects: LCSH: Grange, Red, 1903–1991. | Football players—United States—
    Biography.
Classification: LCC GV939.G7 (ebook) | LCC GV939.G7 W55 2019 (print) | DDC
    796.332092 [B]—dc23
LC record available at https://lccn.loc.gov/2019001926

♾️™ The paper used in this publication meets the minimum requirements of
American National Standard for Information Sciences—Permanence of Paper
for Printed Library Materials, ANSI/NISO Z39.48-1992.

CONTENTS

PREFACE

When I started working at NFL Films, I certainly knew about the career of
Red Grange, but it wasn't until about 1998 that I really started learning
more about this former NFL pioneer better known as the "Galloping Ghost"—
the best nickname in all of sports history. Who knew that some 20 years later
I would set out to write the definitive biography on one of the greatest athletes
of all time. And with the NFL celebrating its 100th season in the fall of 2019, it
was perfect timing to tell the full story of Mr. Red Grange.

During the past two decades I have collected everything I could on Grange,
ranging from programs, tickets, newspaper clippings, books, magazines, ads,
photos, postcards, movie items, game footage, and anything and everything
Grange related. Most of this research has paid off in my biography on the Galloping Ghost. But it wasn't until the thought of the NFL's 100th season coming up that I had the idea of spending a few years researching and writing the
story of the NFL's first superstar. So, three years ago I committed to the project
through my publisher, Rowman & Littlefield. My editor, Christen Karniski,
was enthusiastic about the project, and off I went.

Traveling to several locations where Red lived and interviewing family members and friends, as well as plowing through his archives and newspapers, were
some of the most enjoyable experiences of my career. It was just a three-and-a-
half-hour drive from my house in New Jersey to Forksville, Pennsylvania, the
birthplace of Red Grange. I spent an entire day roaming Sullivan County with
my tour guide, Melanie Norton of the Sullivan County Historical Museum, visiting Red's boyhood home (it's still there) and the cemeteries where his mother,
sister, and other family members are buried. I also spent hours at the Sullivan

County Historical Society and Museum, looking through their library and archives for anything on Red and the Grange family.

My first interview was with Turryann (Welden) Eustice, the daughter of Red Grange's high school coach, Charles Welden. She was just a two-hour drive from me, living in Chevy Chase, Maryland. From there the project continued to take off. I conducted more than 50 original interviews by phone or in person, giving me more insight about a man who had been a part of football for more than seven decades and helped football—the NFL—become the most popular sport in the United States. I also learned about the man away from football with interviews from family members (Rebecca Phillips, Dorothy Flora, Linda Thomas) and friends. This was probably more important than his football accomplishments: the people who knew him, the people who had spent time with him in Chicago or at his retirement home at Indian Lake Estates in Florida.

I spent two weeks traveling throughout Chicago, Wheaton, and Champaign to visit more sites where Grange had grown up, went to school, played football, and made NFL history. While in Wheaton, the town where he moved to when he was six years old, I visited his old homes, his old school, and Red Grange Field at Wheaton Warrenville-South High School and retraced his famous ice route that he worked while in high school and college, becoming the "Wheaton Iceman."

Also in Wheaton I spent several days going through the Red Grange Papers, housed at the Buswell Library at Wheaton College. The special collections staff there—Keith Call, Sara Stanley, and Katherine Braber—were a big help in providing me with more than 50 boxes of material.

In Champaign, where Red went to college at the University of Illinois, I toured the campus, as well as took a walk around Memorial Stadium with Kent Brown of the Sports Information Department, who also allowed me to go through the athletic archives. It was a joy to walk by the stadium every day and stop by the Red Grange statue on the west side of the facility to get closer to the man who meant so much to the sport I love and have enjoyed covering for the past 23 years with the NFL. I also spent some time at the Red Grange Rock, where Red's ashes now rest.

While in Champaign I had an enjoyable two days meeting with Marilyn Coolley-Carley, the daughter of Marion "Doc" Coolley, one of Red's managers during his barnstorming days with the Chicago Bears (1925–1926) after he turned pro. She showed me her father's collection, which features his contract with C. C. Pyle and Byron Moore, creating a new narrative that Red had more than one manager while barnstorming the country.

I also spent a week at the Pro Football Hall of Fame in Canton, Ohio, my favorite place to do research. Going through their many folders and files, including the Dutch Sternaman Collection, I located new information on Red and, in particular, the famous 1925–1926 barnstorming tour.

To complete my research, I watched all the game footage I could find and went through tons of microfilm and made copies of every football game that Red played in (high school, college, pros)—as well as combed through everything online that I could find about the redhead.

I know a few other volumes have been written about Grange, but I hope through my research and writing I can do his story justice and add fresh information to bring the Galloping Ghost to life. He deserves a full-scale biography like the other sports giants of the Roaring Twenties. After 20 years of collecting everything I could of the NFL's first superstar player, I'm grateful to be able to present his story.

ACKNOWLEDGMENTS

More than 20 years ago, I really started researching the life of Harold "Red" Grange, and after completing this manuscript, I still feel I don't have enough words to thank the people who helped me in finishing this book. First and foremost, I want to thank the entire Grange family for their support and generosity. I am extremely indebted to Dorothy Flora, niece of Margaret and Red Grange, for answering my questions about her aunt and uncle, and allowing me to use photos from their collection. I'm also indebted to Linda Thomas, another niece; thank you for taking the time to do an interview with me. Every Grange family member went beyond my expectations, so thank you very much.

Once again, I want to thank the great people at Rowman & Littlefield for believing in preserving the history of professional football. I worked with Stephen Ryan on my first couple of books, and now with Christen Karniski, acquisitions editor. Thank you so much for helping put this book together; you always make the final product better. I also want to thank the rest of the staff at R&L; it is always a joy to work with you, and there's no other publisher I want to work with.

As with my previous projects, my favorite place to visit and do research is the Pro Football Hall of Fame in Canton, Ohio. I want to thank the staff at the Hall—Pete Fierle, Saleem Choudhry, Jason Aikens, and, especially in the research library, Jon Kendle—for all your help. You guys are the best at what you do. Thank you. I also want to thank Joe Horrigan, vice president of Communications-Exhibits, for your support during the past two decades, I really appreciate it.

An extra thank you goes to Melanie Norton, town historian, who showed me around Forksville, Pennsylvania, Red's birthplace, and helped with my research at the Sullivan County Historical Museum. Seeing Red's boyhood home and historical marker was priceless.

I don't know if I can thank him enough, but Joe Ziemba did more for me than anyone I know. Going through a decade's worth of Chicago newspapers to get me everything I needed about Grange, he never failed to deliver. I owe you a lot. Thanks!

Another big thank you goes to Pam Powers, who allowed me to stay at her home outside of Chicago while I did two weeks of research at Wheaton and in the Windy City. I owe you a huge debt of gratitude for your hospitality. Also, thanks to your son Erik, who works with me at NFL Films, for contacting you.

I owe a big debt of thanks to Marilyn Coolley-Carley, daughter of Marion F. Coolley, one of Red's college friends and his former manager during the famous barnstorming tour of 1925–1926. Thanks for talking to me about your father and showing me the family archives during my trip to Champaign, Illinois. Viewing your collection of contracts and photos was a once-in-a-lifetime experience for me as a football historian. I thank you for allowing me to use them for this book. My time spent at the FedEx office—hours—making scans and copies was well worth it. So, thanks! Also, thanks to your daughter, K. C., and your grandson, Nico, for their help.

A huge thank you goes to the staff at Buswell Library on the campus of Wheaton College. The special collections there houses the Red Grange Papers. I got great guidance from Sara Stanley, Katherine Graber (who helped tremendously with my scanning requests, which numbered more than 1,200 scans), and especially Keith Call, who also allowed me to transfer footage of Red's 1978 homecoming visit, which hadn't been seen for 40 years. I thank you all. You made this book better with your help.

Thank you to the staff at the Wheaton Public Library, especially Meghan, Christine, and Donna Freymark (local history). Also, thanks to Chip Krueger, local historian, for his help with the Wheaton High School yearbooks. Kudos to DuPage County Historical Museum (Morgan Valenzuela, Michelle Podkowa) for your help, too.

I would like to thank the University of Illinois athletic department for its generosity in helping with my research, especially Kent Brown (associate director of athletics, media relations) for allowing me to go through material in the archives, as well as for giving me a tour of the stadium and the Red Grange Rock. It was a day I'll always remember. Thanks to Chad Beyler for making copies and scans for me, and thanks also to Ron Guenther, former Illinois athletic director, for talking to me about Red.

I want to give a big thank you to three men who shared one of the most important stories concerning the final resting place of Red Grange—whose ashes are spread out at the Red Grange Rock at Memorial Stadium at the University of Illinois. Thank you so much Mike Pearson (former Illinois sports information director), Dana Brenner (former athletics associate director), and the late Patrick Hayes (former Illinois alumni director) for sharing with me such a special and poignant story. Thanks also for your additional insights on your time visiting Red and hosting Margaret's 1994 visit to campus.

Also, thanks to the staff at the University of Illinois Archives—Linda Stahnke and Anna Trammell, as well as Geoff Ross and Glen Martin (newspapers, microfilm)—who went beyond the call to provide me with the material I requested and made my week there very productive.

A big thank you goes to the staff at Wheaton Warrenville-South High School, who now holds the legacy of Red Grange's high school career. Thank you Dave Claypool (principal), Janet Luckey (secretary), Linda Verstein (staff), and Matthew Stellwagen (assistant athletic director) for helping me with research during my visit to the school. Moreover, thanks to coach Ron Muhitch for spending some time talking to me and showing me around the football stadium and school. I could definitely feel the spirit of Red Grange. Lastly, thanks to John Thorne, former head football coach at Wheaton Central, for his insights on preserving Red's legacy in Wheaton. Another thank you goes to Chuck Baker, former principal at Wheaton Central, for telling me about your history with Red, and especially Margaret Grange. Kudos to the football staff at College of DuPage for establishing the Red Grange Bowl to honor the county's greatest football player and to Matt Foster (head coach, assistant athletic director) and Kevin Willman (multimedia producer/director), in particular, for carrying on Red's legacy.

I want to personally thank the people who agreed to do an interview for this book; I can't thank you enough for giving your time and energy to make this book better. At the top of the list I want to thank Rebecca Phillips, granddaughter of Mildred (Grange) Eston—sister of Red Grange. My afternoon with you at your home in Florida was most memorable. Learning about Mildred, Red, and the Grange family history was priceless. Thanks for allowing me to go through the family archives and use several photos for the book—including the one of Red's mother, Sadie Grange. Thanks to John Haverly, Joan Haverly, and Donna Edwards, who also provided more insight into Mildred and Red.

Another huge thank you goes to Dorothy Flora; I can't thank you enough for answering my questions on the phone and spending an afternoon with me at your home talking about Margaret and Red Grange, your aunt and uncle.

You gave me personal stories—including the one about Margaret saving your life once—and let me go through your collection. I can't thank you enough! I want to thank Linda Thomas, daughter of Beverly DeBaker (sister of Margaret Grange), for talking about your relationship and time with Margaret and Red, as well as e-mailing numerous photos; thanks for all your help.

Thanks to Grange family members Robert Richie, Richard Rinebold, Ray Rinebold, Adele Baldridge, Nancy Hansen, Judy Peterson, Roger Grange Jr., Roger Grange III, John Loyd, and John McVay for your help in understanding the Grange family tree and history.

I would like to thank Janis Franks and John Thompson for talking about their grandfather, L. C. Thompson, and giving me insight into the man who hired Red to be an iceman in Wheaton. Many thanks to Turryann Eustice, daughter of Charles Welden, for spending an afternoon with me talking about her father, who coached Red for two years at Wheaton High. Thanks to your son, Bob Eustice, for setting up the interview. Also, thanks to David Castleman, who talked about this father, Bill Castleman, who coached Red in high school for his sophomore season.

Family members of former Illinois teammates who helped with interviews include Diane Schultz (Emil Schultz), Bernie Oakes Jr. (Bernie Oakes), Craig Mauer (John Mauer), and Dan Umnus and Sue Talo (Leonard Umnus). Thank you. Also, thanks to Julie and Robert Kamins, and Gordon Ingwersen, for their help (Burt Ingwersen).

Thanks to Mike Brown, son of Warren Brown (former Chicago sportswriter), and Liz Tobin, daughter of Mike Tobin (former Illinois sports information director). I also want to thank Debra Gelbert, daughter of Ira Morton, for talking about her father's involvement with writing Red's autobiography and the ensuing friendship that developed between the two men, and for finding the audio interview of Red with her father; many thanks.

I would like to thank Scott Moffatt, grandson of Byron F. Moore, for talking about his grandfather's involvement as one of Red's managers during the famous barnstorming tour of 1925–1926. In addition, thanks to Pam Elster for help with her grandfather, Frank Zambreno. Another big thank you to Chip Shotwell, grandson of Alfred Shotwell, for talking about his family's relationship with Red and the Red Grange candy bar.

Many thanks to the Chicago Bears for helping me with this project. First, I want to thank Virginia McCaskey, whom I have had the pleasure of interviewing twice in my lifetime. They were two of the most enjoyable and memorable interviews I have done in more than two decades of working for the NFL. Thanks to her son, Patrick McCaskey, for his interview and the Bears staff for all their help. Those who gave interviews to discuss former Chicago Bears teammates of Red Grange and to whom I owe thanks include Ed Kopcha (Joe Kopcha), Lynn Meadows and Brenda Stewart (Beattie Feathers), Ann and Kevin Huffman (George Corbett), and Tony Nagurski (Bronko Nagurski). Thank you to Joyce Howe for spending an afternoon with me talking about your father, Joey Sternaman, at your home in Decatur. It was an informative interview about one of the NFL's founding families. Those who gave interviews to discuss former New York Yankees teammates and to whom I owe thanks are Melinda Bricker (Mike Michalske) and Barbara Halse (Eddie Tryon), as well as Don Wilson (Abe Wilson).

I want to especially thank Ann Kakacek, daughter of Jim McMillian, a former teammate of Red's at Illinois and with the Bears. Thanks for allowing me to go through the family's football scrapbooks and make copies of what I wanted. Also, thanks for the pizza. I had a great time in Antioch. A sad thank you to Luke Johnsos Jr., for taking the time to talk about his father, Luke Johnsos. The information on the *Chicago Bears Quarterback Club* show with Red and Luke was priceless. He passed away shortly after our conversation; I hope I helped bring your father to life with his relationship with Red. Thank you to Nancy (Nelson) Wyszynski, daughter of Lindsey Nelson, for talking about her father's relationship with Red.

I want to thank several people who spent time telling me about their experiences with Red during his trip back to Wheaton in 1978. Thank you to David Stamps for your time and thoughtful answers about being Red's chaperone during his visit. You gave many personal accounts of Red that I couldn't have gotten anywhere else, so thanks! Thanks also to Vicky Harrington and Bea Wilson—the widow of D. Ray Wilson—who gave me their insights about that trip.

A big thank you to John Mackovic, former Illinois head coach, for talking to me about his visit to see Red at his home. Also, thank you Lou Tepper, another former Illinois head coach, for his insights on Margaret Grange's visit to the Illinois campus in 1994.

Kudos to the librarians and organizations that helped me during my journey. Thanks to Gerry Smith (Broome County [New York] Public Library); Becky Menzel (Spokane Public Library); Christine Cross, for getting Margaret Grange's high school yearbook (New London [Wisconsin] Public Museum); Don Litzer (T. B. Scott Free Library); David Stevick and Laura Habecker (Houghton College); Jona Whipple (Chicago-Kent College of Law); Urbana Free Library; Maureen Watts (Slover Library); Amy Crow (Claremont [California] Library); Allan Lagumbay (Pomona [California] Library); Hilary Dorsch Wong (Cornell University Rare Books and Manuscripts); Derel Moses (San

Diego Public Library); Leann Stine, for material on Marion Coolley (Danville Public Library); Susan McQuaid (Naperville Public Library); and Jim Jatkevicius (Forest Grove City [Washington] Library).

Thanks to J. Barrett Nelson of Marion Nelson Funeral Home in Lake Wales, Florida, for taking the time to talk to me about his funeral home's handling of the service and cremation of Red and Margaret Grange.

I also want to thank Ancestry.com, eBay, Timeanddate.com, Find a Grave, RMY Auctions, Legacy.com, Newspapers.com, and Newspaperarchives.com for their helpful websites.

More thanks go to the old sportswriters who covered the Chicago Bears, and, in particular, Red Grange. Reading the *Chicago American*, *Chicago Daily Journal*, *Chicago Herald-Examiner*, *Chicago Tribune*, *Chicago Daily News*, and other newspapers from throughout the country gave me information on and insight into who Grange was and how he played the game.

I also want to thank my fellow football historians who helped me with my research: John Richards, Tod Maher (Pro Football Archives website), Jeffrey Miller (Buffalo articles), and Michael Benter (Milwaukee articles). I'd also like to extend thanks to the late Bob Carroll, who passed away in August 2009, for his help and guidance during the 15 years I knew him. Bob published my first-ever article in the *Coffin Corner*—the Professional Football Researchers Association publication—in 1994, and I will always be grateful for his generosity. You are still missed. Lastly, thanks to coach T. J. Troup. I truly enjoy our phone calls and can't wait for the next one.

I want to thank current NFL commissioner Roger Goodell and his staff—Joe Browne, Joel Bussert, and Pete Abitante. I also want to thank fellow authors Sal Paolantonio (ESPN), Allen Barra, John Maxymuk, and Joe Zagorski for their advice—keep up the good work. I would also like to show gratitude toward my colleagues at NFL Films: Dave Plaut (retired), Diane Meo, Pat Kelleher, Ross Ketover, and, especially, Neil Zender. Special thanks to the late Steve Sabol, president of NFL Films, for hiring me 23 years ago. I love being a part of the organization with the best sports filmmakers in the world.

Lastly, I want to thank my family. I want to thank my brothers, Rhu and Adrian, for their support. To my mother, Tina, thanks for all your love and inspiration in helping me finish this book. I know I've couldn't have done it without you. I want to thank my father, Roy Willis, who passed away in 2008. Thank you for giving me my passion for reading and writing as a book dealer for almost three decades. I miss you so much and hope you're proud of this book.

INTRODUCTION

The "Eternal Flame
of Professional Football"

In the fall of 2019, the NFL will celebrate its 100th season of sound and action. The history of the league will take center stage—a celebration of a century of players, coaches, owners, front-office executives, fans, and announcers who have made the story of the NFL a true rags-to-riches tale like none other in American history. But how did the league and, in particular, its players achieve this? Who was the first superstar in the NFL to lay down the blueprint of what the modern NFL player now has the opportunity to achieve—a level of success that makes them some of the most visible sports stars in the world? That blueprint was created almost 100 years ago by a football player who did it decades before it was commonplace.

His name was Red Grange.

Harold Edward Grange was born in 1903, amid the mountains of central Pennsylvania, to an athletic-minded mother and a lumberjack father. Nicknamed "Red" from an early age, because of the auburn shade of his hair, the future football star lost his mother when he was just six years old. Because of this tragedy, Red's father moved his family to Wheaton, Illinois, a small town just 30 miles west of Chicago, to be closer to his brothers and sisters. Red grew up with his brother, Garland, in the shadow of their stocky, hardworking father, who eventually became police chief of Wheaton. Red absorbed many traits from his father. One newspaper in 1925 described Red as a "modest, unassuming chap, who makes friends rapidly—the ideal athlete from every standpoint—a good student—a boy who always stands ready to give his teammates all the credit for his success—a marvel in more ways than one."[1]

The humble, shy, modest, hardworking son of a police chief soon became a superstar athlete at Wheaton High School. This success soon took him to the University of Illinois, where he became an even bigger star because of his football exploits. Red became a three-time All-American halfback under the guidance of the legendary Bob Zuppke, but it was a game against mighty University of Michigan in 1924 that helped him achieve legendary status during the Roaring Twenties. As a junior, Red blazed through the Wolverines defense for five touchdowns, four of them in the first 12 minutes of the game, as he led the Illini to a 39–14 victory. The next day, every newspaper in the country ran articles and headlines describing Red's exploits. The most famous sportswriter at the time, Grantland Rice, wrote a poem that described Red as a "Galloping Ghost" on the gridiron, thus popularizing one of the most famous nicknames in sports history. Red's life would never be the same.

He quickly became associated with the other superstar athletes of the Roaring Twenties, sharing headlines with Jack Dempsey (boxing), Bobby Jones (golf), Bill Tilden (tennis), Johnny Weissmuller (swimming), and the country's most famous athlete—Babe Ruth (baseball). During the Roaring Twenties, the rise of mass media throughout the country, which included newspapers, radio, and newsreels in movie theaters, helped Red become an instant star whom everyone in the United States heard about on a daily basis. His life was soon on the front pages of newspapers and magazines and movie screens everywhere. Although he never did crave the attention or deserve all the credit for his accomplishments, he consistently praised his teammates for his success, a trait that endeared him to everyone he played with. There was one aspect of his celebrity that he did embrace: Red always took his status as a role model seriously, especially in the eyes of the youth of America, becoming a true hero.

Despite his success on the field, he was smart enough to realize it would only be for a brief time. His athletic gifts would not last for long, his popularity would fade, and soon he would be forgotten. So, after his college career was finished, he did the most unpopular thing he could do—he played professional football. He declined other offers in other fields he thought he was unqualified to enter (writing for a newspaper, selling real estate, going into politics, etc.), so he could do the thing he did best, the thing he loved the most—play football.

What he did in 1925 would become the blueprint of the modern NFL player in 2019. The well-groomed, handsome All-American football player who looked like he could find a place in Tinseltown would go on to leave school early, sign with an agent, command the highest salary in football, sign endorsement deals, become a Hollywood actor, become an All-Pro player, and win NFL championships.

After turning pro in the fall of 1925, a day after playing his last college game at the University of Illinois, Red joined the Chicago Bears, owned by George Halas and Dutch Sternaman. Traveling the country on a barnstorming tour, an undertaking that had never before been attempted, Red played in front of massive crowds, setting attendance records in such large cities as Chicago, Philadelphia, New York, and Los Angeles. On one occasion, a pro football–record crowd of 75,000 filled the L.A. Coliseum.

The barnstorming tour of 1925–1926 did not "save the NFL," as some experts might claim, but what it did do was give the young league—only in its sixth year of existence—much-needed star power and publicity as Red joined the pro ranks. Just having the league and pro football in the newspapers, on the radio, and in movie houses throughout the country helped the sport like nothing before. Although football was still decades away from becoming the most popular sport in the world, the Red Grange tour showcased what the future could become and what a superstar NFL player could be.

After retiring from the NFL in 1935, Red once again paved the way for retired NFL players, becoming a coach, a radio and television announcer, a charter member of the Pro Football Hall of Fame, a banquet speaker, president of the Chicago Bears Alumni, a proponent of pensions for retirees, and an ambassador for the NFL.

His blueprint for what a NFL player could become started in 1925, blazing the trails for future stars like Sammy Baugh, Johnny Unitas, Jim Brown, Joe Namath, Joe Montana, Walter Payton, and Payton Manning, and such current stars as Tom Brady, Cam Newton, and Aaron Rodgers, to benefit from their superstar status as some of the most accomplished and most popular athletes in the world.

Throughout his life, Red embraced his status as role model and hero to millions throughout the country. It was a role that he took seriously, and his legacy is still remembered 100 years later. Red never thought he was a big deal; he always thought he would be forgotten. "Today, nobody cares who I was," said Red, at the age of 75, to the Orlando Sentinel in 1978. "They care what I am and how I act. That's the way I like it. It was great. But now I just want to be known as a decent guy." Being forgotten never happened. Even 80 years after he last carried a football, the name Red Grange is still remembered.[2]

In October 1978, Red returned to his hometown of Wheaton for a weekend celebration that was called the "Red Grange Homecoming." During the festivities, he spent time with the man who helped launch his NFL career (and helped found the NFL in 1920) almost 100 years ago, in 1925—George Halas. The two men spent hours reminiscing about the "good old days," when they barnstormed the country to play in front of thousands of fans—mostly fans new to the NFL—demonstrating what the sport could become. In 1978, the professional football was the number-one sport in the United States, surpassing baseball, with more than 13 million fans paying to see NFL games and more than 78 million viewers watching the Super Bowl. After the weekend in Wheaton, Halas wrote a letter to Red in Florida, where the Galloping Ghost was living in retirement with his wife of 49 years, Margaret.

Dear "Red":

It is I who thank you for one of the most memorable days in my life. Being with you on October 28 was a delight, and I am still basking in the euphoria of our visit and chat with the Veyseys at Cantigny. You know, "Red," that was the most private chat we have had in years.

From the moment of your arrival at Cantigny it was *your* day, and not for one second could anyone else claim a part of the day. Even the weather cooperated with one of our most perfect Indian Summer days.

I hear you had the dinner guests in the palm of your hand with your speech, and then, later, at Edman Chapel you held your audience spellbound. "Red" when I said you were "the Eternal Flame of Professional Football," it was exactly how I think of you, and no one else will ever come close to you.

Thanks again "Red" for giving me such a day. Warmest personal regards, and give my love to Muggs.

Sincerely yours,

Geo. S. Halas[3]

One of the founders of the NFL, George Halas always declared that Red Grange was the "Eternal Flame of Professional Football." But today, if you open up the NFL's 700-page *Record and Fact Book*, his name doesn't appear in any of the records. If you look at the Chicago Bears media guide, he doesn't hold a single Bears record; however, if you were writing the history of the NFL, his name might be the first one you start with.

Harold "Red" Grange became the first star of the NFL, and he remains the definition of what a superstar NFL player aspires to be in 2019. Now, with the NFL celebrating its 100th season, it's time to look back at the league's first true superstar. Although he often said he would be forgotten, the Galloping Ghost was wrong. Almost a century since playing his last game, he is remembered as the "Eternal Flame" of the National Football League. This is his story.

PART I

HUMBLE BEGINNINGS
(1903–1922)

1

FORKSVILLE

Before Red Grange became the Galloping Ghost and everyone in the United States knew his name, and more than 100 years before the National Football League was founded in 1920, the Grange family arrived in America. Red's ancestors were originally located in England, living a rather worthwhile but mundane life in Sicklinghall.

Red's great-grandfather, John Grange Sr., born in 1779, lived with his family in Sicklinghall, along with other members of the Grange herd. The village, even to this day, is surrounded by "granges." Most of the town citizens were farmers living in modest country houses. John Grange was one of these citizens. The farmer met his future wife, Jane Midgley, in town, and the two were married on July 21, 1812, in Yorkshire. Soon after the wedding, the two started a family. Three children were born in the next four years—one son, Joseph (1813), and two daughters, Dinah (1815) and Faith (1817).

Just when it looked like life was going well for John Grange, the family was torn apart. According to Roger Grange Jr., grandson of Wallace Grange, one of Red's uncles,

> The reason that John Grange and his family immigrated to the United States was because an older brother of his father had inherited the family property and wanted to sell the property (modest cottage), but somebody in the family was cut out of the will and would not support one or more families. Under those conditions he moved his family and settled in Pennsylvania.[1]

John Grange packed up his wife and three children and headed to Liverpool to take a ship to the United States. The Grange family boarded the vessel *Nancy* and set sail for a new life. Traveling the Atlantic for roughly 11 weeks, the ship docked at the Port of Philadelphia on May 20, 1818. On the port's manifest, the dock official wrote that John Grange and family had with them "two barrels, three boxes, an additional six boxes plus bedding." That's all the Grange family brought with them to America.[2]

After getting through Philadelphia, John Grange took his family some 170 miles west into Pennsylvania, settling in Sullivan County. Knowing a few families in that area, he moved into a house owned by the Fawcett family, who had relatives in Sicklinghall. The stay there was temporary until John soon purchased a farm of his own in Elkland Township, a small town just west of Eldresville (Sullivan County).[3]

After getting settled, John and Jane didn't waste much time restarting their growing family. Six more children were born in Sullivan County, including Mary (1819), Sarah (1821), Anna (1825), Jane (1826), Hannah (1828), and Red's grandfather, John Wesley Grange, in 1823.

John Senior quickly became a successful farmer in Elkland, and Jane made sure the children went to school in town and attended the local Methodist church. John Wesley would follow in the footsteps of his father and oldest brother, Joseph, as a farmer on the family's land. Stoutly built but not too tall, at about 5-foot-10, John Wesley grew up a hard worker and a no-nonsense man. By the time he was in his mid-20s he was a leader of the Grange family.

John Wesley was described as a man who was known to be "antislavery, anti-Mason, antisaloon, and voted his convictions." He also was heavily involved in Sunday school and family worship. In his obituary, it read, "He possessed indomitable will—after his mind was settled he was not easily moved." These were traits that were commonly passed down to the Grange men, including Red.[4]

As much as he worked on the family farm, John Wesley also had time to socialize. It was during one of these outings that he met his mate for life. Eliza Vough was a young, attractive woman who came from a hard-luck family. Born in 1833, the daughter of John and Hannah Vough of Montoursville, Pennsylvania, Eliza's father died when she was very young. Despite being 10 years younger, Eliza quickly fell in love with John, and the two were married on October 30, 1851, in Sullivan County. John bought a farm near Eldresville, and the Grange home soon became populated with the feet of little children. Tragedy struck the young couple when their firstborn, Martha, died two weeks after being born, but that didn't stop the two from wanting a large family. John Wesley and Eliza Grange would have 10 children: Almira (born 1854), Myrtle (1855), Wallace (1857), Luther Hale (1859), Hinton S. (1861), Walter Fremont (1863), Bertha A. (1865), John Nelson Lyle (1867), Arthur (1869), and Ernest O. (1872).

Three girls and seven boys made up the Grange clan. Eliza, with her stern attitude and hardworking determination, managed the Grange home to the best of her abilities—doing the cooking, cleaning, and raising of the children. All 10 Grange children would go to school in town. They would learn to read and write, as well as be physically active. It was John and Eliza's eighth child that would grow up to be the father of the Galloping Ghost.

John Nelson Lyle Grange was born on December 4, 1867. Starting with his grandfather and father's first name, this Grange boy wanted to be different, so he would go by one of his middle names, and most people called him Lyle for the rest of his life. The stocky, broad-shouldered Lyle Grange would grow up to stand a shade more than six feet tall and weigh more than 200 pounds.[5]

After completing his grammar-school education, Lyle went to work. In his early adult years, his red hair thinned considerably and he grew a mustache—like most Grange men—but it wasn't a trait that carried over to his son. His outstanding work ethic would take him to nearby Forksville. Since Lyle loved the outdoors, there was nothing better than being in the beautiful wilderness working long, hard days as a lumberjack. At about this time, Forksville was a small town of roughly two hundred residents (most of whom worked in the lumber yards) and got its name from the confluence of the Little Loyalsock Creek. Writing in his autobiography, Red Grange described Forksville as follows:

> It was situated in a picturesque setting of giant hemlock trees, clear, cool creeks, green grass, and majestic mountains. Forksville was, however, a rustic, isolated community over 15 miles away from the nearest railroad and farther yet from the closet towns of Williamsport and Wilkes-Barre. The town had one ancient-looking hotel, a general store that sold everything from plows to needles, and a schoolhouse with all eight grades in one room.[6]

Lyle Grange loved Forksville and, early on, showed he had a skill for working in the lumberyards. "Lyle Grange and his brothers were the best log cutters of anybody in this (Sullivan) county," recalled Forksville resident Mrs. Bessie Brown in a 1978 interview.[7] In a 1954 book titled *Sullivan County Industries: Then and Now*, the authors wrote about Red's father:

> Lyle Grange was a man of might, skill and, endurance. His record for sustained quality and quantity of bark peel in a season has never been equaled. It took two exceptionally skilled men to peel and pitch to the skid road four cords of bark in

a long day's labor. Lyle Grange and his helper, De Witt Morsey, averaged four times that amount for every day worked in a 50-day season.[8]

Lyle Grange didn't talk much about his lumberjacking days in Forksville, but when Red's football stardom captured the nation's fancy in the fall of 1925, he did speak to Jimmy Corcoran of the *Chicago American*, who specifically asked Lyle about being a lumberjack.

Picture the Chicago River with its surface covered with logs. Multiply by 50 times the current of the river. That will give an idea of the pace of the Loyal Soc. At the start of the long drive the work was not so hard, but as it progressed one needed his spiked shoes and his pike pole to stay on top of the job. . . . As the drive continued down the river everything a man possessed was called into play. There was vaulting to be done, sometimes as many as four or five logs. There were boulders to be dodged and tree stumps to be avoided as one rode along the rumbling, tumbling logs atop the swirling current.

There was danger on every hand, and it required quick thinking and a man that could size up the situation in advance. No time for soldiering. It was beat, beat, beat right along with nature throwing up an obstance ever so often for us to combat.

There were 50 miles of this kind of going every day, and by the time a man had mastered the work he was an accomplished dodger, diver, jumper, and acrobat all combined. In addition to that he was as clear and as keen and sound of mind and body as it was possible for a young man to be. As you rode the logs you had to think. The man who couldn't made his mind and body coordinate wasn't worth a d—n in the logging days around Forksville.[9]

Corcoran also asked Lyle about his athletic background. "I was never an athlete," said Lyle. "I was among the vast majority of what you might call the old-fashioned fathers who had to go out and make enough to raise a little family. . . . Don't ask me if I ever hit a baseball or carried a football in my younger day, I never had a chance to." Although Lyle was never able to experience the athletic glory that his son would, eventually he would enjoy watching him perform more than anything else in the world.[10]

Lyle's special prowess in the lumberyards quickly spread throughout Forksville and Sullivan County, so much so that he eventually became the top foreman in the yards overseeing several hundred men. In later years, Red would tell a story of how one man challenged his father to be the top boss man in the yard:

This man was bigger than my father and fancied himself the town bully. The two men had a showdown one day, battling for six hours in the woods until the bully, battered to a pulp, finally dropped into a state of unconsciousness. After this no man ever dared stand up to my father again.[12]

Lyle's toughness proved to the folks of Sullivan County that he was the right man for the job. He would get the best out of his men, and they would be the most productive lumberjacks in the state.

2

LOSING MOM

Lyle Grange was happy and content in the woods of Forksville. Sullivan County was home to him but not for some of his siblings. Several family members had started to migrate west, finally residing in Wheaton, Illinois, a smallish town of more than 2,300 citizens (1900 U.S. Census) located just 30 miles west of Chicago. Eventually, five of Lyle's siblings moved to Wheaton—Wallace, Luther, Bertha, Arthur, and Ernest.

As his children were scattering around, John Wesley was battling health issues that eventually caught up to him. He passed away at his home in Elkland on August 13, 1896. He was 73 years old. His son Arthur commented on his father's fight to the end, saying, "I was constantly with him during those nights when he could not sleep, and not once at any time did I hear a word of complaint or impatience." After the death of her husband, Eliza decided to leave Pennsylvania too, joining most of her children in Illinois—first living with Wallace and his family, then moving into a house with Luther and Bertha, who were both still single.[1]

With most of his family moved away, Lyle continued his work in the lumberyards. He soon met the love of his life. Just like the Grange's the Sherman family came to Pennsylvania in the 1800s and made their home in Sullivan County. Peter Sherman, a successful local farmer in Forks Township (next to Forksville), married Eliza "Sarah" Mace, and the young couple suffered tragedy, as two of their three children would pass away in childhood. Only their son Adam survived. Growing up on the Sherman farm, Adam learned the trade from his father. Eventually, he married Emma Green (1869) and established his own farm in between Forksville and Forks Township. Unlike his immediate family Adam and Emma raised a fairly large one, having eight children that survived childhood: Ira (1873), Walter (1874), Clinton (1875), Sadie (1877), Stella (1880), Cora (1887), Edna (1888), and Della. All of the Sherman children attended school and church. Most of the boys eventually worked on the farm. Adam and Emma's first daughter would attract the attention of Lyle Grange.

Sadie Ethel Sherman was born on July 19, 1878 (some documents say 1877). She would grow up with three older brothers who made sure she was included in all activities, especially outdoor events. According to one Sherman family member, Sadie was always referred to as a "tomboy with great athletic ability."[2]

The young, athletic, attractive Sadie Sherman caught the eye of Lyle Grange. Rather tall and slim, Sadie grew up to stand about 5-foot-8, with dark, bushy hair, and small, dark eyes, and a round face. It didn't take long for the couple to marry. In 1894, Lyle, age 27, and Sadie, age 17, said their vows in Sullivan County. Lyle bought a house in Forksville to give Sadie a great start to their marriage. This home was two stories tall and had several bedrooms and a small porch. It also had plenty of land surrounding it for a family to play. Soon their first child would arrive. On August 21, 1895, Norma Ethel Grange was born. Three years later, another daughter arrived, when Mildred L. Grange was born on April 12, 1898.

Sadie fell in love with her girls, dressing them up in nice clothes and posing for photos. One family photo had the two girls with their grandmother, Emma Sherman, and another had the two girls posing with a show horse as Norma held the rope around its neck while Mildred caressed the animal. At this time, Lyle was working hard in the lumberyards. He owned his own farmhouse and was happily married with two daughters. Not long thereafter, he would welcome his first son—the Galloping Ghost.

On June 13, 1903, Harold Edward Grange was born at home in Forksville. The newborn had brown eyes and a hair color that would not actually be red but more of an auburn shade, as his sister Mildred would reveal in a 1950 interview: "Harold's hair has a reddish cast. But it is our younger brother, Garland, who has the really red hair. Both boys inherited the red hair from their father."[3] Although mostly everyone would call him Red, the family, including Sadie and Lyle, would always call him Harold. But most kids couldn't say Harold very well, so the nickname, and the closeness of his hair color, gave the Grange boy a moniker for life. "My hair was never bright red. It was kind of an auburn color," recalled Red in a 1973 interview.

You can't expect football players to call you Harold. So, you have to come up with something else. I had kind of an odd name, Harold Edward. That don't sound quite right for a guy that wants to be an athlete. So, they got back to the color of my hair. Of course, I've been called a few other things too.[4]

It would be one of several nicknames that would stand the test of time.

The fourth and last child of Lyle and Sadie Grange arrived on December 2, 1906. Garland Arthur Grange would grow up to have the flaming red hair, not his more famous sibling. Red's auburn hair, which he parted down the middle, eventually became wavy. The two Grange boys would always be close. The Grange family had now reached six members. The four children got along well, as Sadie made sure they attended Sunday School at the local Methodist church and got their early education in the one-room schoolhouse in Forksville. She continued to take photos of the children, once having the four siblings pose together outside the family house. On one occasion, the two girls, Norma and Mildred, stood next to one another in fancy dresses, while Red, wearing dark dress trousers with a long-sleeved collared shirt buttoned to the top, pulled a wagon with young Garland sitting in it for a ride.

Another photo, this one just of Red, shows the future football star in his best Sunday clothes, wearing a nice button-up coat, knickers, knee-high socks, and a small hat, with his floppy auburn hair sprouting out from underneath, while holding a small batch of flowers. In one of the rare interview quotes by Lyle Grange, this time to a *Chicago American* reporter, he talked about his wife Sadie and this particular photo, relating, "This is one of the very few pictures I have of Harold when he was a youngster. His mother tied the little bunch (flowers) together and gave them to Harold so he would look nice when his picture was taken."[5]

When Lyle wasn't working, the family would spend quality time together, although throughout the years since his birth, Red didn't remember too much of his time in Forksville. One of things he did recall in his autobiography was the town's annual county fair:

> I recall how interested I was in the baseball games and track meets that were held at the fair, and how I tried to emulate the older boys who participated in those events. One day after watching one of the track meets I went home and attempted to pole vault with a homemade pole I fashioned from a branch of a tree. The pole snapped when I applied pressure, and part of it ran into my side, breaking two ribs. As far as I know, this was my first athletic injury.[6]

Lyle never scolded Harold when he came home to see the injury. He could see that his son was enjoying being athletic and learning how to compete in athletic competitions, showing him that sports might be a part of his future. Red would enjoy the outdoor life of Forksville, especially fishing and swimming. Another of Red's memories of living in Forksville involved the family dog—Jack—who helped the future football star with some of his natural athletic instincts. "I was crazy about that dog and played with him by the hour," he remembered. "My favorite pastime was to back Jack in the corner of the fence and watch him dodge, fake, and squirm his way out of my grasp. He was unquestionably the greatest open-field runner I ever saw, and I learned things from him I never forgot." But Lyle and Jack weren't the only athletic influences on young Red. His mother might've been the best athlete of the family.[7]

The "tomboy" would encourage her children, especially Harold, to participate in sports. In the July 1951 edition of the magazine *Now and Then* (Muncy [Pennsylvania] Historical Society), one of Sadie's childhood neighbors, H. Delbert Bird, gave an interview talking about her. In an article titled "My Boyhood Days on a Sullivan County Farm," Bird stated,

> In speaking of Red Grange, who is one of the nationally known characters born in Sullivan County, this humble writer went to school with his mother, who was Sadie Sherman. I wore a sore thumb for several years, which I sprained when I ran into Sadie, while playing catcher around the school house. Red probably got his speed from his mother, for she could run like a deer and preferred playing with the boys, and of course she was called a "tomboy."[8]

Red seemed to inherit his father's size and toughness but got his speed and quickness from his mother. The members of the Grange family were happy when they were together. Harold loved his mom and dad very much. He didn't know he soon would be losing his mom for good.

In December 1909, Sadie Grange started to experience some soreness and pain in her mouth. It seemed that one of her teeth was causing too much pain to bear. One of the unfortunate things about living in Forksville was that the town did not have a dentist. So, Lyle had the family look after the children while he took Sadie to nearby Williamsport to get her tooth checked out. He loaded a horse and wagon, and set off southwest for the 35-mile trip.

Once they arrived in Williamsport, Sadie had her teeth looked at. The dentist made the decision that one of them was bad enough to come out. After the tooth was pulled, Sadie started to hemorrhage. The dentist had seen this before, and thinking she wasn't in any serious jeopardy, he thought they could make it home and follow up with a visit to Dr. Davies. Lyle just wanted to get his wife back home. He marched the horse and wagon back to Forksville to make it easier for Sadie. As winter moved on and the calendar turned to 1910, Sadie's health did not improve. Actually, the symptoms got worse. A new physician was brought in to monitor her health. Starting on February 1, Dr. C. M. Bradford looked after Sadie.

Red's mother never did get better. Soon she caught a case of typhoid fever, and then came pneumonia—diseases that are simple to cure now, but in 1910, both were deadly. Showing toughness and bravery, Sadie continued to battle the ailments; however, the time came when she couldn't battle any more. While in bed at her home in Forksville, Sadie Grange took her last breath. At 7:30 a.m. on March 25, 1910, she was gone. She was just 31 years old.[9]

Lyle had lost his soulmate, the love of his life. He would never recover from losing Sadie, as he would never remarry. As for the children, the four Grange siblings would go through the rest of their lives without their mother. Harold Grange wouldn't say much about losing his mom. In the ensuing decades and countless interviews, he would rarely, if ever, mention her. Even in his autobiography, published in 1953, he would only say, "My mother died when I was five." Seven words. Seven words that weren't entirely correct. Harold was six years old and about to turn seven in June 1910.[10]

As the Grange family grieved the death of Sadie, the rest of Forksville read the obituary of the young mother: "Mrs. Grange was a member of the M.E. Church, a kind indulgent mother and an excellent neighbor. She leaves a husband, four children, a mother, brothers and sisters, and hosts of friends to mourn her death."[11]

Described as generous and kind, Sadie Grange died much too soon. Her family would miss her dearly. Since Red Grange never really talked about his mother, who knows what impact her death had on him the rest of his life. She definitely gave her eldest son some of her great athletic ability, as well as a true sense of family, loyalty, love, and kindness. The funeral took place two days later, on Sunday March 27, at the family's Methodist church in Forksville. The Rev. F. P. Hess officiated. After the funeral, Sadie was taken to East Forks Union Cemetery (Warburton Hill) to be buried. Unfortunately, when the headstone was made and placed in the ground the dates were wrong. It read, "SADIE SHERMAN, WIFE OF, LYLE N. GRANGE, July 19, 1877 Mar. 25, 1909." Decades later, when Red Grange returned to his hometown and visited the cemetery, he made sure the headstone was correct. He bought a new one that had the correct dates (1878 and 1910), as well as the names of Sadie's parents, Adam and Emma, and their correct dates. Today the two tombstones sit side by side.[12]

The aftermath of Sadie's death was traumatic for the entire Grange family. Lyle was now a widower in charge of four children who had just lost their mother, the person who took care of them for most of the day when their father was off working. Lyle had to make a decision about what to do next. It didn't take him long to make up his mind. He was going to need help. So, he decided to pack up his family and move from Pennsylvania. He knew what he needed. He needed family.

3

WHEATON

Just a few weeks after Sadie Grange passed away, Lyle packed up his family's belongings and his four children, and headed west. The children followed their father's lead. The Grange family traveled almost 700 miles to Wheaton, Illinois. Lyle's siblings had made a nice home in the tiny town, located 30 miles west of Chicago.

Wheaton was your typical small Midwestern town, with three schools, one college (Wheaton College), two banks, nine churches, four dentists, six physicians, two barbers, a bowling alley, an ice cream parlor, and two tailors. Along Front and Main streets in the business district, the town included such popular retail spots as Rogers's Hardware, Pittsford Dry Goods Co., Dollinger's and Hiatt's & Sons drugstores, the Grand movie theater, a library, two newspapers (*Progressive* and *Illinoian*), Clark's Restaurant, Wheaton News Company, and Central Garage.

When Lyle brought his family to Wheaton in 1910, it had a population of 3,423, which included five of Lyle's siblings—Wallace, Luther, Bertha, Arthur, and Ernest. Also in town were seven law offices, including one owned by Luther, and 10 carpenters and building contractors, two of whom were Arthur and Ernest. Once arriving in town, Lyle agreed to work with his brothers in their house-building business.

While in Wheaton, tragedy didn't escape Lyle. Upon his arrival in town, his mother, Eliza, who had moved to Wheaton after her husband passed away, was already sick. She lived with Bertha and Luther, the two single children, in a home on Wesley Street. On June 5, 1910, Eliza (Vough) Grange died after battling an illness for eight months. Her body was sent back to Sullivan County to be buried next to her husband. She was 77 years old.[1]

Lyle, age 42, Norma (14), Mildred (11), Red (6, would turn 7 in June), and Garland (3) initially rented a home at 511 Ohio Street, near Wheaton College. At first, Bertha looked after the children during the day as Lyle worked. Because of her strict religious beliefs, Bertha, who attended postgraduate school to become an educator and remained single her entire life, made the Grange children attend Sunday school. Church picnics were looked forward to by Red, as he would compete in athletic events, once winning a baseball that became his prized possession. The Sunday school education didn't keep Red from getting into mischief and the occasional fistfight. Red would come home with a bloody nose or a black eye, horrifying Bertha, but Lyle was only interested in hearing if the young boy fought fairly.

Bertha's demands of attending Sunday school did have one additional attraction for young Red. Despite being timid and shy, he started noticing one particular girl in the neighborhood. This girl lived across the street, sporting beautiful brown curls and brown eyes. He never did get the courage to talk to her. Some of Red's timidity and reticence of later years came because his mother was not around to help him. It was this environment in which Lyle Grange fell short. He wasn't equipped to help with the motherly part of parenthood, especially with his two daughters, who didn't embrace Wheaton like Red and Garland.

Compared to Forksville, the two boys appreciated the expansive area where they could play games, with wide-open spaces that weren't enclosed by mountains and water, as well as the closeness of neighbors, with plenty of children to play with who were their own age. Playing tops and marbles, and riding his bicycle, allowed Red to enjoy the town, as well as make friends. One of those friends was Dave Johnson, a young black kid who invited Red to play baseball on his all-black team. Despite being the only white kid, Red didn't have any second thoughts about participating. All he wanted to do was play.

Lyle lost his safety net when Bertha left Wheaton to become dean of women at Houghton College in upstate New York. Lyle moved his boys in with his brother Luther, a bachelor lawyer, in the house on Wesley Street. He thought long and hard about his two girls, who needed a female presence in their lives, and—combined with the financial support of raising four children—made the ultimate decision to send his two daughters back to Pennsylvania to live with Sherman family members.

Soon Lyle escaped the house-building business and gained some financial stability. In 1913, he took a job with the Wheaton police department, earning $75 a month. The stable work allowed Lyle to become more financially independent. The following year, Wheaton mayor H. Ward Mills appointed Lyle as "city marshal," with a raise to $100 a month. It wasn't a rich salary but enough to take care of himself and the two boys. This new police job would keep Lyle busy, as most nights he would be on call for 24 hours.

Lyle finally got a place of his own located at 117 Front Street in the business district, a five-room apartment situated above Dollinger's Drugstore, operated by Charles Dollinger. There was nothing feminine about this apartment, with plain, dark matting rugs on the floors, substantial oak chairs, plain muslin curtains, a few books on the bookshelf, a hat rack, a big heating stove, a dining table and dishes, a cook stove, beds, and a radio. This was now home for Lyle and his two boys.

Before entering sixth grade, Red had achieved a remarkable, rugged physical physique for his age. He was a bit long-legged but had the stamina of good lungs and heart (which would soon be tested). As Red got older, he sought out the games he loved so much, especially football. The town boys would play pickup games in the vacant football field. While playing, some of the older neighborhood boys could see that the young redhead had some promising talent. A trio of boys would make it a priority to look after him: George Dawson, Elmer Hoffman, and his closest friend in town, Lyman "Beans" DeWolf—who would be captain of the 1917 Wheaton High school football team—became mentors to Red. This trio would influence and guide him as an athlete during the next decade, and be his lifelong friends.

Aside from playing the games, Red started to read up on the sports he loved. Flipping through the sports sections of the Chicago dailies, Red read up on the exploits of the local college football teams—Northwestern, Notre Dame, and the University of Illinois—and Potsy Clark and Bart Macomber became some of his first football heroes. "I always had heroes. I remember at the University of Illinois, Bart Macomber," Red recalled in 1978. "I had his picture since I was in eighth grade. And he had a piece of tape over his nose. He had skinned his nose. I would get a piece of tape and hold it for 10 days over my nose, ya know, just to be like him."[2]

Another hero of Red's was George Gipp of Notre Dame. Speaking in 1925, Red talked about the "Gipper":

> I used to read about George Gipp of Notre Dame and marvel at the things he did on a football field. His long runs always thrilled me as I would read of them the day following a game, but the thing that gave me the greatest sensation were the reports of his long dropkicks. Any fellow who can dropkick a football from the 55-yard line must be a wonder, and that were just what Gipp did when he was playing under Knute Rockne.[3]

Despite his growing physique, Red would endure many bumps and bruises as a youth. "The flesh near my eyes were [sic] always getting cut open by some freak of the game in those days, and I remember how often the doctor had to sew me up."[4]

As high school approached, Red was thinking about quitting school. He never really liked doing schoolwork, just enough to pass his classes. But Lyle gave his eldest son an ultimatum.

"You either can go to school or go to work. I want you to go to school, but there will be no loafing," barked Lyle. Even from an early age Lyle treated his sons with respect, regarding them almost as adults. They would make the ultimate decision when faced with an issue. He trusted them to make the right choice. Red thought about it hard, even trying a caddy job at a nearby golf course (which lasted one day of carrying clubs for 72 holes), but he quickly decided he loved playing sports more and having to attend school was worth the price to play.[5]

While growing up, Red would appreciate and welcome his father's guidance, regardless of the subject. "If it had not been for my father during those days, I should have become a bum," he commented.[6] He did not become a bum. He was destined for bigger things. Although Red was not willing to quit school to work, Lyle still wanted his son to learn the meaning of hard work, so he sent his eldest son to live on the farm of his brother Ernest. In his autobiography, Red described the year living as a farmer as such:

> The following was a typical day on Uncle Ernest's farm. Rising at 5 a.m., I'd head straight for the horse and cow barns and put in about an hour's work feeding hay and oats to five horses and milking four cows before sitting down at the breakfast table. After breakfast I had to water the horses, then hitch them to the wagon and drive them into town to deliver the milk to the local dairy. Returning to the farm, I'd get on my bicycle and pedal two miles to school. At night, just before retiring, it was my job to clean out the barns, get the hay down for the next morning, feed the horses and cows again. Needless to say, I earned my keep—and then some. After a year of this my father was convinced Uncle Ernest was working me too hard and took me back to live with him.[7]

Lyle pushed his son to be a hard worker. He saw Red's willingness to get his hands dirty. In 1925, Lyle commented on his son's work as a farmer, saying,

> Harold would have made a good farmer. He likes the farm and farm work. Harold can milk, plow, disc, make hay, and do all farm chores. Several years ago when

we had the exceptional cold weather, Harold was one of the hands on his uncle's farm. The hard physical work of the farm appealed to him.[8]

As Red was getting to know his family in Wheaton, more tragic news would shock the Grange men. This time it came from back home in Sullivan County. When Norma Grange was sent back to Pennsylvania, she grew up in Wilkes-Barre with the family of her mother, Sadie (Sherman). Suddenly, at the age of 21, she became sick with what was described on her death certificate as "toxic jaundice." On October 31, 1916, Norma died at Mercy Hospital from the liver disease. Her body was sent to the East Forks Union Cemetery, where she was buried next to her mother. It is unknown whether Lyle or the boys returned to Sullivan County for the funeral; most likely they did not. In addition to his parents, Lyle had now lost his wife and first child. In the remaining years, the Grange men, especially Red and Garland, made an effort to stay in contact with their sister Mildred, even if they did not see one another on a regular basis.[9]

As for Red and Garland, whom everyone called "Gardy," the two became very close, regularly spending time together playing sports or going to school, something that wasn't Red's favorite part of the day. "I hated school just like any other kid and was resigned to it simply as a duty. The most important part of living came after school when I was able to play football, basketball, and baseball with my pals," recalled Red. Sports, on the other hand, were at the top of the to-do list. Whatever time of year it was, he was excited about playing whatever he could get into—baseball in the summer, track in the spring, basketball in the winter. But it was football in the fall that got his blood going more than anything else.[10] Said Red,

> We used to play football in a vacant lot near the edge of town. None of us had uniforms but improvised by cutting off the pant legs of our oldest trousers and added padding where needed most. The lot we played on was convex in shape, with 50 yards of the field on one side of a hill and 50 yards on the other. On a kickoff the ball would sail up and over the top of the hill, seemingly coming from nowhere. By the time a player tucked the pigskin under his arm and started up the field behind his interference, the opposition would suddenly swarm over the top like "The Charge of the Light Brigade." It was enough to scare the daylights out of a kid.[11]

Red played mainly with the older kids, who gave him a beating. "Many times I got so discouraged I wanted to give up playing football in favor of shooting marbles or playing tops. It was my father who encouraged me to continue. He said it would make a man of me," he remembered. As an eighth grader, Red was given some devastating news. The redhead, who was always active playing any kind of sport or riding his bicycle, received a difficult diagnosis. After seeing the town doctor for a common cold, Red was told he had developed a heart murmur and that he could no longer engage in strenuous exercise. The news shocked Red and crushed Lyle.[12]

The diagnosis did not deter Red. After a few weeks, he began sneaking out to play with his friends in the neighborhood games. This went on for a few months without Lyle suspecting a thing. It looked like everything was fine with the youthful lad until a problem arose that he couldn't hide from his father. During one of his afternoon football games with the older boys, he was involved in a melee and kicked in the spine. Red knocked two vertebrae out of place at the base of his spine. He was unable to sit down for two weeks, trying to hide it from his father. Eventually, Lyle got Red to confess what he had been doing. To Red's surprise, his father did not become angry. Lyle decided then and there that he would support his son's efforts in playing sports, since it meant so much to him that he would jeopardize his health. Lyle was taking a big gamble, but from that day forward Lyle Grange became his son's biggest fan and would remain as such for the rest of his life.

As it turned out, Red suffered no ill effects from the heart murmur. A year later, just before entering high school, he took a physical and was given a clean bill of health. He was now ready to go to high school.

LOVE OF SPORTS

On September 3, 1918, Harold "Red" Grange walked through the front doors of Wheaton High for the first time as a high school student. He was joined by 84 other freshmen, one of the largest classes to enter the high school. The principal, Miss E. M. Gregg, looked after a student body of roughly 300 students in the Longfellow school building, located seven blocks from the Grange apartment on Front Street.

That fall, Red went out for football. He was excited about trying out, joining some of his friends on the football team. Although Beans DeWolf and Elmer Hoffman had just graduated, the Wheaton football team still consisted of some good football players, notably senior quarterback George Dawson.

One of the major reasons Red claimed for going out for the team was that the school supplied uniforms and equipment to the students. "That was my first 'issued' football suit, and it certainly made me feel good," he stated. "Formerly I had been cutting off old pants and sewing them up and so gathering heterogenous outfit together. I felt now that as I had a suit I'd better play."[1]

Maybe having the football uniform made Red try out for the team, but deep down he loved football. He wanted to play the game more than anything in the world. Getting a football suit was just a bonus. But what position would he play? Playing against the older kids in pickup games was completely different than playing in a high school game. He reported to the high school coach, Roy Puckey, who also was the school's new manual training teacher. Puckey asked young Red what position he played. Red, being smarter than the average freshman, responded by asking what position he needed. Puckey said that one of their ends had graduated and he needed an end. Red fired back, "I play end."[2]

Two days after school started, on September 5, Puckey held the first practice for the football team, and 30 players tried out. In Wheaton, it was not "Friday Night Lights" but Saturday morning football that was the norm for the Little Seven Conference (previously the Bi-County Conference from 1918 to 1919). Schools in the Little Seven included Batavia, Dundee, Geneva Community, Naperville, St. Charles, Sycamore, and Wheaton. Those Saturday mornings would be spent playing at the Orchard.[3]

The Wheaton football field was called the Orchard because it was located in a rather large apple orchard field situated east of Gary Street, bounded by Harrison, West, and Jefferson streets. Red fondly recalled playing at the Orchard:

Our football field was located in an apple orchard a mile and half from school. It was no easy task walking that distance every night after a strenuous practice session. The freshman members of the team lined the playing field and cleared away the stray apples on Saturday mornings before the games. Regardless of how careful we were to remove the fruit from the ground, we'd always miss a few. I got juice squirted in my eyes dozens of times falling on those apples.[4]

"The center of the field was bare where the grass had been worn off," recalled Bim Frazer, former high school teammate of Red, in a 1974 interview. "There was nothing ever done to the field to my knowledge. The field was entirely surrounded by a powdered line of lime, and every 10 yards on the field was marked by lime." Crowds of several hundred would attend the games played on Saturday mornings. There were no stands, as people usually just stood on the sidelines to watch the action. Admission was free, but the school usually passed a hat around taking donations, getting 25 or 50 cents per person.[5]

The season started with the school's annual game against the alumni. At the Orchard, the varsity was pounded, 48–0, by the "has-beens." Puckey seemed to be in over his head. Soon it was time for Red's first varsity game. The 15-year-old, 138-pound "rookie" was extremely nervous, as he was the only freshman to start on the varsity team, lining up at left end. "It was so funny to be out on the field before a crowd," Red said. "Everybody seemed to be watching me. I felt so nervous and self-conscious that I wished I hadn't told them I'd play." It might've been the last time he was nervous, because playing football came so natural to him.[6]

A week after the alumni game, the team's performance hadn't gotten any better—it might've gotten worse. Wheaton was hammered, 45–0, at the Orchard by West Aurora High School, and that was followed up by a 36–8 loss on the road at La Grange. The first two games saw Wheaton outscored, 81–8. The *Wheaton*

Illinoian, which was published every Friday and always recapped the previous week's game, stated, "Something is radically wrong with the team . . . let's see some scrap fellows . . . don't let Wheaton be ashamed of the team."[7]

On October 12, Red and his teammates finally tasted victory, defeating conference rival St. Charles, 27-12, at the Orchard. Four different players—Ludgate, Otto, Fischer, and Schussler—scored touchdowns. The *Illinoian* mentioned Red's play for the first time as a varsity player: "They played wonderful ball. (Jake) Miller and Grange played like demons and completely smothered the end runs in their directions." The team celebrated the season's first victory.[8]

After a game with Downer's Grove was cancelled due to an influenza outbreak, Wheaton took on Dundee at the Orchard. The 2:30 p.m. kickoff saw Red starting at left end. The small crowd at the Orchard would stand around in the drizzling rain to witness a hard-fought, low-scoring affair. In the first quarter, after a nice drive, quarterback George Dawson kicked a 30-yard field goal. It would be the only points of the game. The rest of the contest saw many fumbles and sloppy play. Red continued his stellar play at end as the *Illinoian* pointed out more positive action by the freshman. The paper's main sportswriter, John Newman, who wrote a column titled "High School Dope," penned, "Harold Grange was the outstanding figure in the game. His brilliant tackling proved too much for the Dundee backfield. Grange went down the field at an even pace with the ball and, as a result, tackled his man as soon as he caught it."[9]

Now 2-2, the season looked to be a success. But the last two games of the season didn't make anyone want to throw a joyful banquet. Against two tough foes, Wheaton lost games to Batavia (0–16) and Riverside (0–13) by not scoring a point. Red finished his freshman season with a 2-4 record as Wheaton was outscored, 122-38. Overall, Red had a successful freshman season on the gridiron. Despite his youth, the local newspaper coverage of his play was always positive, with most of his success coming on the defensive side of the ball. Tackling was a strength. Although his future as a breakaway runner was just around the corner, young Red learned how to play the line (end play) and what defenses wanted to do to stop end runs. From an early age, Red was becoming a student of the game, a practice he would continue for the rest of his life.

After the football season, Red participated in basketball, track, and baseball, earning varsity letters in each sport. He also was successful in the classroom; aside from passing manual training, shorthand, and typewriting, he received excellent marks in English (84), Latin (90), botany (91), and algebra (94).[10]

While Red was completing his freshman year, things were going fine at the Grange apartment on Front Street. Although their father was on call 24 hours a day, the two Grange boys looked after one another. "I did all the cooking at home, and if I have to say so myself, was a darn good cook," Red declared. "My brother Garland did the shopping and we took turns washing and wiping the dishes. We also did the house cleaning ourselves since Dad was generally too busy to help with any of the chores."[11]

Lyle could see that his two boys were becoming responsible young men. He continued to allow them to learn how to be men and make decisions on their own. Soon Red would be presented with an opportunity to work. He would accept a job that would change his future forever and make him a better football player.

5

THE WHEATON
ICEMAN

After his freshman year, Red was looking forward to a quiet and relaxing summer. Instead, an opportunity to make some money, learn how to do hard work (again), and, by accident, help him become a more physically gifted athlete arose. This opportunity was given to him by a man who was most well-known in town as the man who delivered ice.

Luke Carroll Thompson was born on December 28, 1867, in Wheaton, to Elmer B. and Mary Thompson. Elmer, who went by E. B., was on the Board of Trustees at Wheaton College when the school opened in 1860, starting a relationship with the college that would last for more than two decades. The Thompsons owned 60-plus acres of land next to the school. A religious man, E. B. was difficult to live with. "He (Luke) hated his father because he was so religious," said John Thompson, grandson of Luke Thompson. "His father would go down to the station on Sundays and stand in the middle of the railroad tracks and try to stop trains running through Wheaton. Religious nut."[1]

Growing up in Wheaton, Luke would be called by his initials, L. C., just like his father. Everyone called him L. C. He learned to read and write while completing his grammar-school education, right before his father came up with an outrageous idea. E. B. turned over his 60 acres to the college and took his wife and two boys to the Dakota Territory. In 1881, the Thompson family made their home in Highmore as E. B. became a member of the National Christian Association to be a missionary, helping build churches.

While in Highmore tragedy struck. "In 1885 a huge tornado came out of nowhere," said John Thompson. "Luke, his brother, and his mother all went into the basement of the house, and he (Luke) always told me, 'We just left him.'

He was asleep in the big chair when the tornado hit and took the whole house. The next day they found him a mile away dead."[2] Elmer B. Thompson was found by several town citizens with a broken neck and his face buried three or four inches in the ground. The family didn't cry over the loss of E. B. But they were left with nothing.[3]

Mary decided to return to Wheaton with her two boys and the shirts on their backs. She would try to rebuild her life. L. C. briefly worked at a tin shop in town before making his way back out West, leaving his mother to become a cowboy. The scrawny, brown-haired, brown-eyed, nineteen-year-old, who sported a handle-bar mustache, carried his one piece of luggage to Colorado Springs, Colorado.

The young man from Wheaton seemed to be miscast as a cowboy. His mother warned him not to go, thinking he would be killed by some trigger-happy gunman. L. C. came prepared with his own .38 pistol. "For five years, I rode the range near Colorado Springs. Although I always carried my .38 on my side I didn't have to use it on anyone," he recalled in a 1958 interview with the *Wheaton Daily Journal*.[4] Putting aside the potential of getting shot in the Wild West, Thompson was a die-hard teetotaler, which also didn't sit well in the cowboy town of Colorado Springs. Once, at Christmastime, a group of cowboys tried to force young L. C. to take a drink. "I just patted my .38 and told them they wouldn't be around to try it again next Christmas if they attempted such a thing." Apparently, the group got the hint and never tried again. Although he was young, L. C. became a man not to mess with. "He took pride in that he never took a drop of alcohol in his life," said Janis Franks, granddaughter of L. C. "He was a very strong-willed and very high-morale man."[5]

His five years as a cowboy helped his work ethic and leadership skills in dealing with all kinds of individuals, but soon he missed home and his mother. In 1891, he returned to Wheaton. The following year, he got married to Hattie Barber, had two children (Leon and Helen), and started an ice-delivering business in his hometown. At this time, Thompson stood 5-foot-10 and weighed roughly 165 pounds. "He was small and wirer," Franks continued. "Every time I came to visit him, you had to sit next to him and feel his muscles, because of all those years lifting ice." Delivering ice was not an easy job. When customers wanted ice, they would place a cardboard card in the window by 6:00 a.m. indicating the amount of ice wanted. Ice cakes could be delivered in 25-, 50-, 75-, or 100-pound increments. L. C. and his men would make the rounds to drop off the ice, toting ice cakes weighing as much as 100 pounds on their shoulders and up steps and into people's houses.[6]

"Wheaton (1920) was about 4,500 or 5,000 at the time, which wasn't huge, but he served everybody in town as an iceman," John Thompson stated. "I don't think he had any competition. A lot people owed him money, he didn't care, everybody was a customer, so that's the way it worked."[7]

The L. C. Thompson Ice Company sold ice, coal, and feed, becoming one of the town's most successful businesses. From 1907 to 1930, the company became very profitable for L. C., and during its heyday the business had as many as 19 employees, several trucks, and horses. L. C. was always picky about whom he hired. One ad in the *Chicago Tribune* in 1911 stated, "MAN TO WORK AT ICE BUSINESS: Must be a married man, hustler, and strictly sober, no other need apply. Good wages. L. C. THOPMSON, Wheaton, Ill."[8]

Red knew old man Thompson as the iceman in town but not much more. The summer before his sophomore year in high school, Red came face-to-face with the man who would offer him a once-in-a-lifetime job. One day in town, Thompson wanted to have a little fun with a few of the teenagers, promising a dollar to the boy who could lift a 75-pound ice cake onto their shoulder, knowing full well that most of the them couldn't lift it past their knees. But he didn't know the strength that Lyle Grange's boy had in him. Having some familiarity with using the ice tongs, Red quickly picked up the 75-pound cake and hoisted it onto his shoulder. Thompson was stunned, and as he was a man of his word he handed a crisp dollar bill to young Red. In his autobiography, Red recalled working for Thompson:

> Impressed with my being the only kid able to lift the ice to shoulder height and already having made an investment in me, Thompson invited me to work with him on his ice truck for the entire summer. The job sometimes required working 14 hours a day, from five in the morning to seven at night, six days a week, but I jumped at the opportunity as the weekly wage of $37.50 seemed like more money than I ever dreamed it was possible to earn.[9]

Red accepted the job, mainly for the money. Knowing that his father worked hard to support him and Garland, he wanted to give back to his old man. The weekly salary was good money, even if he had to work hard for it. Red quickly learned the job of an iceman, although he would go through many agonizing moments, jabbing himself with the ice pick, getting the ice tongs stuck in his skin, or dropping the huge ice cakes on his hands, feet, or toes.

Lyle's eldest son knew hard work, learning much from his experience on his Uncle Ernest's farm, so the long days and hours didn't discourage him. Red Grange recalled in a 1977 interview,

We worked six days a week. Monday, Wednesday, and Friday were our busy days. Tuesday and Thursday were light days. I would work from six in the morning til seven at night. And everybody used an ice card. We had a scale on the back of the truck, and we would hang the ice and the tongs on the scale. We never looked at the scale, but nobody knew that, because we knew half of two hundred, and we had it figured out pretty well.[10]

Red quickly learned that spending a summer delivering ice could benefit his athletic career—especially in football. Years later, Red would recall how the job helped him physically:

It is an accepted fact the most important parts of a football player are his legs. Keeping those legs in shape represents the biggest single reasonability of a boy interested in playing football. While working on a road gang, laboring in the coal mines or steel mills is good for general muscle development, it contributes nothing toward keeping a player's legs in condition. One stands still when working at those jobs and doesn't use his legs. Delivering ice, which required my walking miles every day up and down stairs, kept me in all-around fine trim and provided the best possible offseason training for my legs.

The most important thing for a player to remember is that football isn't a game that can be played just three months in the fall. In order to excel in the sport, one must constantly work at keeping his body and, especially, his legs strong the other nine months of the year.

Reporting for football in the fall after a summer on the ice truck, I would be tough as nails and at least four weeks ahead of the other boys in conditioning. My iceman duties made my arms, shoulders, and legs strong and developed my wind. It was, in effect, my own private brand of "spring training" . . . my job on Luke Thompson's ice truck filled the bill to a T.[11]

The summer of 1919 would be the first of nine consecutive summers (1919–1927) where Red would work on the ice wagon. Because of his eventual fame on the gridiron, he would earn the nickname the "Wheaton Iceman," a moniker that would last for the rest of his life. When summer came to end, school was right around the corner. For Red, that meant football season was here. The first big change for him was Wheaton High had a new head football coach.

Wilbur "Bill" Castleman, born in nearby Maywood, Illinois, attended Maywood High School, where he was a member of the football team. "He wasn't a very tall man, maybe 5-feet-8, weighed 170 pounds, with brown hair and eyes," said David Castleman, grandson of Bill Castleman. "But had enormously wide shoulders, which probably led to him having the pleasure of getting into fights. He was a powerful man."[12] The rough and tough Castleman went to Western

State Normal School, now Western Michigan University, where he played as an end on the reserve team, coached by Bill Spaulding. After his graduation from Western State, Castleman joined the U.S. Army, serving in France during World War I. Upon his return home, he accepted the job as manual training teacher and head football coach at Wheaton High School, replacing Roy Puckey. Castleman would use the lessons he learned from Spaulding to help coach his players at Wheaton. He and Puckey, who was more laid back than Castleman, were like night and day, and the intensity he brought to practice and games would help the Wheaton Tigers in the fall of 1919.

Red now had a new coach, and soon he would have a new position. Because of the graduation of his good friend, quarterback George Dawson, who moved on to play football at the University of Illinois, the team had an opening in the backfield. Red had the speed to be a halfback, and everyone knew it. When Castleman saw that Grange's body had filled out and developed after a summer working on the ice wagon, he knew he had a potential star. Grange recalled his developing body:

> Work on the ice wagon made my arms and hands much stronger than they would be otherwise. This came in handy in straight-arming and warding off tacklers. My greatest asset that first season as a halfback was, besides my ability to run fast, my use of the stiff-arm. By building up great strength in my arm working on the ice truck, I was able to push away many would-be tacklers.[13]

First up was the game against the alumni, and this time the varsity put up more of fight, battling to a 21–7 defeat. Red was given high honors by the *Wheaton Illinoian*: "Grange, who has been shifted to half, played a marvelous game. He will develop into the greatest ground gainer on the team this year."[14]

The local paper could see that the high school team had a special player. Red, at just 16 years old, was set to make a name for himself. Two weeks after the alumni game, Wheaton faced off against conference foe St. Charles at the Orchard. It was the coming-out party of Harold "Red" Grange. In the first half alone, he ran for touchdowns of 65, 20, and 12 yards. In the fourth quarter, he added a fourth (20 yards) as the Tigers defeated St. Charles, 25–0. Grange also kicked an extra point, accounting for all points scored. "For Wheaton Grange was the whole show, the speedy right half scoring all the points and advancing the ball every time he was called upon," wrote the *Illinoian*, which reported that Grange accounted for more than 200 yards rushing.[15] Speaking to the *Chicago Daily News* in 1925, Red recalled his first touchdown run as follows:

I had been shifted to the backfield from end and was trying to run with the ball. In one of our early games I tried an end run, and everything piled up in front of me. I ran around it and streaked for the sideline. About five yards from it I started downfield. To my surprise, I got away and made a touchdown.[16]

But in the article Red also gave credit to the ones who made the run happen, adding, "Of course, I could not have gotten away without interference at the start of the run, as my team did its best to get me started." Throughout his life while giving interviews, Red would give others the credit for his success, a trait teammates, coaches, and fans always admired about the redhead.[17]

The following week saw Red eclipse his previous performance. Against a much bigger, heavier squad, Elgin Academy, Red started the game with a 64-yard punt return for a touchdown. With the score tied at 6–6 in the third quarter, Red took over with one highlight after another. A 78-yard kickoff re-turn score to open the second half was followed by a 31-yard touchdown run. After two Bill Fischer scores, Red circled left end for a game-clinching 54-yard touchdown. The *Wheaton Illinoian* reported his total yards at 396 (averaging 16 yards a touch), writing, "He surely has a great future for him in athletics."[18]

The 38–6 victory, in which Red had now scored eight touchdowns and two extra points (50 points total), improved the Tigers' record to 2–0. The next Saturday, Wheaton prevailed over Chicago Austin High, 21–0. The following Saturday, the 3–0 Wheaton Tigers traveled west to play a conference game against Batavia and came away with a 17–0 victory.

After the game, Red's ankle was very sore, but with the team at 4–0, and the next game against Glen Ellyn for the conference championship, he was not about to let his team down by being out of the lineup. A still-hobbling Red and his teammates gutted out a gritty performance. In the first quarter, Wheaton struck first, as Red returned a punt for a touchdown. After having his field goal blocked, Red got mad and responded by sprinting for a 24-yard score to give the Tigers a 12–0 second-quarter lead. "Grange broke away amid deafening roars. Again his straight-arm served the purpose, and he reeled off 24 yards before the crowd got him. When the referee untangled the mass of humans, Grange was grinning through a mask of mud with the ball two feet over the counting mark."[19]

The sprint might've taken something out of him because he missed the extra point. Glen Ellyn got back in the game using the popular Minnesota shift on offense, cutting the lead to 12–7. But right before half, Red ran wild, sprinting 48 yards for a score—his third touchdown of the game. He also had an intercep-tion on defense to close out a 19–7 halftime lead. It would not hold up. Maybe the injuries were starting to affect them, as the Tigers tried to hold on for dear life. Two third-quarter drives helped Glen Ellyn tie the game at 19–19, as both extra points were missed. The game ended in a 19–19 tie, with both teams playing their hearts out. The local paper once again praised the redhead: "Grange, dodging and charging gait with his clever sidestep and wicked stiff-arm, baffled the whole Glen Ellyn team. He was worked hard, but he was game to the core, and every time he responded with everything that was in him."[20]

After defeating Dundee in the season finale, the Tigers finished with a 5-0-1 overall record and outscored their opponents, 132–25. The *Wheaton Illinoian* listed their All-County Team, featuring four Wheaton starters: Whiteley (center), H. Stockton (guard), Miller (end), and Red (halfback). Red was mentioned as well: "Without a doubt he is the star of this selection. He retains his position at right half because in circling left end he uses his right arm for stiff-arming, his greatest assets outside of his long-strided speed."[21]

In his first season at halfback, Red scored 13 touchdowns in just five games (he missed one because of injury) and made First-Team All-County. Red continued his athletic excellence in basketball (being named captain as a sophomore), baseball, and track. His classwork didn't suffer either, as he earned passing grades in English (83), Caesar (81), physiography (91), and ancient history (89).

After a summer of delivering ice, helping him on the football field, Red Grange was about to become the most popular citizen in Wheaton. He was about to do things on the football field that had never been seen before. High school glory was waiting for the Wheaton Iceman.

6

HIGH SCHOOL GLORY

The summer of 1920 saw Red Grange deliver more ice in Wheaton. Herman Otto, nicknamed "Hermie" by his teammates, was helping Red that summer. The two became a perfect team on the ice wagon, talking about movies, girls, and, more importantly, football. Otto, a senior, was going to be team captain so they openly talked about the squad having a special year. Maybe even a conference championship. Then, one day on the wagon, Red had a reckless accident that almost cost him his athletic career. Red recalled the incident as follows:

> This near-tragic accident was the result of a careless habit I had of jumping on the running board of the ice truck while it moved down the street between deliveries. One morning in July, between my sophomore and junior years in high school, the handle alongside the cab of the truck, which I usually grabbed for support when I jumped on the running board, broke off in my hand. I tumbled in the street and under the truck, which was loaded with three tons of ice. Before the vehicle could be brought to a stop, the back wheel ran over the meaty part of my left leg slightly above the knee.
>
> I was momentarily stunned as Herman Otto, who worked the route with me, nervously lifted me into the truck and drove off to the doctor's office. When I got over the initial shock I became almost panic-stricken at the thought that I might never play ball again.
>
> When the doctor first looked at me, he feared the knee was crushed and amputation of my leg would be necessary. Luckily, further examination revealed the wheel missed within an inch of involving the knee joint and there was no need for such drastic action.[1]

The town physician, Dr. Raach, ordered Red confined to his bed for the next month with his left leg "hanging uncomfortably in a sling." In his autobiography, Red recalled the reaction by his boss:

> Fate was kind, for a matter of two or three weeks after I got out of bed I was walking again with little ill effect. Luke Thompson felt particularly bad about the accident (although Red was at fault) and did everything he could to help. He met (paid) all my doctor bills, besides continuing to pay my weekly salary.[2]

Red didn't finish the summer on the ice wagon. Just like he did on the football field, Red had dodged serious harm. As his junior year approached, Red was going get his third football coach in three years. This time he was going to be coached by his first true football mentor, someone who knew a little bit about being a Wheaton high school football star.

Charles Dexter Welden was born on April 21, 1894, in Wheaton, as one of three children of Samuel and May Welden. Charles's father was a builder and house contractor in town, similar to Red's uncles. When Charles turned nine years old, his father suffered a horrible fate. Spending an outing on a boat one winter afternoon, Samuel accidentally fell out of the boat and into the water. He soon caught pneumonia and died, leaving May with three children to take care of.

May found a place to rent off of Front Street. In the 1910 U.S. Census, she is listed as having been a merchant at a candy store. Her son Charles grew up playing sports despite his rather smallish size. "He went by Dink," said Bob Eustice, grandson of Charles Welden. "Everybody called him that. If you knew him you called him Dink."[3]

Dink attended Wheaton High School, becoming one of the school's first great athletes, excelling in basketball, baseball, and, of course, football. On the gridiron, he became the starting quarterback on the football team—maxing out at 5-foot-6 and weighing just 140 pounds. He learned the game at an early age, knowing as much about the sport as the head coach and calling the plays. Before Red came along it, was commonly known throughout town that the best athlete ever produced by Wheaton was "Dink" Welden.[4]

Welden chose to further his education by attending Western State Normal School in Kalamazoo, Michigan—the same school as Wheaton's previous coach and Welden's college teammate, Bill Castleman. Welden played two seasons (1914–1915) under coach Bill Spaulding, lettering both years. His first fall in Kalamazoo, Welden showed some promise on the gridiron, as the school paper wrote: "Welden from Illinois is small, but one of the best tacklers, and though light in weight goes through the line and around the ends with great success." That fall, Spaulding's Hilltoppers had a perfect 6–0 record and didn't give up a single point—outscoring opponents 180–0, including a big 10–0 victory over rival Eastern Michigan.[5]

The following year, Welden was the team's starting quarterback, earning the position for his intelligence. Spaulding allowed his signal caller the freedom to run the show. "Welden used his head, as he always does, and ran the team in fine style," wrote the school paper. After a surprising opening-game loss to Hillsdale (16–20), the Hilltoppers won their last five games to finish 5–1. In Welden's two years at Western State, his team went 11–1. Just like Castleman, Dink learned techniques for both offense and defense play, as well as game planning, motivation, and leadership, from coach Bill Spaulding.[6]

After two years, Welden graduated from Western State in the spring of 1916. He was senior class treasurer, lettered in four sports (football, baseball, basketball, track), and was ready to tackle the world—which, in 1917, literally meant fighting the world. That year, he joined the U.S. Marines, first assigned to 113th Company Marine Barracks, stationed in Santo Domingo City in the Dominican Republic. He wouldn't serve overseas during World War I. The only misstep for Welden in the Marines was a clerical mistake in the spelling of his name, Weldon, instead of Welden, which kept him in the service longer than he was supposed to stay. The following spring, Welden spent time at the Marine barracks in Charleston, South Carolina, reaching the rank of private first class. He was discharged in 1919.

After graduating from college, Welden joined the Marines and served for two years. He then returned to Wheaton to live with his mother. Soon he was recruited to teach and coach at the same high school where he was once a star athlete. The diminutive Welden was excited about the prospects of coaching the current Wheaton squad. In addition to having Red at halfback, he had three other returning letter-winners—seniors-to-be, tackle Lowell "Brute" Reynolds, back Herman Otto, and guard Laurence Henry.

The Wheaton players quickly could see that Welden knew his football stuff. Considering he was just 26 years old, he was right where his players had been just a few years ago—playing football at Wheaton High School. In a 1974 interview, quarterback Bim Frazer spoke of Coach Welden, relating, "Dink was great for being in good physical condition. He was in excellent condition. There was no excess weight on him. He didn't smoke or drink and was in as good shape when he coached us as he was when he was in high school. He also never liked his boys to swear."[7]

The entire team quickly fell in love with Coach Welden. He was almost like one of the boys. Welden even adopted one tradition that his players enjoyed. "The team went down to the (Orchard) field together, and my father always liked that," said Turryann Eustice, daughter of Charles Welden. "They would all run together, including my father, Red, and the team. They all said they liked that. That they all went down at the same time."[8]

The short jog from the school to the Orchard by coach and team made the Tigers a close-knit squad from the start. Behind the coaching of Welden, Red unleashed a combination of speed and creative ball-carrying to have his best year of football. "I changed my style of running a little that year. Formerly I had been doing a lot of stiff-arming. I tried dodging and throwing my hips from the tackler as he was about to hit me, and it worked very well," he said. "Charlie Welden was coaching the team, and he brought me forward rapidly. Our team played together like a bunch of brothers, and it was a pleasure to be on it."[9]

Welden quickly learned that Red was not only his best player, but also a once-in-a-lifetime player. Talking to sportswriter Ralph Cannon of the *Chicago Daily News* in 1924, he discussed about his prized pupil:

> Grange was never any trouble to coach. You'd just tell him what you wanted done, and he'd do it. Maybe you'd go a week without saying anything to him. He was just a natural player. Of course, he never got onto his straight arm the way he has it now until his last year in high school. He'd put his old arm down where they thought his leg would be and step away from them. Nobody in high school could tackle him.
>
> The greatest thing about Red was that he was always the first man on the field and the last one off. He hardly ever missed practice. He was always wanting to learn.[10]

The new coach saw in Grange a burning desire to be a great football player. He saw something in his pupil that burned in most great athletes—the will to succeed. Welden would help Red become a true student of the game, willing to do whatever it took to be the best on the field. Welden wasn't the only one to see the greatness in Red while at Wheaton High. Bim Frazer, starting quarterback in 1920, recalled in a 1974 interview with the *Wheaton Daily Journal* the football abilities of Red Grange:

> Red was a great team player, and everybody, in turn, played for him. His blockers might help him get around the end, but after that, he didn't need any more help.
>
> Red was just a natural coordination with such a deceptive change of pace running. He would run in an upright manner and still be able to change pace while

going full speed. He was very strong for his weight and had powerful legs with long striding. I've seen fast runners who make quick turns, but Red just ran. He was real graceful. The big difference with Red was that he never looked like he was running hard like many runners do. It all seemed so effortless for him.

He knew where the pass plays were going, about all the time, and he'd be there when the ball got there. Red was always a smart player. He had the perception to know where to go or where to be.[11]

On September 25, at the Orchard, Wheaton hosted Wauconda High, a team that had "strength and speed." Hot temperatures greeted Red, who started at quarterback for Welden. After trading touchdowns in the first quarter, Wheaton controlled the rest of the game, with Red scoring three consecutive touchdowns. In the fourth quarter, Herman Otto's touchdown grab gave Coach Welden his first victory, 41–6.[12]

One week after their great win came the lowest point of the season for the orange and black. Traveling to LaGrange to face a "heavy team," outweighing them 15 pounds per man, Wheaton was pounded, 38–0. Welden didn't have any answers for the team from Cook County. "Grange was well watched all the time. The few times that he did get away it was all on his own efforts. He had absolutely no interference. Even with this handicap he stepped off numerous big gains."[13]

Welden had his team right back on the practice field and moved Red to half-back. The extra practice time seemed to pay off. Red's next six games would be unmatched in Illinois high school football history. In the first quarter of their following game, against Geneva, Red ran through the Geneva line for two quick scores. He followed up with two more touchdown runs—including a 48-yard sprint after stiff-arming five men—to help Wheaton to an easy 42–0 victory. Red also made all six extra points, accounting for 30 total points.

The following week saw the Tigers return to the Orchard to face conference rival Batavia. As good as Red had played in the first three games of the year, he was about to get better—much better. On Red's first carry he blazed 53 yards around left end. Although the team didn't score on this drive, it was the beginning of a remarkable day. On the next two drives, he "dodged and stiff-armed men and raced ahead of the field for 76 yards and a touchdown," sidestepping defenders on a 64-yard scoring run. In the second quarter, Wheaton scored three more touchdowns, one of which was a 74-yard run around left end by Red. In the second half, Red continued his scoring spree, rushing for four more scores (22, 52, 1, and 31 yards, respectively). Red would score seven touchdowns in all and was a perfect 10-for-10 on extra points, scoring a total of 52 points in the 70–0 lopsided victory.[14]

On the field that day for Batavia was junior halfback Johnny Mauer, who, two years later, would be Red's teammate at the University of Illinois. As talented as Mauer was, he didn't lay a hand on Grange that day. "This was in high school and they were on opposite teams and he was playing safety on one side of the field," said Craig Mauer, grandson of Johnny Mauer.

> Grange just kept going and running past the defensive back on the other side of the field. So, my grandfather thought he could get him. He said, ah, here comes Grange on the play, and he kind of gave him a hip, as he called it, and he just completely shook him out of his shoes. Kind of neat then a couple of years later here they are teammates at Illinois.[15]

The October 22 edition of the *Wheaton Illinoian* featured the first individual photo of Red Grange in a local paper. Red was in full football uniform, posing with hands on hips, standing in the middle of the Orchard. Wheaton was now 3–1. What would they do for an encore? The next Saturday at the Orchard, Wheaton faced off against Downers Grove. In the opening quarter, Grange ran back a punt 72 yards for one score, followed by a five-yard run. Maloney caught two scoring passes, which were followed by Red's third score of the game, to give Wheaton a commanding 31–0 halftime lead. Red would add two more scores in the second half as Welden's squad won another lopsided game, 51–0. Red scored five touchdowns and kicked three extra points. Since losing to LaGrange, the Tigers had won three straight by outscoring their opponents 163–0. Red himself had accounted for 115 points (16 TDs, 19 XPs). The town of Wheaton was celebrating the football victories. So was Lyle Grange. Most of his attention started to turn toward his son's athletic greatness. He wouldn't miss a game, even if that meant his job duties suffered.[16] Red would later recall the support his father gave him, saying,

> The only relaxation my father had was to attend Wheaton's basketball and football games. Although he never participated in either of these sports as a boy, he grew to be a tremendous fan and to my knowledge never missed a game while I was in high school. He considered attending these contests part of his official duties. It would have been an easy matter to rob a bank while a game was going on . . . he did an awful lot for me. Encouraged me and did everything humanly possible. I certainly owe an awful lot to him.[17]

Ed Corey, a former high school classmate of Red's, remembered Lyle trying to keep fans standing on the sidelines back from the playing field. "Move back please. Give the boy room to run," recalled Corey. "(Red's father) would say move back please."[18]

Lyle had a front-row seat with most of Wheaton for the next game at the Orchard, against Naperville. His boy put on a scoring clinic, as he scored five times in the first half. He ran back the opening kickoff 65 yards, followed by scoring runs of 7, 32, 10, and 1 yards, respectively. Herman Otto capped the scoring with a 5-yard run, putting Wheaton ahead, 41-0, at the half.[19]

The second half saw Red score three more touchdowns, notably a 70-yarder, as Wheaton destroyed Naperville, 83-0. Wheaton scored 12 touchdowns, while improving their record to 5-1. Red had the game of his life. Wrote the *Wheaton Illinoian*, "And nobody stopped Grange yet! He continued his sensational playing and rolled up the largest number of points he has ever scored in one game last Saturday by making eight touchdowns and kicking 11 out of 12 goals, a total of 59 points." It was rather amazing to see that Red was getting better as the season went on. He had played six games and scored 27 touchdowns—an average of four and half touchdowns a game.[20]

Next the Tigers traveled to Hinsdale, where the fans really got on the young superstar, yelling such comments as, "Grange is a college man . . . get that old man." "Red always looked older than his age," recalled Bim Frazer. "People often said, 'Who's that old man out there?'" Yes, Red was more mature and more developed for his age, not your normal looking 17-year-old. His face and body would always look older than his actual age. Maybe Hinsdale paid too much attention to Red, as Welden gave the ball to Frazer and freshmen halfback Vic Gustafson, who accounted for three touchdowns in the first half as Wheaton led, 19-0. In the second half, Red made his presence felt, scoring three times in an easy 46-0 win.[21]

Two weeks later, Wheaton would play for the conference championship against Glen Ellyn—the squad they tied, 19-19, the previous year. Despite favoring his right leg during the game, Red scored three touchdowns, one of which was a punt return for a score in a 73-0 slaughter.

In eight games (7-1 record) in 1920, the Wheaton team outscored its opponents, 406-51, while averaging more than 50 points per game. Charles "Dink" Welden had delivered a winner for Wheaton in his first year as head coach. Red's junior year was truly remarkable. According to newspaper accounts, he had accounted for 33 touchdowns. Red was named First Team All-County, along with five of his teammates.

At the season-ending football banquet, Red was elected team captain for 1921. Following the football season, he led the basketball team to a 17-3 record and a county championship title. In the spring, he lettered again in baseball and track, where he won the state championship in the 220-yard dash and the broad jump. While in the classroom he continued to get strong marks in English (90), plane geometry (92), modern history (92), and chemistry (91).

Because of his athletic success, Red's popularity was growing. The school adored him. The town adopted him as their hero. For many, even teammates and older students, he was their idol. One Wheaton boy who was awestruck by Red was Charlie Crutcher, a young African American, who followed Red on his ice route and was taught how to do the hurdles by Red. "There was something about Grange, because he was willing to spend time with the younger kids teaching them about sports. Most high school kids wouldn't bother," recalled Crutcher.[22]

Even at a young age, Red always took being a role model seriously. He would take pride in being humble and available to anyone. He would take the time to talk to schoolmates, fans, children, or adults who wanted his autograph. Most of his willingness to do so came from his father, who said, "You couldn't be a big shot around him." Red would remain humble despite his accomplishments. His desire to be a good role model for others—especially children—would last his entire life.

The extra attention was not lost on the girls in Wheaton. Red didn't seem interested in dating, although he caught the wandering eyes of many female students at school. One of his high school teachers, Miss Helen Brauns, who taught home economics, remembers Red and his good friend, Larry Plummer, receiving extra attention. She rememebered,

> Red and Larry were at the back door of our class constantly after football practice. They'd want scraps or little leavings we had. I didn't always know it, but the girls would save cookies or other things for them. Red was very popular and got fed many, many times by the girls at football banquets in those days. Red and Larry were always the biggest eaters.[23]

Coach Welden would frequently tell one story of how Red ignored his many admirers:

> One time when we got done playing a game at the old Orchard, a couple of girls were waiting outside the locker room (at the school) to walk Red home. Now Red was very shy with girls for a long time and didn't have much to do with them. In high school he was a very dedicated athlete and was too busy with sports. He didn't have time for the women. He was strictly all business as a kid. I was outside when the girls came by and went back in to tell Red they were waiting on him. He just said, "They're going to have a long wait, because I'm going out the back door."[24]

Red wrote in his autobiography: "I never went out on dates with girls, because I didn't have any money or a decent suit of clothes to wear. The little I earned during the summers working on the ice truck was needed for bare necessities of life."[25] Most of his free time was spent working on the ice wagon for 12 to 14 hours. Despite the long hours, Red would always find time to improve his football skills. Red once talked about the extra time he dedicated to the sport he loved, declaring,

> Regardless of how many hours I put in, after dinner I used to throw a baseball or football around with my brother Garland or close pal (Beans) DeWolf until dark. By 9 p.m. I was usually in bed. As a youngster I wanted more than anything else to be a great athlete, and I realized early that it meant giving up many of the things other kids didn't have to give up to achieve that ambition. Like anything else in life, success in athletics cannot be attained unless one is willing to sacrifice for it.[26]

Aside from Beans, Red also became close with teammate Charles Dollinger, a junior at Wheaton High. The Grange apartment was above Dollinger's Drugstore. Red was always quite fond of the Dollingers, commenting,

> One of the most pleasant recollections of my Wheaton High School days concerns the Charles Dollinger family. The Dollingers were the parents of Charles Jr., a close buddy and teammate of mine on the football teams, and for three years, whenever I wasn't cooking at home, I ate my meals at their house. Mrs. Dollinger was a kindly, gentle women who gave me the mothering a boy of my age needed. Her husband, known affectionately as "Doc" to all the residents of the town, owned the corner drugstore. After a game he would serve free sodas and sundaes to all the members of the team. They were a most generous family.[27]

Emma Dollinger, who served as a nurse in the Spanish-American War, made it a habit to look out for Lyle's two boys, routinely cooking meals, sewing up clothes, and keeping a scrapbook of Red's athletic accomplishments. The Dollingers also helped out the football team. A month before school started, they allowed coach Welden and his team to stay at their summer residence in Powers Lake, Wisconsin—about 90 miles north of Wheaton. The Dollingers had a cottage there that was perfect for Welden to use to help prepare his squad for the upcoming season. According to the *Wheaton Illinoian*, "Welden is putting the men thru daily drills to limber up their bodies. Kicking, passing, and catching is the routine of the days."[28]

Red used these extra practices to hone his skills. Although he was naturally gifted with strength and speed, he worked hard during the summer of his senior year to get better. These natural physical skills paid off under the tutelage of Welden. The trip to Powers Lake was not a vacation for Red; he treated summer camp as a business trip. At about the time when Labor Day rolled around, the team returned to Wheaton. The town was excited about the upcoming football season. Even the Orchard got a makeover, according to the *Wheaton Illinoian*: "A new fence has been constructed around the entire field and should effectually keep the crowds off the field." For Red's senior year, Lyle wouldn't have to ask fans to stay back so his boy could run.[29]

In the September 16 edition of the *Wheaton Illinoian*, it mentioned the redhead: "Grange, the ace of the school and captain of this year's team, will show fans and everybody a great year, as he has been training all summer in rough work in order to get into shape. He says he is in o.k. form and wishes for a game this Saturday." After a summer delivering ice and a couple of weeks at Powers Lake, he was itching to play a game. Welden strengthened up the schedule by adding a tough Cook County school in Chicago Austin and an out-of-state opponent in Toledo (Ohio) Scott.

On September 24, a day before the first game, the *Illinoian* ran a preview of the season opener against Riverside. The article featured photos of Red and Vic Gustafson, while reporting, "Game will be called at 2:30, and if you believe in high school athletes of the clean, healthy brand you won't want to miss a single game on the home grounds or any other if you can possible be there. Give the boys and the school your support. You will get your money's worth."[30]

On a wet and muddy Orchard field, Wheaton rolled to an easy 47–6 victory. A week later, Welden's squad faced off against Chicago Austin, a team that would finish the season as Cook County runner-up. In the first quarter, Red sprinted around end to score the game's first touchdown. The second half saw the ball go back and forth, and there was no score in the half until Gustafson intercepted a ball and returned it for a score, capping a tough 21–0 victory.

Wheaton followed up the win against Chicago Austin with their first road trip to play conference foe Hinsdale. On this Saturday, Red ran beautifully behind his offensive line for four touchdowns in a 47–0 lopsided win. Covering the story, the *Illinoian* wrote, "Harold Grange is a wonder, and after one attempt his opponents seldom tried again to overtake him after he got started." Red also contributed five extra points, giving him 29 total points.[31]

Red had started his senior season on a good note; even his teammates were in awe of what he could do. Backup halfback Charles Gates recalled, "He was sneaky fast, I'd call it. You couldn't tackle that guy. He was smooth as silk, and his swivel movement of the hips was just in him. I think he could do anything."[32]

Wheaton was now 3–0. Next up was nearby Naperville. Despite a wet field, they didn't stand a chance, as the Tigers rolled to a 40–14 victory. The convincing win against Naperville set up the most intriguing matchup of the year: a road trip to Ohio to play Toledo Scott High School—a much larger school, with more than 3,900 students. Scott's line averaged more than 190 pounds, and they had just defeated their first three opponents, Ft. Wayne (55–0), Columbus High (77–0), and Wooster (52–0), in easy fashion without giving up a single point.

The squad left Wheaton at noon on Friday, October 28, as several hundred well-wishers gave coach Welden and his 17 varsity players a "rousing send-off." The game would be a disappointment in many ways. On the opening kickoff, Red booted the ball to Scott halfback Bill Hunt, who sprinted 90 yards for a score. Down 7–0 early on, Red returned the ensuing kickoff 40 yards, helping Wheaton regain some momentum. But it didn't last long. The drive stalled inside the five-yard line as an incomplete pass in the end zone turned over the ball on downs. In the second quarter, Toledo Scott scored again to take a 14–0 lead. Wheaton wouldn't see the end zone all game and was about to lose its main weapon.[33]

In the second quarter, Red would be lost for the game. "Wheaton was going again as the ball was put into play and a pass to Grange was completed, but he was thrown heavily and kicked in the head, putting him out of the game. A bruise back of the ear, which it was feared might prove to be a concussion of the brain, ended his work for the day," wrote the local press.[34]

Charles Gates replaced Red, but the team wasn't the same without him. The hit to the head seemed to be on purpose, as the Scott players wanted him out of the game. Everyone on the Wheaton team knew the Scott men wanted to get Red; one Scott player apologized to a Wheaton player for striking him after a play, saying, "I thought you were Grange." At the sounding of the final gun, Wheaton had lost, 39–0. The trip back to Wheaton was somber, especially for Red, who was in and out of consciousness for a few days.

Grange soon recovered to play the following week against York (Elmhurst) at the Orchard. In the first half, Red sprinted 70 and 80 yards, respectively, for touchdowns, as Wheaton rebounded from their first loss of the season with a 35–13 victory.

Two games remained, with Wheaton still in the hunt for a county championship. Next on tap was a game against Freeport—this would be Red's final game at the Orchard. "A small but enthusiastic crowd braved the elements and slopped around in the snow and mud for an hour and half, and were rewarded for their pluck," wrote the local paper.[35]

Playing on a sloppy, wet field, Red scored his last two touchdowns at the Orchard as Wheaton improved its record to 6–1, with a 21–0 shutout victory. The win set up a county showdown with Downers Grove for the championship. On Thanksgiving Day at 10:00 a.m., Red jogged out onto a high school football field for the last time. It would be a game to remember for young Red Grange.[36]

Wearing his orange and black jersey for the last time, Red sprinted, dodged, and stiff-armed his way to six touchdowns, including an interception return for a score. He also converted all nine of his extra points to account for 45 total points in a 63–14 shellacking of Downers Grove. "It was Harold Grange's best game for his alma mater, and he did his best, fully and completely assisted by his teammates. . . . They were weary and Grange was getting faster on each touchdown. He was also a tower of strength on defense, and his tackling was sure."[37]

Red had given his all in his final high school game. He left nothing to chance. Coach Welden was proud of his entire team, as they claimed the DuPage county championship. "As for Grange, who has played his last football game for Wheaton High, he cannot be replaced, because a competent successor hasn't been born yet," wrote the local paper.[38]

At the season-ending football banquet, Red received his fourth football letter. In his four years at Wheaton High, Grange's teams compiled a record of 21–6–1, while going 14–2 under Coach Welden in his junior and senior years. His teams scored a combined 850 points in 28 games, averaging 30.3 points per contest—while the defense gave up only 286 points, an average of just 10.2 points per game. As for Red, the local paper, the *Wheaton Illinoian*, credited him with 64 touchdowns scored in his three years as starting halfback (22 games), averaging almost three touchdowns a game.

Red always cherished his time playing for Dink Welden. "I learned more football from Welden as you will from a high school coach. He taught the fundamentals of football, and he was great," said Grange in a 1978 interview. The Wheaton Iceman ran the ball like no one had ever done before him. At least 23 of his high school touchdowns went for more than 40 yards or more, bringing the long-distance touchdown run into the sport as a regular weapon—a skill he would soon bring to the collegiate level. Red wrapped up his high school career with 16 varsity letters—four each in football, basketball, baseball, and track. He also was vice president of the Hi-Y club, athletic editor of the yearbook his senior year, and hands down the greatest athlete to ever attend Wheaton High School.[39]

His senior grades were again solid—English (82), geometry (94), advanced algebra (94), physics (86), and American history (93). On his final report card, Red's principal, Principal Gregg, said "his deportment in school has been 'good.'" In the *1922 Wheaton Orange and Black Yearbook*, in the senior class will, Red wrote, "I, Harold Grange, yield my place as hero of the girls of Wheaton High to Victor Gustafson, and award Dingy Mitchell my running shoes to help make his feet fast."[40]

On June 8, 1922, Red graduated, along with 39 other seniors. Just two weeks before receiving his diploma, Red met a man who would guide him in his next chapter, one step closer to football glory.

PART II

COLLEGE (1922–1925)

7

BOB ZUPPKE

Robert Carl Zuppke was born on July 2, 1879, in Berlin, Germany, to Franz and Hermine Zuppke. Everyone would call him Bob. He would have two younger brothers, Paul and Harmon. Bob's parents were one of more than 210,000 Germans who left the Second Reich in 1881, for a new life in America. Franz, who was a jewelry designer in Berlin, settled in a German neighborhood on the southside of Milwaukee—a city that was almost 30 percent German. He opened up his own jewelry store on Grand Avenue.

Bob and his siblings attended grammar school, where German was taught, but his family spoke English. For the rest of his life, Zuppke would speak with a thick German accent, giving colorful quotes to sportswriters throughout his coaching career. Bob regarded his mother as kind and gentle, while his father was a strict disciplinarian. Early on, Bob showed a passion and talent for art. Like one of his coaching colleagues and closest friends, Knute Rockne, Zuppke would always have other interests aside from football, including science, literature, and art.[1]

His father always discouraged him from being an artist; he didn't think he could make a living doing it, particularly at age 13, when young Robert worked as an apprentice in a sign writer's workshop for just 50 cents a week. After one year, Bob went back to school. In 1895, Bob walked two and half miles to attend West Division High School. It was here that he was introduced to a popular game called football. After several injuries to players, the school abolished the sport, but Bob was hooked. He organized and played on an amateur squad—the West Ends football team. "I was an audacious and enthusiastic young fellow in those days," Bob once recalled. "So, I organized a team called the 'West Ends.'

Unhindered by eligibility rules, we were able to get a good 11 together. Since I was head man, I made the team in a breeze. In fact, I was the star defect."[2]

After high school Bob enrolled at Milwaukee Normal School taking American, English, and Greek history courses while also doing several illustrations for the school's yearbook. Outside of the classroom he played quarterback on the football team while also playing basketball and baseball. He had now begun a lifetime affair with football. In 1901 he graduated from Milwaukee Normal School as his teaching training prepared him for a career of instructing athletes and coaches.

Zuppke's first coaching job was with a rural Milwaukee county school for $45 a month. That lasted just one year. In 1903, at the age of 24, he decided to attend graduate school at the University of Wisconsin. While in Madison, Zuppke attended football games, learning more about the sport he loved. In 1905, he earned a Ph.B. in the College of Letters and Science.

Through the University of Wisconsin, his name was brought up for a job at Muskegon High (Hackley Manuel Training) School in northern Michigan, where he would be hired as the new football coach and gymnasium director for a cool $1,000 a year. From 1906 to 1909, Zuppke quickly gained a reputation as a drillmaster. Although he didn't look the part, standing only 5-foot-7 and weighing roughly 140 pounds, he introduced uniforms and shoulder pads to players, while experiencing with new punt formations, spiral passes from center, and "flea-flicker" passes on offense. It was here that Zuppke began to develop the open type of game that he would take to the University of Illinois. In his four seasons at Muskegon High, his teams went 29-4-2. In his first season, in 1906, his team outscored its opponents, 289-6, earning the nickname "adding machines" because of the top-heavy scores they rang up against their opponents.

His success at Muskegon didn't go unnoticed. He was soon recruited by a school in the Windy City. Oak Park High School, located in west suburban Chicago, looked into hiring the fiery little coach with the funny German accent. Zuppke was offered a job coaching five teams (football, basketball, baseball, swimming, and track) and teaching five classes on Greek and Roman history.

The school had a strong sports tradition, which appealed to Zuppke, so when he received an offer of a salary of $2,000 a year, he asked when he could start. Zuppke was about to begin a three-year run that would lead him to the top of the college football world. At Oak Park from 1910 to 1912, his teams won three straight Cook County championships.

Zuppke's star was continuing to rise in the coaching ranks. This time he caught the eye of a Midwest university who wanted to compete with the best football teams in the country. The University of Illinois, originally named

Illinois Industrial University, was one of 37 universities created under the first Morrill Land-Grant Act, signed into law by President Abraham Lincoln in 1862, providing public land for the creation of agricultural and industrial colleges and universities throughout the United States. Among several cities, Urbana was selected in 1867, as the site for the new school. In 1885, the school officially changed its name to the University of Illinois. Located in Champaign–Urbana, the campus rests in east-central Illinois, approximately 140 miles from Chicago.

The school formed a football team that started playing games in 1890, with their first contest on October 2, against Illinois Wesleyan. After losing to Wesleyan, 16–0, the Fighting Illini won the rematch a few weeks later, 12–6, giving the school its first-ever football victory. The school played its home games on campus at Illinois Field, which at its peak had a capacity of 17,000.

On February 8, 1896, school presidents from the University of Chicago, the University of Illinois, the University of Michigan, the University of Minnesota, Northwestern University, Purdue University, and the University of Wisconsin got together to establish rules for eligibility and scheduling, calling their league the Western Conference—the forerunner of the Big Ten. The conference would add Indiana and Iowa in 1899, and Ohio State in 1912.

Right before the turn of the century, a former Illini player, George Huff, became head coach for five seasons (1895–1899). He compiled a mediocre record of 21–16–3, but remained in an administrative capacity that would eventually bring Zuppke to his alma mater. During the early years of the football program, the Illinois faculty ran the athletic program, a practice that was quickly deemed "not faculty business." In 1906, Huff and his Illini coaches were at a crossroads. At this time, the sport of football was being dominated by brute strength, so much so that the key offensive play, the flying wedge, was becoming a dangerous strategy. The flying wedge—and the mass plays it inspired—had deadly consequences. In 1905, there were almost 150 major injuries, and 18 boys died playing football.[3]

On January 12, 1906, football was reinvented at the inaugural meeting of the new rules-making body, which would eventually become the National Collegiate Athletic Association—the NCAA. At the meeting, the following rules were put into place:

The length of the game was reduced from 70 minutes to 60 minutes.

The neutral zone separating the offense from the defense was established.

The distance required to get a first down was increased from 5 yards to 10 yards.

Six men were required on the line of scrimmage (today you must have seven
men on the line of scrimmage).

The forward pass was legalized.

At its inception, the forward pass was subject to severe restrictions. A pass
had to be thrown from five yards behind the line of scrimmage, and an incomplete pass in the end zone that struck the ground turned the ball over to the
defense at that spot. The reforms transformed football from a game of brute
strength to a game in which finesse and quickness also mattered. Requiring
six men on the line of scrimmage eliminated mass plays like the flying wedge.
Increasing the yards needed for a first down encouraged outside runs, and the
forward pass ultimately refocused the entire concept of play. Most importantly,
players stopped dying on the field.

Newspaper dailies started to cover college football more intensely and with
more detail, leaving the lesser and unorganized sport of professional football
in the dust. The "Sunday game" was thought as unprofessional, operated by
scoundrels and played by drunks and hoodlums. The college game increased
its popularity via hiring the best coaches in the country.

Arthur Hall (1907–1912) had the Illinois program going in the right direction, especially in 1910, when the Illini completed their first undefeated season
(7–0). But the next two years saw a decline in the win column, as Hall's teams
had 4–2–1 and 3–3–1 records. The team was also losing the race in the Big
Ten, as such powerhouse teams as Michigan, Chicago, and Minnesota were
consistently producing championship seasons and All-American players. From
1895 to 1912, Michigan, led by the great Fielding Yost (1901, first year), won
82 percent of its games (89 percent of Big Ten games), while the University of
Chicago, led by Amos Alonzo Stagg (first year, 1892), won 81 percent of its
games (72 percent of Big Ten games). This is in comparison to Illinois, which
won 67 percent of its games, while only 49 percent of Big Ten games. At Minnesota, Henry Williams won 81 percent of his games and seven Big Ten titles,
including three in a row from 1909 to 1911.

The in-state rivalry with Stagg's University of Chicago Maroons was one-
sided. From 1904 to 1912, the Illini had a disappointing record of 1–7–1, while
being outscored 214–29, featuring a 63–0 whitewash in 1906. After the 1912
season, part-time coach Arthur Hall resigned after the 3–3–1 campaign. George
Huff, a member of the school's first football team in 1890, had been named the
school's athletic director in 1901. He was now ready to hire not only a head
coach who could coach young boys to be men, but also a man who could beat
the other legendary Big Ten coaches, someone who wasn't afraid to go toe-

to-toe with the likes of Yost, Stagg, and Williams. Huff wanted Zuppke as his next coach. A meeting was set. Zuppke was impressed by his future boss. He commented,

> The thing that really did make a tremendous impression on me was "G" Huff personality. He told me that Illinois hadn't been doing too well in football and that they need a football coach with teeth. He didn't paint a glowing picture of the job; he just dealt the facts face up. He offered me $2,700 a year, and I accepted it. . . . I've never regretted the decision to go to Illinois. It is my home, my life.[4]

On December 12, 1912, the Illinois athletic board recommended a three-year appointment as full-time head football coach at $2,700 a year. The next day, Zuppke signed the contract. Huff would be Zuppke's boss for the next 23 years. The rise of Zuppke from high school football coach in Muskegon to the University of Illinois happened quickly for the 34-year-old coach, but Zuppke was ready for the challenge. He had a coaching philosophy already established and was willing to teach it to his players. In his book *Coaching Football*, Zuppke laid out his "Illini 11 of Coaching."

1. There is no royal way to success as a coach. Properly directed efforts of the squad and yourself, plus hard work, point the way. Cultivate poise.
2. First, you must clearly have in mind what you are going to coach, and secondly, know how to impart that knowledge to the squad.
3. Keep your coaching simple and your English plain. Make sure that the squad understands you. Go from the simple to complex.
4. Learn to select the basic points. Emphasize them! Do not clutter up the main highway with vague, unessential details.
5. Concentrate on important details. Demand perfection. Don't permit careless play.
6. Stress fundamentals. They must be the rock-bottom of your game. To neglect them is to your football structure on quicksand.
7. Learn to turn a defeat in your favor. Don't dodge responsibility.
8. Keep abreast with the game. Don't get sidetracked. There are no copyrights in football. When you see a good point, use it.
9. Too much coaching becomes nagging. Test your squad continually to see if they are mastering their instruction.
10. Develop the spirit of mental and physical aggressiveness in your squad.
11. Put your heart and soul into coaching. Be enthusiastic, encouraging, painstaking, and buoyant.[5]

Zuppke believed in constant motivation of his team. Said Bob, "Don't let your gloom depress the squad. Be a gentleman. Be an inspiration to the boys, both on and off the field. Stress hard, clean playing and good sportsmanship. Be straightforward, impartial, and forceful. The boys should play for the school and not themselves."[6]

Even with only a few years of high school coaching under his belt Zuppke was a master strategist on the gridiron, teaching his players everything about the game—not only how to play the sport, but also how to coach it. He especially loved teaching techniques to his players. Along with praising young men, Zuppke could give his players a good chewing out. One sportswriter labeled him "Little Napoleon." Handling losing was taught just as much as celebrating winning. "A losing squad needs your help more than a winning team," he said. "Bolster them with confidence. Make them feel that you believe in them and will stick to them through thick and thin. Train yourself as well as the men to be loyal—win or lose."[7]

His offensive philosophy on the field was simple. Throughout his time at Illinois he loved running the ball using two formations. The first one was the Illinois formation. The Illinois formation had more line-plunging power than the T formation and was just as deceptive. Zuppke used this formation for strong end running, and it lent itself easily to the development of reverses, hidden-ball plays, and crisscrosses. The backfield is arranged in such a manner as to give added strength to the so-called weak-side attack. In the Illinois formation, the fullback is three yards back of the line of scrimmage, directly behind the seam between strong-side guard and tackle. The left halfback is almost four yards back of the line, directly behind the weak-side guard, and the tailback is four and half to five yards back of the scrimmage line, directly behind the center. Any of the three backfield men can handle the ball.

The second one, the T formation, under Zuppke, was an adaptation of the two-wing formation coached by Glenn "Pop" Warner at Carlisle and later on at Stanford. At the core it was a strong formation, but unlike Warner's system, the fullback didn't need to be the forward passer. His formation gave the advantage of having stronger outside end runs, which would benefit Grange later on.

In Zuppke's T, the fullback was taught to feint, handle the ball dexterously, and run both hard and elusively, while the player lined up a yard or two to his rear was coached to throw passes and run the ends. In this formation, the fullback was lined up three yards back of the scrimmage line, directly behind the strong-side guard. The tailback was four and half yards back of the line of scrimmage and directly behind the fullback. The wingbacks were one yard from the line of scrimmage and to the outside of the ends. Each end lined up a half-yard from his nearest teammates. Later on, the modern T formation would have a quarterback under center.[8]

One of Zuppke's main goals was to beat in-state rival Chicago, led by the game's most famous coach, Amos Alonzo Stagg. In 1913, Illinois lost, 28-7, to Stagg's boys, but the tide was about to turn. From 1914 to 1921 (the year before Red would arrive), Illinois got the best of the Maroons, going 5-2-1, with four shutout wins. In 1914, Illinois won their first three conference games, defeating Indiana (51-0), Ohio State (37-0), and Northwestern (33-0) on their way to winning the Big Ten in just Zuppke's second season. Illinois finished with an unbeaten mark of 6-0, outscoring their opponents 224-22.

Credited with such early innovations as the onside kick, the screen pass, guards pulling to protect the passer, the spiral snap from center, and the huddle, Zuppke had become one of the sport's greatest teachers. In his first eight seasons at Illinois (1913-1920), he went 40-12-5, while going 29-9-5 in the Big Ten. But 1921 saw a setback, as Illinois complied a disappointing 3-4 overall record and tallied just one conference win. After the awful campaign, Zuppke needed to recharge his team. He would do it in a big way.

Zuppke hated to recruit players, relying heavily on alumni, coaching contacts, fraternity rushing on campus, and his yearly visits to the Illinois state interscholastic track meets. From 1914 to 1941, 367 of his players, almost 84 percent, came from the state of Illinois, with 30 percent coming from Chicago and Cook County.[9]

On May 25, 1922, Zuppke decided to attend the state's interscholastic track meet, held in Champaign-Urbana. At this meet, he saw a speedy sprinter from Wheaton who would win the 220-yard dash and finish third in the 100-yard dash. After the meet, Zuppke made it a priority to talk to Red. Said Grange,

> Zuppke introduced himself, and he walked about a half a block with me. Zup was very warm and friendly, and I remember him saying, "If you come down here to school I believe you'll stand a good chance of making our football team." Those words of encouragement from one of football's greatest figures meant more to me at that time than it is possible to express.[10]

Zuppke's words did have a lasting impression on Red. It got him to really think about going to Illinois. The Illinois coach also had another secret weapon at his disposal: one of Red's mentors. George Dawson, who was a member of the Illinois football team, had Red's ear, constantly encouraging him to come to

Champaign. The final straw for Red was that Illinois was the state's university and the cheapest school he could attend. Anything to help his father, who was going to pay for his education.

It was off to college.

8

FRESHMAN TO ALL-AMERICAN

In the fall of 1922, Harold "Red" Grange left Wheaton for Champaign–Urbana. He traveled the 150-mile trip south to the University of Illinois, arriving in town with nothing more than the shirt on his back. "Arriving on campus with the battered, second-hand [*sic*] trunk my father bought for me. I must have looked more like a refugee from Siberia than a university student," recalled Red.[1]

Red and his secondhand trunk headed to the Zeta Psi fraternity house, located at 201 East John Street, northwest of the main campus. He was greeted there by his good friend, George Dawson. Just a few days after getting settled, some of Red's fraternity brothers lined up the pledges to recommend what activities or sports they would be trying out for. Red told his brothers he was going out for basketball and track, thinking those would be the two sports for which he had the best chance of making the teams. His request fell on deaf ears, as the brothers quickly told Red he was going out for football. George Dawson had told them of his gridiron stardom at Wheaton, and the brothers knew having a star football player would help the prestige of the house.

Red then walked to football practice. Once there, he paused, stared out at the practice field, and saw more than 150 freshmen warming up. He quickly turned around and headed back to the frat house. Although he was a star at Wheaton, he thought he didn't have a chance against bigger players from bigger schools. "What chance have I got against all those big guys?" he asked himself. Once again, his fraternity brothers didn't listen to the young freshman. They told him to go out for football or he would have to face the paddle. After hearing the threat of paddling his rear end, Red quickly changed his tune. He returned to practice to take another look at the situation. "When I took a longer look around," he said, "I discovered much to my surprise that although most of the aspirants were much bigger than I, they couldn't run as fast nor handle a football as well. I began to get a little more confidence."[2]

Among the more than 150 candidates on the field, it was Red who quickly made an impression on freshman coach Burt Ingwersen. The 24-year-old Ingwersen played three years for Zuppke (1917–1919), including being a starter at tackle on the 1919 Big Ten championship team. He made All-Conference two years in a row (1918–1919) and graduated in 1920, with an engineering degree. That fall, he played pro football with the Decatur Staleys in the new American Professional Football Association (forerunner of the NFL), coached by former Illinois star and Zuppke man George Halas. The following fall, Zuppke hired Ingwersen away from pro football to be one of his assistants and coach the freshman team.

Red was now a member of the Illinois freshman team, but since he was a first-year player he didn't get the top-notch equipment like the varsity players. Red recalled,

> When I was issued my frosh football uniform equipment neither the shoes nor the uniform fit me properly. Before I could wrangle another pair of shoes, I had developed corns and blisters on my feet. The number on the back of my ill-fitting jersey happened to be 77. It was just dished out to me, I never asked for it. I got to thinking it was pretty lucky and asked to keep it permanently when I returned in my sophomore year.[3]

After hearing about his sore feet, Dawson helped Red get a pair of cleats that fit. Getting number 77 was just the luck of the draw. In later years, Red would claim that he stood in line when the player in front of him got jersey number 76 and the player behind him got number 78. Whatever the circumstance was in how Red acquired the number, he made "77" one of the most famous jersey numbers of all time. Despite his initial reluctance to go out for football, it became apparent early on that Red was going to be the future of Illinois football.

The freshman squad was soon reduced to 60 players. Some of them would help Illinois recapture football glory. Under Ingwersen the team quickly picked up Zuppke's system, so much so that Zup started paying more attention to the squad, leaving his varsity squad neglected. Since the freshman team's main purpose was to prepare the varsity for games, the two units would soon find themselves on the same field.

On Saturday, September 30, the first big scrimmage of the fall took place. Grange lined up as the starting right halfback. The fans saw several big plays by the young freshman. But the highlight for coaches and fans was seeing Red scamper home for a touchdown on a 50-yard punt return. The varsity (1921 record of 3–4), which featured Dawson, Wally McIlwain, Emil Schultz, Len Umnus, and Jim McMillian, had their hands full. The next day, the school's newspaper, the *Daily Illini*, took notice of the redhead from Wheaton, writing, "The chief excitement of the battle coming when Grange circled the varsity ends, when he caught Clark's punt in midfield and zig-zagged [*sic*] 50 yards for a touchdown."[4] Years later, Bob Zuppke would remember this first scrimmage, when he first saw his most prized pupil:

> The first time Grange attracted my attention was when the redhead, then a fresh-man, returned a punt through the varsity for a touchdown in a full-length game between the frosh and varsity. I noticed his high knee action and his extraordinary pickup. He had a pronounced tendency to run wide, toward the sidelines, instead of cutting back. Hence, I told Burt Ingwersen, who was then our freshman coach, to work on Red to help him overcome his fault.[5]

Attending practices became easier for Red since he loved football; even the bumps and bruises were tolerable. Red would be elected captain of the fresh-man team. The *Daily Illini* wrote, "The newly elected captain has ability which is truly exceptional, and his great points have been brought out by coach In-gwersen in his playing against the varsity." Zuppke's attention to the freshman team might have contributed to the Illinois varsity finishing with a disappointing 2–5 overall record (2–4 in conference). It was Zuppke's second straight losing season. That was about to change thanks to the freshman class he was keeping his eyes on.[6]

During his first year at Illinois, Red's social life mostly revolved around the fraternity house. He got along with his frat brothers but was never the "life of the party." Usually he kept to himself, finding time to study and discover ways of getting better at football. "He was very likable, very fine to have around the house," commented Wendall Trenchard, a former Zeta Psi brother, in a 1974 interview with the *Urbana Daily Courier*. "He was reserved and quiet and never let his success go to his head." Red did make one friendship with an older stu-dent who lived outside of the frat house.[7]

Marion Fowler Coolley was born on August 10, 1898, in Newtown, Illinois, to Dr. Elmer B. Coolley and his wife, Mary. Elmer Coolley was the son of a Presbyterian minister who preached religion and education. It was important to him that Elmer get a first-class education. It was an area in which Elmer flourished. He attended grammar school at Cherry Grove School and eventually graduated with honors from Newman (Illinois) High School. After high school, Elmer attended two years of college at Lincoln University in Philadelphia. He parlayed that into a doctorate degree from Rush Medical School, outside of Chicago, in 1889. At the young age of 21, he was a doctor. He returned closer to home in Vermilion County, setting up a practice in Danville, Illinois. It was here that Dr. Coolley would become the most accomplished physician and surgeon in town. He had an office in the Temple Building and was on staff at Lake View Hospital.

After a few years in Danville, Dr. Coolley met his future wife. In 1891, he married Mary Ellen Fowler, whom everyone called "Nellie." The couple would go on to have two boys, Elmer Burt Coolley Jr. (1894) and Marion Fowler Coolley (1898). Elmer Jr. was not very fortunate. He was stricken with tuberculosis and died when he was just 27 years old. For the rest of his life, Dr. Coolley would fight this disease, setting up a sanitorium in Danville to help the cause. Marion's health was only slightly better. He would suffer heart, lung, and other ailments throughout his life. "He had a bad heart and bad lungs," said Marilyn Coolley-Carley, daughter of Marion Coolley. "He had an operation for his lungs later on in life. He eventually never healed from all these surgeries, and the whole time from 1946 to 1956 he spent in hospitals at St. Luke's in Chicago or Mayo to get well. He never seemed to be a healthy man."[8]

In 1905, Dr. Coolley built a home for his family in Danville at 112 Pine Street, which still stands today as a historical home. The Colonial Revival brick house had two floors surrounded by a huge porch leading into the house. On the left side of the home was another entrance leading inside. Inside the home were three bedrooms, two baths, and more than 1,700 square feet. The house was located in one of Danville's nicest neighborhoods.

Marion would follow in his father's footsteps in getting a proper education. He would attend Danville High School, earning the simple nickname "Doc." He would participate in multiple activities, including the spring play, Junior Red Cross, class track, and baseball, and was a four-year member of the Athletic Association (team manager), as well as class president as a sophomore and senior. Before his senior year, Marion tried to join the service for World War I, but because of his health he was turned down several times. Eventually, in June 1917, he was selected to serve in the Ambulance Corp, in the Rainbow Division. He served one month before being dishonorably discharged. He was described as "character very good . . . service honest and faithful. . . . No AWOL."[9]

He returned for his senior year at Danville High, graduating in 1918. In the school's yearbook, *The Medley*, the following appears: "'Doc's a good old boy.

Notorious Doctor of Politics. A little too much so perhaps. Well, we'll forgive him. There's much that's likeable in him."[10]

The following fall, Marion enrolled in classes at the University of Illinois. Standing a shade taller than six feet, with a slender build, the brown-haired, brown-eyed Coolley majored in general business. While on campus he pledged and lived at the Sigma Alpha Epsilon fraternity house. Marion was outspoken and energetic as a student, and he always liked to wear nice clothes, usually a suit and tie, often wearing bow ties. He became involved in several clubs and committees, including the Commerce Club, Mixer Committee, Junior Cap and Prom committees, and Stadium Homecoming Committee.

"He had a great interest in sports but didn't have the health to play. He was not healthy, not even in college," said Marilyn Coolley-Carley. Being seen around campus was also a top priority for "Doc" Coolley. Wanting to be a part of the social scene, he made sure to know the school and the town of Champaign–Urbana very well. Coolley must've really liked campus life, because he was in no hurry to graduate, taking classes at his own pace. His health didn't help the journey either, as by the time Red had arrived on campus Coolley had already had four years of classes. So, he had time to get to know Red and show him around town in his car—something that Red didn't have. The two quickly became good friends.[11]

As for his work in the classroom, Red had his ups and downs throughout the year. In his first semester, he struggled, with several Ds and one failure: accountancy 1A (D), economics (B), rhetoric (D), mathematics 2 (D), mathematics 4 (failure), hygiene (C), physical education (A), military A (A), and military B (B). His failure in mathematics forced Red to retake the class, which he passed in the second semester with a C. His second semester grades were much better, with Red passing economics (B), accountancy 1B (B), physical education (A), military A and B (A), and history 2B (C). His only failure was his rhetoric class, which he retook during the summer at Wheaton College and passed.[12]

As his first year of college was coming to a close, Red had a serious conversation with his good friend, George Dawson. Decades later, Red would always remember his mentor's words: "Red, I'm convinced you have what it takes to become a great football player, but don't ever let it go to your head. Never get to the point where you think you're better than the next guy, because if you do, you'll never go on to realize your full capabilities."[13]

Red returned to Wheaton for the summer. He was back on the ice truck working for L. C. Thompson. His job on the ice wagon continued to help him physically. As the hot summer days passed by, Red got excited about the prospect of playing for Zuppke's varsity team. He was physically ready to show what he could do. Back on campus the excitement for the football season was building. A new stadium, Memorial Stadium, would be ready for the fall, and Zuppke knew he had a promising squad for 1923. The team was built to compete with the best teams in the Big Ten. But the cupboard wasn't bare for Coach Zuppke. He had a top-notch line with team captain Jim McMillian and Roy Miller at guards, Bunny Oakes and Walter "Mush" Crawford at tackle, and V. J. Green at center. Ends were manned by Fred Rokusek, Ted Richards, and backup Emil Schultz. The backfield was young but talented. At quarterback was Harry "Swede" Hall, while the halfback slots were manned by Wally McIlwain (junior) and Red (sophomore), with burly Earl Britton (sophomore) at fullback.

Red and Britton quickly began to build a connection, both on and off the field. On the field, Britton was the lead blocker on most end runs in Zuppke's offensive scheme. His 200-pound frame easily made holes for the swift Red to run through. Red returned the favor as Britton's personal holder when Britton would line up to kick extra points and field goals. Off the field Britton was Red's closest friend. The two came from the same region, with Elgin being just 20 miles from Wheaton. They both enjoyed going to the movies and talking about life. Their friendship would last their entire lives.

During training camp, Red worked hard on his ball-carrying skills, trying to improve every part of his game. One aspect of his game was very obvious: "I've always had good eyes, and I think that they, as much as my speed, helped me," he related, "for I was quick to see what the opposing player was about to do. I depended upon the straight arm a great deal (too)."[14]

As training camp continued, Red's first varsity game, against the University of Nebraska, was fast approaching. Preseason news about the teams of the Big Ten was soon being published by the major Midwestern newspapers. At this time, as the baseball season was ending, most of the Midwest's attention in sports turned to college football—with professional football a distant second. The Big Ten schools, as well as Notre Dame, had major headlines in the Chicago dailies, which included six leading titles: *Tribune*, *Herald-Examiner*, *Daily News*, *American*, *Daily Journal*, and *Evening-Post*. All six wrote about college football. One of the sportswriters covering the college football beat was Warren Brown of the *Chicago Herald-Examiner*.

Brown was born near San Francisco in 1894. He graduated from the University of San Francisco before getting his first newspaper job with the *San Francisco Bulletin*. After serving in the U.S. Army during World War I, Brown returned to the newspaper shortly before taking a job with William Randolph Hearst's *San Francisco Call and Post*. In the early 1920s, he was transferred to New York, where he worked for a year. His final newspaper move was in 1923, to Chicago, to work for Hearst's *Chicago Herald-Examiner*, mainly writing about baseball and college football.

Late in the summer of 1923, Brown was given his first major writing assignment for the *Herald-Examiner*, covering the National Amateur Golf Championship, to be held at Flossmor Country Club in Cook County. Not an expert on golf, Brown decided to do some homework on the sport before covering one of the biggest golf events of the year. Brown headed out to Chicago Golf Club, located in Wheaton. While there, he engaged in a conversation with one of the caddies. Somehow the two got around to talking about football. Brown dominated the conversation, talking about the Ivy League powers from the East he had just seen the year before, for example, Yale and Harvard. He also touted the exploits of such All-American players as Bo McMillian (Centre College) and Brick Muller (California), as well as top coaches Andy Smith (California) and Pop Warner (Pittsburgh).

After hearing that Brown rambled on about players and coaches from the East Coast and West Coast, the caddy brought up a player from Wheaton whom Brown had never heard of. "Wait till you get down to Illinois. They have one of our boys down there this year. His name's Red Grange. Wait till you see him go. I think it was George Dawson who got him to go there," said the caddy. "What does this Grange do?" Brown asked the caddy. "What does he do?" the caddy repeated. "He runs!" Brown would go on to cover every Grange football game at Illinois. He would be the first to write about him on a daily basis.[15]

Illinois's first opponent of 1923 would be the University of Nebraska. On October 6, Red put on his number 77 jersey for the first time as a varsity player. He would stick to a routine when playing games in college. In 1925, Red revealed,

> Before going into practice, I don [*sic*] (a) harness which weighs approximately 15 pounds, consisting of knee and shoulder pads; however, in a game I play without the knee pads and prefer to shed the shoulder armor, for I feel freer without such equipment. Backfield men also guard against ankle injuries by "strapping" or tapping their ankles before games.[16]

With his ankles taped and no knee pads in his football pants, Red jogged out of the locker room for his first college football game. He would be Zuppke's starting left halfback. More than 10,000 fans filled Illinois Field to get their first glimpse of Red Grange. Red was nervous, and his first varsity touch proved that. After the opening kickoff, the Illini defense forced a three and out. On the ensuing punt, Red fielded the ball, then promptly fumbled it away, with

Nebraska recovering. His first varsity touch resulted in a turnover on his own 40-yard line. Red felt miserable. It was not the way he wanted to start his college career. Luckily, the Cornhuskers fumbled it right back. After a sigh of relief, Red went right back to work. His first carry was off tackle for a six-yard gain. He took a hit; now he was ready to go. At the beginning of the second quarter, Red made his first big play. Fielding another punt, he sprinted 35 yards down to the Nebraska five-yard line. On the next play, he circled around left end for his first varsity touchdown. Britton's extra point made the score 7–0. A few drives later, Britton added a 25-yard field goal for a 10–0 halftime lead.

The second half started slow for Zuppke's boys. After an Illinois fumble, Nebraska scored its only touchdown of the game, cutting the lead to 10–7. In the fourth quarter, Red put the finishing touches on an Illinois victory. He caught a 30-yard touchdown pass from Britton and made another highlight-reel play by returning a punt 66-yards for a score, giving the Illini a convincing 24–7 win. According to stats complied by Illinois, Grange played 39 minutes and touched the ball 27 times (20 rushes, 3 receptions, and 4 punt returns) for 208 total yards.

Red scored three touchdowns in his first varsity game. It was like he was back at the Orchard in Wheaton. The following Saturday found Zuppke's boys back out on Illinois Field to face Butler University—a team that had beat the Illini, 10–7, in 1922. It would be the last game at Illinois Field before Memorial Stadium was ready to go.

Zuppke had planned to sit Grange to rest him for the Big Ten opener the following week against Iowa, but the plan didn't work out. After a sluggish first-half performance, the Illini found themselves tied, 7–7. It was time for Red to rescue his team. Sent into the game in the second half, Red showed off his running skills for the second straight game. Running around end and up the middle, he scored two touchdowns in the final period to give Illinois a 21–7 victory.

During this time, Red started a routine after games. Because he didn't care for the attention he was starting to get for his football abilities, he chose to accompany his friend Marion Coolley to see his parents in Danville. The 32-mile trip to the east gave the two time to talk, sharing stories about football, business, and girls. Red would stay for dinner, sometimes spending the night at the Coolley home on Pine Street.

Next up was the conference opener, a road game at Iowa, a team that was 3–0 and had just defeated Purdue. The first half saw a defensive struggle. Red couldn't get untracked behind his blocking. Later on, Earl Britton kicked a 50-yard field goal to give Illinois a 3–0 halftime lead. In the third quarter, Iowa had its best offensive drive of the game. Wes Fry tossed a touchdown pass to Richard Romey to give the Hawkeyes a 6–3 lead.

It was gut-check time for Zuppke's offense. He gave a simple order—get the ball to Grange. With less than five minutes remaining, Illinois took over the ball at its own 19-yard line. On four pass plays, the ball went to Red three times for big yards, notably a 30-yard catch and run. The ball now rested at the three-yard line of Iowa. Red took the handoff and swept around left end for the go-ahead touchdown. Britton, in his excitement, missed the extra point. It didn't matter, as the Illini defense sealed the 9–6 victory.

On campus, more than 3,000 Illinois students and fans packed the Gym Annex to listen to the game on the gridgraph (play-by-play). They went nuts when Grange scored. The *Daily Illini* wrote, "In the delirium that followed Grange's successful run, chairs were smashed, hats lost, and the crowd went wild with delight."[17]

One week after the Iowa game, Illinois faced off against rival Northwestern, a road game in Chicago at Cubs Park (now called Wrigley Field). Overcast skies in the Windy City didn't deter 32,000 fans from coming out to Cubs Park. All the Chicago sportswriters, one of whom was Warren Brown, sat in the press box that day. One special fan who made the trip was Lyle Grange. Getting time off from his police work, he saw his son play college football for the first time. Throughout the game Illinois showed good balance running and passing. Red, from his left halfback spot, ran around right end for the game's first touchdown. Later in the quarter, he again flashed his football brilliance. After fumbling the ball to Northwestern, he made up for the mistake by plucking a Wildcats forward pass at his own 10-yard line. He then sprinted and dodged defenders for a 90-yard interception return for a touchdown. This play really made Warren Brown take notice of the redhead from Wheaton he had heard so much about. Lyle Grange was "overcome with joy and pride."[18]

In the second quarter, Grange's third touchdown, a run off right tackle, gave Illinois a 22–0 halftime lead. The ballgame was over. Warren Brown was convinced he was watching the best player in college football. In the October 29 edition of the *Chicago Herald-Examiner*, Brown wrote an entire article on Red. His headline read, "Watch Grange! Now Slogan of Big 10 Coaches; Illini Star Has Scored 54 Points This Season; Which Proves Zuppke Was Right, That Wheaton Boy's Attack Demands Attention." He also wrote, "Grange is the center ring performer of the Zuppke circus." At about this time Brown would refer to Grange as a "Galloping Ghost." In several interviews later in his life, Grange would give Brown credit for giving him the iconic nickname, including in a full-scale interview with *American Heritage* in 1974. It was at this time that the Galloping Ghost was born.[19]

Grange had played just four varsity games and scored nine touchdowns. He was tops in the Big Ten in scoring. Next up was the toughest opponent on the schedule: the University of Chicago, coached by Amos Alonzo Stagg. The Maroons were also undefeated at 4–0, with two conference wins over Northwestern and Purdue. During his time at Chicago, Stagg hired advance scouts to help him with his opponents. In 1923, he had as many as five different scouts attend Illinois games to write up reports on Zuppke's team. Among those who scouted Illinois's first four games were N. H. Norgren, E. D. Huntington, H. A. Mefford, Terry Hitchherd (who was captain of the 1905 Chicago football team), and H. O. Crisler.

Crisler played for Stagg as a starting end from 1919 to 1921. Stagg nicknamed him "Fritz." In 1922, he was hired by Stagg to be one of his assistant coaches (1922–1929). After leaving the Maroons in 1930, Crisler went on to coach 18 seasons as head coach of Minnesota (1930–1931), Princeton (1932–1937), and Michigan (1938–1947). He compiled an overall record of 116–32–9, winning almost 80 percent of his games at Michigan, including three national championships. Crisler was in the stands at Cubs Park to watch Illinois destroy Northwestern. After the game, he wrote his scouting report, featuring his opinion of Red Grange:

> To me Illinois seems to be a one-man team with everything built around Grange. During the first half it was the feats of Grange which were directly responsible for Illinois' scores. After Grange was taken out, Illinois seemed to weaken, and they were held almost nip and tuck by Northwestern.
>
> Grange, of course, is a remarkable player. On his runs around defensive end and tackle he is led almost a yard by center. He runs from five or six yards back and prefers to go around. He would start out almost directly at the end and then give ground for three or four yards as he was outrunning the defense. Not once did I see him cut back; when forced in he would pass the line of scrimmage and would still bear outwardly. He was used on runs to the weak side as readily as on the strong, but about 90 percent of the time he was used on the wide side of the field. He feints very well, dodging either in or out, but prefers to dodge so he finally can use his left arm as a stiff arm. He decidedly likes to run to his right because his left stiff arm is much more natural and effective than his right. He does not stiff-arm well with his right. All his long gains were made around Illinois' right. He was used to punch into the line but without much success.[20]

Another scout, H. A. Mefford, after watching the Butler game, wrote,

> At that time, the Illinois team looked very much like the Zup teams of the past two seasons with the exception of Grange, who appeared to be a whiz. . . . Grange is what I call a knifer. That is, he goes in a straight line and never cuts back but drives and tries to knife out using his speed to outrun the defensive men coming up to meet him.[21]

Stagg was preparing to stop Grange. He would have a hard time doing it. As both teams were game planning to battle one another, news of new Memorial Stadium was making headlines everywhere. College football facilities were now being built by many schools following the rise in popularity of the sport. The East Coast establishment, which helped popularize the game, had several models to choose from—Harvard Stadium (40,000 capacity), the Yale Bowl (61,000), and Palmer Stadium on Princeton's campus (42,000)—which had already generated additional revenues for their schools. Ohio State University built Ohio Stadium in 1922, with a capacity of almost 70,000. The Big Ten would see a flurry of new stadiums in the Roaring Twenties—Purdue and Minnesota in 1924, Northwestern in 1926, Michigan's "Big House" in 1927, and Iowa in 1929.

Zuppke, athletic director Huff, and school president David Kinsley helped the school garner more than $1.7 million in donations from more than 2,100 students, alumni, and fans to help build the new facility. Memorial Stadium was named as a memorial to the Illinois men and women who gave their lives for their country during World War I. Their names appear on 200 columns that support the east and west sides of the grounds. It took more than 2,700 tons of structural steel, 1,000 tons of reinforcing bars, 4.8 million bricks, 50,000 barrels of cement, 404 miles of lumber, and 17 miles of seats covered with 21 acres of paint to complete the stadium. It was a beautiful new facility for the school. The university's athletic publicity man, Mike Tobin, would write several of the passages on the columns. The U-shape design mirrored the construction of Harvard Stadium and the newly built Ohio Stadium. The original capacity was a little more than 55,000, with the ability to have standing room only.[22]

The Friday night before the Chicago game, Zuppke took his players to Champaign Country Club—a routine for home games—to run a short walk-through and eat dinner. These private gatherings on Friday afternoons allowed the players to get their minds set for Saturday games. On game day, the city of Champaign–Urbana was buzzing with excitement. Alumni and fans were making their rounds throughout the new stadium. A record crowd was expected.

Even the city of Wheaton was planning to be there. More than 200 citizens—including Mayor Marion J. Pittsford—made their way south. They were there to support Illinois but mainly to cheer on their native son.

A light drizzle fell as the new stadium opened. Illinois ticket manager Frank Beach announced that 61,305 spectators attended the first-ever game at Memorial Stadium. It was another defensive battle, as neither team gave any ground on the new field, made sloppy by the weather. Stagg's scouting reports helped slow down Red some, as his famous end runs were stopped, but after a scoreless half Red led the most important drive of the game. Midway through the third quarter, the Illinois offense took over the ball at its own 37-yard line. Using Zuppke's power formations, the offense ran the ball on 10 consecutive plays, with McIlwain carrying the ball four times and Red carrying it on six occasions. On the 10th play, Red wormed his way through the middle to cross the goal line from three yards out. It would be the only score of the game, as Zuppke again got the best of Stagg. Red was the difference in the game.[23]

After the Chicago game, Red wasn't quite done with all the attention. When he returned to the Zeta Psi house, many former brothers, fans, and alumni, as well as the big congregation of folks from Wheaton, had gathered out front of the house in the rain for a chance to meet Red. Being polite, he stood out in the drizzling rain for more than an hour, greeting and shaking hands with everyone. Everyone wanted to talk about the game, and Red obliged, mainly by shaking his head. He was usually embarrassed and uncomfortable talking about his accomplishments.[24]

Two days after the game, Warren Brown was still writing about his prized celebrity. "So much for what 'Red's' mud galloping did last Saturday for his conference, his team, and his coach," said Brown. But the nature of all this attention would soon change. By the time his next game rolled around, Red's name would be seen in a different light—a negative one.

A report surfaced out of Madison, Wisconsin, that Red had played professional football with the Green Bay Packers—coached by Curly Lambeau. Pro football, and the first few years of the NFL, which was organized in 1920, had battled the problem of their teams paying college players to play pro ball. But this particular rumor was untrue.[25]

The rumor that had been reported had Red playing with the Packers under the last name "Smith." The Packers denied that Grange had ever played for them. Red spoke out about the allegation. "I have never played football any place in the world except Illinois and at Wheaton High School. Why I don't think I even know where Green Bay is," he said, laughing.[26] Mike Tobin issued a statement: "The United Press rumor about Grange playing professional football is absolutely false, and it will be a crime against the greatest player in the west to 'play this up.'" This was Red's first go-around with being associated with professional football. It wouldn't be the last.[27]

On November 10, Illinois hosted Wisconsin at Memorial Stadium. The crowd gathered was not quite as large as for the Chicago game, but 35,000 fans assembled to witness another great Grange performance. Early in the first quarter, Red was dominant. Four carries around end netted 13, 11, and 30 yards, and the final sprint of 26 yards resulted in a touchdown. Moments later Britton, booted a 34-yard field goal. The 10-0 lead held up for the rest of game. The Illini remained undefeated, at 6-0.

After the hard contest against Wisconsin, Coach Zuppke decided to rest Red in the next game. Britton and McIlwain played only a quarter against nonconference foe Mississippi A&M (now known as Mississippi State). Coached by first-year head coach Earl Able, the Aggies were 4-1-1, with their only loss to Tennessee. Not quite as strong as the Big Ten teams they were playing against, Zuppke wanted to give Red a rest for the season finale against Ohio State. The backups did well, pounding the Aggies, 27-0, with more than 17,000 filling Memorial Stadium.

The Illini football team then traveled to Columbus, Ohio, to face off against the Buckeyes, who were 3-3-1 overall but just 1-3 in conference. A crowd of more than 42,000 fans filled Ohio Stadium. The Buckeyes defense came ready to play, slowing both the running and passing game of the Illini. After a scoreless first half, Zuppke adjusted the game plan. The Illini defense started with a goal line stand, and then they had their best offensive drive of the game. Helped by a 16-yard run around right end by Red, the drive ended with a 37-yard field goal by Britton and a 3-0 lead. Red started gaining bigger chucks in the fourth quarter. One drive ended with him galloping 32-yards for a touchdown. Despite a missed extra point, Illinois escaped with a 9-0 victory and a share of the Big Ten championship, sharing the title with Michigan, which defeated Minnesota, 10-0, at home to finish with an 8-0 mark. Illinois finished with a 5-0 league record, while Michigan finished 4-0. Because of bad scheduling the two best teams in the Big Ten did not play one another. It would set the stage for an incredible matchup in 1924—a game that would change the life of Red Grange.[28]

Red finished the season leading the Big Ten in scoring with 72 points (12 touchdowns). The player closest to him was halfback Earl Martineau of Minnesota, with a distant 43 points. Red would be selected to numerous First Team All-American teams as a sophomore. Two of the more prestigious were Walter Eckersall's squad for the *Chicago Tribune* and the Walter Camp All-American team. The father of American football, Camp wrote about Grange when naming his squad of the best players in the country:

> Grange of Illinois is the star backfield man of the middle west conference, and that means traveling in high class. . . . Grange not only is a lone smasher of great power, but also a sterling open field runner and has been a great factor in the defense of Illinois through the middle west conference. He is classed as the most dangerous man in that section, and probably the country over, when all kinds of running must be considered.[29]

One glaring omission of Red's 1923 season came from the *Michigan Daily*, the school newspaper for the University of Michigan. The paper's sports editor left Red off of his First Team All-American squad, claiming, "Although Grange is a great star at carrying the ball it is his only real accomplishment."[30] Instead they selected Earl Martineau of Minnesota and Harry Kipke of Michigan.

The *Daily Illini* didn't take too kindly to this jab at Grange's football skills. In the December 5 edition of the paper, sports columnist Tom Morrow wrote in his column, "Bunking the Line," one of the greatest all-time comebacks in sportswriting history. After listing the First Team and Second Team selections of the *Michigan Daily* he penned, "You're right, Sister Annie. The above selection of All-Conference tars is from the *Michigan Daily*. AND ALL GALLI-CURCI CAN DO IS SING." In all caps, Morrow made his point. It would be one of the most famous quotes attributed to Red for the next eight decades. If the *Michigan Daily* didn't think Red was worthy in 1923, they would have a front-row seat to his greatness in 1924. As for Tom Morrow, after graduating from Illinois, he would go on to work for more than three decades writing for the *Chicago Tribune*.[31]

Red was now getting attention from a variety of publications. In the November 24 edition of the *Chicago Evening American*, Joe Wayer, a fraternity brother of Red's at the Zeta Psi house, wrote an article entitled "Grange's Roommate Tells What Real 'Red' Is Like." In the article, Wayer, a senior from Goshen, Indiana, wrote,

> Grange is not a huge man but is powerful built. In street clothes he is merely trim and husky—stripped he is a surprising example of physical development. Although only 20 years old, he seems extraordinarily mature in every way. His features perhaps give that impression; his face is deeply lined and in repose is almost severe. Grange dresses quietly, neatly, and without ostentation. He is well groomed. . . . He is the gentlest, most assuming, most retiring man I have met in college. With strangers he is almost shy, although polite. He dislikes meeting

people and is annoyed by congratulations, although he never appears irritated or displeased when people praise him to his face.[32]

The attention Red received in 1923, as a sophomore All-American, was about to get even crazier in the years to come. Two days after Christmas, the town of Wheaton held a celebration for their newest star at the Clubside Inn. Both Wheaton High School, with coach Dink Welden, and Wheaton College football teams attended. Everyone sat down to eat a large turkey dinner served with coffee and ice cream. Most of the men fired up a cigar to celebrate the evening. The town of Wheaton honored Red throughout the night. Speakers included Dr. George Dyche, president of the Lions Club; Frank Herrick, who talked about Red's childhood in Wheaton; Charles Hadley, an attorney in town; and Jack Conley, Wheaton College head coach. The final speaker was Reverend E. C. Lumsden of Gary Memorial Methodist Church, who praised Red for his achievements at Illinois, telling him how the entire town wanted to show their "token of esteem and love, full of good wishes from every man, women, and child of Wheaton." He finished his speech by saying, "We care and love you, Harold Grange."[33]

After the applause died down, Lumsden presented Red with a fantastic gift. He handed Red a silver loving cup. Red rose from his chair to a thunderous round of cheers. When he spoke, he hesitated modestly and quietly expressed his thanks to everyone. He talked briefly about hard work and preparation at Illinois, and that he had great teammates and coaches. "All that I can (say) is that I am proud to come from Wheaton," he declared. Then he sat down. Lyle was never prouder of his eldest son. Although he didn't say many words, he beamed the entire night.[34]

Getting the urge to compete again, Red combined his participating in spring football with playing on the baseball team as an outfielder. He would earn a varsity letter. As for his schoolwork, Red's sophomore year was much better than his freshman one. In the fall semester, he had two As (physical education and military 3A), three Bs (public speaking 1, military 3B, and economics), one C (history 2A), and one D (history 3A). In his second semester, Red had one A (military 4B), two Bs (public speaking 2 and military 4B), and four Cs (home economics 3 and 3B, and history 1B and 3B).[35]

After his sophomore year was finished, Red returned to Wheaton to watch Garland graduate from Wheaton High School. In the school's yearbook, Garland was quoted as saying, "Three things shine—the sun, the moon, my hair." Garland never lacked a sense of humor. Gardie would join his big brother at Illinois to play for Bob Zuppke.[36]

9

12 MINUTES TO IMMORTALITY

Throughout the summer of 1924, Red could only think about two things. While working on the ice truck, his thoughts drifted to football and the University of Michigan. Bob Zuppke wanted it that way.

> I had hardly arrived in Wheaton. In June I started receiving letters from Zuppke about the game coming up that fall. And in all these letters he would say what (Fielding) Yost had been saying about the Illinois team. He said we weren't fit to be in the Big Ten. And every week I'd get the letter. Well, eventually you get aw-fully mad . . . not at Michigan, but at Yost. And that went on all summer. I went back for practice in September, and I found most of the other squad had been getting these and, boy, they were hopped up on Yost. Later I found out that Yost had been in Europe all summer, hadn't even been in this country. But that was when the buildup started.[1]

Also, that summer Grange worked on becoming a better passer. Zuppke had given Red a few footballs to take home so that he could work on his throwing skills. He wanted Red to be more of a threat to pass so that the opposition wouldn't be sure of him when he got the ball. "I started out by winging baseballs to my brother Garland for hours at a time until I developed near-perfect control and the ability to throw on the run," he said. "Then I switched to throwing a football. It got so I could pass with a high degree of accuracy at 20 or 30 yards."[2]

Red spent more time with his brother during this summer than he had ever done before. Garland had just graduated from high school and would work the ice route with him to prepare for his freshman year at Illinois. The two made the job fun, acting like typical siblings. In a 1978 interview, Red remembered clowning around with his kid brother:

> We used to have some of the greatest arguments, Gardy and I, when working on the ice truck. We're out in the country, and I remember this so well, we stopped the truck and turned it off and got out into a field. We had the doggonesdest fight you ever saw. We both are bloody. We clean up and get back in the truck and go to work. We work all day together the both of us.[3]

In the fall, Garland would be on the freshman team and live at the Zeta Psi frat house with his big brother. Lyle would now be paying for two college tuitions. Even though he wasn't with his players, Zuppke pushed his team mentally throughout the summer by using the letters as motivation to help his squad prepare for the upcoming matchup against Michigan. Zuppke could see how special Grange was. "Grange has absolutely no lost motion," he commented. "He doesn't take an unnecessary step. He is the fastest man I ever coached. He has the ideal football physique, stocky thighs, long, muscled calves, and a man-sized foot that enables him to keep his balance even when he is hit hard."[4]

Grange had filled out physically. His body dimensions were recorded by the University of Illinois as follows:

Height-weight: 5-foot-11, 170 pounds stripped
Neck: 15.6 inches
Wrist: 8 inches
Biceps: 14¾ inches
Chest 38 inches; 44 expanded
Waist: 35 inches
Thigh: 23½ inches
Calf: 16 inches
Ankle: 10 inches
Foot size: 9
Reach: 74 inches[5]

Zuppke could also see Red's football IQ growing. Speaking to Grantland Rice in 1934, Zuppke talked about Red's football intelligence, relating, "Red had one of the quickest competitive minds I've ever known. He could size up a situation in a flash, and action was almost instantaneous with thought. It was like setting fire to a pile of powder."[6]

On September 15, the team arrived on campus for their first practice. Zuppke had lost a few good men on the line, most notably All-American guard Jim McMillian. Returning lettermen included C. A. Brown (tackle), Roy Miller (guard), Leonard Umnus (center), Clarence Muhl (end), Fred Rokusek (end), and the entire starting backfield of Red, (left halfback), Harry Hall (quarterback), Wally McIlwain (right halfback), and Earl Britton (fullback).

Expectations were high in Champaign. Most experts were picking Michigan to win the Big Ten, but Illinois was right with them, and even Knute Rockne picked them as the "class of the Big Ten." Excitement for a special season in 1924 became even more present for Illinois after defeating Nebraska and Butler.[7]

At 2–0, the season was off to a successful start. It was now Michigan week. The most important week of the season began with one of the Grange boys suffering a setback. On Monday, October 13, at practice, Gardie dislocated his right shoulder while making a tackle. He would miss the rest of the season. Red made sure his attention was now on the Wolverines. Most of the school and the fans were gearing up for the game of the year.

During the summer, Zuppke had sent letters trying to prepare his team for the emotional nature of the game. He had them so fired up he knew they would be ready to play. He then turned his attention to the mental aspect of the game. His game plan called for his All-American halfback to do something he had never done before: he wanted Red to use the cutback when carrying the ball. Up until that point, Red had been effective in using his speed by going around the end on most of his runs. With his speed, he could gain ground by just trying to beat them to the edge. Red recalled,

> This game he had worked all week and most of the year with me to try to get me to cut back . . . drawing it up on the blackboard to show the simple fact that this is the smart way to run, not to run down the sidelines. Because, as I say, it's easy to push you out (of bounds), and they have the angle on you. So, each time I could make it on the end, or off-tackle, I would cut wide, and then, cut right back across the field.[8]

The day before the game, Illinois ventured out to Champaign Country Club to run its final drills. Afterward, the squad ate dinner at the club, a rare streak for Red, relaxing after going through a grueling week of practice. Michigan came into town and stayed at the Urbana Country Club. Yost was confident his team would win, proclaiming, "Stop Grange and we win."[9]

The following morning, Zuppke's men traveled nearly two miles from the country club to Memorial Stadium. Already arriving was the big contingent of press members.

More than 50 newspapermen packed the press box, some of whom were Chicago beat writers Warren Brown (*Herald-Examiner*), James Crusinberry (*Tribune*), and Ralph Cannon (*Journal*), as well as national writers Frances Powers (*Cleveland News Leader*), Henry Farrell (*United Press*), Lawrence Perry (*Consolidated Press Associated*), and Charles Dunkley (*Associated Press*). They were about to witness a performance like none other on a football field.

The game against Michigan was going to be the day that the school dedicated Memorial Stadium. Forty special trains were ordered to travel to Champaign to help with the arrival of the sold-out crowd. In the end, the new facility cost $1.7 million, with a capacity of about 68,000. This would be one game that would be remembered for a long time. As the teams took the field, Red realized it was going to be a different kind of game. "I'd never played before a crowd like that," he remembered. "We walked out into the stadium and you look around and there's 68,000 people out there, and they looked as though they were right down on top of you. Gosh, when I was at Wheaton, I never played before 200 people before."[10]

In the locker room after warm-ups, Zuppke looked at the team and made an odd request. "Okay fellas, let's take off the stockings. It's hot out there and without those heavy socks you'll feel a lot fresher and cooler," said Zuppke.[11] He later said, "There's nothing in the rule book that says you have to wear your stockings so I told the players to take them off. They were reluctant—Grange, I think was the last to do it." The players peeled off their socks. Trotting back onto the field, Michigan coach George Little and athletic director Fielding Yost became suspicious. In full view of the sold-out crowd, Yost and Little ordered team captain Herb Steger to feel the Illinois players' legs to see if they hadn't greased up their legs to get an advantage. He found no grease. No rule prohibited the removal of socks, so the Illinois players were free to play without wool stockings.[12]

The gate for the game would add up to $148,667.50. Illinois would split the gate 50–50 with Michigan, which meant George Huff's athletic department would clear $74,126.61. The decision to build the stadium had paid off. At midfield, Illinois captain Frank Rokusek won the toss and elected to receive. Michigan decided to defend the south goal. The hype and buildup from the past year was now gone. It was time to see who was the best team in the Big Ten.

Wearing his number 77, Red trotted out to the north-end goal line. For the next 12 minutes, he would change the course of college football history, and his life would never be the same. Michigan team captain Herb Steger, starting left halfback, booted the kickoff high into the sky. The ball landed in the arms of Grange at the five-yard line. Said Red,

> Running straight down center, I cut wide to the right to avoid a host of tacklers at about the 30-yard line. From the extreme westside I cut back across the field and headed up the east sidelines, crossing the goal line a fraction of a second after Wolverine quarterback Tod Rockwell made a frantic dive to get me.[13]

Red had taken to heart Zuppke's advice about cutting back. Starting down the right sideline and working back toward the middle of the field, he went 95 yards untouched for a shocking touchdown less than 10 seconds into the game. The team's perfect blocking weighed on Red's mind. "I remember the thing went through my head, after 10 guys got me this far, wouldn't it be awful if this one fella tackled me here about the five yard line? Well, I got by him and scored the touchdown," recalled Red.[14]

Red caught his breath and then held on the point after for his good buddy Earl Britton. Less than 10 seconds into the game, Illinois led, 7–0. In 1924, the NCAA had a rule where after a touchdown was scored, the team on defense could choose to accept the ball on a kickoff or kick off back to their opponent, the thinking being you would pin the offense deep into their territory, force them to punt out of trouble, and win the battle of field possession. Michigan didn't think Illinois or, in particular, Red Grange would continue to return kicks for touchdowns. So, they choose to kick back to Illinois. This time they stopped them. But after punting back to the Illini, it was again time for the Galloping Ghost to take over.

Illinois took over at its own 30-yard line. After a McIlwain three-yard run, Red took off. This time he sprinted through the Michigan defense for a 67-yard score. "On the next play I got away again as I stepped around left end, cut back, then circled behind my interference," recalled Red.[15] Illinois's "rooters swayed from side to side and rocked in sound."[16]

Michigan decided to kick off back to Illinois. After another exchange of punts, Illinois took over at its own 44-yard line. All it took for Grange was one play. Once again, the redhead went untouched for a 56-yard score. "I was given the ball on Illinois' 44-yard line and took off around right end," he related. "When my blockers allowed the Michigan secondary to get outside of them, I cut back to the center of the field, where I had a clear path to the goal line." Britton missed the extra point. That didn't stop the Illinois faithful from celebrating another Grange touchdown, as the fans "brought pandemonium" inside the stadium. The score was now 20–0.[17]

Illinois took the next kickoff, but Britton was forced to punt. Michigan's Rockwell promptly fumbled the ball away, setting up the Illini at the Wolverines 45-yard line. You can guess what happened next. "On the next play we tried the identical maneuver that resulted in my last touchdown. Running wide around right end I cut back when the Michigan secondary was again drawn over to the sidelines. After sidestepping a few stray would-be tacklers in midfield, I found easy sailing to another tally," recalled Red. Britton made the extra point to make it 27–0. The crowd was so loud that the noise could be heard in Chicago.[18]

Red had scored four touchdowns in the first 12 minutes. A legend had been born. He was also dead tired. At this point, quarterback Harry Hall called a time-out. When Matt Bullock, the Illinois trainer, came out with water, he asked Red how he was doing. "I'm so dog-tired I can hardly stand up. Better get me outta here," Grange replied. Zup obliged and sent in backup Ray Gallivan to replace him. The crowd cheered and applauded Red as he trotted to the Illinois bench.

As Grange jogged to the Illinois bench, he was "given a cheer such as no football player got in a decade," wrote the *Chicago Tribune*. Zuppke's game plan to have Red cut back had been a stroke of genius. For most of his sophomore year, Red had gone around end, using his speed to get to the corner. This was the first time he used the cutback, and Michigan had no answer for it. The first-quarter stats were unheard of. In the first 12 minutes of action, Red had touched the ball eight times (three kickoff returns and five runs). He had gained 262 yards (averaging 32.7 yards per touch) and scored four touchdowns. Red remained out of the game through the second quarter. Illinois took a 27–7 lead into halftime.[19]

In the third quarter, Red returned to the field. It was like he never left. Completing passes (three completions for 18 yards) and rushing for chunks of yards, he scored his fifth touchdown from 11 yards out. Midway through the fourth quarter, Red tossed an 18-yard TD pass to Benny Leonard. After all the hype and buildup, the final score read Illinois 39, Michigan 14. Red recalled, "When we defeated Michigan, we did it because Zup keyed us up to the point where we believed the fate of the nation hung upon the result. If we lost, Yost and his demoniac Wolverines would overrun the face of the earth; humanity would be doomed."[20]

Grange's performance goes down as the greatest single-game performance in college football history. According to the University of Illinois sports information department, Grange totaled 402 yards. He had 15 carries for 212 yards, passed for 64 yards (completing 6 of 8 passes), and had 3 kickoff returns for

126 yards. He accounted for six touchdowns.[21] In his autobiography, Red recollected what happened after the game:

> Bedlam broke loose in our locker room after the game. The place was jam-packed with excited reporters and photographers. Everyone was yelling, jumping up and down, and running around slapping everyone else on the back. All I wanted to do was lie down and rest, but the newspapermen proceeded to surround me and ask an endless number of questions. It was nearly an hour after all the other players had departed before I was able to tear myself away. Even then I found it necessary to leave by a side door to avoid a large number of Illini rooters waiting for me on the outside.
>
> When I got back to the fraternity house the place was in an uproar. The walls were literally bulging with alumnus, friends, Zeta Psis from the Michigan chapter, and more newspapermen. Escaping from all this posed a greater problem for me than eluding Michigan tacklers.
>
> Finally, I managed to get up to my room and, after changing clothes, slipped out the kitchen door with one of my more understanding fraternity brothers. We had dinner by ourselves, then took in a movie. Returning about 10:30 that night and finding conditions somewhat more peaceful, I went straight to bed.[22]

Just hours after his great performance, all Red wanted to do was eat dinner and go see a movie. He wanted nothing to do with the extra attention. The Michigan game would not only change Red Grange's life but would also validate an entire program. "The Illinois team was higher for this game than any game we played during my three years," said Red more than 50 years later in a 1978 interview. "I've often said, and I believe it's true, that on October 18, 1924, I don't believe any college team in the United States could have licked the University of Illinois on that day." For the rest of his life Red would give his blockers all the credit for his remarkable performance.[23] He continued,

> I think I was very fortunate in that game. I carried the ball. I've often said, the ballcarrier is the most unglamorous fella on the team. But the fellas that really count and always have in my book, this goes back to my grade school days, are the other 10 fellas, the fellas that do the blocking. I think blocking is the toughest job on a football field. You get absolutely no pats on the back, or no headlines, because you're a blocker.[24]

Grange knew his teammates were equally responsible for his performance, but the press only gave credit—and huge headlines—to one man—the Galloping Ghost. Just hours after making history, the name Red Grange was appearing throughout the country. Newspaper headlines giving his name and accomplishments against Michigan were plastered on front pages and sports pages everywhere. Mass media at this point in history was at its highest point. Newspapers and radio were the main avenues of getting and hearing the news. By 1925, almost 40 million Americans were reading newspapers; there was no television or internet yet, so printed newspapers were the main source of news.

In the Windy City, the *Chicago Tribune* headline read, "Illinois Buries Wolverines 39 to 14; Grange Thrills Huge Crowd by Racing to Five Touchdowns." The sports page also included a panoramic photo of the sold-out crowd at Memorial Stadium. James Crusinberry wrote, "He (Red) stamped himself as one of the greatest football stars of all-time, east or west." He also compared Grange to former Michigan All-American great Willie Heston, who, with Jim Thorpe and Walter Eckersall, was arguably the greatest football player up to this point. "Grange is a big fellow like (Willie) Heston and runs like him and plunges like him," continued Crusinberry. "Only it's doubtful if Heston ever was as fast. Grange seems to have the size and strength of a Heston and the speed and dodging ability of an (Walter) Eckersall."[25]

A few pages into the sports section, readers saw several photos of Red in action. At this point in time in newspapers, it was common to see photos of games or events that had occurred the previous day, just another way of getting the reader closer to the action and allowing them to view people from throughout the world. The *Tribune* photos included several of the greatest images of Red in action. One photo had him carrying the ball in his left arm, being led by his lead blocker, Britton, on the opening kickoff. The caption below said, "Notice the bare legs of the Illini." Two other photos show Grange carrying the ball on his other touchdowns.[26]

Newspapers and sportswriters from throughout the country now made Grange their top priority, especially the writers who were there to witness his performance. Some of the best sportswriters in the Midwest lauded the Galloping Ghost. Warren Brown (*Chicago Herald-Examiner*) wrote, "Grange, the unstoppable, is the most amazing runner who ever trod a gridiron." H. G. Salsinger (*Detroit News*) opined, "Grange established himself as the greatest runner in football in the Michigan game. His performance finds no equal in football history. Here indeed was a superman, a player that could not be stopped." Wrote Francis Powers (*Cleveland News Leader*), "Let the dust of glorious memory settle forever on the deeds of Eddie Mahan, Jim Thorpe, Chic Harley, and other football heroes of the past. For a new superman has come to rule the gridiron, and today fans are calling 'Red' Grange the greatest running back of all time."[27]

Major newspapers throughout the United States, including the *St. Louis Star-Times, Detroit Free Press, Los Angeles Times, Oakland Tribune, Pittsburgh*

Post-Gazette, Philadelphia Inquirer, Minneapolis Star-Tribune, and *Baltimore Sun* ran full-page recaps of Grange's performance and photographs from the game. Even sportswriters who didn't attend the game started to inquire about Grange's performance; they couldn't believe one player, especially one from the Midwest, could perform like that. One writer who wasn't at the Michigan–Illinois game was the most famous and influential of them all—Grantland Rice. That Saturday, Rice had attended the equally attractive Notre Dame–Army matchup. The following day, he wrote one of the most beautiful poems and created one of the most popular sports nicknames of all-time: "Outlined against a blue-gray October sky, the Four Horsemen rode again. In dramatic lore they are known as Famine, Pestilence, Destruction, and Death. These are only aliases. Their real names are Stuhldreher, Miller, Crowley, and Layden." But after reading and hearing about the play of Red Grange, he quickly saw an opportunity to pen another poem that would stand the test of time. In his column "The Sportlight," he wrote,

Red Grange of Illinois
A streak of fire, a breath of flame,
Eluding all who reach and clutch;
A gray ghost thrown into the game.
That rival hands may rarely touch;
A rubber bounding blasting soul
Whose destination is the goal.[28]

The nickname Galloping Ghost now had a noticeable following, being used almost daily when writing about Red Grange. The press was going nuts over Red. His name was now being used in the same sentence with Bobby Jones, Jack Dempsey, Earl Sande, Bill Tilden, and the great Babe Ruth as the country's most popular athlete. With all the commotion, Red just wanted to be left alone. In the end, it was the *Daily Illini* that got the last dig at Michigan. Sportswriter Tom Morrow couldn't help himself by taking a shot at his counterparts at the *Michigan Daily.* He started his game recap simply by writing, "All Grange can do is run. But that was plenty. Four times yesterday in the first 12 minutes the redheaded lad cut loose for the goal line, and four times he went as far he could within the fence."[29]

Walter Camp was even writing about the redhead, saying, "He is fast and has a remarkable ability to dodge, pick his openings, and shake loose from tacklers. The records thus far demonstrate that the only way to accomplish this would be to hire an assassin and get him somewhere off the gridiron!" Soon, Camp would see the Galloping Ghost up close and personal.[30]

A day after the Michigan game, Red got a visit from one sportswriter, and it hit close to home. James Crusinberry, of the *Chicago Tribune*, was assigned to write an exposé on the country's newest sports celebrity. He would spend time with Lyle Grange in Wheaton and meet with Red at the fraternity house. He compared getting to Red to trying get an interview with President Calvin Coolidge or the Prince of Wales. He approached the house nervously, "but after talking to this famous athlete for one minute all that nervousness leaves one, for young Mr. Grange is just a big, bashful boy . . . he thinks of himself just as Red Grange, the Wheaton boy who played football in high school there."[31]

In a write-up that took up almost a full page, Crusinberry's title was "Red Grange, Off Grid, Is a Big Bashful Boy; Loves Football but Hates to Talk about It." It gave a little insight into what Red was dealing with just a few hours after the Michigan game. People wanted to talk about football, but they also wanted to know who Red was, what he was doing, and how he was feeling. His father Lyle was quoted as saying his son "was the most bashful lad he has ever seen while in high school." He added, "And he's self-effacing." Red was no longer just a football player or student. To the public and press, he was a superstar, and they wanted to know everything about him. His life would never be the same.[32]

After the school's biggest victory ever, Zuppke gave his starters some much-needed rest before the next game against tiny De Pauw. Led by sophomore quarterback Ray Gallivan's three touchdowns, the backups looked like the starters as Illinois crushed the Tigers, 45–0. Next up was a tough matchup with Iowa. In 1924, Burt Ingwersen took over as the new head coach for the Hawkeyes. Zuppke hated to see him leave; now the two would square off. Four minutes into the game, Red smashed through right tackle to score on an 11-yard touchdown run. On the next drive, Red snuck through the line to score from two yards out. Britton would add another touchdown before the end of the first quarter to give the Illini a 19–0 lead. Zuppke's boys continued their scoring spree in the second half, as Illinois cruised to a 36–0 beatdown of their former freshman coach. "Despite the absence of long runs, Red proved himself great by smashing through the tackle and hurling accurate forward passes about the lot," wrote the *Daily Illini*.[33]

Grange's all-around play of running and passing was improving each week. His ability to throw had given the Illinois offense another weapon. Defenses would not jam the line of scrimmage to stop Red. Preparing for Illinois, Maroons coach A. A. Stagg once again relied on his scouting reports to help him. His top assistant, Fritz Crisler, scouted the famous Michigan game, praising the

Illinois aerial game: "Illinois passing attack has been very successful to date. Grange threw all the passes in the Michigan game. He is protected well and given lots of time to get them away. . . . The most successful way of stopping Grange is to keep Illinois on defense." Fellow scout Hal Mefford wrote, "I think putting two men should be delegated to take Grange and the slogan should be to 'Put Grange on the ground every play.' If we stop Grange, the entire Illinois team will disintegrate as they cannot play football when he is absent."[34]

Stagg trusted his scouting reports, but he wasn't quite sure as to which Grange he would be getting—the one who loved to run around the ends, the one who would cut back, as he had done against Michigan, or the one who had shown improvement passing the ball. Stagg could see that Grange was a special player. He stated,

> Grange is not tearing along at breakneck speed all the time; quite the contrary, he changes his pace to suit the conditions. When he has to outrun somebody, he is able to do so. He always has something left for that big effort, and invariably he knows when it is time to make that big effort. That judgement, that knowledge of just what to do and just when to do it is, in my opinion, Grange's greatest asset.[35]

The Illinois team traveled by train into Chicago on the Illinois Central Railroad. Zuppke had the team stay at the South Shore Country Club on the Friday before the game. Waiting outside the country club were a few newspaper writers. One was Sonia Lee of the *Chicago American*. She wanted a quick interview with Red. Staying close to his teammates, he eventually gave in to the request. Lee asked a few questions about the upcoming game against Chicago, then fired off a few more "personal" questions about the country's biggest sports star. Red answered them politely, saying, "You know, not nearly all of the stories about me are true. Somebody sprung one about my taking a girl to the movies and being afraid to take her in the house because her dad wanted to talk football. I'm not afraid to call for a girl or take her home, either."[36]

Then the *Chicago American* writer got a big idea. There was an ice truck nearby with blocks of ice in back of the wagon. She suggested that Red pose for a photo of him picking up a block of ice to show how he spends his summer vacation. In his suit and tie and backward hat, Red grabbed the ice tongs, clipped off a 100-pound chunk of ice, and hoisted it onto his shoulder with no trouble. He did a short turn toward the photographer and, with a small smile, posed for the photo. After putting down the chunk of ice, he made one last comment, this time about his health: "Feeling fine! A bad ankle, but I'll forget about it in the game." That night's *Chicago Evening American* featured the article on Red written by Lee, and accompanying the article was the photo of Red resting the chunk of ice on his shoulder. This was the first photo taken of Red performing his summer job, but it would not be the last time he was asked to pose as the "Wheaton Iceman."[37]

After dinner, the players sat in on skull meetings to make some final adjustments to the game plan. Red was in bed shortly after 8:00 p.m. The game would have one special guest. Walter Camp arrived in Chicago the day before the game. It was a big get for western football, as Princeton was battling Harvard in Cambridge that same day. Camp's main reason for traveling the almost 900 miles was to see Red Grange in person.

More than 32,000 fans filled Stagg Field. The November air was damp and chilly, biting the fans through their overcoats and gloves. Red jogged out wearing his now-famous 77 jersey. Instead of using the Michigan game plan of pummeling Red, Stagg wanted to keep the ball away from the All-American. They held the ball throughout the entire first quarter, without Illinois running one offensive play from scrimmage. On the first drive, the Maroons took 11 plays, putting the ball down at the Illinois seven-yard line before fumbling the ball away. After Britton punted away on first down, the Maroons marched nine plays for the game's first touchdown. Zuppke decided to pin the Maroons back, so he decided to kick off back to them. Once again, they couldn't stop Stagg's boys, as the Maroons offense took 14 plays to score their second touchdown on the first play of the second quarter. After one quarter and one play in the second, the Maroons had run 34 offensive plays to zero by Illinois, taking a 14–0 lead. The game looked to be a blowout, but Red and his teammates wouldn't go quietly. This time, Zuppke decided to take the football. He wanted Red to handle the pigskin.

On the ensuing drive, Red carried the ball five times for 18 yards and competed three passes for 56 yards to set up his own four-yard touchdown run around right end. Britton's extra point made it 14–7. The Maroons marched right back down the field to add another touchdown. Then Stagg's biggest fear came alive. The Galloping Ghost became unstoppable. Red touched the ball eight times on the next drive, resulting in his second touchdown of the game. The 21–14 score held going into halftime.

The entire stadium was being entertained, even Walter Camp. In speaking with Fred Young, the head lineman, he told the official that "he had seen more real football in 30 minutes than he has witnessed all year on the Atlantic seaboard," which was saying something.[38]

Midway through the third quarter, Red brought the sold-out crowd to its feet. After getting perfect blocking around left end, he galloped and dodged

Maroons defenders for a spectacular 82-yard touchdown run. After the extra point, the game was tied. The *Urbana Daily Courier* wrote, "It was a great run, and the stands trembled as both the Illinois and Chicago fans cheered. The thousands who were in the stands came here to see a run of this kind by Grange."[39] Grange had done it again. It was another coast-to-coast run to add to his highlight reel, this time in front of the "Father of American Football"— Walter Camp.

The rest of the game saw the two defenses finally showing some teeth. Both teams tried to get into scoring range but failed. The final gun sounded with the scoreboard at Stagg Field reading 21–21. Grange would always claim this was the toughest game he ever played in. "The Illinois–Chicago classic of 1924 was the toughest football game I ever played in college," he declared. "Every time I was tackled I was hit hard by two or three men. At one point in the game I was so exhausted I fell flat on my face as the Maroons were running off a play."[40]

His statistics that day reflected a young man who gave his all to help his team win. According to the University of Illinois athletic department, he had 27 carries for 196 yards, caught 2 passes for 40 yards, returned 3 punts for 8 yards, and completed 5 of 10 passes for 86 yards for a total of 330 total yards. Even Walter Camp was impressed by the game. Said Camp, "The Illinois–Chicago game here Saturday was one of the most wonderful football games I have ever seen on any field anywhere. It was worth coming a thousand miles to witness."[41]

A few days after the tie game, Zuppke made a big announcement. Illinois would play the University of Pennsylvania in 1925. Red would make an appearance on the East Coast in his senior year. Next up for Illinois was Minnesota. The Golden Gophers were having a down year, with an overall record of 2–2–2, going winless in Big Ten play, at 0–2–1. For Illinois, another Big Ten title was just two games away.

A sluggish first half saw the Illini trail 20–7 at halftime. Just as the third quarter closed Illinois lost its top weapon. On an interception return, "(Red) grabbed the ball and started one of his specialties, but somebody caught him and threw him out of bounds on his own 29-yard line. Somebody else piled on him after he was down, and Minnesota was penalized," wrote the *Chicago Tribune*. It took a while for Red to get to his feet; however, he stayed in the game. On the next play, he completed a pass. But a play later he tried to throw again; his right arm hung down to his side. Zuppke knew something was wrong and took his star out of the game.[42]

Red suffered a serious injury. X-rays showed a strain ligament in his right shoulder blade. "I am unaware of any dirty playing on the part of any Minnesota player. It's all in the game and should be looked at in that light," said Red to the press after the game. Minnesota had pulled off a huge 20–7 upset. The loss did do one thing: it virtually eliminated Illinois from winning the Big Ten title.

The attention on Red didn't wane, even with an injury. The press also reached out to other members of his family. In Wheaton, Lyle Grange was hounded. Margaret Dale of the *Consolidated Press Association* visited Red's father at the Grange apartment on Front Street. She wanted to interview the man who helped raise the Galloping Ghost. Dale arrived in Wheaton to find that young Red was the "best loved man in Wheaton." She reported on the Grange men's "bachelor apartment on the second floor" and that Lyle had raised Red to be a "regular man."[43] Lyle showed the writer newspaper clippings he had kept that were hanging on the apartment wall. According to Lyle,

> I pasted the clippings there; my son Harold, that is, "Red," would not have done it. He's too modest. He does not like all this adulation anyway. And if there'd been any women here they probably would have put them in a scrapbook somewhere. But I like them where they are. They're finer than paintings to me, and they make this look like a regular he-man's apartment.[44]

It was obvious to Dale that Lyle was extremely proud of his son, as well as the fact that he had raised his two boys to be successful college students. "Fathers ought to play more with their sons and encourage them in good athletic games. It keeps them out of mischief, both the sons and father, and where athletics and studies are linked together the boy has more interest in the latter. And I did it without any women's help," Lyle said pridefully. The Dale article was picked up nationally, appearing in newspapers throughout the country.[45]

While Lyle Grange was gaining some notoriety, his son was dealing with an injury to his right shoulder blade. Although he would recover quickly, the injury would keep him out of the season finale against Ohio State. Without their star halfback in the lineup, the Illini struggled on offense. Zuppke's squad showed enough grit on defense to pitch a shutout. Ray Gallivan plowed over from inside the five-yard line to give Illinois a 7–0 victory. Despite the sluggish ending to the season, the Fighting Illini finished with a 6-1-1 record and a tie for second with Iowa, just one game behind Stagg's Chicago Maroons, at 3-0-3. In his first two varsity seasons at Illinois, Red had been part of a team that had gone 14-1-1.

The liberal arts major struggled with his classes during the fall of his junior year. After the Michigan game, it was hard for Red to find quality time to study. Aside from the press, the entire university seemed to want some of his time. He passed all five of his classes. He earned a D in history; three Cs, in economics, geology 1, and history 51A; and a B in public speaking.

Shortly after the season, Red was honored as one of the best college football players in the country. Walter Camp once again placed him on his First Team All-American squad. Camp wrote,

> Harold Grange is the marvel of this year's backfield. His work in the Michigan game was a revelation, but his performance in the Chicago game went even farther . . . he is elusive, has a baffling change of pace, a good straight-arm, and finally seems in some way to get a map of the field at starting and then threads his way through his opponents . . . we have in Grange probably the best all-around ground gainer we have had for a long time.[46]

Red had another tremendous honor bestowed on him when the *Chicago Tribune* started a new award to honor the Big Ten Player of the Year. Grange was the first receipt of what is now the Big Ten MVP Award. He would be given a full-size silver football trophy. After the season, Red was never bored. On November 24, the Illinois football banquet was held at the Champaign Country Club. Red received his second varsity letter and was elected team captain for the 1925 season. A few days later, his hometown wanted to honor him in a big way. Just like the previous year, Wheaton set up a celebration for its hometown hero.

On November 28, at the Masonic Temple in Wheaton, Red and his father Lyle showed up for what was being billed as "Red Grange: Home-Coming Banquet." More than 250 people filled the banquet hall, sitting at six large rows of tables, with each guest wearing a carnival hat. Small souvenir programs (4 x 6 in size) with Red's photo on the cover were handed out. Food was served by ladies of the Eastern Star café, and the menu featured oyster cocktail and southern baked ham or salmon loaf, with sides of escalloped potatoes, corn, and cabbage salad. Apple pie a la mode and coffee were served for desert.[47]

Music was played throughout the night by a hired orchestra. Wheaton mayor Marion Pittsford served as toastmaster. "Wheaton has never had such advertising in its history as it is getting now with Grange in Illinois backfield," spoke Pittsford. Wheaton High School coach Dink Welden praised Red as a hero for young kids in town to idolize. "Grange, the greatest we've ever had here and honor his as such," he said.

At the end of the evening, Red was presented with a pair of silver ice tongs as a token of the town's sincere gratitude and appreciation of the fame he had brought to the city. As Red rose to accept the award, the crowd came to their feet to give their guest of honor a round of applause. Not one for long speeches, Red spoke a few words of thanks. He finished his speech by saying,

> I'm proud I'm from Wheaton, and every game at the Zeta Psi house there's a regular homecoming of Wheaton folks on the lawn with citizens from this city of ours attending the game. I appreciate the honor bestowed upon me, and I like the spirit of support I'm getting from my hometown.[48]

After Red sat down there were calls for Lyle Grange to speak. He responded by merely bowing his head in acknowledgment. The town of Wheaton was falling in love with Red. He would always be their hero. The homecoming banquet was a pleasant experience for the Grange family. Red was grateful that his hometown would take the time to honor him. Because of his newfound celebrity status as the country's biggest sports star, Red would soon meet a man who would change his life even more—a man who was like no other individual he had ever met.

10

C. C. PYLE

R ed Grange was a simple, shy, humble, athletically driven 21-year-old boy from a small Midwestern town. Who knows what he thought when he first met the man who would change the course of his life. That man was Charles C. Pyle—a man who came from the same small-town Midwestern roots as Red.

The Pile family settled in Van Wert, Ohio. Charles's father, William, a farmer who was in poor health with a weak heart when Charles was young, moved his family to Van Wert to take a job as a minister. Soon after arriving there, the family changed its name from Pile to Pyle. In 1876, William married Sidney McMillan, and the couple went on to have three children—Anna, Ira, and Charles. Charles Cassius Pile, or Charles Clifton Pile (referred to both ways in historical documents), was born on March 25, 1882, in northwest Ohio. The spelling of the family's original last name, Pile, may explain why he always took pains to remain well-groomed. Pile is slang for hemorrhoids, and for most of his life Charles would go by the initials C. C.[1]

By 1889, William had moved his family to nearby Delaware. Charles's father traveled to churches near his family's home, filling in for various congregations. It was at this time that Charles saw that a man didn't have to work a farm or in a factory to make a living, that one could make a respected income by talking about something he believed in, and for much of his childhood his mother encouraged him to be a preacher—like his father.

William Pyle had a gift for conversation, a skill he passed on to his son. William died in 1890, when Charles was eight years old, from tuberculosis. From this point onward the Pyle family struggled to make ends meet. Pyle's mother worked as a dressmaker, while her three children also found work to help pay the bills. In 1894, when Charles was 12, he and his brother Ira, who was 14, served as a travel agent for one of his father's churches and accompanied members of the congregation as train butchers, a common term used at that time to describe the people who sold passengers candy, fruit, and cigarettes.

Charles got his first taste of football by going to games at Ohio Wesleyan University, located in Delaware. The coach at Wesleyan was 26-year-old Fielding Yost, who, in 1897, guided OWU to a 7-1-1 record before leaving for Michigan. Yost was Pyle's first hero. Years later, he talked worshipfully of Yost's skill in rousing players and how he pushed his teams to victory when defeat seemed pending. Pyle also became a decent athlete himself—performing well at basketball, boxing, and bicycle riding—although pleurisy and a genetically weak heart ended any chance of him becoming a college or professional athlete.

By 1900, Charles, then 18, clerked on weekends at a grocery store, where he spent time thinking about his future. Would he go to college at Ohio Wesleyan to become a preacher, like his mother wanted, or leave home to make something of himself? Deep down, Pyle wanted to become rich and famous, he just didn't know how he was going to do it. Then came the opening that would change his life, a diagnosis by his doctor that the weak respiratory condition that he had inherited from his father would be eased somewhat by the fresh-air climate of the Pacific Coast. So, Pyle headed west.[2]

Taking a job selling Western Union time-service clocks for a commission of two dollars each, Pyle used Western Union passes to travel the railroads throughout the West. First landing in California, Pyle eventually made his way to Silverton, Oregon. It was there that he started his own theatrical company. To cut expenses, he became his own leading man starring in such plays as *The Golden Giant Mine* and *The Tennessee Partner*. On one of his tours, Pyle met Dorothy "Dot" Fischer, a 17-year-old performer whose father owned the local hotel in town. In 1905, Pyle, age 23, and Dorothy, age 21, were married. By now Pyle had joined a troupe, making $10 a week working as an advance man by traveling ahead of the actors and wheeling and dealing with theater and opera house owners. The job required C. C. to become a jack-of-all-trades by posting the handbills, drumming up publicity, and making stagecoach and hotel reservations.

Shortly after marrying Dot, her father passed away while the troupe was stationed in California. Hearing the news, C. C. and his wife remained in the small town of Eureka, where Pyle purchased a theater in town. As with the rest of his life, Pyle didn't stay still long. In 1907, he moved to Oakland, managing two theaters. At this time, Pyle's mother and siblings, Anna and Ira, moved out west. Pyle soon found himself smothered. He felt restless. He didn't want to be tied down, so he divorced Dot and abandoned her and their young daughter. While touring with the troupe, the group had a performance in Boise, Idaho. While standing on Main Street downtown, Pyle got his next big idea. He was going to open the first movie theater in Boise. Despite losing money, the theater went up and became a hit, but in a pattern that would engulf his entire life, Pyle became restless in Idaho. He wanted out.

Boise couldn't hold Pyle's attention, so once again he had to leave. In 1910, he left for the Windy City. In Chicago, Pyle quickly established himself. He landed a position with the Essanay Manufacturing Company, a film studio founded by George Spoor and "Bronco" Billy Anderson. While at the studio, Pyle fell in love with Martha Russell, a dark-haired vaudeville star. Assuming duties as her business manager, C. C. overflowed with ideas. But nothing hit it big, and the marriage ended quickly.

Pyle had now thrown away two wives, a daughter, and lots of money. After a second failed marriage, the 32-year-old Pyle hastily fell in love a third time, this time to "Effie" Arnold, a 27-year-old divorcee from St. Louis with two small children. Returning to Chicago, Pyle took a more stable job selling insurance to help his new family; however, he soon got the itch to get back into the game. In about 1918, Pyle took a job as a salesman with the Barton Musical Instrument Company, which made elaborate pipe organs for movie theaters. After two years working for Barton, Pyle made a connection that would lead him to football's biggest star.

The sandy, gray-haired Pyle grew up to be 6-foot-2 and 175 pounds, with broad shoulders and a sharp smile. He always dressed impeccably, usually sporting a black suit and black derby. He had his trademark short mustache trimmed weekly, but it wasn't his appearance that made him convincing. The man could talk. "He is a Scotch-Irishman with twinkling gray eyes, who immediately takes you in, in the warmth of his greeting and his general good fellowship," said one newspaper. Pyle looked like a man of money and influence, and he was, after years of trying. His initials, C. C., sportswriters joked, meant "Cash and Carry," and Pyle embraced the nickname.[3]

As the Roaring Twenties began, things were looking up for Pyle. He met Almon Stoolman, a Champaign contractor, who decided to partner with Pyle in building a lavish movie theater in the central college town where the University of Illinois was located. Pyle divorced again and moved into the Beardsley Hotel to start his newest project. In 1921, the newly minted Virginia Theater, named after Stoolman's daughter, opened in grand style, featuring a live stage show of the hit mystery *The Bat*. The next night, the Virginia showed its first feature film, *The Boat*, starring Buster Keaton. At this point, Pyle was flourishing.

Managing the Virginia in Champaign, he expanded his enterprise in the next few years to include a second theater, the Park, in Champaign, as well as one in Kokomo, Indiana, called the Victory Theater. Pyle was making a living, but deep down he wanted a shot at the big time. He was about to see it come walking through his doors at the Virginia.

When and how Red Grange actually met C. C. Pyle for the first time is somewhat of a mystery. For most of his life, Red said that he first met Pyle right before his senior season in the fall of 1925, at the Virginia Theater, but research proves this not to be true. They met almost a year before that historic meeting. Pyle always wanted a shot at the big time, especially in the entertainment field, but he needed a star to make him rich and famous. After the Michigan game, Red had hid from the public at a movie house, most likely the Virginia Theater on West Park Avenue, which was a little more than a mile walk from the frat house on East John Street, north of campus. Since Red enjoyed going to the movies, along with his good buddies Earl Britton and Doc Coolley, this is probably why for years Red mentioned that he met Pyle here before his senior year was to begin. Coolley knew everyone in town and might've introduced the two to one another.

Pyle knew a star when he saw one, and Red was now a superstar. The Virginia Theater even showed the newsreel of Red's superhuman performance against Michigan a week after the game. Once Red had become the biggest name in sports after the Michigan game, Pyle took notice of him. Red Grange was going to be his meal ticket to get rich. Red was immediately taken by Pyle. He liked him from the start and was especially impressed by his appearance.[4] Said Red,

Pyle was about 45 when I met him. He was a shade over six feet tall and weighed about 195 pounds. He had gray hair and a neatly trimmed mustache. An immaculate dresser, his clothes were made to order by the most exclusive tailors. He always carried a cane, wore spats, a derby, and a diamond stickpin in his tie. He was suave, brilliant, and perhaps the greatest super-salesman of his day. Pyle came up with more ideas in one day than most men come up with in a lifetime.[5]

Once his junior year on the gridiron was finished, Red kept busy. Just two days after his big homecoming banquet in Wheaton, Red was back on the move. This time he was headed to the Windy City. On November 30, Red was spotted at an NFL game. This was probably the first time he attended a pro football (or NFL) game. Red began thinking about his future—or maybe after meeting Pyle he was getting several opportunities to do something to capitalize on his growing fame. His public profile was growing. He was starting to become a celebrity and not just a 21-year-old student-athlete, so he wanted to see what the pro game was about.

On this day the Milwaukee Badgers were playing the hometown Chicago Bears at Cubs Park. Red sat in the stands with roughly 1,000 other fans, shivering on a cold and windy Sunday afternoon. The Bears were loaded with former Illinois players who had played for Bob Zuppke. The co-owners of the team, George Halas and Dutch Sternaman, were also the starting right end and left halfback, respectively. Other Illini alumni playing for the Bears included Oscar Knop (fullback); Vern Mullen (end); Dutch's younger brother, Joey Sternaman (quarterback); and Red's good friend, Jim McMillen, who was starting at right guard. Red's appearance at the game was reported in the *Chicago Herald-Examiner*:

> In a game full of forward passes the Chicago Bears thumped the Milwaukee Badgers, 31 to 14, at the Cubs' Park yesterday afternoon. It was the most spectacular clash of the season on the North Side, open football being turned on until the air seemed teeming with footballs.
>
> While this was going on, making the half-frozen spectators almost forget the cold, Red Grange, Illinois captain, sat in the stands and took it all in. It was something new for Red, seeing a gridiron battle without any work to do.[6]

There was no mention of who was with Red on this day. Maybe C. C. Pyle, Doc Coolley, Beans DeWolf, or his brother Garland. Who knows. But one thing was for sure, Red was thinking about playing professional football.

During the winter break, Red continued to keep busy. Soon a story came out that had all the fingerprints of C. C. Pyle. The report out of Champaign told of a rumor that Red would sign a contract to do movie work that would pay him $5,000 a week for five weeks. Headlines throughout the country read, "Grange to Make $25,000." The initial report said that "university officials had given concession" for Red to work. The offer came from Fine Arts Picture Corporation of New York. Pyle had a connection with the company through his theater work and encouraged his "star" friend to take the job. Red was reluctant to agree. He was nervous about jeopardizing his eligibility for his senior year. Illinois officials were equally nervous. "There is no truth in the report that we have granted Grange permission to accept a movie contract and absent himself from his schoolwork," declared Illinois athletic director George Huff.[7]

Red would turn down the offer and the money. This would be Pyle's first attempt at getting his newest "client" into Hollywood. Pyle was just getting started with his influence on Red. Shortly after the supposed movie offer, an advertisement was seen in a Seymour, Indiana, newspaper for "Red" Grange socks. The Hub clothing store in Seymour advertised "Red Grange college sox for high school boys." The cost was 25 cents. Pyle could have arranged this, but maybe the store just wanted to capitalize on Red's name. This would be an issue that Pyle wanted to tackle head-on.[8]

Back on campus, Red received a letter from a dear friend. Lowell Reynolds, a former teammate of his from Wheaton High School, was currently the head football coach at Richmond High in Richmond, Michigan. Reynolds invited his good friend to Richmond to speak at his team's annual end-of-year football banquet. He had talked to his team throughout season about his connection with Red and thought having him make an appearance at the banquet would thrill his players. Red couldn't say no to his friend. It would be the trip where he almost died.

Red left Champaign on the afternoon of February 4, to head north on the 420-mile trip to Michigan. Richmond was located 40 miles north of Detroit, so he made a pit stop in the Motor City that night to meet some special people. That evening, Red was a guest at the home of E. G. Miller. While at the "informal reception," Red was introduced to Willie Heston, the former Michigan halfback everyone was comparing Red to. Heston was practicing law near Detroit and eventually would serve as a state court judge. But on this night, Heston, 46 years old, and Red, 21 years old, were just two athletes talking football. The two then played a game of billiards. "Heston won, but Harold (Red) Grange was a good loser." Red was thrilled to have met Heston.[9]

Grange left Detroit at about midnight to travel the remaining 40 miles to Richmond. He would stay at the home of Lowell Reynolds. The small town of Richmond had a population of less than 1,500 citizens. Since hearing that Red would be coming to speak, the townspeople had gone all out to make him feel welcome. Getting to bed well after 1:00 a.m., Red slept in the following morning, waking up around 10:00 a.m. He soon complained of a sore throat. A doctor was immediately called on and gave Red the bad news. He was diagnosed with mumps. For the next few hours, his face was "swollen to unnatural size."[10]

Throughout the afternoon Red stayed in bed, only rising twice. Although very sick, he wanted to make an appearance at the banquet, since he had committed to being there. Somehow he gathered the strength to get to the Hotel Lenox, where the banquet was being held. More than 300 guests jammed the banquet hall.

The crowd was stunned by the appearance of Red. They had heard he was too sick to attend, but the Galloping Ghost slowly walked in to speak at the podium. The large banquet crowd rose up and gave him three cheers. He didn't say much, mostly hello and then good-bye. Red then returned to the guest bed at the Reynolds house. During the next few days, Red's condition got worse. His fever was high, his face was still swollen, and he was only able to sit up in bed once or twice a day. Just when it looked like he could go home, he had a relapse, with another high fever and chills. Richmond physician Dr. J. F. Mc-Carthy was brought in to attend. He told the press that Red was a "very sick man." Soon Red started to show signs of improvement. "Mr. Grange passed a restful night," claimed Lowell Reynolds to the press. "His fever is down, and his pulse has decreased. The cough which he has had throughout the siege, however, is still with him, but he is as well as can be expected."[11]

It had been two weeks. Red had not only been sick, but also missed two weeks of classes. He was itching to get back to Champaign. As soon as he felt better, Grange was moved into the home of H. A. Simmons, whose son, Walter Simmons, was a former track star at the University of Michigan. With help from a nurse, Red was ready to leave. He told her, "I hope I never see a bed again as long as I live." Three weeks after arriving in Richmond, Red was finally healthy enough to go back to school. "I'm going right back to Champaign," Red said to the press in Richmond. "And get back to my studies. I've missed three weeks of work and will have a job on my hands getting caught up." As he returned to campus, he announced that he would not play baseball in the spring; he needed to focus on school and getting healthier.[12]

As he got back to his studies, his relationship with Pyle continued to grow. He trusted him. Red, Doc Coolley, and Pyle soon would come to an agreement to join in a partnership. Pyle knew he wanted to look after Red's future, but he needed additional help with the potential earnings that would come down the road. Since he wasn't a great businessman or financial wizard, he needed someone to look after that end of the agreement. Pyle turned to another movie theater manager for help. He went to see Byron F. Moore.

"My grandfather was of fairly good stature," said Scott Moffatt, grandson of Byron Moore. "He had a mustache, black hair combed straight back, stood about 5-foot-10, in that range, not overweight, of medium build." The outgoing, intelligent Moore had spent his early adult life operating theaters in Richmond, Indiana; South Bend, Indiana; and Champaign, where he started a friendship with Pyle. He would spend a lifetime in the movie business, eventually working for Warner Brothers running theaters in St. Louis and Pittsburgh. "My mother always bragged about that," said Moffatt.

These movie stars traveled in those days, came to Pittsburgh, and visited my grandfather and his Warner theaters; stars such as Humphrey Bogart, Clark Gable, would come into town to sign autographs, and my father would take care of the Vaudeville or live acts. The Orpheum in Champaign was live shows before the movies.[13]

Moore was just a theater manager operating the Orpheum Theater in South Bend at the time Pyle brought up the opportunity to help with Red Grange. How could he say no? "He was a pretty outgoing guy, and my mother was excited about the Red Grange connection," said Scott Moffatt. "She believed that it was a lucrative arrangement for my grandfather. He wasn't rich, but I think he thought the idea was a very good money-making thing for him at the time. That connection with Red Grange economically was a pretty good move for him."[14]

Now on board to look after Red's affairs was a trio of men—Pyle, Moore, and Coolley. The group reached out to H. L. Jones, a Champaign lawyer whose office was located just two blocks from the Virginia Theater, at 112 West Church Street, in the Trevett-Mattis Banking building, to help them hammer out an agreement. The 46-year-old Jones had plenty of law experience with contracts since becoming a private attorney 20 years earlier. He drew up a contract for the four men. The contract was six pages in length and dated March 27, 1925. It was typed up on H. L. Jones's stationary paper. According to the contract the first party was the trio of Pyle, Moore, and Coolley, and the second party was Red Grange. The contract had 13 individual items that were agreed on.

H. L. JONES; CHAMPAIGN, ILLINOIS

"Articles of Agreement, made and entered into this 27th day of March A.D. 1925, by and between Chas. C. Pyle and Byron F. Moore, of Champaign, Illinois, and Marion F. Coolley, of Danville, IL, parties of the first, and Harold E. (Red) Grange of Wheaton, IL, party of the second. Witnesseth that for and in consideration of the respective promises and agreements hereinafter set forth, the respective parties here to agree as follows:

1. Party of the second part (Red) hereby agrees to give the parties of the first part (Pyle-Moore-Cooley) exclusive rights to manage and contract for the public exploitation, personal/public appearances and appearances in motion pictures, theatrical performances, professional football exhibitions/or otherwise . . . (also) for the use of his name in advertising ventures, including the advertisement of his appearances in motion pictures, theatrical

performances, professional football exhibitions/or otherwise . . .
(and) the exclusive rights and privileges in motion pictures, theatrical performances, professional football exhibitions/or otherwise
of contracting for the publications of newspaper or magazine
articles or stories published under the name of the party (Red)
. . . (and) further agrees that he will make no appearances and will
not permit the use of his name in any manner other than as in this
clause provided without the unanimous consent of the parties of
the first part during the period of this agreement which shall commence upon the date hereof and continue for, during, and until
March 27, 1928.

2. Said party of the second part hereby to agree to appear and fill all
engagements arranged and contracted for by the first parties of the
first part . . . there for, inevitable accident, illness, or other invol-
untary incapacity expected, provided however, said second party
(Red) not be obliged to make any appearances or conduct any
performances as hereinbefore above provided prior to the close of
the 1925 University of Illinois football games or prior to the 1925
football season closing on Saturday prior to Thanksgiving day in
the year 1925, and further agrees to do nothing whatever prior to
that time which would render himself subject to classification as a
professional athlete or football player.

3. Said second party (Red) further hereby agrees to exert his best
endeavors during the 1925 season to retain the popularity of his
name and make the use of same more effective for the purpose of
this agreement.

4. Said second party (Red) agrees to be governed by the rules and
regulations prevailing in the several localities where he may appear
under this contract/respect to the time of rehearsals and giving appearances.

5. Said second party (Red) hereby agrees that the first parties (Pyle-
Moore-Coolley) have exclusive rights to contract for display of his
name, pictures, and personal appearances in public or otherwise
for profit in such advertising ventures, motion pictures, theatrical
productions, football exhibitions, etc., during the entire period
covered by this contract . . . (close of 1925).

6. And that in event of the failure, default, or refusal upon the part of the part of the second part (Red) to perform the terms and conditions of his agreement, that the parties of the first part (Pyle-Moore-Coolley) shall have the right to sue for damages for the breach of this contract.

7. Said second party (Red) further hereby agrees to that he will promptly deliver over to the parties of the first (Pyle-Moore-Coolley) part all letters or other communication which may be received by him containing offers for his services or for the use of his name in any manner hereinthefore specified are to co-operate with the parties of the first part in carrying out this agreement for the mutual advantage and benefit of both parties hereto.

8. It is further hereby mutually agreed that the actual expenses of promotion and obtaining and making any necessary expenses of manager and second party (Red) in filling engagements contracts under this agreement, the said expenses to be itemized and an account thereof kept by the parties of the first (Pyle-Moore-Coolley) part for the benefit of both parties hereto, shall be paid out of the gross receipts.

9. And the parties of the first part (Pyle-Moore-Coolley) hereby agree to accompany said second party (Red) and personally represent him at each place he might be required to appear under the terms of this agreement.

10. Said parties of the first part (Pyle-Moore-Coolley) further hereby agree that they will do nothing under this contract on or before Saturday prior to Thanksgiving Day 1925, which would render the said party of the second part (Red) subject to classification as a professional athlete or football player.

11. Said parties of the first (Pyle-Moore-Coolley) part further hereby agree to use their best efforts to promote and exploit said party of the second part (Red) through the use of his name, pictures, and newspaper or magazine articles under his name and to do the other things herein before provided to be done by them.

12. The parties of the first part further hereby agree that the said Charles C. Pyle shall, and he hereby authorized by all of the parties here to personally negotiate and execute any and all contracts which may be obtained, negotiated, and concluded by or for the

parties of the first part (Moore-Coolley) pursuant to the terms of this agreement.

13. It is further hereby mutually contracted and agreed that the net proceeds or net profits derived from these engagements, performances, ventures, or undertakings, conducted pursuant to this agreement shall, upon receipt, therefore be divided among the several parties hereto as follows; 40 percent (40%) thereof shall be paid to the party of the second part (Red); 25 percent (25%) thereof to the said Charles C. Pyle; 17½ percent (17.5%) thereof to the said Marion F. Coolley; and 17½ percent (17.5%) to the said Byron F. Moore, settlement upon that basis to be made by such of the parties of the first part (Pyle-Moore-Cooley) as shall be present at the respective appearances or engagements of the party of the second part (Red) as his representative at the time in connection therewith.

WITNESS the hands and seals of the respective parties hereto this 27th day of March A.D. 1925.
Chas. C. Pyle (signed in purple ink)
Byron F. Moore (signed in black ink)
Marion F. Coolley (signed in black ink)
Harold E. "Red" Grange (signed in blue ink)
(all signed and sealed)[15]

This was a historic contract. Never before had a college football player signed with an "agent" to help represent him. In 1925 there was no NCAA rule against signing with another person to represent you. This was more of a "power of attorney" contract for the future, not a contract to play pro football. Red was clearly aware of what he was doing, so much so that he put in the contract, items 2 and 10, a clause that nothing was to be done until after he completed his senior season at Illinois. He did not want to sign any contracts with pro teams or Hollywood studios, or take any money. The split of the net profits would come later, with the split as follows: Red Grange, 40 percent; C. C. Pyle, 25 percent; Byron F. Moore, 17.5 percent; Marion F. Coolley, 17.5 percent. This would eventually change.

Last but not least, this contract shows proof of who represented Red Grange. It appeared that only C. C. Pyle was Red's manager; however, this was not true.

Red would be represented by three men. Three men who would watch over his business affairs and split the net profits with Red. The contract, signed in March 1925, would be kept by the Marion F. Coolley family for almost 100 years.

After regaining his strength, Red participated in spring ball. While Grange got back on the football field, the Pyle group looked to capitalize on his popularity. Pyle's first big scheme came out a few weeks after the agreement with Red. He and Coolley took Red into Chicago to take a photo at Society Brand, a line of men's suits manufactured by Alfred Decker & Cohn of Chicago. A company founded in 1902, by Alfred Decker and Abraham Cohn, the company building was located at 416 South Franklin Street and was one of the largest manufacturers of men's wear in the country. While at Society Brand, Red was dressed in an immaculate suit and tie, a vest, a white collared shirt, and shining dress shoes for a publicity photo. This photo was then seen in an ad for the Mayer Bros. Company of Lincoln, Nebraska.[16] The ad ran for a few weeks in the *Lincoln Evening Journal*. Below the photo it read, "Red Grange: Famous Football Player—seen in action at the New Stadium last fall. This photo shows Mr. Grange in one of the new 'Sandtones' as tailored by Society Brand, Alfred Decker & Cohn, Chicago."[17]

Who knows if this advertisement was completely Pyle's idea or whether Red got paid, but it definitely had the influence of Cash and Carry. Pyle continued to work with his contacts in Hollywood to get Red a chance at being in the movies. Red went along with Pyle's next attempt at the big time. This time Pyle took Red, Coolley, and Harry E. McNevin, who was the former manager of the Rialto Theater in Champaign and secretary-treasurer of the Stoolman–Pyle corporation, on a road trip. In 1925, McNevin was also working as a cashier at the Illinois Savings and Trust Bank in Champaign. He was Pyle's money man.

On May 12, the foursome arrived in Milwaukee, Wisconsin, to attend a three-day convention of the Motion Picture Theatre Owners of America. They would stay at the Hotel Pfister, where the convention headquarters resided. The annual convention was sponsored by Universal Studios, which had several big-name actors and actresses attending, including Virginia Valli, Louise Dresser, Jack Daugherty, cowboy Hoot Gibson, William Desmond, and stuntman Al Wilson. Red was thrown into the Hollywood world for the first time. Although shy by nature, he soaked in the atmosphere.

Pyle was there to mingle with the Hollywood executives and theater owners, but he was also there to show off his prize recruit. Throughout the day he and McNevin kept bragging about Red, saying he would be the next Wallace Reid, one of Hollywood's best silent-movie stars, referred to as the "screen's most perfect lover."[18]

Red knew his future was on the football field at Illinois, but he wanted to see what the movie industry was all about. He agreed to take a "screen test" and have some publicity photos taken. He was paired up with actress Virginia Valli, an attractive young brunette, who had appeared in a dozen silent films and just finished a picture entitled *The Pleasure Garden*, which was the directorial debut of Alfred Hitchcock. Valli taught him to put on makeup while the photographers took pictures. "You are an awfully smart boy on the football field, but you don't know anything about lipstick," Valli scolded Red. "You'd be surprised," retorted Red, as he promptly kept his lips pursed for the application of the red salve from Valli, who laughed. Red was hamming it up for the photographers and the Hollywood crowd.[19]

A few Milwaukee newspapermen soon surrounded Red to get some answers. Was he going to Hollywood? "I am here as the guest of Mr. Pyle, simply to meet some of the men engaged in the picture business," he said. "I do not expect to go into any business this summer, until after I finish my college work at Illinois."[20] Does he have the required temperament and love for the ladies to make him a matinee idol? "The first will come easily as the salary mounted, the latter I have always had," Red responded.[21] Does attending this convention mean that you are leaving Illinois? "I haven't signed anything and don't expect to sign any contracts except for my usual summer work in the ice business in Wheaton," he declared. "After I have finished my college work, there's time to talk about that."[22]

The newspapermen wrote that Red had turned down Hollywood to remain an iceman. The headlines, probably encouraged by Pyle, read that he turned down a $300,000 movie offer. For the second time in five months, Red had turned down Hollywood.

After returning from Milwaukee, Pyle took Red to Kokomo to show him off in the town where he owned the Victory Theater. For a weekend, Red was paraded around as Pyle's big star. On Friday, May 22, Red was one of the special guests for a local youth jamboree sponsored by the Kokomo Rotary Club. The event was held at the local high school auditorium, where almost 1,000 boys, ages nine to 14, attended. Along with Roltaire Eggleston, the famous magician, and William Herschell, the Hoosier poet, Red was a big hit with the kids. Pyle introduced his star to the crowd after giving a brief outline of Red's life. Red then gave a "short but pleasing address" to the boys. "You and I are both happy school will soon be over," Red said. He also talked about being part of a team and following the "rules laid down for athletic training."[23]

The *Kokomo Daily Tribune* wrote that Red was a "likeable chap," adding, "He is a modest, likeable fellow and is out to learn all he can wherever he goes."

The paper also wrote that after a roar of applause Red "blushed like a schoolgirl at the ovation." The following day, Red made two appearances at the Victory Theater for Pyle. Showing that day was the movie *Percy*, starring Charles Ray and Betty Blythe. Red greeted moviegoers at the matinee and evening showings. After the weekend in Kokomo, he returned to Champaign to finish out the semester.[24]

Red struggled with his second-semester classes, albeit this was understandable with missing three weeks because of the mumps. But his time with Pyle also didn't help. He finished with a B in geography 3; a C in business administration; two Ds, in history 61B and history 22B; and one F in transportation 1. The school allowed him to make up the failure in transportation by taking a special exam during the summer. After a trying junior year, Red returned to Wheaton for the summer. He and Garland would work the ice truck for L. C. Thompson.

In the middle of his summer break, Red received a request from Pyle. He wanted to take another road trip. Nothing got under Pyle's skin more than the use of Red's name for advertisement. Right after the famous Michigan game, the Wills-Sainte Claire Car Company of Marysville, Michigan, a small town located about 55 miles north of Detroit, had started to run full-page ads claiming their cars were the "Red Grange of Traffic." One ad stated, "Suddenly out of the inextricable tangle, with utter unconcern and the dash of a 'Red' Grange, there emerges *One Car*." This ad, which appeared in approximately 20 newspapers, soon caught the attention of Pyle. He wanted to take a stand. He got in touch with Homer McKee of Indianapolis, who handled the company's advertising, complaining about the use of Red's name in the ads. After talking with McKee, Pyle learned that he would have to broach this subject with the president of the company, C. Harold Wills.[25]

From an early age, C. Harold Wills had a way with metal and a love for cars. Trained as a machinist, Wills worked during the day at the Boyer Machine Company, and, in 1899, he began moonlighting for Henry Ford—for free. Like Ford, Wills learned by doing. But unlike Ford, who worked instinctively, Wills worked effectively with blueprints and was a brilliant draftsman. Together they made a perfect team. Following the success of the "999" and "Arrow" race cars, the Ford Motor Company was founded in 1903, with Wills as chief engineer. Wills's continued studies and experiments led to new steel alloys, allowing Ford to make lighter, smaller, and stronger parts. Wills even designed the script for Ford's famous company emblem. Eventually, Wills's earnings at Ford enabled him to form his own company in 1921—the Wills-Sainte Claire Car Company. Wills had worked for many years alongside the perplexing Henry Ford. Thus, dealing with a superagent wasn't something he was worried about.

Using letterhead of the Victory Theater, Pyle sent a letter to Wills, dated June 9, 1925.

My Dear Mr. Wills:

I called on Homer McKee, of Indianapolis, a few weeks ago as a representative of "Red" Grange, football star of the University of Illinois. My interview with Mr. McKee was in reference to an advertisement which was carried in all the metropolitan newspapers last year, headed the "Red Grange of Traffic."

After having a very satisfactory interview, Mr. McKee assured that he would write to you and arrange an appointment with you so that Mr. Grange and myself could state to you personally our complaint. We felt that it was only fair to both sides, and if a satisfactory adjustment could be made, it would not be necessary to turn it over to place it in the hands of our attorney.

After waiting several weeks, I have just received a letter from Mr. McKee suggesting that I write you direct, as his company is no longer handling your account. I desire to make an appointment with you with Mr. Grange and myself in Chicago at your convenience, or if you prefer it, we will come direct to Marysville. You will find us fair in our dealings.

A letter addressed to me in care of this theater or Hotel Beardsley, Champaign, Ill., will receive my immediate attention. (Signed) CHARLES C. PYLE.[26]

Wills responded to the letter by agreeing to a meeting to discuss the complaint. Pyle responded with a short telegram, which stated the following: "Mr. Grange and myself will call on Mr. Wills next Tuesday morning accordance with your letter." The meeting was set for June 22. Red traveled with Pyle. How much Red wanted to handle this situation is unclear, but Pyle was in charge.[27]

The two arrived in Marysville at the showroom of C. Harold Wills. Pyle did most of the talking. He showed Wills a scrapbook of Red's accomplishments, claiming that he was bigger than Babe Ruth and that the "free" advertisement of his name probably helped sales. Speaking to the *Detroit News*, Wills recalled Pyle's demands:

(Pyle) then asked "how much they thought the damage would amount to." . . . Pyle replied that he thought it could be settled for two automobiles, one for

Grange, the other for himself. Then I asked them if they wished to see the factory. I had a man take them through the various departments while I got in communication with Mr. Butzel (his lawyer) over the telephone. When, after a half-hour or so, Grange and Pyle returned in very good spirits, they announced they had selected their cars. Each had selected a roadster. I told them that I would not give them their automobiles and to get out, or words to that end. That was the last I have seen of them.[28]

Wills also told the *Detroit News* about his impression of Red Grange. He related, "He is a big, boyish fellow, rather silent. Pyle did practically all the talking. Once in a while Grange would nod his head as if to back him up, or add a few words to whatever Pyle said."[29]

Pyle tried his best to talk his way into getting cars for Red and himself, but it didn't work. Wills had called his bluff. Pyle was not about to tie himself up in court to win two cars. In the end, it was just a waste of time. The failure of Pyle to obtain the cars didn't change Red's feelings toward Pyle. He liked his flamboyant style. He would eventually get things done for the redhead. He could see it.

During the previous seven months, Pyle, Coolley, and Moore had exercised a tremendous influence on Red. They were steering him toward the movies, advertisements, and public appearances, although none of this involved any money. Red was tired. He wanted to concentrate on his senior season. If he failed to produce on the field, no one would want to pay to see him play as a professional later on. He still needed to excel on the field. He still needed to be an All-American.

Even with all the traveling and summer work Red was able to pass his transportation class. He was now eligible to play. As Red was turning his focus to playing his senior year at Illinois, Pyle was brainstorming his next big idea. He knew that Red was reluctant to capitalize on his fame in areas that he was uncomfortable in, like acting or vaudeville. Red wanted to play football. Pyle started to think about the biggest, greatest football tour of all time. It would be Red doing the thing he did best. People would come out in the thousands to see him perform. This was what Pyle needed to make himself rich and famous. It was time to tell Red about his plan.

This is where Red's version of what happened next with Pyle is factual. Red walked to the Virginia Theater to see a movie, but Pyle wanted to talk with him in his office. Speaking to Myron Cope for his book *The Game That Was*, Red recalled,

Well, the first words Charley Pyle said to me were "Red, how would you like to make $100,000, or maybe even $1 million?" I couldn't figure what he was talking about. But he said, "I have a plan. I will go out and set up about 10 or 12 football games around the United States. I can talk George Halas and Dutch Sternaman of the Chicago Bears into making their team available, and as soon as the college season ends, we will make this tour, and I'll guarantee you that you'll make at least a hundred thousand out of it." Of course, I was flabbergasted. But Charley made good his word.[30]

For most of his life, this is how Grange told the story of how Pyle revealed his idea of playing professional football in his office at the Virginia Theater. Red loved football and wanted to play pro ball, but he never would have thought about trying to set up a barnstorming tour just after his last college game. He loved the idea. He also trusted Pyle, who told Red not to sign any contracts or accept any money until after his final college game on November 21, just like their agreement said. Pyle said he would handle the details. He just wanted Red to play football.

Red thought his life was crazy then, but in three short months his life would change again, getting crazier than ever. He would soon experience the ride of a lifetime by touring the country playing pro football.

11

EAST COAST INVASION

After spending most of the spring and summer getting to know C. C. Pyle and agreeing to have him as his comanager, along with Doc Coolley and Byron Moore, Red started to concentrate on football. He needed to be in shape if the plan of playing professional football was to play out. He had to be the same superstar player he was in 1924.

On September 15, Coach Zuppke had more than 70 players out for the team's first practice. The roster had some key losses, especially his linemen, and those remaining didn't have much experience. Zuppke knew his squad might struggle more than they did in 1923–1924. He did have one young player who he was eager to see on the field.

Garland Grange was finally ready to contribute to the varsity team. Unfortunately, he never got the opportunity. During one of the team's early scrimmages against the freshmen, Garland reinjured his bad shoulder. This time it was serious. X-rays proved extensive damage to the shoulder, requiring surgery. At St. Luke's Hospital in Chicago, Garland had his shoulder operated on. He would miss the entire 1925 season.

On September 30, the *Chicago Tribune* published a headline stating, "Pro Football Leaders Seek Red Grange for Eastern Games." The article, written by James Crusinberry, revealed that a few New York city sports moguls wanted to bring the redhead to the Big Apple to play professional football. That was the first big exposé about Grange's future plans. In writing the article, Crusinberry traveled to Champaign to talk to Red. For more than an hour, Red discussed some of the so-called plans with the eastern pro teams:

I haven't made any plans whatever to play professional football. I haven't signed a contract with anyone nor have I made a verbal agreement to play, and right now I really don't know whether or not I would accept an offer to play for money.

No one has talked to me about playing with the Four Horsemen in New York, but I have heard that Col. Ruppert of the Yankees is expecting to put on professional football games at his stadium. . . . I am not opposed to college men playing professional football after they have finished their college career on the gridiron. I guess a lot of us need money and can't well afford to turn down big offers because of sentiment.[1]

"The Western Conference is one of the cleanest organizations in the country, and it will hurt us if Grange turns pro," said Major John L. Griffith, commissioner of the Big Ten, who responded to the report. "Of course, we cannot prevent him from doing as he chooses, but if he plays after the Ohio State game on Nov. 21, the conference faculty committee may take some drastic action to prevent such a thing happening in the future." The water was starting to boil in the battle for football's soul. Colleges versus pros. Red would be stuck in the middle.[2]

Sportswriters throughout the country wanted to check out the Illini football team and, in particular, Red Grange. Two well-known East Coast writers, Grantland Rice (*New York Herald-Tribune*) and Herbert Reed (*Universal Services*), traveled to Champaign to see Illinois's first game of 1925. For the third straight season, the season opener was against Nebraska. This time the Illini would not cross the Cornhuskers' goal line. In front of a crowd of roughly 25,000 at Memorial Stadium, the Fighting Illini offense, with Red, was stopped by a smothering defense led by All-American tackle Ed Weir. On a muddy gridiron, Red committed the game's first big mistake. Dropping back, he misguided a pass that Nebraska halfback Frank Daily intercepted and returned 38 yards for a score. The Cornhuskers would go on to post a 14–0 win, handing the first setback to Zuppke's squad in Memorial Stadium. "We were beaten by a superior team," said Zuppke after the game.[3]

The rest of the country would so be getting more of Red Grange. In their October issue, *Sportlife* magazine wrote a three-page article entitled "How'd You Like to Be the Iceman?" Another article about Red came from a magazine that was fast becoming one of the country's most popular publications.[4]

Time magazine was founded in New York by Henry Luce as the country's first weekly news magazine, combing politics, newsmakers, entertainment, and sports in one volume. Luce called it *Time* because the thought was that a reader could save time in reading the magazine in one hour. Launched in 1923, the magazine became an instant hit. Famous personalities graced the cover from the start. In 1925 alone, the likes of Henry Ford, Thomas Edison, Winston Churchill, Charlie Chaplin, and golfer Bobby Jones were featured on the cover. On the front of the October 5 edition was a head shot of Red Grange. Inside, the one-page article was titled "Enter Football." The seven paragraphs spoke briefly of college football and its biggest star. Grange would be the first football player to be featured on the cover of *Time*. He wouldn't be the last.[5]

The following week, Illinois rebounded with a nice 16–13 victory against Butler. Red, who had been battling a cold all week, returned to his usual ways scoring on a 60-yard punt return and a 10-yard run. The next two weeks would be the toughest of Red's career. First, Zuppke switched Red to quarterback but only by name. He would still line up at his traditional left halfback spot, but now Red would call the signals. Talking to the *Chicago American* during the 1925 season, Zuppke praised his team captain's football IQ, saying, "Grange is a great runner and a sturdy back, but two-thirds of his success is due to his football knowledge. He studies the game. He knows it thoroughly. He is a football strategist of the first water—and a leader par excellence."[6]

Although he was just 22 years old, Red had learned much about the game of football from his previous mentors. Going back to high school with Charles Welden and in college with Burt Ingwersen and Bob Zuppke, Red was already on his way to earning a PhD in football strategy.

Next on the schedule was Iowa, a team that had won its first two games, against Arkansas and Saint Louis. Burt Ingwersen prepared his team well to face his former boss. Against his former freshman coach, Red would suffer his toughest defeat. A sold-out crowd at Iowa Field did get to see one of Red's trademark coast-to-coast scores. On the opening kickoff, he dodged and sprinted through the entire Hawkeyes cover team untouched for a remarkable 83-yard kickoff return touchdown. Red's score gave Illinois an early lead that held up into the fourth quarter, 7–6. Helped by a roughing the passer penalty, the Hawkeyes made one last drive. After a 10-play march, Iowa capped the drive with a one-yard touchdown run by halfback Nick Kutsch for the deciding score. Red played all 60 minutes against the Hawkeyes, only to come up short in a 12–10 defeat.

Zuppke's squad was now 1–2, with more losses than the previous two years combined. Next for the Illini was Michigan. This was the game the town of Wheaton wanted to see, so much so that Wheaton mayor Marion Pittsford proclaimed the day of the game "Red Grange Day":

I, Marion J. Pittsford, mayor of the city of Wheaton, Illinois, do hereby declare and proclaim Saturday, the 24th day of October, A.D. 1925, a holiday in honor of Harold Grange, a citizen of this city, in order that those citizens so desiring may avail themselves of the opportunity of attending the ceremonies to be held at the University.

M. J. Pittsford.[7]

Businesses were closed so that employees could to go to the game. This included law enforcement, which meant that Lyle Grange could travel to Champaign to watch his son play. More than 400 citizens of Wheaton made the trip south to Champaign. Sitting mostly in one section of the stadium, the joyful and vocal group wore bright orange caps with Wheaton written across the top. Lyle sat nervously in section M, waiting to watch his son play. Also in the stands were Illinois lieutenant governor Fred Sterling and state senator William McKinley, a graduate of Illinois.

At Memorial Stadium, the two teams played a defensive slugfest. Another muddy field limited Grange's speed. Midway through the second quarter, the Wolverines put together their best drive of the day. Quarterback Benny Friedman booted a 25-yard field goal to give Michigan a 3–0 lead. The score would hold up. Yost got his revenge by beating Zuppke. Despite the lack of wins and big highlight runs for touchdowns, Red was still in demand—especially with the Chicago press.

Behind the guidance of Pyle, Red was asked by two Chicago newspapers to help write his "story." Dueling "life stories" or "as told to" articles were featured in two Windy City newspapers. First was the *Chicago Daily News*. In a series of articles titled "Red Grange: His Story" written by James Braden, a former All-American fullback with Yale from 1916 to 1919, the Illinois star sat down for 17 different stories that would run in the *Daily News*, as well as in newspapers throughout the country, including the *Los Angeles Times*, *Tennessean*, *Minneapolis Star-Tribune*, *Pittsburgh Post-Gazette*, and *Detroit News*.

At the beginning of each story appeared the line, "This is my real story. I have authorized it for publication—Harold Grange." The 17 articles chronicled Red's life, starting with his birth in Forksville and continuing on to his life in Wheaton, his high school glory days, his arrival at Illinois, and the past four years as a football phenom. The articles included a few quotes from Grange, but they were mostly more encyclopedia-ish and, quite frankly, a little boring. One gem he told Braden about himself was as follows:

There is only one way I know to become an athlete. Gets lots of sleep and live a regular, normal, healthy life. Keep away from the white lights, and eat plain food. Don't eat too much meat. Any vegetable is good. Spinach and potatoes are excellent. Chew the food well. Don't smoke. Don't drink liquor. Don't be a loafer on the street. Think that you will come to the top and you will get there.[8]

In the last article, Red talked about the game he loved so much:

It's the best game ever invented. It demands more than any other game from the players. It gives little in a material way but everything in a spiritual way. I'm sure I'm a better man for having played. Most of the credit for my individual performance should go to Bob Zuppke and the members of the Illinois football squad.[9]

The second series of articles was written in the *Chicago American* by one of its ace sportswriters—Harold Johnson. These were "as told to" articles and gave more insight into the 22-year old superstar who was making daily headlines throughout the United States. From October 29 to November 21, 18 separate stories were written by Johnson. These articles featured a few photos, while also digging into more personal aspects of Red's life.[10]

Typically, Johnson would meet with Red at the fraternity house to have dinner and interview the redhead in a session he called "fanning the bee." The veteran scribe quickly found Red charming and a good storyteller, saying, "He tells it in a straightforward, sincere manner that cannot be bettered. . . . He will not talk about himself unless you peck, peck away. If you praise him, he'll give a look and say the word 'baloney.'"[11]

The early articles featured many stories about how Red handled being a celebrity and the tons of letters that were sent to him. Said Red,

If I were to show you some of the communications that arrive in the mail, there were more than two bureau drawers full of letters from all parts of the country, some of them very interesting and appreciated. But then there were lots and lots of them of the mushy types from girls. One very attractive young woman wrote from a small town in Massachusetts and enclosed a photograph of herself standing under a tree alongside her pet pony. If I tried to answer all the letters that come here I'd never have a chance to attend classes, study, or practice. Last year, at the height of the season, I got as many as 20 letters a day.[12]

Red told Johnson that he always made it a priority to answer the letters from the young boys who wrote to him. "They want my autograph, and I always get a laugh out of it," he said. One letter arrived from boxing champion Jack Dempsey—one of the other sports stars of the Roaring Twenties who shared headlines with Red. "I take my hat off to you, Red," Dempsey wrote. "I meet only one man and usually have difficulty in getting the decision. You, with only one arm free, usually pound through 11 men. Take it from me, you're a marvel. How you do it is a mystery to me."[13]

"I believe it is a good idea to make as many people happy as you can," said Red to Johnson for the November 5 article. "Probably I won't have this chance after I am out of school and the people have started to forget about me."[14]

In the November 10 article, Red described his typical day as a college student:

> I'm up every morning at 7 o'clock, whether I am at school or home. At 7:30 I answer the bell for breakfast at the Zeta Psi fraternity house and at 8 o'clock start to my classes at the university. As a rule I devote three hours each morning to studies, returning to the fraternity house for luncheon from 12 until 1 o'clock. During the next two hours I engage in classwork, and at 2:30 p.m. I go in for football practice.
>
> We usually take it easy on Monday following a hard game, but on the afternoons we drill from 3 o'clock until long after dark, practicing under arc lights when dusk settles about us. Occasionally, after practice I slip off to a motion picture theater but always make it point to be in bed not later than 10 o'clock.[15]

In one of the last articles, Red commented on being a college football player:

> You know, you can't beat the training you receive on a university football squad to prepare you for the hard knocks of the future when you go forth to earn a livelihood. That training makes real men of the boys. It puts you in the very best physical condition so there isn't any reason for whimpering when you are nailed hard by an opposing tackler.[16]

In his four years at Illinois, under the guidance of Bob Zuppke, Red had learned much about being not only a great player, but also a man. He definitely didn't regret his decision to attend the University of Illinois. After the tough loss against Michigan, Red was thinking about the team's upcoming game against Penn. "Tell the alumni in the East, who, I understand, will be at Franklin Field by the thousands next Saturday, that we will do our best, and I personally hope they will not be disappointed," he said. "I was sure glad when Zup told me we were going to play Penn. Now I want to do something out there so they won't think I am a terrible bust."[17]

The Illinois season was going down the drain fast, with the team sporting a record of 1–3, but Zuppke knew the season would hinge on one game—the East Coast trip to battle the University of Pennsylvania—so much so that the athletic department spent $5,015.38 for the trip. It was money well spent. Lou

Young's Quakers were one of the best teams in the country. In 1924, they had gone 9–1–1, with their only loss coming in a New Year's Day setback against the Cal Bears in California. So far in 1925, they were undefeated, at 5–0, with wins against Brown and Yale, and a week earlier they had beaten Stagg's Chicago squad, 7–0. They were huge favorites going into the game with Illinois.[18]

Zuppke had a plan. He had been scouting the Quakers for years. In a 1978 interview, Red recalled his coach's game plan against Penn:

> Let me give the coaches credit. (Illinois) scout came back, and each time he would tell us that Pennsylvania had a great defensive team but that they overshifted all the time. Now, in my day, we used what we called an unbalanced line. We would have four men on one side of center and two men on the other. And we would line up our backfield strong to the four-man side. And that's called a "single-wing back."
>
> Well, we found when other teams playing Pennsylvania would shift to the right, Pennsylvania would shift its whole defense over in front of the strength. Now, Zuppke had never run a lot of weak-side plays. By that, I mean, run back, the ball would come to the tailback (he was four and a half yards back of the center and instead of going back to the strong side, where we had four linemen, go back to the weak side where we had two linemen). So we decided the only way we could beat Pennsylvania was by running weak-side plays.[19]

The team left Champaign at noon on the Thursday before the game. Thirty-five strong, the Illini were confident that they would bring a victory back to campus. An enthusiastic crowd of several thousand fans cheered the athletes on their way east. The team arrived in Philadelphia on Friday morning. After a short lunch Zuppke took his squad out to see Franklin Field, where the game would be played. Snow was coming down, and the groundskeeper made no effort of trying to cover it up. It would be another sloppy, muddy field. Zuppke had his players check out the dressing quarters and went through a "dummy scrimmage" on the wet gridiron. Reports said the "workout was short and snappy." The squad then continued on to the Manufactures Country Club, where they would stay the night.[20]

Red had waited an entire year—maybe his entire life—for this game, hoping for a stage like this. Zuppke would not let his prized pupil down. He would feed him the ball. The game plan featured weak-side runs. At Franklin Field, the press box was jammed with almost 100 newspapermen. The usual Chicago–Champaign suspects were there—Warren Brown (*Herald and Examiner*), James Braden (*Daily News*), Jimmy Corcoran (*Chicago American*), Kenneth Fry (*Evening Post*), Tom Morrow (*Daily Illini*), and Eddie Jacquin (*Champaign*

News-Gazette)—but the East Coast heavyweights also took their seats, including the three most important eastern sports scribes, Grantland Rice (*New York Tribune*), Ford Frick (*International News*), and Damon Runyon (*Universal News Service*). Also covering the game were Frazier Harrison (*Big Ten Weekly*), Ross Kaufman (*Pittsburgh Press*), Parke H. Davis (*Pittsburgh Press*), Ed Pollack (*Philadelphia Public Ledger*), Gordon Mackey (*Philadelphia Enquirer*), Harry Cross (*New York Times*), W. B. Hanna (*New York Herald-Tribune*), Davis J. Walsh (*International News*), and Henry L. Farrell (*United Press*), and from down south, Jack Bell of the *Miami Herald*.

A crowd of 63,000 filled Franklin Field. The hometown fans wouldn't have much to cheer about it. On a muddy gridiron, Red again proved to the critics that he was the best football player in the country—and made a case as the best football player of all time.

Zuppke's game plan of having Red run to the weak side quickly paid off. Decades later, Red would recall his coach's instructions moments before kickoff:

(Zuppke) told me before the game, "If we receive, I want you to line up strong either right or left. Run (Earl) Britton into the strong side first two times. The third time, I want ya to line up strong one way, generally, to the short side of the field. Then I want you to take the ball and go to the weak side." And sure enough, we received, and it turned out just as Zuppke said it would. We took the ball. . . . I ran Britton strong into the strong side, and each time, he made one yard and lost a yard once. And the third play coming up I was the one to take. I shifted strong to the right. I let our backs run to the right. I touched the ball down the ground, and I went back left. I went 56 yards to a touchdown, and there was not anyone over there. I never was as lonesome. I could be in Wheaton at 12 o'clock midnight and they'd have more people in front of me than I did there.[21]

After the kickoff, Red lined up in his usual halfback position (although he was the starting quarterback). Just like Zuppke wanted, Red called for a run by Britton to the strong side of the line. Red called another strong-side run. Neither play generated positive gains, so Red called for a punt. After one play from scrimmage, the Quakers punted the ball back to the Illini. Now it was time for Red to keep the ball and go back to the weak side. On the first play, he sprinted through the mud 55-yards for a touchdown. Britton missed the extra point. The sold-out crowd and onlookers in the press box were stunned by the quick score.

The Quakers, just like Michigan in 1924, decided to kick off back to Illinois for field possession. Bad idea. Red took the kick back 57 yards, down inside the Quakers 20-yard line. After nine straight runs, Britton plowed over for another score. He missed his second extra point, giving Illinois a 12–0 lead.

As the snow came down the field got muddier, but the slick gridiron did not slow down the Galloping Ghost. Red recalled,

> In those days they had no cover for the gridirons except straw. They had put hay and straw on the field. And a couple of hours before game time they took the straw off. And it was bad mud. We used mud cleats, which is [*sic*] a little bit larger than a regular cleat. And mud never worried us any. I kind of like to play in the mud! As a kid, I liked to play in the mud puddles and things; it never affected me in any way. . . . I always took high steps, as long as I could get my footing. I don't think mud had anything to do with it. It didn't affect the game in any way. Playing on a dry field, we would have played the same way.[22]

Later, in the second quarter, the Quakers blocked a Britton punt through the end zone for a safety. It would be their only score of the day. After an exchange of punts, the Illini offense took over at the Quakers 38-yard line. Red carried the ball three times, reaching the 12-yard line, where he ran weak side again for another touchdown. "The redhead, covered with mud, from head to foot, was accorded a deafening ovation as he trotted to the sidelines."[23] Fans and those in the press box knew they were witnessing a once-in-a-lifetime player making history—again.

Early in the third quarter, the Quakers punted out of trouble to near midfield. This time the offense got a little fancy and tried a flea-flicker. Britton handed off to Chuck Kassell, who tossed the ball to Red. Grange sprinted 20 yards for his third touchdown of the game. It was a rout. The Fighting Illini trounced the Quakers, 24–2. "You know I starved the team for this game. Three nights I sent them to bed hungry and gave them lots of tea—that helped them on edge," said Zuppke after the contest.[24]

According to the University of Illinois, Red had 363 total yards in the game (28 carries for 237 yards, 2 catches for 35, 2 punt returns for 12, and 2 kickoff returns for 79) and 3 touchdowns. After the game, while the Illini locker room rejoiced, the Quakers locker room was silent. Coach Lou Young sang the praises of Red. "Grange, in my estimation, is the greatest football player in the game," he commented. "They can compare him with any of the greats of the past, and they can place him alongside of Thorpe and others, but to me he stands out alone." Young would know, as he played on the 1912 Pennsylvania team that faced off against Jim Thorpe's Carlisle Indians at Franklin Field, a contest the Quakers won, 34–26. Young continued,

> I saw Thorpe play in his heyday, when he was the hardest man in football to stop. But I firmly believe that Grange eclipses anything Thorpe ever did. The manner

in which Grange ran that ball, the way in which he pivoted, used his straight-arm, shook off tacklers, made me feel that he was virtually unstoppable. His change of pace, in addition to all his other attributes, puts him in a class by himself among the football carries.[25]

In the visitors' locker room Red was quickly surrounded by reporters, who wanted his opinion of the game. Red gave credit to his teammates for his remarkable performance:

The interference the entire team gave me was marvelous. Many times Britton and the rest of the boys opened huge places around the ends for me. . . . My running mates in the backfield also played bang-up football. Dougherty, Gallivan, and Britton carried the ball in splendid style, while their defensive work was remarkable. . . . There certainly was a great crowd at the game. I hope I looked good to them, for if I ever wanted to get loose it was on Franklin Field. You know this was my first game in the East and my first visit to Philadelphia since I was a boy.[26]

The writers continued to ask Red about how he was able to be the star of the show, but all Red wanted to do was talk about his teammates. He added, "Let's not talk about my playing any longer. There were 15 other men in the game, and everyone deserves great credit." Most of Red's teammates passed by him saying, "Great game Red." Red would shoot back, "Great game yourself."[27]

Zuppke told the press how he really felt about his prized pupil, relating, "There is no comparison to be made, Grange is always a great player. He has gained wonderfully all year, but he has not had the interference he had today. My only regret is that he will soon graduate and his wonderful ability will have to leave the college gridiron."[28]

The next day, the only thing that seemed to matter in the country was what Red Grange did to the poor Pennsylvania football team. Newspapers everywhere praised the redhead from Wheaton. The *Chicago Tribune* had full coverage, with three photos of Grange in action and a game recap by Walter Eckersall, referee for the game. Jimmy Corcoran of the *Chicago American* wrote, "He dazzled the stands with his dodging, his slants, his stiff-arming, and his great speed. He was the greatest football player of the day in his elements, and conditions for him never were worse."[29]

The East Coast writers were more impressed—since they were the bigger skeptics. Damon Runyon wrote, "This man Red Grange of Illinois is three or four men and a horse rolled into one for football purposes. He is Jack Dempsey, Babe Ruth, Al Jolson, Paavo Nurmi, and Man o' War. Put them all together, they spell Grange."[30]

Ford Frick wrote,

There goes the redhead!

This writer has never specialized in naming great figures of sport. But a year ago, writing of "Red" Grange, he referred to him as football's will o' the wisp. That still goes. As elusive as a ray of light, as hard to fathom as the wayward spark, he dances and darts his way to greatness. Perhaps there have been greater backs; perhaps other men have been as scintillating and as brilliant. But this writer has never seen them.[31]

But Harry Cross of the *New York Times* nailed Red's performance like no other East Coast writer could:

The speed, cleverness, and uncanny intuition of any other football player have never made such an impression on the Eastern gridiron as Grange's meteoric flights over a slippery, muddy field this afternoon.

The East has heard of the great achievements of this football player and has taken them with a grain of salt. They did not believe that he could be as great as the Middle West said he was. But he is. That is the strange part of it. Red Grange is human. He is not a myth. He dashes and dodges over the gridiron with a speed of foot and an alertness of mind which set him high up on a pedestal among this generation of football players.[32]

Red had now played two "games of his life." Most players never even have one. He and his teammates had never had a sweeter victory. They would celebrate on the train ride back west. Arriving on campus on Sunday night, they saw a scene out of a movie. An estimated crowd of 10,000 fans had gathered at the Illinois Central train station to greet the team upon its arrival. As the train was pulling in just after 10:00 p.m., chants of "We want Red and Zuppke!" could be heard. Fireworks were shot off into the night's sky. The howls and cheers from the loud student body even made Zuppke smile.[33]

Hearing the commotion and seeing the large crowd, Red tried an end around and left through the last coach of the train. He made it more than a block away until the mob saw him. He was promptly picked up by the crowd and carried on people's shoulders. Traveling through the business district, the mob took Red all the way to the Zeta Psi frat house, and Red went inside. Even then, the crowd refused to leave until Red made a speech. Chants of "We want Red! We want Red!" could be heard throughout campus. The bashful redhead finally appeared out of a second-story window. Almost tongue-tied from embarrassment, Grange finally spoke, stating, "We, er, had a fine visit down East. I don't know how to thank you fellows for everything, but the team deserves the credit. And we're certainly going to do everything in our power to lick Chicago next Saturday." Red then ducked back inside, refusing to come out again. The party on campus lasted into the morning.[34]

The day after Red thrilled 63,000 screaming college football fans in Philadelphia, the Chicago Bears played the Rock Island Independents in an NFL game in front of 8,000 customers at Cubs Park in Chicago. Despite no offensive fireworks—little offense at all, in fact—the Bears won a defensive struggle, 6–0.[35] In three weeks, the future of pro football and the NFL would change forever.

12

RUMORS SWIRL
AND RED'S LAST
GAME AT ILLINOIS

Two days after the Penn game, Red was sitting at the dinner table at the Zeta Psi house with Harold Johnson of the *Chicago American* to continue their interviews for the paper's series of articles. Johnson quickly asked about the shocking victory in the East. Red thoughtfully said what was really on his mind:

> We were all fired up with only one thought. All we were thinking of was how we were going to beat Penn. Franklin Field was muddy, but I have played on worse gridirons than that. We all wore long, round cleats on our football shoes, and while things may have looked comical to the rooters they were not to the Illinois boys. . . . All I want the public to know is that Illinois has 11 men in every game. So much has been written to the effect that it was a one-man game that I am pretty sore. Please set the folks right, will you? We had 11 men on that field, and they all worked their head off to win for Illinois. I was only one of the 11.[1]

Red knew he wasn't the only player on the field. It was a team effort. He wanted his teammates to get the credit they deserved. Sports fans, as well as the rest of the country, were starting to know the name Red Grange. His monikers, the Galloping Ghost and the Wheaton Iceman, were now sharing newspaper headlines with the likes of such sports stars as Babe Ruth, Jack Dempsey, Bobby Jones, Bill Tilden, and the horse-racing champion Man o' War. Newsreel footage of the Illinois–Penn game, shot by *International News Service*, was being shown in movie theaters throughout the country. During the Roaring Twenties, Red would forever be linked with the greatest sports stars of the golden age of sports.

Red tried to put the Penn game behind him, along with the other distractions of being one of the country's biggest sports stars. He turned his attention to one of Illinois's biggest rivals—the University of Chicago. "I have been thinking of this game all season, and I am going to toss everything I have into it," said Red to Jimmy Corcoran of the *Chicago American*. "Of course, I can't promise to run up and down the field, but there may be a few thrills. Maybe I'll produce them—probably someone else will."[2]

Memorial Stadium was covered by hay for a few days before the big matchup, but a steady rain fell throughout the morning of the game to create a gridiron on a day that was described by the *Chicago Daily News* as a "fine day for penguins."[3] Inside the stadium, a crowd of 69,000 sat down to witness Red's last home conference game. At the game was Red's father Lyle, who brought along Dr. Davies, the Forksville physician who had brought Harold into the world.[4]

On a day where the sky was filled with gray clouds, a drizzling rain continued to fall throughout the game as fans tried to cover their heads with canopies, oil cloths, bed sheets, and pillow cases from hotel rooms. Red looked up at the rain drops and smiled. "We have played most of the season in the rain, so we are getting used to it," he said. "Besides, it is just as bad for the other follows."[5]

Throughout the game, Stagg's boys slowed him down, but eventually Red guided his team to a victory. Behind touchdowns by Earl Britton and end Art D'Ambrosio, the Illini squeaked out a 13–6 win. Red went unbeaten against Stagg in his three years, going 2–0–1. "And I want the whole world to know that was the greatest team that I have ever been up against," Grange said in the locker room.[6]

At the fraternity house after the game, Red entertained family and friends. He ate dinner with his father and Dr. Davies. But the celebration was short-lived, as Red's life, if it hadn't been already, was about to be turned upside down—by rumors, followed by more rumors. The first gossip to come out was a report that he had signed a contract to play three pro football games in New York for $40,000. The NFL's New York Giants, owned by bookmaker Tim Mara, were interested in having Red in the Big Apple. Mara told the press,

> In the first place we are limited under the league rules in the amount of money we can pay a player, and for three games this limit would not reach $1,000 much less $40,000. In the second place we are under agreement not to tamper with football players while they are in college, and I believe in the rule.[7]

The rumors of Red playing professional football were coming more and more each day. John L. Griffith, commissioner of the Big Ten, was not pleased with hearing them. He did not want to see Red turn pro. Griffith commented,

> The college spirt is lacking in professional football. The players are not willing to risk injury to themselves just to enable an outstanding star to make a good show-

ing. . . . Grange needs perfect, well-timed interference to enable him to get away on his thrilling runs, and he will not get this in a professional game. They will simply hand him the ball and say to Grange there it is, now see what you can do.[8]

With daily rumors of Illinois players turning pro, Zuppke tried to keep his attention on coaching his team. His stars would mostly sit out the next game against Wabash. On November 14, Red ran out onto the field at Memorial Stadium for the last time. After warm-ups, it looked like that would be the only time he would see the field. After three and half quarters of cries from the stands to see Grange in action, Zuppke finally relented. According to a newspaper report, "Red entered the game for a short time in the fourth quarter, not once carrying the ball. When he left the field, the 20,000 rooters stood in tribute."[9] Red had been on the field for just three plays, but he got a standing ovation from the hometown fans. The backups cruised to a 21–0 victory against Wabash, improving the Illini record to 4–3.[10]

In the dressing room after the game, Red sat in front of his locker, slowly pulling off his number 77 jersey. He took a look at it, inspecting the famous numerals. A photographer's flashbulb went off, preserving a special moment in college football and Illinois football history. The historic photo appeared in the *Chicago American* on November 17.[11] Red had just one more week as an Illinois football player. His playing career couldn't be over, could it? He was just 22 years old, and his best days as a player had to be ahead of him. He knew what he wanted to do with his future. It was almost time to tell the world.

Everyone had their opinions on what Red should do next. Most college coaches were on the same page—Red shouldn't play professional football. Michigan's Fielding Yost said, "I'd be glad to see Grange do anything else except play professional football. I don't think he'd be much of a success as a professional. I'd rather see him go into the movies or write then turn professional."[12] Both Zuppke and George Huff wanted Red to stay away from pro football. "I hope these reports are not true and that Grange will not play professional football. I shall talk with him after the Ohio State–Illinois game." said Huff.[13]

Lyle Grange agreed with the college coaches. He didn't want his boy playing pro football. "Every time I read in the paper that Harold has accepted a contract from this or that team, it gives me a shock," Lyle commented to the press. He continued,

I sincerely hope that he does not do this, although he has not confided in me what his plans are. I have a notion, however, that he will drop out of school for a while after the football season and accept one of the offers made to him. I think he's entitled to "cash in" on the long runs his gridiron fame have brought him. It has been expensive for me to send Harold and his brother, Garland, through the university. We are not rolling in wealth, and I think the public would approve of anything Harold does.[14]

In the end, Lyle left the decision up to his eldest son.

After hearing more rumors about pro football, Zuppke quizzed his team on the hearsay of some of his players signing contracts to play football for money. His interrogation was really meant for two players—Red Grange and Earl Britton. Zuppke wasn't happy about hearing the whispers about his program and, in particular, his most famous pupil. He barked at them, "If you are ineligible, then turn in your suits." Red and Britton had a private chat with the coach, who quizzed them at length about their plans of playing pro football. Zup had heard the gossip. He wanted answers. Both denied the reports of signing contracts with pro football teams.[15]

Huff, as well as Zuppke, knew this was taking a major toll on Red. He didn't seem to be in any kind of condition to play a game, with the next contest just a few days away. Both men recommended that Red go home to see his father. They excused him from practice on the Tuesday before the Ohio State game, and Red borrowed Doc Coolley's car to get him to Wheaton.

Wearing a newsboy cap and an ankle-length racoon-skin coat, Red arrived in his hometown. He first went to track down his brother Garland. Don Maxwell of the *Chicago Tribune*, after receiving a tip, also arrived in Wheaton. The sportswriter headed straight to the Grange apartment. Lyle invited him in. When Red and Garland arrived at the apartment, Maxwell asked, "The newspapers are full of stories about what you're going to do. What have you got to say?" Red answered, "I'll tell you, if you'll go down to the restaurant with me. I'm half starved."[16]

Red, Garland, and Maxwell headed downstairs to grab a bite. Red was comfortable in his hometown, so much so that he started explaining the current situation to the writer and about a half-dozen Wheaton folks listening in from the next table. Red spoke with conviction in his voice.

You don't know what a tough place I'm in. Everybody's saying this and that about me turning pro and throwing down Illinois. I don't know what to do. I've tried to keep clean on this amateur stuff. I haven't taken a cent from anybody, and I haven't signed a contract with anyone.

Folks have said I got money playing football for Illinois. That's all bunk. The only money I got I earned working on an ice wagon in the summer, and the rest my father has given me.

Dad's not got much. You can see that. Now if I can go out and make a lot now it would help him out. . . . I know what the fellows down at the university will think. They'll say I'm throwing my school down. But should I take advice from them? Most of the fellows who are telling me not to earn anything on pro football will have forgotten all about me by next year. If I'm broke then I don't suppose they'd loan me a dollar.

The whole situation is like this. I'm going back to Illinois tomorrow and practice for the Ohio game. I'm going to play Saturday and play my best for the school. After that game I'm going to listen to these offers. Maybe I'll accept one of them. I can't tell you now which one it will be. But you can be sure I haven't signed a scrap of paper with anybody, and I haven't told anybody what I'm going to do.[17]

Garland sat down next to Red. "If I eat it's on you, Red," said Red's kid brother. "I'm broke." Smiling, Red responded, "Go ahead kid, I guess I can stand it." Red finished a bowl of tomatoes, and then the party strolled out onto the street to say good-bye. The redhead was totally honest with Maxwell, revealing a stressed-out 22-year-old student-athlete. He was ready to make a decision about his future. He just had to wait a few more days. The rest of the night Red talked to his father about his plans. He knew what he wanted to do. That night he slept in his own bed.[18]

The following day, on November 18, on the sports page of the *Chicago Tribune*, the paper ran a huge headline: "I'll Not Sign Until Saturday—Grange." The accompanying article was written by Don Maxwell. Also in the paper were two photos, one of Lyle Grange in a white dress shirt and tie, reclining in his chair at the DuPage county jail, and the other featuring Red, wearing his fancy racoon-skin coat, shaking hands with his brother Garland. The following morning saw more Chicago reporters invade Wheaton, one of whom was from the *Chicago American*. That morning Red was having breakfast with his brother in the same restaurant next to Dollinger's Drug Store, surrounded by several sportswriters who didn't want to get outscooped by the *Tribune*. Red remained chatty, talking to the press about the rumors of his future.

I may play professional football. You know a football player when he has left his team is as dead as yesterday's newspaper. If I am to make any money playing football I have got to do it now. I can't wait. I need the money, I'll admit that. Father has helped me, and he's in ordinary circumstances. You may tell the readers of the *American* that I have not signed any contract to play. Nor have I talked over any of their propositions with them. That would be unfair to Coach Zuppke and to my university. You know I owe something to him and to my school.

I suppose that my friends on the campus hate to see me turn "pro." Well, a year from now none of them would loan me a dollar if I was down and out. It's up to me. If, after Saturday's game, I have a chance to play football, I may take it.[19]

The young football star once again demonstrated his mind-set at the time. First, he wanted to take advantage of his popularity by cashing in on it. By waiting, he could be forgotten or suffer an injury, and then no one would pay to see him play football. He had to act now. Second, and more important to Red, he wanted to act quickly so that he could repay his father for everything he had done for him. He could make money for himself, but he could also set up his father for life. This was a chance to do that. After breakfast was finished, Red and Garland headed over to the jailhouse to visit their father. After a short conversation, Red went downstairs and got into his car, en route to Champaign. That afternoon's *Chicago American* had the headline, "'I Haven't Turned Pro Yet,' Grange." The city of Chicago, as well as the rest of the country, was keeping up on the daily reports speculating on Red's next move.[20]

The offers were plenty, whether through Pyle or directly to Red. He could get paid in Hollywood, be a real estate agent (a company in Florida offered him a job for $20,000), write for newspapers, or run for political office, but Red already knew what he wanted to do. He wanted to do what he did best and the thing he loved the most—and that was play football.

While Red returned to Champaign, more reports were coming out. The press even stayed in Wheaton to interview Lyle, who was asked about his son's visit. Lyle replied,

When Harold was here yesterday (November 18) he told me he had not signed a contract with the Chicago Bears or any other team. I am sure he would not tell me anything that is not so. I have my own opinion what Harold is going to do, but I do not care to express it. You see, this is a very trying situation for Harold. He has to be careful. I cannot talk for him. I have a whole lot of faith in him, and I am satisfied that he will do the right thing. The boy cannot be easily fooled. He has a good head, and his head is good for business, too.[21]

Red jogged back onto the practice field on Thursday, November 19, two days before the Ohio State game, only to see a group of reporters. He commented,

I'm due out there at the field for practice. Ohio State, you know, is an old rival of Illinois, and we've got to lick them. That's the chief thing on my mind right now. As for professional offers, I'll be ready to discuss them after the game. I'm just one of the 11 regulars on our college team until then.[22]

Later on, Red would open up about his trip home to see his father. "I'm still pretty much of a kid," said Grange, smiling. "My dad and I have been pals. He has paid my way through school, and I wanted to talk it over with him before making my decision. But I haven't signed a contract for anything," he stated positively. Red continued,

> It would be a violation of the university's rules, and until Saturday's game is over I'm going to be loyal to my school and give it everything I have. . . . Well, I've had a lot of offers, but I don't like to sell things. I think I'm a rotten salesman. But I do like to play football. . . . I'm not saying that I won't (play pro football). Some of my advisers have frowned on professional football, but the way I figure is that's my own business and my father has left it to me to decide. After all, I'll soon be forgotten down on the campus, and some of the fellows who are now my best friends wouldn't loan me a dollar 10 years from now if I was broke. And I haven't much money.[23]

Hearing the latest rumors, Zuppke still supported his star player, although he felt he was losing him to the pros. Speaking after practice on Thursday, Zuppke defended Red but made it clear what he thought his player should do after his last college game:[24]

> We would rather Grange wouldn't play professional football for his own good. But we have no control over his private affairs. Grange has no more bound to parade his private affairs than any other person.
>
> Grange would be eligible if he had signed a contract. That is the point that everyone has overlooked in the present professionalism argument. Any conferences we have had with Grange have been held with the purpose of keeping him from making the mistake of quitting school, with the rosy promises of penniless promoters as the bait. We have at no time been worried about any supposed contracts.[25]

Later that night, the Illinois squad left Champaign on two special Pullmans on the Illinois Central. When Red stepped off the train in Columbus, Ohio, he was swamped by newspapermen and chats of "Grange! Grange! Grange!" Photographers fetched him into the sunlight to get a photo, but he was grabbed by the coattail by Zuppke and jerked away. "I'm tired of all this notoriety," said Red to the press. "I have had an awful week of it. Almost got kicked out of school and everything. This excitement and everything is more than I can stand. I do not know what I'm going to do." Red was quickly put into a cab and whisked off to the Southern Hotel, where the team would be staying. Red had a restless night. He knew that in just a few hours he would be playing his last college football game and his life would change forever. He knew what he was going to do, even if he wasn't ready to say it to the world.[26]

The following day saw a record crowd of 85,500, the second largest crowd to ever see a college football game, jam Ohio Stadium. Most were there to cheer on the Buckeyes, but others were present to watch Red play in an Illinois uniform one last time. In the press box there were more than 100 newspapermen, notably the great Grantland Rice, who couldn't wait until the game was over to ask Red the "million-dollar question."

Red led his team out onto the field for warm-ups. "As Grange ran out of the southwest tower of the stadium to perform one last time as an amateur, the spectators scrambled to their feet, splitting the air with a deafening roar in a mighty tribute to Grange, the hero of gridiron heroes," wrote the *Chicago Evening Post*. He was quickly swarmed by movie cameras and photographers. For several minutes, they followed the redhead around like lost puppies, chronicling his every move. Red remained stoic throughout the warm-ups. He was on a football field, his favorite place to be. Now it was just about playing football.[27]

Early in the first quarter, after an interception by Bernie Shively, the Illini offense went on a 10-play drive that resulted in a short Earl Britton touchdown run. His extra point gave Illinois a 7–0 lead. Ohio State generated a safety in the second quarter to cut the lead to 7–2. Later in the quarter, Red broke off one of his longest gains, a 26-yard scamper, which set up one of his beautiful halfback passes to Chuck Kassel for another score. At the half, Illinois led, 14–2. Red had only 30 more minutes to play. Then the storm clouds would hover over him.

In the third quarter, the Buckeyes scored on a touchdown pass to cut the deficit to 14–9. Red wanted to end his career on a high note. The Illini defense would help him get it. Late in the fourth quarter, the Buckeyes tried one last march. On the last play of the game, Ohio State halfback "Cookie" Cunningham heaved a pass downfield. Red, playing center field, leaped for an interception, preserving the victory. His last play as a collegian was a pick to help his team win. Red smiled while celebrating with his teammates. They had just won their fourth straight game to finish the season with a 5–3 record. The hard work and sacrifice had paid off to give Red and his teammates a successful year. Soon, Red was being mobbed on the field as he tried to make his way to the locker room with at least 50 newspapermen trailing him. As soon as he reached the dressing room, Grange announced his plans for the future.

> I plan to organize a football team of my own, of which I will be the manager. I probably will take Earl Britton with me and several of Notre Dame's Four Horse-

men of last year. I will take no man who has not completed his college football career.

We will play our first game on Thanksgiving Day. It may be in Chicago, but we have not decided yet. We will play in Florida during the Christmas break.

My back was injured in the first half, and I did not want to go back into the game. But I had to call on every one of our resources to keep Ohio in check. I hope the doctors will put me in shape by Thanksgiving Day.[28]

Most of what he said was true. He was going to play professional football, and he was going to play in Florida on Christmas. Everything else was just hearsay. He wasn't aware of everything Pyle was doing, he just knew it was a relief to finally come out with the truth. He was ready to move on. After he got dressed, Red was kidnapped, not by the press or some agent, but by his coach. Zuppke wanted to speak with him. They hopped into a nearby cab and took off. Red recalled the conversation they had as follows:

Zup, visibly disturbed by the news, drove with me from the stadium to the hotel. Mrs. Zuppke was along, and we spent an hour in a cab as Zuppke ordered the driver to "keep driving" while he tried desperately to make me change my mind. "Keep away from professionalism and you'll be another Walter Camp," he pleaded. "Football isn't a game to play for money." My reply summed up what I believed all along. "You get paid for coaching, Zup, why should it be wrong for me to get paid for playing?"[29]

Red's conversation with his coach reaffirmed his decision to play pro football. Zup couldn't answer a simple question: "You get paid for coaching, why should it be wrong for me to get paid for playing?" Red knew he was making the right decision, even if some didn't agree with it.

Red returned to the Southern Hotel. He ran into more reporters, one of whom was Tom Morrow of the *Daily Illini*. "I don't care what they print, let them write anything they want to," Red declared. It looked like Grange was going to stay with the team in Columbus. He spent a quiet evening having dinner at the Neil House with Mike Tobin, Illinois athletic public relations director, and a few other Illini personal. Red was tired of the attention. "You'd think I was president of the United States the way they flock after news of what I am going to do," he said as his parting shot.[30] But the attention and the media circus were just getting started.

Red headed up to his room. He started to pack. There was no looking back now. He was off to Chicago.

PART III

BARNSTORMING WITH THE CHICAGO BEARS (1925–1926)

13

GEORGE HALAS AND DUTCH STERNAMAN

Professional football had been around since 1892, but an organized league would take almost 30 more years to come to fruition. It happened at the start of one of America's most fruitful and entertaining decades. From the beginning, the Roaring Twenties lived up to their name. With the world safe for democracy after World War I, the United States discarded its battlefield persona and replaced it with an excess of fun and leisure. Prosperity fueled the celebration. Famed writer Paul Gallico wrote, "We had just emerged from a serious war and now wanted no more of reality but only escape therefrom into the realms of the fanciful." In 1920, prohibition went into effect, American women got the right to vote, radio was popular, Warren G. Harding was elected president, and, yes, 10 professional football owners gathered in a Canton, Ohio, automobile showroom to organize the American Professional Football Association (APFA). Two years later they renamed the league the National Football League (NFL).[1]

The NFL was established during the age of flappers, jazz, the Charleston, Lindbergh, speakeasies, Capone, flaming youth, Chaplin, and sports of all sorts. For the first time, the world of sports captured the public's eye and pocketbook. In the words of one historian, "Next to sport of business, Americans enjoyed the business of sport." Most Americans enjoyed the economic boom following World War I, and much of that was spent on sports tickets, as people flocked to stadiums and arenas in record numbers. Sports heroes emerged in every field of athletics. Such names as Jack Dempsey in boxing, Knute Rockne and the Four Horsemen of Notre Dame in college football, Lou Gehrig in baseball, Helen Wills and Bill Tilden in tennis, Bobby Jones in golf, and Johnny Weissmuller in swimming simply made this the golden age of sports.[2]

Gallico, who followed all the sports giants of the 1920s as a columnist and sports editor for the *New York Daily News*, said "Sports and sports stories and sport characters who were almost magical in their performance provided much of that escape" for Americans to enjoy their free time. Throughout the 1920s, professional football was an unloved child in the family of American sports. Baseball was indeed the national pastime. Baseball occupied the nation's conscience and the biggest stadiums, and it had the biggest name in sports during the Roaring Twenties, Babe Ruth. If baseball didn't fascinate you, there was always college football. College football had its well-established traditions and its rah-rah attitudes, which would make front-page headlines. On the other hand, professional football and the NFL went mostly unnoticed. Professional football was truly unloved.[3]

But what was it really like in the early days of the NFL, when the game was played in an era before television, million-dollar contracts, fantasy football leagues, domed stadiums, and field turf? What was the "Old Leather" era truly like, when footballs were fashioned from canvas and leather, and the game was played on a dirt field. In *The Football Encyclopedia*, football historian Jordan A. Deutsch wrote,

> We can get a front-row seat for one dollar. If we're at Canton's Lakeside Park to watch the Canton Bulldogs, a mere 4,000 fans would pack the bleachers. A program would cost 10 cents. There are no souvenir or beer stands, but you could bring your own liquor flask for later. You could also make a friendly bet on who would win with your neighbor sitting next to you. Usually five dollars would do the trick. Other spectators would be wearing suits and ties, no outrageous costumes with team logos. No cheerleaders or banners to help pump up the crowd. These fans come to see the game, not to be seen.
>
> The field is your familiar 100 yards long, laid out in five-yard segments, with real grass, or more likely, real dirt. It has no hash marks. Not until 1933 will the ball be brought in towards the middle of the field when a play ends near the sidelines or out of bounds. The bench area is just that, a wooden bench with maybe a bucket of water for a drink at halftime. The goalposts are roughly 20 feet high and stationed at the front of the goal line.
>
> When the teams take the field, we notice that there are only 16 players on each squad. By 1930 the league votes to expand the roster to 20. Most players are paid about $100 a game, while some star players might make up to $150. Both teams wear dark jerseys, giving fans a tough time telling them apart. The uniforms show little individuality, except for maybe a logo or letter on the front. The faded jersey might have a number on the back, but the practice wasn't yet standard.
>
> The trousers are made of canvas, worn with hip, thigh, and knee pads. Each player wears black high-top shoes with rectangular cleats and wool socks, if they

had their own socks. The jersey was pulled over a flimsy set of shoulder pads that didn't seem to protect anything. The same could be said for the helmet, which was made from leather and called "head helmets." Some players didn't bother to wear one. No rule requiring a player to wear a helmet was passed until 1943. The NFL in the Roaring Twenties had a rag-tag [sic] look to it.

Instead of a whole set of officials, we only see three that govern the action. An umpire, a linesman, and a referee. The officials also keep the game clock on the field, no fancy scoreboards here. From our bleacher seat we see that the ball is made of leather and is fairly round. Easy to dropkick but difficult to pass. By the end of the decade the ball is slimmed down, making passing easier.

After a coin toss at the center of the field, we see a kickoff at the 40-yard line. All 22 men who were on the kickoff teams stay on the field, no substitutes. Each man plays both offense and defense. Most plays are called at the line of scrimmage instead of a huddle. The head coach doesn't send in plays, and little time is spent in between plays. There are also no television timeouts. Most lineman weigh about 200 pounds, with most backs being much smaller.

Passing was restricted because of the rather fat ball. Some teams passed more than others, but the early pro game was built around the power running game. Also, most rules still handicapped the passing game throughout the 1920s. Until 1933, the forward pass had to be thrown from five yards behind the line of scrimmage. Until 1934, an incomplete pass in the end zone was an automatic touchback and gave the ball to the opponent. Also, most coaches didn't have the time to practice the passing game since most teams only practiced once a week.

Most professional teams used the single wing or Notre Dame box, a predominately rushing offense. Defensively, most teams used the six or seven-man fronts to counter the rushing attacks of early NFL teams. Regardless, both offenses and defenses were so close to start a play, that when the ball was snapped 22 men would converge on the ball, and after the dust settled we could see the ballcarrier usually only gained a few yards.

Punting was the key to the outcome of most games. The way to victory was not to possess the ball, but to give it to your opponent deep in their territory and let him make a mistake. An amazing number of punts occurred on third down, as teams played for field position. With defense so emphasized, low-scoring games dominated the early days of the NFL. Some games would end in a 0–0 tie. If you were lucky enough to see a touchdown, you definitely didn't see any end zone celebrations from the players. The game usually lasted about two hours and ended with a gunshot from the referee.[4]

Representatives of pro teams were under the gun in 1920, when they met in Canton, Ohio, to organize what would become the NFL. The pro game was beset with three major problems: Salaries were skyrocketing, players hopped from team to team during the season to play for the highest bidder, and too many teams padded their rosters with moonlighting collegians playing under assumed names. A league needed to be formed.

They had good reason to meet in Canton, now the site of the Pro Football Hall of Fame. Ohio was the geographical center of professional football at this time. Proximity was important in that era when teams traveled by train and team managers sought games with opponents in cities in Ohio and the Midwest, which could be easily reached by rail. Thus, only a few East Coast teams played during the NFL's early years, and the too-distant West Coast would not be home to an NFL franchise until after World War II.

When the league was formed in 1920, the newly established organization elected the biggest name in pro football to help guide the league. His name was Jim Thorpe. But he was a great athlete, not an administrator, so in 1921 the young league elected Joe F. Carr as its new president. Carr had a great sports background, being a former sportswriter and editor for the *Ohio State Journal*, as well as team manager of the highly successful Columbus Panhandles pro football team. He was the right man for the job. One of the men who attended the NFL's inaugural meeting in Canton would have one of the biggest impacts on the life of Harold "Red" Grange. That man's name was George Halas.

George Halas, a baseball and football star at the University of Illinois, never forgot what his coach, the great Bob Zuppke, had said: "Why is it that just when you players are beginning to know something about football I lose you and you stop playing. It makes no sense. Football is the only sport that ends a man's career just when it should be beginning."[5] He would remember these words for the rest of his life.

George Stanley Halas was born on the northside of Chicago on February 2, 1895, as the eighth child of Bohemian immigrants Barbara and Frank Halas. Out of the eight children, only four would survive beyond infancy. Frank was a tailor, and Barbara would make buttonholes for him in the shop. Halas's early childhood revolved around school, church, work at the shop, and sports. George described his father as "frail," adding that he "ran a strict household," while his mother "had meals on time and was an excellent cook." George's favorite dish was "duck cooked Bohemian-style." The family moved to 18th Place and Wood, where they resided in a three-story structure. Each floor had an apartment to rent and a large corner shop for the business, which mainly became a grocery store and dairy for Barbara.[6]

Young George's evenings were spent studying. Education was preached to him by his parents. In 1909, he entered Crane Tech High School weighing just 110 pounds. The following year, George lost his father on Christmas Eve. His mother would continue with the store, as well as rent out the apartments. She had one main rule: her children would go to college.

While his mother saved money for college, George enjoyed playing sports for Crane Tech. He participated in football, track, and baseball. In the fall of 1914, after a successful athletic career at Crane Tech, Halas enrolled at the University of Illinois and went out for the football team, coached by Bob Zuppke. Playing for Zup made a tremendous impression on the young man. "He was a careful teacher," said Halas. "He knew how to get the best out of young men." Throughout time Halas would use many of Zuppke's teachings, especially the T formation, in professional football. Freshmen weren't eligible for the varsity, so Halas reported to Ralph Jones, the freshmen coach. Jones, like Zuppke, made a lasting impression, as the young freshmen would hire him years later to coach the Chicago Bears.[7]

As a sophomore, Halas played end. During his junior year, he suffered a broken leg. With the war raging in Europe, Halas joined the U.S. Navy. The University of Illinois made arrangements for him to get his diploma while he served as an ensign. Halas reported to Great Lakes Naval Station near Waukegan, Illinois, for officers' training. While at Great Lakes, Halas played on the football team, which also featured future pro stars Paddy Driscoll and Jimmy Conzelman. That season, Great Lakes earned an invitation to the 1919 Rose Bowl, where Halas earned MVP honors by catching a touchdown pass and returning an interception 77 yards in a 17–0 win against the Mare Island Marines of California.

In March 1919, Halas was given his military discharge. Shortly thereafter, he signed a Major League Baseball contract with the New York Yankees for $400 a month. According to Yankees manager Miller Huggins, the right-handed-hitting Halas could hit a fastball but not the curve. In spring training against the Dodgers, Halas drilled a ball to deep left-center field. Sprinting around the bases he slid into third base awkwardly. After gathering himself up, he started experiencing pain in his hip, which lingered for the rest of the season. Stationed in right field, Halas played in just 12 games, going 2-for-22 at the plate. The Yankees soon replaced him in right field with a converted pitcher they bought from the Boston Red Sox. His name was Babe Ruth.

Although his baseball career was over, Halas still wanted to play the game he truly loved. Later that year, he played pro football with the Hammond (Indiana) All-Stars, earning $100 per game from owner A. A. Young. While playing with Hammond, Halas took a job working for $55 dollars a week as an engineer, designing bridges at Chicago, Burlington & Quincy Railroad (CB&Q). "I was really impressed by the $100," admitted Halas. "That was almost twice as much money as I made in a week for the railroad."[8]

At this time Halas was 25 years old, stood six feet tall, weighed 182 pounds, and was at the peak of his athletic prowess. The Hammond team practiced every Thursday evening, while playing their games on Sundays. In late 1919, two November games at Cubs Park drew 10,000 and 12,000 paying spectators, respectively. "The six games I played for Hammond that fall sold me on the future of pro football," said Halas. "I figured that a sport which could attract such fine players as (Paddy) Driscoll had a real future."[9]

In March 1920, Halas received a phone call from a Mr. George Chamberlain, who offered him a unique job that would eventually give the NFL its "Papa Bear." Chamberlain was a superintendent at the A. E. Staley Manufacturing Company, a starch business located in Decatur, Illinois, about 172 miles southwest of Chicago, in corn country. Augustus Eugene Staley was the founder of the Staley Company and always believed sports was a positive force for developing human character and stimulating a wholesome attitude of spirited competition for his employees. He fielded successful sports teams, especially baseball squads, managed by former major-league star Joe "Iron Man" McGinnity. In 1920, he wanted his football team to be just as successful as his baseball squad, so he sent Chamberlain to Chicago to talk to this passionate football star who played brilliantly for the University of Illinois.

"Chamberlain made a date with me, and we met at the LaSalle Hotel. He asked if I would like to move to Decatur to work for the Staley Company," Halas would write in his autobiography. "I would play on the baseball team and manage and coach the football team, as well as play on it. I don't know how much money he offered. It may have been a little less than the $55 the railroad paid me. The magnet for me was the opportunity to build a winning team."[10] Halas asked Chamberlain for three things: could he recruit players who had made a name in college, at Great Lakes or on semipro teams; could he offer the players full-time jobs with the company; and could he and the team practice daily on company time for at least two hours? Mr. Chamberlain said yes to all three. "I was elated. I saw the offer as an exciting opportunity but did not suspect the tremendous future Mr. Staley was opening for me," recalled Halas.[11]

Halas rented a small room on the second floor of a boarding house near the streetcar line that led to the factory at the edge of town. When Halas arrived at the plant, he began his work as a scale house clerk, responsible for weighing deliveries of corn; he also began checking into the credentials of those employees who had played amateur football for the company. After playing baseball in the spring, Halas quickly turned his attention to football. Halas recalled that first year as follows:

> All summer I worked out plays learned at Illinois from Bob Zuppke. He used the T formation, the oldest in football, although most colleges had gone to the single wing or the double wing. Notre Dame and Minnesota had their own formations. In a little clothbound notebook, I diagrammed plays, one to a page, properly numbered and coded.[12]

Halas was now in charge of his own pro football team and went about signing players for his squad. With the resources provided by Mr. Staley, Halas would sign a team full of former All-Americans, including Hugh Blacklock (Michigan State), Jimmy Conzelman (Washington of St. Louis), Burt Ingwersen (Illinois), George Trafton (Notre Dame), and Guy Chamberlin (Nebraska), who played for the Canton Bulldogs in 1919.

Wearing five hats—employee of the Staley starch works, athletic director, football coach, football player, and talent scout—the young Halas wanted his squad to play the best teams in pro football. He found out about the beginnings of a pro league in Ohio, and after writing to Ralph Hay of the Canton Bulldogs, he boarded a train with fellow Staley employee Morgan O'Brien, an engineer, to see about this new league.

On September 17, a hot and muggy Friday night in Canton, Ohio, 10 professional football teams convened at the automobile showroom of Mr. Hay. It would be a historic meeting in the annals of sports history. Hay didn't know how many owners would actually show; his small office soon filled to capacity and was too small to have the meeting, so they moved into the spacious showroom where the cars were on display. It was quite a scene as these milestone men met in the showroom of an automobile dealership. In his autobiography, Halas described the experience:

> Morgan O'Brien, a Staley engineer and a football fan who was being very helpful in administrative matters, and I went to Canton on the train. The showroom, big enough for four cars—Hupmobiles and Jordans—occupied the ground floor of the three-story brick Odd Fellows building. Chairs were few. I sat on a running board.[13]

After some informal discussion, the meeting started at 8:15 p.m. What they did decide was to name the organization the American Professional Football Association (APFA). The managers might have felt that the use of the word *association* was looser and more general than using a word like *league*, perhaps denoting less of a commitment. Several managers urged Hay to take the association's presidency, but he realized that the organization needed a bigger name to earn respect from the public and the nation's sports pages. So, they choose the biggest name in pro football to be president—Jim Thorpe.[14]

The group decided to charge a $100 fee for membership, but this was just for show. "We announced that membership in the league would cost $100 per team. I can testify no money changed hands. I doubt if there was a hundred bucks in the whole room. We just wanted to give our new organization a façade of financial stability," Halas would admit. The rules were not discussed, as the pro game still used the same ones the colleges made up. George Halas was about to begin a lifetime affair with the NFL that would last for the next 63 years.[15]

Throughout their first season in the APFA, Halas drilled his men hard on the practice field during company time. "The value of our daily practice sessions quickly showed up when the season started," said Halas. "We were easily the best-conditioned team in the circuit and probably the best organized." The extra practice paid, off as the Staleys (10–1–2) played hard throughout the 1920 season, finishing in second place, behind the Akron Pros (8–0–3). The following year found Halas's team right at the top.

With a roster that featured Chic Harley, Pete Stinchcomb, Hugh Blacklock, Guy Chamberlin, and Dutch Sternaman, the 1921 Decatur Staleys were a talented and very expensive team. After beating Waukegan American Legion to warm up for the APFA season, the Staleys prepared to play the Rock Island Independents at Staley Field. Then Halas was summoned to the boss's office to discuss the football team. Halas remembered,

> Mr. Staley asked me to come to his office. I had no idea what he wanted. We talked only on the field, but there was no question in my mind that the sports program would continue. Mr. Staley greeted me warmly and said, "George I know you are more interested in football than starch. As you know, there is a slight recession in the country. Time lost practicing and playing costs a huge amount of money. I feel we can no longer underwrite the team's losses. George, why don't you take the team to Chicago? I think football will go over big there. Professional teams need a big city base. I'll give you $5,000 seed money to pay costs until the gate receipts start coming in. I ask only that you continue to call the team the Staleys for one season." I said I will do it. Thank you, thank you, thank you very much. We shook hands.[16]

A written agreement was signed on October 6, by both Halas and Staley, stating the following:

A sum of $3,000 was given in return for two pages of advertising in team programs, plus pictures and 100-word biographies of the chief Staley company officers.

The other $2,000 would be paid at the rate of $25 dollars a week per player up to a total of 19 players.

The team would operate in Chicago as the "Staley Football Club."

That new arrangement would terminate at the end of the 1921 season.

After signing the written agreement, Halas immediately telephoned William Veeck, president of the Chicago Cubs, and asked if he could see him. Veeck said come on in. Halas took the train into Chicago and laid out the situation. "I'm bringing the Staley team to Chicago, and I would like to use Cubs Park as our home, for practices, as well as our home games," Halas recalled. Veeck welcomed the idea, as his ballpark would be empty after the baseball season. Halas asked the terms. Veeck said 15 percent of the gate and concessions. "I considered that very fair and rejoiced silently," Halas said. "All right, providing I can keep the program rights, which sold for 10 cents in those days. He said done, and I left the park a happy man." After playing the Rock Island Independents at Staley Field in front of just 3,600 fans, Halas's team played their first game in Chicago against the Rochester Jeffersons on October 16. Almost 8,000 customers saw the new, permanent Chicago team win a thrilling 16–13 game over the Jeffs.[17]

Once in Chicago, Halas set up headquarters at the Blackwood Apartment Hotel at 4414 Clarendon, where he rented 10 rooms ($2 a week for the players) and was a mile and a half from Cubs Park. According to Halas, "The hotel was cheap, clean, decent, and within walking distance of the field." He also picked out the Staleys' uniform colors—orange and blue—the same colors as his alma mater, the University of Illinois. But Halas recognized the many problems of running a team and decided to take on a partner. As he remembered in his autobiography,

> I wanted Paddy Driscoll, but he wasn't available (Driscoll was under contract with the Chicago Cardinals), so I looked around the team and I settled with Dutch Sternaman. I offered him a 50-50 partnership. He and I agreed to take $100 each game, same as the players, if any money were still in the bank.[18]

In 1921, Halas and Sternaman guided the Chicago Staleys to the APFA championship, with a 9–1–1 record. Halas had his first championship. The following summer, newly elected NFL president Joe Carr announced that the next league meeting would be held on June 24–25, 1922, in Cleveland. It would be another productive and historic meeting. Eighteen teams arrived at the Hollenden Hotel to discuss the association's business. First up was the small but groundbreaking discussion to change the name of the organization. On a suggestion by Halas, the owners decided to change the name of their "little group" to the National Football League. Halas would recall,

> I lacked enthusiasm for our name, the American Professional Football Association. In baseball, "association" was applied to second-class teams. We were first class. The Chicago Cubs baseball club belonged to the National League, not the American League. "Professional" was superfluous. I proposed we change our name to the National Football League. My fellow members agreed.[19]

The "Football" was true enough, and so was the "League." But "National" it wasn't. With New York and Washington out, the farthest eastern team was Rochester, and the same was true for Louisville, as the most southern team. Rock Island was the farthest west. Despite the technicality, it was a thousand times better than the awkward and lengthy American Professional Football Association.

Although George Halas's Chicago-based team was a first-rate outfit in 1921—best in pro football—he did not actually own the franchise. The Chicago Staleys were still the property of starch maker A. E. Staley. Halas and his partner Sternaman were managers of the team (as well as coaches and star players), but old A. E. still had the official ownership according to the NFL. Based on the agreement between Halas and Staley, the two owners needed to secure the franchise after the 1921 season. At the meeting, Bill Harley wanted a team for Chicago, too, and applied. So did Halas and Sternaman. Having been on the scene since 1920 gave them the inside track.

Carr telephoned Staley in Decatur to get his version of the 1921 arrangement with Halas. "A. E. said he had transferred the team to me the previous fall. The company, he said, was quitting all paid athletes," Halas would write in his autobiography. "The members debated throughout the day and into the evening. Said Halas, "In the end, they decided to vote on whether the franchise should be given to Sternaman and me or to Bill Harley. Eight votes for us, two for Harley." George was elated that he still had his team, but he needed a new name. "I considered naming the team the Chicago Cubs, out of respect for William Veeck, who had been such a great help," he added. "But I noted football players are bigger than baseball players, so if baseball players are cubs, then certainly football players must be bears. The Chicago Bears were born!"[20]

Despite coming up short in the NFL standings in 1922, the Bears were not doing too bad at the box office. After the season, Halas was giddy after seeing the bank account numbers and recalled telling his mother,

> On the last day of 1922 I drew up the financial accounts. We actually made a profit! A profit of $1,476.92! We were offered $35,000 for our franchise. We turned it down. With pride I showed the accounts to mother. She looked at the bottom line, shook her head sadly and said, "George, go back to railroad, dear. You'll have a steady income there."[21]

Despite the meager financial earnings and the dismay of his mother, Halas was in the pro football business for life. He and Sternaman always found time to talk football even if it wasn't their full-time employment. Former Bears lineman Hunk Anderson remembered the duo's passion for the sport:

> In those days, with the Bears paying what was considered top salary per game, Halas was lucky if the club broke even financially. He made Dutch Sternaman his partner in the club, and both of them had to find jobs to keep their heads above water. Halas would sell cars, and Dutch would work at his gas station, and George would come by in a demonstrator to the gas station to his "board meeting" with Sternaman.[22]

During the next three seasons, the Chicago Bears played great football but could not regain the title. For three straight years, they finished in second place. Halas had built a talented team, but his men couldn't win the big game at the end of the season. He and his partner started to really think about making their team a success.

Edward Carl Sternaman was born on February 9, 1895, in Springfield, Illinois. From an early age, everyone called him "Dutch." His father was a pattern maker in town. Dutch was five years older than his brother, Joey Sternaman, who would follow in his footsteps many times. The Sternaman house in Springfield was old-fashioned. The home had an outhouse out back; it wasn't until 1910, when Dutch was 15, that the family put a bathroom upstairs and a toilet just off the kitchen. Out front, the house had vacant lots on each side with cherry and apple trees nearby. The vacant lots gave the Sternaman boys plenty of room to play sports.

Dutch honed his athletic skills by throwing and kicking footballs through the trees, a skill he passed down to Joey. After graduating from Springfield High School, Dutch moved on to the University of Illinois. He was 5-foot-8 and weighed 176 pounds. He played three years of varsity action at halfback for Bob Zuppke and became one of the best all-around players in the Big Ten. One of his teammates there was George Halas. Sternaman soon left Illinois to join the U.S. Army, missing the 1918 season. He was assigned as the physical director at Camp Funston in Kansas. When the war ended, he returned for his senior season. After graduating from Illinois with a degree in engineering, Sternaman was contacted by an old friend about a great opportunity to work and play pro football.

In the summer of 1920, Dutch received a phone call from his former college teammate, who had just been hired earlier that year to work at the Staley Manufacturing Company in Decatur. Halas offered Sternaman a job working in the starch factory and a spot on the team. Sternaman said yes. Dutch became Halas's closest confidant, becoming his partner when the team moved to Chicago.

Two weeks after Red's historical performance against Michigan in 1924, George Halas decided he had to see the Galloping Ghost in person. On November 1, Halas and his wife invited his good friend, Ralph Brizzolara, and his girlfriend, Florence, to join them for a road trip to Champaign to watch Illinois play the University of Iowa. Halas remembered the trip to his alma mater to see the Galloping Ghost.

> Ralph borrowed his father's open touring Hudson and picked up Florence. She wore a new fur coat. Min thought it would be a shame to get the coat wet, but Florence said animals stay out in the rain so a little water wouldn't hurt the coat. Min had made egg sandwiches. Mrs. Bushing had agreed to watch baby Gin (his daughter Virginia) until we returned the next day. During the drive I was in the pink. I belted out my favorite song, "Alice Blue Gown," alternating now and then with the old Illinois college song "Hail to the Orange, Hail to the Blue."
>
> When we arrived, the park was already full. Rain was falling. We soon were soaked. We brushed the rain off our faces and shouted all the louder for Red. . . . It is strange I don't remember the game. Perhaps I was living in my dreams. I assume Illinois won. I do know that evening, Florence and Min talked about the exciting, handsome Red. We had seen the "Galloping Ghost" in the flesh. As an owner, manager, coach, and player, I was determined to have Red on the Bears.[23]

On that day, in the rain, Grange scored two touchdowns, leading the Illini to a 36-0 victory against Iowa. The following day, Halas's Bears played in front of 10,000 fans at Cubs Park against the Rock Island Independents. Jim Thorpe, at 37 years old, and Joey Sternaman traded field goals in a 3-3 tie. In 24 hours, Halas had seen pro football's past (Thorpe) and future (Grange). After the 1924 season, Halas became even more obsessed with signing the Galloping Ghost.

After Red's famous meeting with Pyle at the Virginia Theater before his senior season, Pyle set off on a chain of events that would lead the Galloping Ghost to the Windy City. Red must have mentioned to Pyle that the Bears would be the ideal team for him to play for. Starting their own team would have required more time and resources, while playing for the Bears would mean little in the way of organization or expenses. Pyle just had to negotiate with Halas and Sternaman. Plus, the Bears had several ex-Illinois players, including the two coowners of the team, and Red's good friend, Jim McMillian, who was the starting right guard. And since Halas and Sternaman learned under Bob Zuppke, they ran some of the same offensive and defensive schemes. Red would be familiar with them; it was a perfect combination. Pyle quickly got to work. On a letter dated August 9, 1925, on stationary from the Victory Theater, addressed to Dutch Sternaman, he typed up his initial plan for his client—Red Grange.

Edward Carl Sternaman
c/o Federal Electric Sign System
9700 Blackstone
Chicago, Illinois

Dear Mr. Sternaman

I desire to meet you within the next week or ten days in reference to a tour that I am interested in arranging for Red Grange this winter or as soon as his season with Illinois is over.

   Please write me to Beardsley Hotel, Champaign, Illinois, when and where I can reach you at the time I am in Chicago.

Very Truly Yours,
Chas. C. Pyle (signed)[24]

This letter got the ball rolling for Red in pursuing his goal of playing pro football after his senior year was completed. While Red's college career was coming to an end, Halas was approached by an unknown theater owner who wanted to talk about the famous redhead. "One day late in October of 1925 a Chicago man named Frank Zambreno approached me. He was a manager of a movie house and distributed films," Halas related.

He told me about a friend in Champaign named C. C. Pyle, who had been in vaudeville and now owns a movie theater in the college town. Pyle was thinking of being Red's manager. Zambreno said Pyle wanted to know if, were he successful, would I be interested in having Red play with the Bears and, perhaps, make a big tour after our season. I told him I liked the idea. Zambreno carried messages back and forth.[25]

A few days after the messages were sent, Pyle traveled to Chicago to meet with the two owners of the Bears. One day after defeating the Frankford Yellow Jackets, 19–0, in front of 5,000 fans at Cubs Park, the two parties met. The course of NFL history was about to change. Knowing they couldn't be seen together, Halas reserved a room at the Morrison Hotel, where Pyle sat with Halas and Sternaman to discuss the signing of Red Grange. "Pyle was an interesting man. I noted how carefully he dressed and how well-tendered was his mustache. His shoes were brilliant. He spoke well. He was suave. I felt I was in the presence of a born promoter," Halas said.[26]

Pyle laid out his plan for Red signing with the Bears. He would finish out the regular schedule with the Bears, plus a few additional games on the East Coast, followed by a barnstorming tour of exhibition games down South and out West. Halas and Sternaman were blown away. "It was a powerful idea," George declared. "I wouldn't have dared think of a sweeping enterprise. But Pyle had unlimited vision. I asked who would make the arrangements. Pyle said he would." The trio then started to discuss who would pay for what and how the earnings would be shared. Halas recalled the negotiating:

> It was obvious all of us had to share earnings. I could not possibly make a cash offer. I had no idea how much the tour would bring in. I had no spare cash for advance. I said I thought a two-to-one split would be about right. Pyle agreed, much to my surprise. Without a word, a single word. I anticipated at least some discussion. My astonishment may have stirred my generosity, because I then volunteered that the Bears would pay costs. "Of course," Pyle said. I said I hoped Grange would find the arrangements acceptable. "He will," Pyle said.
>
> A sense of uneasiness came over me. The negotiations had moved too easily. I thought I should begin again. "All right. It is agreed the Bears will get two-thirds and . . . Pyle cut me short. He said, "Oh no, George, Grange and I will get two-thirds. The Bears will get one-third."
>
> I said that was impossible. After I paid the players and the tour costs, I'd be lucky to break even. The sweetness went out of the discussions. We talked through the afternoon and the evening and the night and the next morning and on into the afternoon. After 26 hours, we did come to an agreement. We would split the earnings 50–50. I would provide the Bears and pay the tour costs. Pyle would

provide Red. Red would provide the crowds. It was a fair arrangement. . . . We put it in writing. The last clause stated if any of us were asked about a contract we would declare none existed. The date was November 10, 1925.[27]

A three-page contract was typed up for Red's first pro game against the Chicago Cardinals on Thanksgiving Day 1925. It stated the following:

This agreement made and entered into at Chicago, Illinois, this 10th day of November, 1925, by and between the Chicago Bears Football Club, an Illinois corporation, hereinafter referred to as the "Club," and Charles C. Pyle of Champaign, Illinois, hereinafter referred to as "Pyle."

WHERE AS, The said Club maintains a football team known as the "Bears" and is desirous of engaging the services of Harold E. "Red" Grange to play with its team against the team known as the "Cardinals" scheduled for Thanksgiving Day and (inserted in black ink Nov 26, 1925, C.E.S. GST, CCP, Nov. 10, 1925)

WHEREAS, the said Pyle is the manager and attorney in fact of the said Grange and is authorized to execute this contract on his behalf.

Nine separate clauses followed:

1) Red would report to practice and for the Cardinals game on Thanksgiving Day, November 26th, 1925.
2) The Club agrees to pay for the appearance and pay an equal amount to 35 percent of the total receipts at the box office after first deducting park rent, and U.S. tax, hereby guaranteeing that said payments shall not be in any event less than $1000.00, and after allowing to the two Clubs participating in said game the sum of $14,000.00 for both.
3) Practice period will use reasonable care to prevent injury to the said Grange and during the game will lend every assistance and full co-operation to allow the said Grange to properly display his playing ability.
4) The Club hereby gives the right and authority to the said Pyle to have credited agents in the several box offices during the sale of tickets and will permit at any reasonable time a full and complete inspection of its books and records pertaining to the receipts of said game and will immediately at the conclusion of said game submit a statement of the total receipts of said game together with the amount of money due and payable as above specified.
5) It is mutually agreed by the parties that this contract shall be confidential and that no report thereof shall be made to anyone until Nov. 22nd, 1925, and that for publicity purposes the parties hereto shall if interviewed deny the existence of any contract before said date.
6) Pyle agrees that the said Grange will completely sever his connection as a student with the University of Illinois on or before November 26th, 1925. The

Club allowing to the said Grange if he believes proper a personal visit to the University on November 23rd (crossed out in black ink, handwritten 24th, ECS, GSH, CCP, Nov. 10th) 1925, for this purpose.

7) The Club will furnish the usual and proper uniform and it—cross out and written—it is agreed to designate him on the playing field by the number "77."

8) The Club hereby grants to Pyle the right to place vendors of a book on the *Life of Grange* for sale to the spectators at said game.

9) Simultaneously with the execution of this contract the said club has paid to the said Pyle the abovementioned guarantee of $1000.00 in the form of its check, the receipt whereof is hereby acknowledged, said check being dated November 26th, 1925, and Pyle hereby agrees that in the event that the said Grange shall not report for said game barring accidents, acts of God, or any other contingency beyond his control that he will forfeit to the said Club the sum of $1000.00 as damages.[28]

The contract's last paragraph read,

IN WITNESS WHEREOF, the said Club has caused these presents to be signed by its duly authorized agents and officers and the said Pyle has placed his hand and seal hereon the day and year first above written.

Chicago Bears Football Club, Inc.
By Edw. C. Sternaman (signed in black ink)
By Geo. S. Halas (signed in black ink)
Charles C. Pyle (signed in light black ink) SEAL[29]

Pyle seemed to want more money at the gate. The second clause, written in black ink, stated, "15 percent on $10,000 and 20 percent if receipts exceed $10,000—signed in black ink with the initials of E. C. S., G. S. H, and C. C. P."[30]

After signing the contract for the Cardinals game, both parties also signed a contract for the game on November 29, against the Columbus Tigers at Cubs Park. This time the gate was split: 10 percent of the first $5,000, 20 percent of the next $5,000, and 40 percent of everything else, with $2,000 guaranteed up front.[31]

The historic contract would make Red Grange a member of the Chicago Bears five days after his last college game. Pyle got his client the money he was seeking and made sure he had his famous number "77" jersey to wear, as well as the ability to sell a souvenir booklet titled *Life and Football History of Harold E. "Red" Grange*. The 12-page booklet was published by Bentley, Murray & Company, out of Chicago. It featured a close-up image of Red on the cover (below the image was written "Under Management Chas. C. Pyle") and included 12 photographs inside with Red doing several different football poses. It also featured his life story, football accomplishments, and college stats, as well as quotes from a few well-known sportswriters. On the back was the number "77" in quotation marks. The booklet measured 9 × 12½ and sold for 50 cents at stadiums.[32]

Pyle had done his job. Now both parties had to keep quiet for another two weeks. They had to make sure that clause number five, the confidentiality clause, was followed. For Pyle it would be tough; he had more work to do in setting up his barnstorming tour. He headed straight for Florida to start planning games in the south. As for the two Bears owners, they found themselves in the spotlight too, as rumors of Red turning pro were surfacing. George Halas told the *United Press*,

> I have no contract with Grange, but I am extremely hopeful that he will play with the Bears on Thanksgiving Day. I shall talk business with him right after the game at Columbus Saturday.
>
> I know that several eastern teams have offered him $40,000 to play three games. We cannot meet this figure, but most of the men on our team are former University of Illinois players, and I hope that sentimental consideration will sway Grange to play with us for a smaller figure.[33]

As Red was getting settled in Columbus for his last college game, more rumors were swirling in Chicago. The day of Red's last college game, Jimmy Corcoran of the *Chicago American* talked to Dutch Sternaman.

> You see we are not in Columbus. We have placed a bid for Grange's services, and we hope we can get him. We will await the trains from Columbus, and we will watch the auto routes. If Grange comes to Chicago tomorrow we will be here to meet him and again offer our terms. If he accepts, we will be only too proud to shout the good news from the house tops and if possible will have him at the game tomorrow afternoon.
>
> But there is no certainty of this. New York has made him a better offer than we have, and Rochester would pay him more. Detroit is also after him. I'll not believe he is our man until he puts his name to the contracts we have ready for him.[34]

The NFL office in Columbus, Ohio, was also asked about the Red Grange rumors. Under the weather after an attack of appendicitis, Joe Carr released a statement:

> No college player may participate in any game of the National League while he is still eligible to play on his college team and that he cannot play in the same year in which he finishes his football career, in the event he remains in college.

Of course if Grange retires from school after Saturday's game he is a free agent and cannot be restrained under the rules of the National League. It would be absurd for the National League or any other organization to try and restrain any athlete from capitalizing his ability when he is no longer a member of any amateur organization and has retired from college.[35]

Carr, who was a stickler for rules, uncharacteristically opened the door for NFL teams to sign Red. He knew the colleges wouldn't be happy about this, but it was a decision he approved of. Deep down Carr knew this might be the NFL's one shot of getting the greatest college football player ever to play in the league. The wording of the rule against college players playing in the NFL would be dealt with later.

On November 10, just hours after signing the contract with Halas and Sternaman, Pyle traveled by train to Florida to negotiate for three exhibition games in Miami, Tampa, and Jacksonville. He spent $357.10 of his own money on expenses, which was for railroad transportation, hotels, taxis, telegrams, telephone calls, and meals with promoters and city officials. Pyle returned to Chicago on November 20, just one day before Red played his final collegiate game.[36]

The stage was now set. Pyle was back in Chicago at the Morrison Hotel. Halas and Sternaman were at their homes in Chicago on the eve of their game against the Green Bay Packers. Both parties now waited. It was like the night before Christmas for all three men. The Galloping Ghost was headed their way.

14

SIGNING WITH THE CHICAGO BEARS AND FIRST PRO GAME

Red left the Southern Hotel in Columbus with little fanfare. "One guy gave me a wig and I had a cigar in my mouth, I had never smoked in my life, and I went out the back door. Nobody recognized me, and I got on the train to Chicago," he recalled in a 1978 interview. With his beat-up suitcase in hand, wearing his ankle-length racoon-skin coat and newsboy cap, Red traveled by train overnight to the Windy City. He checked into the Belmont Hotel since the press and fans were staked out at the Morrison Hotel.[1]

On the morning of Sunday, November 22, Red would make his way to the Morrison. Located downtown in the Loop, the Morrison was a high-rise hotel at the corner of Madison and Clark. The recent expansion of the hotel had just been completed in 1925, to give the hotel 46 stories and almost 2,000 rooms. The stylish hotel was the perfect headquarters for C. C. Pyle. In rooms 1739 through 1941, "Cash and Carry" was ready for the morning show. Red, wearing a light-colored suit, vest, striped tie, and white-collared dress shirt, with his auburn hair slicked back and parted down the middle, knocked on the door of room 1739. Red entered the suite and greeted George Halas and Dutch Sternaman for the first time. Red was quickly impressed by Halas. Said Grange,

> I was impressed with him because he did everything himself. George was a one-man gang. He was his own press agent, his own coach, he played right end, he ran the ballpark, looked out for security, he signed the players, he did his own scouting, he did everything there was to do around the football team.[2]

After a few pleasantries, Pyle got the circus started. The eager promoter brought in the press and photographers. The moment everyone had been waiting for had arrived. In the suite, the four men sat down at a round glass table. The contracts and several pens were lying there, ready to make history. Red, sitting in the middle, had Pyle to his left and Halas to his right, with Sterna-man sitting next to Halas. The foursome posed as Red held pen in hand, ready to sign his first pro contract. Through a haze of smoke, following a broadside of flashlight powder from cameras, Red signed his name. With the press surrounding him, Red said a few words:

> Why I can't see that there is any difference between the game as it is played on college gridirons or on the fields used by men who turn their attention to the sport for financial rewards. I am at a loss to comprehend all the fuss that has been made in my case simply because I propose to capitalize on such success as I have attained while playing at the University of Illinois.
>
> There are scores of baseball players who were mighty good men on college diamonds who upon leaving their universities have entered professional baseball and are now earning comfortable livelihood through their skill at pitching, fielding, or batting. No one ever criticized those fellows for signing pro baseball contracts.[3]

Red then released a more complete statement, dated November 22, to the press on why he choose to play pro football.

> Yesterday I played my last college football game. Today, I am looking forward to my future. I alone must determine my career of tomorrow. No longer can I turn my eyes to those sterling American gentlemen and sportsmen, Huff and Zuppke, for the assistance they contributed so wholeheartedly in my development as a football player. My teammates who stood by me in the thick of conflict are now separated. No longer can they join with me with their splendid cooperation in the execution of the play as they did when we held aloft the colors of our beloved University of Illinois. No more will the liberal and generous press feature my deeds as a college football player. The plaudits of the student body and the public can no longer acclaim me for exploits upon the campus.
>
> There remains uncharged my obligation to my father. Possessed of a scant supply of this world's goods, he has given me an opportunity for an education at a great sacrifice. Then there is still imposed upon him the burden of my brother's education. . . . In what manner can I best perform my duty to my father and my brother? This is the question I have been turning over in my mind and seeking for an answer in my conscience for many days. Trained and developed in the game of football and achieving some success as a player, there is where my best talent has been revealed.
>
> I have received many alluring offers to enter fields of enterprise in which I have had no training or experience. But I believe the public will be better satisfied with

my honesty and good motive, if I turn my efforts to that field in which I have been most useful, in order to reap the reward which will keep the home fires burning.

There are countless thousands interested in football who seldom have an opportunity to see a college game. These devotees of the sport cannot take Saturday off and make a long trip to Champaign or some other point, in order to witness a college game. Many are excluded from college games, too, because of the limited number of tickets available to the public. These people in order to satisfy their desires must perforce attend professional football games which are held on Sundays, when and where it is convenient for them to go.

Therefore, I have resolved that I will play professional football. I will play with the Bears because they are a Chicago team, many Zuppke trained at Illinois University—some of them predecessors as captains of the team.

I signed a contract today to play with the Bears on Thanksgiving and other days. This is the first contract I have ever signed to play professional football. I preserved my amateur standing spotless until my college career as a football player ended.

Mr. Pyle has acted within the recent few weeks as my good friend and adviser. Today he is my manager.

To Messers, Huff, and Zuppke, and my teammates, to the student body and alumni, to the public, and to the press I give my thanks out of the depths of a grateful heart for the splendid support and encouragement extended to me throughout my college football career.[4]

Simultaneously with the Grange's statement, Pyle issued a few words of his own:

Considerable speculation and misinformation have been going the rounds during the past several days as to my relations with Harold Grange. As his friend, I undertook to act for him as an advisor and emissary.

With all the numerous offers being made to Mr. Grange, it was necessary to reduce them to a sensible selection. Recognizing this need, I visited the managers of professional football teams in Florida, advised with promoters and schemers, as well as bona fide producers of motion pictures, interviewing them by scores, ascertained their offers and ability to make good, and in every way I attempted to ferret out the good prospects from the worthless ones.

I traveled a great deal, spent much time, and defrayed all my own expenses, in order to make this investigation. After considerable work and examination, I came to certain conclusions as to what Harold Grange's future course should be. I laid my conclusions before him, and he is now making his decision in respect to them.

He has appointed me his manager. Today we have entered into several contracts for professional football to be played in Chicago and other cities.

Mr. Grange has at no time sullied his pure amateur standing by any act of professionalism. He waited until his last game was played, and today the contracts for his future services were drafted and entered into. I believe Harold Grange has made a wise decision in following up his splendid spectacular college career by engaging in professional football while his popularity is at its zenith.

Joining the Chicago Bears, Mr. Grange will be continuing to play under the same teaching he received at the University of Illinois. He will give the lovers of the professional football game the same sterling efforts he gave to the followers of the college game. He is destined to be great as a success in his newly chosen field as he was in the one just brought to a very successful conclusion.[5]

At the same time that Red was signing his contract with the Bears, he also redid his deal with Pyle, Coolley, and Moore, but he made one big change to the original contact drawn up in March 1925. The four men agreed to change the percentage of net profits. On the original contract, Red crossed out the March 27 date and wrote November 23. Then, under item number 13, the original split of the net profits was crossed out and written was the new split. Red would get 50 percent of the net receipts. The new numbers were Harold (Red) Grange, 50 percent; Charles C. Pyle, 25 percent (no change); Byron F. Moore, 12½ percent (down from 17½); and Marion F. Coolley, 12½ percent (down from 17½). So, the group decided to give Red half of the net profits, with Coolley and Moore getting only 12½ percent each. It was only fair, since Red was the one who was playing football.[6]

Both Grange and Pyle's full statements would be used by newspapers throughout the country. The dynamic duo of Grange and Pyle had completed a journey that had started almost a year earlier after Red's headlining performance against Michigan. Red's first big financial move following his newfound fame and wealth was paying off his racoon-skin coat. It cost him $500. Red, wearing the coat, was now off to Cubs Park. He would attend the Bears game against the Green Bay Packers.

The game seemed secondary to the presence of Grange. A crowd of 7,500 fans, above average for an NFL game, filled the stands at Cubs Park. That attendance figure was about to go up. After the game started, Red took a seat on the Bears bench. Looking more like a movie star, sporting his fur coat and cap, he leaned forward to watch the action while rolling up the game program in his hands. In the first half, a *Chicago Tribune* photographer snapped an image of Red on the bench, sitting between tackle Ralph Scott and end Vern Mullen. Red's Hollywood star power came out in full array in the photo, which was featured in the *Tribune's* photo section the next day. Behind a stifling defense and three touchdowns by the offense, the Bears cruised to an easy 21–0 victory against the Packers.[7]

The photo of Red sitting next to Pyle, with Halas and Sternaman, at the Morrison Hotel, signing his pro contract, was featured in newspapers throughout the United States, usually with a bold headline announcing the big news. The headline in the *Chicago Herald-Examiner* read, "Red Grange Signs Fat 'Pro' Contract."[8]

Influential sportswriters the likes of Billy Evans and Westbrook Pegler supported Grange's right to choose his career, but not everyone was happy with Red's decision to play pro football. Obviously, college coaches and administrators were upset with his decision to drop out of college to turn pro. Fielding Yost and Pop Warner took shots at Red. "I'm sorry that he is in the hands of managers who would exploit him for their own benefits," said John L. Griffith, commissioner of the Big Ten. But there wasn't much they could do about Red's decision. He recalled,

> You see, all the college coaches and athletic directors, they were 100 percent against professional football. They thought anybody connected with it was going to hell, you might say. When I joined the Chicago Bears, as far as the University of Illinois was concerned, I would have been more popular if I had joined the (Al) Capone mob.[9]

Red heard the criticism about his decision to turn pro. Sensitive to the talk, he knew deep down he had made the best decision for himself, and he had to live with his choice. The only person he had to answer to was his best friend—his father. Lyle Grange trusted his son to make a good decision, but he wasn't happy with the choice of a business manager to help guide him. Speaking to the *Chicago Herald-Examiner*, Lyle was quoted as saying, "I'd rather that my boy had turned to something that would have allowed him to stay in school, if that was possible. . . . I want to say here and now, though, that I want my boy to have nothing to do with that Pyle, and you can go as strong as you like about that."[10]

Eventually, Lyle Grange would come around. On November 23, the day after Red signed his pro contract, he woke up early for his first practice with the Bears. According to his contract, Red was to practice in the morning, then be allowed to travel to Champaign to attend the football banquet at Illinois. At about 11:00 a.m., Red walked into Cubs Park as a pro football player. He greeted his teammates, as well as a host of newspapermen, photographers, and newsreel cameramen. Halas placed Red at left halfback on offense. Red was joined on the field by no less than seven former Illini players—George Halas, Dutch

Sternaman, Joey Sternaman, Jim McMillian, Oscar Knop, Vern Mullen, and Laurie Walquist. He was in familiar surroundings.

The Bears made sure a number 77 jersey was ready for him to wear. "Seventy-seven was awfully good to me in college, and I do not wish to change my luck at this time," said Red to the press. Harold Johnson attended the practice for the *Chicago American*, reporting that "Red was usually frisky and consumed with learning and mastering all the plays and formations." Halas was pleased with how quickly Red was picking up everything. "Gee, he is a wonder at mastering plays," said Halas to Johnson after Red grabbed a pass from Joey Sternaman. "Let me explain this to you in detail," suggested Halas to Red during one play from scrimmage. "That's all right George, I got it the first time," responded Red. After running the play again, Red swept through the play in perfect fashion.[11]

All the major Chicago daily newspapers covered Red's first practice. In the afternoon edition of the *Chicago Daily News*, the paper recapped the event, as well as published three photos: Red in full football uniform (no helmet), Red posing with the Bears offense, and a posed shot of Red in a huddle with Halas and Sternaman. The *Chicago American* ran an exclusive photo of Red as a ballcarrier behind lead blocking by Dutch Sternaman and Laurie Walquist, with Joey Sternaman calling the signals and George Trafton, who had just snapped the ball to Red. Meanwhile, the *Chicago Evening Post* wrote, "Red absorbed some of the Bears signals and plays today and went thru a snappy workout. In passing the ball around the players, there were plenty of comments on the heaving of Grange. . . . Grange went at his new job as if he meant business."[12] Accompanying the article was a photo of Red with Pyle, with the caption, "Pyle and His Meal Ticket," taking a shot at old Cash and Carry.

Ever since Red announced he was signing with the Chicago Bears, tickets to his debut game against the Chicago Cardinals on Thanksgiving Day were a hot commodity. Tickets were being sold at Cubs Park and the A. G. Spalding & Company sporting goods store at South State and Adams streets. The Bears owners decided not to raise ticket prices, which turned out to be a smart move. From the start they sold like hotcakes. Prices were $1.75 for a reserved seat and $2.00 for a box seat.

That Monday, fans lined up for blocks to get tickets to see the Galloping Ghost. As the *Daily Illini* wrote, "Nobody wanted a ticket because it was the Bears or Cardinals playing—they all wanted tickets for 'the Grange game.'" Fifteen police officers were called in to calm the "riot," as reported by the *Chicago Herald-Examiner*. Jimmy Corcoran of the *American* wrote, "The panic is on! Pandemonium has broken loose. The town has gone NUTS in Harold Redhead

Grange, the flaming phantom of the greensward. Everybody wants tickets, tickets, TICKETS!" The *Herald-Examiner* ran on the front page of the paper (not just the sports section) the big bold headline, "RIOT FOR GRANGE GAME SEATS: Ticket Line Fights Keep Police Busy." Within the first three hours, all 20,000 tickets were sold. Halas got busy printing more.[13]

Pyle was happy to hear about the long lines for tickets, but while Red was at practice, Pyle was negotiating another game that would kick off his grand plan of a football barnstorming tour. St. Louis sports promoter Bud Yates came to Chicago to secure a game for his city with the Galloping Ghost. He spent all day in the Windy City across the table from Pyle. Shortly before midnight, Yates had his game, which was scheduled for December 2, a Wednesday afternoon contest right before the Bears were slated to head east to play the Frankford Yellow Jackets on Saturday, December 5, and the New York Giants on Sunday, December 6.

Pyle had one of his lawyers from Brundage & Gorman in Chicago type up a two-page contract for the Bears to sign. In the contract, it said, "Grange agrees to participate in said game for a period of not less than twenty-five (25) minutes." Pyle then took advantage of the Bears owners by "agreeing to pay the second party (Bears) the sum of money equal to twenty-three (23 percent) of the gross receipts, of the sale of tickets for said game (St. Louis)." A 77–23 gate split didn't seem to be fair for the Bears. But what could they do about it? Pyle could see the money adding up, even if he didn't understand the toll that playing football games on an almost-daily basis would take on his client or the Bears. "Let's get the money boys" was his motto.[14]

A few hours after his first practice as a pro, Red drove to Champaign to attend the annual season-ending football banquet held at the Champaign Country Club. It would be a disaster for the Galloping Ghost. Red stepped into the banquet hall, greeting teammates and alumni. During the dinner, he spoke briefly about how there was nothing better than playing for the University of Illinois and how he was now doing the next best thing by playing on a team with old Illinois men. "That can't compare with the pleasure of three years under coach Zuppke," remarked Red.[15] Although Red was playing nice with his words, Zuppke would not. Soon the coach's fiery remarks toward Red and professional football resounded throughout the banquet hall. In what was called a "verbal spanking" by the *Chicago American*, Zuppke did not hold back on Red and his decision.

> Remember, Harold, I have no fight with professional football, and if you choose to enter it, that is your business. But Grange is green, greener than when he first came here to Illinois. He must watch out for persons who will try to make their own fortunes out of his tact and his talent.

Suppose he does get $60,000 for his professional football services? Will he be able to guard that from those who will seek to take it away from him? Wouldn't he be better off, in the long run, if he took up some additional business and profited by it? He must remember that old saying of "Easy come, easy go." But above all, he must be careful of his companions, his associates. He must not fall into the hands of yes men who are eager to use him for their own advantages.

The Grange we know, and the Grange we have watched for three years, is a myth. As time goes by those runs of his will grow in length with the telling. And soon they will be forgotten.

Grange will pass on. He will be forgotten.

I tell you that no other $100,000 player is going to be on one of my teams.[16]

Zuppke's strong words were met with silence in the banquet hall. He had made his point. He did not appreciate that his most prized pupil had gone against his strong wishes, and he had a strong distaste for Red's "entourage." Zup had no time for "Doc" Coolley or "Cash and Carry" Pyle. As for Red, he didn't make it to the end of the heated speech. He was so upset with Zuppke's remarks and tone of voice that he left the banquet in the middle of his coach's rant. Red was not happy with what he had heard. He commented,

I don't think those remarks were called for. I acted according to my own judgement. Zuppke advised me against professional football, and I decided to go into it. Naturally he was peeved. . . . I wonder what Zuppke would do if somebody came along and offered him many thousands of dollars to go elsewhere and coach. Suppose he were offered $20,000, as I have been guaranteed for one game in Florida. Would he turn that down and stick to Illinois?

I'm not so dumb as a lot of people think I am. I not being fleeced by any promoter or going into anything with my eyes shut. I know just what I am doing, what I am getting, and what everybody else is getting. They are not playing me for a sucker, in any way at all. I am satisfied with the arrangement I have made, and I don't see why anyone else should be worried about it.

I went down to that dinner because it was for my team. I had to drive all the way, after practice with the Bears, in order to get there. I wouldn't have missed it for anything in the world. I am not sore at Zuppke. I just feel hurt at the whole matter. I have the greatest respect for him, and I consider him the greatest coach in football today.

I could have left the University of Illinois a year ago, had I desired. The offers that were made to me this year were no greater, or no more numerous, than they were at the close of the 1924 season. If I were as anxious to get away from Illinois as some people say I was, how do they account for the fact that I came back for this season? I could have plenty of money today, instead of just starting out to get it, if I didn't have a sense of loyalty.[17]

After the banquet, reports came out about a feud between Red and Zuppke. The relationship was broken, and the two weren't talking to one another. The two bull-headed men would have time to think about what had just happened. Zuppke was wrong about one thing in his speech—Red Grange would not be forgotten.

Not everything at this time was being written about the famous redhead. The *Danville Commercial-News* published a headline titled, "Coolley Looking Out for Grange." In the article, the paper wrote about their local boy's connection with the country's most famous sports star.

> The story goes that (Marion) Coolley, a college chum and close friend of the famous Illini star, is handling one of the managing of the famous redhead, although the senior (Dr. E. B.) Coolley intimated Monday noon that his son is just watching out for Grange's interests from the standpoint of a personal friend.
>
> Grange and Coolley had been very close friends for nearly four years, and since early fall rumors have been circulated around Champaign and Danville that Coolley was to be one of Grange's managers. . . . It was young Coolley who accompanied Grange to Wheaton last week for the star's preprofessional debut conference with "Father" Grange. Scarcely a weekend has passed that did not see Grange accompany Coolley to Danville to spend Sunday visiting at the Coolley home.[18]

With the support of his managers, Red turned his focus away from his former college coach's remarks to prepare for his first pro game. He had the support of his Bears teammates. "We want the redhead to go, and you can bet every last one of us will see that he gets every chance," declared Bears tackle Ed Healey to the *Chicago Daily Journal*. As game day approached, scalpers were having a field day. News reports came out that the $1.75 grandstand seats were fetching as much as $20. The crowd at Cubs Park was looking to set a record for a pro football game. The city assigned almost 300 police officers to stand watch during the event, and automobiles were parked for 10 blocks in every direction around Cubs Park.[19]

On the day of the game, Irving Vaughn of the *Chicago Tribune* wrote, "Grange is the man who has stood the town on its beam end as no other athlete ever had done, and he's the man those 35,000, most of whom have never cast eye on him, want to watch." The *Tribune* also wrote,

> No previous sporting event in the history of the Midwest has stirred up a city as Chicago has been stirred since the roaming redhead broadcast word that he had hung up his hat alongside those of other stars who had deemed it fitting to turn their varsity fame and ability to the making of a honest dollar. . . . No event here

ever caused a ticket turmoil such as broke loose when Red was formally received into the ranks of those who draw pay for their play.[20]

The city of Chicago was ready to see Red Grange. The gates opened at 9:00 a.m., with kickoff at 11:00 a.m. Fans filled the park by the thousands, while outside programs featuring Red smiling in his Bears uniform on the cover were sold for 10 cents. In the press box were all the big Chicago sportswriters—Irving Vaughn (*Tribune*), Harry MacNamara and W. V. Morgenstern (*Herald-Examiner*), Robert McBroom (*Evening Post*), and Harold Johnson and Jimmy Corcoran (*American*). Newspaper accounts of the game reported a crowd of 36,000 to 40,000.

Wearing his famous number 77 jersey, Red jogged out onto the field at Cubs Park as a member of the Chicago Bears for the first time. He would be starting at left halfback, with Laurie Walquist at right halfback, Dutch Sternaman at fullback, and Joey Sternaman at quarterback. Starting on the line would be Frank Hanny (left end), Ed Healey (left tackle), Bill Fleckenstein (left guard), George Trafton (center), Jim McMillian (right guard), Don Murry (right tackle), and George Halas (right end).

Lost in the excitement of Red's pro debut was the Bears' opponent. The Chicago Cardinals, led by All-Pro halfback Paddy Driscoll, were 8–1, and at the top of the NFL standings. They were fighting for a championship, but on this day they would take a backseat to the greatest football player on the planet.

As for the game, it was nothing to write home about, but tons of sportswriters tried their best to describe the action. The five major Chicago daily newspapers—*American, Daily Journal, Daily News, Herald-Examiner,* and *Tribune*—wrote plenty about Red's daily actions to their almost 2 million readers in 1925. The game quickly became a defensive battle with neither team giving an inch. Red was able to have a few good kick returns, three of the them going for more than 20 yards, but those were his highlights for the game. Throughout the contest when Red retired to the bench, he took a seat next to Pyle, who was trying to stay warm bundled up in his overcoat and fedora. Several times you could see Red and Pyle chatting away.

In the third quarter, the usually reliable Driscoll missed two field goals from 43 and 50 yards, respectively. Red continued to plug along with few chances to succeed. This day he wouldn't give the fans a big reason to cheer. He did have an interception in the red zone to help stop a Cardinals drive. The game ended in a 0–0 tie. While leaving the field, Grange was surrounded by a huge rush of fans. "He was almost carried off his feet by the rush after the final whistle, and it took a flying wedge of bluecoats (police) to get him off the field."[21]

Red finally arrived at the Bears locker room only to be greeted by newspapermen. Sporting a large red bump under his left eye, he was exhausted as he talked to the press. He related, "They are two great teams, the Bears and Cardinals. They are better than any college team I ever played against . . . this was the hardest game that I was ever in, but it was clean. It was much cleaner than most college games. I got this bump when I ran into a player." Red was asked about the interference he was given by his teammates. He responded,

> The best I ever got. The Bears did all they could for me today, but it's different blocking out these players than it is in college. It is a lot harder to do. I knew what this game was when I went into it, and it was just about as I expected. But I like it, as I expected to like it, and I intend to keep on going.[22]

The main story line in most game recaps was Driscoll's decision to punt away from Red. The future hall of famer became the villain. Jimmy Corcoran of the *Chicago American* wrote, "Paddy Kicks 'Em O.K. but Not towards Red-Head; Paddy Driscoll—Shame on You!"[23] Fans might have been disappointed with Red's play, as well as Driscoll, in the scoreless tie, but none of that mattered to one spectator—C. C. Pyle. He was overjoyed with seeing a sold-out crowd. "Charlie Pyle, after a while, saw a fella coming through the gate with the gate around his neck, and he said, 'I knew we'd sold out. They broke the gates to get in,'" recalled Red in a 1978 interview.[24]

Both Pyle and Red knew they needed someone to help look after the gate receipts that would be coming in. If Pyle was good at his job, then the money would be coming in like water flowing from a spout. Pyle recommended one of their partners to help on a full-time basis. Byron Moore was the man for the job. "Moore was hired by Grange and myself to check up on the gate receipts at the various games because of his experiences in handling such matters," said Pyle to the press.[25]

As for the Chicago Bears, Dutch Sternaman was in charge of supplying the Red–Pyle group with the exact box-office statements. He would provide the figures to them on typed-up stationary, whether it was in Chicago or on the road. Sternaman kept these statements, as well as the game contracts, his entire life. The documents were eventually donated by the Sternaman family to the Pro Football Hall of Fame in 2011.

Although Red might not have been a success on the field, he sure was a winner at the gate. Red, Pyle, Coolley, and Moore received a typed-up letter on Chicago Cubs National League Ball Club stationary with the gate numbers

Table 14.1. Cardinals at Bears, November 25, 1925

Tickets	Gate Receipts	War Tax
9,237 @ $1.61	$16,718.97	$1,755.03
13,503 @ $1.59	$21,469.77	$2,160.46
8,440 @ $1.36	$11,478.40	$1,181.60
Ex5 @ .452.25.25 = $31,180	$49,669.39	$5,097.36
Cubs 20 percent	$9,933.88	$39,735.51

Source: Marion F. Coolley Family Collection and Dutch Sternaman Collection, Pro Football Hall of Fame.

for Red's pro debut against the Cardinals. The numbers were staggering (see table 14.1).

Based on the gate receipts, the actual paying crowd was 31,180—a record for a pro game. Free passes and gate crashers probably pushed the crowd to more than 36,000, which was reported in the newspapers. The total gate amounted to $49,669.39, of which $9,933.88 was paid to the Cubs for use of the ballpark and expenses. Based on the contract Pyle had negotiated with Halas and Sternaman two weeks earlier, the Red–Pyle group received $9,007.43 for the game (15 percent of the first $10,000 and 20 percent of everything thereafter). Halas and Sternaman paid Grange and Pyle with two checks (#3029 and #3030). The Bears also paid the guarantee for each club ($14,000), the three game officials ($120), and printing of tickets ($114.44). Based on the contract written up between the four men, the total split of $9,000 for Red's first pro game would've been Red ($4,500), Pyle ($2,250), Coolley ($1,125), and Moore ($1,125).

Halas was also ecstatic. "There had never been such evidence of public interest since our professional league began in 1920," he recalled." I knew then and there that pro football was destined to be a big-time sport." The attendance figure was a record for a pro football game. The record wouldn't last long. The only person who was a loser in the money department was Cardinals owner Chris O'Brien. Not expecting the massive crowd, O'Brien decided to take the $1,200 guarantee instead of a piece of the gate, a move that backfired.[26]

Red enjoyed the next two days off to rest his body. He would need it. The barnstorming tour was just getting started. While relaxing at the hotel, he met up with a close friend. Earl Britton had arrived in the Windy City after dropping out of Illinois. The burly fullback soon started contract negotiations with the Bears. Hours before the Bears played the Columbus Tigers, he signed a contract to play pro football. He would sit out the game before making his debut in St. Louis. Now the Bears would have eight former Illinois players.

At this time, through one of Pyle's connections, Red agreed to be a guest referee for a semipro championship football game between the American Legion and Jonesboro teams in Kokomo, Indiana, on December 14. Red told Pyle he would donate his appearance fee to charity. It was the right thing to do.

A snowstorm hit Chicago right before Red's second pro game against Columbus. The bad weather didn't deter the fans interested in seeing the Galloping Ghost. An attendance figure of 28,000 was reported by the press. Red again played his left halfback position. On a snow-covered gridiron at Cubs Park, he performed much better in his second game with the Bears.

The opponent, the Columbus Tigers, was one of the worse teams in the NFL. They were winless, at 0–8, and had been outscored 15–110. Despite the lack of talent, the Tigers gave the Bears all they could handle. In the second quarter, Red started to help the Bears move the ball on offense. After returning a punt to the Tigers 38-yard line, Red had four carries for 26 yards to help put the ball at the one-yard line, where Joey Sternaman took it over for the score. Later in the quarter, Red threw a 37-yard scoring strike to Laurie Walquist. According to the *Chicago American*, in the first half, Red had carried the ball 11 times for 77 yards and had one kick return for 38 yards, two catches for 30 yards, and one touchdown pass. Up 14–0, it looked like an easy victory for Halas's squad, but the Tigers battled back. Right before halftime, Bob Rapp snared a pass from Dom Albanese to cut the lead to seven at the half. Then, in the fourth quarter, the Tigers pushed across another score, but the extra point was missed. The Bears controlled the ball the rest of the way to squeak out a 14–13 win.

The Columbus gate figures were just as impressive as those from the Cardinals game. Again, they were typed up on Chicago Cubs stationery (see table 14.2).

Based on the gate receipts, Red's second game made $41,643.16. After paying the war tax, park rental, the two teams, and game officials, the Red–Pyle group cleared $8,825.80 (after subtracting a $2,000 advance). Once again, Halas and Sternaman paid the duo with two checks (#3070 and #3071).

Two games as a pro saw an estimated 64,000 fans come out to see the Galloping Ghost. His pro debut saw 36,000 spectators—a record for a pro football game—and 28,000 for his second game. The actual paid figures come to 56,465. During that time, those numbers were unheard-of for a pro football game. In 1925, when the largest NFL crowd was approximately 10,000 to 15,000 and the average crowd was about 6,600, these two games blew those previous highs away. Even if fans hadn't been to a pro football game or were only there to see Red Grange play, the Galloping Ghost turning pro helped the sport reach an unprecedented level of success.[27]

Table 14.2.   Tigers at Bears, November 29, 1925

Tickets	Gate Receipts	War Tax
9,231 @ $1.61	$16,708.11	$1,753.89
13,509 @ $1.59	$21,479.31	$2,160.46
2,539 @ $1.36	$3,453.04	
Ex6 @ .452.70.30 = $25,285	$41,643.16	$5,097.36
Cubs 20 percent	$8,328.63	$33,314.53
10 percent	$5,000 = $500	
20 percent	$5,000 = $1,000	
40 percent	$23,314.53 = $9,325.80	
Total	$10,825.80	
Paid in advance	$2,000	
Balance due	$8,825.80, Chicago Bears Football Club, Inc.	
Geo. S. Halas		
Edw. C. Sternaman (Signed in black ink)		

Source: Marion F. Coolley Family Collection, Pro Football Hall of Fame.

As for the Red–Pyle, group the first two games had made them a net total of $17,833.23. In 1925, the average yearly salary for a manufacturing job in the United States was $1,267. Today that amount would be roughly $255,000 for two games.

For all parties involved, it would only get better.

⑮

EASTERN BARNSTORMING TOUR (NOVEMBER 22, 1925– DECEMBER 20, 1925)

Red's first two professional games proved to be a gold mine for the 22-year-old from Wheaton. The games also put pro football and the NFL on the front pages of newspapers and the lips of sports fans and Americans throughout the United States for the first time. Both parties would benefit from this relationship. It was just two games, but it was about to get better.

Red's life was now a whirlwind. Before the grand tour started, he wanted to see his best friend. He went to visit his father. It was time to repay the man who had given him so much. A few days after Red turned pro, Lyle was paid a visit by Jimmy Corcoran of the *Chicago American*. He told the sportswriter about Red's surprise visit the day after the Bears defeated the Columbus Tigers.

I guess a lot of people thought that Harold would let the dollar go to his head and be swallowed up in his new life. Well, Harold isn't that kind of boy. This is what he did. He came to Wheaton the Monday after his first two professional games. I was at the jail, and a neighbor told me that he was in town. For a minute I was afraid he wouldn't come over to see me, but sure enough he did. Harold put his arms around me and said, "Here dad, is a little present for you!" He handed me ten $100 bills. I didn't want to take the money, but Harold insisted. And it was the first time that I ever saw tears is his eyes since I tanned his hide for some misdemeanor not so many years ago. Harold said that it was the first $1,000 that had been paid to him from his professional work.

Yes, there has been talk that Harold will build a fine big house in the country where I can spend my next years like a king. Well, I don't want that, but I don't suppose it will stop Harold. He always wanted a big house for us. If his mother were alive things would be different. She would have taken great pride in the way that Harold has conducted himself. But . . . (almost stopping) I've worked too hard to stop now. I've worked ever since I was a boy. I'm still a young man at 58. Ought to be about 10 years of work left in me yet.[1]

Red promised to repay his father, and he did, handing his old man the first $1,000 he earned from playing pro football. He took care of his younger brother too, by giving Garland a crisp $100 bill. Corcoran also asked Lyle if he was still upset at Mr. Pyle being his son's manager. "No, I am not," replied Lyle. "He has played square with my boy. That is all I can ask. Harold is satisfied that he is getting a square deal from his manager." Although he might've accepted the fact that Red was not being taken advantage of by his agent, Lyle still wanted his son to be around more people who could watch out for his best interests. This would be a subject that he would revisit.[2]

Red left Wheaton behind to see the country and play football. The first stop would be St. Louis. Newspapers throughout the country started calling the upcoming Bears schedule the "greatest barnstorming tour in football history." Combining the Bears' remaining NFL games with Pyle's "money-making" exhibition games, the tour's eastern schedule now looked like this:

Wednesday, December 2, at St. Louis All-Stars
Saturday, December 5, at Frankford Yellow Jackets (NFL game)
Sunday, December 6, at New York Giants (NFL)
Tuesday, December 8, at Washington All-Stars
Wednesday, December 9, Providence Steam Roller (NFL)
Thursday, December 10, Pittsburgh All-Stars
Saturday, December 12, Detroit Panthers (NFL)
Sunday, December 13, versus New York Giants (NFL, in Chicago)[3]

At one point in the tour, they would play six games in eight days. There was no rest when it came to making money. On the night of December 1, the team gathered at the Dearborn train station in Chicago to leave on a barnstorming tour, something that had never before been attempted in football history. With the addition of Earl Britton, the Bears had 20 players along for the ride. Before leaving the Windy City, the team gathered at the rear of the train to pose for a team photo. More than half the team stood on the tracks in back of the train. Marion "Doc" Coolley was on the far right wearing Red's racoon-skin coat. Standing above them on the caboose of the train from left to right were Earl Britton, Red, C. C. Pyle, George Halas, and Dutch Sternaman. It was a historic moment in NFL history and the beginning of a journey that would last the next two months. The photo would appear in the *Chicago Tribune* above the headline, "Grange Opens Barnstorming Tour in St. Louis." Also traveling were Chicago sportswriters Irving Vaughan and Westbrook Pegler of the *Tribune* and Harry MacNamara of the *Herald-Examiner*, who, along with Pegler, would make the journey east with the tour. The traveling football circus would pick up many more scribes along the way.[4]

The train moved south until its first stop at Forrest, Illinois. Several hundred fans, mostly children, gathered at the station to get a glimpse of Red. MacNamara of the *Herald-Examiner* wrote, "Grange was lunching in the diner but stepped out onto the platform so that the kids might give him the once over. . . . Redhead seemed very much pleased over his reception."[5]

ST. LOUIS GAME
WEDNESDAY, DECEMBER 2, 1925
BEARS VERSUS DONNELLY'S ST. LOUIS ALL-STARS
(NON-NFL), AT SPORTSMAN'S PARK

The St. Louis team was organized by Art Donnelly, a local mortician and sports promoter, who helped fellow promoter Bud Yates with the $2,000 guarantee (some news reports say it was $5,000) to get Red and the Bears to come to St. Louis. Because of the hastily put together game, the squad was mostly comprised of local talent from St. Louis University. Yates was able to attract former Cornell All-American halfback Eddie Kaw, former Michigan star center Ernie Vick, and Detroit Panthers player-coach Jimmy Conzelman to play for St. Louis. They only had a week to get ready.

The Bears arrived the evening before the game at Union Station in St. Louis just after 6:00 p.m. local time and were greeted by several hundred fans and the press. Conzelman also showed up to greet his former teammates with the Staleys—Halas and Sternaman—as well as meet Red for the first time. The team was taken to the Coronado Hotel, where they stayed the night.

The game was played on a Wednesday afternoon at Sportsman's Park—home of baseball's Browns and Cardinals—on the city's northside. Tickets were sold at the ballpark and Leacock's, the city's leading sporting goods store. Prices were set at $4.40 for box seats, $3.20 for the grandstands, and $2.20 for bleachers and the pavilion, plus tax. Ads in the *St. Louis Star and Times* read as follows:

RED GRANGE
At Sportsman's Park
Wednesday, Dec. 2
Tickets at Leacock's (10th and Locust); and Sportsman's Park.[6]

There was no mention in the ad of the Bears or Donnelly's All-Stars, just the Galloping Ghost. "For those games left on the Chicago Bears schedule, the posters read, 'See the Chicago Bears with Red Grange,'" recalled "Beans" DeWolf in a 1987 interview. "But when they began the barnstorming trip, the posters were changed to read, 'See Red Grange with the Chicago Bears.'"[7]

Kickoff was set for 2:30 p.m. Local sportswriters John Alexander of the *St. Louis Post-Dispatch* and Ted Drewes of the *St. Louis Star and Times* joined the Chicago writers in the press box. The press reported that 8,000 fans braved the 40-degree "cold" afternoon contest. Pyle was disappointed with the turnout.[8]

As for the game, it was a lopsided affair. With only a few days of practice, Donnelly's All-Stars looked more like duds. Red gave the small crowd plenty to cheer for while playing a little more than a half of football. On the first two drives of the game, the redhead scored touchdowns. Bears fullback Earl Britton would make his professional debut by replacing Dutch Sternaman in the second quarter. The scoring continued in that quarter with another TD by Red, as the Bears took a 27–6 halftime lead. In the fourth quarter, Red scored his fourth touchdown of the game as the Bears cruised to an easy 39–6 victory. The *Chicago American* wrote that Red "was in great form and ran wild early in the game."[9] Alexander of the *Post-Dispatch* wrote,

> It is hard to describe that action. Essentially, it seems to be the ability to make tacklers miss him completely without forcing him to lose headway and to shake them loose once they catch hold. . . . One such run as yesterday's is worth the price of admission. One does not often see a player who can run into an apparent muddle of enemies and shake them from his shoes like so much mud. Grange does that. His footwork is deft and artful, and when he breaks loose in an open field, he resembles nothing so as Eliza skipping over the ice floes with the bloodhounds baying at her heels and a child tucked under one arm, changing pace and varying her course slightly each successive hop.[10]

Red was a success on the field this time, albeit against an inferior team, but it was the first time he was a failure at the box office. Shortly after the game, the gate receipts "officially" came out. Promoter Yates announced the paid attendance at 5,032, with a total gate receipt of $13,657. Based on the report, the Grange–Pyle–Bears group got $7,834, while the local team got $1,547.

The Bears left St. Louis Thursday morning at about 9 a.m. to head to Philadelphia to play the NFL's Frankford Yellow Jackets. Dutch Sternaman paid $1,183.36 for 27 train fares, which included 20 players plus C. C. Pyle, Doc Coolley, trainer Andy Lotshaw, and Harry MacNamara of the *Chicago Herald-Examiner*. On the train headed east, the Bears passed their time playing cards. Frank Hanny and Jim McMillian held court at the card table, while Johnny Mohardt "lectured Red and George Trafton in the observation car on the human anatomy." After his football career ended, Mohardt would go on to become a doctor and one of Chicago's leading brain specialists.[11]

PHILADELPHIA GAME
SATURDAY, DECEMBER 5, 1925
BEARS VERSUS FRANKFORD YELLOW JACKETS (NFL),
AT SHIBE PARK

The Grange–Bears barnstorming tour arrived at the Broad Street Station in Philadelphia on the morning of Friday, December 4. After getting settled at the Robert Morris Hotel, the team went to Shibe Park for an hour-long walk-through, as Halas wanted to "get the boys acquainted with the mud." A steady rain would continue through the night and into Saturday. Later that evening, Red was invited to attend a show at the Earle Theater. He brought the entire Bears team with him. As he entered the theater, he was "given a rousing reception."[12]

Because of the Sunday blue laws in Pennsylvania, the Frankford Yellow Jackets played most of their home games on Saturdays and then would travel to play a road game on Sunday. Because of the potential for a large crowd, the Frankford Athletic Association, which operated the team, moved the contest from their home field at Frankford Stadium to the larger Shibe Park—home of the American League's Philadelphia A's—with a capacity of almost 35,000. Led by player-coach Guy Chamberlin, the Yellow Jackets were 11–5 and one of the best teams in the NFL. Tickets were sold at Gimbel's Department Store,

National Ticket Agency, Robin's Cigar Store, and the Capitol Theater box office. The following ads appeared in the *Philadelphia Evening Bulletin*:

FOOTBALL TICKETS
SEATS AT $2.50 and $3.50
Red Grange with Chicago Bears
vs. Frankford Yellow Jackets
NATIONAL TICKET AGENCY[13]

Ticket prices were $4.00 to $5.00 for field seats, $3.50 for reserved box seats, and $2.50 for general admission. The press reported a crowd between 35,000 and 36,000, which more than doubled the Yellow Jackets' previous high of 15,000 fans. The sold-out crowd almost set another record for a pro football game, matching Red's debut just nine days earlier. It was on the East Coast that several of the country's greatest sportswriters joined the barnstorming tour. Chicago beat writers Westbrook Pegler and Harry MacNamara now sat in the Shibe Park press box with the likes of Richard Vidmer of the *New York Times*, Marshall Hunt of the *New York Daily News*, Damon Runyon of *Universal Service*, and local writers Perry Lewis of the *Philadelphia Inquirer* and Ross Kaufman of the *Philadelphia Evening Bulletin*. Lewis's preview of the game in the *Inquirer* stated, "This is the morning of professional football's greatest day in Philadelphia. . . . In those crowded stands will be thousands who never saw a professional football game before, and they will judge the sport in its entirety by what they see today."[14]

Before the game, Red jogged out to midfield to greet Frankford captain Guy Chamberlin. The two shook hands. The duo then shook hands with Philadelphia mayor W. Freeland Kendrick as photographers and newsreel cameras shot the moment. Red was also presented with a phonograph and a few records, one of which was an album of songs of the University of Illinois, including "Hail to the Orange" and "Illinois Loyalty."[15] "Grange, who is very fond of music, appeared delighted with the gift," wrote the *Daily Illini*.[16]

As was the case when Red visited Philly in late October to play Penn, the city of brotherly love, there were plenty of rain showers. Rain continued to come down throughout the game, making the field a "waterlogged gridiron." Neither team got off to a fast start on the muddy field. After nine punts, the Bears finally mounted a drive. On the first play of the second quarter, Red capped an eight-play, 47-yard drive with a 2-yard touchdown run. Joey Sternaman's extra point gave the Bears a 7–0 lead. The Yellow Jackets would continue to struggle on offense, throwing three interceptions in the first half as the game stayed 7–0 at halftime.[17]

In the second half, the stadium lights were turned on so that the wet crowd could get a better look at the action, as the Yellow Jackets gave the hometown fans more to cheer about than just seeing the Galloping Ghost. Midway through the third quarter, Hust Stockton completed a pass to Ben Jones, who weaved for a 40-yard touchdown. The extra point tied the game at 7–7. Red, who sat out the third quarter, returned to action in the fourth, as the sold-out mob "stood up and bellowed" for him. He would give the crowd more to applaud.

Late in the game, Red completed a 17-yard pass to Johnny Mohardt to put the ball at the Yellow Jackets 36-yard line. Red sprinted for 14 yards and Mohardt rushed for 19, to put the ball at the 3-yard line. Two plays later, Red plowed over for the go-ahead score. Leading 14–7, the Bears defense denied the Yellow Jackets on two straight drives, forcing five consecutive incomplete passes. It was a hard-fought win for Red and his Bears.[18]

The local press praised Red. Perry Lewis of the *Philadelphia Inquirer* wrote,

He proved it. The "He" we refer to is that Galloping Ghost of the gridiron, Red Grange. . . . Red was in that game just about 30 minutes of the 60 minutes of actual play. But while he was there he enveloped his entire team with an atmosphere of quiet confidence. Without him the Bears played magnificent football, football that appeared to be mechanically perfect, against a machine equally as good. With him in there they *did* things. His mere presence appeared to spur them to deeds that otherwise would have been beyond them.[19]

Shortly after the game, the team sprinted to the train station wearing their muddy uniforms for their 6 o'clock train to New York. On the ride to the Big Apple, Pyle told Halas, "This tour will make you so wealthy Halas, that next year you'll be able to afford two sets of uniforms."[20]

After a disappointing gate in St. Louis, the trip to Philadelphia was much sweeter. The typed-up statement for the Frankford game revealed a paying crowd of 25,408 fans. The total gate was a remarkable $81,069. The breakdown was as follows:

Total gate receipts: $81,069.00
War tax (possible): $7,424.10
20 percent park rental: $16,213.80
Pyle's share (27.5 percent): $17,835.18 (paid by check #3084)

Expenses of Bears: $2,000

Expenses of Frankford: $2,000[21]

The Bears received almost 50 percent of the gate, based on the standard NFL game contract, while the Red–Pyle group took home $17,835.18. The pace was picking up. Starting with the Frankford game, the Grange–Bears squad would play five games in the next six days. Dr. Harry March, a front-office executive for the New York Giants, was worried about Red's schedule. "He played Wednesday in St. Louis; he plays Saturday in Philadelphia; he goes to a banquet Saturday night; he plays again Sunday in New York, Tuesday in Washington, and Wednesday in Boston," declared March. "If he doesn't slow up, he'll blow up. This isn't baseball."[22]

The main organizers of the tour—Pyle, Coolley, and Moore—were looking out for Red, or more likely themselves. As the tour marched on, Westbrook Pegler started to take notice of the trio. He called Pyle the "manager" and Coolley the "deputy manager." No mention is made of what he called Moore. Pegler wrote, "Mr. Pyle is concerned with the big affairs of getting the money and Doc Coolley with seeing that none of it gets away from them at the turnstiles." "It's not true that we are cutting our share down the middle," said Pyle to Pegler. "Red gets more than I do." This was true, as Red got more than Pyle.[23]

The train carrying the team arrived in New York on Saturday night, just in time for Red to attend the All-American team football banquet, sponsored by the *New York Sun*. Red was selected as one of the First Team All-American backfield players. After a busy day of playing football in Philadelphia and seeing the nightlife of New York, Red finally went to sleep in his bed at the Astor Hotel. In a few hours, he would have to play his best game in front of the biggest crowd to ever see a pro football game, in the entertainment capital of the world. He had to be at his best.

NEW YORK GAME
SUNDAY, DECEMBER 6, 1925
BEARS VERSUS NEW YORK GIANTS (NFL), AT THE POLO GROUNDS

From the start when Red signed his contract to play pro football, the game in New York was going to be a big event in the Big Apple. The New York Giants announced early on they would not increase ticket prices for the "Red Grange Game." Regular prices ranged from $.50 to $2.75. It was a smart move by Giants owner Tim Mara. On Sunday, November 29, just three days after Red played his first pro game on Thanksgiving, during the game against the Dayton Triangles, nine booths were opened at the Polo Grounds as the Giants sold more than 15,000 tickets to the Grange game. Later, during the week, additional tickets were sold at the Giants ticket office and the Polo Grounds. On December 4, advance sales were reported to be more than 45,000 tickets. On three separate occasions, new tickets had to be printed to meet the demand. In almost every mention of the contest, the event was being called the "Red Grange Game," with slight mention of the Bears.[24]

Throughout the week, the New York newspapers wrote about Red Grange. It was an event worthy of the Big Apple. Ford Frick of the *New York Evening Journal* wrote, "Not since Mr. Babe Ruth went on his home run rampage a few seasons ago has any athlete attracted so much attention as Mr. Grange. Almost single-handed he has filled stadium after stadium. . . . Like Ruth, he is a hero whether he runs for a touchdown or is thrown for a loss."[25]

Tim Mara needed this type of game. He had been losing money throughout the season, with reports stating he had a financial deficit of about $40,000. Mara had been rethinking his investment in an NFL franchise in New York, but the early sales of the Grange game picked up his spirits.

On the morning of the game, the rain had stopped on the East Coast, and the sky was clearing. Mara knew this could be a day that could save his team. Said Mara, about seeing the massive crowd arrive, "When I saw that crowd and knew half the cash in the house was mine, I said to myself, 'Timothy, how long has this gravy train been running?'" The gates at the Polo Grounds opened at 11:30 a.m., with a 2:00 p.m. kickoff. At 1:15 p.m., the Bears jogged out onto the field. What they saw was another record crowd for a pro football game. Newspapers reported the attendance at between 65,000 and 70,000, which matched the Army–Navy game held at the Polo Grounds a week earlier. "I don't think there were too many rabid fans one way or the other," recalled Wellington Mara, son of Giants owner Tim Mara. "We hadn't had time to build up that much of a following. I think they were there to see Red Grange perform, without any questions."[26] Inside the stadium, bunting decorated the stands, and it was a perfect day for a football game, "bright and balmy," wrote the *New York Times*.[27]

In the press box, the ever-growing number of sportswriters was increasing. Almost 100 newspaper writers crowded the box, including some of the most influential sports scribes in the country—Westbrook Pegler (*Chicago Tribune*), Harry MacNamara (*Chicago Herald-Examiner*), Harry Neily (*Chicago American*), Richard Vidmer (*New York Times*), Allison Danzig (*New York Times*), W. O. McGeehan (*New York Herald-Tribune*), Marshall Hunt (*New York*

Daily News), Frank O'Neil and Ford Frick (*New York Evening-Journal*), Bill Cunningham (*Boston Post*), Roger Batchelder (*Boston Globe*), Damon Runyon (*Universal Service*), and Lawrence Perry (*Associated Press*).

Red had now played four games with the Bears. He was plenty involved in the offense and had played well on defense, but, more importantly, he had proved to his new teammates that he was a team player. Joey Sternaman recalled the game plan in using Grange.

> Well, when he [Red] came with the Bears I was the play caller, and I said to him, "Are you interested in doing well for yourself or are you interested in winning ballgames?" After all, he'd been used to an offense down at Illinois that was built solely on opening a hole for him. Everything was geared to that. Well, we had a lot of different things, and we need them in the pros. We had quick opener that would work well with Red, but we also had a lot of deceptive plays that we used. We were not just going to blow open a hole for Red Grange.
>
> Well, Red was honestly interested in winning games, and, as I found out, he was one of the finest team players around. So, what I did a lot after Red came with us was use him as a decoy. I'd fake handing the ball off to him, and hell, I'd be bootlegging around the other end or off on the other side passing it to one of our ends. We used a lot of deception, and it worked well. And Red took a real beating, especially that first year, but he never complained, just played his best.[28]

Red the decoy would take center stage in the entertainment capital of the world. The Bears faced off against a good Giants football team that was on a roll—having won seven straight NFL games and outscoring their opponents 84–15 (five shutouts). The Bears got off to fast start by establishing a tough running game. With Red being a decoy in the red zone they scored twice, with Joey Sternaman carrying the ball over for both scores to take a 12–0 first-quarter lead. The Giants cut the lead to 12–7 at the half. In the second half, the two defenses played tough. When Red wasn't in the game chants from the stands of "We Want Grange!" rang throughout the stadium. Finally, in the fourth quarter, Red gave the massive crowd what they had come to see—a thrill—when he returned an interception 30 yards down the sidelines for a game-clinching touchdown. The Bears left the Polo Grounds with a 19–7 victory. The game ended at 4:25 p.m., as the New York crowd left the stadium with a lasting highlight from the Galloping Ghost.[29] Red recalled the game in the following way:

> Although we had won, it was one of the most bruising battles I had ever been in. I especially remember one play when Joe Alexander, the Giants' center, almost twisted my head off in making a tackle. . . . It was clear we were all beginning to

show the wear and tear of our crowded schedule. After that encounter with the Giants, the Bears were no longer able to field a team free of injuries.[30]

Red always remembered the Giants game as one of the most physical games of the barnstorming tour. He would leave the game with numerous bruises and was kicked in the arm by Giants lineman Tommy Tomlin. Whatever money he was able to walk away with was definitely earned. As for the New York press, they wrote glowingly of pro football and the Galloping Ghost. Allison Danzig, one of the lead sportswriters for the *New York Times*, wrote,

> New York saw red yesterday; not the red that causes the eye to flame with anger, but the Red who inflames the imagination with the heroic proportions of his deeds on the football field and the glamour that surrounds the most celebrated figure the game has known. For three years New York has heard about Red Grange, read about him, talked about him. Yesterday it saw him.
>
> To call these 70,000 spectators football followers needs correction. There were thousands in that tremendous assemblage who probably never saw a game before, who did not have the slightest idea of what the proceedings were all about. They knew only that Grange was out there on the field among the 22 young warriors clad in moleskins, and they wanted to see what were the things he did and how he did them to differentiate him from the 21 others and win him such renown.[31]

George Trevor of the *Brooklyn Daily Eagle*, who would become one of the greatest college football writers for the *New York Sun*, simply wrote, "There is an indefinable something about Grange that stamps him as one among many. Babe Ruth has it. Man o' War had it, Jack Dempsey has it. Even while he was being effectively bottled up, Grange looked the part of a master player. Class sticks out all over him."[32]

The *New York Daily News* had full coverage of the game in a recap by Marshall Hunt that included a five-page photospread on the back page under the bold caption, "70,000 See Grange Star."[33] The great Ford Frick of the *New York Evening Journal* wrote,

> Well, Mr. Red Grange has come and gone. So has some $30,000 of good money which was last seen being stuffed into the professional sock of the professional Red Head himself. But it was worth it. National hysteria always is; all the Red Grange hysteria is one of the noblest brands this writer has ever been privileged to witness.
>
> During the first part of the game the Red Head failed to distinguish himself unduly, and there was considerable jeering. This however turned to cheers as he

snatched that final Giants pass out of the air and galloped to a touchdown—and everyone left the field happy and contented.[34]

Frick would be mesmerized by the Galloping Ghost, so much so that he would follow the rest of the eastern barnstorming tour for the next week. He would travel with the Bears, writing every day about the goings-on of the tour and its superstar. No pro football or NFL game had ever been covered by the press like the Grange game in New York. Lastly, even the Giants players were impressed by Red. Giants right tackle "Babe" Parnell said, "He's just about the best backfield man I've ever seen play."[35]

The *Chicago Tribune* reported that Grange earned roughly $30,000 from the gate (from a total gate of $120,000), while Pyle stated to the press that the amount was $36,000. This was one of the few games for which Dutch Sternaman didn't keep a gate statement. Whatever the total, you can be sure it was the biggest gate for a professional football game up until this point.[36]

Later that night, just after 10:00 p.m., Red agreed to give a speech on New York radio station WEAF to help raise money for the Near East Relief Fund. He spoke at length about football.

Football, I am convinced, is the best game invented. It demands more than any other game from a player, and the rewards of it are spiritual rather than material. . . . I am sure that I am better a man for having played this game. The big thing I have won from football is not the fortunate break which has enabled me to earn certain monetary rewards, but rather the more permanent matter of training in courage, stamina, and ability to use mind and muscle more effectively.[37]

Yes, Red loved the game of football and everything about it; he always did and always would. But the money he collected in his first 10 days as a professional football player would take center stage. His bank account was about to grow even bigger. The day after the successful game at the Polo Grounds was a day off for the Bears, but it was not a day of idle play for Pyle and Red. "Cash and Carry" set up shop at the Astor Hotel to make even more money. He had planned it this way. With the day off, he and Red would stay in the Big Apple to reap more rewards.

Pyle's headquarters was located in the east ballroom of the hotel, a perfect spot to listen to endorsement deals and take advantage of Red's name. Early that Monday morning, the Galloping Ghost entered the ballroom, passing by a large group of newspaper writers and photographers. "Grange, dressed very natty, in a double-breasted dark suit set off by a brilliant red necktie, was all smiles when interviewed by reporters today. He was still shy, still reluctant to talk," wrote the *New York Sun*.[38] Pyle did most of the talking. He was in his element, and product owners were ready to spend their money. "Don't be impatient gentlemen," said Pyle loudly to the group of men lined up. "Everybody will be heard in due course." One by one the checks were signed to Pyle and Red to help endorse such products as a sweater ($12,000), a doll ($10,000), shoes ($5,000), ginger ale ($5,000), a cap ($2,500), souvenir footballs ($2,000), and tobacco ($1,000).[39]

Red never smoked, but he agreed to a testimony with the Murad Turkish Cigarette company, saying, "If I smoked, I choose this brand." For almost 90 minutes, the money kept flowing. The morning was capped by Red signing a movie contract. Pyle brought the photographers into the ballroom to snap an image of Red signing another historic contract. Walter E. Shallenberger of Arrow Picture Corporation negotiated the deal with Pyle to pay $300,000 for Red's initial appearance in a Hollywood movie. The large check was flashed to the press, with Red holding it. The contract made headlines throughout the United States, and it was just as Pyle wanted it. On the back page of the *New York Daily News*, the headline read, "Grange in Movies—$300,000," with a photo of Pyle and Red together. For 24 hours in New York, the Pyle–Grange duo was on a roll. Between the game and the endorsement deals, they collected $373,500 in the Big Apple.[40]

But saving money wasn't lost on young Red. Pyle told the press of Red's allowance: "A week ago Saturday I gave Red a $100 bill. Yesterday, thinking he might be in need of some change, I asked him if he wanted his $100. 'Oh no,' he answered, 'I still got $70 left, and the trainer (Andy Lotshaw) owes me $10.'"[41]

Lyle Grange was concerned. He had heard the reports of the money coming in and the people his son was surrounding himself with. He was uncomfortable, so he decided to talk to one of Red's closest friends. Beans DeWolf, who was working as a salesman for the Union Tool Company, was asked by Lyle to watch after Red on the tour. DeWolf's main job was to "keep undesirables away from Red." DeWolf would join the tour once it returned to Chicago on December 13. At 2:00 p.m., the Red–Pyle–Bears tour took a train to Washington. Arriving in the evening, the group checked into the Lee House and went straight to bed. While the team headed to the nation's capital, Pyle left the tour to head back to Chicago. He left Red in the hands of Coolley and Moore. Back at the Morrison Hotel, Pyle told the press of his next move:

> We got so many remarkable offers from the Coast, four of them from Los Angeles alone, that I decided it would be best for me to go out there and make the contracts after I had a chance to look things over. . . . We had no idea that Grange's

success would be what it is. I know something about showmanship, but the developments since Thanksgiving have been remarkable. I do not know how to account for it except that Grange has great publicity and has the knack of being popular. He is clean-cut and honest, he was a poor boy, and he had to work through school—those are qualities that seem to have a tremendous appeal. He is a great hero with boys and girls, and that means a lot.[42]

Pyle, along with his attorney, H. L. Jones, traveled out West to secure a promoter for the game in Los Angeles, as well as to find a suitable director for Red's Hollywood debut. What Pyle didn't know was that his star client was about to break down.

WASHINGTON GAME
TUESDAY, DECEMBER 8, 1925
BEARS VERSUS WASHINGTON ALL-STARS (NON-NFL),
AT GRIFFITH STADIUM

After a day off, the Grange–Bears tour was back on the field, but only after an impromptu visit to the White House. On the morning of the game, Red got a unique request. Illinois senator William McKinley, who was a graduate of Illinois and had seen many Illini home football games in which Red had played, and William Holaday, a representative in the House of Representatives from Illinois, who also played a little college football at Penn College and Missouri, and received his law degree from Illinois, invited the redhead to the White House to meet President Calvin Coolidge. Red quickly said yes. Joining Red would be George Halas, Doc Coolley, and Byron Moore.

Red, dressed in a dark winter overcoat with quarter-size buttons, a fedora, and a suit and tie, with a stripped scarf around his neck, wanted to look like an average 22-year-old. He allowed his good friend Coolley to wear his trademark raccoon-skin coat. The foursome was picked up by the senator and transported from the Lee House to the White House. After posing for a few photos outside the famous building, the men went inside. Red said of meeting the president,

> I remember our game in Washington very well. Senator McKinley called George Halas and asked us if we'd like to meet the president. And, of course, we were flattered and thrilled to have the opportunity to meet President Coolidge. And the Senator picked us up and took us to the White House. And I remember so well as if it was yesterday. He said, "Mr. President, this is George Halas and Red Grange

with the Chicago Bears." I remember President Coolidge saying, "Young men, I'm very happy to meet you, I always did like animal acts."[43]

A few minutes later, the group left the White House. In newspapers everywhere, it was reported that Red had meet the president. In every article it was mentioned that he briefly met Coolidge, who shook his hand, asked him where he was from, and wished him good luck. It was obvious that the president didn't know who Red was, since he had to ask where he was from. Most sports fans and citizens knew that the redhead was from Wheaton. This meeting became a banquet story told by Red and Halas for decades. Now it was on to the game.[44]

The Washington game was set up between Pyle and local sports promoter Al Stern, who agreed to give "Cash and Carry" 60 percent of the gate. Tickets were sold for $2.50 (general admission), $3.85 (grandstands), and $5.50 (box seats) at Griffith Stadium and Spalding's Sporting Goods. Stern and Pyle also agreed to offer 5,000 tickets at $1.00 to prep school, high school, and college fans. Advertisements in the local papers announced, "Red Grange at Griffith Stadium," with no mention of the Chicago Bears or Washington All-Stars.[45]

As for the team Stern had organized, it was a rather rough and tough group of players. Because of the haste, Stern was only able to sign a few quality pro football players, including Jack Hagerty, former Georgetown star who played for the New York Giants (1926–1932), and Les Hawes (Dartmouth), who also played for the Frankford Yellow Jackets. Most of the roster was made up of semipro players from the area.

The Bears were starting to feel the strain of playing several games in a row, as tackle Ed Healey and center George Trafton would sit out with nagging knee injuries. But Red would spend his allotted time pleasing the fans. Most contracts drawn up by Pyle had him obligated to play at least 25 minutes. In the press box would be the usual suspects—Pegler, MacNamara, and Frick—but this time they would be joined by local writers Ross Conklin of the *Washington Times*, Frank Young and Walter Haight of the *Washington Post*, and Arthur Chamberlin of the *New York World Service*. The crowd was disappointing for both teams. It also didn't help that the game was scheduled on a Tuesday afternoon, with a 2:00 p.m. kickoff. Newspapers announced that there were as many as 15,000 onlookers and as few as 5,000, but there were most likely 5,000 people in attendance.

Most spectators sat in the cheap seats, paying $1.00 in the southeast corner of Griffith Stadium. The first half became a slugfest with no scoring. Red did nothing to separate himself from the other players. "When he retired early in the second quarter, probably for the first time in his young life he was greeted with several raspberries," wrote the *Washington Post*. The Bears then suddenly started to make some plays in the second half, this time on defense, as Duke Hanny (30 yards) and Johnny Bryan (65 yards) returned interceptions for touchdowns. The Bears won, 19–0.[46]

Red struggled mightily against the Washington team, rushing for less than 10 yards. The local press wasn't kind to the redhead. The headline of the *Washington Times* article written by Ross Conklin read, "Red Shows Nothing Here: Other Players Far Outshine Chicago Bears' Big Drawing Card," and in the piece Conklin called him a "bust."[47] Walter Haight of the *Washington Post* wrote, "Red a Sheep in Bear's Clothing: Merely 'Puts in Time.'" The *Post* recap had three photos, one of which was an image of Red being tackled hard and another showing Grange sitting on the bench between Jim McMillian and Don Murry. Frank Young, also of the *Post*, wrote about the prospects of pro football in Washington:

> True, Grange himself proved quite a disappointment when the game actually staged, but fans could not anticipate this in advance and the fact that such a small number showed up proves conclusively that no matter what the attraction, as long as it is pro football, Washington fans are not interested.[48]

The Grange tour had demonstrated that pro football was a game that could entertain and be a business—the games in Chicago, Philadelphia, and New York had proven that. The nation's capital would be slow in recognizing the popularity of the pro game. Not every stop on the tour would be successful in spreading the NFL's propaganda. Washington wouldn't embrace the NFL until 1937, when the Redskins arrived in town. After the game, Al Stern reported that Red and company had collected $6,752.52, while the gate brought in between $11,000 and $12,000. Stern claimed he broke even. As for Red, he was beat up. He was not only dead tired, but also had suffered a bruised nose, badly hurt mouth, and wrenched left arm. At 7:00 p.m., the tour boarded a train headed for Boston.

BOSTON GAME
WEDNESDAY, DECEMBER 9, 1925
BEARS VERSUS PROVIDENCE STEAM ROLLER (NFL),
AT BRAVES FIELD

The management of the NFL's Providence Steam Roller, led by Charley Coppen, handled ticket sales and advertisements, with help from Eddie Riley, secretary of the Boston Braves baseball team. The Steam Roller usually played home games at the Cycledrome, a bicycle stadium in Providence, but since Red was coming to town, the game had been moved to Boston and Braves Field, home of the National League's Boston Braves. Braves Field had a seating capacity of 40,000, and Coppen and Riley hoped to fill it up. Tickets were set at $2.00 for rush seats, $3.00 for reserve seats, and $3.50 for box seats, and were sold at Wright & Ditson Sporting Goods store, Horace Partridge Company, the Huntington Club, and Ryan's Cigar Store in Pawtucket. To accommodate the Providence fans, Steam Roller management provided buses from Providence to Boston for a price of $2.00 round-trip.[49]

The ads in the *Boston Evening Transcript*, *Boston Globe*, and *Providence Journal* revealed ticket prices for the "Red Grange Game" but did not mention the two teams.[50] News coverage of Grange had been appearing on the front page—not just the sports page—of the *Boston Globe* ever since Red announced his plans to play pro football. On December 9, the paper wrote,

> Grange at Braves Field has been the talk of the town. That is the reason many of the folks, some of whom never saw a football game, want to get a peek at the athlete who has relegated Jack Dempsey and Babe Ruth to the background. They want to get a closeup of the "Galloping Ghost."[51]

It seemed all of Boston was interested in seeing Red. "Francis Ouimet, whose keenness for football is second only to his love of golf, was the first of Boston's prominent citizens to purchase a box seat for the Wednesday contest," wrote the *Boston Evening Transcript*.[52] The team arrived at the Back Bay Station in Boston in the early morning hours of Wednesday, December 9, to check into their headquarters at the Hotel Brunswick. Sternaman paid the hotel $65.00 for 26 rooms ($2.50 per man).[53] Upon their arrival, Red and George Trafton got breakfast at Child's Restaurant on Boylston Street near the hotel. Red ate a stack of pancakes and drank coffee. While the men were dining, several reporters surrounded the famous football player to ask a few questions. Red seemed tired and gruff while answering. "Suppose you hadn't eaten a decent meal since yesterday morning and had spent a restless night on the sleeper? Wouldn't you be tired?" he implored. The reporters agreed. Red continued,

> Don't believe half these stories you read about my income. I can't actually tell you how much money I've made and I haven't much idea of what I'm going to do with it, but I do know that I've got a long climb yet before reaching the half-million mark. I knew the figures have been exaggerated.[54]

Red went to his suite at the Brunswick, room 460, for a few hours of sleep before the afternoon game at Braves Field. While in his room he was again surrounded by sportswriters, including Ford Frick, Westbrook Pegler, and Charles Merrill of the *Boston Globe*. Red's brown eyes and young face looked tired as his muscles twitched in front of the scribes. "It isn't the playing but all this fuss that goes with rushing around the country," he said. "I don't have a minute's peace." Asked how he felt, Red responded, "Oh, not so good. I'm all bruised up."[55]

While still at the hotel, Red got a famous visitor. Babe Ruth, the man whom Red had been sharing national headlines with, stopped by the Brunswick to meet the Galloping Ghost. After exchanging a few words about baseball, the two posed for a photo while sitting on the bed. Both stars of the Roaring Twenties smiled happily for the camera. Frick, in his daily column, wrote about Ruth's advice to Red:

Don't be too thin-skinned. You've got to expect a lot of knocks in the professional racket, and you've got to take a lot of criticism and a lot of insults that you didn't get before. But keep your head up, and don't be afraid to say "no" when the pressure gets too rough . . . get the dough while the getting is good, but don't break your own heart trying to get it.[56]

After Ruth left, it was off to play another game. The weather was not ideal, not even 20 degrees, and a raw wind from the northwest made it feel even colder. The baseball field was still frozen at 2:00 p.m., for the kickoff. In the press box, regulars Pegler, MacNamara, and Frick were joined by local sportswriters A. J. Monahan and Melville Webb of the *Boston Globe*, Bill Cunningham and Fred Hoey of the *Boston Post*, and George Carens of the *Boston Evening Transcript*. Doing double duty was John Hallahan, who not only wrote for the *Boston Globe* but also was the referee for the contest. The crowd at Braves Field was announced by multiple newspapers at 15,000.[57] Despite the full-scale coverage by the *Boston Globe*, the city of Boston didn't show up in full mass. Once again, the midweek afternoon kickoff set up by Pyle, as had been the case in St. Louis and Washington, didn't help the gate one bit.

The Steam Roller, led by quarterback Curly Oden, halfback Cy Wentworth, and recently signed halfbacks Don Miller and Jim Crowley, two members of Notre Dame's famous Four Horsemen, as well as halfback Fritz Pollard—one of the early black players in the NFL—added more star power to the game.[58]

Red lined up again at his left halfback position; this would be a game he would want to forget. The two teams were evenly matched, as the Bears kept the game close in the first half. But feeling the effects of playing their fourth game in five days, they had a punt blocked for a safety and a fumble returned for a touchdown to trail 9–0 at the half. In the third quarter, Red tossed an interception before leaving the field for the bench. Boston fans weren't too happy about seeing the famous football player take a seat in the dugout. According to the *Providence Journal*, freezing fans "booed, hissed, jeered (Red) . . . cries of 'get the ice tongs' . . . were yelled at Red, who sat in the dugout." The Bears showed some life late in the fourth quarter, when Joey Sternaman connected with Johnny Bryan for a 35-yard score to cut the lead to 9–6, but the offense failed on two drives to end the game. It was the first loss for Red Grange in his seventh game as a pro.[59]

"Red's showing was a bitter disappointment to football enthusiasts who made the trip to the Wigwam to watch the Galloping Ghost in action," wrote the *Providence Journal*. Bill Cunningham of the *Boston Post* wrote, "Red was bad, and his team was worse."[60]

After the game it didn't get any better for Red, as he was mobbed by fans. Grange recollected,

> I was booed for the first time in my career in the Boston game. It made me aware of something I had never thought of before—that the public's attitude toward a professional football player is quite different from the manner in which they view a college gridder. A pro's performance is evaluated much more critically, and he is less likely to be forgiven when a mistake is made. A pro must deliver, or else.[61]

Sternaman did not receive a typed-up statement for the Providence game. Newspaper accounts wrote that the gate receipts were $40,000. The breakdown was Red–Pyle, $14,000; Bears, $12,000; Steam Roller, $7,000; and Braves Field, $7,000.[62]

It was a tough game for Red and the Bears. They had been defeated for the first time since Red turned pro, and their bodies were starting to break down. Red was sore, and his left elbow was hurting, so much so that he had a hard time holding the ball in his left arm so that he could use his right to stiff-arm. The tour was becoming a grind, but it was still going. At about 5:00 p.m., the team was back on a train heading for Pittsburgh. One positive of the tour was the money being collected. Coolley and Moore were making sure the checks were being properly deposited. Everything was being sent back to Champaign to Harry McNevin, cashier at Illinois Savings and Trust. "We are receiving checks made out to Grange every day from the East. Sometimes there are three or four in every mail," commented McNevin to the press.

PITTSBURGH GAME
THURSDAY, DECEMBER 10, 1925
BEARS VERSUS PITTSBURGH ALL-STARS (NON-NFL),
AT FORBES FIELD

The Pittsburgh game was the result of a deal made between C. C. Pyle and Barney Dreyfus, owner of the Pittsburgh Pirates baseball team. The game was scheduled not long after Red turned pro and would be played at Forbes Field, home of the Pirates. Dreyfus put together an all-star squad that featured Andy Gustafson, star fullback from the University of Pittsburgh; halfbacks Karl Bohren, of Pitt, and Jimmy Robertson, former star of Carnegie Tech, who also played for the Akron Pros (1924–1925); and center Herb Stein and tackle Russ Stein, who were playing for the Pottsville Maroons in 1925.

After arriving in Pittsburgh, Red quickly hopped off the train, turned up his coat collar to cover his ears, got into a cab, and was driven to the Schenley Hotel, where the team was staying. While at the hotel, Red gave a short interview to a reporter from the *Pittsburgh Press*:

> Interviewing is harder than playing football. I don't mind the newspaper folk. It's the idle curious who masquerade as newspaper people that worry me. The newspapers have been good to me, and I want 'em to know I appreciate it. . . . Movie contracts, repudiations, sore arms, women who are foolish enough to lose their heads over a little publicity—gosh, it's a tough game. I wish I knew just how long I'm going to keep my head clear.[63]

Still following the tour were Pegler (*Chicago Tribune*), MacNamara (*Chicago Herald-Examiner*), and Frick (*New York Evening-Journal*), as well as local sportswriters Regis Welsh (*Pittsburgh Daily Post*), Ralph Davis (sports editor of the *Pittsburgh Press*), and Chester Smith (*Pittsburgh Post-Gazette*). Outside Forbes Field, programs were being sold for 10 cents as a disappointing crowd of 5,000 fans was reported by the newspapers.[64]

The field was frozen and covered with snow for the Thursday afternoon kickoff, scheduled for 2:00 p.m. Speaking of the gridiron, Grange said the "playing field became like a ripped-up concrete road." By the end of the first quarter, Red's good fortune was about to change. On an interception return by Johnny Mohardt at his own 20, Red threw a block, during which his left arm hit hard on the frozen field. In severe pain, Red tried to ignore the discomfort to stay in the game. After a few more plays, the quarter ended. Red had been through enough. Wincing in agony he grabbed his left elbow; he instantly knew something was wrong. As Red left the field his head was down, and he was holding his left arm like it had been shot off his body. Johnny Bryan sprinted onto the field to replace him. On the sidelines Doc Coolley greeted Red and walked him off the field and into the locker room. A minute later, Coolley was back on the field to beckon Dr. Gustave Berg, the Pittsburgh Pirates' team physician. After looking at Red's left arm, he diagnosed him with a torn muscle and a broken blood vessel, which was causing some hemorrhaging.[65]

After Red left for the locker room, the Bears seem to lose interest in the game. The Pittsburgh squad rolled to a 24–0 victory. The *Pittsburgh Daily Post* featured three action photos of the game, played in ankle-deep snow. Regis Welsh of the *Daily Post* wrote,

> "Red" Grange's lust for money has been halted—temporarily. Battered and bruised from the almost inhuman task of playing football daily, mentally distraught by the fuss being made over him since he became the most talked-of athlete in modern times, Grange, with a painfully bruised arm, a swirling head, and a tired body 'neath his heavy uniform, walked off Forbes Field yesterday before the termination of the first period, the muscles of his left arm dislocated, a broken blood vessel in his forearm, and countless bruises on his body.[66]

Ralph Davis, sports editor of the *Pittsburgh Press*, called the game a "financial bust" and an "artistic bust," adding, "It didn't take a second look at the Chicago Bears, when they came upon the field before the game, to impress one with the fact that they are overfootballed, if we may use the expression."[67] The gate receipts were typed up on letterhead of the Pittsburgh Athletic Company baseball team. Official attendance was 4,498, with a total gate of $11,041. After the park rental (15 percent), the split for the game was Red–Pyle $3,910.36 and the Bears $2,346.21.[68]

Back at the hotel, Red was miserable. He wasn't thinking about gate receipts. His left arm was twice its normal size, and the thought of playing another game in two days, in Detroit, was making his head spin out of control. At least he didn't have to get on a train, as the team stayed overnight in Pittsburgh. The following morning, after a night of restless sleep with a bad left arm, Red and the Bears hopped on a noon train to travel the 300 miles to the Motor City. No decision was made as to whether Red would play against the Detroit Panthers on Saturday, December 12.

Before leaving the hotel in Pittsburgh, "Doc" Coolley sent communication to Jimmy Conzelman of the Detroit Panthers that Red "would be in uniform but probably not in the starting lineup." Conzelman said he would give refunds if Red could not play.

DETROIT GAME
SATURDAY, DECEMBER 12, 1925
CHICAGO BEARS VERSUS DETROIT PANTHERS (NFL),
AT NAVIN FIELD

The Grange–Bears tour arrived in Detroit on Friday evening. Red had never played in the state of Michigan, as both games against the University of Michigan were held in Champaign, so Red really wanted to make his debut. It was not meant to be. The team checked into the Webster Hall Hotel. In room 944, Red was surrounded by his managers, Doc Coolley, Byron Moore, and Frank Zambreno, who had joined the tour. The left arm was still swollen to twice its size. Red couldn't stop rubbing it. That night, Red was visited by Dr. George Waldbott, a local physician, who examined his arm to see if he could play. It was obvious his arm was in no shape to take the pounding of a football game. Also in the room were several members of the local press. "Grange looked weary and drawn. Deep lines in his face showed the strain to which he had been subjected," wrote the *Detroit News*.[69] Red was asked, "I suppose you don't want to disappoint the crowd?" "No, I don't want to disappoint the crowd," he answered. "But I don't want to permanently injure myself either."[70] Red then related how his arm had been injured.

> It all started from a small bruise in that St. Louis game on December 2. It didn't look serious and wasn't painful, so I had it rubbed and used hot applications. In Washington it was bruised again, and in the Boston game it gave me a lot of pain. I'd be all right if I hadn't played that game in Pittsburgh. I went in hoping I could protect myself, but the first time I was hit hard the pain came back and at the end of the first quarter I couldn't raise my arm. . . . The bump I received in the first quarter caused everything to darken in front of me, and I finally had to leave the game. I'm sorry I can't play in Detroit, for I'd like to do good here.[71]

After the examination, Dr. Waldbott pronounced Red's arm in danger of blood poisoning if the bruised arm and ruptured blood vessel were not properly taken care of. The doctor put Red's arm in a splint to help it heal properly. "All right, put it in splints; do anything so I can get some sleep. I have not had a bit of sleep for two nights because of the pain in my arm," said Red. He would not play in the game against Detroit.[72]

Once news came out that Red wouldn't be playing, a long line of fans stood at the box office at Navin Field to get a refund. More than half of the 15,000 tickets sold were turned back in. "People like football, but they like Grange better," wrote Irving Vaughn of the *Chicago Tribune*.[73] Newspapers reported that only

6,000 fans attended. Despite Red's absence on the field, the tour writers were joined by Detroit's finest sportswriters, including W. W. Edgar of the *Detroit Free Press* and Lloyd Northard and Kendrick Kimball of the *Detroit News*.[74]

Red initially sat on the sidelines, dressed in a suit, a blue-gray winter overcoat, and a fedora, with his swollen left arm in a sling. It seemed football was the last thing on his mind. "A good night's sleep looks better to me than $5,000," Grange said yearningly to Kimball of the *Detroit News*, "or even $10,000."[75] After the game started Red, along with Coolley and Zambreno, strolled over to the dugout to take a seat. Saying a few works to Zambreno, the worn-down football star sat mostly in silence. At halftime, Red was introduced to the crowd. The field announcer yelled, "The gentleman on my right is Red Grange, football's most famous player." The small crowd let out an enthusiastic cheer. W. W. Edgar, of the *Detroit Free Press*, wrote,

> The injured player appeared distressed, his left sleeve hanging empty at his side. But whatever pain he may have been suffering was forgotten when the hero-worshippers came rushing to greet him. From all parts of the stands they raced to get a "close-up" of the most widely heralded player of all time. They were eager to grasp his hand, but this one thrill was denied them when police, fearing that someone might bump the injured arm, served as a bodyguard and opened a path for him to the Bears' dressing quarters.[76]

The Panthers dominated the worn-out Bears, cruising to an easy 21–0 victory, the Bears' third straight loss. Without Red on the field, the game in Detroit was a box-office disaster. The actual paid attendance was 4,111, with the total gate at $9,263.63.[77]

NEW YORK GAME
SUNDAY, DECEMBER 13, 1925
BEARS VERSUS NEW YORK GIANTS (NFL), AT CUBS PARK

The eastern part of the barnstorming tour was now on its last train ride—back home to Chicago. On Sunday, December 13, the Bears were to face the New York Giants at Cubs Park. Again, Red would not play; he needed rest. Although he wasn't in uniform, the city of Chicago still came out. Despite more refunds, a crowd of 15,000 fans braved a chilly day to get a glimpse of the redhead. For the second straight game, Red watched from the sidelines, wearing his overcoat, arm in a sling. "Feel as good physically as I ever did," commented Red to Jimmy

Corcoran of the *Chicago American*. "This bad arm is the only thing that bothers me. If anyone says I'm through they're as wobbly as my old ice wagon."[78]

Playing with more effort and heart, the Bears still came up short in a 9–0 shutout loss as the Giants got their revenge for the defeat in New York one week earlier.

Many Bears players were ailing: George Trafton and Ed Healey (knee injuries); Laurie Walquist (fractured toe, in Boston); Johnny Mohardt (bad shoulder); Joey Sternaman (sore knee); Dutch Sternaman (shoulder); Milt Romney (sprained ankle); and George Halas (boil on neck). Everyone needed a break. "Undoubtedly they are about convinced that one must be a superman to play football five times a week," wrote the *Chicago Daily News*. The Bears finished their NFL season with a 9–5–3 record (17 games)—a seventh-place finish in the 20-team league. The crosstown Chicago Cardinals won the NFL championship with a 11–2–1 mark.[79]

A few hours after the Giants game, Red was looked at by Dr. E. B. Coolley, who tried to relieve the pain in Grange's left arm. He ordered Red to come to Danville the next day to get more treatment. But first, Red had to keep a prior engagement. The Monday after watching his Bears lose to the Giants, Red, Doc Coolley, and Beans DeWolf took a train from Chicago to Kokomo, Indiana. A month earlier, Pyle had arranged for Red to appear as a guest referee for the semipro football game between the Kokomo American Legion and the Jonesboro Flyer—billed by the local press as the "state semipro football championship." A rather decent crowd of almost 2,000 spectators—in a town of roughly 30,000—paid $1.00 a ticket to show up at Expo Park for the 2:00 p.m. kickoff. Minus the arm sling and bandages, Red wore a white wool sweater, white knickers, striped wool socks, and cleats as he did his duty as referee. His pal Beans lent a hand as head lineman. Both men gave their pay for the game to various local Howard County charities. The Legion won easily, 28–0, making the hometown fans happy.[80] The *Muncie Star-Press* gave a glowing review of Red's work as a referee:

> Grange was more than successful in handling his first job as referee despite the fact that the two teams on the field were bitter rivals and play at times was exceedingly rough with many heated arguments. He was called upon to render many close decisions and at one time was forced to banish one player for fouling.[81]

As soon as the game was over the three men took off for Danville. After spending the night at the Coolley home, Red felt energized. The following morning, he headed to Lake View Hospital to see Dr. Coolley. Even in the small town of Danville, everyone wanted to know what Red was doing and what he was like. The nurse, Miss Leeper, talked about the famous sports star.

> I never believed those stories about Harold Grange being so modest and so bashful. Now I know they are true. Whoever heard such a thing, a world hero of the sport world who can crowd President Coolidge off the front page of newspapers of whatever town he happens to be in, why the great big bashful boy—how do they get that way? I should like to know. . . . I'll tell the world he's a bashful boy, and modest too.[82]

Red spent an hour at the hospital. The left arm was feeling better. "We will do everything possible to have him in shape for the trip South," said Dr. Coolley. After the tests and treatment, Red was finally given some good news. Dr. Coolley announced that if he continued to rest the arm, Red would be able to play on Christmas Day in Florida. Dead tired, Red went to bed at 9:00. The next morning, he was feeling much better from the treatments he received from his pal's father, so much so that he, Coolley, and DeWolf traveled back to Chicago the next day.[83]

The time off and treatments made Red feel like a million bucks. "The arm is almost back to normal, and by the time of our game on Christmas Day at Miami, Florida, it should be as strong as ever," said Red to the press. To demonstrate how strong his arm was feeling he staged a short wrestling bout with his buddy Doc Coolley. The arm did not seem to bother him.[84]

Christmas Day was right around the corner, and the second leg of pro football's greatest barnstorming tour was about to begin.

16

SOUTHERN BARNSTORMING TOUR (DECEMBER 21, 1925– JANUARY 10, 1926)

A s the first leg of the barnstorming tour ended, Red continued to rest his arm, trying to get some much-needed peace and quiet. Throughout the country he was still on the minds of sporting fans, as well as other football players. Talking to Lawrence Parry of the *Associated Press*, Guy Chamberlin of the Frankford Yellow Jackets, spoke about Grange.

> The day that the famous Illinois star stepped on the professional field is one that will be regretted a long time by the followers of the commercial game.
>
> Grange broke down mentally and physically because more was asked of him than any human being could perform. The pro players on other teams were affected by the Grange splurge and the public disillusioned. Nonetheless, there is much to be said in justification of pro football. It should have a legitimate place in the sun. It does a lot of good in certain sections of the country. It seems to me that those connected with professional football are to blame for this. If the National League of Football lived up to the rules of prohibiting a college player from signing with a pro team before he had been graduated, the game would now be in better favor.
>
> Professional football can be fostered in a way that would appeal to most thinking persons, but it can also be killed dead as a stone.[1]

Yes, Red left school early to play pro football and was handsomely paid, but he did not harm the sport or the NFL. Most 22-year-old football stars would have taken the money. In his mind, Red knew he made the right choice. He was taking advantage of his skills on the gridiron and his popularity, as well as helping his family. He did not regret his decision to turn pro one bit. He would once again reward his family. This time he bought a car in Chicago and drove home to Wheaton in style. He splurged for a Nash Special Six roadster, with a price tag of $2,000. "I wanted to have a nice new car to show the folks at home. Besides, I guess I can afford to own one now," said Red to the Chicago press. The car was a Christmas gift for Garland.[2]

Red, Pyle, and the rest of the Bears reconvened back in Chicago. On December 16, 1925, Pyle and Red met with George Halas and Dutch Sternaman to hammer out the details for the southern and western tours. Pyle had arranged for nine games to be played, so he wanted to get a contract signed with the Bears owners. The four-page contract contained agreements that the Bears would provide the players (standard NFL players' contract salaries); Pyle would pay the players' expenses (transportation, hotels, meals); and both the Bears and Pyle would keep accurate expenses and gate receipts. Then came the big decision—how to split the gate profits. It was here that Pyle took Halas and Sternaman behind the woodshed for a good spanking. The two parties agreed to the following:

> The first party (Pyle) will pay to the second party (Bears) for the faithful performance of its covenants herein contained, an amount equal to 10 (10%) percent of the first three hundred thousand ($300,000) dollars of net profits and of any excess of and over said three hundred thousand dollars, an amount equal to seven and one-half (7½%) percent.
>
> Net profits shall be that amount which shall remain, after deducting from the total receipts, the salaries, bonus to players, if any, cost of equipment, transportation, hotel, meals, and all other expenses of the first party.[3]

In the end, Pyle was able to get a 90–10 split on the net gate receipts for the first $300,000 of the tour—a number that the second tour wouldn't come close to netting. This time around, Pyle did a better job of scheduling games for the southern and western tours. He had learned his lesson. When Red played his first pro game on Thanksgiving Day in 1925, he went on to play eight games in 15 days (November 26–December 10). The schedule for the south and west would mostly be one game a week, with just three instances where the team would play back-to-back games. All games would be played on the weekend, with no weekday afternoon games. The schedule was as follows:

Friday, December 25, 1925, at Coral Gables (FL) All-Stars
Friday, January 1, 1926, at Tampa (FL) Cardinals
Saturday, January 2, 1926, at Jacksonville (FL) All-Stars

Sunday, January 10, 1926, at New Orleans All-Southerns
Saturday, January 16, 1926, at Los Angeles Tigers
Sunday, January 17, 1926, at San Diego California All-Stars
Sunday, January 24, 1926, at San Francisco Tigers
Saturday, January 30, 1926, at Portland All-Stars
Sunday, January 31, 1926, at Seattle Washington All-Stars

A couple of the Bears players couldn't make the trip. Milt Romney (coaching basketball) and Johnny Mohardt (premed classes at Northwestern) stayed home, as well as comanager Byron Moore. He would monitor the cash flow from afar. With permission from NFL president Joe F. Carr, George Halas was able to recruit a few more players to add to the roster, giving the team depth to overcome injuries. He recruited a backup for each position on his team. Halas added tackle Link Lyman from the Canton Bulldogs–Frankford Yellow Jackets; guard Hec Garvey, who had played for the Chicago Bears in 1922–1923; center Ernie "Dutch" Vick of the Detroit Panthers; end Paul Goebel of the Columbus Tigers; and halfback Hal Erickson of the Chicago Cardinals. They would play with the team in the south and west.

At noon on Monday, December 21, the Chicago Bears reunited as a team at Chicago Illinois Central Station on 12th Street to take the trip down south. The group boarded a train called the "Floridan." In addition to 22 players, Red was joined by Pyle, Doc Coolley and his father, Dr. E. B. Coolley, as well as Harry McNevin and his good buddy Beans DeWolf. "I'm not taking any chances with this injured wing this time," Grange told the press. "Doc Coolley is going along to see that I don't overexert." The group looked happy, acting like a bunch of young schoolgirls. They were leaving the harsh Chicago winter to head for the sun and fun of Florida. Even Red left his trademark racoon-skin coat behind with his brother.[4] Covering the Bears at the train station, the *Chicago Daily News* wrote,

> The Wheaton Iceman didn't wear his coonskin coat, and he wasn't as bashful and shy as on other occasions. He smiled, laughed, and greeted his many friends cheerfully. He stood out from the rest of the players in a light hat and navy blue overcoat. The crowd that had assembled in the train shed yelled encouragement to him. . . . The former Illinois captain waved his hand in appreciation of the good wishes and promised to do his best.[5]

The Floridan motored south, making a short 10-minute stop in Columbus, Georgia, as the team detrained for a short walk-through. The squad could feel the sunshine; they were no longer in the Windy City.

After World War I, the state of Florida saw an unprecedented land boom in real estate. With more time and money to spend, Americans ventured to Florida to buy up land in the Sunshine State. By 1925, the state's population had exceeded 1.2 million. It was an area that was growing. Pyle saw it as an atmosphere primed for making money by presenting events—pro football games—to well-to-do customers.

CORAL GABLES GAME
FRIDAY, DECEMBER 25, 1925
CHICAGO BEARS VERSUS CORAL GABLES ALL-STARS,
AT CORAL GABLES STADIUM

Back in November, when Pyle traveled to Miami, he met with Henry C. Dutton, recreational director for the city of Coral Gables. After 48 hours of negotiating, the two finally came up with an agreement. Dutton said, "We feel justified in predicating that Coral Gables will be able to stage the greatest program of post-season football in the history of the game." Tim Callahan, a former Yale guard who was team captain in 1920, was hired by Dutton to coach the team. The plan was for Coral Gables to build a stadium that would have a capacity of 20,000.[6]

As for the split of the gate, Pyle held all the cards. He had the "star" everyone wanted to see. Dutton gave in to the demands. Pyle drew up a standard three-page contract—which he would do for every stop on the southern and western tours. For this stop, he asked for a guarantee of $25,000, an unheard-of sum for a pro football game. Pyle asked for $5,000 up front on the day the contract was signed and the rest to be deposited in Illinois Savings and Trust by December 19. Pyle then got 66 percent of the gate receipts.

Because of the large guarantee, ticket prices were set high, at $5.50, $8.80, and $11.20 for end seats, and $13.20 for center and midfield. Ads in the *Miami Herald* and *Miami Daily News* read as follows:

> ### FOOTBALL GAME
> "Red" Grange and his team of ex-college stars versus
> CORAL GABLES Collegiate All-Stars
> Christmas Day, December 25th at
> Coral Gables Athletic Stadium; Game Called 3 p.m.[7]

Tickets could be purchased at Tiny Parker Reservation Agency, located in the lobby of the Alta Vista Hotel. Arriving in Coral Gables, a town roughly six miles from Miami, Red and the Bears stepped off the train at 4:30 p.m. on December 23, as the team was met by fans and a police escort to the hotel.

The following day, the Bears conducted a workout. When they visited the empty field where the game was to be played, they found hundreds of busy workers building a stadium on four and half acres of land. Work had started on the stadium just two weeks earlier, but it wasn't until December 16 that the construction crew got really busy. Crew supervisor J. W. Ricketts oversaw 82 large trucks, hauling lumber and supplies to the site. His staff included 400 workmen working eight-hour shifts to have the stadium ready by Christmas Day. A chef was hired to prepare sandwiches and hot coffee for the laborers. Each day saw 100,000 feet of lumber sawed and put into place, with 35 tons of cast iron pipe laid. By the time the stadium was finished, 600,000 feet of lumber and 250,000 riveted bolts had been used. The U-shape arrangement of seats stretched 1,120 feet around the eastern, northern, and western sides of the stadium in 17 sections. Coral Gables Stadium was completed at midnight on December 23, with the final touches to the stands, which could seat 16,000 spectators. Seats rose up 24 rows, some 66 feet from top to bottom, with a press box.

At Red's first workout since injuring his arm, he suffered a black eye. During one play he smacked into the elbow of one of his teammates. The swelling under his left eye was proof that the sport wasn't any easier to play in the Florida sun. The Coral Gables All-Stars were handpicked by Tim Callahan and featured some talented players from three NFL teams—the New York Giants, Pottsville Maroons, and Frankford Yellow Jackets—most notably tackle Bull Behman and fullback Jack McBride.

Game day had arrived. The Christmas Day crowd was a big disappointment. Newspapers reported that only half the stadium was filled—8,000 spectators. In the press box to cover the game were Larry Dailey of the *Chicago Herald-Examiner*, Jack Sell of the *Miami Herald*, and Steppy Fairman of the *Winnipeg Tribune*. At the time of kickoff, 3:00 p.m., the air was warm and the newly sodded field more filled with sand than grass, as players would call for the water bucket many times.

As for the game, the small crowd saw a defensive battle with little thrills—although they were given a chance to have better seats. Midway through the first quarter, the Bears called a time-out. Larry Dailey of the *Chicago Herald-Examiner* wrote, "The spectators on the end section ($11.20 tickets) were invited to occupy the middle stands (midfield seats at $13.20), which were not half occupied, and they made a wild scramble for more advantageous seats."[8] After just one carry in the first quarter, Red came alive in the second. His first big carry went for 22 yards. To finish off the drive, he plowed through for a 4-yard touchdown. That would be all the scoring for the day. In the second half, Red thrilled the fans one last time with a 52-yard scamper. The Bears won, 7–0.[9]

The *Miami News* reported that the game "proved dull and uninteresting to the small crowd of football fans who braved the top prices of $5.50 to $13.20. which were tacked up as an entrance fee." But it did praise the redhead, commenting, "Dixie has seen the most talked of football player in America in action, and Dixie was not disappointed. Grange is still Grange, there is no other."[10]

Although the crowd was small, Red, Pyle, and the Bears still made out. The $25,000 guarantee made sure of that. The typed-up statement had the total gate at $20,725.91, of which 66 percent went to the Red–Pyle–Bears group. In the end, Coral Gables and the city of Miami refused to pay the obscene ticket prices to make a bigger gate. The guarantee was enough for the tour to make a profit, but Dutton and the city of Coral Gables did not. After the game, the stadium was torn down to make way for more housing. The tour was now headed to Tampa.[11]

TAMPA GAME
FRIDAY, JANUARY 1, 1926
CHICAGO BEARS VERSUS TAMPA CARDINALS, AT PLANT FIELD

The train carrying the team traveled almost 300 miles to the west side of Florida, arriving in town on December 27. The team stayed at the Tampa Terrace Hotel. Pyle negotiated the deal to bring a game to Tampa with local promoter J. Burris Mitchell. The original contract—signed on November 17—had Mitchell agreeing to pay a guarantee of $15,000. The first payment was to be paid on December 19, to Harry McNevin of Illinois Savings and Trust, with the second payment, of $10,000, to be received by December 26. The Red–Pyle group would get 60 percent of the total gate.[12]

As the game approached, money became a problem for Mitchell. He needed help with the guarantee. Enter Dr. H. E. Opre. A Chicago surgeon, Opre had recently gotten involved in local real estate transactions in the Tampa area, one of which included him becoming owner of the Tampa Smokers baseball team in the Florida State League. Instead of cancelling the game, Opre put up the rest of the guarantee to pay Pyle. The night before the contest, Pyle, Opre, and A. H. Bowlby, manager of the Rock Island Independents, who was providing most of the players for the game, signed a new contract. Opre agreed to pay $13,000 of the guarantee, with $10,000 going to the Pyle–Red group and $3,000 to Bowlby so he could pay the players for Tampa. The game was still on.

The Bears would have a few days to practice and enjoy the Tampa area. Red took advantage of the free time to play some golf at Temple Terrace Golf and Country Club. On one outing at the club, Red was introduced to several other sporting stars who were in Tampa at the same time: Jim Barnes, British Open champion in 1925; Helen Wainwright, an Olympic swimming champion who participated in the 1920 and 1924 Olympic Games; and Johnny Farrell, a golf pro from New York who would go on to win the U.S. Open in 1928.

The foursome spent the afternoon at the country club promoting sports in the Tampa area. The group was dressed in their Sunday best, with Red wearing a dark sweater with a collared shirt underneath, golf knickers, and golf shoes. While at the course, they paused for a few photos, one where they struck golf poses and one where they lined up in a football formation. From left to right in the backfield were Barnes, Wainwright (behind center), and Red in his usual left halfback spot, while Farrell was in a center stance with his hands on a football, ready to snap it, all wearing big smiles.

After posing for the photographs, the athletes met up with Joe Mickler, director of public relations for the Greater Tampa Chamber of Commerce, who offered to take them to town to pick fruit from a nearby orange grove. Mickler had a new 12-cylinder Packard car. Seeing the beautiful vehicle, Red convinced Mickler to let him drive it to the grove. Red took the wheel while Wainwright sat in the front seat, with Mickler, Barnes, and Farrell sitting comfortably in the rather large back seat. Red pushed on the gas pedal, quickly accelerating the car to 65 miles an hour. It didn't take long for him to be noticed. A motorcycle cop, H. G. Gillette, of the county traffic department, pulled over the car just after the group exited the golf course. The cop presented Red with a ticket for speeding. Red paid the $25 bond in cash. While Red was pulled over on the side of the road, the photographer who had taken photos at the country club happened to be following them. He snapped a photo of Red being handed the ticket by the police officer. This image would be published in newspapers throughout the United States.[13]

The game in Tampa was played on New Year's Day at Plant Field, the first athletic venue in the city. Not starting from scratch like in Coral Gables, the stadium in Tampa did get some additional seating, putting the capacity at 15,000.[14] Jim Thorpe, age 37, was signed to play for and coach the Tampa Cardinals. The Tampa promoters billed the game as "old vs. new." With permission from Bowlby, Thorpe brought his former Canton Bulldogs teammate Pete Calac to play fullback, as well as a few other Rock Island teammates, including quarterback Rube Ursella, halfback Johnny Armstrong, end Joe Little Twig, end Joe Rooney, tackle Chet Widerquist, and guard Joe Rooney.

Tickets were slightly less than Coral Gables, with prices set at $2.20, $5.50, $7.00, and $10.00, and fans could purchase them at United Cigar stores and Hunter's Recreation Hall, and in room 315 at the Tampa Terrace Hotel. The lower prices didn't help the gate. Newspapers reported 8,000 fans. In the press box was Marvin McCarthy of the *Tampa Tribune*, as the southern tour did not have the crowded press box full of sportswriters like on the eastern tour. In the stands were special guests Jim Barnes, Helen Wainwright, and boxing champion Gene Tunney.[15]

Thorpe started at right halfback, but after fumbling the ball a couple of times he was replaced by Calac, who moved over from fullback. Red wasn't impressed with Thorpe: "Thorpe was about 41 years old at that time and hadn't played much in the past several years, but it was thought to be a good publicity stunt to bring him down to Tampa for this contest," he said. "Pathetically out of shape, the once-fabulous Indian athlete fumbled several times and had a terrible time trying to move around with his old-time speed." This would be the only time Red would play against Thorpe in his career—but not the only time their paths would cross.[16]

Red played 30 minutes against Tampa, giving the crowd a few highlights. The *Chicago Tribune* reported that Red had seven carries for 88 yards. It was another defensive struggle, as the game went into the fourth quarter tied at 3–3. Then the Galloping Ghost gave the fans something to cheer about. Taking the ball around left end, Red sprinted past the Tampa defense on a 60-yard touchdown run. Some reports had it as 70 yards. Joey Sternaman scored on a five-yard TD run late in the fourth quarter to seal a 17–3 Bears victory. The *Tampa Tribune* wrote, "(The) Illinois Flash gave a beautiful exhibit of offensive football . . . as spectators find that pro grid game is not so insipid after all."[17]

Two games into the southern part of the tour, Pyle had seen two disappointing crowds. But he was still making money with two large guarantees totaling $40,000.

JACKSONVILLE GAME
SATURDAY, JANUARY 2, 1926
CHICAGO BEARS VERSUS JACKSONVILLE ALL-STARS,
AT FAIRFIELD STADIUM

The next day was another game. The team took a short train ride on the Floridan to Jacksonville—some 200 miles. This game had another big star, as Red's influence had spread countrywide. Playing pro football was now "cool." Jacksonville promoter John S. O'Brien was able to recruit another big-time football player to face off against Red. Ernie Nevers, an All-American fullback at Stanford, was a 205-pound bulldozer who had earned headlines as the best player on the West Coast. After seeing Red turn pro, he was also ready to cash in.

Nevers's contract was reported to be signed for $25,000 for several exhibition games in Jacksonville. The Jacksonville squad also included backs Charley Bowser (Pittsburgh), Red Barron (Georgia Tech), John Shirey (Auburn), Jim Kendrick (Texas A&M), Jack Sacks (Pitt), and Jim Lawson (Washington & Jefferson). Nevers taught the squad the plays of Pop Warner, whom he had learned from at Stanford. O'Brien promised Pyle a big crowd:

> It should be the battle of the century, Mr. Pyle. I aim to cover the South with announcements that no red-blooded man should miss the titanic struggle between the Galloping Ghost and the Lion of the Sierras—Red and Ernie. It will be a sellout with lamentable numbers turned away at the gate.[18]

Promotion included local female aviator Mabel Cody dropping leaflets advertising the game to citizens of nearby towns. Tickets were sold at the Mason Hotel, ranging from $1.50 for standing room to $10.00 for field boxes. A few sportswriters attended the game, including Paul Ferris of the *Florida Times-Union* and Walter Davenport, managing editor of *Liberty Magazine*. The attraction of Red and Nevers did not help the gate. Newspapers reported a crowd of 6,700 at Fairfield Stadium. For a town with almost 100,000 residents, it was a disappointing gate. O'Brien estimated that he lost $12,500.[19]

After a scoreless first quarter, the Bears scored at will in the second. Red got the scoring started with a perfect 30-yard scoring toss to Verne Mullen. Two plays after the ensuing kickoff, Nevers fumbled. Hal Erickson returned it for another score. Jacksonville decided to kick off to the Bears and play for field possession, which was not a good idea. The Bears decided to work on their passing game. Joey Sternaman completed a pass to George Halas for 25 yards, followed by another pass, this time to Paul Goebel, for 15 yards, as the drive was finished off by Sternaman on a 30-yard run. The Bears led, 19–0, at the half.

Nevers seemed to outplay Red, rushing for 46 yards, completing 8 of 16 passes, intercepting 2 passes on defense, and stopping Red on two breakaway runs. He also punted six times for an average of 53.3 yards per punt. But Red's squad came up with the victory. Nevers's late touchdown in the fourth quarter made the final score 19–6. Most game recaps and headlines praised Nevers's performance, and the headline for the *Chicago Tribune* was, "Nevers Stops Red, but Bears Win, 19–6."[20]

After almost two weeks in Florida, the Red Grange–Chicago Bears tour was leaving the Sunshine State. The team embarked on the 550-mile train ride, lasting roughly eight hours, to New Orleans.

NEW ORLEANS GAME
SUNDAY, JANUARY 10, 1926
CHICAGO BEARS VERSUS NEW ORLEANS ALL-SOUTHERNS,
AT HEINEMANN PARK

The day after playing in Jacksonville, the tour arrived in the Crescent City, population approximately 400,000, as Red felt very welcome. The team was housed at the Roosevelt Hotel. Said Grange,

> I am glad that the team that we are going to oppose will be mostly local boys and especially Southern boys. I have heard so much of the great teams that are being turned out in the South. . . . Playing against a team that comes from here makes the game a real big punch for me. It will be like the days up at Illinois when we go to Chicago, Michigan, or Pennsylvania.[21]

The game in New Orleans was organized by one of Pyle's good friends, W. H. Pickens, former manager of race car driver Barney Oldfield, and his partner, G. H. Dorward. No guarantee was paid, as the contract was signed to give Pyle 65 percent of the total gate. The two promoters recruited Lester Lautenschlager, a former Tulane University star halfback who had just completed his senior year, to build a team to battle Red. The talented Lautenschlager had just guided the Green Wave to a 9–0–1 record under head coach Clark Shaughnessy. He organized a roster of local stars. Such former Tulane stars as Johnny Wight (end), Eugene Bergeret (guard), William Bessleman (center), and "Brother" Brown (halfback) were joined by fullback Tommy Ryan of Vanderbilt, tackle Art Swanson of Louisiana State University, and end Gene Walet of Loyola.

On Wednesday, January 6, Red attended an event for the Young Men's Business Club, and a record crowd of 400 filled the banquet hall. Red gave a short speech, saying he was glad to be away from Florida and felt he was among friends in New Orleans. He was given a round of applause. The next day, Red spoke to a group of students at Boys' Commercial High School after getting an invitation by Mrs. Gardner, the school's principal. "'Red' was the biggest kid of the whole bunch. He actually blushed as he was introduced by his manager and Mrs. Gardner, and, of course, 'Red,' the hero of every small boy in the nation, was given his supply of applause. And then he blushed some more," wrote the *New Orleans Times-Picayune*. Red said,

> Football is the best game that there is for young boys. What is more wonderful than a young boy trying to become an athlete? There's only one way I know to become an athlete. Gets lots of sleep and live a normal, regular, healthy life. Keep away from the bright lights and eat plain food. Don't eat too much meat. Any vegetable is good. Spinach and potatoes are excellent. Don't smoke. Don't drink liquor. Don't be a loafer on the street. Think, dream, and believe that you will come to the top and you'll get there.
>
> Football is like life. One fellow carries the ball and gets most of the credit. Yet 11 men have helped him push through, and without them he would not have gained an inch.[22]

Game tickets were priced at $2.20, $3.30, and $5.50, and sold in room D of the Roosevelt and Mayer Israel Clothing Store. The city of New Orleans did not buy. Newspapers reported a crowd of just 6,000 fans at Heinemann Park. Some rain showers during the week made the gridiron at Heinemann muddier than expected. After having the week off, Red played almost the entire 60-minute game. In the second quarter, the Bears scored first when Ernie Vick broke through the New Orleans line to block a punt; his recovery for a touchdown made the score 7–0.[23]

In the fourth quarter, Red gave the fans the biggest thrill of the game. Fielding a punt, he sidestepped a half-dozen players on a 51-yard return. "Down the field '77' tore, dodging, twisting, sidestepping tackler after tackler as the white marks passed swiftly beneath his flying feet," wrote the *Chicago American*.[24] A questionable clipping penalty brought the ball back 15 yards, but a few plays later Red went over for the final touchdown of the game as the Bears won for the fourth straight time, 14–0. The paid attendance was officially at 4,533, with a total gate of $12,213.00, after the war tax.[25]

The tour had now played its fourth and final game in the South. For Red, Pyle, and the Bears, it was a win–lose trip. The automatic guarantees for the games helped fill bank accounts, but the disappointing crowds—likely influenced by high ticket prices—showed that professional football had a long way to go in getting established in Florida or Louisiana. The four games combined for just 28,700 spectators: Coral Gables (Miami), 8,000; Tampa, 8,000; Jacksonville, 6,700; and New Orleans, 6,000.

17

WESTERN BARNSTORMING TOUR (JANUARY 11, 1926– FEBRUARY 4, 1926)

The tour was now off to the West Coast. Good-bye to the South. The tour also said good-bye to a few of its members. "Doc" Coolley and his father, Dr. E. B. Coolley, left to return to Danville. Pyle had realized that he no longer had a use for Coolley; he could handle the business deals from here on out. Pyle no longer wanted to share money with Coolley or Byron Moore. He was working too hard to share the wealth.

Red said good-bye to his good friend; to show his appreciation the redhead had George Halas, Dutch Sternaman, and the entire Chicago Bears team sign a football to be presented to Doc. Also appearing on the ball were the scores of the four games played in the South. Doc appreciated the gesture and would keep the football for the rest of his life. The signed ball is still in the family, almost 100 years later.

The daily coverage of Red in the newspapers was still a regular occurrence throughout the country, but the crowds in the South hadn't been anything to write home about. The trip to the West Coast would be different. People living there were ready to see the Galloping Ghost.

LOS ANGELES GAME
SATURDAY, JANUARY 16, 1926
CHICAGO BEARS VERSUS LOS ANGELES TIGERS,
AT LOS ANGELES MEMORIAL COLISEUM

After three days of traveling, the tour arrived early in Los Angeles on the morning of Thursday, January 14, pulling into the Southern Pacific Station at 7:30 a.m. local time. The players and other members of the tour were met by a large crowd of fans, newspapermen, photographers, and one enthusiastic marching band. "Red Grange Is Haled by Throng; Ready for Big Coliseum Game: Famous Football Flash Is Given Rousing Welcome," was the big headline in the *Los Angeles Evening Express*. "Gee! This is the greatest welcome I've ever had. Even greater than after the Pennsylvania game back in college," Red told the massive crowd.[1]

At the station was promoter P. H. Halbriter, accompanied by the University of Southern California marching band, which "swamped Grange and Pyle to [*sic*] music and cheers." Red, wearing a gray newsboy cap, gray overcoat, and suit, and sporting a flashy bow tie, shook hands with fans and then grabbed the baton from Howard Roberts, USC band director, for the benefit of photographers. "Other members of the team (Bears) were pushed into the background, and all eyes focused on the 'red phantom,'" wrote the *Evening Express*. For a few minutes the members of the band blared their horns and pounded their drums as Red waved the baton in the air, not knowing what he was doing. All the while Pyle and Halbriter smiled at the scene.[2]

When Pyle traveled to the West Coast in December, he and his attorney, H. L. Jones, spent a week in California setting up games in Los Angeles and San Francisco. According to the expense account he kept, Pyle spent $1,495.90 of his own money during his trip. Included in the total was railroad fares ($472.06), his four-day stay at the Biltmore Hotel in Los Angeles ($298.15), his three-day stay at the Palace Hotel in San Francisco ($25.94), meals ($97.00), telegrams and stenographer fees ($73.75), taxis ($4.50), and tips ($27.50).[3]

While in Los Angeles, he met with several promoters, at least seven different men, but it was Halbriter who won him over. Percy H. Halbriter had been a local prep star at Los Angeles High, class of 1907, who went on to make his money owning a successful men's furnishing store, Halbriter's Inc., located in the city at 633 South Olive Street. With his additional wealth, Halbriter got heavily involved in promoting sports, including football, baseball, wrestling, and auto racing. He was general manager of the Vernon Tigers baseball club in 1919, when the team won the Pacific Coast League championship. It was this experience that attracted Pyle to him. He had the money and connections in the city to pull off promoting a game with football's biggest star.

Dealing with Halbriter proved to be a challenge for Pyle. Pyle was used to being the one to set the terms of his agreements, but Halbriter held his own against Cash and Carry, so much so that the two agreed to spread the wealth. They agreed that 25 percent of the gate would go to local charities selected by the five major newspapers in town—the *Examiner, Herald, Times, Express,* and *Record.* While finalizing the deal with Halbriter at the Biltmore Hotel, Pyle was visited by Braven Dyer, the top sportswriter of the *Los Angeles Times.* Dyer wrote, "Mr. Pyle is okay. . . . There was a stack of telegrams on the table, a secretary to answer the phone, take dictation and attend business matters, not to mention another gentleman (H. L. Jones), whose name we have forgotten who is employed in an official capacity." Pyle then told Dyer what the past two weeks had been like since Red turned pro.

> Grange gets between 300 and 400 letters per day. We have an average of 50 telegrams each day and something like 140 phone calls. The first eight days after he turned professional were the busiest days of my life. Playing football takes up only a small part of the day. During the rest of the time he is besieged with requests to endorse everything from socks to cigarettes. There are an average of 40 interviews requested of him each day. It is physically impossible for "Red" to attend to all these matters, and if you could take his place for a day I know that would agree with me.[4]

Halbriter put up $17,000 of his own money to bring the game to Los Angeles. From the train station, the Bears followed five traffic policemen, who escorted the team to the Biltmore Hotel, where they would be staying.

Dyer would shadow Red for his entire stay in town. He was quickly impressed by the young superstar athlete, writing,

> All this stuff about "Red" being modest, retiring, and easy to talk to is absolutely true. He keeps in the background as much as possible, shoving his teammates to the front whenever he gets a chance. His voice is soft, and he talks without stuttering or groping about for stock phrases to make an impression.[5]

Halbriter recruited Sid Nichols to coach the team, which was named the Los Angeles Tigers. Nichols had a connection with Red, as he also had been coached by Bob Zuppke at Illinois. A star quarterback, Nichols lettered in 1917, as a teammate of George Halas. After leaving Illinois, Nichols went on to play two seasons of pro football with the Rock Island Independents (1920–1921). In

1924, he traveled West to become head football coach at Occidental College in Los Angeles. That season they went 3–4, but in 1925, he guided Occidental to a 6–3 record, with tough losses to Hawaii, Stanford, and UCLA. The Illinois connection made it easier for Halbriter to bring Red on board for the "Red Grange Game." Then the Tigers would get a big star of their own.

George "Wildcat" Wilson was an All-American halfback at the University of Washington who, in the fall of 1925, had guided his team to an unbeaten record of 10-0-1. On January 1, the Huskies played Alabama in the Rose Bowl in front of 45,000 fans. Wilson was the best player on the field, despite the tough 20–19 loss. Since Wilson was interested in playing pro football, he was able to negotiate his own deal. It was reported that he was paid $5,000 for games in Los Angeles and San Francisco. He also committed to playing in Portland and Seattle. "No I didn't need the money badly," he declared. "I turned professional in order to meet Grange on the gridiron. It has long been my ambition to play against him, and now that it is about to be realized I am ready to give my best to make him taste defeat."[6]

Wilson was a competitor, and playing against the great Red Grange was a chance he couldn't pass up. He might have downplayed the money he got to play, but you can bet it played a big part in Wilson deciding to turn pro. Either way, Red had influenced another All-American player to join the ranks of professional football. Also recruited by Nichols were several USC stars, including halfback Roy "Bullet" Baker, tackle Bill Cole, and halfback Hobo Kincaid, as well as fullback Bill Blewett of California, guard Paul Minnick of Iowa, guard Felton McConnell of Georgia Tech, tackle Harry Shipkey of Stanford, center George Baker of Stanford, and quarterback Chuck Winterburn of Pittsburgh.

Halbriter handled the game details in Los Angeles. Tickets were set very reasonably, at $1.50, $2.50, and an entire section for children at $.50. They were sold at two locations by the Gittelson Brothers Ticket Agency—one at the Biltmore Hotel and the other at the Lankershim Hotel. Ads would appear locally touting, "Best Seats for 'Red' Grange vs. George Wilson."[7]

While in Los Angeles, Red was able to mingle with some of Hollywood's biggest stars, including Douglas Fairbanks and Harold Lloyd. He also met his Hollywood crush, actress Marion Davies, at MGM Studios in Culver City. Photo opportunities with the stars allowed Red to pick the brains of the famous actors. In just a few months, he would be appearing in front of camera, so he needed all the help he could get.[8]

The night before the game, Red attended an Illinois alumni banquet at the Windsor Tea Room with more than 300 alumni. Also there was Bob Zuppke, who was in California visiting his parents, who lived in Long Beach. It would be the first time both of them would be in the same room since Red walked out of the Illinois football banquet as his coach was ripping him a new hide about turning professional. Everyone in the room could feel the tension. What would happen? The moment arrived when Red entered the room. With some difficulty, Red eventually made his way to the head table, where Zuppke greeted him with a healthy handshake.

"Hello, Red," said Zuppke. "I am glad to see you. I wish you the best of success in professional football and especially in your game tomorrow." "Hello, coach," returned Red. "Have you tickets for the game? If not I want you to sit on the bench with the Bears." "Thanks, but I have sat on the bench too often," replied Zuppke. "Tomorrow I wish to sit in the stands and enjoy myself." Red's college coach would attend the game sitting in the stands as a spectator. The two then said their good-byes. The short meeting began a slow repair of their relationship. The two would later become very close friends.[9]

On the day of the game, everything was perfect. The sun was shining, and the city of Los Angeles was buzzing about Red Grange. Unlike the South, the City of Angels was excited about the prospects of seeing the Galloping Ghost. Programs were sold for 25 cents and featured a drawing of a football player wearing an orange jersey with number 77 on the back, running the ball behind two blockers trying to be tackled by two players in blue jerseys. The game was broadcasted on KNX radio. Newspapers reported that a capacity crowd of 75,000 filled Memorial Coliseum. This time the reports weren't exaggerated. For the third time on his barnstorming tour, Red Grange had set a new attendance record for a pro football game—topping the previous marks in Chicago (36,000) and New York (70,000).[10]

In the stands were some of Hollywood's biggest stars and executives. They wanted to see Red in action. Looking around a fan could see Marion Davies, Charlie Chaplin, John Gilbert, and Lew Cody in one section. In another section one could spot Douglas Fairbanks and Mary Pickford, who "had plenty of friends" with them. Film producers Irving Thalberg and Louis B. Mayer of MGM, as well as Joseph Schenck of United Artists, had front row seats. In the press box were George Shaffer (*Chicago Tribune*); Lincoln Quarberg (*United Press*); and Damon Runyon (*United Service*), who had rejoined the tour. Local sportswriters included three from the *Los Angeles Times*—Braven Dyer, Bill Henry, and Paul Lowry—and two from the *Los Angeles Herald-Examiner*. Harry Culver and Leo Calland were ready to cover the big game.[11]

After a scoreless first quarter, the Bears came alive after recovering a George Wilson fumble near midfield. The drive started with a Laurie Walquist pass to Red for 16 yards, followed by runs by Walquist (13 yards) and Joey

Sternaman (16 yards) to put the ball on the Tigers 4-yard line. One play later, Red plowed over right guard for a touchdown. After hitting the ground, his helmet came flying off. "The crowd gave him an ovation," wrote the *Oakland Tribune*. Joey Sternaman's extra point gave the Bears a 7–0 halftime lead.[12]

Throughout the week and during the game, Braven Dyer of the *Los Angeles Times* paid close attention to Red on the field, whether it was his passing or running abilities. He wrote,

> (Red) draws his arm back easily, with a swinging motion, and then sweeps the ball away without the slightest hint of a jerk. It sails straight and true, with maybe just a wee bit less speed than when tossed by the blonde Husky (George Wilson) from the northwest. . . . He runs with an easy motion of the legs, his strides being long and his hips swaying as he goes. It's easy to see where he gets that "Galloping Ghost" appellation. He seems to glide down the sidelines so rhythmical in his coordination.[13]

In the third quarter, Joey Sternaman dropkicked a 15-yard field goal to increase the lead to 10–0. Red came back into the game late in the third quarter to give the fans one last thrill. After completing a pass to Verne Mullen, the Galloping Ghost slipped off tackle for his second touchdown of the game. The Tigers scored late, as the Bears won, 17–7. All in all, the Bears put on quite a show for the 75,000 fans in the stands. Afterward everyone praised a great game.

Said Grange,

> I think that George Wilson is one of the greatest backs I have ever played against. He is a wonder at running with the ball and great on defense. Roy Baker also looked good to me. It was a wonderful crowd, and I'm sorry that I could not turn in a long run for them. However, I think it was a fine game and that the fans got their money's worth.[14]

George Wilson, halfback for the Los Angeles Tigers, commented, "Grange is a wonderful player. He plays a clean, hard-hitting game and is a square shooter. He is the hardest man to tackle I ever played against. He is fine as an opponent; he never 'crabs' and is just out there to play the game." Roy "Bullet" Baker, back for the Tigers, declared, "It was a great game. Grange is all that they say he is, and little Joe Sternaman is another real halfback. It was a great game, but I'd like to play the Bears again. I think we could give them a tougher battle if we had about two weeks more practice." Paul Minnick, the Tigers' left guard, said, "Grange's ability to elude tacklers is due, I think, to his tremendous speed and uncanny sidestepping. He can also hit hard when necessary." The promoter for the Tigers, P. H. Halbriter, exclaimed, "Fine crowd! Great crowd! Wonderful crowd! Great game! The boys did fine! Great crowd!"

The local coverage of the game in Los Angeles was impressive. The *Los Angeles Times* ran several pages that featured four photographs—three action photos and one panoramic photo of the large crowd—as well as full play-by-play charts and full statistics of Red and Wilson.[15]

The *Los Angeles Herald-Examiner* also ran multiple pages covering the game, Harry Culver's recap, with a few photographs—one photo of Red's touchdown, with another showing Hollywood stars and executives Irving Thalberg, Louis B. Mayer, Marion Davies, Charlie Chaplin, and John Gilbert sitting in the front row. It wrote of the game, "The crowd itself was a spectacle not soon to be forgotten."[16] The *Times* also included the figures for the total gate receipts, with the Bears getting 10 percent; Halas pocketed almost $5,000 for his players. The total gate amounted to $144,556.66. In today's value, the gate would have exceeded $2 million. The breakdown was as follows:

Pyle gate: $47,711.84 (split with Red Grange and 10 percent going to the Bears)

Halbriter gate: $39,483.63 (his expenses, $25,000)

Government tax: $12,944.56

Coliseum rental: $11,580.60

Charities (five newspapers): $39,483.63 (five each getting $6,560.62; might be $32,803.10)[17]

Pyle was giddy about the results. Speaking to the press he stated,

Los Angeles is the sports center of the United States. This is the best city we have ever played in . . . the crowd was wonderful, the biggest Grange has ever played before. Naturally we are all very much pleased. Our combined three games in Florida were witnessed by about half as many fans as turned out for the one contest here.[18]

Unlike in Florida and New Orleans, professional football and Red Grange were a success in Los Angeles.

After the game, Red got a pleasant surprise. Back in his room at the hotel, he was visited by his Aunt Mabel and two cousins—Pearl and Arline. Mabel was the wife of Ernest Grange, one of Red's uncles, who had lived in Wheaton when Lyle brought his family back there in 1910. When Ernest passed away in 1921, Mabel had moved to California with her two daughters. This was the first time Red had seen them in years. "As a boy, Harold made his home with us (in Wheaton) after his mother died. He worked on an ice delivery route for the purpose of defraying his school expenses," said Mabel to the press at the hotel. She mentioned that Red might visit her in Ontario when he returned to California to shoot his movie. "Harold's plans are indefinite. His time is really not his own," she added. Yes, Red had little time for himself, but he always found the time to visit with family, something he would make a priority for the rest of his life.[19]

The Bears hopped on the train to head to San Diego.

SAN DIEGO GAME
SUNDAY, JANUARY 17, 1926
CHICAGO BEARS VERSUS CLINE'S CALIFORNIANS ALL-STARS, AT (SAN DIEGO) CITY STADIUM

A day after playing in front of 75,000 fans in Los Angeles, the Grange–Bears tour headed 120 miles south to San Diego. While in Los Angeles trying to find a promoter, Pyle met George Cline, who owned a well-known sporting goods store, Dyas-Cline Sporting Goods House. Cline had contacts in San Diego to help Pyle organize a team there and promote a game in that city. Since he missed out on promoting the game in Los Angeles to Halbriter, Cline jumped at the chance to help Pyle in San Diego. The team would be called Cline's Californians All-Stars.

Cline recruited mostly USC players, including several who played against Red in Los Angeles the day before. Halfback Roy "Bullett" Baker, tackle Bill Cole, end Newt Stark, center Whitey Baker, guard Paul Minnick, and team captain John Hawkins would play back-to-back games against the Galloping Ghost. After several conversations, the three-page contract between Pyle and Cline was signed on January 14, just three days before the game. Pyle felt a little more generous with Cline, agreeing to split the gate 50–50, with payment to be made after the game. Tickets were priced at $1.00, $1.50, and $2.00, with children's tickets set at $.50, and on them it said the "Red Grange Football Game," with no mention of the Bears or Cline's Californians All-Stars. They were sold in San Diego at Hazard-Gould Sporting Goods and the Theater Music Company.

The Bears arrived in San Diego to less fanfare than in Los Angeles, as the team made its way to the U.S. Grand Hotel. The game would begin at 2:15 p.m. At City Stadium, a rather disappointing crowd came out to see Red and the Bears play. For a city of almost 100,000 residents, game recaps in the newspapers reported a crowd of 10,000. It would be much smaller than that. In the press box was George Shaffer, who continued his coverage on the West Coast for the *Chicago Tribune*, and Ted Steinmann of the *San Diego Union*.

Because of a late cancellation, Red's good buddy, Beans DeWolf, would fill in as head linesman. As for the game, it was a lackluster affair by both teams. The Bears jumped out to a 7–0 first-quarter lead behind an Oscar Knop seven-yard touchdown run. In the fourth quarter, after a Bears interception by Knop, the crowd cheered as Red went over for a 12-yard touchdown run, capping a Bears 14–0 victory. The *Chicago Tribune* reported that Red had 12 carries for 53 yards and one touchdown, while getting 30 minutes of action. Despite the lack of fireworks, San Diego fans seemed to enjoy watching pro football. Ted Steinmann of the *San Diego Union* wrote that Red "showed his stuff to the satisfaction of the crowd of about 10,000 assembled in the bowl. And everyone went home happy. . . . The game gave San Diego its first look at professional football. It proved a good demonstration."[20]

The field conditions in San Diego's City Stadium were weighing on the minds of Red and Pyle. "All the stadium needs is a turf field to complete it," remarked Red. "A football team cannot play a hard, lively game on a skin field as hard as this. There is too much danger of injury. The men almost afraid to fall," barked Pyle to the press.[21]

After the gate was counted up, Dutch Sternaman received the typed-up statement (on Grant Hotel stationery), which had only 5,482 tickets sold and a total gate of $7,678.00 The statement was signed by George T. Cline. Because of the 50–50 split, Pyle received a total of $3,839. The game seemed to please the crowd but not the pocketbooks of Pyle, Cline, or Halas.

After spending the night in San Diego, the tour returned to Los Angeles for one more night before heading to San Francisco, the last stop in California.[22]

SAN FRANCISCO GAME
SUNDAY, JANUARY 24, 1926
CHICAGO BEARS VERSUS SAN FRANCISCO TIGERS, AT KEZAR STADIUM

On Tuesday, January 19, the tour traveled north 380 miles to arrive in the city by the Bay. San Francisco would be the third and final stop in California. The team arrived at 9:30 a.m., at the Third and Townsend street train depot, greeted by George "Wildcat" Wilson, fans, newspapermen, and Edward Rainey, secretary of San Francisco mayor James Rolph. The Bears were provided a dozen Studebaker cars to parade them up Third Street to Market Street, down California Street, through the financial district, and all the way to city hall. A small crowd had gathered on the steps of city hall to welcome Red, Pyle, and the Bears. "It's better looking than the national capital," said Red to the crowd. After a short visit with Mayor Rolph, the group split up. The Bears went to Kezar Stadium, where the game was to be played.[23]

Pyle had negotiated with promoter Mervin S. Cowen to organize the game in San Francisco. The two had signed the game contract in December, when Pyle was in California after the eastern barnstorming tour ended. Pyle was able to get 60 percent of the total gate. The game was scheduled to be played at Kezar Stadium, a sports facility that had just opened that May. While the Bears checked out the stadium, Red and Pyle proceeded to the Shrine Hospital for Crippled Children, where they handed out several dozen miniature footballs to more than 70 crippled children. Wrote the *Oakland Tribune*,

> Grange enjoyed the best half-hour of his day at the hospital. He moved from bed to bed bestowing the famous smile that all but erased the harassed, tired look that two months on the professional gridiron had worn into his eyes. He didn't say much to the kiddies, nor did they say much to him. It was one of those cases of mutual enjoyment when no words needed to be said.[24]

Cowen built his team around George Wilson, adding some talented supporting players. This included center "Buck" Bailey (Olympic Club); tackle Harry Shipkey (Stanford); quarterback James "Rabbit" Bradshaw (Nevada); halfback Houston Stockton (Gonzaga), who had played against Red for the Frankford Yellow Jackets in December; and fullback Bob Fitzke (Idaho). Tickets were set at $1.00, $2.00, $3.00, and $5.00, and were sold at the Cabin Sport Shop and A. G. Spaulding and Brothers. Ads in the local papers read as follows:

FOOTBALL
RED GRANGE and the CHICAGO BEARS vs.
BUCK BAILEY and GEO. WILSON'S TIGERS of San Francisco
KEZAR STADIUM; SUNDAY JANUARY 24—2 P.M.[25]

This time ads mentioned the two teams and the stars of the game. A day after arriving, Red, Pyle, and most of the Bears took some time to see the town. After attending a luncheon of the Santa Rosa Rotary Club, most of the team paid a visit to

Luther Burbank, the noted botanist who had developed more than 800 strains of plants in a 50-year career. The "Wizard of Horticultural" was thrilled to meet the Galloping Ghost and his Bears teammates, 14 total, along with Pyle, Lotshaw, and DeWolf. During the visit, Red, who wore a Chicago Bears sweatshirt and knickers, was photographed several times with Burbank. In one photo, the 77-year-old Burbank was in a center stance hiking the ball to the football star. Red asked, "Ever grow one of these things Mr. Burbank?" pointing to the football. "No, but I can try. But I understand that these are raised by the toe," replied Burbank with a smile. It would be a shock for Red and his teammates when three months later, Burbank would pass away from a heart attack caused by colon trouble.[26]

On January 21, Pyle sent off a Western Union telegram to his partner, Doc Coolley, updating him on the tour:

> Marion F. Coolley; 112 Pine St.; Danville, IL.
> LA 47 grand for us. SD only 38, our share looks good here (San Francisco). Everybody good shape, Harold feels great. Watch us Sunday we play Portland Jan. 30, Seattle, 31st, then Chicago. Regards from Red, Beans, (Dinty), and Self. Stopping Palace Hotel here . . . Chas.[27]

On game day, newspapers reported a crowd of between 20,000 and 25,000, which was an above-average crowd and the second-best crowd during the Southern–Western trip behind the huge crowd in Los Angeles. In the press box at Kezar were Braven Dyer (who made the trip from Los Angeles) and local sportswriters Pat Frayne, Rene Cazenave of the *San Francisco Call*, William Leiser of the *San Francisco Examiner*, Harry Smith, Ed Hughes of the *San Francisco Chronicle*, Harold Lehman, Al Santoro of the *Oakland Post-Enquirer*, and Harry Borba of the *Oakland Tribune*.

After a scoreless first quarter, the Tigers put together a scoring drive. After recovering a Bears fumble, the Tigers ran the ball nine straight times. On 4th and goal from the 1-yard line, fullback Fitzke plowed over for a touchdown, giving the Tigers a 7-0 lead. Midway through the third quarter, the Bears finally got a break when they recovered a Fitzke fumble at the Tigers 20-yard line. This led to a Joey Sternaman 20-yard field goal, cutting the lead to 7-3, but near the end of the quarter the Tigers marched back down to the Bears 1-yard line. On the first play of the fourth, quarter Stockton plowed over for a score. The Tigers now lead, 14-3. Later in the quarter, the Bears finished off a nice offensive drive when Joey Sternaman completed a pass to end Paul Goebel. A missed extra point left the score 14-9. That is how the game ended. It was the first loss by the Bears on the second part of the tour after winning six straight games.

The *San Francisco Examiner* wrote, "Red was not called on often enough to satisfy the crowd." The *San Francisco Call* reported that Red touched the ball seven times for 40 yards and passed for 30 more yards, while Wilson had 14 touches for 70 yards. Pat Frayne of the *Call* penned, "Grange had a lackadaisical air about him in the game, although he did show activity." The *Call* also published three action photos from the game taken by staff photographer Joe Marron. Harry Smith of the *San Francisco Chronicle* produced the headline, "Jimmy Bradshaw Was Real Hero of the Day," adding, "Red Grange very much of a disappointment."[28]

As for the gate, paid admission was listed at 17,060, with a total gate of $40,858.00. Red was a hit in San Francisco but not so much on the field. After spending the night in the Bay area, the team was back on a train headed to the Pacific Northwest.[29]

PORTLAND GAME
SATURDAY, JANUARY 30, 1926
CHICAGO BEARS VERSUS PORTLAND ALL-STARS,
AT VAUGHN STREET PARK

Despite playing in Portland, the Bears took a train—some 800 miles—to Seattle, spending a few days there before their game in Portland, a town of 250,000, on Saturday, January 30. Red stepped off the train wearing a dark suit, wide trousers, rainbow socks, a "gaudy striped shirt," and a "still wider necktie," with a raincoat that he bought in New Orleans to cover him from the light rain. Despite the wet conditions, many fans, photographers, and the local press were there to greet him. The team would stay at the city's plush Olympic Hotel.

The first day in Seattle, Red gave a speech at Broadway High School and attended a luncheon at the hotel in his honor given by the Young Men's Business Club. At the luncheon was Seattle mayor Edwin Brown, who gave praise to Red and Wilson. Said Brown, "No matter what anyone has said against professional football, they can say nothing against Grange and Wilson, and when fine young men of their type enter the game, I believe in the sport and in its future." Red then spoke:

> I don't know what the future of professional football will be, but it is my guess that the game has come to stay and that it will soon be one of the recognized sports of the country. . . . We are all tired. Smashing against men like Wilson very often naturally makes one tired. I know, too, that the Chicago Bears have one more

good game in their bag for Seattle Sunday, tired or not. It's our last, and if there is anyone skeptical about what professional football is watch the boys play it Sunday and then I will be willing to leave it to you to judge the sport.[30]

The coverage of Red's first day in Seattle was extensive, especially in the *Seattle Post-Intelligencer*, which ran full-page coverage, with three photos taken by staff photographer Jerry Eaton. There was one of Red on the telephone in his hotel, one of Red shaking hands with George Wilson, and one with Red reading a textbook surrounded by seven female students from Broadway High. Meanwhile, the *Seattle Daily Times* ran a photo of Red getting off the train with the bold headline, "Here Is Red."[31]

Pyle had organized the Portland game with the help of Tom Turner, president of the Portland Beavers Baseball Club of the Pacific Coast League. He was able to get a whopping 65 percent of the gate. The game would be played at the Vaughn Street Park, which had a capacity of roughly 12,000.[32] "I figure Portland sport followers are just as eager to get a glimpse of the most sensational football player in the history of the United States as were the fans elsewhere in the United States, who turned out in record numbers to see the 'Galloping Ghost' of the gridiron," said Turner to the local press. They would not fill up the Vaughn Street grounds.[33]

Ticket prices were set at $1.50 to $2.00 for bleachers, $3.00 for reserved covered grandstands, and $.50 for kids 13 and younger. Portland fans could purchase them at the Portland Baseball Office, Spalding's Sporting Goods, and Rich's Cigar Store. Ads in the local paper read, "GRANGE–WILSON FOOT-BALL GAME," with kickoff at 2:00 p.m.[34]

Tom Turner didn't have much time to put together a team. He, however, did have one big piece, "Wildcat" Wilson, who would be playing in his third game on the tour. Turner also added Houston Stockton, who traveled with Wilson from San Francisco, as well as end Dick Reed of the University of Oregon. But most of the team was built around players from the Waterford Athletic Club, a semipro football team in the city, led by their big tackle, Red O'Keefe, who never played college football.

Just like in San Francisco, Pyle sent off a Western Union telegram, dated January 29, 1926, to Doc Coolley.

Chicago papers reference impending break is bunk. Never had more harmony. Tough breaks, lost Frisco game, our share almost 25. Looks small here (Portland), big in Seattle. We are all pretty tired, glad to get home. Arrive Thursday, meet you Morrison Hotel. Regards from Red, (Dinty), Beans, boys, and self . . . (signed) Charles C. Pyle[35]

Pyle's reference to the impending break was vague. Was that the relationship of Red and the Chicago Bears? Or was it the relationship of Red–Pyle–Coolley–Moore? On January 28, the *Chicago Tribune* wrote in a small article that "ill-feeling between Pyle and the Chicago Bears would result in a breakup." Either way, all parties would have a reckoning when the greatest football barnstorming tour of all time was finished.[36]

On the day of the game, the press box was filled by Reuel Moore of the *United Press* and local sportswriters James McCool and L. H. Gregory of the *Oregonian*. Newspaper reports had the crowd listed at 5,000. Red's good pal Beans DeWolf once again filled in on the field, this time as umpire. The game was not even close. The hastily put together Portland All-Stars were over-matched throughout the game, as the Bears thumped them, 60–3. Running on a muddy field, Red played almost half the game, contributing two touchdowns, while Earl Britton scored three. Laurie Walquist, Joey Sternaman, Hal Erickson, and Verne Mullen turned in one each.

L. H. Gregory of *the Oregonian* wrote of the game,

> This writer confesses to having got a real kick from the exhibition despite the lopsidedness of the 60-to-3 score. It was so different from what we had expected. . . . Part of the kick, of course, was in watching Grange and Wilson perform; but it was almost as interesting to see those behemoths of the Bear lineup at their work.[37]

The local paper also published two photos of the game—an action photo of Walquist being tackled to the ground and another showing Red, in full uniform, wearing a sideline jacket and helmet, sitting on the bench between Walquist and Halas. The Portland crowd had just 3,254 paying customers, with a gate of $6,284.50.[38] After the convincing win, Red was thinking about going home. "The last game of the trip will be played here (Seattle), and I am glad of it," he said. "Professional football is all right and I am glad I went into it, but I have played 24 games of football this season and I am ready to rest."[39]

The tour was off to its last stop.

SEATTLE GAME
SUNDAY, JANUARY 31, 1926
CHICAGO BEARS VERSUS WASHINGTON ALL-STARS,
AT SEATTLE BALLPARK

Shortly after the Portland game, the tour members traveled the 175 miles back to Seattle. When setting up the Seattle game, Pyle had contacted Charles Lockard, president of the Seattle Pacific Coast League baseball club, who offered his playing stadium to host the game. Once again, Pyle was able to get 65 percent of the gate.[40]

The Seattle team was organized by Lorin Solon, a former Minnesota All-American end-fullback coached by Henry Williams, who played under Walter Camp at Yale. Williams guided the Golden Gophers to eight conference championships, while posting a 136–33–11 record in his 22 seasons at Minnesota (1900–1921). He was elected to the College Football Hall of Fame in 1951. While at Minnesota, Solon lettered three years (1913–1915), becoming a two-time All-American (1913 and 1914). Solon was now an assistant coach at the University of Washington, while also playing pro football with the West Seattle Athletic Club. He would build the team that would face Red in Seattle. "I want to give Seattle the best 11 possible for the game," said Solon to the *Seattle Post-Intelligencer*.[41]

George Wilson agreed to play his fourth game on the tour, making his way close to home and his college stardom at the University of Washington. Solon recruited mostly local players, signing Gonzaga stars Marlon Ashmore (tackle), Gil Skeats (halfback), and R. Allerdice (quarterback), as well as Washington fullback Elbert Harper and a few teammates from the West Seattle Athletic Club in ends B. Osterman and Rollie Corbett.

Tickets were priced at $1.50, $2.00, and $3.00, and $.50 for youngsters, and sold at the ballpark, Spalding's Sporting Goods, Pursley's Cigar Stand, and Scobey's Cigar Store in Tacoma. The Seattle ballpark did not see a large crowd, as newspapers reported just 5,000 fans. In the press box for the last game on the tour were local sportswriters George Varnell (who played football for A. A. Stagg at Chicago) of the *Seattle Daily Times* and George Scherck of the *Seattle Post-Intelligencer*. Scherck would go on to become a well-known sportswriter and racing editor for the *Oakland Tribune*.[42]

Just like in Portland, the game was played on a muddy gridiron, but that didn't slow down the Bears. In the first half, Red scored two touchdowns, both on 30-yard runs, as the Bears rolled to another easy victory, 34–0. Late in the fourth quarter, one of the Seattle players suffered a gruesome injury. End Rollie Corbett suffered a broken right leg. No one felt good about the injury, since there were just a few minutes until the tour was over. Pyle was generous, chipping in $100 toward Corbett's medical expenses. Charles Lockard matched the total, and George Wilson chipped in an additional $50.

The small crowd and local press were not impressed by the performance. "Seattle's first view of professional football was a disappointment. . . . If the pro game ever had a chance they sure killed the bird that laid the golden egg at the ballpark yesterday," wrote George Scherck of the *Post-Intelligencer*.[43]

The official statement released after the game reported just 3,837 tickets sold for a total gate of $7,136.50. The final game of pro football's greatest barnstorming tour was over. It was time to go home.[44]

18

IMPACT OF THE
BARNSTORMING TOUR

The tour was a success in many ways. "It turned out better than Pyle or I expected, in a financial way," said Red to the *Chicago Herald-Examiner*. Red Grange and the Chicago Bears, as well as opposing players, all got paid. In 1925, a good lineman in the NFL probably received about $100 per game, while a good back was paid $125 to $150. Most players received between $50 and $75. Red blew those numbers out of the water and he knew it. C. C. Pyle had promised him. Red turned pro mainly to make money, although he loved to play football. The game made him feel free and happy—although the tour tested that love—but it was the money that drove him, and he didn't hold back when talking to the press or the public.[1]

While in New Orleans during the tour, Red gave an interview with Meigs Frost of the *New Orleans States*.

I'm tired of being a target. I want to do a little shooting myself. I've got a few things I want to get off my chest.

My father's income as deputy sheriff never was more than $200 a month. He borrowed money from the bank to help me through college, and I earned $40 ($37.50) a week summers as an iceman. I took all the hammering they could give me through three years of varsity football. Football is the thing I do best in the world. I gave the best I had to the university. Why shouldn't I give it to the public now when the public is willing to pay to see it?

What's the disgrace of being a pro, I'd like to know? You never heard a howl about Christy Mathewson or Eddie Collins or any other college man playing professional baseball. What's (Bob) Zuppke but a professional? Does he feel that he owes so much to the University of Illinois that he wouldn't leave them at the end of his contract if some other university offered him $5,000 a year more to coach for them?

Nobody would have said a word if I'd started out as a bond salesmen when I left college. . . . Nobody would have kicked if I had started out at an office boy's pay in some business. But here I had an asset worth thousands of dollars, over the limited period of a couple of years. Ask any business man what he'd call me if I left it go to waste. He'll tell you I would be a darned fool.[2]

In today's NFL environment, Red would fit in nicely. He would leave school early, sign with an agent, sign a pro contract with the NFL team that drafted him, sign endorsement deals, sign a contract for a Hollywood movie, and play in front of sold-out crowds for a record rookie salary. The only thing is that Red did this in 1925—almost 100 years ahead of his time.

TOUR MONEY

According to the expense sheets and statements kept by Marion "Doc" Coolley (through Pyle and Moore), the group received two checks in December with the following breakdown:

First entry:
Harold E. Grange......Dec. 7, '25......$30,000.00
Chas. C. Pyle............Dec. 7, '25.......$15,000.00
M. F. Coolley...........Dec. 7, '25......$7,500.00
Byron F. Moore........Dec. 7, '25......$7,500.00

Second entry:
Harold E. Grange......Dec. 21, '25.....$20,000.00
C. C. Pyle...............Dec. 21, '25.....$10,000.00
M. F. Coolley...........Dec. 21, '25.....$5,000.00
B. F. Moore.............Dec. 21, '25.....$5,000.00[3]

By the end of the first part of the tour, Red had earned $50,000, while Pyle ($25,000), Coolley ($12,500), and Moore ($12,500) also made out. The second part of the tour generated more income for the group. The final net profits were almost identical to those from the first part of the tour.[4] In his autobiography, Red remembered what he made on the tour, relating, "I received my second $50,000 check from Pyle immediately after the game in Seattle. Counting the money I drew weekly, I had earned nearly $125,000 in my first season as a professional football player. Charlie had kept his word."[5]

The numbers aren't "official," but in the two months he toured the country playing pro football, Red Grange most likely earned more than $125,000. In 2019, that amount would be almost $2 million. Pyle had delivered on his promise—Red would earn more than $100,000.

As for the Bears, they profited too. George Halas claimed that the Bears came away with a profit of $14,675, after paying players, for the 1925 season. The players also benefited from the tour. In his memoir, Bears guard Hunk Anderson wrote that he made $1,800 for the tour. "I have to chuckle in reminiscing about my first contact with the redhead," wrote Anderson. "He was resplendent in an almost floor-length racoon coat—the style of the day—and resembled a simian on a sabbatical from the zoo. The redhead proved to be not only a great football player, but a congenial, levelheaded youngster, and none of us on the squad resented him."[6]

ENDORSEMENTS

Aside from the net profits from the football tour, Red earned more income from endorsements, a movie deal, and sales of the publication *Life History of Red Grange*, for which he earned $1,411.25. In New York, Red was able to accumulate roughly $37,500 in endorsements. After the tour ended, such items as a Red Grange doll, a Red Grange football, and a Red Grange sweater hit the stores.

The F. A. Kalil Company of New York paid $12,000 to Red to produce a Red Grange sweater. The official Red Grange "77" sweater hit stores in early 1926. The V-neck sweater was made of wool and had elastic cuffs, and came in two sizes—one for boys and one for men. Newspaper ads appeared nationwide for department stores selling the garment. They read, "Woven of all-worsted yarns with a slight mixture of rayon which tends to brighten their attractive color combination of powder blue, buff, and grey. Bright jacquard designs. . . . Every sweater bears the 'Red Grange' label and is packed in the 'Red Grange' box."[7]

The souvenir box had emblazoned on it an image of Red carrying the football in his left arm, while his right arm is extended for a stiff-arm. Stores throughout the United States sold the sweaters at $3.95 for boys and $4.95 for men.[8]

The Red Grange football was produced by Wilson Sporting Goods Company, which paid $2,000 for the rights. Wilson released the football in a souvenir box with Red's image on it, and the ball featured Grange's signature overlapping the number 77 in the background. On the box was a quote from Red: "I believe this football fills the need of every American boy." The football sold for $5.00 for a ready-laced version with a pump and $2.00 for a junior-size cowhide version, and came with a souvenir studio close-up photo with Red's facsimile signature.[9]

The Red Grange doll was produced by Live Long Toys, based in Chicago, and designed by Eileen Benoliel. The manufacturers of Skeezix Dolls, oilcloth dolls, Live Long mostly made dolls of cartoon characters—Little Orphan Annie, Skeezix baby, Herby, Kayo, and Sandy. The Red Grange doll measured 18 inches tall and had a blue or red sweater with 77 on the back, a helmet, canvas pants, blue socks, and brown cleats. The helmet was removable, revealing red hair underneath. The doll held a football in its left arm with "Red Grange 77" written on it. It sold for $1.95 in stores.[10]

Red soon signed contracts with Yeast Foam Malted Milk; Arnold Bros. Meats, a meatpacking company in Chicago (earning him $1,000); and the *Chicago Daily News*, which paid him $1,000 for his "life story." But the biggest pay day came from another Chicago business that opened up its checkbook for the Galloping Ghost.

The Shotwell Candy Company was an institution in the Windy City producing yummy treats for the youth of America. Owned and operated by Alfred Shotwell Sr., the Shotwell Manufacturing Company had been producing "checkered candied" popcorn, marshmallows, and candy bars for almost 20 years.[11] "Chicago was the candy capital of the country at this time," said Chip Shotwell, grandson of Alfred Shotwell. According to Chip, there were "several candy companies in Chicago, one being Curtiss Candy Company, which was owned by the Schnering family, who made the 'Baby Ruth' candy bar." He added, "So, my grandfather was well regarded in the city of Chicago." In 1916 alone, Shotwell was shipping eight million pounds of raw corn yearly to its popcorn factory.[12]

Companies like Shotwell and Cracker Jack had started to insert free promotional items in their products—rings, plastic figurines, stickers, and trading cards. When Red Grange turned pro, Shotwell took note of the popularity of the football star. Since he was popular with the young kids of Chicago, it would be a slam dunk to get Red to help sell candy bars. Shotwell agreed to produce a "Red Grange Candy Bar," a milk chocolate nut bar that would be sold for five cents. Shotwell ads for candy stores to buy the tasty treat read, "Another Shotwell success; a big two oz. maple caramel cream nougat center rolled in peanuts and chewy caramel with milk chocolate coating; lithographed glassine wrapper with individual picture of Red Grange; 24 bars in Red Grange display box."[13]

Promotional boxes were produced, with the candy bars to be sold at candy stores. "Remember at this time there were candy stores everywhere," said Chip. "So, you put a display up, and my grandfather had salesmen who would travel around to these stores to sell candy and you go in and show it to the proprietor and ask for some space to set up your display and so forth. The nicer they were, the more eye-catching it was."[14]

The candy bar would come in a Red Grange wrapper and within that wrapper would be a collector's card. In early 1926, Shotwell produced a 12-card set of Red Grange cards. The cards measured 2 x 3 1/8 inches and pictured Red in different football poses—passing, running, catching, kicking—plus images of him as the "Wheaton Iceman" and wearing his famous racoon-skin coat. Today, in good condition, the cards can fetch between $200 and $300 each. In 1926, the card cost just five cents and came with a delicious chocolate nut bar.

According to the cash statement expense sheet kept by Doc Coolley, Shotwell initially paid Red $12,000 for the right to use his name and images for their products.[15] According to the Shotwell family, after the retainer fee, Red was paid $62,000 by Alfred Shotwell. "It involved some royalties. He was paid $62,000 dollars, which was a hell of lot of money back then," said Chip.

> Oh yeah, my grandfather would go to the games and take my dad with him. Red called my father "Shotsie." Dad always loved to visit and stop by to see Red (when he retired in Florida). He was the salt of the earth. The nicest guy you would ever meet. And very quiet about his history and his accomplishments he did, about how great he was, he didn't do any bragging, he was very humble.[16]

"It's exciting," continued Chip. "He was a figure in the history of Chicago, University of Illinois, and the history of the NFL. To have a family connection to that is very exciting. It's some history that is really pioneering. Who knew the NFL was going to make for two seasons. You know. It did. It's exciting."[17]

IMPACT ON THE NFL

Red Grange did not "save" the NFL, as some headlines or historians have claimed. His most important impact on the young league was that he gave the sport respectability with its players, as well as popularity and exposure. No other NFL or pro football player, not even the great Jim Thorpe, provided the sport the media attention that Red Grange was able to generate. The two months that he spent touring the country playing pro football enabled the sport to achieve mass-media coverage. Newspapers, radio, newsreels, and magazines all covered the tour and its star.

The large attendance figures and massive crowds wouldn't hold up, but they did show the leaders of the NFL that the sport could be a viable business, if properly operated. The crowds, especially in the big cites, could support the sport. After the Portland game, L. H. Gregory of the *Oregonian* interviewed George Halas about the tour and what it had done for professional football. Halas stated,

> We have been doing well in professional football and making money for several seasons. We were gaining ground steadily but slowly. Then comes Grange and focusses attention on pro football. The public has turned out in droves, not only to see Grange, but to attend other professional football games. Now professional football is on the map. It will get bigger and bigger.
>
> The real difference between professional football and college football is about that between a major-league team and a minor-league team. . . . The Bears hasn't a weakness, whereas every college team I ever saw has weakness. We are strong at center, strong in the line, strong on the ends, and strong in the backfield, and every man knows his football and must be smart.
>
> Professional football will never replace college football, and we don't want it to. The college and pros have no quarrel. Professional teams of today are recruited almost entirely from the best college players, and it is absolutely against our rules to do any "raiding" of the colleges. They must have completed their three years before we talk to them, and it is likely that a rule will be adopted requiring that a college player must have graduated.[18]

Halas was right, pro football—and the NFL—was attracting a higher caliber of player. Slowly the sandlot rough-and-tumble player was becoming extinct. The more skilled college player who had a regional, sometimes national reputation like Red was filling up the rosters, and it was being done on the up and up, and not by the college player using an assumed name to conceal his identity. Red had made it easier for some of the major college stars to choose pro football as a viable option for making an income. In his first two months as a pro, Red was able to play against some of the greatest players of the early days of professional football, including seven future hall of famers: Paddy Driscoll (Chicago Cardinals), Jimmy Conzelman (St. Louis All-Stars), Guy Chamberlin (Frankford Yellow Jackets), Link Lyman (Frankford Yellow Jackets), Fritz Pollard (Providence Steam Roller), Jim Thorpe (Tampa Cardinals), and Ernie Nevers (Jacksonville All-Stars). He was also able to match his skill against such

All-Pro–caliber players as Pete Calac, George "Wildcat" Wilson, Frank Nesser, and Houston Stockton.

Combing the caliber of players he was competing against in an insane number of games per week, it's easy to see why Red did not dominate in his first foray into pro football. At the time of the tour, college football was seen as superior to pro football. The coaching was better, the players cared more because they weren't just playing for money, and the pubic accepted the collegiate game as gospel. The colleges and universities created and organized the game, while the pro game slugged its way to a cheap paycheck. The barnstorming tour proved that there were more good football players out there, and they could stop the great Red Grange. He did not get off on as many of his signature long runs, demonstrating to the public and the press that maybe the pro players knew what they were doing. If they could stop the Galloping Ghost, they could stop any great back. Red had given the NFL and the sport a map to follow to be successful. It would just take some time to get there.

ATTENDANCE

One thing for sure was that Red brought fans out to the games. The majority of them were just there to see Red, but they got to see an NFL game up close and personal. Some would come back, most didn't. But the NFL and pro football were on the center stage of sports more than ever before.

Table 18.1 shows the numbers. According to local and national newspaper reports, the massive attendance numbers proved that Red was a bona-fide sports attraction. The actual game receipts kept by Dutch Sternaman and Doc Coolley give a more realistic view of the number of fans in attendance, but either way the figures are close, showing that spectators came out in droves to watch Red perform. Compare those figures to the NFL's figures from 1920 to 1925 (see tables 18.2 and 18.3).

The spike in the number of fans was due to the barnstorming tour featuring Red. The much-needed media exposure helped the NFL achieve a new level of acceptance. Red's decision also helped pave the way for other college All-Americans to choose the same route. Pro football had always had college players and All-Americans playing the sport, but Grange's entry convinced even more quality players to join the pro ranks. In just two months after he turned pro, the likes of Ernie Nevers (Stanford), George Wilson (Washington), Earl Britton (Illinois), and Lester Lautenschlager (Tulane) got paid to play professional football. Perhaps they never would have played pro ball had it not been for Grange.

Table 18.1. 1925–1926 Red Grange–Chicago Bears Barnstorming Tour

Date	Opponent	Newspaper Attendance	Actual Attendance	Total Gate (tour expense sheets)	Red–Pyle Split (tour expense sheets)
Eastern Tour					
November 26	Chicago Cardinals	36,000	31,180	$49,669.29	$9,007.43
November 29	Columbus Tigers	28,000	25,285	$45,914.25	$10,825
December 2	St. Louis All-Stars	8,000	5,032	$13,057	$5,000 guarantee
December 5	Frankford Yellow Jackets	35,000	25,408	$81,069	$17,835.18
December 6	New York Giants	70,000	70,000	$120,000	$25,362.94
December 8	Washington All-Stars	5,000	5,000	$12,000	$6,763.62
December 9	Providence Steam Roller	15,000	15,000	$40,000	$23,101.65
December 10	Pittsburgh All-Stars	5,000	4,498	$11,041	$3,910.36
December 12	Detroit Panthers	6,000	4,111	$9,263.68	$911.52
December 13	New York Giants	15,000	15,000	n/a	$3,000
Totals		223,000	200,514	$382,014.22	$105,717.70
Southern and Western Tours					
December 25	Coral Gables All-Stars	8,000	8,000	$20,725.91	$25,000 guarantee
January 1	Tampa Cardinals	8,000	8,000	n/a	$9,500
January 2	Jacksonville All-Stars	6,700	6,700	n/a	$20,000 guarantee
January 10	New Orleans	6,000	4,533	$12,213	$7,938.45
January 16	L.A. Tigers	75,000	75,000	$144,556.66	$47,711.84
January 17	San Diego All-Stars	10,000	5,482	$7,678	$3,839
January 24	San Francisco Tigers	20,000	17,060	$40,858	$24,514.80
January 30	Portland All-Stars	5,000	3,254	$6,284.50	$3,770.70
January 31	Seattle All-Stars	5,000	3,837	$7,136.50	$4,281.90
Totals		143,700	131,866	$239,452.57	146,556.69
Grand Totals		366,700	332,380	$621,466.79	$252,274.39

Lyle Grange, father of Red, head portrait, circa 1908. *Courtesy of Rebecca Phillips*

Sadie (Sherman) Grange, mother of Red, poses for portrait, circa 1908.
Courtesy of Rebecca Phillips

Lyle Grange, first row far right with hat, poses with fellow lumberjacks in the woods of Sullivan County, circa 1909. *Courtesy of Rebecca Phillips*

Red Grange, age three, holding flowers, Forksville, Pennsylvania. *Courtesy of University of Illinois Athletics*

The four children of Sadie and Lyle Grange, circa 1909, in Forksville, Pennsylvania. From left to right, Red, Norma, Mildred, and Garland (sitting in wagon). *Courtesy of Rebecca Phillips*

Red (left), age 11, and Garland (right), age 8, dressed in cowboy outfits at their home on Ohio Street in Wheaton, Illinois, circa 1914. *Courtesy of Rebecca Phillips*

Red Grange, far right, sitting in classroom at Wheaton (Illinois) High School, circa 1918–1919. *Courtesy of author's collection*

Red Grange, sitting for 1920 Wheaton High football team photo at the Orchard in Wheaton. *Courtesy of Buswell Library, Special Collections [SC-20], Wheaton College, Illinois*

Red Grange (left) with L. C. Thompson (right), owner of L. C. Thompson Ice Company in Wheaton. Here he presents Red with special silver ice tongs, 1926. *Courtesy of author's collection*

Red Grange on his ice route in Wheaton, not a posed photo or staged one, circa 1927. *Courtesy of author's collection*

Red Grange poses with football in hand at the University of Illinois, circa 1923. *Courtesy of University of Illinois Athletics*

Red Grange (left) with his brother Garland (right) at practice at the University of Illinois, circa 1924–1925. *Courtesy of University of Illinois Athletics*

Red Grange studying at the University of Illinois, 1924. *Courtesy of University of Illinois Athletics*

Red Grange, wearing a suit by Society Brand, a line of men's suits manufactured by Alfred Decker & Cohn of Chicago, 1925. *Courtesy of Marilyn Coolley-Carley*

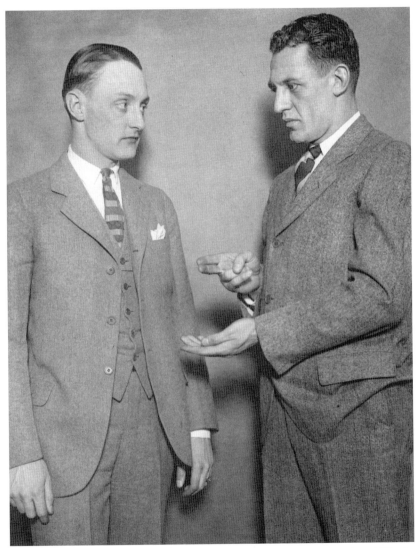

Red Grange with college buddy Marion "Doc" Coolley at the University of Illinois, 1925. *Courtesy of Marilyn Coolley-Carley*

H. L. JONES
CHAMPAIGN, ILLINOIS

paid to the party of the second part; twenty-five per cent
thereof to the said Charles C. Pyle; seventeen and one-half
twelve
per cent thereof to the said Byron F. Moore and seventeen
twelve
and one-half per cent thereof to the said Marion F. Coolley,
settlements upon that basis to be made by such of the parties
of the first part as shall be present at the respective
appearances or engagements of the party of the second part
as his representative at the time in connection therewith.

WITNESS the hands and seals of the respective
parties hereto this 27th day of March A. D. 1925.

Chas C. Pyle. (SEAL)

Byron F. Moore (SEAL)

Marion F. Coolley (SEAL)

Harold E. "Red" Grange (SEAL)

In March 1925, Red Grange signed a contract with C. C. Pyle, Marion F. Coolley, and Byron F. Moore, making the trio his comanagers. This is the last page of the contract, which shows the four men's signatures, as well as the updated date of contract, November 23, 1925, just two days after playing his last college game at Illinois. The original contract has been in the Coolley family collection for almost 100 years. *Courtesy of Marilyn Coolley-Carley*

Red Grange poses for a pregame photo before his last college game for the University of Illinois, against Ohio State. On November 21, 1925, Grange would play his last collegiate game at Ohio Stadium. *Courtesy of University of Illinois Athletics*

On November 22, 1925, one day after playing his last college game with Illinois, Red Grange signs a contract to play pro football with the Chicago Bears. Sitting at the table, from right to left, are C. C. Pyle (Red's manager), Grange, George Halas, and Dutch Sternaman (owners of the Bears). *Courtesy of Buswell Library, Special Collections [SC-20], Wheaton College, Illinois*

Souvenir program titled "Life and Football History of Harold E. 'Red' Grange," published in 1925, and sold for $.50 at stadiums during the 1925–1926 barnstorming tour. *Courtesy of author's collection*

In Wheaton, Red shakes hands with his father, Lyle, while wearing his famous $500 raccoon fur coat, 1925. *Courtesy of Buswell Library, Special Collections [SC-20], Wheaton College, Illinois*

This photo was taken outside the White House in Washington, D.C., on December 8, 1925. Red would shake hands with President Calvin Coolidge. From right to left are Byron Moore (Red's comanager); Grange; William McKinley (Illinois senator); William Holaday (representative in the U.S. House of Representatives from Illinois); and Marion "Doc" Coolley (Red's friend and comanager), who wears Red's famous raccoon fur coat. *Courtesy of Marilyn Coolley-Carley*

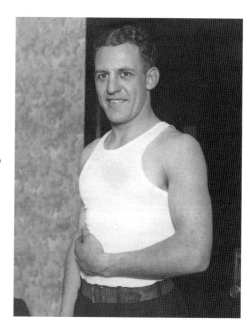

Red Grange poses for the press with his bad left arm, injured on the barnstorming tour. This photo was taken at a Detroit hotel, December 1925. *Courtesy of author's collection*

On December 14, 1925, Red Grange was a guest referee at the Kokomo Legion–Jonesboro Flyers semipro football game played in Kokomo, Indiana. In this photo Red wears a white sweater, football pants, and high-top football cleats. *Courtesy of author's collection*

In this photo Red Grange rides a horse in Northern California during the famous barnstorming tour, January 1926, outside of San Francisco. *Courtesy of Ann Kakacek*

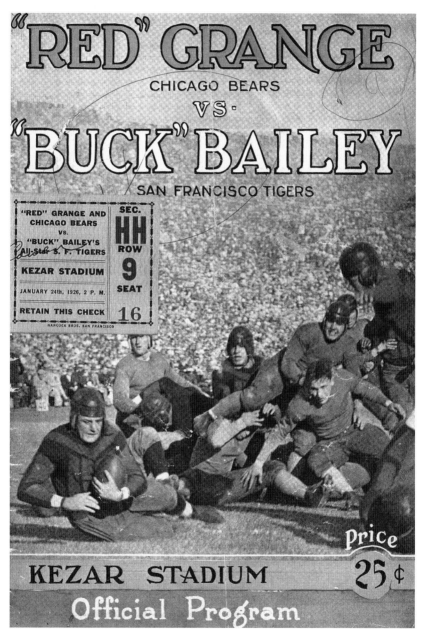

"RED" GRANGE

CHICAGO BEARS

VS.

"BUCK" BAILEY

SAN FRANCISCO TIGERS

"RED" GRANGE AND
CHICAGO BEARS
VS.
"BUCK" BAILEY'S
All-Star S. F. TIGERS

KEZAR STADIUM

JANUARY 24th, 1926, 2 P. M.

RETAIN THIS CHECK

SEC.
HH
ROW
9
SEAT
16

HANCOCK BROS. SAN FRANCISCO

Price

25 ¢

KEZAR STADIUM

Official Program

One of the barnstorming tour game programs for the contest in San Francisco on January 24, 1926. The program and ticket stub was part of a crowd of 20,000 fans who attended the game at Kezar Stadium. *Courtesy of author's collection*

During the 1925–1926 barnstorming tour, Red Grange agreed to endorse many products, including a football, meat loaf, a candy bar, a doll, and a sweater. This image is the box cover for the Red Grange "77" Sweater, sold in 1926. *Courtesy of author's collection*

In this photo, Red Grange (left) sits next to C. C. Pyle (right), who would be Red's manager for three years (1925–1928), while they take a train ride during the barnstorming tour of 1925–1926. *Courtesy of Buswell Library, Special Collections [SC-20], Wheaton College, Illinois*

During his heyday Red appeared in three movies in Hollywood, including two silent movies (*One Minute to Play* and *The Racing Romeo*) and one talkie (*The Galloping Ghost* serial). In this photo, Red poses at one of the studios with a fake mustache. *Courtesy of author's collection*

In Wheaton, Red talks with his father, Lyle, who points to their new home, 1926.
Courtesy of author's collection

In August 1926, Red took his father to visit his birthplace in Forksville, Pennsylvania, where he spent a week in Sullivan County visiting old friends and family. In this photo are Red (seventh from right), "Beans" DeWolf (Red's friend, next to him), and Lyle Grange (Red's father, third from left, holding hat in hand). *Courtesy of University of Illinois Athletics*

In 1926, Red Grange and his manager formed a rival league called the American Football League. Red's team was the New York Yankees. In this publicity photo, Red is wearing his Yankees sideline jacket, eating an apple with Myrtle Valsted, who was named Miss Chicago. *Courtesy of author's collection*

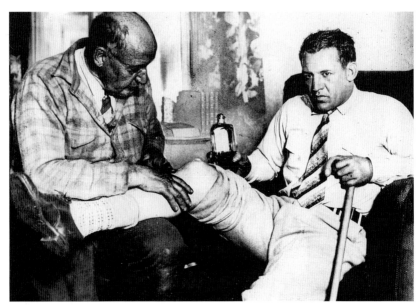

In 1927, while playing with the New York Yankees, Red Grange injured his right knee in a game against his old team—the Chicago Bears. In this photo, Red is sitting at home resting while his father, Lyle, examines his knee. *Courtesy of author's collection*

Red Grange (left), with Bears owner and head coach George Halas, poses during a Bears practice in 1934. *Courtesy of author's collection*

In January 1934, the
Chicago Bears starred in
an MGM short produced
by Pete Smith titled *1934
Pro Football*. While in
Hollywood, Red posed
with two young actresses
for several publicity
photos. *Courtesy of
author's collection*

For four decades, Red
Grange broadcasted
college and pro football
games, as well as hosted
and appeared on radio-TV
shows. In this photo, Red
is behind the mic for
WJJD of Chicago, circa
1931. *Courtesy of author's
collection*

Margaret Hazelberg (1917–1997) was an intelligent, outgoing, accomplished professional before she met her famous husband, Red Grange. This photo is her headshot when she worked at United Airlines as a stewardess, circa 1939. *Courtesy of Dorothy Flora*

On October 13, 1941, Red Grange married Margaret Hazelberg in Crown Point, Indiana. This photo was taken at the county court house moments after getting married. *Courtesy of Dorothy Flora*

Red Grange (standing) poses with his brother Garland at Richards Department Store in Miami, Florida, where Garland was a credit manager, circa 1958.
Courtesy of Dorothy Flora

From time to time, Red and his wife would travel to his birthplace in Forksville to visit family and attend reunions. These photos, circa 1950, were taken by family members on one of those visits. On left, Margaret Grange; on right, Red Grange.
Courtesy of Ray Rinebold

Red Grange in the broadcast booth with partner Lindsey Nelson. The duo did the *College Football Game of the Week* for NBC for five years. *Courtesy of author's collection*

In 1978, Red Grange returned to his hometown of Wheaton, Illinois, for a "Homecoming" weekend. These two photos, taken during this visit, show Red speaking to a youth football team and signing autographs. *Courtesy of Buswell Library, Special Collections [SC-20], Wheaton College, Illinois*

After retiring from broadcasting, Red Grange spent his remaining years living in a golfing community in Indian Lake Estates with his wife of 49 years, Margaret. In this photo, from 1990, the couple poses with one of Red's scrapbooks, this one featuring letters from former president Gerald Ford. *Courtesy of University of Illinois Athletics*

In October 1994, Margaret Grange made her first and only visit to the University of Illinois, the campus where her husband Red starred as an All-American football star. During the pregame of the Michigan–Illinois matchup, she was introduced to the crowd, and she also flipped the coin. *Courtesy of University of Illinois Athletics*

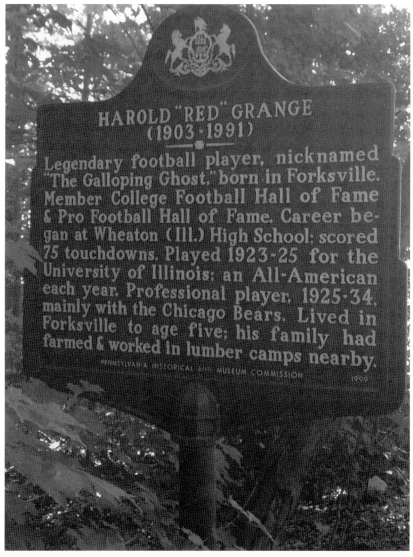

In 1997, the town of Forksville unveiled a historical marker just down the road from the house that Red Grange was born in. *Courtesy of author*

The Red Grange Rock, which sits inside Memorial Stadium on the campus of the University of Illinois. In 1994, Red's ashes were spread at the base of the rock by his widow, Margaret Grange. In 1997, her ashes were also spread at the base of the rock. *Courtesy of author*

Table 18.2.   NFL Attendance Figures (1920–1925)

Season	Number of League Games	Number of Fans
1921 APFA	66	172,804 (36 out of 66 games reported in papers)
1922 NFL	74	187,752 (42 out of 74 games)
1923 NFL	88	252,596 (57 out of 88 games)
1924 NFL	80	292,444 (61 out of 80 games)
1925 NFL	103	680,361 (74 out of 103 games)

Table 18.3.   Average Attendance per Game

Season	Fans per Game
1921 APFA	2,618
1922 NFL	2,537
1923 NFL	2,870
1924 NFL	3,655
1925 NFL	6,605

The floodgates would remain open, with the NFL drawing high-quality players to the league.

TRAVEL

The barnstorming tour was also pioneering in its widespread travel throughout the country to play pro football games. Most NFL teams traveled by train to just a few games, and most of these games were played in their region of the country. The Grange–Bears tour traveled 10,896 miles, visiting 12 states. Ann Kakacek, daughter of Bears guard Jim McMillen, recalled her father going on tour:

> He thought it was an exhausted time. Played so many games in a short amount of time. Barnstorming tour, they spent a lot of time on the train. They did put their clothes out of the window to let them dry. I think they were basically exhausted. Because it was a tough tour.
>
> It changed the face of football. Red Grange changed the face of football. It was minor back then, kind of like minor leagues today in the country. They would get a little bit of attention but not a lot. Pro football was like that, up til now. Grange just attracted so many people that it changed the whole thing around. Once television came in the 1950s even better.[19]

MEDIA ATTENTION AND SPORTSWRITERS

Probably the most important impact that the tour had, especially for the NFL, was the amount of media attention Red and associates received. Radio, with more than 650 stations and more than three million Americans owning listening devices, followed Red's exploits while on tour. Daily articles in newspapers throughout the United States were written by some of the best sportswriters in the country. Red spoke of the writers on the tour, relating,

> You'd have a little clipping, it would be on the third or fourth page of the sports section, and nobody paid attention to it. Thanks goodness (George) Halas was the one that got a little publicity in it (from Chicago writers). But when we arrived in New York, the first time we had ever had any big-name reporters follow professional football. And I knew we had made it.
>
> Westbrook Pegler, Grantland Rice, who was the biggest sportswriter in the nation in those days. Ford Frick, who later became president of the National League, and Damon Runyon. Those four fellas out of New York, they followed us around for nearly a week. And we knew if we could have the ability to attract fellas of that type, from then on we really got back in the front pages.[20]

The list of sportswriters who followed the tour, covered the games, or wrote daily articles on Red and colleagues was impressive. No other pro football or NFL game or event had that many sportswriters punching away on their typewriters. Locally, in Chicago, or nationally, the sporting press couldn't get enough of Red. The list of sportswriters was extensive:

Boston Globe: John H. Hallahan
Boston Post: Bill Cunningham
Chicago American: Jimmy Corcoran, Harold Johnson
Chicago Daily News: James Braden
Chicago Evening-Post: Robert McBroom
Chicago Herald-Examiner: Warren Brown, Harry MacNamara
Chicago Tribune: James Crusinberry, Don Maxwell, Westbrook Pegler, Irving Vaughn
Detroit Free Press: W. W. Edgar
Detroit News: Lloyd Northard
Los Angeles Evening-Herald: Harry Culver
Los Angeles Times: Braven Dyer
New York Daily News: Marshall Hunt
New York Evening-Journal: Ford Frick

New York Herald-Tribune: W. O. McGeehan
New York Times: Allison Danzig, Richard Vidmar
Philadelphia Inquirer: Perry Lewis, Gordon Mackey
Pittsburgh Post-Gazette: Chester Smith
Pittsburgh Press: Ralph Davis
San Francisco Chronicle: Ed Hughes, Harry Smith
San Francisco Examiner: William Leiser
Seattle Post-Intelligencer: George Scherck
St. Louis Post-Dispatch: John Alexander
Universal Services: Damon Runyon
Washington Post: Frank Young

Accompanying these articles were photographs of not only of Red—although there were tons of them—but also the NFL and pro football. Rare action photos were taken during games. Most NFL games covered in 1925 and earlier had scarcely more than a few paragraphs taken during the span of a game, let alone a photo with the game recap. That all changed with the barnstorming tour, as most games on the stop had game previews, rosters, ads to buy tickets, and game recaps (with photos), which was uncommon for most NFL games. Even national publications picked up on the Red Grange story. Full-scale articles appeared in *Physical Culture* (by Daniel Mann, February 1926); *Success* (by Tom Morrow, January 1926); *Liberty Magazine* (by Walter Davenport, February 20, 1926); *Collier's Weekly* (by John B. Kennedy, January 16, 1926); and *Outlook* (by Herbert Reed, January 20, 1926). Red's popularity had surpassed sports stars the likes of Bobby Jones, Jack Dempsey, Bill Tilden, Lou Gehrig, Earl Sande, and even Babe Ruth.

NEGATIVES OF THE TOUR

The truly negative aspect of the tour was the scheduling of games—carried out by C. C. Pyle. The eager promoter wanted to get as much money as possible, giving little thought to the health of his superstar client—or any of the Chicago Bears players for that matter. In his column written on December 14, 1925, famed writer Ford Frick didn't hold back on his opinion of Pyle's scheduling prowess:

A month ago "Red" Grange was the most popular figure in athletic history, heralded everywhere as the wonder of the age. Today he's a broken, tired youngster, his arm in a sling, his golden future stained and rusty with the ashes of a dream gone wrong.

And it's Pyle's fault!

It was Pyle who arranged that hectic schedule of eight games in 10 days! It was Pyle who couldn't see tomorrow's dollar in the shadow of today's dime!

In the last three games in which Grange appeared he played like a man in a trance. He was weak and tired and worn. He heard the boos and jeers of a disappointed fandom ringing in ears that yet echoed the applause of a few weeks ago—and he had no comeback. That's tragedy!

For, this writer is convinced, Grange could live up to all the fine things said about him—if he were only given a fighting chance. Never did nervier youngster step on the gridiron or more likeable chap figure in a nation's publicity. And he is a good football player—make no mistake about that! Given half a chance and he would thrill spectators at professional games as readily as he thrilled them in undergraduate days when his name was on every tongue. . . . But he never had a chance.[21]

Red and the team broke down during the latter half of the eastern tour because of Pyle's greed and lack of football knowledge when scheduling games. Pyle learned his lesson when organizing games for the South and West.

FUN AND CELEBRITIES

It was a once-in-a-lifetime tour for Red and his teammates. Along the way he met the president of the United States, Calvin Coolidge, as well as Babe Ruth, Luther Burbank, Douglas Fairbanks, Harold Lloyd, Johnny Farrell, Pop Warner, and many more athletes and celebrities. He spent time in St. Louis, Philadelphia, New York, Washington, Boston, Pittsburgh, Detroit, Miami, Tampa, Jacksonville, New Orleans, Los Angeles, San Diego, San Francisco, Portland, and Seattle.

Not only did Red enjoy the tour, but also his Bears teammates. Seeing the country, especially in the South and out West, was truly a joy for them. Joey Sternaman recalled taking his first airplane flight while on the tour:

The second tour lasted five weeks, a lot easier than the first one of two weeks. I think through it all I got $200 a game. Red, of course, got much more, thousands, I believe, but he was the drawing card. It was quite something, and we all enjoyed it, the second tour, that is. We saw the nightlife of New Orleans and a lot of the stars in Hollywood, and there was always something going on. Pyle saw to that. I had my first airplane ride while I was on it. Up in Portland, Oregon, there was this fellow, Oakley Kelly, I believe his name was, and he took me up in an open-cockpit plane. I was sitting on a parachute while we flew over the city. That was really something in 1925. That Kelly was the first man to fly across the country, coast to coast, from dawn to dusk.[22]

The Grange–Bears barnstorming tour stands as one of the single greatest achievements in NFL history—as well as sports history. Red might not have "saved" the NFL, but he certainly put the league on the map—the national map. Almost 100 years later, the impact of the tour endures.

Total games: 19
Red Grange games: 17 (missed two due to injury)
Total travel days: 66 (November 26, 1925–January 31, 1926)
Miles traveled: 10,896
Hours traveled: 171
Bears record: 13 wins, 5 losses, 1 tie
Bears points for: 283 (14.8 points per game)
Bears points against: 129 (6.7 points per game)
Red Grange rushing touchdowns: 15
Red Grange receiving touchdowns: 1
Red Grange interception return touchdowns: 1
Red Grange passing touchdowns: 2

PART IV

HOLLYWOOD AND THE "GRANGE LEAGUE" (1926–1927)

19

WAR WITH THE NFL
The Grange League

After barnstorming the country playing pro football in front of large crowds, the Red–Pyle duo was set to face off with the NFL establishment. During the trip back home from Seattle, C. C. Pyle huddled with George Halas and Dutch Sternaman to discuss Red's plans for the 1926 season. The Bears' owners thought the 1925 deal heavily favored Pyle, but they were willing to accept the same arrangement to keep Red in a Bears uniform. Pyle was amenable to a 50–50 split, but he also asked for one-third ownership of the franchise. Halas and Sternaman said no way. "No, no, no! In no way. No, first, last and always! The matter was not negotiable. A percentage of earnings, yes, that was negotiable, but a share of ownership, no!" Halas wrote in his autobiography. The Red–Pyle team then parted company with the Bears. Pyle was lookig to get his own team for Red.[1]

On February 4, the tour arrived back in the Windy City at the Chicago and Northwestern train station. They were greeted by the Chicago press and photographers. "Whew, a fellow can't keep this up for a long time," muttered Red. "It sure has been a grind. It will be great to get home again." Red was picked up by his brother. Before leaving the station, Grange posed for a few photos—one with his brother and another of him about to get into the car he had bought Garland right before the holiday. After a night at home in Wheaton, player and agent were back on the move.[2]

The NFL's winter meeting would be held on February 6–7, in Detroit, Michigan. The most important topic was, of course, the NFL's relationship with the colleges and universities throughout the country. NFL president Joe F. Carr and owners George Halas and Tim Mara knew they had to regain (or, in some opinion, acquire) the trust of the coaches and athletic directors who ran college football. Failure to do so could make life very difficult. It was time to get the "specific wording" correct and iron-clad so that there would be no argument. After getting the input they needed, the NFL came up with the answer they were looking for.

At 2:00 p.m. at the Hotel Statler, President Carr called the league meeting, with 20 NFL teams in attendance. First up, the NFL presented a new resolution that would state the eligibility of college players coming into the NFL in a clear and concise manner:

> We believe there is a public demand for professional football, as has been clearly demonstrated by the wide interest manifested notably throughout the past season, and, to the end that this league may not jeopardize the amateur standing of any college player, it is the unanimous of this meeting that every member of the National Football League be positively prohibited from inducing or attempting to induce any college player to engage in professional football until his class at college shall have graduated, and any member violating this rule shall be fined not less than One Thousand Dollars, or loss of its franchise or both.[3]

The NFL had finally gotten the "specific wording" right, and it seemed that the new resolution would stand up. After the meeting, Carr spoke to the press about the resolution:

> What more could we do to prove our regard for college football than rule that a lad who matriculates in any institution of learning cannot play in our league *until his class has graduated*? This means that if a boy enters the University of Pennsylvania, say, this fall, joins the freshman squad, and quits college two weeks after he matriculates, *he cannot play football in the National League until 1930.* That may work a hardship on some boys. I could cite several cases where it has appeared to be a little harsh already. But it is the only way we can prove to the college men that we are not going to do anything to weaken amateur athletics as the recreational part of higher education.[4]

In what would become known as the "Grange Rule," the new bylaw became one of the NFL's proudest badges of altruism. The league had always taken pride in its "class-has-graduated" rule as an example of how it protected college football. Sixty years later, some student-athletes would be willing to challenge that rule in the courts as a violation of their right to earn a living. Just when it looked like the NFL was feeling good about itself, another war was about to start.

Pyle and Red had arrived in Detroit to apply for an NFL franchise, but Cash and Carry never did anything by the books. Pyle took the floor and announced that he and Red had just secured a five-year lease for Yankee Stadium for every Sunday and the holiday dates from October 15 to December 31. "I have the biggest star in football and I have the lease on the biggest stadium in the country and I am going into your league," Pyle boldly announced. They proposed running their own franchise right there in New York. Pyle painted a convincing picture, touting the biggest stadium in the country with the biggest star in football playing in it. All the league members stood to profit greatly—except one.[5]

Pyle hadn't discussed his idea with Tim Mara, who just a year earlier had purchased his Giants franchise with the thought that he was buying an exclusive franchise in New York. Wasn't that the purpose of a franchise? In the name of profit, would the league set aside Mara's territorial rights and allow a new franchise in Yankee Stadium just across the Harlem River, less than 1,000 yards from the Polo Grounds? Several owners didn't think twice before jumping on the Grange bandwagon. A. H. Bowlby of Rock Island bubbled over; Dutch Sternaman went for it; and Halas was noncommittal, knowing that Red in the league would only help the NFL. But as much as the other owners wanted Red in the NFL, he couldn't be in New York unless Mara said okay.

Mara didn't care for the way Pyle had moved into his territory and assumed the league would just give him a franchise. He told Pyle no way. That evening, some of the owners attempted a compromise. Perhaps Mara would be willing to countenance a Grange franchise in Brooklyn. Perhaps Pyle would be willing to back off and go to Ebbets Field, some 10 miles from the Polo Grounds. Pyle dug in for a fight, saying to Red, "No blasted Irishman is going to keep me out of New York!"[6]

After roughly five hours of discussions, a meeting was arranged between Mara and Pyle. It was doomed. Mara had developed a dislike for Pyle's arrogance, and now C. C. was treating him as a tiresome obstacle to more "riches." According to one witness, Mara came close to punching Pyle. In the end, it looked like Mara would get his wish for no NFL franchise for Red–Pyle. Mara's refusal to acquiesce to Pyle's demand was well within his rights, and Carr backed his owner 100 percent. He, like Mara, didn't care for the way Pyle did business. Everyone knew that Pyle was only trying to capitalize on Red's fame, something that every man in the room was anxious to do, the only difference being that, unlike the others, Pyle was determined that Red receive the biggest share of the capitalization. Carr couldn't bankrupt his league so that Pyle could become rich. Everyone in the league had to follow the same rules, right?

That Mara's refusal to be bulldozed was fueled by self-interest goes without saying. He saw no profit in allowing his Giants to become New York's "second" team. But beyond that, he could think of long-term profits as opposed to quick riches. If the league caved this time, what would happen when next year's "Grange" came along and wanted a slice of Chicago? The year after that would Philadelphia be given away to another college star? Mara, Carr, and the other owners had to ask, who was running this show anyway, the league or the stars? This was a battle worth fighting for.

The first day of the winter meetings ended with Pyle being shut out of the NFL. "The National League needs 'Red' Grange. He contributed to the big success that pro football achieved last season, and if the league doesn't think that he is still an asset another one will be formed," barked Pyle to the press. He and Grange knew the door was pretty much closed, so Pyle did the only thing he knew how to do and that was think big. Pyle slowly got the word out that he and Red were going to organize their own league, with Red's team playing in New York at Yankee Stadium. The entire dynamic of professional football was about to change, and the NFL was about to face a war against what historians called the "Grange League."[7]

Tim Mara began the struggle with a war of words.

Red Grange is fine type and a great athlete, but he has fallen into the hands of the Philistines. If he comes into New York for a professional football war, he'll lose his shirt and that magic "77" along with it. All that money he is supposed to have made this year will float right out the window. . . .

Incidentally, I'm far from alone in my stand against an invasion of New York territory. President Carr has telephoned me with the assurance that the league is behind me to a man. As for the report that Grange and his manager, Pyle, might persuade the Chicago Bears to desert in a body, I am pleased to say that they have told me they are with the New York Giants 100 percent.

If Grange carries out his threat to promote a team in New York and conflicts with our Sunday dates, neither one of us will make a nickel. But we are in a better position to survive, as we are in an organized league and any other team that invades our territory without a franchise will have to play as an outlaw.[8]

Dr. Harry March of the Giants was a little more diplomatic, saying, "Competition is the backbone of all sports, and the New York football Giants welcome the coming of a new league in this city."

Even Red talked the talk. Speaking on KYW radio in Chicago, the redhead spoke up for himself:

I cannot understand why the league doesn't want to allow me to buy a franchise. Football is my profession, a profession I am going to follow as long as there is any fight left in me. I love football, love to play it, and play it clean. I have given the game my best and have put it on a high plane. . . . With C. C. Pyle, my manager, I went to Detroit and asked for a franchise. I was declined recognition.

I want to play football, and I'm going to play. When the doors of the pro league were closed to me, there was nothing left for me to do but listen to the appeal of the New York interests who would join me in putting another team into New York and if necessary another league.

It has been said we will be a failure if we start. I don't believe so. The public will support teams that give them real football, and I feel the men we will get together will play real football. I am sorry to be put to this test by men I gave my best to. I am entitled to a place in football other than that of just a player. . . . Fortunately, I am in a position where I can be an owner, as well as a player, a position I have made through hard work on the gridiron. I am entitled to be a little more than just a player under the dictates of some manager.[9]

Pyle began to organize his new league. He set up shop with an office in New York at the Hotel Astor. On February 17—eight days after his negotiations with the NFL broke down—Pyle announced that his league, which would be called the American Football League (AFL), would have 10 teams and start play that fall. The first four teams would be located in New York, Boston, Newark, and Milwaukee. Other possible cities included Chicago (to compete with the Bears and Cardinals); Brooklyn; and a West Coast city, with team to be led by George "Wildcat" Wilson. Pyle also talked the talk:

Our league will be limited in the number of clubs. It will follow a schedule that is arranged before the season opens, and there will be no deviation from this schedule, no games tossed in, or out, as the race is underway. We intend to have one of the most influential figures in the football world as the head of our league. We will insist that each club given a franchise put up a substantial sum, which will go into a sinking fund.

We are not preparing to start a football "war," as has been announced, but if there has to be a "war" our army will be strong enough to win it.[10]

There was no doubt professional football was about to see a "war." To make a big splash, Pyle announced the hiring of William "Big Bill" Edwards, the former Princeton All-American tackle, who had held jobs as collector of internal revenues and street cleaning commissioner in New York, to be the president of the AFL. Pyle signed Edwards to a three-year contract at $25,000 per year. Edwards ascended to his office with a ringing speech about preserving "high-class football" and "red-blooded sport." The huge salary made big headlines, but it also turned off potential investors. At the same time they announced Edwards as president, the AFL revealed that teams would play an 18-game schedule, adopt the NFL rule that no college player could play until his class had graduated, set player rosters at 18 men but with no salary limit, and finalize the league's by-laws. Moreover, according to the bylaws each franchise would "deposit $3,000 to guarantee appearances and take care of fines and other financial matters under the circuit's supervision." Whether the teams paid this fee is unclear.[11]

While fighting the NFL, Pyle was also fighting his partners. Doc Coolley and Byron Moore knew they were on the outs, but they still had a signed contract—a signed contract for two more years. Pyle had already started to negotiate a settlement with the two men. On March 17, 1926, Pyle shot off a Western Union telegram to Coolley in Danville expressing his feelings. "No definite payment was agreed upon," he wrote. "I am treating you fairly. Doing everything possible for me to do. Wire answer, Regards, Chas."[12]

The breakup was near. Pyle wanted all the money for himself, and he was about to get it. Red seemed to be more comfortable with Pyle running the show, so he had no objection to having Cash and Carry push Coolley and Moore aside. A year after agreeing to be Red's managers, the trio of Pyle–Coolley–Moore was officially about to split up. A three-page contract was typed up. It was pretty much a divorce, but Coolley and Moore would not go away empty-handed.

AGREEMENT

This agreement, made this fifteenth day of March, 1926, by and between CHARLES C. PYLE, MARION F. COOLLEY, and BYRON F. MOORE. WITNESSETH:

WHEREAS, the parties here to are the same parties who heretofore entered into a contract with HAROLD E. "RED" GRANGE, wherein and hereby they acquired certain percentage rights as manager of the said H.E.R.G. in and to the proceeds arising out of the exhibition, performance, and activities of the said GRANGE.

WHEREAS, the said Pyle is desirous of purchasing the interest of the said Coolley and Moore, and the said Coolley and Moore are desirous of selling the same to said Pyle.

NOW, THEREFORE, for and in consideration of one dollar ($1) and the other good and valuable consideration each to the other paid, the receipt whereof by each acknowledged; the parties agree as follows:

The said Marion F. Coolley and Byron F. Moore do hereby sell, transfer, and assign all of their respective rights and interests in and to their contract with the said Harold E. "Red" Grange to Charles C. Pyle.

Charles C. Pyle does hereby agree to pay to the said Marion F. Coolley and Byron F. Moore each the sum of twelve thousand five hundred dollars ($12,500), payable to each five thousand dollars ($5,000) upon the execution hereof and the balance (a note for) seven thousand five hundred dollars ($7,500) due on or before July first, 1926, in full payment for such assignment. . . . The said Pyle claims responsibility for all claims, demands, and liabilities.

IN WITNESS WHEREOF, the parties hereto have placed their hands and seals hereon, the day of and year first above written.

Charles C. Pyle (signed, black ink)

Marion F. Coolley (signed, black ink)

Byron F. Moore (signed, black ink)

I hereby accept and approve the terms of the above and foregoing contract and do release Marion F. Coolley and Byron F. Moore of and from all further duties and obligations under the certain contract between them and myself as therein above referred to:

Harold E. Grange (signed, black ink)[13]

The original contract had two items crossed out in black ink. First, in the opening line, the date of March 15 was crossed out for March 26. The second item crossed out was the due date for the second payment by Pyle. He had agreed to pay Coolley and Moore $12,500 each for the right to be Red's only manager. On the day of the contract, he paid each man $5,000. But instead of on or before July 1, written in black ink was May 1. So, Pyle would be under the gun. He would only have five weeks to pay off the remaining money. Pyle would eventually make the payments. As of March 26, 1926, C. C. Pyle was Red's only manager.

As for the two men who were also Red's managers during the famous barnstorming tour, they went their separate ways. Byron Moore would get back into the theater business, eventually working for Warner Bros. theaters in St. Louis and Pittsburgh. Coolley would go on to law school, graduating from Cornell University, class of 1927, and then work for years as a loan officer for

Northwestern Mutual Life. Coolley married Helen Yaeger and had one child, a daughter. Marylin Coolley-Carley remembered growing up hearing about Red Grange.

> My father had a good sense of humor, that's for sure, and he had a lot of friends. He had all of these people over, and the most exciting thing when I was about 13, we had the first TV on the block, and all the boys came over because they wanted to watch any of the sports that were on. And the boys were at my house all the time, because they wanted to talk to him about Red Grange. My teenage friends were there all the time.[14]

Throughout the years Red would kept in touch with Doc Coolley, visiting him in Danville and mailing him a signed copy of his autobiography. Coolley never could shake his health problems. Because of his heart issues, he passed away on April 10, 1955, at the age of 56.[15]

The war with the NFL was just beginning. The Rock Island Independents (who were 5–3–3 in the NFL in 1925) defected to the AFL. Pyle then tried to woo Chris O'Brien and his Cardinals to the new league as an anchor franchise in Chicago. Even though the Cardinals were not the moneymaker they once were, the loss of the 1925 NFL champions would have hurt the older league. O'Brien was loyal to the NFL, forcing Pyle to make his arrangement with Joey Sternaman and taking "Little Joey" away from the Chicago Bears to run the Chicago franchise. The NFL kept Paddy Driscoll, who was sold to the Chicago Bears, and beat Pyle's AFL in signing Ernie Nevers. The Duluth Eskimos and Ole Haugsrud (a former high school teammate of Nevers's) signed the great fullback for $15,000 and a share of the bigger gates, making him the highest-paid player in the NFL. Carr's league was feeling good about boosting their membership to 22 teams. The president's strategy was to fight the AFL with numbers—teams in the league, players under contract, and games available to fans.

On July 17, Pyle issued a statement saying that his new AFL would have nine teams and start play on September 26. He was able to recruit a few owners to get his new league up to nine franchises.

New York Yankees (Red Grange, C. C. Pyle)
Chicago Bulls (Joey Sternaman, C. C. Pyle)
Los Angeles Wilson's Wildcats (George Wilson, C. C. Pyle)
Brooklyn Horsemen (Humbert Fugazy, boxing promoter)
Newark Bears (W. J. Coughlin, theater executive and head of the New Jersey Athletic Association)

Boston Bulldogs (Robert McKirdy, boxing promoter)

Philadelphia Quakers (Leo Conway, football promoter)

Cleveland Panthers (Charles X. Zimmerman, president of Amiesite Asphalt Company)

Rock Island Independents (A. H. Bowlby, football promoter)

The league consisted of three teams clustered around New York; Pyle's New York Yankees, featuring Red Grange; the Brooklyn Horsemen, so named because the team signed two members of the famous Four Horsemen of Notre Dame (Elmer Layden and Harry Stuhldreher); and the Newark Bears. Other franchises included the Boston Bulldogs (a team of former Ivy Leaguers); Philadelphia Quakers; Cleveland Panthers; Rock Island Independents; and Los Angles Wildcats, a traveling team named after their star attraction—George Wilson.

Pyle was supposedly no more than the owner of the New York franchise, but that was just for public consumption. The Wilson's Wildcat franchise was definitely his concoction, and the Chicago squad was likely being funded by Cash and Carry. He owned nearly a third of the league. The public and press thought of the AFL as the "Grange League." Although Red put up his share of money, in reality it was Pyle's. As the war continued to rage on, Red Grange headed to Hollywood.

20

ONE MINUTE TO PLAY

While C. C. Pyle did most of the legwork in organizing the new professional football league, Red was keeping busy. He spent most of his time in Wheaton taking care of his father and brother. Red spoiled his old man. Keeping his promise, Red bought his father a three-story house in town. Located at 314 North Main Street, the Grange men remodeled the outside with stucco and had Marshall Field and Company furnish the interior. Lyle picked out the furniture for the house—a maple bedroom suite, tapestry-upholstered easy chairs, hand-carved cabinets, and walnut and mahogany tables. Upstairs Red made sure his father had plenty of space to entertain friends. "The den on the third floor was like a private club. It had wood-paneled walls, leather coaches and chairs, a pool table, poker tables, and a bar. Dad particularly enjoyed entertaining his cronies up there," wrote Red in his autobiography.[1]

Red also built a four-car garage for the new cars that he was about to buy. The Grange men loved their automobiles. In addition to the Nash he bought for his brother, Red, with his newfound wealth, bought a Lincoln for his father and an Auburn 8-88 for himself. They would now drive around Wheaton in style. The three men loved to drive fast. Garland would get many speeding tickets throughout the years, while Red wasn't too far behind him in that category. Red would tell a story about how once his Aunt Bertha was visiting and he took her out for a drive in his new Auburn roadster:

> I remember she came back when I bought my first automobile, and I took her for a ride. I rode around and I was very careful, cause Aunt Bertha was getting up there in years. She said, "Red, can't this car go any faster than 40 miles per hour."

"Yea, but I didn't think you wanted." She said, "Yes, let me see how fast you can go." She was a great sport.[2]

In the end, reports came out that Red had spent $25,000 on the new house. Just as the Grange men were getting settled into their new home, they were visited by Roy Gibbons, a writer from Newspaper Enterprise Association (NEA). Gibbons wanted to write an exposé on Red's relationship with his father. Red spoke glowingly of his old man, relating, "He's the real boss. I'll follow his advice because he's everything I got. Nothing else counts much. I've got him fixed now. He's never have to worry. I'm satisfied." Red was sincere in his words to Gibbons. After the hassle and negativity toward him when he signed to play pro football, it had been worth it to see his father happy. Papa Grange was then asked how he raised his son.

> I was raised in Pennsylvania and in the lumber camps of Sullivan County when I lived in Forksville, and when I worked as foreman it was necessary for a fellow to be a regular he-man if he wanted to get along. That's how I raised Harold, and that's how I'm raising Garland. I've tried to put real spunk and character in them, and I've tried to give them chances to be what I always wanted to be but never had the opportunity. . . . Harold will never be a playboy. His money will never bother him. He's got the Grange spirit too deeply planted in him.[3]

Red smiled as his father praised him for his modesty. He truly loved his father, the man who had given him so much. Red was also realistic about his time as a "famous celebrity."

> I know this can't last forever. But I've got everything I've ever wanted, and I'm going to make the best of what's at hand while it's here. . . . My dad and brother Garland mean everything to me. I'm going to see the kid through school, and I'm going to make the dad take it easy if I can. But I doubt that. He just insist on working at something.[4]

Both Red and Lyle posed for a few photos for the article. They each sat on the bumpers of their cars, posed with a bucksaw while cutting a log, and used a shovel to dig up some dirt. While digging Lyle said, "It's a mighty fine house. And Harold's a son to be proud of, just like his brother Garland. Character and not money is what the world needs today. Money is nice. But between the two, character is the most important." Lyle had raised his son right, giving him the tools necessary to handle being one of the most famous athletes in the world. As proud as he was of his son, Red was even prouder of his father.[5]

Red and his family didn't have to worry about money, but his acting career in Hollywood would need some help. Arrow Pictures Corporation had run into financial problems, declaring bankruptcy. The $300,000 "retainer" check sitting in the bank in Champaign would be worthless. So, Pyle had to go looking for another studio. They found Film Booking Offices of America (FBO), which had just been purchased by Joseph P. Kennedy, the father of John F. and Robert Kennedy. The Boston native made a name for himself as a successful stock broker with Hayden, Stone & Co., eventually becoming a multimillionaire with his own investment company. Kennedy parlayed his fortunes into owning a few film studios, one of which was FBO, a small Hollywood studio known for making cheaply produced Westerns. He saw the star power of Red and put up the money for his movie debut, tentatively called *The Halfback*.

It was now time for Red to head back out West. The Galloping Ghost would take Hollywood by storm. Just like on the barnstorming tour, Lyle Grange wanted his son to be surrounded by people he trusted. Beans DeWolf would go on the trip to California. The two Wheaton boys arrived in Los Angeles in mid-May. Pyle had gone out a few weeks earlier to make the necessary arrangements. He rented two luxury suites at the Ambassador Hotel, one for the living quarters and the other for an office. The Ambassador would be Red's home for the next two months. He quickly jumped into the glamour of La La Land, meeting one of his movie idols. Said Grange,

> I happened to drop in to an exclusive haberdashery shop which was owned partly by Douglas Fairbanks. Sr. Doug was in the store at the time and offered to match me double or nothing (coin flip) for a tweed suit I picked out. When I won, Fairbanks wrote on the inside label, "This suit is on you, but it's on me." I proudly kept that suit for nearly 15 years.[6]

Before filming started, Pyle had set up some speaking engagements in town for Red to appear at. After being introduced by Pyle, Red would usually give a short speech during these appearances. Speaking mostly to high school football players, Red made stops at San Bernardino High School, Redlands High School, and the Santa Ana Junior Chamber of Commerce. His talks would be about how the game of football had taught him to be a confident man: "Football teaches youth not to be discouraged. The players get knocked down and banged around but usually come up smiling. Being batted around and forced to smile will make a hero out of any man." Just like in high school and college, Red took his position as a role model seriously; he always wanted to pass along his advice to the youth of America.[7]

Red jumped right into being a Hollywood actor. The movie title would be changed to *One Minute to Play*, written by Byron Morgan. It was your typical college rah-rah story, a genre that was becoming popular—*The Quarterback*, starring Richard Dix, and *Brown of Harvard*, starring William Haines, would also be released in 1926. The plot deals with the adventures of a young high school football player whose success on the field was much greater than his success in the classroom. Upon finishing high school, his father sends him to college to focus on going to school, and he is ordered not to play football. But due to a mix-up on the train taking him to college, the main character, "Red" Wade, ends up at the wrong school, where he subsequently breaks his promise to his father. While at college, Wade falls in love and becomes the star of the football team. When his father learns of his son's escapades, he descends upon the school to prevent his son from participating in the sport he loves; however, in the end, he relents, as the boy plays in the closing minute of the big contest and single-handedly wins the game.

The cast was filled with Hollywood veterans. Charles Ogle (Mr. Wade) and Edythe Chapman (Mrs. Wade) played Red's parents. Lee Shumway (Tex Rogers) was the football coach, and Jay Hunt (President Todd) was the college president. Red's costar and love interest was played by Mary McAllister, a 16-year-old brunette with brown eyes. Standing 5-foot-2, McAllister started acting at six years old and, at that point in her career, had appeared in more than 30 silent movies. The twosome made an adorable on-screen couple.

Sam Wood was hired to be the director. The 42-year-old Wood had directed more than 25 silent films in Hollywood, working with the likes of Gloria Swanson and Wallace Reid. He would bring the film in under budget, spending less than $100,000. Wood had his work cut out for him dealing with Red. Several pro athletes had tried their hands at acting. Babe Ruth, Jack Dempsey, and Charley Paddock had appeared in movies, with disappointing results. Red would try to change the industry's attitude—something that was quite difficult since he was a "pro football" player. The virgin actor would get plenty of help from his director.[8] "I became particularly fond of Sam Wood and often thought he would have made a great football coach because he could get a lot out of you the easy way," wrote Red in his autobiography. "During my first summer in Hollywood I rarely did anything but work. The only relaxation I had was when Director Wood let me off early a few afternoons to watch the Los Angeles Angels play ball."[9]

Charles G. Clarke was hired to be the cinematographer. One report claimed that Clarke used as many as 30 cameras during filming, mostly for the football scenes. The movie was shot on the campus of Pomona College, located in nearby Claremont. The cast and crew worked hard on the film, sometimes laboring for as many as 16 hours a day. The movie was faced with a big dilemma. The script called for the big game at the end of the film to be played on a Saturday in late fall; however, it was the middle of June in Hollywood, with temperatures hitting highs in the 90s. The film's producers wanted to shoot crowd shots of fans watching the game, but how would they do it?" Red wrote in his autobiography,

> Since the game was supposed to be played in the Midwest on a fall afternoon, the crowd couldn't be shown in such attire. Charles Pyle came up with the solution to the problem. He induced the studio to put advertisement in one of the Los Angeles papers that George Wilson's team would play Red Grange's team in a regulation game, and admission was free to anyone who came dressed in fall apparel. The results of Pyle's brainstorm were unbelievable. Fifteen thousand die-hard football fans turned out in felt hats, scarves, coats, and jackets, and when seen on the screen couldn't be distinguished from a crowd on a chilly fall day in Ohio or Illinois.[10]

Pyle was a genius. Admission to the grandstand was free to fans with a ticket, with tickets given out by the Santa Ana Chamber of Commerce and the San Bernardino County Chamber of Commerce. A few days before the game, the *San Bernardino County Sun* wrote, "Persons with straw hats will not be admitted. This is because motion pictures will be taken of the crowds and, because football is played in the autumn, straw hats would seem out of place in the motion picture production in which the game (fall game) will be a principal feature."[11]

At 10:00 a.m. on June 19, the game between Red Grange and George Wilson was staged at Alumni Field on the campus of Pomona College. Pyle announced that the game would not be a "fake game" but would be played "just as hard fought as any game the Wheaton Iceman ever played in." More than 3,000 fans—not quite the 15,000 that Red wrote about in his autobiography—came from Los Angeles, San Bernardino, and Claremont to help fill the stadium. For the purpose of the movie, the local team (Red's) was called "Parmalee College," and the visiting team (Wilson's) was called "Claxton College." A local band played music to create a college football atmosphere. Red, wearing his famous number 77 jersey, had his squad, and George Wilson had his. Wilson's team also included tackle Bill Cole (University of Southern California), center George Baker (Stanford), and guard Bert Lembeck (UCLA). The rest of the players, at least 14 of them, were recruited from Pomona College. The big scene of the film was for "Red" Wade to run 90 yards for a touchdown. Two days before the game, Red told the local press,

Every opposition player has been told to down me and down me hard. A bonus has been offered by the movie director to those who tackle me and prevent me from making that long run. So you can see there is nothing "phoney" about it, and what's more its business with me. I'm going to try and get away with that run just as quickly as I can, as I realize the longer I put it off the harder it will be.[12]

The game was a success. Director Wood and his cinemaphotographer, Clarke, got the shots they needed, as well as the most realistic football game shot on film for a Hollywood movie. After almost two months of work, Red was getting antsy about going home. He wanted to see his father and get ready for the football season. "Red says he's pretty soft, and he's coming back to the ice wagon for what he says is the best conditioning work in the world," said Lyle Grange to the press. L. C. Thompson was eager to get his best iceman back. He sent out a wire: "Holding your old job open at the regular salary. You are the best iceman we ever had, even if you did play football."[13] Red responded to the local press by saying, "I've got to get in training for my football next fall. I can't keep in trim making love to your pretty girls. I've got to heave a few cakes of ice this summer and get back into physical condition. I'm leaving at noon tomorrow, and I'm not coming back."[14] Despite being tired and homesick, Red did have one fan in Hollywood—Joseph P. Kennedy. "Young Grange screens unusually well and responds readily to direction, and our company would be very glad to have him for a heroic lead in romantic stories," said Kennedy to the *Film Daily*.[15]

Red was frustrated and tired when he told the press he was not coming back to Hollywood. He would return. Red recalled his first movie experience in Hollywood, reflecting,

> Making *One Minute to Play* was the worse drudgery I'd ever experienced. It took us a little better than four weeks of actual shooting time to complete the movie. To do the football sequences I spent 10-straight scorching hot days in front of the camera from dawn to sundown in full football regalia. By the time I got back to the hotel at night I cared about nothing except falling into bed. I was so tired and bored that I counted the days until the film was completed so I could get back to Wheaton.[16]

Pyle was convinced that Red was going to be a Hollywood star. "That Grange is a real actor," he said to the press. "He is taking the city of Hollywood by storm. Why, all the critics thought that he would not be much on the screen, but he is making a tremendous success. It is unbelievable. He dominates every scene in which he plays."[17]

After two months in Hollywood, Red and DeWolf arrived back in Chicago, greeted by Lyle and Garland. Red, wearing a light-colored suit, striped tie, and new hat—a fancy pith helmet—proudly shook his father's hand when he greeted him. Soon the Grange party was surrounded by photographers. There was no break from being famous. Red would spend the night at his father's new home. He would return to his work on the ice wagon, making L. C. Thompson very happy. Red had missed spending time with his father. So, the two planned a unique trip. They would take a week to visit Red's birthplace, Forksville. It would be the first time in 16 years that father or son had been back home. Garland wanted to stay in Wheaton, so DeWolf joined the two on the trip east.

In late July, the three men loaded into one of the Grange cars to drive the 680 miles to Forksville. It didn't take long for the party to get pulled over. Behind the wheel, Red was caught speeding through Justice Park, a small town just 20 minutes outside of Wheaton. The police officer clocked him going 45 miles per hour. Despite the objection of the Wheaton police chief, Red paid the $25 bond.

The first stop on the trip was Johnson City, New York, to visit family. It had been a long time since Red had seen his sister. The same was true for Lyle and his daughter. Mildred was 28 years old, married to Alvin Haverly, and raising two boys (Ray and Cleon). The family was back together. This was what the trip was all about. After spending the night at his sister's house, Red took his father and DeWolf into Forksville. They would stay the rest of the trip at the Lake Wesauking Lodge and spend most of the time fishing, relaxing, and meeting Lyle's old acquaintances and family. One evening, the Grange party had dinner in Blossburg with Dr. John Davies, the doctor who brought Red into the world.

While in Forksville, Red was invited to participate in a few local events. He attended a baseball game between Towanda and the South Waverly Tigers. Red and Beans were asked to play, but the two decided to volunteer as umpires instead. The other event was much bigger. When word got out that Lyle Grange was coming home and bringing his son with him, the town wanted to celebrate. Their famous son was returning. Since the local county fair was coming up, they decided to merge the two events. On August 4, the Sullivan County Farmer's Picnic was held at the Forksville fairgrounds. Several ads appeared in the county papers.

The picnic started early in the morning, with Red and his party arriving around 10 o'clock. "When he (Red) came upon the grounds, men, women, children flocked around him, shaking hands." More than 3,000 residents— mostly young boys and girls—of Sullivan County came out to the fairgrounds, which was decorated with bunting, American flags, and signs. A large white

"County Wide Farmers' Picnic
Wednesday, August 4
On the Fair Grounds at Forksville, Pa.
HAROLD "RED" GRANGE

National Football Star of Wheaton, Ill., will be there. The management of the picnic is making this a "Welcome Home" for the "hero of the gridiron," thus giving the people of Sullivan and adjoining counties an opportunity to meet the "Wonder Football Player of the World."[18]

banner hung in the middle of the grandstands. Roughly six feet in length with red lettering, the banner read, "Welcome Home Red Grange." On that warm summer day, Red wore a long-sleeve white dress shirt, a bow tie, dress trousers, dress shoes, and a baseball cap off and on to shield his head and eyes from the beaming sun. The afternoon was filled with music, provided by the Boys Band of Canton, and such amusement games as soft drink and watermelon-eating contests. "Red was very much pleased with the music," wrote the local press. At lunchtime, Red, Lyle, and Beans were joined by Mildred and her family, as well as Dr. Davies. Father and son were having a great time with family and friends.[19]

Red gave a short speech to the picnicgoers. "Never say you can't do a thing until you try," he opined. "Always do your best, and the results will be surprising. Above all, play clean and fair, either in sports or in business, and your opponents are bound to respect you." Red then urged for the making of a playground at the Forksville school so that boys and girls could engage in clean sports to go along with their education. "However, with the thousand and one requests for pictures, signatures, etc., he never for one instant lost his good humor."[20]

Just after three o'clock, the Grange party left. It was time to head home. Red and his father had enjoyed every minute of their trip to Forksville. It had been a once-in-a-lifetime trip for both of them. In the ensuing decades, Lyle would not return, but Red would make the effort to return to his roots. As for the town of Forksville, they loved their famous son. The small town would always revel in the notoriety that they were the birthplace of Harold Edward Grange. Even in the years to come, when most sportswriters and historians would claim that he was born in Wheaton, they were quick to correct, as did Red himself, saying that Forksville was his place of birth. The "welcome home" picnic was a tremendous success, so much so that the white and red "Welcome Home Red

Grange" banner was kept as a souvenir. It survives and is proudly displayed at the Sullivan County Historical Society and Museum, located in LaPorte.[21]

Once back in Wheaton, Red threw himself into his work on the ice wagon. He only had a few more weeks until the football season was set to commence. He needed to be in shape. As the summer came to an end, the AFL and NFL were preparing to do battle on the field. The 1926 professional football season would have two leagues, 31 teams, and more than 600 players. The only question was would paying fans show up?

21

1926 PRO FOOTBALL SEASON

I t was a busy summer for Red Grange. He had made a Hollywood movie, visited his birthplace, and worked his summer job as the "Wheaton Iceman." It was time to get back to playing football. Despite losing Paddy Driscoll and Ernie Nevers to the NFL, Pyle and the AFL were able to steal a few player-coaches of their own.

The Philadelphia Quakers stole head coach Bob Folwell and tackle Century Milstead from the New York Giants, while also picking up tackle "Bull" Behman from the Frankford Yellow Jackets, giving the Quakers the best line in the AFL. Cleveland was able to sign veteran guard Al Nesser, who had played with his brothers for the Columbus Panhandles and, in 1925, was on the NFL's Cleveland Bulldogs. The Chicago Bulls not only stole Joey Sternaman from the Bears, but also signed end Eddie Anderson, who had played the past three seasons for the Chicago Cardinals, and halfbacks Johnny Mohardt and Roy White, previously on the Bears roster. The Brooklyn franchise signed Red's buddy, fullback Earl Britton, and former Decatur Staleys–Canton Bulldogs guard Tarzan Taylor, adding more star power to backs Elmer Layden and Harry Stuhldreher, two of Notre Dame's Four Horsemen. The Newark Bears were able to sign former Georgia Tech star halfback Doug Wycoff (who would go on to play six seasons in the NFL).

Wilson's Wildcats, led by George Wilson, signed George's brother, Abe Wilson (Washington) to play guard. "That first season with the AFL, my dad, Abe, was paid $100 a game as a lineman, and George (Wilson) made $125 a game as a back," said Don Wilson, son of Abe Wilson. "It was a fantastic experience. They both got to see a lot of the country. And he really enjoyed the football aspect of it, he loved the game, and loved playing it." Wilson and Pyle were also able to recruit a few players who had played on the West Coast during the barnstorming tour of 1925–1926, including quarterback Jim Bradshaw, end Jim Lawson, and tackle Harry Shipkey.[1]

As for Red's New York Yankees, Pyle was able to recruit a star-studded team. It was his league and he had the money to spend, so it made sense that he would give Red the best team in the league. First, Pyle snagged tackle Ralph Scott from the Bears to coach the team. On the line, he signed future Hall of Fame guard Mike Michalske from Penn State and ends Red Maloney, who played with the Providence Steam Roller in 1925, and Paul Goebel, who had played the past three seasons for the Columbus Tigers. From the college ranks, Pyle added fullback Pooley Hubert (Alabama), quarterback George Pease (Columbia), halfback Wes Fry and center Hal Griffen (both from Iowa), and end Art Coglizer (Missouri). The biggest get for Pyle was signing former Colgate star halfback Eddie Tryon. One newspaper reported that Tryon's contract was for $6,000 a season for two years.[2]

On September 2, Red attended a preview of *One Minute to Play* at the Orchestra Hall in Chicago. A crowd of 600 theater managers, looking to book the film, joined Red inside the establishment. The redhead sat "slumped down in a back seat" while watching himself on screen. "I like the movies better than football. You don't get smeared around the field so much," said Red jokingly after the show.

A few days later, Red was off to the Big Apple for another premiere. On September 5, Red attended the New York premiere of his movie at the Colony Theater. Located on Broadway and 53rd, the Colony was decked out for the big premiere, decorated with a three-story movie billboard featuring Red in a kicking pose. Moviegoers were surrounded by college pennants (one with Red Grange, another with *One Minute to Play*), fraternity ensigns, and ushers wearing football sweaters. Tiny footballs were dropped down from an airplane, some containing order forms for a Red Grange sweater from Davega's Sport Store. Sold-out crowds arrived throughout day, with three lines of moviegoers prepared to watch the Galloping Ghost in his movie debut. Red was present for most of the day, hanging out with C. C. Pyle, Sam Wood, and Byron Morgan. After each showing, he made a few comments in front of the moviegoers. He talked about how uncomfortable he was putting "paint on his lips" and that he hoped the audience enjoyed watching the film as much as he enjoyed acting in it.[3]

The movie's run at the Colony was a huge success. The managing director of the theater wrote a letter to Joseph Kennedy, holding nothing back in stating his enthusiasm for the film.

September 7, 1926
Mr. Joseph P. Kennedy
Film Booking Offices of America
1560 Broadway, N.Y.C.

Dear Mr. Kennedy:

It gives me much pleasure to inform you that Red Grange in "One Minute to Play" broke all opening day records at the Colony Theater on the occasion of its world premiere, Sunday, September 5. It topped by $250 the opening day receipts of Harold Lloyd in "The Freshman," thereby establishing Red Grange as the greatest box-office draw in the history of the screen.

This astounding record was made despite the downpour of rain that would have washed out the average show.

Yours very truly,

H. Gittleson, managing director[4]

The first week at the Colony was a record-breaking debut for *One Minute to Play*. It earned $39,428, with more than 100,000 tickets sold—the most ever for a film shown at the Colony. In 2019, that would equate to roughly $561,000. The Colony Theater ran the movie every day from noon until 11:00 p.m. for more than three weeks. Soon theaters throughout the United States were premiering *One Minute to Play* to large crowds.[5] The reviews came out in bunches. Red was a hit in Hollywood. In the *New York Times*, movie critic Mordaunt Hall wrote,

> In his first screen touchdown "Red" Grange demonstrated his ability to tackle the role of a college hero and portray it far more convincingly than most of the handsome young men who are thoroughly accustomed to greasepaint and facing the camera. Mr. Grange's performance in "One Minute to Play" is pleasingly natural, and it is agreeable to observe that he has not copied the conventional tactics of the ordinary actor. He has an ingratiating appearance, and the idea that he is actually a football player adds to the thrill of this gridiron story.[6]

Movie critic Edwin Schallert of the *Los Angeles Times* opined, "The general impression of his (Red's) portrayal is pleasing. And the climaxing portion of the picture has been filmed with an intensity that grips."[7]

Oscar Cooper of *Motion Picture News* wrote, "Football's Galloping Ghost steps onto the screen and scores a decisive hit. . . . Grange himself as a movie actor puts some of the big stars to shame . . . the football game with remarkable angles and action shots. The excellent supporting cast, the refreshing story, far out of the beaten path of film stuff."[8]

Even New York mayor James Walker, who had a private showing in the FBO projection room, praised the film. "The greatest ever! Red marvelous! Wood's direction revelation! Morgan's story superb!" he said. "It is the everlasting credit to have produced such a motion picture, and it is most gratifying to know that the entire city of New York shares my enthusiasm." Aside from the positive reviews, movie audiences everywhere were spending their money to see Red perform as an actor. Movie theaters throughout the country were giving out Red Grange candy bars and footballs at openings, as well as Red Grange paper megaphones bearing an image of him in a kicking pose. FBO produced movie packets for theaters featuring more than a dozen different styles of ads that could be used in the theaters or published in newspapers. Posters, lobby cards, colored slides (glass), and postcards were also distributed. *One Minute to Play* and Red Grange were everywhere.[9]

According to IMDb, the movie grossed $247,334 during its run.[10] In today's (2019) inflation, the movie would have made approximately $3.5 million. Red's public profile was still growing. Shotwell continued its relationship with Red by releasing a new 24-card set that featured different scenes from the movie. Selling for $.05, these cards, with blank backs, came with a Red Grange candy bar. Grange was even rumored to be engaged to his attractive costar. "I get engaged to somebody every once in a while without having anything to say about it," he said to the press. "I know Miss McAllister very well, but as far as getting engaged is concerned I haven't even a prospect."[11]

After the hoopla in New York concerning *One Minute to Play*, it was time to return to the gridiron. For their first AFL game, the Yankees played a road contest against the Cleveland Panthers. At Luna Park, a crowd of 22,000 got Pyle's war with the NFL off to a good start. If only the Yankees had played better. The backfield of Grange and Tryon did nothing as the Panthers pulled off the upset, winning 10–0. "My team will concentrate on cooperation from now on. The urge to star individually is hampering the progress of the Yankees," Red commented after the game. The team had only been together a few weeks, so time was needed for the squad to congeal into a real team.[12]

The Yankees rebounded after the loss to the Panthers, easily defeating the Rock Island Independents, 26–0, behind two touchdowns by Red and an 82-yard interception return for a score by Wes Fry. The game was played in Moline at smallish Browning Field, attracting only 5,000 fans. "I don't want the fans to believe the Yankees have a one-man team, for we have several backs, and one is just as good as another," said Red after the game to the *Moline Dispatch*. Just like at Illinois, Red didn't want all the attention; it took 11 men to play football.[13]

Six days later, the Yankees took care of the Boston Bulldogs at Braves Field, winning 13–0, and improving to 2–1. The next day, the Yankees played a nonleague game in Hartford, Connecticut, against a team called the All-New Britain—a squad made up of mostly local semipro players. Pyle negotiated with All-New Britain managers Edward Dailey and Peter Perakos to get the game in Hartford, as the local team guaranteed $10,000 for the appearance. In the contract, it was stated that Red had to play at least 25 minutes. Tickets were priced at $2.30 and $3.45, and sold at the Tobacco Shoppe, located on Pearl Street in town. On a cold, wet day, a crowd of just 4,000 fans filled Clarkin Field. It was an easy contest, as the Yankees breezed to a 19–0 victory.[14]

Encouraged by Joseph P. Kennedy, Red remained in Hartford after the game to attend the premiere of *One Minute to Play* at Poli's Capitol Theater. "Tremendous ovations greeted him as he walked on the stage following introduction by (theater) manager James Clancy," wrote the *Hartford Courant*. Red said a few words.

> I like to play football; it is a great game. But you know I can't keep playing it forever. Twenty-five to 30 games in a season is no joke; it is a darn tough grind. . . . Making motion pictures is a lot of fun, but it is also a lot of work. Gee, I never knew before I made my first picture how much work there really is in making a film. They keep you on the jump all the time. We played football six consecutive days in California. The temperature was around 100 degrees. That was real fun![15]

Red stayed and watched the entire film.

Just when it looked like the Yankees had become a dominant team, they ran into Joey Sternaman's Chicago Bulls. On October 17, more than 16,000 fans showed up at Comiskey Park to watch the Bulls stun the Yankees, shutting them out, 14–0. Red's former teammate with the Bears, Johnny Mohardt, stole the show by scoring both touchdowns. Red played three quarters, rushing for 128 yards, but it was not enough. That same day in the NFL, the Bears battled the Cardinals. A mere 12,000 fans filled up Wrigley Field to watch Paddy Driscoll score all the Bears' points in a 16–0 victory. In what was supposed to be the biggest day for pro football in Chicago, the two games combined for only 28,000 customers. Red, in his pro debut, attracted 36,000 onlookers. The two teams were both disappointed with the gate receipts. One month into the season the Yankees were just 2–2.

But the tide was about to change for the Yankees. In the next month they wouldn't lose a game. The winning streak started on October 24, against George Wilson's Wildcats, based in Los Angeles. After playing their first four games on the road, this would be the Yankees' first home game at Yankee Stadium. New York sportswriters would cover the AFL and, in particular, Red's Yankees pretty regularly. The *New York Times* assigned veteran scribe Richard Vidmer to cover the team, while the *New York Daily News* assigned C. A. Lovett to do the same. Each recap would be detailed, even listing the attendance of each and every game. Ads for the games that appeared in the *Times* had Pyle selling "20,000 tickets for 50 cents," and tickets were sold at the Yankee Stadium box office and Schumm and Snyder's Hat Store.[16]

As New York was preparing to watch the Yankees play at Yankee Stadium for the first time, Red was looking out for the city's youth. Through the cooperation of President William "Big Bill" Edwards and Pyle, he began a series of talks to high school boys, given on Saturday mornings at the stadium prior to the team practice. The demonstrations started at 9:00 a.m. and were free to attend. "Grange, unquestionably one of the most colorful and popular figures in football, intersperses his talks with practical demonstrations as far as possible," wrote the *New York Daily News*.[17]

A steady rain kept the first home game to just a little more than 11,000 fans. The sloppy field made it impossible for the offensives to move the ball. The game remained scoreless into the fourth quarter, when Eddie Tryon made the play of the game. Tryon broke loose on an 80-yard touchdown run to save the game, as the Yanks won their home opener, 7-0.

Five games into the season, the AFL showed its first cracks as a league. The Newark Bears, owned by William Coughlin, called it quits. After playing in a downpour in front of just 400 paying customers at home against the Rock Island Independents, Coughlin had experienced enough. He had lost too much money. The victory against the Wildcats carried over into the next week, when the Yankees played their best game of the year, facing the best team in the AFL, the undefeated Philadelphia Quakers (4-0), who had outscored their opponents 30-3, without giving up a touchdown. Ads in the Philly papers announced, "He Is Coming! Red Grange: The Galloping Ghost, the greatest football player ever developed in the stadium." The Quakers sold tickets for $1.65, $2.20, $2.75, and $3.30, at Gimbels Department Store, Conway's, and Spalding's Sporting Goods. In front of 30,000 fans at Sesquicentennial Stadium, the Yanks rolled to a convincing 23-0 win, crossing the Quakers goal line for the first time.[18]

Just a few hours after the Yankees' biggest win, the AFL suffered another casualty. After their 6-0 defeat by the Los Angeles Wildcats, the Cleveland

Panthers called it quits. Only 1,000 fans came out to Luna Park, not enough to support a pro football team, as Panthers management didn't even bother to pay the players.

Because of heavy rains—a staple for every Sunday football game in the fall of 1926—the Yankees game against Rock Island was moved to Tuesday, November 2. "I'll never forget that it rained every Sunday all fall. I don't think we had one sunny Sunday," Red would recall about the bad weather.[19] Back at Yankee Stadium to face the Rock Island Independents, the large crowd was reported at 30,000. It was another easy win for the Yanks. Behind two touchdowns by Tryon and one each by Red, Pooley Hubert, and Larry Marks, Pyle's boys cruised to a 35-0 win, the third straight win by shutout. The following Sunday, the Yankees continued their winning ways, defeating the Brooklyn Horsemen, 21-13, in front of another stellar crowd, reported at 28,000. Tryon continued his great play with two touchdowns, while Red chipped in a TD run.[20]

It would be a bittersweet game for the Brooklyn Horsemen because soon after the loss to the Yankees they would say good-bye to the AFL. Instead of folding, they added insult to C. C. Pyle's pocketbook by merging with the Brooklyn Lions of the NFL. The team was called the Brooklyn Horse-Lions. The AFL was down to six franchises.

The Yankees' four-game winning streak was impressive, outscoring their opponents 85-13, with three shutouts. They also were attracting fans, more than 104,000 for the four games. But the Yankees and the Quakers were the only AFL teams attracting fans. The day after the Brooklyn win, the Yankees traveled north to play another game. On Monday, November 8, the Yankees played Wilson's Tigers in Toronto. One news report claimed that the Yankees got a $10,000 guarantee to play the game in Canada. The crowd at Maple Leaf Stadium was announced at 10,000. After a scoreless first half, Red gave the Canadian fans something to cheer about. The Galloping Ghost sprinted 60 yards for the game's first score. The Yanks scored three more touchdowns to win, 28-0.

At about this time, Red engaged in another business venture that would help him years later as a member of the media. Pyle was able to get Red a paying job with *Universal News Service*, writing a series of articles about the game of football. Red would write at least 25 articles for *Universal*, with each article around 1,000 words, covering two to three columns. It's not known if Red had a ghostwriter; most likely he had someone help him. But unlike Babe Ruth, who had Christy Walsh help him, or Jack Dempsey, who had the assistance of Ned Brown, Red had a passion for writing. He also had opinions on everything to do with football and wanted to share them. To introduce the series Red wrote,

Writing a series of articles on football has long been a pet idea of mine. So I welcome the opportunity afforded me to give my views on various angles of the game in this series for *Universal Service*. I have learned, particularly during the past year, that the public is intensely interested in many phases of the game which have been discussed but little, if at all. These will be the topics which I will discuss.

For his 25 articles, Red used such titles as the following:

November 6: "Red Grange Believes Too Many Penalties Hold Football Back"

November 8: "Red Grange Discusses Huddle System"

November 13: "Line Overlooked by Sports Writers, Red Grange Says"

November 16: "Early Training for Football Necessary, Red Grange Holds"

November 26: "Pro Football Here to Stay, Red Grange Says in Defending Quality of Games"[21]

The series of articles were published in the *Chicago Herald-Examiner* and newspapers throughout the United States that carried *Universal Service*. Many times during the next four decades Red would try his hand at writing about the game of football; sometimes he had help, and sometimes he wrote it himself. It would be a way of keeping close to the game.

The following Sunday, the Yankees made it six wins in a row. At Yankee Stadium, 18,000 fans watched Red have his best game of the year against the Boston Bulldogs (2–3). In the first half alone, Red scored three touchdowns— a 5-yard run, a 35-yard run, and a dazzling 55-yard interception return for a score—helping the Yanks cruise to a 24–0 victory. This would be the last game for the Boston Bulldogs, as owner Robert McKirdy, who was a boxing promoter, "threw in the towel." For four straight weeks, the AFL had witnessed the collapse of a franchise due to financial problems. Pyle's league was down to just five teams.

As the AFL plugged along, the Yankees were looking to win a championship. As of November 15, after six straight wins, they were in first place in the AFL standings. The standings were as follows:

New York Yankees, 8–2

Philadelphia Quakers, 5–2

Cleveland Panthers, 3–2 (folded)

Chicago Bulls, 4–3–2

Wilson's Wildcats (Los Angeles), 4–5–1

Boston Bulldogs, 2–4 (folded)
Rock Island Independents, 2–5–1
Brooklyn Horsemen, 1–3 (folded)
Newark Bears, 0–3–2 (folded)

On November 21, the Yankees, at 8–2, hosted George Wilson's Wildcats, at 4–5–1, a team that Red's squad had defeated twice already. On this day, with snow flurries falling, 19,000 fans packed Yankee Stadium. It would be the toughest game of the year for the Yanks, as well as Red. In the first half, the Wildcats scored early and often, taking a commanding 16–0 lead. Then Red suffered a bruised left side after being tackled hard. He would miss the rest of the game. In the second half, the Yankees cut the deficit to 16–6, but they couldn't get any closer. It was their first home loss at Yankee Stadium. That same day, the Rock Island Independents played their last game, a pathetic 3–0 setback against the Chicago Bulls in front of just 1,800 fans at Comiskey Park. It was the fifth team to fold their franchise in Pyle's league. Only four teams—New York, Philadelphia, Chicago, and Los Angeles (all financed by Pyle)—would finish the season.

The Yankees' home loss to the Wildcats snapped the team's six-game winning streak, putting the Yankees (8–3) a game behind the Philadelphia Quakers (6–2). As the schedule shaped up (or by default), the Yankees would play a home-and-home series with the Quakers, on Thursday, November 25, at Yankee Stadium, and Saturday, November 27, in Philly. The AFL was about to crown a champion.

On Thanksgiving Day in New York, Yankee Stadium saw 22,000 fans show up for the AFL's game of the year. They would see the best team in the AFL win. What they didn't see was Red Grange play. Because of the injury suffered to his left side, Red was unable to enter the game. The Yankees rallied around their fallen star to go toe-to-toe with the Quakers, but it wasn't enough, as they lost to the Quakers, 13–10. Two days later, the Quakers won another tough one, 13–6, while Red sat out again. The Philadelphia Quakers would win the 1926 AFL championship with an 8–2 record. At the end of the day, the Quakers were the better team.

The final game of the AFL season was played on December 12, as Red returned to Chicago to play the Bulls. "I never felt better in my life. Put it down now that I'll show the Bulls more heels than they ever saw before on one man. I feel it will be a bitter game, and the score will be close, but the Yanks are out to win," said Red to the *Chicago American*.[22] In front of 8,000 fans at Comiskey Park, the last game of the 1926 AFL was won by the Yankees, 7–3. The season bankrupted Joey Sternaman. "We actually had a pretty good team, but we didn't get the crowds," Sternaman recalled in a 1983 interview. "We sure tried. But everywhere in that league it was tough. We had plenty of big names and fellows who tried to make it work. But it went under at the end of the year. I came out broke after it; it was a bum gamble."[23]

The Yankees ended up playing 15 AFL games, finishing with a 10–5 mark, good for second place behind the Quakers. They outscored their opponents 212–82, becoming the top-scoring team in the league. Eddie Tryon outplayed Red on the field, leading the AFL in scoring, with 72 points. Joey Sternaman was second (52) and Red third (50). The teams in the AFL were undercapitalized, and when the league didn't capture the fan's interest, the owners—meaning Pyle—couldn't cover the promised salaries. A particularly rainy autumn compounded the problem. Plus, most of the teams in the AFL weren't very good. They had been hastily assembled, lacked acceptable linemen, and were badly coached. The games, although often close, were always low-scoring or dull affairs.

Most of the problems that afflicted the AFL were also present in the NFL. Talent was spread thin, and most of the 22 teams were weaklings. The traveling Louisville Colonels didn't score a point in their four league games, and Hammond scored only a field goal in their four contests. Neither those two teams nor Racine or Milwaukee finished the season. Akron, Brooklyn, Canton, Columbus, Dayton, Detroit, and Hartford limped to the end.

Ernie Nevers's Eskimos drew fans here and there but not enough to offset the heavy losses for even the stronger teams. Tim Mara's Giants, going directly against Grange's Yankees, reportedly lost $40,000. In Chicago, where three teams squared off, both the Bears and Cardinals were badly hurt. Halas wrote in his autobiography, "I wasn't happy. We were back to the small gates, the search for fans, the pinching of the penny. Mara learned the Red Grange euphoria had vanished. The Giants drew only 3,000 or 4,000. Mara would look through binoculars at Yankee Stadium and say, 'There's no one over there either.'"[24]

Ironically, the NFL had a strong finish to the season. By the end of November, the Bears were undefeated (11–0–2 record) and the Frankford Yellow Jackets had one loss (12–1–1), setting up a winner-take-all game on December 4, when the Yellow Jackets pulled off a 7–6 "miracle" win. Philadelphia added the NFL crown to the AFL's Quakers.

Although it looked like the NFL had won the war against the Grange League, it definitely lost its share of money. "The National League must have lost at least $250,000. I am sure that 11 of its 22 teams lost $150,000 among them. Our club finished the season at least $35,000 in the red," said Jack McDonough, manager of the NFL's Los Angles Buccaneers. "Tim Mara was a heavy loser. Only four clubs in our organization made money, the Philadelphia Yellow Jackets, the Chicago Bears, the Providence Steam Roller, and Green Bay Packers."[25]

Just a year after rejoicing the big crowd of the Grange game, Mara's heavy losses in 1926 made him rethink his involvement in the unpredictable sport of professional football. "Many times my father had second thoughts about football, advancing money, and writing off losses. His friends told him he was foolish to keep the Giants, but he stayed firm, I am sure, because my brother Jack and I were so interested in the sport," remembered Wellington Mara. In the end, Carr's more structured league was better prepared to lose money and still be able to survive than Pyle's AFL. But it also proved to Carr, Mara, and Halas that the franchise—not the star—would guide the league and be the most important property.[26]

After the AFL season was done, Red, Pyle, and the Yankees went on a barnstorming tour throughout the South and West. Trying to capitalize on Red's name and popularity, Pyle was hoping for more big paydays. The Yankees would play against George Wilson's "Pacific Coast All-Stars." The two teams would play five games against one another in five different cities in a span of two weeks.

December 14, at Atlanta, Georgia (tie, 7–7; 4,000 in attendance)
December 16, at Birmingham, Alabama (Yankees won, 14–3; 5,000 in attendance)
December 19, at Dallas, Texas (Yankees won, 17–14; 5,000 in attendance)
December 22, at Beaumont, Texas (Pacific Coast All-Stars won, 34–0; n/a in attendance)
December 26, at San Antonio, Texas (Yankees won, 20–14; 3,000 in attendance)

Red played at least three quarters in each game, giving the fans a chance to see him perform. Most of the games received mixed reviews. One reporter wrote about the Birmingham game, "It was a high-class brand of football that pleased the fans, who evidenced their approval by hearty cheering, and should the pros comeback, even greater number will see them play."[27] About the Atlanta game, the *Atlanta Constitution* wrote, "Two great football teams were seen in action at Spiller's Field Tuesday, and they put out some real football, but give me college football for mine." Red did suffer a left knee injury, causing the tour to cancel a game on Christmas Day in Waco, Texas. He was able to return to the field the next day for the game in San Antonio.[28]

The highlight, or lowlight, of the trip was the arrest of several players in Dallas. At 4:00 a.m. on December 20, just hours after playing a game, Red and three of his Yankees teammates—Ralph Scott, Bill Oliver, and Pooley Hubert—were arrested at their hotel for intoxication and disturbing the peace. Red and his teammates were allegedly making too much noise, and a proprietor at the Ritz Hotel called the police on them. The five men spent three hours in a Dallas jail. Red told the press his teammates were not drunk and that no liquor was found on them. Because of their next game in Beaumont, Red decided to pay the $10 fine for each man, but they declared themselves guilty of nothing more than "maybe making too much noise last night." Red continued, "We had no idea it would turn into such a hullabaloo as this. If we had felt guilty we could easily have given fake names."[29]

After the five games in the South, the tour headed out West. They would have more luck in California. The Yankees would play four games (three in Los Angeles and one in San Francisco). The crowds were much better.

> January 16, at Los Angeles Buccaneers, Wrigley Field (Yankees lost, 30–6; 20,000 in attendance)
>
> January 23, at Hollywood Generals, Wrigley Field (Yankees won, 48–6; 3,000 in attendance)
>
> January 30, at Los Angeles Buccaneers, Wrigley Field (Yankees won, 14–0; 10,000 in attendance)
>
> February 6, at Los Angeles Buccaneers, San Francisco, Ewing Field (Yankees lost, 7–6; 8,500 in attendance)

The West Coast games averaged more than double the games played in the South, almost 10,000 a game, but not quite like the games played by the Red–Bears tour the previous year. Instead of the Coliseum, the three LA games were played at smaller Wrigley Field. The Yankees lost two of the three games to the NFL's Los Angeles Buccaneers, loaded with Western stars, including former University of California All-Americans Harold "Brick" Muller (end) and "Tut" Imlay (quarterback). Red played four nonspectacular games. After one game, Braven Dyer of the *Los Angeles Times* wrote, "Grange's defensive playing was even better than his offensive work. . . . Grange did a lot of good tackling which was not noticed by most of the fans."[30]

After playing 27 games in 1926–1927, the New York Yankees were finally headed home.

22

BACK TO HOLLYWOOD

The Racing Romeo

After a grueling football season Red Grange seemed to have had enough. Talking to reporters in Texas on the Southern leg of the tour he was asked, "What do you think of the future of professional football?" Red vented his frustrations concerning the sport he loved.

> Well, I'm just about disgusted with the whole thing. I've lost money on it this season, and I don't see any chance to get it back. Of course, I'm still on the black side of the ledger because I piled up some dough by making a movie, and I have royalties coming in from several manufacturers who are using my name on their products.
>
> But the future of pro football isn't so bright now. Maybe I'm a little pessimistic because I've been down-hearted over a bad knee that has kept me from showing my real form in our southern barnstorming game. . . . We have our followers, of course, but they're not in the majority, taking football fandom as a whole. Will I play next season? Well it's according to what turns up between now and then. Maybe I'll steer clear of the magnate's part. I've been playing just because of the boys, playing for a guarantee.[1]

After some rest and relaxation in Wheaton, Red was looking forward to seeing the sunshine of California. He would return to Hollywood. FBO would produce Red's second silent movie. His newest film would be far different than his first. For starters, it wasn't a college or football film; it would be a built around auto racing, something that Red was very excited about doing. Once again, Byron Morgan would write the script and Sam Wood would direct. Red's costars were Walter Hiers (Sparks, his best friend), a popular comedian at the time, Trixie Friganza (Aunt Hattie, the aunt of his girlfriend), and Ben Hendricks (Rube Oldham, a rival racer). Red's love interest this time around was the beautiful Jobyna Ralston, a 27-year-old brunette who had become famous for her on-screen chemistry with Harold Lloyd, notably costarring in the popular *The Freshmen*, released in 1925.

Red would play "Red" Walden, a down-on-his-luck racer who owns his own car garage, struggling to make ends meet so that he can marry his girlfriend. The movie was originally titled *The Motor Maniac*, but the title was quickly changed to *The Racing Romeo*. The main plot has Walden losing out in the annual town motor race when Aunt Hattie Wayne and her niece Sally advise him to pay more attention to his garage. Six months later, as he is preparing for marriage to Sally, she breaks a mirror and fears that bad luck will follow. Then Red, driving Aunt Hattie down a country road, crashes into a tree and is sent walking for help; a wild chase follows when Red is given a ride by Sally's maid. Asserting himself, Red prepares to enter the motor sweepstakes against Rube Oldham, a champion driver. Red arouses Sally's jealousy by flirting with Lorraine Blair, the leading lady of a motion picture company, but he wins Sally back when he wins the race.

Red would make sure this time around that he didn't work so hard. "The first summer I did little else besides perform my various chores at the studio and engaged in little or no contact with the film folk," he recalled. "I still worked hard to be sure but began to get into the swing of Hollywood's social whirl. And I loved every minute of it." This time Red, Pyle, and Beans were joined by Ralph Scott, Yankees head coach. Instead of the hotel, the four men rented an elegant 10-room house on fashionable Gramercy Place, replete with a houseboy and cook. Soon, Scott got mad and fired the cook, which Pyle didn't take too kindly to, so he made Scott the full-time cook. He remained on the job the entire stay. The group soon was inoculated into a weekly poker game that included Red, Pyle, Scott, and a group of Hollywood actors. This included Red's costar, Walter Hiers; Tom Gallery; Adolph Menjou; Lloyd Hamilton; and LA-based sportswriter Mark Kelly. The group would stay up all night dealing cards. Red and colleagues were also weekly guests on Sunday nights at the home of Tom Gallery, former actor and sports promoter, and his wife, stunning actress Zasu Pitts, who was mostly known for her role in the hit film *Greed* (1924). Red called these gatherings "shindigs," saying there "was so much fun to be had at those parties we never missed one." Red was definitely enjoying Hollywood more the second time around.[2]

Filming of *The Racing Romeo* began in the early spring of 1927. Red was dead set on trying to race as fast as he could. He would get the best coaching from Hollywood stunt driver Cliff Bergere and racing professionals Babe Stapp, Lou Moore, and Freddie Frame, who would go on to win the Indianapolis 500 in 1932. Famed race car driver Barney Oldfield was also brought in as a technical advisor. "I wanted to do my own stunt driving, but Sam Wood insisted that Cliff Bergere do the dangerous bits. He didn't want to risk the chance of my getting hurt," Red remembered about wanting to do his own driving.

> However, I drove in all the close-up shots. We had some of the fastest cars in the country on hand for *Racing Romeo*, and I got a terrific kick out of getting behind the wheel of those souped-up jobs. I often remained at the track hours after everyone went home in order to take some extra turns on my own.[3]

The majority of the racing scenes were shot at the fairgrounds racetrack at Seaside Park in Ventura, about 60 miles north of Hollywood. Wood had his drivers push the limits while speeding as fast as 65 to 75 miles per hour. "We've got to have that stuff. The races Sunday will be the most thrilling ever staged on a dirt track in California," said Wood to the press. The producers of the film invited fans to watch the racing in Ventura, charging no admission so that they could shoot fan cutaways. Ads appeared in the *Oxnard Press-Courier* encouraging fans to come out to Seaside Park to watch Red Grange drive.[4] One newspaper reported that a crowd of 10,000 fans came out to see a day of racing.[5] Sometimes the driving got intense. One driver, Richard Perry, was injured in a crash when he lost control of his car and careened off the track, plowing through a fence. He suffered a fractured jaw and a cut on his head. Shooting *The Racing Romeo* took more than five weeks. The time flew by for Red.[6]

In the end, *The Racing Romeo* fell flat. It didn't do as well as *One Minute to Play* did at the box office. Red blamed Pyle's contract negotiations with Kennedy for more money, saying they hurt the promotion of the film. It didn't get the red-carpet treatment that *One Minute* received. The reviews were mixed. *Photoplay Magazine* wrote, "Another of the motor maniac yarns where the hero just must win the race. The story is slim, and the comedy gags obvious. The chief claim to your attraction is Red Grange and a cute little pup. Jobyna Ralston is the girl. As you might suppose, this is very poor entertainment."[7]

Variety was much more positive, writing,

> The picture has its best fast stuff in the race scenes, with the speeding cars shot from all angles spewing clouds of dust into the air. Several wrecks are shown, one looking as though it hit the camera shooting. . . . (Red) Grange would have looked

much better in a football picture, but he manages to act more convincingly than you'd expect a football player could.[8]

In all, *The Racing Romeo* was considered a box-office disappointment.

Later in the summer, Red returned home to Wheaton. Football season was right around the corner.

PART V

NFL CAREER (1927–1935)

23

1927 NEW YORK YANKEES

The NFL had won the war but lost lots of money. The league needed to downsize. President Joe F. Carr fought the AFL with more teams and games, and now it was time to cut his losses. The NFL would only field teams that were financially stable—or ones that had owners who could lose money and still survive. That meant franchises in the big cities, similar to Major League Baseball. Carr reduced the NFL from 22 teams to 11. Once that was settled, Carr and the owners, mainly Tim Mara, had to figure out what to do with the Brooklyn franchise. This is where C. C. Pyle comes in, since Cash and Carry still had the most famous football player under contract—for one more year—and the NFL was willing to negotiate. But this time the NFL held all the cards.

Tim Mara intensely disliked Pyle, but Mara was no fool. He knew Pyle still had Red Grange, a football team, and a lease on Yankee Stadium. By taking Pyle into the NFL, Mara could put a leash on him. As an outsider, Pyle could have scheduled independent teams throughout season for Yankee Stadium, cutting into attendance for Mara's Giants, but once inside the NFL Pyle was stuck with whatever Mara wanted him to do. In mid-August, the two groups met at Saratoga Springs Racetrack to discuss the matter. Mara, Pyle, AFL president Bill Edwards, and, by request of Carr, William Veeck, president of the Chicago Cubs, attended the meeting. The four men hammered out an agreement for Pyle's team to join the NFL.

Mara dominated the discussion, as the two men agreed to pretty much everything he wanted. The Yankees would be kept out of New York and on the road, playing only one date in New York at the same time as his Giants. The Giants and Yankees would then play a home-and-home series on December

4 and December 11. In 1927, the New York Yankees became the NFL's 12th team. Newspaper reports called it a "merger" of the NFL and AFL, and while technically correct, the only team to join was Pyle's Yankees. Some of the players from the AFL's Chicago Bulls were divided among the Cardinals and Bears. Joey Sternaman returned to the Bears. George Wilson was signed by the Providence Steam Roller, while the New York Giants inked a trio of AFL free agents: Century Milstead (Philadelphia Quakers), Doug Wycoff (Newark Bears), and Al Nesser (Cleveland Panthers). The three men would help Mara's squad to the top of the NFL standings in 1927. Other stars who signed with the NFL were Bull Behman (Philadelphia Quakers) with the Frankford Yellow Jackets; Duke Slater (Rock Island) with the Chicago Cardinals; and Red's good buddy, Earl Britton, with the Dayton Triangles. But the biggest signing in the NFL was Michigan's All-American quarterback, Benny Friedman, who joined the Cleveland Bulldogs. The 5-foot-10, 180-pound Cleveland native went home to play pro ball. He would take the league by storm, throwing for 11 touchdowns and bringing the forward pass as a first-down weapon to the pros.

As for the AFL, it lasted only one year. Throughout history the league has been called the "Grange League" because of the involvement of football's most famous player; however, both Red and C. C. Pyle should get credit for starting the league, and both men should also share the blame for its failure. Pyle did not think it through and was ill-equipped to organize and run a pro football league. He failed to recruit financially stable owners; overspent on a league president (Edwards did not get all his money); and, once again, scheduled way too many games. Some of the teams had good players (Red, Wilson, Joey Sternaman, Ray Flaherty, Duke Slater, Doug Wycoff), but the weather also hindered attendance. The only games that were a success were those contested by Red's Yankees and the Quakers. Rock Island, Newark, Boston, and Brooklyn were poor choices. As for Red, he trusted Pyle too much on this venture. He spent some of his own money organizing the Yankees and lost most of it. If he wanted his own team, he should have done a better job of dealing with the NFL rather than bulldozing the league.

Red was back in the NFL. He was 24 years old and at the height of his physical abilities. He once again put in more than a month on the ice wagon to get himself into shape for the long season. Who knew this would be his last summer working as the "Wheaton Iceman."

Before he left for training camp, Red received some good news about his brother. Garland was finally healthy enough to play football. With his shoulder completely healed, he would play his senior year for Bob Zuppke at Illinois. Red was very proud of his younger brother, always instilling confidence in him and building up his self-esteem. It wasn't easy being the brother of Red Grange. "I don't see why he shouldn't be a great football player. He has a swell build, he can run the hundred in 10.1, and he has the finest hands you'd want to see. I know just how big he is, for he wears all my clothes," laughed Red to the press. He continued,

> And if anybody ever had intestinal strength, Pinkey has. When we were kids he used to tackle guys in the neighborhood that I didn't care to run into. That was when we played on a corner lot across the street. Garland's hands are his great asset, and he can pass mighty accurately. His hands are about the biggest I have ever seen, much bigger than mine. The baseball managers that cry for men with big hands should see Garland's claws.[1]

Most of the 1926 New York Yankees backfield returned for the new season, with Red, "Bullet" Baker, Wes Fry, Larry Marks, and Eddie Tryon back in the fold. At end, Red Maloney returned, along with linemen Mike Michalske, Bill Oliver, Dick Hall, and player-coach Ralph Scott. Red and Pyle then looked to upgrade the roster. They quickly signed a few players from some of the defunct AFL teams, including star end Ray Flaherty (Wilson's Wildcats), guard Ray Stephens (Wilson's Wildcats), and center Louie Kolls (Rock Island Independents). They also signed three key rookies from the college ranks: Montana halfback "Wild" Bill Kelly, St. Mary's guard Fritz Kramer, and University of Southern California end Morris "Red" Badgro. Red felt good that he had a quality team that could compete with any NFL team.

The Yankees played their first-ever NFL game against the Dayton Triangles in Dayton. The Triangles were a founding member of the NFL in 1920, but the team had fallen on hard times, winning only three games in the past three seasons. They were mainly a traveling team, as their game with the Yankees would be their only home game in 1927. Triangles manager Carl Storck had posted ads for the game in both local papers, selling tickets ranging from $.50 for children to $1.00 for general admission and $2.50 for box seats.[2]

The attraction of Red Grange induced a rather large crowd of 6,000 fans to come out to Triangle Park. Red lined up at his normal left halfback position. Facing off against his good buddy Earl Britton, the game was a close one. In the second quarter, Britton kicked a 40-yard field goal to give the Triangles a 3–0 lead. Then, midway through the third quarter, halfback "Bullet" Baker returned a punt 72 yards to the Triangles 2-yard line. Two plays later, Wes Fry plowed over for the game-winning score.

The 1–0 Yankees proceeded to win back-to-back games against the Cleveland Panthers and Buffalo Bisons, setting up the game of the year for Red Grange. His Yankees would play the Chicago Bears in Chicago. It would be the first time Red would play against his former team. It also would be the game that would end the legend of the Galloping Ghost. Heading into the game, both teams were undefeated, the Yankees at 3–0 and the Bears at 2–0. George Halas's squad was coming off a tough 7–6 victory against the Green Bay Packers. They were excited about playing against Red.

The city of Chicago was also ready for the big matchup. The *Chicago Tribune* and *New York Times* reported a crowd of 30,000 fans at Wrigley Field. The Bears outplayed the Yankees the entire game. In the second quarter, Paddy Driscoll, even at the age of 32, showed his greatness by scoring on a touchdown run. Instead of taking the ball, the Yankees decided to kick off to the Bears. Driscoll took the kickoff deep into Yankees territory, where Red made a touchdown-saving tackle, but that was futile, as Bill Senn scored a few plays later. The Bears' 12–0 lead held up into the fourth quarter.[3]

Then the unthinkable happened. With the game seemingly out of reach, the Yankees tried to mount a drive. Eddie Tryon heaved a pass downfield for Red. "We were playing in a game against, of all teams, the Chicago Bears at Wrigley Field," Grange told author Richard Whittingham in 1984.

> I had my cleats dug into the ground, and it was a kind of wet day and somebody fell over my knee. It was nothing deliberate, just one of those things. I was hit from the side by somebody (George Trafton), and boom, out went my knee. Knees and shoulders, those were the two places a ballplayer got hurt the most seriously in those days. After the injury I was just another halfback.[4]

Red was carried off the field. "The stands cheered and hundreds formed lines between which the Yankee leader was hurried to the dressing room," wrote the *New York Times*.[5] No more would Red be able to go 80 yards consistently in one sprint to thrill fans. On October 16, 1927, at Wrigley Field, where Red had played his first pro game, the Galloping Ghost as a runner died. After the doctor examined his knee, Red was told that he had torn a tendon. Although Red knew the injury was serious, he never blamed his former teammate for the hit. "It was one of the cleanest football games I ever played in," said Red on the trainer's table after the game. For the rest of his life, he would talk about Trafton's hit as being part of the game, always taking the high road.[6]

The torn tendon in his right knee made it almost impossible for Red to walk. He was given a cane to use. "For years I longed to carry a cane. But I was too shy," proclaimed Red to the press. "Now I can carry one, but I'm not so keen about the condition which makes it necessary. A torn tendon is bad."[7] The Yankees lost not only the game to the Bears, but also their star attraction.

The next game was in Green Bay against the 4–1 Packers. Red would dress in his football uniform but would not play. He limped around the field with the use of his cane. Surprisingly, 11,000 fans came out to see the matchup. It would be the largest crowd to see a Packers home game up to that point. (The previous high of 7,000 was achieved twice, on October 18, 1925, versus Rock Island and September 26, 1926, versus the Bears.) In their first five home games of 1927, the Packers averaged just 4,420 fans, with a high of 5,500 for the Bears game on October 2. They doubled their average for Red's Yankees. Red's star power was still evident, especially in Green Bay, a city that hadn't had the opportunity to see Red, even the nonplaying version. Red's only appearance on the field was walking out to midfield during halftime to be introduced to the crowd. As for the game, the hometown Packers took it to the visiting Yankees, shutting them out, 13–0. In the next day's *Green Bay Press Gazette*, the paper ran a photo of Red wearing his Yankees sideline jacket walking with his cane in his right hand, head bowed. The caption read, "Poor Old Red."[8]

After suffering consecutive losses, and losing Red to injury, the Yankees rebounded with a tough 7–6 victory against the Chicago Cardinals (2–2). The following week, Red would miss his third straight game, a 15–0 setback against the Cleveland Bulldogs. Benny Friedman tossed a pair of touchdowns. Two days later, the sometimes offbeat scheduling of the NFL reared its ugly head again as the Yankees were preparing for their rematch against the Bears. The game would be played on Tuesday, November 8, this time at Yankee Stadium. It would be the Yanks' first home game of the season—as Tim Mara made sure that Pyle's team did not invade his territory for almost two months.

The Bears were still unbeaten, at 5–0–1, while the Yankees were just 4–3. Red wasn't about to miss this game. Although he did not start, he did replace "Bullet" Baker at left halfback in the second and fourth quarters. With their backs against the wall, the Yankees would play their best game of the season. The first half saw the two teams go back and forth, trading touchdowns until Ray Flaherty took over. He caught three touchdown passes to give the Yankees a convincing 26–6 victory. Red, who would mainly start at quarterback for the rest of the season, wasn't asked to run the ball at all. He would contribute as a passer. Red played his best game of the season so far, providing a spark on offense and playing great on defense.

Following their big victory against the Bears, Red's Yankees played two games in three days, winning both—defeating the Pottsville Maroons, 19–12, on

Friday, November 11, in Pottsville, and easily beating the Chicago Cardinals, 20–6, on Sunday, November 13, at Yankee Stadium. Eddie Tryon scored three of the Yankees' six touchdowns in the two wins. The Yankees were now an impressive 7–3, only two games out of first place.

But the team was getting beat up, as the heavy scheduling was taking its toll. Red was still limping badly on his bum right knee, while "Bullet" Baker had sore ribs and Tryon was carried off the field against the Cardinals. Pyle could see that Red needed more rest when he was diagnosed with "water on the knee." He needed his star attraction on the field to make sure fans continued to come out for the games. They had 11 days before their next game. During that time, Red had his right knee put in a plaster cast that extended from the middle of his thigh to his calf. He was stuck in bed at his hotel for most of this time, as Dr. John Lawlor, the team physician, monitored him.

On Thanksgiving Day, November 24, the Yankees faced off for the third time against Benny Friedman's Cleveland Bulldogs. The two teams had split the previous two games. A nice crowd of 15,000 showed up at Yankee Stadium— much better than the turnout in Chicago for the Cardinals–Bears game (6,000 fans), or at Frankford Stadium for the Yellow Jackets–Packers contest (9,000), or at tiny Minersville Park for the Pottsville Maroons–Providence Steam Roller matchup (4,000). This game would finish the Yankees' season.

The hometown crowd saw the Yanks jump out on top early. A Kelly touchdown run was quickly followed by a Tryon fumble recovery of a Friedman muffed punt for a score. The Yankees were up, 13–0. But it was downhill after that. The Bulldogs scored 30 unanswered points, and a late Yankees touchdown made the final score 30–19.

Red's boys would never recover from the loss. They would not win another game the rest of the season. Even with five games remaining, the Yankees were out of the championship race. They would lose back-to-back games against the Providence Steam Roller (14–7, 9–0, respectively) scoring only one touchdown. On December 4, the Yankees played their first game in a home-and-home series with the crosstown New York Giants. Tim Mara's squad was the best team in the NFL, with a 9–1–1 record. Plus, Mara again wanted to stick it to C. C. Pyle.

A disappointing crowd of just 10,000 fans—with Babe Ruth and Lou Gehrig in the stands—came out for the event. On the opening kickoff, halfback Hinkey Haines returned the kick 75 yards for a score. The Yankees were done, losing 14–0. A week later, the Giants won the rematch, 13–0, at Yankee Stadium, in front of just 8,000 fans. The Giants finished the season as NFL champions, with an 11–1–1 record. "Last year I lost $69,000. We are going into the last game of the season even to play," said Tim Mara to the local press. He was happier that he beaten Pyle's team twice.[9]

The Yankees limped to the end, finishing in sixth place in the NFL standings, with a 7–8–1 mark. Red had also limped to the end of the football season. Feeling the pressure of having to play in games for the gate to be in the black, his knee never fully recovered. He made it worse. Instead of calling it quits after the NFL season, Red and Pyle agreed to play a few barnstorming games on the West Coast to try and make up for some of the money that had been lost during the season.

After a game in Stockton, California, the rest of the tour consisted of a round-robin schedule of games with four teams: Red Grange's Yankees, George Wilson's Wildcats, Benny Friedman's Bulldogs, and the Tut Imlay–Ernie Nevers Giants. Red's Yankees would play six games—two at Ewing Field in San Francisco and four at Wrigley Field in Los Angeles.

Meeting on Sundays for six straight weeks, the play lacked offensive fireworks, as most of the games saw only one or two touchdowns scored. The play was somewhat uninspiring, as crowds of roughly 10,000 West Coast fans watched pro football again.

As for Red, he must have spent most of his free time in California thinking about his future—a future without football.

24

OUT OF FOOTBALL

Red's 1927 season ended badly—about as bad as it could get—while Garland's senior year at Illinois was much more successful. Red's younger brother had filled out physically, standing six feet tall and weighing 170 pounds; he had shown Coach Zuppke that he was worth the wait. Wearing Illini jersey number 22, he started every game at end, helping Illinois to a 7–0 record and winning the Big Ten championship. As for Red, he had his worst year playing football. He mostly limped through 13 NFL games and scored one measly touchdown. Playing several months with a torn tendon in his right knee, he made the injury worse. It would cost him the 1928 season.

After finishing the football season on the West Coast, Red decided to stay in Los Angeles to help his manager with his next big promotional event. Pyle had come up with the idea of a cross-country race from Los Angeles to New York involving runners who would be pushed to their physical limits to achieve this incredible feat. He called it "C. C. Pyle's International-Transcontinental Footrace." The race would cover 3,400 miles, and each day the runners would travel roughly 30 or 40 miles, making daily stops in different cities throughout the United States—the runners would run, jog, or walk, or any combination of the three, to make it to the next assigned stop. At the end of each stage, the runners' times would be recorded by the race official. The daily times then would be added together to make a cumulative time. The runner with the lowest total time into New York would be declared the winner. Along the way, Pyle would sell programs for 25 cents and other souvenirs to make money.

The winner would get $25,000, with second place getting $10,000, third $5,000, fourth $2,500, and fifth through tenth $1,000 each. The total purse was

$48,500. On March 4, the assistant race director, Red Grange, lit the starting firecracker to begin the race. As many as 100,000 spectators lined the route to see the 199 runners begin their journey to New York. "Today the eyes of the world are watching the greatest, most stupendous athletic accomplishment in all history," declared C. C. Pyle.[1]

For the next three months, Red would accompany Pyle on his foot race throughout the country—a race the press called the "Bunion Derby." They would travel in style. Pyle would make sure of that. Grange told Myron Cope in *The Game That Was*,

> He went up to Oakland to a bus company and had a bus custom made for $25,000. I've never seen anything like it. It slept eight or nine. He had a shower bath and a galley and berths and a radio. It was the most palatial thing you ever saw, and that was the way we traveled from Los Angeles to New York.[2]

The "cruising coach" was constructed by the Fageol Motors Company in Oakland. Reports said that Pyle paid $25,000 for the luxury vehicle. Red's main job was getting spectators out to watch in each city. He brought star power to the "show." As runners struggled through the grueling race, Pyle was losing money. The programs didn't sell as well as he thought they would. After 84 days, the race limped into New York, with only 55 runners completing the challenge. Andy Payne, a 20-year-old from Oklahoma, was the winner—finishing the race in 573 hours, 4 minutes, 34 seconds. "Say, maybe you think I ain't glad this thing is over," said Red to the *United Press*. "I never was so tired of anything in my life. They nearly ran me crazy in the small towns. I'm going back to Wheaton for a little rest as soon as this crazy thing is over." Red didn't even run in the race but was tired from the experience.[3]

While in New York, Red had one more thing to take care of before heading back to Wheaton. Red's three-year contract with Pyle had expired in March 1928, so he and Pyle had a serious heart-to-heart meeting in the Big Apple. Red had decided on his future. The two men, who had been linked together for the past four years, mutually agreed to go their separate ways. The two released a joint statement to the press: "We are severing our business relations under the friendliest feelings. Our contract has expired. We have various interests to look after personally and therefore deem it inadvisable to sign a new agreement."[4]

Red also announced his football plans for 1928: "Grange had retired permanently from football owing to the condition of his knee. He feels he does not care to play unless he can give the public his best."[5]

Red had always cherished his relationship with Pyle, never once voicing a bad word, even when others spoke negatively of his manager. Pyle had always been honest with Red, as well as fulfilled his promise of getting the youngster money if he left school to play pro football. Pyle had his flaws—using Red to make money being one of them—but he never treated Red unfairly. Although they didn't see one another often in the ensuing years, the two men remained friends for life. "He was a fellow you would like," said Red to author Myron Cope in 1970. "The greatest mixer, a great storyteller. He loved to sit around and have a drink with anyone. A loveable guy. I never met anyone who did not like Charley Pyle. He was a great guy to have on our side. He was a good-time guy. They don't make 'em that way anymore."[6]

Pyle moved on to other money-making promotions—conducting a second transcontinental race and promoting professional tennis with French star Suzanne Lenglen—but he would never make it back to the top once he stopped being Red's manager. He was always losing money.

In addition to walking away from Pyle, Red also made a decision about his football future. He was done. His knee wasn't responding to rest or anything else for that matter. He knew he couldn't compete the way he wanted to, so he decided to walk away. "In those days we did not have the know-how of operating on knees as they do today," said Red in a 1978 interview. "And I was told I might never walk again if I was operated on. So, I never took the chance." If playing in 2019, Red would have had surgery on the knee and been back in the game in six to 12 months, no big deal. But in 1928, that was not an option. Surgery was thought of as a last resort, a risky procedure, especially for an athlete. Red was much better playing on a bum knee rather than having surgery. He simply stepped away from football.[7]

Red returned to Wheaton. He became reacquainted with Frank Zambreno, the theater manager and Pyle's good friend, who set up Red with his next job. Acting as Red's representative, Zambreno was able to get his client a role on a vaudeville tour for the fall of 1928. Instead of Hollywood, Red turned to the stage. He joined a vaudeville group that would travel the next nine months, performing an original skit focused on the ex-football star. First titled 77, then changed to *Come On, Red*, the stage show featured a number of performers, college girls, songs, and musicians. The entire program would last twenty minutes, performed right before the main motion picture was shown.

The program was broken into three scenes. For his first appearance on the stage, Red is greeted by a flock of girls in college outfits, with a college campus background. His second appearance on stage finds him disheartened because for some reason he is out of the game. One of the college boys comes running on stage, telling Red to hurry up and get in the game, as the team is losing and in need of his help. For his third appearance, Red is seen running, making a touchdown, and winning the game. "Tricky lights made this scene go over," wrote the *Exhibitors Herald and Moving Picture World*. In between Red's appearances were songs, dancing, and other entertainment, with Red sometimes joining the other actors. After the program, Red entertained the audience for a few minutes, telling stories about football and his Hollywood experiences. On the tour he would work with such vaudeville music stars as Paul Ash, Mark Fisher, Al Morey, Joane Gaylord, Harriett Hutchins, and Evelyn Zambreno, the daughter of Frank Zambreno. The tour would take Red to major cities in the East and Midwest.[8] Cities included on the 1928–1929 *Come On, Red* tour were as follows:

Boston, MA (August)
Stanford, CT (August)
Hartford, CT (September)
New Haven, CT (September)
New York, NY (September)
Indianapolis, IN (October)
Chicago, IL (October–November)
St. Louis, MO (November)
Detroit, MI (December)
Cedar Rapids, IA (January)
Brooklyn, NY (February–April)
Philadelphia, PA (April)

The show was popular in most cities, but reviews were mixed. For the New York show at the Auburn Theater, *Variety* wrote, "With the football season here, Grange ought to draw in the neighborhoods. His personality and appearance are in his favor, and a talk at the close on his Hollywood experience had the audience forgetting the thin act. If they can induce Grange to lecture before city high school squads it ought to increase his b.o. (box office) value."[9]

For the Detroit show, *Exhibitors Herald and Moving Picture World* wrote,

Without criticizing Red too much, it might be said that he gets along better on the football gridiron than on the stage, and he has sense enough to realize it. So he contents himself, in the main, with wearing his football togs and letting the audience get a look at him as he was in the days of his All-American fame.[10]

The biggest shows were in Chicago, as the tour performed for three weeks at five different Balaban & Katz theaters in the Windy City: the Oriental, Paradise, Harding, Norshore, and the Tower. *Variety* reported that the show at the Oriental Theatre made $44,000 (*Docks of New York* was the headline movie). "Hard to guess just how much of it Grange drew, but apparently he was responsible for some," wrote *Variety*. Another review of the Chicago show performed at the Oriental went as follows:

> Grange personally may be let down as a performer. Histrionic talents not usually expected of athletic heroes, especially those whose stage experience is as limited as that of Grange. Considering this, Grange makes a well-formed impression on general conduct, while not scoring any touchdowns with his talk and a few light steps with a girl. He does not attempt vocalizing.
>
> As a drawing card Grange's name should attract. In his first appearance at the Oriental, no question but that some edge must come off with Paul Ash the kingpin in this house and also a redhead. Ash gave a showmanlike performance with this show and did his utmost to put Grange over, while not forgetting the others. He left little for himself but satisfied.[11]

The *Chicago American* wrote, "The college show supplied as the background for Red's activities isn't anything to rave about, but he isn't a half-bad actor and so it all goes over."[12] Once, in between curtain calls in Chicago, Red thought about the game he loved.[13] "Sometimes I think I'd like to play one more game, and sometimes I'm not so sure," he said. "But I suppose I'll wind up by crashing into a game sometimes before the season is up. My leg that was hurt in a professional game last fall is all right, and I am in good condition."[14]

While performing on stage, Red had his most trying time. In late October, he was arrested on a paternity charge. A former coat clerk at the Morrison Hotel accused Red of fathering her child. Helen Flozek (née Morrissey), a 22-year-old woman with black hair and a round face, was already married with one child. Her husband had deserted her and she was desperate. Because she had briefly met Red at the Morrison, she tried to carry out a scheme to get money. She named her seven-month-old child, who happened to have flaming red hair, Haroldine, although Red's hair was an auburn tint.

From the start Red denied the charge. He knew it was a money-making scheme. Grange commented,

> There is nothing in this case but an attempt at blackmail. The only knowledge I have of this case comes from the representative of a women attorney who visited me that the girl was hard up and would settle for $800. I am told that this girl was

an employee of the Morrison Hotel during the period I was stopping there. If so she is just one of a large number of employees with whom I had merely a chance acquaintance. I will fight it most strenuously, in order to vindicate my reputation. I want the right to be unmolested by people seeking easy money.[15]

Mrs. Mary B. Quinn, an aunt acting as Flozek's attorney, put Red on the defense. "I told him that under the law a paternity case could be settled out of court for $800, but that if fatherhood was proved in court it would cost him $1,100." Everything about Flozek came across as desperate.[16]

Red left the charge up to his attorneys, knowing he did nothing wrong. According to the Grange family, this was not a happy time for Red. "Those newspapers reports and charges were simply not true," said Linda Thomas, niece of Red Grange. In the end, Flozek got her money. Red paid $900 for the case to be dismissed.

As Red continued on his vaudeville tour that fall, Pyle's New York Yankees were grinding through a football season without their superstar player. The 1928 Yankees finished with a 4–8–1 record and a seventh-place finish in the NFL (out of 10 teams). On December 16, Pyle finally got the last word against Tim Mara, as his Yankees defeated the Giants, 7–6, at Yankee Stadium. It would be the last football game Pyle would ever be involved in. After the season he would turn in his franchise to the league.[17]

When the vaudeville tour stopped in Detroit, Red found another avenue to make additional income. Since he would be spending two weeks in the Motor City performing at the Capitol and Fisher theaters, he was asked by the *Detroit Free Press* to write a series of football articles. Assisted by Harry Bullion, sports editor of the *Free Press*, Red wrote a summary of the past football season, gave his opinion on several football topics, and selected an All-American team. From December 8 to December 21, Red contributed 13 articles for the *Free Press*.

Red enjoyed sitting down every day with Bullion at the *Free Press* offices to put his thoughts on the game he loved on paper. He clearly was missing the sport. His articles were a hit with Detroit readers. Writing to young football players he opined,

Work is the secret of success in football. As in any line of endeavor the most important element to determine success or failure is the amount of effort given. Anyone hoping to become a star of the first magnitude in the football world must resign himself to plenty of work.

Before ending I would like again to advise the youngster on football. As I said in an earlier article hard work is the principal element. Obey your coach. He has been through the mill and knows how to handle each situation. Drill at all phases of the game. Learn the fundamentals and then learn the technique of each play. And when a little success comes your way don't get the swell head. It will do you more harm than anything else.[18]

After nine months on the vaudeville tour, Red was finally ready to take a break. He had worked hard to make a living. One newspaper reported that Red was getting $2,500 a week for appearing on stage. In his autobiography, Red declared,

> I was deeply concerned about the prospect of being washed up as a player but managed to keep my mind temporarily off my troubles by going on a vaudeville tour that Frank Zambreno lined up for me. I did a football skit that was given the corny title *Come On, Red*. The act was given top billing all over the circuit, and I earned a nice piece of change for my efforts.[19]

By the summer of 1929, Red was at another crossroads in his life. This time an old friend would help him get back into the game he loved.

25

HALAS BRINGS BACK THE GHOST

Bouncing around in show business wasn't what Red truly wanted to do. Although he liked the challenge of performing in front of an audience, he always seemed to be a fish out of water with his acting skills. He missed the game he loved. The fall of 1928 saw Red without football for the first time since he was a youngster back in Wheaton. He craved getting back on the field but didn't have the confidence. He needed someone to believe in him. That man—the man who signed Red to his first pro contract—would soon knock on his door.

Deep down, Red wanted to prove to himself that he could make it in pro ball. He had not played up to his standards. He wanted to give it another try, and George Halas gave him that opportunity. Halas had heard that Red was thinking about playing football again. That's all he needed to hear. Through Frank Zambreno, the Bears owner wanted to meet with his former player. At first Red was reluctant to put the pads back on. He thought he had nothing to offer. "I finally went to see George and, much to my surprise, found him very enthusiastic about the prospect of my returning to the Bears as a player," recalled Red.[1] Halas knew that fans would still come out to see the Galloping Ghost play. "I realized he would no longer gallop for touchdowns, but I liked his intelligence, his determination, and his desire. I thought he still had a great contribution to make to football. Too, there was still magic in the Grange name," remembered Halas.[2] "In spite of my doubts I agreed to give it a whirl, for deep down I wanted to get back into football in the worse way," Red said.[3]

In the summer of 1929, instead of working on the ice wagon, Red headed back to Hollywood. Zambreno had negotiated a deal that would have Red back in the movies, starring in a talkie. Or so he thought. This time around Red only brought his father with him to California. He thought the sunshine would help his father relax and adjust to not working a job for once in his life following his retirement from police work. Father and son would spend quality time together. As for the movie deal, it was not set in stone. The producers had difficulty final-izing the story, which was to be entitled *The Varsity Show*. With more free time on his hands, Red continued to get treatment for, and advice on, his bum right knee. After a year and half of limping around, Red finally caught a break. He remembered dealing with his bad limb:

> I walked on crutches for eight months. The doctors would tell you that if they operated, they couldn't guarantee anything, and you might have a stiff leg or not even be able to walk again. I went to doctors coast to coast. One of them put my leg in a barrel of ice. Another fellow put it in a cast. All of those doctors told me to stay off it.
>
> So that's what I did. It puffed up. I had water on it. But finally, I got out to Los Angeles, still getting around on crutches, and went to a Dr. Spencer. He said, "Do you play golf?" I said, "Well, I hack around a little." And he said, "I want you to go out and play golf." I told him I couldn't even walk, that I was on crutches, but he said, "I don't care if you're on four pairs of crutches. Go out and start playing golf. If you don't use that knee, you'll never walk again."
>
> So, I went out and hobbled around the golf course, and inside of a few months I was walking fairly good again.[4]

Red's inactivity had hampered his recovery. He would hit the links to get better. While playing golf in Los Angeles, Red was sometimes joined by col-lege coaches Bill Spaulding (Charles Welden's old college coach) of UCLA and Howard Jones of the University of Southern California, as the trio would tee it up often at the California County Club. Said Grange,

> I need the outdoor exercise. At the studio they had me stripped to the waist, shoe-ing a horse, for a publicity shot, but that's too dangerous. I might put the shoe on the wrong foot. As long as I play golf with men who shoot as well as Jones and Spaulding doing the training isn't apt to be dangerous unless I should hit myself in back of the head with one of my own hooked drives.[5]

During one outing on August 3, Jones shot an 83, Spaulding an 84, and Red a 95. Red was feeling "content," according to Braven Dyer of the *Los Angeles Times*, who followed the foursome, which also included Fay Coleman, the country club's best golfer, who shot a "snappy 74."[6]

After a few months of waiting, Red decided to head back home to get ready for the football season. He would leave Hollywood with no movie deal. The trip wasn't a total waste, however, as golfing had helped Red's knee heal enough that he gained the confidence to play football again. Still, the redhead was nervous. He hadn't played football in a year and didn't know if the knee would hold up. He was eager to prove himself.

Red also helped his younger brother get into pro football by convincing Halas to sign Garland to a contract with the Bears. It would be the first time Red would get to play organized football with his brother. Because of their age difference, and his shoulder injury, Garland never got the chance to play with Red in high school or at Illinois. This would be a special time for the Grange boys. In his autobiography, Red recalled how Garland was as a player on the field:

> My brother was an entirely different type of personality on the football field than I. While I was a quiet sort of player who could feel it inside, he could stimulate the entire team with his enthusiasm. He breathed fire and brimstone, and before a game we almost wanted to tie him up for fear he might go out on the field and kill somebody.[7]

As player-coach, George Halas guided his Bears to a 7–5–1 record in 1928, fifth place in the NFL standings. After the season, Papa Bear retired as a player. Red was joining a Bears team that included some familiar faces: a 34-year-old Paddy Driscoll, who was playing in his final season in the NFL; quarterback Joey Sternaman; halfback Laurie Walquist; center George Trafton; tackle Don Murry; and guard Bill Fleckenstein. Other returning Bears players were backs Roy White and Bill Senn, and newly signed veteran end Cookie Cunningham.

Aside from Garland, Halas and Dutch Sternaman signed a few more promising rookies who would contribute for the next several years. Because the NFL didn't have a draft, each team was free to sign whomever they wanted for the most money. Fullback Walt Holmer (6-foot-0, 185 pounds) and end Luke Johnsos (6-foot-2, 195 pounds) came from nearby Northwestern, while tackle Packie Nelson (5-foot-11, 205 pounds) had played for Bob Zuppke at Illinois. Guard Jules "Zuck" Carlson (6-foot-0, 208 pounds) arrived from Oregon State, center Bert Pearson (6-foot-0, 206 pounds) from Kansas State, and guard Joe Kopcha (6-foot-0, 220 pounds) from Tennessee-Chattanooga. These seven rookies would play a combined 33 years for the Bears.

At 26 years old, Red was back with the Bears. Competing at training camp in early September, he felt right at home; this was where he was supposed to be. Knowing he couldn't cut and swerve like he used to, Red showed off his pure speed for Halas. He could still run. Halas also asked Red to work on his passing skills. He wanted to use Red more as a passer than a runner. Red usually started the game at left halfback, playing the first and fourth quarters, while Garland was a substitute end, replacing Cunningham midway through each game.

The Bears' first game, on September 22, was against the Minneapolis Red Jackets in Madison, Wisconsin. A crowd of 6,000 fans watched Red and Garland play their first NFL game together. Red put on his Bears number 77 jersey for the first time since the famous barnstorming tour. It felt nice to pull it over his shoulder pads again. After trailing 6–0 at the half, the Bears turned on the offensive power to coast to a 19–6 victory.

The following week, the Bears traveled to Green Bay to play the Packers (1–0). Some 12,000 fans—the most ever to see a Packers game—packed City Stadium. Because he missed playing in Green Bay in 1927 with the Yankees, Red asked to speak to the crowd via the PA system. "He said he was glad of the opportunity to play in Green Bay and hoped that the best team would win," wrote the *Green Bay Press-Gazette*. It would be a historic year for the Packers, as they would win their first NFL championship in 1929, setting the stage for a remarkable three-year run as NFL champion. On this day, they rolled to an easy 23–0 victory.[8]

After defeating the Red Jackets for the second time in three weeks in a 7–6 win, the Bears played their fourth straight road game, this time facing the Buffalo Bisons at Bison Stadium in front of 5,200 fans. For the first time all season, Red helped his team find the end zone. In the second quarter, he threw a touchdown pass to Bill Senn, as the Bears won, 16–0, to improve their record to 3–1. Then the Bears hit a wall, winning only one more game the entire season. After playing a 0–0 tie against the crosstown Chicago Cardinals in front of a nice crowd of 20,000 at Wrigley Field, the Bears faced off against the Red Jackets for a third time. It would be a historic game for the Grange family. Just like the previous two games, the Bears rolled over the Red Jackets, winning 27–0, but it was a play in the fourth quarter that made Lyle Grange the proudest. The Bears' final touchdown of the game came courtesy of a Red Grange touchdown pass to Garland. This would be the only time they would connect on a scoring pass in their NFL careers.

The following day, the *Chicago Daily News* recap of the game had the headline, "Grange Plays Brilliantly at Wrigley Field." The paper continued, "The galloping Red did about everything one expects him to do, including brilliant broken field running, accurate pass tossing, and excellent catching of teammates' passes. It was he who placed the ball where his teammates carried it over." The *Chicago Evening Post* wrote, "There were many fine executions of grid ball by the Bears, but the brotherly act of Red and Garland Grange far excelled in color with their successful passes."[9]

As the Bears were rejoicing in their victory against Minneapolis, the rest of the country was about to hit rock bottom. The Stock Market Crash in late October sent the entire population into a panic. By 1933, almost half of all U.S. banks had failed, and unemployment was approaching 15 million people, or 30 percent of the workforce. The Bears, as well as the NFL, would try to survive the Great Depression.

The Bears were now 4-1-1. The next Sunday, they played the New York Giants, who were 4-0-1. "Fans are looking forward to the duel between the great Benny (Friedman) and 'Red' Grange. Grange is in top form and anxious to 'steal the show' from the visiting star. He demonstrated to the fans last week that he is the Galloping Ghost of old," wrote the *Chicago American*.[10] A Bears season-high 25,000 fans packed Wrigley Field. Early in the first quarter, the Bears recovered a Friedman fumble. They capitalized on the turnover when Red scored on a two-yard run—his first rushing score of the season. After that the Giants took control of the game, scoring 26 answered points. A late Bears score made the final 26-14.[11]

Red suffered a painful shoulder injury after "making a flying tackle in the first quarter." It would keep him out of the next game, a loss to the powerful Packers. He would return, but the Bears continued to struggle, losing three straight games, including a terrible 19-7 loss to the Buffalo Bisons, who were 0-7-1 at the time. Four days after the awful Buffalo loss, the Bears bottomed out. In their annual Thanksgiving Day game against the cross-town Cardinals, Halas's squad was embarrassed. In front of a small crowd of 7,000 fans at Wrigley, Ernie Nevers put on a one-man show for the ages. The burly fullback scored an NFL-record six rushing touchdowns, while also kicking four extra points—scoring all the points in a 40-6 beatdown. Nevers's 40 points scored is still the most points by a player in a single game in NFL history.

The Bears wrapped up the season by losing eight of their last nine games, going 0-8-1 in those nine contests. They finished with a 4-9-2 record, good for ninth place in the NFL standings (out of 12 teams). The Packers won the 1929 NFL title with a 12-0-1 record—defeating the Bears three times. They only gave up 22 points on defense the entire season, while the Bears surrendered a league-high 227 points. Opponents were impressed with Red. Speaking to the *Green Bay Press-Gazette* after the December 8 game at Wrigley Field, Packers center Jug Earpe said,

There isn't a cleaner player in the professional league than Red Grange. He tackles cleanly, and no one has ever known him to pull a "shady" play. When he is hit by a blocker or when he is tackled hard he never "crabs," but gets to his feet without a word and tries all the hardest to get through the next time.[12]

Red had a successful season, missing just one game. His knee had held up. According to the Bears balance sheets kept by Dutch Sternaman, by the end of the season Red had been paid a salary of $3,337.75, which in 14 games averaged out to $238 a game. It is the one time his salary had been published. Garland's salary was $1,631.66 for the season ($108.00 per game).[13] One thing that Red didn't care for was the extra attention by the press. He got most of it even if he didn't deserve it. Newspaper accounts always described what Red did in the game: "Red Grange Still Pulls the Crowds,"[14] "Packers Smother Galloping Ghost,"[15] "Red Grange's Pro Team Loses to Yellowjackets."[16]

After the season his Jekyll–Hyde persona with the press got the best of him. As much as Red didn't like to take all of the credit, he didn't mind telling his story to the reading public. His rags-to-riches story was always good copy, especially in Chicago. In December 1929, Red sat down with Westbrook Pegler of the *Chicago Tribune* to write a series of articles titled "Red Grange's Own Story." For four straight Sundays, Red's story was published under the byline "By Red Grange, as told to Westbrook Pegler."[17]

Red mostly talked about his upbringing with his father and brother in Wheaton, his time at Illinois playing under Bob Zuppke, his relationship with C. C. Pyle, the barnstorming tour, and how much money he made. The articles were published in such other national newspapers as the *St. Louis Post-Dispatch* and *Los Angeles Times*. The articles were also filled with photos of Red at different stages of his young life. The four installments were popular with Chicago readers. The best stuff was centered on Red's personal thoughts about his relationship with Pyle. He mentioned how they first met in Champaign. This time Red said they met because he was overwhelmed by the letters and telegrams he was receiving—roughly 5,000 of them—asking to capitalize on his fame and for the use of his name. Because he didn't want to jeopardize his amateur status, he visited Pyle for help. Red wrote,

> "Have you corresponded with any of these people?" Pyle asked. "No," I said. "I wish you would take all this detail off my hands. It's driving me crazy."
>
> "Then, go on back to the team," Pyle said, "and do not sign anything or promise anything that would affect your amateur standing." I left him with the understanding that I would turn pro under his management when the season ended.[18]

It was still a version of the story that he met Pyle at the Virginia Theater. Red also mentioned that he thought he made approximately $250,000 on the barnstorming tour. He also gave a few other financial nuggets. He revealed that he and Pyle each lost about $15,000 running the AFL in 1926. "It was a crazy promotion and we were badly beaten, but I don't blame Charlie Pyle," said Red. "I was for him when he was making money, and I couldn't turn against him merely because he showed me the way to a loss."[19]

As for Hollywood, Red wrote that he received a cash advance for $50,000 from FBO studios for *One Minute to Play*, while he got another $50,000 cash advance for *The Racing Romeo*, although this time Red wrote that because of their losses from the AFL, they had to use $30,000 to pay expenses. The two then split the rest, with each man getting $10,000. Red gave his share to his father. Red wrapped up the series writing about Pyle: "We are friends still. He was honest with me, and I never knew any man who would go deeper into his pocket to help a friend in trouble. We made a lot and lost a lot together, and if the losing ideas were his so were the winners."[20]

The losing season in 1929 didn't sit well with Halas or Sternaman. The two men also couldn't agree on how to run the offense. "We had two offenses," recalled one Bears player. "The Halas offense and the Sternaman offense."[21] The duo knew something had to be done. It didn't take them long to decide what to do. First, they fired themselves as head coaches. "The time had come for Dutch and me to stop coaching, or, more accurately, miscoaching. We had to put coaching under one mind. We decided to bring in someone who would pull the team together," wrote Halas in his autobiography.[22]

Second, they hired an old mentor to fix their team. Ralph Jones had been coaching football since he was 18 years old after graduating from Shortridge High School in Indiana. He had stints at Crawford (IN) High School, Butler, and Wabash, but it was at the University of Illinois where he established himself as a premier teacher of football strategy. For eight seasons (1913–1920) he was an assistant under Bob Zuppke, helping the Illini through their glory years. It was during this time that he helped coach Halas and Sternaman. The Bears owners knew Jones to be a great teacher of the game and that he would emphasize intelligence as much as toughness.

In 1920, Jones was hired away from Illinois to be the athletic director and head football and baseball coach at Lake Forest Academy, a prep school located on Chicago's North Shore. Jones compiled a record of 82-8 in his 10 years (1920–1929) as head football coach. Dominating teams at the prep level, Jones sometimes had to schedule games against such college freshmen teams as Yale, Princeton, Notre Dame, and Marquette. It came as a surprise to everyone in Chicago and in the media that the Bears would hire a prep football coach, but the owners knew what they were doing.

On December 27, 1929, Halas and Sternaman signed Jones to be the Bears' next head coach. Newspapers reported that Jones was to be hired for a yearly salary of $12,000. In his autobiography, Halas said the salary was $7,500. Whatever the price, the Bears had their man. Halas knew it. "Ralph Jones was a sound strategist. He believed muscle, guts, and spirit was not enough," said Halas. "He believed it also took brains to win games. Brainwork reduced the amount of profitless and painful crashing, and thrashing about, if properly applied, could add excitement and make the game more attractive."[23] Jones was excited about coaching the Bears. He declared to Halas, "I'll take the job if you two stay put in the front office, let me do things my way, and I'll win the championship in three years."[24]

T FORMATION SYSTEM

The diminutive Jones, standing 5-foot-7 and weighing 150 pounds, quickly went to work revamping the Bears offense. The prevailing offenses in the NFL at this time were the single- or double-wing formations, which focused on sheer power-running and an occasional forward pass thrown in to surprise the defense. But under Jones, the T formation, which had been around since the 1880s, would be emphasized as the primary offensive formation. Although this formation was considered outdated in 1929, Jones made up his mind that it would work for the Bears.

By "reintroducing" the T formation, Jones's streamlined, multifaceted offense would attack defenses that would be spread out to defend an offense against what it thought it would do. To accomplish this, Jones increased the splits for the offensive line and was very precise about how each of his backs lined up. The idea was to spread out the defense. Deception was added by snuggling the quarterback under center to take the snap, hiding the ball sooner and longer in the backfield.

But Jones's key innovation to the T formation was his man-in-motion concept. At this time, the NFL had a rule stating that one man could be in motion at the snap of the ball. In the single- and double-wing formations, backs would shift but had to be set for one second before the snap. Thus, the man-in-motion created quite a stir with defenses trying to defend the more wide-open T formation with a man-in-motion.

The Bears' T formation was taking shape. For running plays, holes to the right were odd numbers (1, 3, 5, 7, 9), and holes to the left were even numbers (0, 2, 4, 6, 8). Backs were numbered: left halfback (#2), fullback (#3), and right halfback (#4). So, if the running play called was 31-26, the fullback (#3) would get the ball and go through the one hole between center and guard; the left halfback (#2) would go in motion to the right, and the ball would be snapped on six.

Jones had his backs lined up precisely. Fullbacks were four yards directly behind the ball. The right halfback lined up straddling the outside leg of the right tackle; the left halfback straddled the outside leg of the left tackle, with each halfback placing his heels in-line with the fullback's toes.

Although Halas had incorporated studying film and learning opponents' game plans into the Bears' system, Jones increased the volume of information. Every Monday before the next game, the coaches would break down the next opponent's defense and prepare a "short list" of plays that they thought would work—a dozen pass plays and a dozen run plays. The plays—the game plan—then would be given to the players on Tuesday. The team would practice the plays twice a day throughout the week to familiarize the players with the specific plays. At night, the players would have to diagram the plays so that they knew their assignments.[25]

The Bears would play much better in 1930. As for Red, his knee did hold up again, and he missed only one game in 1929, due to a bad shoulder. Physically he was fine. It was time to contribute more. In the summer of 1930, Red returned to Los Angeles to spend time with his father, who was staying in California. To make some extra cash, Red decided to take a job as a host for a local nightclub. Working evenings at the Cotton Club in Culver City, he was still able to mingle with the Hollywood crowd. "I have what some people think is a funny job for a football player, but I like it," said Red to a reporter from *I.N.S.* "I meet the local celebrities, and the celebrities meet me. My job is to introduce these 'hot' celebrities when they come into the place and kid them along. They like it, and so do the customers." No more than a summer job, Red was soon back in Chicago. It was time for another football season. He would return to the Bears.[26]

The NFL accepted applications for a few new franchises for 1930, adding the Brooklyn Dodgers, Portsmouth Spartans, and Newark Tornadoes (replacing the Orange Tornadoes), and giving the league 11 teams (gone were the Boston Bulldogs and Dayton Triangles). The Bears made a few changes to their 20-man roster, the NFL limit. Retiring was Paddy Driscoll. Red and Garland would be joined by backs Joey Sternaman, Laurie Walquist, Walt Holmer, and Bill Senn; end Luke Johnsos; and linemen Don Murry, Bert Pearson, George Trafton, and Zuck Carlson. Guard Joe Kopcha would take the next two years off to attend medical school.

Returning to the Bears was tackle Link Lyman, who would add much-needed strength on the line. Halas also signed guards Dan McMullen (5-foot-8,

230 pounds) and Paul Schuette (6-foot-0, 220 pounds) away from the New York Giants. The rookie class would add some impressive names, including quarterback Carl Brumbaugh (5-foot-10, 170 pounds) from Florida, half-back Joe Lintzenich (5-foot-11, 187 pounds) from St. Louis, halfback Dick Nesbitt (6-foot-0, 205 pounds) from Drake, end Hoot Drury (6-foot-4, 189 pounds) from St. Louis, tackle Larry Steinbach (6-foot-0, 214 pounds) from St. Thomas, and guard Babe Frump (6-foot-0, 225 pounds) from Ohio Wesleyan. But the gem of the rookie class was a fullback from Minnesota.

Bronko Nagurski was a 6-foot-2, 226-pound physical freak who would take the NFL by storm. Jones would pair the burly fullback with Red in his T formation backfield, along with quarterback Carl Brumbaugh and right halfback Joe Lintzenich. For most games, Garland would join his older brother in the starting lineup at right end, playing opposite Luke Johnsos. Jones's first training camp started just after Labor Day at Mills Stadium in Chicago and lasted two and half weeks. "Red Grange, who reported in excellent condition, showed his old-time skill in practice during the past couple of weeks, and Jones believes the famous redhead will clip off many yards in the campaign," wrote the *Chicago American*.[27]

The Bears' 1930 season got off to a slow start. They did nothing in a score-less tie against the Brooklyn Dodgers and lost a tough 7–0 game in Green Bay against the defending champion Packers. On October 5, the Bears played their best game, beating up on the Minneapolis Red Jackets, 20–0. Nagurski scored two rushing touchdowns, while Red caught a 30-yard scoring pass from Joey Sternaman. "The redhead seems to have taken a new lease on life under the tutelage of Jones," wrote the *Chicago Herald-Examiner*.[28]

The win was short-lived, as the next week they suffered a 12–0 defeat at the hands of the New York Giants despite a nice crowd of 12,000 fans at Wrigley Field. The following Sunday against the Cardinals, the Bears played their most complete game of 1930, with Red doing some of his best work. In the first quarter, he sprinted 38 yards for the first score of the game. "Grange's mates furnished ex-cellent blocking for the run, but he evaded the last two tackles much in the manner of five years ago when he ran for Illinois," wrote the *Chicago Tribune*. Moments later, after a Bears interception, Red galloped around left end for a 15-yard score. Walt Holmer proceeded to score three more touchdowns to close out a dominat-ing 32–6 victory. A year removed from being embarrassed by the Cardinals, when Ernie Nevers scored 40 points, Halas and Sternaman rejoiced in getting the best of their crosstown rivals. Hiring Jones seemed to be paying off.[29]

Red could see that Jones was making a big impact on the team. Players had to be not only physically strong, but also mentally tough. In 1933, Red wrote:

Every player on the Chicago Bears is required to make a written report immediately after each game. He must write his observations of the opposing team, particularly in regard to his individual opponent. He describes his opponent's style, charts the positions he assumed on offense and defense, the plays which worked, or failed, against him, and records any weaknesses he may have revealed. These reports are filed and used for blackboard reference before the next game with the same team. Special plays are planned to take advantage of weaknesses disclosed in the preceding game.[30]

Three days after the big victory against the Cardinals, the Bears played a Wednesday night road game against the newly formed Portsmouth Spartans. After trailing 7–0 for most of the game, the Bears scored a late touchdown when Joey Sternaman connected with Luke Johnsos for what looked to be the tying score. Instead, the younger Sternaman missed the extra point. The tough 7–6 loss left the Bears with a 2–3–1 record.

Ralph Jones knew his squad was playing well, just not well enough to win games. He pushed them harder in practice. The extra work would pay off. They would rebound with a nice 13–7 win against the Frankford Yellow Jackets and a more impressive 20–7 victory against the Red Jackets. "Red Grange was the liveliest member of the Bears against Minneapolis," wrote the *Chicago Tribune*. Against the Red Jackets, Red caught a 25-yard touchdown pass from Walquist and ran 14 yards for another score.[31]

After the two-game win streak, next up for the Bears was the best team in the NFL—the Green Bay Packers. Curly Lambeau's squad was rolling along with a record of 7–0, outscoring their opponents 140–32. They had just pummeled the Spartans, 47–13. The Bears once again gave them a close contest. This time Bears fans came out to Wrigley, with more than 22,000 spectators passing through the turnstiles. Both teams traded touchdowns, as the ballgame was tied, 6–6, heading into the fourth quarter. The Packers struck first, as Red Dunn connected with Verne Lewellen, and the extra point made it 13–6. The Bears marched right back downfield, as Walquist plowed over for the score. But just like against the Spartans three weeks earlier, the Bears missed the extra point. It would cost them the game, with the Packers going for the win, 13–12.

A few days after the setback against the Packers, Red gave an interview with George Kirksey of the *United Press*. He openly talked about his play on the field:

In college I used to think the ballcarrier was the most important man on the team, but I've changed those ideas now. The ballcarrier is just one-eleventh of the team, and he can't do a thing unless his interference and linemen get him past the line of scrimmage. There must be somebody out there blocking out the tackle and knocking down the end and halfback.[32]

At 28, Red was growing up as an NFL player. He was becoming a better all-around player—not just an open-field runner. He could make a difference on the field as a blocker and a passer, and on defense, excelling in pass defense. "The hardest thing about pass defense is to stay where you are," Red once said in an interview. "It's the most natural thing in the world to want to dash over and help the other fellow. Then the first thing you know, they've thrown the ball where you should have been."[33]

The following week behind two Nagurski touchdown runs, the Bears defeated the New York Giants, 12–0, at the Polo Grounds. The following week against Frankford, Red had his best game of the year. In the first quarter, he sprinted around left end 51 yards for a touchdown. In the second quarter, Red again blazed through the Yellow Jackets defense, this time galloping 75 yards for the score—this would be the longest touchdown run by Red in his NFL career. It was the first time that he looked like the Galloping Ghost of old. The headlines in the next day's *Philadelphia Inquirer* read, "Ghost's Long Runs Conquer Frankford: Red Dashes First 51, Then 75 Yards to Spread Terror and Devastation in Ranks of Hornets as Bears Gambol to Win."[34]

At 6–4–1, the Bears finished the season strong with three consecutive wins. They finished the season with a 9–4–1 record, good for third place in the NFL standings behind the Packers (10–3–1) and Giants (13–4). The defense gave up only 71 points, second best in the league (with the Dodgers in first, with 59 points) and much better than the abysmal 227 they gave up in 1929. Ralph Jones had worked his magic, and the Bears were on their way to being one of the best teams in the NFL.

As for Red, he was better in 1930 than in 1929. He scored eight total touchdowns (six rushing, two receiving) to lead the Bears in scoring, with 49 points (he also had one conversion catch). Attendance for the Bears was sporadic at best in 1930; according to newspaper reports the two Packers games at Wrigley attracted 44,000 fans, while the other four home games averaged 7,500 fans. The Bears played 14 games, averaging approximately 9,691 fans per game, which was above average for an NFL game in 1930, at 7,027 (513,000 fans, based on newspaper reports of the 73 league games). "We are bringing out a new type of spectator," said Red to Les Conklin of *I.N.S.* "These new fans are being educated to the gridiron sport and should increase in numbers every year. Chicago, Green Bay, and New York already are good pro towns." Red could see that the NFL was making strides each year to gain a foothold in the sporting scene. Crowds were getting bigger each year.[35]

Just when the Bears thought their season was over, they played one more game. This time it was for a good cause. Tom Henage, secretary of the Chicago Athletic Association, and George Getz, chairman of the Illinois Governor's Commission of Unemployment and Relief, came up with the idea to play a charity football game in Chicago. Henage and Getz approached the Bears and Cardinals about playing in the game. Along with Dr. David Jones of the Cardinals, Halas and Sternaman quickly said yes. Anything to help the city battle the grips of the Great Depression. The game was set for Monday, December 15.

Because it was mid-December in the Windy City, the owners were concerned about the weather. The two teams agreed to play the game indoors at Chicago Stadium—the home of the Chicago Blackhawks, the city's hockey team. One small obstacle would be presented to the group. The Blackhawks had a game scheduled for Sunday, December 14, against the Montreal Maroons. So, the plan was, moments after the hockey game was finished, for the arena crew to break down the ice on the floor and have six five-ton trucks deliver more than six inches of dirt onto the 47,500 square feet of space that constituted the playing surface inside facility.

Another obstacle was the size of the football field. Because of the small confinement, the gridiron would only be 80 yards long, with one goal post. The two teams agreed to kick off from the goal line, and once the ball reached midfield it would be moved back 20 yards. The rafter was 94 feet from the dirt surface, so punts would be fine to execute. Tickets were sold at the arena, the Chicago Athletic Club, and the Illinois Athletic Club, with prices ranging from $2.00 to $3.00 (mezzanine seats), to $1.50 (first balcony), to $1.00 (second balcony). After paying the stadium rental, officials, and players, who would play for half their salaries, proceeds from the game were to go the Governor's Unemployment Fund, with the funds from the game to be dispensed in Cook County.

On December 15, a near-capacity crowd of 10,000 fans came out to Chicago Stadium. Referee Bobbie Cahn was the star of the game, "marching back and forth to mark the ball." In the first quarter, Brumbaugh connected on a long pass to Johnsos to set up a Lintzenich score. In the second half, the Bears defense tackled Nevers in the end zone after he fumbled a center snap to take a 9–0 lead. A late Cardinals touchdown closed the gap, but the Bears held on for a 9–7 victory.[36]

The true winner was the relief fund. The total receipts from the game amounted to $16,012.50, after expenses, which included stadium rental

($3,500), ticket sellers and ushers ($404), officials ($85.00), other expenses ($109), and the salaries of the two teams ($10,000). The game generated $2,014.50 for Cook County. It doesn't sound like much, but in 1930, every little bit helped.

Red's body needed a little rest. He stepped away from football to be part of another vaudeville show. He visited such Midwest cities as Dixon, Illinois; Belvidere, Illinois; Manitowoc, Wisconsin; Valparaiso, Indiana; Marion, Ohio; Circleville, Ohio; Middletown, Ohio; New Castle, Pennsylvania; and Altoona, Pennsylvania. After three months of touring, from January to March 1931, Red returned to Chicago. He soon had a tryout with WJJD radio in Chicago to do Cubs and White Sox baseball games. "He's now at the Cubs Park everyday handling play-by-play reports for the game. And he doesn't confuse punts and forward passes with base hits and outfielders' pegs to home, either," wrote the local press. Red got his feet wet in the radio business doing a few baseball games. It would be a career that he would revisit.[37]

After a busy spring, Red chose to spend his summer in Hollywood with his father and make another movie. This time, Frank Zambreno was able to negotiate a Hollywood deal with Nat Levine of Mascot Pictures for Red to appear in a 12-part serial titled *The Galloping Ghost*. Levine founded Mascot in 1927, producing serials and B-Westerns. In 1929, he produced *The King of the Kongo*, the first serial with sound. *The Galloping Ghost* would be Red's first talkie. "Making *The Galloping Ghost* was, without a doubt, the most strenuous work I have ever done in my life," Red declared. "What made it even more difficult was the task of learning spoken lines for the first time. Talking pictures were still new (1931), and it was a difficult adjustment for even the most seasoned actors in Hollywood."[38] The *Motion Picture Herald* reported that Grange would receive $50,000 for his work.[39]

Produced by Levine, *The Galloping Ghost* was directed by B. Reeves Eason (some research says that Eason was eventually replaced by Benjamin Kline to finish the serial) and written by Ford Beebe, Wyndham Gittens, and Helmer W. Bergman. Red would play himself, Red Grange, a college football star thrown off his college football team at Clay College after being framed for throwing a game for gamblers. His costars included Francis X. Bushman Jr. (Buddy Courtland, Red's friend), Dorothy Gulliver (Barbara Courtland, Red's girlfriend, Buddy's sister), Tom Dugan (Jerry, comedian, cabbie driver), Gwen Lee (Irene Courtland, Buddy's blackmailing wife), Theodore Lorch (Dr. Julian Blake, villainous brain surgeon), Ed Hearn (Clay College coach), and Walter Miller (George Elton).

One of the major criticisms with Red being cast in *The Galloping Ghost* was that he was 28 years old playing a college student-athlete. Levine didn't care, he had his star. Most moviegoers overlooked the easy mistake. The full-plot was an industry standard "unjustly accused" theme that was guaranteed to arouse audience sympathy. In the film, Red's college roommate, Buddy Bushman, takes a bribe from gamblers to throw a game. Buddy, it seems, got drunk one night and secretly married Irene (Lee), which, according to a rule, will get him kicked out of school. She blackmails Buddy, asking for $1,000 to keep the truth a secret, so Buddy is asked to throw the game. Red tries to stick up for his teammate but is accused of throwing the game himself and expelled. The rest of the serial has Red put in several hair-raising predicaments while trying to clear his name. He solves the case just in time to rejoin the football team to win the big game. Loaded with breathtaking sequences of motorcycle and speedboat chases, automobiles plunging off cliffs, Red jumping from one airplane to another, and bruising street fights between rival taxi gangs, *The Galloping Ghost* contains no dull moments.

Red spent roughly five weeks in Hollywood shooting the serial, mostly at Tec-Art Studios. Doing most of his own stunts, he kept in good shape for the upcoming football season. "To finish the picture in that short time we worked seven days a week, sometimes as much as 18 hours a day," Grange remembered. "Levine would call for me every morning at five o'clock, and we'd stop in the coffee shop near the studio for breakfast. As soon as it was light outside we were on the set ready for action. Levine had every movement of his movie so carefully planned there was never a minute wasted." By the time *The Galloping Ghost* wrapped, it had 12 chapters. Each chapter is about 20 minutes in length (226 minutes total). "It will be just what the kids, especially, will want to see," said Red to the Hollywood press. "Since the talkies replaced the silent films the kids haven't had much except comedies to amuse them. They want some drama, too, and I'm going to give it to 'em."[40]

Red's time in Hollywood went by quickly, returning to Chicago just in time for training camp. For the 1931 NFL season the league dropped two franchises, Minneapolis and Newark, and added just one, the Cleveland Indians. The league now had 10 teams. Despite the Great Depression infecting the country, the NFL looked to stable its organization. The Bears, always a brick of stability, showed a crack. Before the season started, Dutch Sternaman was feeling the crunch of the Depression, so he decided to sell his interest in the Bears to his partner. "In the summer of 1931, my partner, Dutch Sternaman, couldn't meet mortgage payments on his apartment house and his gas station. His only asset was his partnership in the Bears. He asked if I would buy him out for $38,000, enough to meet his financial needs," recalled Halas in his autobiography. "I did want control of the Bears. My faith was boundless." Eventually Halas borrowed $5,000 from good friends Ralph Brizzolara, Jim McMillen, and Charlie Bidwill. He also borrowed $20,000 from the mother of George Trafton and a small amount from his mother. "On July 3, 1931, I did buy out Dutch. I paid him $25,000 in cash and promised to pay $6,000 on January 25, 1932 and the final $7,000 on July 31, 1932," remembered Halas. Halas was now running the show all by himself.[41]

Red was entering his sixth season of professional football. Bears programs had him listed at 182 pounds, while Garland was listed at 178. The roster Halas had built was primed to compete for a championship. Hiring Ralph Jones kept Halas busy scouting for talent. In 1930, he hit it big, especially with Nagurski and Brumbaugh. In 1931, the Bears didn't lose many players. Returning were Carl Brumbaugh, Laurie Walquist, Joe Lintzenich, Dick Nesbitt, and Bronko Nagurski in the backfield, as well as linemen Link Lyman, Don Murry, Larry Steinbach, Zuck Carlson, Dan McMullen, Paul Schuette, Hoot Drury, Luke Johnsos, Bert Pearson, and George Trafton.

Veterans added were guard Bill Buckler, who had played for the Bears from 1926 to 1928; tackle Cookie Tackwell from the Frankford Yellow Jackets; mid-season signee fullback Herb Joesting from the Minneapolis Red Jackets; and Keith Molesworth from the semipro Ironton (Ohio) Tanks. Molesworth was a unique find. Late in the 1930 season, the Bears played the Tanks in an exhibition game at Crosley Field in Cincinnati. Molesworth helped lead the Tanks, who also had halfback Glenn Presnell, who signed with the Portsmouth Spartans in 1931, to an upset victory against the Bears, 26–13. Halas was so impressed with Molesworth that when the Tanks folded after the season, he quickly signed him. Two other rookies were signed: tackle Jesse Hibbs (6-foot-0, 195 pounds), who played for Ralph Jones at Lake Forest and college ball at the University of Southern California, and massive tackle Lloyd Burdick (6-foot-4, 250 pounds), who played for Zuppke at Illinois.

Camp was the usual grind. Players practiced for almost two weeks at Loyola Field in Chicago. "Red Grange is in better condition than at any time during his career. From his position at left half Red is expected to get away on running plays, while he also will be depended upon for a major portion of the forward passing," wrote Wilfrid Smith of the *Chicago Tribune*.[42]

The Bears' second season under Jones got off to a fast start, with the team hosting the newly organized Cleveland Indians on a Friday night in Chicago—the first-ever night game for the Bears in the Windy City. More than

6,000 fans came out to Loyola Stadium for the 8:15 p.m. kickoff. Red got the scoring started with a short touchdown run, while scores by Lintzenich and Senn capped a 21-0 shutout victory. The win set up an early matchup with the Packers in Green Bay. "They have got the strongest squad they ever had in the National Professional Football League," said Ralph Jones to the *Chicago Evening-Post*. Once again, the fans would come out, with 13,500 onlookers watching another close, bruising contest between two teams that were now bitter rivals. Neither team backed down. In the end, the Packers squeaked out a 7-0 victory.[43]

Two weeks later, the 1-2 New York Giants came to Wrigley. In a defensive battle, Red was able to provide the only score of the game, a 1-yard touchdown run around right end in the second quarter as the Bears held on for the 7-0 win. Jones's boys would next square off at Comiskey Park against the crosstown Cardinals (0-2), featuring the great Ernie Nevers. It would be Red's best offensive game of the year. After trailing 7-0 at the half, Red took over the game. In the third quarter, he scored twice—a 25-yard run off right tackle and a 20-yard catch. After a beautiful 62-yard touchdown rumble by Nagurski, Red capped off the Bears scoring with his third touchdown of the game—a 10-yard run. The Bears rolled to a 26-13 victory. "Old Red just would not be stopped, and with the assistance of the big Nagurski, who bowled over the opposition as interference, the redhead, at the end of the 60 minutes, had crossed the Cardinal goal line three times," wrote the *Chicago Herald-Examiner*.[44]

The Bears were now 3-1. Jones's T formation offense was very productive, scoring 54 points in the first four games. The next two weeks would be both good and bad for the Bears. Playing both games at Wrigley Field, the Bears lost two nail-biters. Against the Frankford Yellow Jackets on October 25, the Bears' Achilles heel—placekicking—popped up again. In a back-and-forth game the Bears scored a late fourth-quarter touchdown by Nagurski to pull to within one point, 13-12. As in previous years, the extra point was missed, and another chance at a tie or victory was lost. "He is still the Galloping Ghost as far as I am concerned," said Yellow Jackets center Nate Barrager. "I tried tackling him several times and missed as often as I connected. He has a way of slipping by that was the most baffling thing I have ever come across in football."[45]

One week after that heartbreak, the Bears hosted the two-time champion Green Bay Packers on November 1. As had been the case two months earlier, the game was bitterly fought. In the second quarter, the Packers' all-world guard, Mike Michalske, intercepted a Brumbaugh pass and sprinted 80 yards for the game's only touchdown. The Bears forced a safety in the second half but came up short again, losing 6-2. Head coach Jones was criticized for passing at that time. "I have heard many arguments in which it is contended that the Bears, making their gains and downs, should not have passed," said Garland Grange to the *Chicago Herald-Examiner*.

> Last year, in the game between the Bears and Packers, this same Brumbaugh received the ball and, not once, but twice, passed to Johnsos for a touchdown, and he was proclaimed a hero. It's the break of the game. Had Brumbaugh's pass to Johnsos been completed last Sunday there would have been much cheering for Carl.[46]

Since Red rejoined the Bears in 1929, he had played eight games against the Packers; the Bears were 1–7 and had been outscored 35–95. If they were going to compete for an NFL championship, they had to find a way to defeat Curly Lambeau's Packers. The Bears were now just 3–3. Coach Jones rallied his troops. Red had gotten banged up against the Packers, but he would be ready to answer the bell against the streaking Portsmouth Spartans. The small-town Ohio team had hired former Zuppke protégé Potsy Clark as head coach. Clark signed former Colorado College All-American Dutch Clark to run his single-wing offense. The Spartans roared to an 8–1 record, suffering their first loss of the year against the New York Giants. The Bears rebounded in the win column behind a field goal by Johnsos and a touchdown run by Brumbaugh for a hard-fought 9–6 victory against the pesky Spartans.

A week later, the Bears traveled east to play the Giants at the Polo Grounds on November 15. The attraction of Red and Nagurski brought out a crowd of 20,000, with New York mayor Jimmy Walker and former New York governor Alfred Smith in attendance to see an exciting game, with Grange making the key play of the contest. After trading touchdowns with missed extra points, the two teams were tied, 6–6, late in the fourth quarter. After a huge interception by the Bears, the clock showed less than one minute to play. The Bears called a pass play. Brumbaugh fired a short strike to Garland Grange, who did the rest, sprinting 28 yards for the game-winning score. The newspaper headlines read, "Red's Kid Brother Steals Show."[47]

By the end of the 1931 season, Ralph Jones had his team playing good football. The Bears were set to play the Packers for the third time. In front of 15,000 fans at Wrigley, the Bears would make all the plays. Early in the first quarter on an icy surface, they pushed across a touchdown when Lintzenich caught a scoring pass. After the score, Tackwell booted the extra point. In the second quarter, Red slipped in pass coverage, allowing Johnny "Blood" McNally to catch a touchdown, but Grange's mistake didn't have a permanent impact, as the Packers missed the extra point. The 7–6 lead would hold up. Red would help clinch the victory with a fourth-quarter interception. "Red Grange played a steady, if not brilliant, defensive game all afternoon," wrote the *Chicago American*.[48]

The Bears finished the 1931 season with an 8–5 record, good enough for a third-place finish in the standings behind the Packers (12–2), who won their third straight NFL title, and the Spartans (11–3). Red had another solid year, scoring seven touchdowns (five rushing, two receiving) and leading the Bears in scoring for the second straight year with 42 points. Red was selected First Team All-NFL by George Kirksey of the *United Press*.

"Whitey" Calhoun of the *Green Bay Press-Gazette* also had Red on his First Team All-Pro squad at left halfback. "Grange had another great year, gaining lots of ground on the attack and proving a 'Bear' on defense," Calhoun declared. Since rejoining the Bears three years earlier, Red had proven to the NFL, his critics, and himself that he could be an All-Pro player. He was also a member of an elite NFL team. It was time to become a world champion.[49]

26

INDOOR MADNESS

On September 1, 1931, *The Galloping Ghost* serial was released in theaters throughout the country. Reviews were positive. "And you will see, too, that Grange can do many things besides football, for in this picture he essays the type of role that made Douglas Fairbanks famous in his first screen productions," wrote the *Gaffney* (South Carolina) *Ledger.* "Interesting and exciting serial in which Red Grange, in trying to save his friend from a football gambling ring, is himself accused of taking bribes. The last episode is unusually good," wrote the *National Board of Review Magazine.* The *New Movie Magazine* wrote, "Some of the stunt stuff is well contrived, and the trick photography is first rate."[1]

Some NFL players didn't miss the redhead on screen. Red remembers getting asked about the serial during games:

> After I made the serial, I was playing in New York against the New York Giants at the Polo Grounds, and Steve Owen, the big tackle, hit me and I was never hit so hard in my life. And I'm layin' on the ground and he's on top of me. He said, "Don't try to get up. What happened when you fell out of the airplane? I missed the final episode."[2]

Even the Halas family made time to see the shows. "My mother took us every Saturday afternoon to the Nortown Theater because it was a 12-part serial," says Virginia McCaskey, daughter of George Halas. "Each week the end of the episode ended with a cliff-hanging situation of some kind. So, everybody would be back the following week to see how he got out of that. It was really a lot of fun."[3]

The Galloping Ghost continued to be shown in theaters for months. Even decades later, the serial would sometimes pop up on television. It can be bought on DVD. Although Red would never act in another feature film, he enjoyed his time in Hollywood. He reflected,

> In looking back upon my experiences making motion pictures and appearing briefly in vaudeville, I've always felt it represents one of the most memorable and worthwhile chapters on my life. When I first reported for work in the film capital back in 1926, I was a shy, bashful, small-town boy despite the national prominence I had achieved for my football playing. Facing cameras, live audiences in the theaters, and mixing with all the stimulating people connected with show business did something for me. It gave me confidence and poise and made me feel a little bit more like a man of the world.[4]

Red's offseason had no vaudeville tour or postseason exhibition games. He would take it easy, spending time with his father and brother. But while he was relaxing, his boss was under the gun. On July 31, George Halas was facing a big deadline. In the agreement he had signed the previous year to buy out Dutch Sternaman, his last payment of $7,000 was due. On that day, Halas was short $5,000. According to the agreement if Halas didn't make the payment, Dutch would assume control of his stock and the team. Dutch's lawyer sent Papa Bear a letter stating that Dutch was putting his stock up for public auction. Desperation set in for Halas, as he only had until noon to gain full control of the Bears.

"I tried everywhere to raise the $5,000. I called everyone I knew. No one could help me. Many banks were closed, and those open would make no loan. I was desperate. At noon I would lose my Bears," Halas remembered in his autobiography. He continued,

> About 11 o'clock Mr. C. K. Anderson, the president of the First National Bank in Antioch, phoned. He said he understood I needed $5,000 urgently. "How true! I must have the money by noon or I will lose my Bears!" He said he would lend me the money. I raced from my office at 111 W. Washington to his Chicago office at Randolph and LaSalle Streets and collected his check, with grateful but quick thanks, and then ran to the lawyer's office and handed in a check. It was 10 minutes to noon. . . . I had firm control of the Bears.

Halas had avoided disaster and was now the sole owner of the Chicago Bears.[5]

After a strong 1931 season, the Bears were looking to take the next step toward a championship. For Halas, the losing season of 1929 seemed a distant memory, as the hiring of Ralph Jones, plus the addition of Nagurski,

Brumbaugh, and Molesworth, had stabilized the team. Halas felt that he could finally get back on top, something he hadn't done since 1921. First, his squad would have to dethrone the Green Bay Packers. The 1932 campaign would be a special season for the Bears.

The NFL was entering its 13th season. The league would finally decide to keep official statistics for the first time. In the middle of the Depression, money was still scarce, as the NFL dropped from 10 franchises to eight. Gone were two former NFL champions–the Frankford Yellow Jackets (1926) and the Providence Steam Roller (1928). Also saying good-bye was the Cleveland Indians franchise, gone after just one year (2–8 record). The only addition was the big-city Boston Braves, owned by a group of businessmen led by the brash George Preston Marshall, who made his wealth from operating more than 50 successful laundromats in the Washington area. Marshall's group paid $2,500 for the franchise fee. The newly minted Boston Braves made the NFL a strong eight-team league.

Halas put the NFL's business behind him to concentrate on evaluating his roster. After playing three seasons with his older brother, Garland Grange left the Bears. He didn't quit pro football, eventually signing with the St. Louis Veterans, a non-NFL team, as player-coach. The younger Grange installed Ralph Jones's T formation and played right end. He would guide the Veterans to a 2–2–1 record. He finished the season playing for the Memphis Tigers.

In addition to starting end Garland Grange, Halas lost several key contributors. Also leaving were end Hoot Drury (retired) and tackle Jesse Hibbs (retired), as well as key starters Link Lyman (tackle), Joe Lintzenich (halfback), and Laurie Walquist (longtime quarterback, retired). Walquist was the easiest to replace, as Keith Molesworth was ready to step in. Lintzenich was replaced by Dick Nesbitt. The backfield now had depth and versatility. Led by Red, the unit would feature Nagurski (fullback), Nesbitt (halfback), Molesworth (quarterback), Brumbaugh (quarterback), Paul Franklin (halfback), and Herb Joesting (fullback). Returning on the line would be Lloyd Burdick (tackle); Don Murry (tackle); Bill Buckler (guard); Zuck Carlson (guard); Luke Johnsos (end); Cookie Tackwell (end); Bert Pearson (center); and George Trafton (center), back for his 12th season with the Bears.

The rookie class would once again be the best in the NFL. Halas signed guard Gil Bergerson (6-foot-6, 245 pounds) from Oregon State; halfbacks George Corbett (5-foot-9, 179 pounds), from tiny Millikin College, and John Doehring (6-foot-0, 216 pounds), who didn't play college football; and tackles Harold Ely (6-foot-2, 268 pounds) from Iowa and "Tiny" Engebretsen (6-foot-1, 238 pounds) from Northwestern. But it would be three other rookies who would make the most impact—each playing five seasons with the Bears: center Charles "Ookie" Miller (6-foot-0, 209 pounds) from Purdue, halfback Johnny Sisk (6-foot-2, 197 pounds) from Marquette, and end Bill Hewitt (5-foot-9, 190 pounds) from Michigan. This would be the squad that would help restore the Bears' championship ways.

Training camp was held for two weeks at Logan Square Baseball Park in Chicago. For the third straight year, it would be conducted under the direction of Ralph Jones. Red arrived in tip-top shape, weighing 185 pounds. Jones and the Bears selected Red as team captain. While at camp, Grange gave an interview to Jack Cuddy of the *United Press*, relating his views on the pro game.

> Weather has been the greatest obstacle to the professional game's progress since its beginning 10 years ago. In spite of this the sport has made such rapid strides in the last three years that promoters will take steps shortly to eliminate this uncertainty. . . . Already some of them are making plans to build mammoth indoor plants where the game can be played at night during five months of the year—from September to late February. Then, it can rain or snow, but the fans will be there just the same.[6]

Red reminded the sportswriter that the success of the college game was based on advance ticket sales to alumni regardless of the weather, whereas the pro game's ticket sales were usually on the day of the contest:

> Commercial football is catching on amazingly. There are three reasons for this: (1) The professionals play better football than collegians, (2) It gives the chap who hasn't gone to college a team to cheer for, and (3) The prices are within reach of the average man.
>
> The most important of those reasons is that the butchers, bricklayers, plumbers, mechanics, truckdrivers, and their wives get a team they can call their own. A team they can root for on Sunday. Most people haven't gone to college so why should they get all excited over a college game? But give them their Dodgers, Giants, or Bears, and they're out there yelling their heads off as loudly as any alumnus cheering for the Dear Old Ruggies.

The NFL was attracting consistent crowds—loyal fan bases in their eight cities, hardworking citizens who didn't mind spending their money to attend a NFL game on a Sunday afternoon.[7]

The season opener was against the three-time NFL champion Green Bay Packers. More than 13,000 fans at Green Bay's City Stadium saw a defensive battle, so much so that neither team scored, in a 0–0 tie. The lack of offense would haunt the Bears for the first half of the season. "Yes, we have a good team.

They haven't been working together very well yet. But we should have beaten Green Bay, and we'll start clicking soon. Then watch out," said Ralph Jones to the *Chicago American*.[8]

The next two games also ended in scoreless ties, against the Staten Island Stapletons and the Chicago Cardinals. "Some Sunday in 1932 the Chicago Bears are going to score a point. But you can't prove this by past performances," wrote the *Chicago Evening Post*. The Bears had played three NFL games and scored zero points. Ralph Jones was miffed at the fact that his squad couldn't get the offense moving. To top things off, Red dislocated his right shoulder in the first quarter of the game against the Cardinals. He would miss the next game—the rematch against the mighty Packers.[9]

Playing the Packers at home, the Bears were looking to make a statement. A crowd of roughly 20,000 fans filled up Wrigley. Present was NFL president Joseph F. Carr. In a game described by the *Chicago American* as a "bitter, slugging dogfight," the two rivals fought toe-to-toe for four quarters. The only score came in the second quarter, when Packers right end Tom Nash broke through the Bears line to block a Dick Nesbitt punt. The ball went through the end zone for a safety. The tough 2–0 loss would have deflated most teams, but not the 1932 Chicago Bears. Although it didn't look like a championship season in the Windy City, the winds were about to change. The setback against the Packers on October 16 would be the last game the Bears would lose.[10]

The Bears' next game was a rematch against the Stapletons. This time the Bears didn't mess around. Five minutes into the first quarter, Red got the scoring going with a TD catch from Keith Molesworth. After 245 minutes of action, the Bears scored their first points of the 1932 season. Two Nagurski scores and another by Nesbitt led the Bears to a convincing 27–7 victory. The meaningless Stapletons touchdown was the first one given up by the Bears defense. They would only surrender six touchdowns the entire year.

Red was smack in the middle of another productive year, playing his best football. He was also thinking about life after football. Grange gave an interview with the *United Press*. In it he said, "I'm 29 now. I'm getting around the age where a man gets brittle. There's no use playing football after you lose the edge for the game. Football has been good to me. I want to leave it while I still like it."[11]

During this time Red took on another role—as sportswriter. In 1932, he met a man who would help him develop his voice away from the gridiron. George Dunscomb came from a newspaper family. The son of a newspaper publisher, George Sr. was the publisher of the *Windsor* (Illinois) *Gazette* and grandson of the founder of the *Moultrie County-News*. Dunscomb went on to attend Milliken

University in Decatur, where he played on the basketball team, before transferring out West to Berkeley, California, to live with his uncle Charles, who ran the *Berkeley-Gazette*. George went on to graduate from the University of California in 1921.

Dunscomb returned to Illinois to write for the *Decatur Daily Review*. He also penned freelance articles that would appear in *Collier's* and *Red Book*. He then went to work as an advertisement agent in Chicago for McCann-Erickson, Inc. Dunscomb soon became acquainted with Red. With his help, Dunscomb wrote a fictional article that appeared in multiple issues of *College Humor* magazine, published monthly by Collegiate World Publishing, located in Chicago. Well-known contributors to the publication would include Robert Benchley, Groucho Marx, Heywood Broun, and F. Scott Fitzgerald. Titled "77: A Novel Dedicated to Red Grange," the story first appeared in the October issue and continued through the January 1933 issue.[12]

At the same time that the fictional story came out, Red joined forces with Dunscomb to write a series of articles about football that would appear in the *Saturday Evening Post*, the country's most widely circulated weekly magazine. By the early 1930s, the magazine would reach almost three million weekly readers, featuring covers by well-known artist Norman Rockwell. In the fall of 1932, Red and Dunscomb wrote two articles: "Lo! The Poor Tackle" (October 8, 1932) and "The College Game Is Easier" (November 5, 1932).

The articles were roughly four pages in length and contained 2,500 to 3,000 words. In "Lo! The Poor Tackle," Red emphasized that there was "no tougher job in football—than playing tackle." He then went into detail, spanning four pages, about how teams tried to attack the (defensive) tackle position, either from the double-wing offense (the Pop Warner system) or the Notre Dame system. Red was always fascinated by the strategy of the game, and passing on his knowledge to fans was intriguing to him. The articles included photos and several diagrams of the plays and techniques he was talking about to give readers a better understanding of the sport. Giving his take on playing tackle, Red wrote, "Their huge hands and there never was a great tackle with small 'dukes'—seem always ready to ward off an attack from the side, front, or rear. At that, I can't go around an inconvenient chair without suppressing a desire to straight-arm it."[13]

The second article, "The College Game Is Easier," received more publicity because Red gave his honest opinion of the two games. After being asked whether a good college team could beat a good NFL team, Red wrote, "My reply is that I believe the college 11 would have little, if any, chance of winning. The margin of victory be more than a touchdown." Red went on to give the pros the edge in blocking, tackling, and general defense, "which is far superior" and "headwork and in cool sureness in utilizing every ounce of immense brawn, the pros have an advantage."[14]

He did give college football the advantage in pregame frenzy, "but a fanatical desire to win and the inspiration of a coach won't take a halfback over, around, or through a hard, fast line which averages 220 pounds from end to end." He added, "That's what you face when you line up against the Green Bay Packers." Red did say that it was a toss-up as to which game was superior when it came to ball-carrying. Red truly believed the pros could defeat any college team by at least a touchdown. He had personally seen the effort these men put into the pro game. "They are out there to win," he declared. "In the dressing room I've seen hulking pro gridders shed childish tears after losing a bitterly fought game. I've shed a tear or three myself when the Bears have dropped a close one."[15] During the next couple of years, the two authors would go on to write six articles for the *Saturday Evening Post*.

The team was soon headed to the East Coast for back-to-back road games in Boston and New York. In the first game, against the Braves (1–2–1), the two teams traded touchdowns—with Red scoring on a seven-yard end run—but neither team could break the tie. In front of 12,000 at the Polo Grounds, the Bears played their most complete game of the season against the struggling Giants (1–4–1). It was Red's best game of the year. The Galloping Ghost accounted for three scores (two receiving and one rushing), which led to a 28–8 win against the Giants.

One of Red's touchdowns demonstrated the play-calling abilities of the Bears. Giants head coach Steve Owen had his defensive unit in a 6–3–2 alignment to take away the power running game of the Bears. Writing for the *Saturday Evening Post* in 1933, Red described the scoring play as follows:

> Our left end hiked downfield, heading outward at full speed, and the opposing quarter (def. halfback) covered him. Our right end did the same thing, and the opposing left half, also playing deep, went with him. I headed straight toward the defending right half; approaching him, I feinted toward my left, and as he turned to go with me, I cut back toward the middle. That's the advantage the potential receiver has over the defender—you know where you're going; he doesn't.
>
> Bronko Nagurski had taken the ball from center and threw the pass. Meanwhile, the opposing center (like a middle linebacker down the middle of the field) was backing up to cover the territory toward which I was headed. I was running forward while he was running backwards, so it wasn't an even race. Bronko threw the ball over the center's head and about a yard and a half ahead of me, so that I took it in full stride. There wasn't anyone near enough to bother me, and I had no trouble going on to a touchdown.[16]

The day after the Bears defeated the Giants, the *Chicago Daily News* wrote, "The return of Red Grange to peak form has been the greatest single factor in the rejuvenation of the Chicagoans' offense. His running has been of high order, and last Sunday he grabbed two passes and turned them into touchdowns."[17]

The big victory had the Bears record at 2-1-4. For the next three weeks, the Bears would be at home in Wrigley. Despite having only two wins, George Halas was giddy about his team. In speaking with Jim Gallagher of the *Chicago American*, the Bears owner didn't hold back.

> Boys, we're just starting to click. I know it was disgusting to watch those score-less ties, but watch our smoke from now on. Red Grange has recovered from his shoulder injury, and he's playing marvelous football.
>
> Can we beat Green Bay? Boy, we're going to knock Green Bay right out of the league when they come back here in December. They're the luckiest team in the league to have a win and a tie over us in the two games we've played already.[18]

Next up was their toughest opponent since playing the Packers four weeks earlier—the Portsmouth Spartans. The Ohio team was 4-1-2, led by their All-Pro back, Dutch Clark. The press billed the contest as a duel between Clark and Grange, only Red didn't make it to the field. While walking out of the dugout runway at Wrigley Field with his mud cleats, Red slipped, felled down, and injured his ankle. He would miss the game, being replaced by George Corbett.

A smallish crowd of just 5,500 huddled together at Wrigley Field. In the first quarter, both teams traded touchdowns. The Spartans crossed the goal line again to take a 13-7 halftime lead. In the fourth quarter, the Bears fought back. Nagurski capped off a drive with a short TD run. The Bears' kicking woes, which looked to be behind them, popped back up again, as "Tiny" Engebretsen missed the extra point.

The 13-13 game had suddenly clogged up the tie column. The NFL had to do something about all the tie games, which were detracting from the entertainment value of pro football. Red's preseason comments were not coming true. The next two weeks saw the Bears play great on both sides of the ball. The defense had been solid throughout the year, but they further elevated their play. The Bears easily took care of the struggling Dodgers. Red, who scored a TD run, returned to help the Bears shut out Brooklyn, 20-0. Four days later, on Thanksgiving Day, Halas's men crushed the crosstown Cardinals, 34-0.

Because the NFL did not count ties when calculating winning percentages in the standings, all three NFL teams at the top on November 25 still had a chance to claim the title. The NFL schedule worked out perfectly, setting up a showdown with the Spartans in Portsmouth on November 27. A nice crowd of 7,000 watched in "subfreezing weather" as the teams turned in a hard-fought tie, 7–7. It was the Bears' sixth tie of the season. It would not be the last time they would see the Portsmouth Spartans.[19]

With two games remaining on the schedule, the Bears were still in the mix. The next game was against the New York Giants on December 5, at Wrigley Field. The Giants were just 4–5–2, but they had given the Packers their only loss of the season. Coach Jones knew they would be a tough bunch to beat. "It looks as though the Giants have at last struck their stride," Jones said to the *Chicago Herald-Examiner.* "If we are to beat them it will be after a terrific argument." The coach was right. It would be a dogfight. The Bears defense dominated, but it was the Bears offense that got off to a quick start. In the first quarter, after forcing a Giants punt, Molesworth returned the pigskin to midfield. Molesworth connected with Red for 18 yards, then completed a strike to Johnsos, who carried the ball 29 yards for the game's only score. The Bears defense did the rest, sealing a 6–0 victory. The win made the Bears 5–1–6.[20]

On the same afternoon in Portsmouth, the Spartans trounced Curly Lambeau's squad, 19–0, ending the Packers' three-year run as NFL champion. The NFL title was now within reach for the Bears. If they could defeat the Packers in Chicago the following week they would tie the Spartans for first place in the standings. Despite one last game on the schedule, the Packers were out of the championship race. The NFL standings as of Monday, December 5, were as follows:

First: Portsmouth Spartans, 6–1–4 (.857 winning percentage). Regular season completed.

Second: Green Bay Packers, 10–2–1 (.833 winning percentage). Next game on December 11, at Chicago Bears

Second: Chicago Bears, 5–1–6 (.833 winning percentage). Next game on December 11, versus Green Bay Packers

The three-team race was down to one last game. Both teams couldn't have had different emotions going in—one playing for a title and a proud champion not. How would each team play? The Bears coach knew his squad was ready. "We know these boys are tough," said Ralph Jones to the *Chicago American.*

We've tried to develop a defense against any eventuality, but when you're up against a smart, big, fast team like Green Bay, you never know what will happen. We have a few surprises for them, but if the weather is cold, we may not be able to do much. One thing is for sure—the team is in great shape, and we'll give them a real battle start to finish.[21]

Mother Nature did not cooperate for the home team. Green Bay faced the Bears at Wrigley Field in a heavy snowstorm. A mere 3,000 die-hard Bears fans filled the stands. Knowing this was the most important game of his NFL career, Red found the energy to play all 60 minutes. The Packers offense was stifled by the Bears defense, but after three quarters the score stood at 0-0. Then, in the final quarter, the Bears scored twice, a field goal by Engebretsen and a 56-yard touchdown run by Nagurski to give them a hard-fought 9-0 victory, bringing the Bears (6-1-6) and Spartans (6-1-4) into a tie for first place. Despite the disputed championships in the league's first dozen years, this was the first race to actually end in a tie.

Had the league compiled its standings as it does now—counting a tie game as a half-win, half-loss—the championship would've gone to Green Bay; however, the rules established in 1921 were in effect. Winning percentage, based strictly on wins and losses, determined the order of finish; ties were simply ignored.

Right after the Bears defeated the Packers in the snow, Halas conferred with Spartans owner Harry Snyder about playing a playoff game to decide the NFL title. They agreed that it would be the best thing for the NFL. Halas then called President Carr to ask if this game could take place. Carr was on board with the idea and gave the two teams permission to play the game at Wrigley Field the following Sunday, December 18. After playing one another twice during the regular season, the Bears and Spartans would face off again for the NFL title.

The decision to play the game would make history, as the NFL was about to play its first-ever postseason game. Although the game would be an extension of the regular season rather than a "championship game," the playoff would count in the standings, which meant the loser would slip to third place behind the Green Bay Packers. The season would now hinge on one last game. For Halas and his Bears, the journey would not be easy.

The first obstacle was the weather. The Bears had played the Packers in a driving snowstorm in front of just 5,000 fans, and the week of the playoff game it didn't get any better. Bitter cold and heavy snow continued to pound the Windy City, and the possibility of playing the game at Wrigley Field—with any type of fan support—looked to be a bad idea. Halas remembered his team and the Cardinals playing a charity game indoors at Chicago Stadium in 1930, and he suggested to the Spartans that the game be contested at that site if the snow continued to fall.

Although the weather looked to be the biggest problem for the Spartans, they had their own dilemma. On the Tuesday before the game, it was announced that star halfback Dutch Clark would not be able to play. Clark was scheduled to go back to his alma mater, Colorado College, to start his duties as head basketball coach. Since the playoff game wasn't on the original schedule, the Spartans didn't foresee this being a problem. Management contacted the school's athletic director and asked for permission to allow Clark, just this once, to show up late so that he could play. They rejected the request.

The Spartans were dealt a big blow even before the game started. Despite the loss, Spartans coach Potsy Clark was still confident his squad could pull out the victory. "I'll have the boys clicking again, and we know the offense of the Bears and will plan to break it up. If the boys play any kind of ball at all, we should win," he declared. The two teams played twice during the regular season and tied both games—13–13 on November 13, and 7–7 on November 27.[22]

President Carr arrived in Chicago late in the week, and on the Friday before the game, he announced that the game would be played indoors at Chicago Stadium because of the snowstorm. Red's preseason prediction of the NFL moving into indoor stadiums had proven accurate—if for only one game. Chicago Stadium was the perfect size to host events for its usual tenants—hockey teams and circuses. As in 1930, the field was absurdly small for football—only 45 yards wide (53 one-third yards) and 80 yards long, figuring in the end zones. Fortunately for the players, a circus sponsored by the Salvation Army had just performed in the arena the week before and left a six-inch bed of tanbark dirt on the cement floor. Chicago Stadium superintendent Marty Doherty told the *Chicago American* that the surface was a "very swell brand of dirt."[23]

More than a few players and fans noted the peculiar aromatic quality of the playing surface. "It was stinking and dirty," recalled Charles "Ookie" Miller, Bears center. "One of our players got sick in the stomach and threw up. Oh it was bad. I could tell you something else. We had a couple of nips the night before. That smell wasn't too good either. I could hardly get my head in that huddle."[24] "It was dirt. It wasn't grass, believe me," recalled Red in a 1978 interview.[25]

"I remember being there, because I was nine years old. I remember the odor," said Virginia McCaskey. "The field was not your ideal field. It certainly was a lot more comfortable than being at Wrigley Field that particular week."[26] "It didn't smell very good," remembered Glenn Presnell, former Spartans halfback, who replaced Dutch Clark in the starting lineup.[27]

Because of the confined playing environment, several rules were put into place to make the game easier. Little did the league know these rules would open the eyes of everyone involved in the NFL. To accommodate football indoors, the two teams agreed to the following stipulations:

1. The field would be only 80 yards long, including the end zones (which were half-moon shaped), with a single goal post placed at one goal line. Kickoffs would originate from the defensive team's 10-yard line. Field goals were prohibited.
2. When a team crossed midfield, it immediately was set back 20 yards.
3. Because a solid fence surrounded the field only a few feet from the sidelines, the ball was moved in 15 yards (some reports say 10) after each out-of-bounds play instead of starting the play right at the sideline with a loss of down. This would be the first time "hash marks" would be used in a NFL game.
4. In case of a touchback, the ball would be brought out to the 10-yard line.

The game was set for Sunday, December 18, with kickoff at 8:15 p.m. (CST). The capacity crowd of almost 12,000 battled the elements to attend the NFL's first-ever playoff game. Outside the arena it was 15 degrees with chilly winds; inside it was a comfortable 70 degrees.

Fans came and stayed warm, but they didn't see much action. The confined conditions, as well as the sloppy dirt, limited the play on the field. "It was very treacherous footing," remembered Spartans halfback Glenn Presnell. "My favorite play was an off-tackle dive. One time we were close to the goal line, I ran off-tackle; as I planted my foot, it skidded out from under me and I went down. There was a hole there. I would've scored a touchdown."[28]

In the first quarter, Red got smeared by two Spartans defenders, whose hard hit knocked him from the game. George Corbett replaced Red. Despite missing Dutch Clark, the Spartans held tough and fought the Bears on even terms for three quarters. "The line play and the open-field tackling were accurate and hard," wrote the *Chicago Tribune*. Neither team had scored heading into the final quarter. After resting, Red returned to the game. With less than five minutes remaining, Bears halfback Dick Nesbitt made a leaping interception of an Ace Gutowsky pass, returning it to the Spartans' 7-yard line before being knocked out of bounds. Because of the special rule, the ball was brought into the field 15 yards, costing the Bears a down. On second down, Bronko Nagurski blasted 6 yards to the 1; on third down, Nagurski tried again, but this time he lost a yard. On fourth down, the game's pivotal play was about to take place, and the NFL would never be the same.[29]

It was fourth and goal from the 2. Red lined up at his left halfback position. Nagurski was at fullback and Nesbitt at right halfback. Nagurski got the ball a third time, faked a line smash, retreated a few steps, and fired a pass to a wide open Red in the end zone. Referee Bobbie Cahn signaled touchdown. "I lined up four yards back. Red went in motion. The ball came to me. There was no way I could get through. I stopped. I moved back a couple of steps. Grange had gone around and was in the end zone, all by himself. I threw him a short pass," recalled Bronko of the touchdown.[30] "Nagurski was not the greatest passer in the world," Red said about the game-winning toss. "He threw me a great end-over-end pass. I had blocked, or tried to block for someone, and Bronk went for a jump pass. He threw me the ball."[31]

Spartans coach Potsy Clark stormed onto the field, protesting that Nagurski was not five yards behind the line of scrimmage when he threw the pass, as the rules required. "We were sure that he was going to make a line plunge. He wasn't anywhere near five yards back of the line of scrimmage, which was a rule in those days," said Presnell. "It was an illegal pass. He wasn't five yards back. Of course he lined up about five yards back, but when he took the ball he stared to plunge into the line. Then he jumped up. They counted it anyway."[32]

"Well, I'm right in the middle. As I recall he started up and then jumped in the air and threw the pass," remembered Ookie Miller. "They complained of course. They claimed it was illegal, but Nagurski claims he backed up far enough that he was five yards back. I know we were working on that play for months." Cahn was unmoved by the protesting and held up the score. Engebretsen converted the extra point. A few moments later, the Bears got a safety on a bad Spartans center snap through the end zone. The Bears finished the game strong to win the 1932 NFL title with a 9-0 victory.[33]

"After 11 years the Bears were again champions!" wrote Halas in his autobiography. "Ralph Jones had delivered. Everybody acclaimed him. The modern T formation with man-in-motion had delivered."[34] Halas had title number two. The best thing about the game was the amount of press the game received, as almost every newspaper ran articles on the Bears' big victory. Kenneth Fry, writing for the *United Press*, described the "indoor madness":

Chicago Bears defeated the Portsmouth, Ohio, Spartans on the indoor gridiron at the Chicago Stadium last night, 9 to 0, for the professional football championship. . . . The playing field was six inches of dirt and tanbark spread over the stadium's concrete floor. The field itself was 60 yards long, 40 yards short of the rule book length. Players standing on their own goal lines punted into the other team's end zone all evening. Punts from the middle of the field landed in the mezzanine balcony and adjacent territory. One kick knocked the "BL" out of the Black Hawks hockey sign. Another hit a sour note on the organ, as the organist was playing, for obscure and undetermined reason, a song about "Cutting Down the Old Pine Tree."

The organist played "Illinois Loyalty" when Red Grange caught a forward pass for a touchdown. By mutual agreement neither team attempted field goals. Windows cost money. . . . Only one punt was caught and returned during the entire contest. One went out of the bounds, one was downed. The rest landed against the walls or sent spectators scurrying for cover. Officials spent more time picking large clinkers out of the soil than they did blowing whistles.[35]

The *Chicago Tribune* had Wilfrid Smith's detailed game recap, along with a photo from the game. The only known image of action from the contest shows Nagurski, as ballcarrier, being tackled by the neck by Spartans halfback Glenn Presnell in the first quarter of play. Smith revealed that the gross receipts from the game "were in excess of $15,000."[36]

The *Portsmouth Times* called it a "sham battle on a Tom Thumb gridiron," although they did say the fans "enjoyed immensely the spectacle of an outdoor sport performed indoors."[37] For the past month, rumors had been circulating that this was going to be Red's last game. The *Chicago Tribune's* sports editor, Arch Ward, wrote,

If Grange has played his last game it can be said that he passed out as dramatically as he entered. He was all but knocked out in the first half with a blow on the head that temporarily deprived him of his senses. . . . He came back in the closing moments to score the touchdown that clinched the championship for Chicago. . . . They say that no man is a great fighter until he gets off the floor to carry on to victory. They can say the same about Red Grange, the football marvel of his day.[38]

Red had finally made it to the top. He was a world champion. "It was a good football game, and the attendance was good. We had a sellout," recalled Red in a 1978 interview. "The people loved the game, because they were right up on the field and could see the blocking and tackling, and all the maneuvering. Everyone enjoyed it, it was quite a football game."[39]

Red received his share of the headlines in newspapers throughout the United States. The *Chicago Tribune* wrote, "Grange Hero as Bears Capture 1932 Pro Diadem," while the *Green Bay Press-Gazette* ran the header, "Grange Closes Grid Career in Hero Role."[40] Everyone involved in the NFL's first-ever postseason game benefited. The bottom line was that the indoor game had more significance than its immediate effect on the NFL standings. It would be one of the NFL's most important games.

A couple of days after the indoor game, several writers and fans still weren't satisfied with the outcome. Tom Swope of the *Cincinnati Post* penned the headline, "Pennant Decided in Joke Contest" and called the charity exhibition game between the Bears and Spartans in Cincinnati the true championship contest. President Carr put to rest any potential controversy by saying,

> You fellows decided to play for the championship in the Stadium. You knew in advance the field was small. You should have known that the smallness of the so-called Stadium gridiron would preclude real football and prevent both sides from executing many of the plays at your command. But since you announced that the championship would hinge on the indoor game, the Bears must be declared champions of our league.[41]

Despite the negative tone put out by some members of the press, the NFL was able to gain great insight as a result of the NFL's first-ever "playoff" game—there was unbelievable interest generated among fans and the media by playing a game for all the marbles at the end of the season. The owners would also see the positive impact of the indoor game, and they would respond quickly.

27

THE NFL GROWS UP

At the end of the 1932 season the NFL coaches selected an All-League Team. Red was selected to the Second Team. Although he missed out on First Team honors, Red was pleased that three of his teammates—Carlson, Johnsos, and Nagurski—made the list. Art Bystrom of the *Green Bay Press-Gazette* had Red on his 22-man All-NFL team. He was joined in the backfield by quarterbacks Dutch Clark (Spartans) and Molesworth (Bears); halfbacks Bob Campiglo (Dodgers), Ken Strong (Stapletons), and Glenn Presnell (Spartans); and fullbacks Clarke Hinkle (Packers) and Nagurski.

Red was now considered one of the best players in the NFL. Packers coach Curly Lambeau thought highly of the aging superstar:

> Let me tell you the difference between pro ball and college ball. Red Grange was a riot at college. He was a wonder. Then he came into our league, and in his first year he was a flop. We found that we could pass him dizzy. We could run by him. He was only a ballcarrier. But then, Grange started to learn football. He knew he couldn't get by just on his ball-carrying ability. Today? Today, Grange is the best defensive player and the best blocker in the league. He does not make many 80-yard runs, maybe, as he did when he was at Illinois, but he's a far greater ballplayer—can do anything. Grange is smart.[1]

It was the ultimate compliment from a future Hall of Fame coach. Red had proven to the league and himself that he was a great professional football player—but more as a defensive player than the great open-field runner he was in college.

About to turn 30 years old, Red was considering retiring. "I'm beginning to get a little too old to undergo the bumps like I once did," said Red to the press. He was thinking about coaching. One rumor circulating was that he was in the running for the head job at Oregon State. But first he joined the Green Bay Packers squad out West to play in a few exhibition games. His name would help draw more fans out to the games, while filling the pocket of his rivals' bank accounts. Red and his manager, Frank Zambreno, drove his automobile to California to play for Curly Lambeau. The first stop would be San Francisco.[2]

The games were sponsored by the Knights of Columbus with some of the proceeds turned over to several Catholic charities. In their first game against Ernie Nevers's Pacific Coast All-Stars, Red started at left halfback in the same backfield as quarterback Roger Grove, right halfback Arnie Herber, and full-back Clarke Hinkle. It must have felt strange for the redhead playing for a squad that featured his bitter enemies of the past four seasons. He adapted. In front of a large crowd of 30,000 fans at Kezar Stadium, Nevers got the best of Red's team, winning 13-6.

Red's contract called for him to play at least 20 minutes. For the most part, he played well, helping his squad on both sides of the ball. But Red was thinking more about his football future. "I think this will be my last game. I've contemplated quitting for some time. I'm on the lookout for a coaching job. I have several angles now and may line up before the 1933 season starts," said Red while playing in Los Angeles. Another rumor was reported that he was a candidate for the Wyoming coaching job.[3]

While Red was thinking about joining the coaching ranks, his current mentor with the Chicago Bears was calling it quits. Ralph Jones had accomplished what he wanted to do. The one thing that he promised George Halas he would do in three years—deliver him a championship—had been accomplished. Because he had reached his goal with the Bears, Jones decided to walk away from the pro game. He returned to Lake Forest to help coach young boys into men. After a futile search, Halas reinstated himself as head coach. Despite the championship season Halas had lost money—$18,000. It was a problem worth having.[4]

Once he returned to Chicago, Red was interviewed by Kenneth Fry of the *United Press*. The Ghost, "wearing the lopsided grin so familiar to sports page readers," reflected on his future and love for the game of football. "Right now I believe I'm through," he pronounced.

But when next fall comes around, I might give in and try football another year. It isn't easy to give it up. . . . I loved football, both as college and professional player. Many lads like football because of the headlines their deeds bring the next

morning. Those players have no business continuing in the game after college. . . .
Don't go into the game of pro football for the glory. It's hard work.[5]

Red retuned to Wheaton to visit his father. In 1931, Lyle had returned full-
time to the small town in DuPage County, resuming his job as chief of police,
working harder than he ever had. Before long, Red's free time was being spent
back in show business. He toured the country with a vaudeville group of 65
singers, dancers, and comedians performing in a show called *Earl Taylor's
Vanities*, also featuring Mildred Harris, the first wife of Charlie Chaplin. Acting
since she was 11, Harris had appeared in more than 100 films. She and Red
would headline the tour. Acting as master of ceremonies, Red introduced the
show's acts and entertainers. A dancing "beauty chorus" was the main part
of the 90-minute show. The tour made stops in small towns and county fairs
throughout the United States. It appeared in such cities as Logansport, Indiana;
Green Bay, Wisconsin; Manitowic, Wisconsin; Escanaba, Michigan; and even
Winnipeg, Canada, at the West and Old Kildonan Fair.[6] Reviews were mostly
positive. The *Green Bay Press-Gazette* wrote,

> The stage show, lasting over an hour, played to a capacity crowd last evening and
> kept the audience in a good mood throughout the entire run of the program. . . .
> The finale of the show is a dandy with the "Galloping Ghost" encasing a football
> in his hands while he starts out on an imaginary long, sweeping run for a distant
> goal. His interference takes out all would-be tacklers, and "Red," it is safe to say,
> chalks up another touchdown for his side.[7]

In late April, the tour made a stop at Red's old college hangout. For four
days, the show appeared at the Virginia Theater in Champaign. In the same
place that C. C. Pyle had discussed his plans for Red turning pro and going on
a once-in-a-lifetime barnstorming tour, the Galloping Ghost performed a song
and dance show. Red visited with friends, as well as saw his old coach, Bob
Zuppke. The two men started to repair their relationship. Zuppke could see that
pro football had not harmed the college game and wanted to get back on good
terms with his greatest pupil. Speaking to the *Daily Illini*, Red was eager to talk
about football. He commented, "Football's the thing. I don't know what I'd do
if I couldn't play the game or be connected with it in some manner." After thinking about his future, he put off coaching to play another year with the Bears.
The Ghost would be back on the gridiron for the 1933 season.[8]

While Red was dancing on stage, planning his return to the gridiron, the
NFL was going through some massive historical changes. In 1932, the NFL
had seen more progress, with an increase in the average attendance per game.

A total of 599,561 fans had passed through the turnstiles in 48 NFL games (47 regular-season games and one postseason game). The league saw an increase from 9,727 fans per game in 1931, to 12,490 fans per game in 1932, and with the additional positive press coverage of the season-ending playoff game, the NFL owners felt the future was bright.

During the 1932 NFL season, as well as during the indoor playoff game, league president Joe F. Carr and the other owners saw that the play on the field was getting stale. As a group, they began discussions about how to improve the game. The first thing to be examined was what to do about the significant number of tie games. Of the 47 regular-season games in 1932, 10 (21 percent) had ended in a tie.

During the 1932 season, the NFL saw just *six* field goals made—Dutch Clark (Spartans) led the league with half of them, with three. In comparison, the NFL saw *seven* safeties, eight if you count the one in the indoor playoff game. When the stats showed that teams had scored more safeties than field goals, it became clear something had to be done. Scoring had to be encouraged by more scoring, which, in theory, would reduce the potential for low-scoring tie games. President Carr agreed, saying,

> Spectators are opposed to drawn-out games. They want rapid action, intermingled with thrills and glamour, which have made football such a great spectacle. If the new rules detract from the glamour of the game, we will have to revise them to suit our needs. It is our desire to open up the game and give the public as much action as possible. Our greatest appeal to the public is the speed with which a professional game moves.[9]

Carr could see that something had to be done and that the league couldn't wait until the summer to discuss the issues facing the owners. In addition to the efforts to make the NFL more fan friendly, Carr had several new franchise applications land on his desk. Several cities wanted in, including Philadelphia, Cincinnati, Cleveland, and Pittsburgh. The Steel City had several different promoters interested, so Carr decided to kill two birds with one stone and called for a special league meeting, set for February 25 and 26 in Pittsburgh.

On the first day, Carr called the meeting at 1:00 p.m. in the conference room at the Fort Pitt Hotel. Eight teams and their owners gathered for a session that would change the course of professional football. One of the first owners to talk was Boston owner George Preston Marshall, who, after just one year as an NFL owner, wasn't shy about expressing his feelings. "Gentleman it's about time we realized that we're not only in the football business. We're also in the entertainment business," he stated.

> If the colleges want to louse up their game with bad rules, let 'em. We don't have to follow suit. We should do what's best for us. I say we should adopt rules that will give the pros a spectacular individuality and national significance. Face it, we're in show business. If people don't buy tickets, we'll have no business at all.[10]

After the lengthy discussion, the owners adopted the following three resolutions:

1. Motion by George Preston Marshall, seconded by George Halas, that goal posts be placed back at the goal line, instead of back of the end zone. Motion carried.
2. Motion by George Preston Marshall, seconded by George Halas, that the rule covering the use of the forward pass, five yards behind the line of scrimmage before he can pass the ball, be changed, permitting the passer to pass the ball from any point behind the line of scrimmage. Motion carried.
3. Motion that when the ball is within five yards of being out of bounds, the ball would be moved into the field of play 10 yards (hashmarks). Motion carried.[11]

The owners, led by the two Georges, had made some important and much-needed changes, and they were also about to separate their game from the collegiate one. Ever since the National Football League was founded in 1920, as the American Professional Football Association, it had followed the rules of college football, but, in 1933, they made important decisions and rule changes that redirected the course of the league. The NFL needed to make its "product" more exciting and more marketable. This was a big start, but the owners weren't done remaking the league.

While in Pittsburgh, Carr also meet with potential investors for an NFL franchise to be located in the western Pennsylvania city, as well as in Philadelphia. The team's admission into the NFL was predicated on the removal of the state's blue laws, which made it illegal to hold professional sporting events on Sundays. For years, the state's baseball teams had suffered under the restrictions of the laws, but baseball could be played any day of the week, to numerous crowds. Because pro football teams normally played only one game per week, they needed to draw large crowds on weekends, and Saturdays belonged to the colleges. The new law allowing Sunday games in the state of Pennsylvania would go into effect that November. Carr selected Art Rooney to be the Pittsburgh owner and Bert Bell and his partner, Lud Wray, to be the Philadelphia owners. Rooney, a former boxer and semipro football player, named his squad the Pittsburgh Pirates, while Bell, a former star player at the University of Pennsylvania, christened his team the Philadelphia Eagles.

Four months later, the owners met in Halas's hometown to further grow the league. Held at the Blackstone Hotel in Chicago on July 8 and 9, the league met again. On the second day, the owners were fixing to make more history. For years, they had bounced around the idea of splitting the NFL into divisions, similar to baseball's American and National leagues. It was time to take that leap. In a motion brought up by George Preston Marshall, it was suggested that the NFL be split into two divisions. The East would consist of Boston, Brooklyn, New York, Philadelphia, and Pittsburgh. The West would be comprised of the Chicago Bears, the Chicago Cardinals, Cincinnati, Green Bay, and Portsmouth.

But Marshall wasn't done with his idea of how the new NFL should look. He brought up another motion suggesting that the winner of each division meet in a championship game.

It was about time. For almost a dozen years the NFL hierarchy had talked about arranging itself into two divisions so that it could have a season-ending championship game. A championship game would do away with unseemly postseason arguments about which team had actually won the title. Disputes had erupted in 1921, 1924, 1925, and 1931. In 1932, the Spartans and Bears were tied at season's end, and the NFL couldn't expect the outcome to always be so straightforward. The new setup would give the league a "second" pennant race. In theory, you only had to be good in your division. Moreover, the championship game at the end of the season would bring in more money. The NFL now had its version of baseball's World Series. After 13 seasons in operation, the NFL was all grown up—on the right track toward separating itself from the college game and creating its own image and brand.

As for Red, he still wanted to be part of the league he helped foster. He wasn't ready to step away or take on a coaching job. In August, he signed his Bears contract and sent it to Halas. "Although I'm traveling around the country in a show, I am keeping in condition and never felt better. I'm down to playing weight and can't wait to get into that old '77' jersey again," he said.[12]

The Bears roster had stayed much as it was for the 1932 championship season. Losses from the year before were center George Trafton, who finally retired, and fullback Herb Joesting. The biggest position hit was at tackle, as the Bears lost Lloyd Burdick, Tiny Engebretsen, Don Murry, and Harold Ely.

Halas would need a whole new set of tackles. He started with an old friend. Link Lyman decided to rejoin his old club. Halas then would add veteran Ray Richards, who played for the Frankford Yellow Jackets, and tackle Dick Stahlman (6-foot-2, 219 pounds) and guard Joe Zeller (6-foot-1, 203 pounds), both former Packers and also seasoned vets.

Returning on the front line would be ends Luke Johnsos, Bill Hewitt, and Paul Franklin; guards Zuck Carlson, Joe Kopcha, Bill Buckler, and Gil Bergerson; and centers Ookie Miller and Bert Pearson. In the backfield Red was joined by halfbacks George Corbett, John Doehring, Dick Nesbitt, and Johnny Sisk; quarterbacks Keith Molesworth and Carl Brumbaugh; and the league's best fullback, Bronko Nagurski. Once again for the fourth straight year Halas signed a great rookie class. On the line he added end Bill Karr (6-foot-1, 190 pounds) from West Virginia and massive tackle George Musso (6-foot-1, 262 pounds) from Milliken University. In the backfield he added halfback Gene Ronzani (5-foot-9, 200 pounds) from Marquette, a teammate of Johnny Sisk, and fullback Jack Manders (6-foot-1, 203 pounds) of Minnesota, who also kicked, solving a longtime problem for Halas. These four men would play a combined 34 years for the Bears.

For the first time since 1929, Red was not starting; he would come off the bench to replace Gene Ronzani at left halfback.

The season opener was against their bitter rivals—the Packers. Almost 12,000 fans jammed into Green Bay's City Stadium to witness another tightly fought contest. After a scoreless first half, the Packers jumped out in front with a touchdown in the third quarter. Late in the fourth, the Bears shocked the hometown team with two great special teams plays. First, Hewitt blocked a field goal attempt that led to his scoring toss to Johnsos. Then, after a three-and-out with one-minute remaining, Hewitt crashed through the Packers line again to block a Packers punt and then recovered it for a game-winning touchdown. According to the *Green Bay Press-Gazette*, Halas was seen on the bench "acting like a wild man, jumping and dancing after the score." The Bears' improbable 14–7 victory started a season of fantastic comebacks and fourth-quarter thrills. "I've been waiting six years for this day," said Halas after the game. "It's been a long time since we beat the Packers here, but this game makes up for the lean years we have had here."[13]

The following week, the Bears fought their way to a tough 7–0 home victory against the Boston Redskins, behind a fourth-quarter scoring run by Johnny Sisk.

Back-to-back wins against the Brooklyn Dodgers (10–0) and the Chicago Cardinals (12–9) had the Bears undefeated, at 4–0. The fast start set up a quick rematch with the Packers in Chicago. Once again, the Bears snatched victory from their rivals. This time the clock showed just less than four minutes remaining, with the Bears trailing 7–0. The Bears offense finally woke up when Red tossed a 24-yard lateral scoring strike to Johnsos. With time running out Jack Manders kicked a 30-yard field goal to send the hometown fans home into a frenzy.

One week later, the Bears faced off against the Giants (4–2), and a season-high 28,000 fans came out to Wrigley. Red was full of energy, starting at left halfback and playing the entire 60 minutes. The first half saw each team trade touchdowns. Then, in the fourth quarter, Ken Strong kicked a 26-yard field goal to give the visiting Giants a three-point lead with less than five minutes remaining. But this was just where the Bears wanted them. Just like in the season opener against the Packers, special teams came up big. After stopping the Giants just past midfield, Strong stepped back to punt, trying to pin the Bears back. Instead, Luke Johnsos crashed through, partially blocking the kick. Hewitt scooped up the ball, rumbling all the way to the Giants 18-yard line before being tackled. After gaining one first down, the game-winning play was a passing play designed by Halas worthy of the highlight reel.

The ball was snapped to Keith Molesworth, who faked a handoff to halfback Johnny Sisk, then tossed a lateral to Bill Hewitt, who came from his end position behind the halfbacks. As he ran behind the line of scrimmage—the defense thinking it was an end-around run play near the goal line—the other end, Bill Karr, drifted downfield. Taking a glance to see Karr, Hewitt, surrounded by several Giants defenders who were thinking it was a run, tossed a lazy spiral downfield to Karr, who caught the ball one step from the goal line and scored an easy touchdown. Wrigley Field erupted with cheers. The miracle Bears had pulled off another victory.

For the fifth time in six games, the Bears had mounted a comeback in the fourth quarter after being tied or trailing. It was becoming a special season on the North Side of Chicago. The Bears then traveled east for a three-game road trip. The seemly invincible Bears came away with no wins. The hometown Boston Redskins handed the Bears their first loss of the year, 10–0, as 23,000 watched. The following week in Philadelphia, the Bears played their first game against the newly formed Eagles—a game that ended in a 3–3 tie. The final game of the trip saw the Bears lose, 3–0, to the Giants on a Ken Strong field goal in front of 22,000 screaming fans at the Polo Grounds. The Bears limped home with a 6–2–1 record, leading the Portsmouth Spartans by just one game in the Western Division. But like the champions they were, the setback against New

York would be their last loss of the 1933 season. As of November 20, the 1933 NFL standings were as follows:

Eastern Division	Western Division
New York Giants 7–3	Chicago Bears 6–2–1
Brooklyn Dodgers 4–2–1	Portsmouth Spartans 6–3
Boston Redskins 5–4–1	Green Bay Packers 4–5–1
Philadelphia Eagles 2–3–1	Cincinnati Reds 2–5–1
Pittsburgh Pirates 3–5–2	Chicago Cardinals 1–8

The refocused Bears arrived at Wrigley Field to face the Portsmouth Spartans for the first time since the indoor game. The Spartans had suffered a key loss when All-Pro Dutch Clark decided to retire, sticking to coaching in Colorado. He was replaced by the equally tough Glenn Presnell. The Bears jumped out quickly, scoring on a Manders field goal and a Hewitt touchdown pass to rookie Bill Karr, but the always tough Spartans came roaring back. Presnell and fellow halfback Ernie Caddell both hit pay dirt to give the Ohio team a 14–10 lead in the fourth quarter. But for the third time Hewitt would block a kick that would change the outcome of the game.

Charging the line from his end position Hewitt stepped in front of an Elmer Schaake punt, smothering the ball against his arms. The ball bounced crazily up the field until finally being recovered by Zuck Carlson at the Spartans 29-yard line. On the next play, Nagurski sprinted around left end behind perfect blocking for the go-ahead score. The defense did the rest, preserving a 17–14 hard-fought win. The Bears were now in the driver's seat in the Western Division.

In addition to playing games for the Bears, Red continued to contribute to the sport off the field. He resumed his relationship with George Dunscomb, writing two more football articles for the *Saturday Evening Post*. The first article, titled "The Easy Way to Score," in the October 28 issue, went into detail about using the passing game to score quick touchdowns. Grange described the best way to attack a 6–3–2 defense. "Of all the departments of football, I like the forward pass best. There's a little baseball involved in it, and to me it is the most interesting phase of the game," wrote Red. The second article was titled "Outguessing Them," in the November 25 issue. In this one, Red got technical, explaining why the game of football is the best strategic sport. He called the game a pure "clash of wits . . . attempts to outguess, outthink, or out maneuver your opponent." He also called the game a "chess match." He gave examples of certain Bears plays that proved his point and also praised some of the smartest players in the NFL, including Bronko Nagurski, Benny Friedman, and Mike Michalske.[14]

Four days after defeating the Spartans, the Bears tangled on Thanksgiving Day with their crosstown rivals the Cardinals, who were a disappointing 1–8. The game was no contest. Halas's squad took care of business, dispatching the Cards, 22–6. "Red Grange, who showed flashes of his old elusiveness, provided most of the thrills," wrote the *Chicago Daily News*.[15]

The Bears were now 8–2–1 (first in Western Division), with two games to go. If they defeated the Spartans, they would clinch the division and play in the NFL's first championship game. Halas also knew that if they had the best record of the two division winners they would host the title game. "If the choice is ours, we'll play here," said Halas to the local press. "The Chicago fans have supported us wonderfully this season and deserve the chance to see the title game."[16]

Traveling to southern Ohio to play in front of 10,000 screaming fans at Universal Stadium to defeat the Spartans wasn't going to be easy. Potsy Clark's squad was well rested, having not played on Turkey Day. The Bears didn't show the effects of the short rest. Controlling the ball on offense with a potent passing attack, the Bears got touchdowns on pass plays to Hewitt and Molesworth—who caught his toss from Red. The Bears' 17–7 victory clinched the Western Division. That same day, the New York Giants defeated the Pittsburgh Pirates, 27–3, to wrap up the Eastern Division. The NFL's first-ever championship game was set. It would be the Eastern Division's New York Giants against the Western Division's Chicago Bears.

On December 5, league president Joe F. Carr announced that the NFL's first championship game would take place on Sunday, December 17, at the home field of the division winner with the highest winning percentage. That meant if the Bears defeated the Packers in their season finale, they would host the game at Wrigley Field; if they lost and the Giants won their game, the big game would be at the Polo Grounds.

Newspapers nationwide ran headlines calling the game "Pro Football's World Series." The game was getting top billing throughout the country. The title game was set, and when the Bears defeated the Packers, 7–6, on December 10, it was determined that the NFL's first championship game would be played at Wrigley Field a week later.[17]

After the last regular-season game against the Packers at Wrigley, Red was asked if this would be his last game. "I think this will be my last year as a player," said Red. "It's getting to be a pretty tough grind, and I'm about ready to call it quits and take something softer." After a season of bumps and bruises, you couldn't blame the 30-year-old football warrior for wanting to call it quits, but the Galloping Ghost still had one more big game to play, and one more memory to put into the history books.[18]

The two division winners had met twice in the regular season, with both teams winning at home, the Bears 14–10 at Wrigley and the Giants 3–0 at the Polo Grounds. Wrigley Field would be the site of the NFL's first championship game. The Bears had been undefeated at home (6–0), outscoring their opponents 67–46, while the Giants were just 4–3 on the road, outscoring their opponents 90–75.

Wanting to avoid ending the game in darkness, Carr told the teams and the press that the game would begin at 1:45 p.m. (CST) instead of the original 2:00 p.m. kickoff—which was the time on the game tickets that Halas had printed up. The Bears were a 7-to-5 favorite to retain the championship.

On December 17, on a cool and damp Chicago afternoon. the two teams arrived at Wrigley Field to find perfect football weather. Programs were being sold for 10 cents, and the few remaining tickets went up for sale at the box office. The press box was filled to capacity with sportswriters, and the game would be broadcast locally on radio by WGN. Although the field was soft and slippery with a stiff wind coming out of the northwest, it wouldn't hinder the offensive fireworks that were about to happen.

Wrigley Field was jam-packed with 26,000 fans who had no idea what they were about witness and would be talking for years to come. At kickoff, fog hung low over the field as the Bears took an early 3–0 lead on a Jack Manders 16-yard field goal. As the second quarter began, Manders kicked a 40-yard field goal—thanks to owners for moving the goal posts up—to give the Bears a 6–0 lead. Then Giants quarterback Harry Newman got his high-scoring offense on the board. Throwing passes through the mist, Newman connected with Red Badgro for 29 yards to score the first touchdown in NFL Championship Game history—giving the Giants a 7–6 halftime lead.

Both teams seemed to be feeling one another out. The second half would be a different story, as the fans and the rest of the country would get a chance to see the future of the NFL. Coach Halas rallied his troops. "Halas says, 'We can win this ballgame. We've just been making a few mistakes out there. Just play the kind of ball that we're capable of playing and there'll be no doubt you can win this ball game,'" recalled Bears tackle George Musso in a 1999 interview.[19]

In the second half, the lead bounced back and forth with one exciting play after another. In the third quarter, Manders kicked his third field goal to give the Bears a 9–7 advantage. The Giants came roaring back with a 61-yard drive ending with a one-yard Moose Krause touchdown plunge to regain the lead at

14–9. The scoring had just begun, but one spectator thought his team was in good enough shape to win. "I used to sit on the bench in those days," recalled Wellington Mara, the son of the owner. "I remembered they kicked a field goal, kicked two field goals. We scored a touchdown. They kicked a field goal. We scored a touchdown. I remember saying, 'Boy this is great. We'll trade a field goal for a TD anytime.'"[20]

The Bears quickly retaliated by scoring on a play made famous one year earlier in the "indoor circus." Deep in Giants territory, Halas called a line-plunge by Nagurski, who would stop short and take a few steps back to toss a pass to rookie Bill Karr. It worked perfectly for an eight-yard score. Now that you could pass from anywhere behind the line of scrimmage, this play didn't cause any uproar from the Giants. As the third quarter ended with the Bears leading 16–14 and the Giants driving again, 26,000 spectators had just witnessed three lead changes in one quarter. Both offenses were playing the wide-open, exciting, entertaining game that the owners envisioned when they made the rule changes just 10 months earlier. Fans at Wrigley Field were on the edges of their seats waiting to see how this great game would end.

On the first play of the fourth quarter, with the ball at the Bears eight-yard line, Ken Strong took a handoff but became trapped near the sideline and lateraled the pigskin to a surprised Harry Newman. "Ken Strong took the ball, and he went across the field. [But] he couldn't find an opening," remembered Giants quarterback Harry Newman in a 1999 interview. "Meanwhile, I'd gone to my right. He threw me the ball back to me. The Bears all followed me. I tried to go through, find a hole. I couldn't find one. I started back. I looked, and there was Ken waving his arms over the goal line. I threw the ball back to him for a touchdown."[21]

The remarkable touchdown caused the hometown crowd to moan and groan—but also ooh and ah—because the lead had once again changed hands. Late in the fourth quarter, down 21–16, the Bears came back one final time. Just like they had done throughout the season, the Bears gathered up the energy for one more fourth-quarter comeback. After a Keith Molesworth pass to Carl Brumbaugh brought the ball to the Giants 33-yard line, the next play saw the Bears pull off one of the most amazing plays in NFL history.

Nagurski took the handoff and threw a quick jump pass to a helmetless Bill Hewitt from his left end position. After gaining 14 yards, two Giants defenders converged on his left. Hewitt saw teammate Bill Karr coming hard on his right and, in a split second, lateraled the ball to Karr. Caught by surprise, the Giants watched the rookie from West Virginia sprint the remaining 19 yards for a stunning touchdown.

The Windy City crowd erupted, as did George Halas on the sidelines. "We called it 'Little Pea Pass.' It worked for us many a times that play," recalled Musso.[22] It was the sixth lead change of the game, and it gave the Bears a 23–21 lead late in the fourth quarter.

When the Giants got the ball back again there were only a few seconds remaining. Newman faded back and threw his 12th completion for the day (on 17 attempts) to wingback Dale Burnett, who broke open in the Bears secondary. Racing a few steps behind him was All-Pro center Mel Hein. Standing in between the two Giants players was Red Grange, and he knew quickly what Burnett wanted to do. He had just seen the Bears pull off a lateral, so Red wasn't about to see the NFL title slip away on a repeat move.

"I could see he wanted to lateral, so I didn't go low. I hit him around the ball and pinned his arms," said Grange after the game. "It was just one of those things. Anybody could've done the same thing, and would've done the same thing. But we won the ballgame." After the two men fell to the ground, the gun sounded, ending the game. The crowd let out a big gasp and roared for joy, as the Bears had won their second straight NFL title and the league's first championship game. "Red Grange saved the game for Chicago . . . that quick thinking prevented a score on the last play," said Tim Mara to the press after the game.[23] George Halas would always say, "That play Grange made was the greatest defensive play I ever saw."[24]

Throughout the years Red always said that the game-saving tackle in the first NFL Championship Game was one of his greatest thrills in pro football.[25] "To this day I still say it's the greatest football game I ever saw or ever participated in," Red said in a 1973 interview.[26]

The two teams left Wrigley Field knowing that they played the best they could have played. The public and press agreed, as the NFL's first championship game was a big hit nationwide. The headlines and game recaps throughout the United States proclaimed the action on the field:

National Pro Football Honors Won by Bears in Spectacular Aerial Struggle—The struggle was a revelation to college coaches who advocate no changes in the rules. It was strictly an offensive battle, and the professional rule of allowing passes thrown from any point behind the line of scrimmage was responsible for most of the thrills.—*New York Times*[27]

Game Thrills Crowd—Even several college coaches who sat in the press box were left shaking with excitement and suggesting that the colleges adopt the pro league's forward pass rule, which made those thrill-packed minutes possible.— Howard Roberts, *Chicago Daily News*[28]

Universal comment on Sunday's game was that the Giants and Bears staged the greatest offensive battle in modern football.—Wilfrid Smith, *Chicago Tribune*[29]

The game was a brilliant display of offensive power . . . in one of the most spectacular games ever witnessed.—*Associated Press*[30]

The NFL's first championship game was a huge hit. The hard work of the NFL in the past 12 months, most notably taking a risky chance of establishing new rules to break away from the more popular college game, had paid off in a big way. After the game Carr broke down the gate receipts and announced the good news to everyone involved. The net receipts of the game, after paying the government tax, park rental of Wrigley Field ($3,170.77), and expenses of staging the game, totaled $14,606.92. Of this amount, 60 percent was to go to the players based on the meeting in Columbus. The Bears would take a 60–40 split of that pie for winning, and that would come out to $210.84 per player. The Giants got $140.22 per player.

Halas also awarded trainer Andy Lotshaw and assistant Laurie Walquist a share of the earnings. Halas wanted to give all the credit to his players. "I really had little to do with it," he said to Howard Roberts of the *Chicago Daily News*. "The real reason the Bears won is that the squad was composed of 22 fellows who love to play football. With a bunch of fellows like that to work with it's not hard to produce a winner."[31]

The money was secondary, although Red and his teammates enjoyed the extra cash. The tremendous publicity by the press and the enthusiasm for a title game shown by the fans proved to everyone involved in the NFL that the league could have its own identity and something to sell to the public.

After the big game Red jumped right into another business opportunity, investing some of his money in a nightclub named after him. The new "77 Club" was located on the North Side of Chicago at 1116 Leland Avenue, near Broadway. Ads featured throughout town read,

> You'll find "Red" Grange's 77 Club the newest and coziest equipped dine and dance place on the North Side. Splendid entertainment and popular prices will prevail. We feel confident that you will enjoy the atmosphere of this newest of Chicago nightclubs. Come tonight and join in on the grand opening festivities!

Pabst Blue Ribbon beer was served for the opening ceremonies, which took place just a few days before New Year's Eve. Matchbook covers were given out bearing a picture of Red in his Bears uniform, wearing his white number 77 jersey.[32]

Having grown out of his shy stage from high school and college, Red had learned to enjoy mingling with people, he just wasn't the biggest fan of the drinking scene. "I never took a drink in my life," said Red to the press covering the opening of the club.[33] "We once had a party for the Bears there," he recalled in a 1976 radio interview. "I had the thing for about three months, broke about even. But I learned all the headaches in that job."[34] The opportunity to own his own nightclub seemed to go against his character. It would be just that. Seven months later, Red would sell his interest in the establishment. "I can't run a nightclub and try to play football too," he said to the local press. "I'd rather play football."[35]

28

THE GALLOPING GHOST WALKS AWAY

After defending their crown as NFL champion, Halas treated his squad to a vacation—to play more football. Traveling out West and down South, the Bears would try to cash in on their championship reputation. The 1933–1934 postseason exhibition schedule was as follows:

St. Louis Gunners, St. Louis, Missouri, December 24, 1933
Southern Methodist University Ex-Letterman, Dallas, Texas, January 6, 1934
Erny Pinckert's All-Stars, Los Angeles, California, January 14, 1934
Pacific Coast All-Stars, San Francisco, California, January 21, 1934
National All-Stars, Los Angeles, California, January 28, 1934
Erny Pinckert's All-Stars, San Diego, California, February 4, 1934
Western All-Stars, San Francisco, California, February 11, 1934
Arizona All-Stars, Phoenix, Arizona, February 14, 1934
Orleans All-Stars, New Orleans, Louisiana, February 18, 1934

Playing nine games in the span of two months, the Bears' schedule wasn't a walk at the beach. They earned their extra money. They also didn't take it easy on their opponents. After a 0–0 tie against the St. Louis Gunners in front of 13,000 spectators a week after winning the NFL championship, the two-time NFL champs won every other game (8–0), outscoring their opponents 212–34. For most of the stops, the Bears were offered a $2,500 guarantee, or 30 percent of the gate. Red started most games at left halfback. Throughout the tour, he was more than happy to help promote the professional game, giving local interviews to help the NFL cause. In Dallas, Red praised the sport, saying the following:

> The handwriting is on the wall. Professional football is demanding and getting the spotlight. I really believe that if the present trend of favor continues our game will crowd baseball for the favored professional ranks.
>
> We have opened up the game so that it may be played as spectators want it played. Folks don't want to watch a purely defensive battle between two teams which literally crawl in one direction, with few, if any, scores. The customers want thrills, action, speed, touchdowns—and, most of all, they want surprises, and that's just what professional football offers them.[1]

Red was becoming an ambassador for the NFL. He could see the potential of the sport, just like the owners—Halas, Mara, Rooney, Bell, and Marshall. While in California, Red and the Bears spent time mingling with Hollywood royalty, hanging out with comedian Joe E. Brown, and actresses Madge Evans and Mae West, who was named official "mascot" for the Bears. Brown purchased 400 tickets to the January 14 game for Warner Bros. employees so that they could enjoy the game. Against Erny Pinckert's All-Stars at Wrigley Field, Red scored two rushing touchdowns, one of which was from 67 yards, in front of 20,000 fans. In attendance were Hollywood stars Joe Brown and Will Rogers, as well as Northwestern head coach Dick Hanley.[2]

Before one game in Los Angeles, Red sat down with several reporters at a luncheon to talk football. "Yes, I'm getting along in years, but I love football," he said. "The game has been good to me, and I still get a big kick out of going into action. The bumps hurt more now than they did 10 years ago, but I can still take 'em if they don't come too frequently."[3]

Halas remained one of Red's biggest fans. "We'll play Red Grange at least long enough to win the game," said the Bears coach to Phil Ray of the *Oakland Tribune*. "Red is in great form and as hard to stop as he was in the days of his prime with Illinois."[4] The game on January 21, in San Francisco, attracted 35,000 spectators to Kezar Stadium. Organized by the Knights of Columbus, some of the gate went to local charities. The Bears came away with a 21–7 victory as the "Ghost received a big ovation from the crowd."[5]

While in Los Angeles, the Bears were hired by Hollywood to star in their own film. Halas negotiated a deal with MGM studios to appear in a "short reel" production produced by Pete Smith. Smith had been working for MGM in Hollywood since the early 1920s, eventually becoming the producer of short subjects that would be called "Pete Smith Shorts." During a period of 30 years, he would produce more than 150 shorts for MGM, one of which featured the

Chicago Bears in 1934. Titled *Pro Football*, the short was nine minutes in length and directed by Ray McCarey.

The football scenes were shot on the football field at Loyola University (now Loyola Marymount). Accompanied by music and Smith's corny narration track, the Bears performed several football plays for the film. The opening scene starts with George Halas, wearing a Bears sweatshirt, blowing his whistle to gather together his team. The Bears are identified by name. Lyman, Musso, Miller, Carlson, Ronzani, and Hewitt are shown in close-up shots wearing their helmets. Nagurski is shown running the ball, Manders kicking, and Brumbaugh and Doehring passing. Doehring is also shown throwing a pass behind his back for 50 yards.

But the star of the show was Red Grange. The Galloping Ghost is introduced by showing the back of his famous 77 jersey, then taking a handoff and running the length of the field, with the narrator saying, "And now the famous number 77 . . . football's superman. . . . He's still the fastest heavyweight player to streak down the field with the ball, straight-arming as he goes, aided by swell blocking, he crashes through for a touchdown . . . who is he? Red Grange, the one and only." Red runs the length of the field, dodges defenders, gives a stiff-arm, and gets toppled over at the goal line into the end zone for a touchdown. As he sits up and turns to the camera, he gives the viewers that Hollywood smile.[6]

Director McCarey definitely made Red the star of the film, as he is mentioned more than any other player. Unlike Nagurski, who didn't want much to do with the production and is mentioned only once in the picture, Red appears everywhere. Music and slow-motion action shots of the Bears' famous jump-pass and lateral plays gave the film much added production value. The *Hollywood Reporter* wrote, "While the picture was on a three-day schedule, there were only six actual hours of shooting."[7]

After finishing the MGM short, the Bears played their last exhibition game in California on February 11, in San Francisco. They would make two more stops, playing games in Phoenix and New Orleans, both to crowds of just 3,000 fans, before heading back to Chicago. Red would take the entire offseason to rest his body. He needed time to think about his next career move.

As for the NFL, the 1933 season was its most successful. The league increased the number of games played from 48 to 58, with attendance increasing as well, from 599,561 in 1932 to 657,594 in 1933. The average per game fell slightly, from 12,490 to 11,337. Despite the improvements, there still was plenty of work to do for the owners.

The NFL had a tremendous jump in field goals made, from the embarrassing 6 in 1932 to a whopping 39 (including the three kicked in the NFL Championship Game) in 1933. The league scoring average jumped from 16.4 points per game to 19.4, and the tie games went down from 10 to just 5. The new rules would pay off in a big way in 1934, when the NFL didn't have a single tie game.

The big franchise moves saw the struggling small-town Portsmouth Spartans relocate to the Motor City and the addition of the Cincinnati Reds, which made the NFL an 11-team league (six teams in the Western Division). The newly named Detroit Lions were established by George A. Richards, a millionaire who made his money in the automobile industry but at the time owned and operated several radio stations, notably WJR in Detroit and WGAR in Cleveland. He would be another flamboyant owner to join the NFL. One of his first "ideas" to surface was asking George Halas if he would bring his mighty Bears to Detroit on Thanksgiving Day. Richards wanted to have the NFL's best team in town so that he could market the event on his radio stations, making the game available nationally on NBC radio. It was the first NFL game to be aired coast to coast and would be the beginning of another bitter rivalry for Halas's Bears.

As for his squad, Halas had a loaded roster—a championship roster. Most of the Bears players would return. Halas was able to add one big veteran to the group, signing guard Walt Kiesling (6-foot-3, 260 pounds), out of St. Thomas. Nicknamed "Keys," the massive Kiesling had played eight years for three different teams, standing as one of the best guards in the league. For the last five seasons he had played for the Chicago Cardinals. Center Eddie Kawal was added, too.

The Bears owner also added a few rookies to his veteran team. He signed tackles Art Buss (6-foot-3, 220 pounds) from Michigan State and Ted Rosenquist (6-foot-4, 222 pounds) from Ohio State, and quarterback Bernie Masterson (6-foot-3, 195) from Nebraska. But it would be a rookie halfback who would make the biggest impact in 1934. Halas scouted and signed Beattie Feathers (5-foot-10, 185 pounds), out of Tennessee, to do one thing—replace Red at halfback. Grange was quickly impressed by the rookie who would take his job. "Belying his name, Feathers is a hard, heavy runner and appears to be traveling much slower than he really is, as many speed merchants who have been outdistanced by him will testify," said Red, who added, "He is the best cutback artist I have ever seen."[8]

Red thought about his future in football. "Yes, I think I'm about as fast now as I was then," he said to the press. "I'd get a kick out of handling a college squad and trying to pass along to them some of the things I've learned in about 200 pro games." Red's name came up for college coaching jobs with San Diego Military and Naval Academy and Kansas State, but he was looking to get back onto the playing field. He would sign a contract with Halas for another year—his seventh with the Bears.[9]

On July 6, 1934, the pages of the *Chicago Tribune* carried an announcement of what the newspaper described as the "most unusual football game ever scheduled." This game would be played on the evening of August 31, at Soldier Field. The two participants would be a professional team, the NFL champion Chicago Bears, and a squad of college All-Americans made up of players who had just completed their eligibility the previous season.

The man behind this idea was Arch Ward, the esteemed sports editor of the *Chicago Tribune*, who had established Major League Baseball's All-Star Game the previous summer. When Chicago's Century of Progress World's Fair was extended into 1934, Chicago mayor Ed Kelly asked Ward to arrange yet another unique sporting event. When the announcement of the game appeared in the *Tribune* on July 5, Ward said, "The game will stand as football's contribution to the Century of Progress Exposition."[10]

The game was to be sponsored by the *Tribune* and the proceeds donated to Chicago-area charities. Ward announced that major newspapers throughout the country would be conducting a national vote by fans to select the College All-Star Team. Many conferences objected to the game, but most college coaches felt it was a great honor. Thirty newspapers worked with the *Tribune* in carrying out the vote. For the player poll, the two individuals at each position receiving the highest vote totals would be invited to the team, with an additional 10 or so players joining as backups.

The Bears would hold training camp at Lane Tech High School, Halas's alma mater, and finish up practices at Dyche Stadium on the campus of Northwestern. Red reported at 194 pounds, slightly heavier than he wanted to be. "I've worked Red as hard as anybody on the squad," said George Halas to George Kirksey of the *United Press*. "Probably harder than I should, but I haven't heard a word of complaint from him. He has as much enthusiasm as any player on the team and is still a great football player. You don't find many like him." The 31-year-old would spend the next two weeks getting into better shape.[11]

On August 31, a massive crowd of 79,432 jammed Soldier's Field to watch the first-ever College All-Star Game. The rather large crowd didn't see any scoring, as the two teams battled to a 0–0 tie. "The snap, precision, and fire was lacking, and without those factors the outfit (Bears) was sluggish," wrote Howard Roberts of the *Chicago Daily News*. Halas said, "They had a great team and were in better physical shape than we were. The Bears have always been slow to develop in the early season." It would be the last time the Bears would come unprepared to play a game in 1934. After the game, the *Tribune* had $21,000 left to distribute to three local charities. The exhibition game was a complete success. The College All-Star Game would last for more than 40 years, until 1976, when the series was cancelled.[12]

Before the season opener, Red took on a few new roles—as a member of the press. First, he was hired by the Newspaper Enterprise Association (NEA), a news service, to write a series of articles during the football season about Big Ten football. The weekly articles were about two columns in length, containing roughly 800 to 1,000 words. He might have gotten some help from an NEA writer, but for the most part Red wrote his own articles. Because of his name, Grange started to make connections within the football landscape, talking to coaches, players, and game officials to get more insight into what was happening in the game of football. Red would enjoy his first foray into covering the sport, even while trying to play for the Bears.

Second, Red was hired as a football commentator for CBS to do several football shows slated to air on radio three times a week—Thursday, Friday, and Saturday—at 6:00 p.m. Titled *Football Forecasts*, the 15-minute shows would have Red previewing games on Thursdays and Fridays, and recapping college games on Saturdays, as well as offering gridiron gossip and forecasts of games. Sometimes he would offer up his weekly picks for the college games. Locally, in Chicago, CBS station WBBM carried Red's show. In conjunction with the radio show, Shell provided "score sheets" to help listeners pick games based on Red's comments and insights. These score sheets could be picked up at any Shell gas station. On the front of the sheet were columns for each game for listeners to write in their scores and Red's prediction, as well as the score from 1933, if the two teams had played one another. On the back of the sheets were diagrams and drawings on how to play the game of football—for example, the "dos and don'ts of how to punt or placekick." One newspaper reported that Red was paid "$500 a week for broadcasting."[13]

Red and his Bears teammates were ready for the regular season to start. This would be Red's 16th year of organized football, dating back to his freshman year at Wheaton High. It would be his last. After a few exhibition games, the Bears were prepared to defend their title. The season opener would be against their biggest rival. Almost 14,000 fans packed Green Bay's City Stadium. In a back-and-forth tussle, the game went into the fourth quarter knotted up at 10–10. But the final quarter was dominated by the NFL's best player—Bronko Nagurski. The bruising fullback took over the game by pounding up the middle against Lambeau's front line, scoring two touchdowns (including a 40-yarder) to secure a 24–10 victory. It was the Bears' fifth straight win against the Packers. The following week, the Bears traveled to Ohio to play the Cincinnati Reds. It was not a close contest. Behind the all-around play of the Bears backfield, Chicago came away with an easy 21-3 win. Rookie halfback Beattie Feathers had 140 rushing yards, while Red and Nagurski joined Feathers in scoring touchdowns.

The schedule would pick up mightily, as Halas's squad would play three games in the next eight days. They showed no ill effects of the hectic schedule, dispatching the Brooklyn Dodgers (21-7) and Pittsburgh Pirates (28-0) on the road, before shutting out the crosstown Cardinals, 20-0, at Wrigley. The Bears were now 5-0, outscoring their opponents 114-20.

Red collaborated again with George Dunscomb for another article for the *Saturday Evening Post*. Titled "Future Football," the four-page piece talked about the wide-open game being played by NFL teams, especially how the passing game was making the sport more thrilling for paying spectators. He wrote about the 1933 championship game, saying that it was a "really excellent preview of football of the future . . . it was the most exciting, harrowing, and dramatic game within my experience."[14]

Red also enjoyed the release of the MGM short *Pro Football*, which was being shown in theaters throughout the United States. "The film shows the pros as super-footballers. They show the colleges the way to scoring possibilities of super thrills that would make the sport infinitely more thrilling for the spectator," wrote one newspaper review. Several newspaper ads read, "Red Grange (and the Chicago Bears) in Pro Football," giving the aging superstar top billing. It would be his last venture in Hollywood.[15]

On October 21, the Bears raised their championship banner in front of 10,000 fans at Wrigley Field. The two-time champs stomped the lowly Reds, 41-7, scoring all of their points in the first three quarters of action. Jack Manders and Beattie Feathers scored twice, while Red chipped in with a 10-yard touchdown reception and an 18-yard scoring toss to Bernie Masterson. The undefeated Bears (6-0) prepared for their rematch against the Packers. Feathers dominated the action, scoring two touchdowns in a 27-14 victory.

The Bears kept rolling in November, easily dispatching the Giants, 27-7, at Wrigley, followed by shutting out the Boston Redskins, 21-0, behind two touchdown catches by Bill Hewitt. Then it was on to the rematch with the Giants. On November 18, at the Polo Grounds, the Bears faced off against the Giants in front of a large crowd of 55,000 onlookers—the largest NFL crowd since Red's visit to the Polo Grounds in 1925. Tim Mara's boys would finally give the mighty Bears a close game.

In the first three quarters, it looked as if the Giants would finally give Halas's team its first loss of the season. A Ken Strong touchdown run and a safety on defense gave the Giants an insurmountable 9–0 lead heading into the fourth quarter. Then the champions came to life. The running game clicked behind the blocking of the NFL's best line, as Feathers's score cut the lead to 9–7. As time was clicking down, the Bears made a last-ditch drive, giving Manders a shot to win the game. His 24-yard boot split the uprights to give the Bears a 10–9 comeback victory. It was the Giants' only home loss in 1934.

Feathers was close to making history. Newspaper reports stated that he had 962 rushing yards. He was about to top the 1,000-yard mark. The Bears were now 10–0. As they were rolling along, so were the Detroit Lions, behind the superb play of All-Pro Dutch Clark, who returned after missing one year. They, too, were undefeated, at 10–0. Despite the challenge by the Lions, the Bears looked to be a cinch to win their third straight NFL championship.

The Cardinals gave the undefeated Bears a serious tussle. The Cards were just 4–5, but the team was coming off a big upset victory on the road against the Green Bay Packers. A crowd of 13,800 came to Wrigley Field to see the two Windy City rivals play. Jumping out early, the Bears cruised to a 17–6 victory. During the game, rookie halfback Beattie Feathers made history by increasing his season rushing total to 1,004 yards, becoming the NFL's first-ever official 1,000-yard rusher. But it came at a cost, as Feathers suffered an injury to his shoulder. Early in the first quarter, he was tackled hard out of bounds by three Cardinals defenders and would miss the rest of the season.

On the same day that the Bears defeated the Cardinals, the Lions suffered their first loss of the season, falling 3–0 to the Packers. Despite the setback, the Thanksgiving Day game would still decide who would win the Western Division.

On Wednesday, the Bears left the Windy City to travel to Detroit. On the day of the game, *Detroit Free Press* sportswriter W. W. Edgar praised the growth of the league, as well as the Galloping Ghost: "When the players dash by Red Grange this morning as he sits, huddled in a blanket, on the bench of the Chicago Bears, they can look at him and realize that he, more than anyone else, has put their game—professional football—on the high level it enjoys today."[16]

On November 29, in Detroit, a large crowd of 25,000 and broadcasters for 94 nationally syndicated radio stations settled in to watch the NFL's two best teams slug it out. Early on, the Lions built a 16–7 lead, and the home fans were going crazy. In the third quarter, Jack Manders kicked two field goals to narrow the lead to 16–13. Then the Bears pulled off the biggest play of the game when guard Joe Zeller intercepted an Ace Gutowsky pass and returned it to the Lions four-yard line. Brumbaugh then called for the play that had won the 1932 indoor game, when Nagurski faked a line plunge, stepped back, and fired a touchdown pass to Bill Hewitt. The Bears held on and won, 19–16, clinching the Western Division for the second straight year.

Three days later, the rematch with the Lions was held at Wrigley Field in front of a massive crowd of 34,412 fans. The Bears won, 10–7, completing an undefeated season in the NFL, at 13–0. In the NFL's first 15 years, no team had completed a season unbeaten and untied. Halas's squad had just one game to go, a championship game rematch with the New York Giants. The Giants had their own injuries, losing star quarterback Harry Newman to a cracked vertebra. Backup Ed Danowski took over. "Look out for this guy Danowski, fellows," yelled Halas to his squad early in the week. "He's a more dangerous passer than Newman." On Friday, the Bears loaded up on a train to head to the Big Apple.

"It was a confident but not cocky group of athletes that started out east on the title quest," wrote Howard Roberts of the *Chicago Daily News*. They had beaten the Giants twice during the regular season, 27–7, at Wrigley, and the tight 10–9 game at the Polo Grounds. Confidence levels were high. The day before the game, the Bears had a practice at the Polo Grounds. This would be Red's last official practice as a Bears player. Playing mostly on the scout team, Red played the role of Giants star halfback Ken Strong. "I know we're favored, and I guess on the strength of our record that's right," said Halas during practice. "But we've never beaten the Giants three times in a league season, and if you're asking me that's even too much too hope for."[17]

While the Bears were preparing for the biggest game of the year, Red had made a decision on his future. He would retire as a player. "Yes, it is really definite this time," said Red to the press. "I think I have outlived my playing usefulness. You know, I'm 31 years old, and that is rather elderly for a football player. I have in mind a coaching job and I have three or four tempting propositions, but I may not do anything about them for some time, likely in the spring."[18]

Going into the game, the Bears were a heavy favorite. The Giants had won the East Division with just an 8–5 record, with two of those losses against the Bears. The 1934 NFL Championship Game would feature two Hall of Fame coaches (Halas and Steve Owen), and 10 future Hall of Fame players—the Bears with six—(Grange, Nagurski, Hewitt, Kiesling, Lyman, and Musso), while the Giants had four (Mel Hein, Ray Flaherty, Ken Strong, and the injured Red Badgro). The game would feature one of the strangest midgame adjustments in the history of pro football and the most explosive fourth-quarter scoring spree in NFL Championship Game history.

The night before the game, freezing rain and cold temperatures that would top off at 28 degrees at kickoff made the home turf at the Polo Grounds a sheet of ice. Any speed the Bears thought they had would be negated by the frozen field. The crowd was tallied at 35,059 brave fans. While the spectators took their seats, the Giants brain trust was about to make a decision that would go down in NFL lore.

Giants end Ray Flaherty started to kick at the icy turf and then approached his coach, Steve Owen, with an unusual idea. "[Coach] it may sound crazy, but one day when I was playing for Gonzaga the ground was just like this. We switched from cleats to basketball shoes and got some traction." Owen thought it couldn't hurt, so he summoned clubhouse attendant Abe Cohen and gave him the task of going to Manhattan College to gather up all the basketball sneakers he could find. Just before kickoff, Cohen took off to get the sneakers.[19]

As for Red, he never left the bench. He would just be a spectator for one of the most memorable games in NFL history. The game began with the Bears taking an early lead behind the power running of Nagurski. The Giants seemed to be on their heels, sliding backward throughout the first half as Halas's boys went into halftime with a 10–3 lead. The Bears were one half—30 minutes—away from a perfect season. But the game was about to change.

The Bears had increased their lead to 13–3 when Cohen arrived with a big box of sneakers. The Giants grabbed them and put them on as the fourth quarter was about to start. Using their newly acquired footwear, the men from New York exploded with a barrage of big plays. Rookie halfback Ed Danowski, the man Halas was concerned about, threw a 28-yard touchdown pass to Ike Frankian. On their next possession, after taking over on the Bears 42-yard line, the Giants needed only one play to score as Ken Strong burst up the middle for a touchdown. A short while later, Strong scored again on an 11-yard run but missed the extra point. It didn't matter, the Bears were done. To finish the scoring, Danowski stunned the Bears with a 9-yard dash around right end. After it was all said and done, the Giants and their "magic sneakers" had scored a remarkable 27 fourth-quarter points. No other world championship game or Super Bowl has seen that many points by one team in the final quarter. For the first time in three years, the Bears failed to close out a big game in the fourth quarter.

Tim Mara's Giants were world champions for the first time since 1927, spoiling the Bears' undefeated season. "I never was so pleased with anything in my life. In all the other contests with the Bears I always hoped the whistle would blow and end the game. Today I was hoping it would last for a couple of hours," said Mara to the *New York Times*. Did the sneakers really help the Giants win? After the game, there was a difference of opinions. "I think the sneakers gave them an edge in that last half, for they were able to cut back when running with the ball, and we couldn't cut with them," said Nagurski. Said Neil Cohalan, the Manhattan basketball coach, "I'm glad to hear our basketball shoes did the

Giants some good. The question now is, did the giants do our basketball shoes any good?" "I don't think the shoes made that much difference. Any back can run through a hole," declared Ken Strong.[20]

Whether or not the sneakers helped, the bottom line was that the Giants won, 30–13. The game has simply become known as the "Sneakers Game." Halas hated the outcome but was gracious in defeat. He stated, "They deserved to win because they played a great game in the second half. My team was under a terrific strain, however, trying to maintain a winning streak. . . . After all we've caused a lot of headaches, so I suppose we can stand one ourselves."[21] The fans got their money's worth for the second straight championship game. "It was an uninterrupted parade of thrills, and for professional football it was a brilliant climax to its most successful season—a season that established the game as a major sport," wrote the *Chicago Daily News*.[22]

But the disappointing end to the season was short-lived, as Halas had organized a few exhibition games to make some extra cash for his players. The first stop was in Philadelphia, to play a game against the Eagles. Tickets were sold at anywhere from $0.55 to $2.20. The game program featured Red on the cover, with the caption, "Farewell to Red Grange!" in the upper left-hand corner. Only 7,500 paying customers came out to Phillies Ball Park to watch. Red didn't start but played the final three quarters as the Bears won, 28–14.

The tour then continued on to Knoxville, Tennessee, where Beattie Feathers, back from an injury, performed in front of his college home crowd as the Bears defeated the Brooklyn Dodgers, 20–6, with Red catching a TD pass. But Red suffered a broken toe against the Dodgers that would keep him out of the next game, a 30–13 victory against the Memphis Tigers. Rehabbing his toe, Red joined the Bears as they headed out West. He would finish his career playing three games on the West Coast.

The Bears checked into the Hollywood Plaza for their stay in Los Angeles. Red had mixed feelings while in LA, the city where he had played in front of 75,000 screaming fans, as he wrapped up his football career. It was an unsettling time for the Galloping Ghost, both mentally and physically. Before the first game against the Chicago Cardinals, Grange suffered through a case of ptomaine poisoning. Halas kept him on the bench to watch his Bears lose, 13–9. Hollywood stars and sports celebrities the likes of actor Joe E. Brown, pro golfer Walter Hagen, and mascot Buddy Shaffer watched from the Bears bench. While out West, Red reflected on his career, saying, "I'd probably do the same thing. I wouldn't sell the friendships and contacts I've made in pro football for anything. . . . My radio, newspaper, and magazine work will bring me more money than I can get from coaching, but I want to stay in football if I can."[23]

The second game saw the Bears play more like themselves, pounding the Pacific Coast All-Stars, 26–7, in front of 10,000 fans. Even C. C. Pyle was on hand for the contest. Red started at right halfback, playing most of the first quarter and some of the second. He would now prepare for his farewell game. Halas, Red's teammates, the press, and the fans all knew he would be playing in his last game.

On January 27, 1935, in Los Angeles, Red Grange arrived at Gilmore Stadium. In the locker room, he placed his famous number 77 jersey over his shoulder pads for the last time. Red would line up across from the New York Giants, the team that had denied the Bears a chance at an undefeated season and a third straight NFL championship. The Bears won the game, 21–0, getting revenge on their defeat from one month earlier, but this game was all about sending Red out on a high note. He played a few minutes in the first half while the Bears had the ball in Giants territory, but there was no touchdown for the redhead. Once he reentered the game in the fourth quarter at left halfback, the Bears wanted to get him a touchdown. Taking the ball over on their own 20-yard line, the "fix" was in—without Red's knowledge. The Bears had set up the Giants to let Red sprint for a long score, sending the Ghost out on a high note. Everyone seemed to know what to do except Giants tackle Tex Irvin. On the play, Red took a handoff and sprinted right up the middle through the Giants front line. Red recalled,

> I took the pigskin and behind perfect blocking broke loose and got as far as mid-field, but my legs kept getting heavier and heavier as I ran. I just about reached the Giants' 39-yard line after a 41-yard run when Cecil Irvin, a 230-pound tackle, pulled me down from behind. Almost 32 years old, and more than 11 years since I played my first college game, it was obvious I had hit the end of the trail.[24]

Several Bears, notably Art Buss and Luke Johnsos, were furious that Irvin had tackled Red. They threw their helmets to the ground in disgust and started to cuss out Irvin. The 41-yard run would be the last time Red Grange would carry the football.

In the locker room after the game, Red talked to Paul Zimmerman of the *Associated Press*. He related,

> I'm earnest about it. I'm through, definitely through this time. The legs haven't got it anymore. I'm 31 now, and it's time to quit when a back gets that old. I'm getting out of this game before I get killed. If I had scored on that run, I would have grounded the ball behind the goal posts and walked off the field. I'm leaving the game with many regrets, but my failure to score on that run probably will

remain as the greatest. . . . What will I do now? Coach, I hope. I am considering two offers and several promising business ventures, but I won't know definitely what my next move will be for several months.[25]

On that sunny day in Los Angeles, the Galloping Ghost walked away from the NFL as a player.

PART VI

COACHING, RADIO AND TELEVISION, AND MARRIAGE (1935–1962)

29

COACHING AND BROADCASTING

After retiring from the Chicago Bears as a player, Red had time to figure out the next step in his life. "I am closing out as a player," said Red to Francis Powers of the *Chicago Daily News*. "I still love football and never can be happy away from the game. That is why I want to coach." While in New York for the NFL Championship Game, the redhead met with Pittsburgh Pirates owner Art Rooney to discuss being the Pirates' next head coach. Rooney was disappointed in his team's play in 1934, under Coach Luby DiMeolo, as the Pirates went 2–10 in their second season in the NFL.[1]

The two men spent several hours having dinner to discuss the position. At the end of the meeting, Rooney offered Red the job. Red paused. He needed time to think it over. "We didn't come to an agreement yesterday," said Rooney the next morning. "But I'm going to see Grange again today." Just hours after losing the "Sneakers Game," Red was about to make a decision on his next career move. He told Rooney, the man who would eventually win four Super Bowl titles in the 1970s, that he would pass on the job.[2]

At this point, Red was all in for coaching, although he didn't seem all that interested in selecting a place where he was at the helm. Rumors abounded. His name was mentioned for head coaching jobs at four schools—Florida, Missouri, George Washington, and Stetson. Whether he had doubts about coaching or was waiting for the right situation, Red took his time in deciding on his next venture. He turned to his mentor and good friend—George Halas. During the summer, Red was offered the head coaching job for the Chicago Bears. It was a flattering offer, but Red turned down Halas. It was too much for his first coaching job. "(I) hadn't enough experience to handle the team alone," he said to the *Chicago Tribune*.[3] Instead, Red accepted the position of backfield coach. He would work for Mr. Halas, who also hired Luke Johnsos—replacing Laurie Walquist—to coach the ends, making the Bears a three-man staff for the 1935 season. "I know one subject, football," commented Red. "I'm sure I can do one thing well, coach football. I've learned this old game. I'm going to stay with it." One thing was for sure, Red was a football lifer. It was his passion.[4]

Red's first batch of backs would include all his old teammates—Nagurski, Manders, Masterson, Feathers, Ronzani, Corbett, Sisk, and Molesworth. The first-time coach would have the best backfield in the NFL. Red was a quick study, learning everything he could about the game. "I'm only now learning how to build defenses and other vital features of the strategy of the game," Red admitted to the Chicago press. Deep down, he preferred the pro game to the college game. "Professional players study the game scientifically over a period of years and know it in all departments. They probably are among the best-equipped men available for coaching," said Red at a dinner banquet in Bloomington, Illinois.[5]

Despite leading the NFL in rushing (2,096 yards) in 1935, the Bears finished 6-4-2 and out of the title hunt. But Red knew he had made a good choice in joining the coaching ranks. Writing for *Saturday Evening Post* in 1935, in an article entitled "Little Things Make Touchdowns," Grange wrote,

> Now my playing days are definitely over. I am continuing in football as a coach and as a commentator. This I know, the next best thing to playing football is coaching it—passing on to kids bursting out of their skin with health, vigor, and bounce some of the things you pick up about the game as you go along."[6]

This would be the last article for *Saturday Evening Post* that Dunscomb and Red would collaborate on.

In 1936, Red took on more responsibilities outside of coaching. That fall he agreed to do a series of three broadcasts on NBC Radio. These three spots would air on NBC stations throughout the country on Friday, Saturday, and Monday nights beginning on September 4 until November 28. The radio show was sponsored by Sinclair Oil, which, according to several newspaper reports, paid Red $12,000 for the 12-week run.

Red's show, similar to one in 1934, would have him comment on upcoming games for the weekend on the Friday show, while on Saturday night he would recap the college football games, finishing up with the NFL games on Monday. He would provide his expert opinion on players and coaches while dissecting key matchups. He also gave his picks for the weekend, and Sinclair Oil would hold a weekly contest to see if customers could beat Red's choices. At any Sinclair station, a customer could pick up a weekly forecast sheet listing the games. They were to make their selections for the winner of each college football game in the hopes of besting Red's choices each week. The person selecting the most correct winners and coming the closest to the correct scores would win prizes, including radios, footballs autographed by Grange, and the grand prize—a choice of one of three automobiles. It was called the "Red Grange Football Radio Contest."

Red's show was popular with football fans nationwide. According to *Broadcasting* magazine, more than three million fans sent in filled-out score sheets, with more than 1,400 weekly winners. Entries were received from all parts of the country—from 86,740 entries in the first week for games on September 19, to 424,631 entries for the November 21 games—the highest total for any week.[7] "Red Grange electrified the world as a football player. And he has given to network listeners splendid service as a football commentator. We hope his sponsors bring him back next season," wrote the *Pittsburgh Press*. He would be back the next season.[8]

At about this time Red accepted another job, adding to his already busy schedule. In Chicago, he became friends with Jim Peterson, a former University of Illinois Law graduate, class of 1922, who attended every game Red played in at Illinois. Peterson quickly became a fan of the Galloping Ghost. After graduating from Illinois, Peterson became president of Hinckley & Schmitt, a nationally known water mineral company based in the Windy City. Peterson was head of the company for almost three decades.

In 1937, Peterson hired Red as a sales promotion manager for a reported annual salary of $7,500. According to George Schmitt, grandson of the founder of Hinckley & Schmitt, Red primarily visited the downtown office managers who were buyers of the water cooler services provided by the company. Being a spokesperson to attract buyers came easy for Red; all he had to do was talk about football and potential buyers were hooked. It was a win-win for both partners.

Later that same year, Red and George Dunscomb collaborated to write a book about Bob Zuppke, who was celebrating his 25th year at the University of Illinois. The book, titled *Zuppke of Illinois*, was published by A. L. Glaser, based in Chicago. The book was 179 pages in length, with 23 chapters and 24 photos. The foreword was written by Grantland Rice. The volume was filled with interview quotes from Zuppke based on interviews done by both Red and Dunscomb, who did most of the heavy lifting in writing the work.

Red enjoyed spending time with his old coach; he loved hearing Zuppke tell his old football stories. "Victory in football is 40 percent ability and 60 percent spirit," said Zuppke to Red. His former coach also gave his thoughts about how he coached the Galloping Ghost: "You were sensitive—you were a lone wolf type. To ride you would have been fatal. It was only necessary to explain to you the how and why of things and to convince you that you really could do what I told you you could."[9]

Zuppke also compared the two Grange brothers, saying, "Red was exceptionally fast, but he wasn't quite as speedy on the straightway as his brother, Garland. Gardie didn't have Red's elusiveness—no player has ever had it—nor did he have Red's pickup. He had more dash and fire. Red was a soundless rocket."[10]

The book was published in hardback with a dust jacket featuring a head shot of Coach Zuppke. It sold modestly for $2.00, mainly to Illinois alumni and fans. The book review in the *Chicago Tribune* went as follows: "Subject and author of this book, one of the most informative and entertaining treatises of the sports year, form one of the most famous twosomes in football history."[11]

The Bears cruised to the Western Division title, winning the division by three games over the Packers, but in the NFL Championship Game they ran into the league's best quarterback in the Washington Redskins' rookie signal caller, Sammy Baugh, who threw three touchdowns to upset the Bears, 28–21.

The following season, while also coaching the Bears backfield, Red continued to do radio. This time his football forecast show was sponsored by Pure Oil and heard on CBS stations. He appeared on the radio for two spots in the evening, Thursdays to preview and predict the games, and Saturdays to recap games with scores of the college football matchups. At this point in his life, Red was content with just being an assistant coach. "I've got a good business connection, and I like my coaching job with the Bears. But none of that head coaching stuff for me," he announced to the press. "Boy, think of the grief those guys have to take and then wind up getting fired."[12]

On February 3, 1939, news came out that C. C. Pyle had died of a heart attack in Los Angeles. He was 56 years old. Newspapers throughout the United States carried the news, and several of them, including the *Chicago Tribune* and *Los Angeles Times*, had photos of Red together with Pyle to accompany the articles. Red was heartbroken when he heard the news. Speaking to the *Chicago Tribune*, he said, "I'm sorry to hear Charlie's gone. Gosh, that's terrible. He was the greatest promoter of all time but not the greatest businessman. He had more ideas than any man I ever knew. He was always completely honest with me." Red deeply cherished his relationship with Pyle, never once speaking a negative word about the man who guided his career into pro football. Although they had drifted apart in the past decade, Red grieved for his good friend.[13]

That fall Red coached the backs, as the Bears finished with an 8–3 record, one game back of the Packers in the Western Division—who went on to defeat the New York Giants for the NFL championship.

That fall Red continued his radio work, this time doing a weekly spot called *Red Grange Football Gossip*, sponsored by his employer, Hinckley & Schmitt. Every Friday for 15 minutes, from 5:30 to 5:45 p.m., on WGN radio, Red would give insight into the upcoming weekend games. The show lasted 13 weeks.

In 1939, the NFL had its most successful season to date. The league surpassed 1,000,000 paid fans in attendance for the first time, with 1,071,200, in 55 regular-season games, despite the tragic loss of NFL president Joe F. Carr to a heart attack. Because of the financially stable owners he had chosen to run the big-city NFL franchises, the future looked bright for the league.

Red would coach backs with the Bears through the 1940 season. The Bears squad was about to change the NFL landscape.[14]

Halas now had a staff of four men, hiring Red (backfield), Carl Brumbaugh (quarterbacks), and Hunk Anderson (line) to be his assistants. He also got some help refining the T formation from Clark Shaughnessy, who at the time was head coach at Stanford. The single-wing offense was used by most teams in the NFL, but Halas continued to use the T formation with his newest star signal caller, Sid Luckman, signed out of Columbia in 1939. By 1940, he was ready to unleash the T formation on the NFL.

That fall, Red's attention turned away from coaching to focus more on his role as a radio personality. His radio show, *Red Grange Forecasts*, was picked up by the Mutual Broadcasting System (MBS) and would air twice weekly, on Fridays from 6:15 to 6:30 p.m. and Saturdays from 5:45 to 6:00 p.m. The 15-minute shows were sponsored by the National Refining Company (Pure Oil), and once again his picks were part of a national radio contest where listeners could win such weekly prizes as a new car—a Chevy, Ford, or Plymouth.

On weekends, Red started to broadcast college football games or do his radio spots from stadiums. He would travel to the games—mostly in the Midwest—on Fridays, spend Saturdays at the game, and come back to join the Bears on Sundays. In the fall of 1940, he made stops at the following locations:

October 19, Minnesota at Ohio State, Columbus, Ohio
October 26, Notre Dame at Illinois, Champaign, Illinois
November 8, Iowa at Nebraska, Lincoln, Nebraska

November 16, Northwestern at Michigan, Ann Arbor, Michigan
November 23, Indiana at Purdue, West Lafayette, Indiana

On Fridays, Red would preview the games for the weekend, sometimes interviewing the college coaches of the game he was at, while on Saturdays he would recap the games with scores and more interviews with coaches at the game. This was Red's first experience broadcasting football games on the road. He instantly liked it. This would be his football future.

The Bears (8–3) won the Western Division by a game and half over the Packers. They would face the Washington Redskins (9–2) in the nation's capital for the NFL championship. Three weeks earlier, the Redskins had defeated the Bears in a close matchup, winning 7–3. After the game, Redskins owner George Preston Marshall opened his big mouth, claiming that the Bears were a "bunch of crybabies." This comment didn't sit well with Halas or his players.

The NFL Championship Game would see a different outcome. Led by Sid Luckman, a powerful running game, and a stifling defense—which returned three interceptions for touchdowns—the Bears made Marshall eat his words in a 73–0 beatdown of his Redskins. The T formation was a resounding success on the biggest stage. Because of the impressive victory, NFL teams, as well as college and high school teams throughout the country, would soon adopt the formation as the primary offensive formation in football—making the single-wing almost extinct within a decade. For Red, the 1940 NFL championship would be his last as Bears coach.

Red wrapped up his shows on MBS by announcing his College All-American Team and his NFL All-Pro squad. Coaching and broadcasting, as well as working for a mineral water company, kept the former football star busy after hanging up his cleats. In the middle of all this hard work, Red would meet the love of his life, a woman he would share the next 50 years with.

30

MARGARET
"MUGGS" GRANGE

After the 1940 season, Red Grange stepped away from coaching. He went out on top, as the Bears thrashed the Washington Redskins to win the NFL championship. Although he enjoyed being around the guys, his passion for the game of football steered from the playing field to the broadcast booth. He could see that the game of football was becoming more popular with fans, and the NFL, which once again topped 1,000,000 paying customers in attendance, with 1,063,025, was steadily growing. Wanting to be around the game, Red thought that being a broadcaster would do the trick. He could talk to coaches and players, as well as cover the sport from every angle, without the stress and mental pain that came with coaching. He now had a specific career path in mind, one that in 2019 would be the next logical step for a former NFL superstar. Today, once a player retires, he goes straight to the broadcast booth, but for Red in 1940, he was a trailblazer in this area for future former players to find employment. It was the decision to be a broadcaster that led the Galloping Ghost to the love of his life—Margaret Hazelberg.

The Hazelberg family came to the United States from Norway in 1850, settling in Iowa, Minnesota, and Wisconsin. Most family members became farmers. Tobias Hazelberg, Margaret's grandfather, was born in 1862, outside of Moscow Township, Iowa County. His family moved to Granite Falls, Minnesota, where he attended high school. Education was preached to the Hazelberg children. Tobias went on to further his education at Miller's Commercial School in Keokuk, Iowa, which led him to find employment in several different areas—insurance, a produce business, and a furniture business—while living in Granite Falls. In 1884, Tobias married Helen Jargo, a schoolteacher, and the young couple would go on to have six children—Marion (1885), Esther (1887), Karl (1889), Ella (1891), Hubert (1894), and Miles (1897)—all born in Granite Falls.

In 1900, with his rather large family by his side, Tobias moved to Barron County, Wisconsin. He bought 240 acres of land, erecting a modern farmhouse and barn, which would be rebuilt several times. On his land, Tobias did general farming and dairy work. Described as a "man of force, personality, and decided qualities of leadership, it is natural that he should have taken an interest in public affairs from the time of his first residence here." Tobias jumped into civic duties by becoming town clerk (1902-1905), town chairman (1905-1911), county clerk (1911-1919), and state prohibition commissioner (1919-1921). "In all of these positions he served with credit to the community and with honor to himself."[1]

Every one of Tobias and Helen's children attended school in Barron County, graduating from Rice Lake High School. The third child, Karl Hazelberg, was born on July 8, 1889, in Granite Falls. "He was average height, about five-feet-nine, had light brown hair and blue eyes," said Dorothy Flora, granddaughter of Karl Hazelberg. "He was outspoken, opinionated, sometimes didn't show love as much as he could have."[2]

Young Karl was baptized at Granite Falls Lutheran Church and learned quickly that education was the key to his future. "He was such an avid reader, he just loved to read," said Linda Thomas, niece of Margaret Hazelberg.[3] He attended Rice Lake High School, like his siblings, which led to him being hired as a schoolteacher in 1910. While teaching, Karl also worked on the family farm. In 1911, he married a local woman, Olga Hanson. "She was very beautiful and very petite," said Dorothy. They would go on to have three children—two boys, Scott (1913) and Robert (1914), and one girl.[4]

Margaret Helene Hazelberg was born on January 6, 1917, in Stanley, Wisconsin, located east of the center of Barron County. The Red Cedar River flowed from north to south across the western side of the town, where the Hazelberg family farm resided. Growing up, Margaret spent most of her time attending school and the local Lutheran church with her two brothers. The three siblings got along well, staying close for the rest of their lives. "Just a wonderful relationship that they had with each other, nothing negative, every time we were together we had fun," Dorothy added.[5]

Similar to Red's upbringing, Margaret's world would be shattered at an early age. In September 1924, Olga Hazelberg died at her home from tuberculosis. She was just 33 years old. "The floral offerings were exceptionally many, which speaks for itself as to the high esteem in which Mrs. Hazelberg was held," read the local obituary. Just like her future husband, Margaret, at the age of seven, was growing without her mother.[6]

Karl (age 35) quickly rebounded after losing his wife. The following year, he remarried Clara Amundson (age 25), 10 years his junior. Four years later, the couple would have their only child, a daughter, Beverly Bernice Hazelberg, born April 13, 1929. Despite being 12 years older, Margaret would always look after her baby sister, as the two would become best friends. The group of siblings enjoyed being around one another, especially spending time outdoors. The Hazelberg family eventually bought 160-plus acres of land at Bush Lake, Michigan, building a family home. Margaret enjoyed playing sports, fishing, and ice skating. It didn't matter what time of year or the weather conditions, she relished being outside or at the lake.

During the next couple of years, Margaret found herself to be a traveling nomad. In 1928, when she was 11, Karl got a high-paying job with Darling & Company, based in Chicago, as a traveling salesman. He would be gone for stretches of time, selling commercial fertilizer, bone meal, and other products in different areas of the heartland. They would live in several cities, including Concord and Garner, Iowa, where Margaret started high school. During the middle of her junior year at Garner High, her father was transferred to New London, Wisconsin. Instead of moving with her parents again, she convinced her father to stay in Garner so that she could finish her junior year. The determined scholar stayed with the Peterson family, Irving Peterson, the county's assistant superintendent, being a family friend. After the school year was finished, Margaret reunited with her family.[7]

Her senior year would be spent at a new school—New London High School. Despite the changing of schools, Margaret was an above-average student, while participating in the glee club for two years, as well as drama and the declam club for three years. She was very personable and able to talk to anyone. At New London she was able to make friends and joined the extemporaneous reading club. She graduated from New London in 1934. In the school's yearbook a short quote next to her senior photo says, "A wandering girl, but she always comes back."[8] Yes, Margaret had been to many places, but she never quite called any of them home.

The following fall, she enrolled at Lincoln County Normal School in Merrill, Wisconsin. A teacher's school, Margaret joined 22 other students to learn the teaching vocation. While at Lincoln County, Margaret became involved in several activities. She participated in a school play titled *All of a Sudden Peggy*, playing the lead role of Peggy. The three-act comedy, in which Peggy finds love, was a hit with the student body, getting a full-page write-up in the yearbook.

Margaret also worked on the school's yearbook staff, collaborating with classmate Ruth Marquardt on the calendar section. In the "Last Words" section, she is quoted as saying, "Say, listen!" After one year at Lincoln County, she graduated in 1935, with her first-grade teaching certificate. But Margaret dreamt of something more than her mundane Midwest life. She loved her family and her siblings, but she wanted to see the world. People around her knew it. It was no secret. She had plans.[9]

She decided to go to the big city, enrolling in a nurse training course at the Lutheran Deaconess Hospital in Chicago. She worked hard during her training, a smile always on her face. Her nursing skills were quickly put to good use. Dorothy Flora, niece of Margaret, recalls her aunt's heroic effort:

> Fond memories of her, so very giving. She saved my life when I was two years old. I got double bronchially [sic] pneumonia and almost died; my heart stopped for about a minute. Margaret became an RN, and she flew in. The doctors tried to revive my heart, and she came to see me and to support the family. When she arrived was when they couldn't do anything more, but she had them make black coffee and they poured it down my throat and revived my heart. My heart started beating. I woke up, my eyes opened and looked straight ahead and at the foot of my bed were my two brothers and my parents, and I felt hungry so I turned my head and at the side of the bed was a little table and had a bowl of fruit and there was an apple and took a big bite out of it . . . so she saved my life.[10]

Margaret received her RN degree in 1938. Staying in Chicago, she turned her attention to another career path. Wanting to see more of the world, Margaret applied for a job with United Airlines to be a stewardess. At this time, stewardesses were only required to have a nursing degree, so she was instantly qualified. Most airlines hired good-looking women, representing the All-American girl more so than the "showgirl type." They were selected for not only their intelligence, but also their characteristics. A 1936 *New York Times* article described the requirements as follows: "The girls who qualify for hostesses must be petite; weight 100 to 118 pounds; height 5 feet to 5 feet 4 inches; age 20 to 28 years. Add to that the rigid physical examination each must undergo four times every year, and you are assured of the bloom that goes with perfect health."[11]

The first female flight attendants for United Airlines wore green berets, green capes, and nurse's shoes. They were responsible for seeing to passenger needs—for example, helping them board the aircraft, assisting with baggage, serving refreshments, and assuring that passengers put out their cigars and cigarettes. They also helped comfort passengers, as most of the airplanes were DC-3s, which were nosy and bumpy.

In 1939, Margaret started working for United Airlines as a stewardess. Staying in Chicago, she got a roommate, Ada Maranda, a fellow United stewardess, to rent an apartment on South Woodtown Avenue. She earned a steady paycheck of $100 a month, more than most female nurses, teachers, or clerical workers were making. She mainly worked flights on the Chicago-to-Denver-to-Cheyenne line.

"Margaret was the funniest lady I ever met," said Linda Thomas, niece of Margaret Hazelberg. "She always had a smile on her face. She had this beautiful smile with deep dimples. Just a gorgeous lady. She just enjoyed being around people."[12]

She was only 22 years old, but Margaret had already accomplished a lot in her young life. Some biographers, in writing about Red's future wife, only mention that she was a stewardess. But Margaret Hazelberg was much more than that. She was an intelligent, educated, driven, successful woman who had achieved many things in her life long before she met her famous husband.

In early November 1940, Margaret showed up to work a United Airlines flight from Chicago to Omaha, Nebraska. Red boarded that flight en route to Lincoln to cover the Iowa–Nebraska football game. The future lovebirds were about to meet for the first time. In his autobiography, Red wrote,

> I boarded an Omaha-bound United Airlines plane in Chicago, and, although I didn't realize it at the time, that flight turned out to the greatest break of my life. . . . The stewardess on the plane was an attractive, friendly girl named Margaret Hazelberg. We got involved in conversation, and she expressed a desire to see a Bear game in Chicago, where she was headquartered. By promising to get her some tickets, I wrangled her phone number. Within a few weeks we had our first date.[13]

As soon as he entered the airplane, Red noticed the attractive stewardess. Margaret was 5-foot-4; weighed 120 pounds; and had dark, bushy brown hair and bluish-green eyes. She was the most beautiful woman Red had ever seen, even counting all the Hollywood and vaudeville stars he had met. Margaret also would remember meeting Red for the first time. In a letter she wrote in September 1991, to Kathy McKenna, a teacher at Wheaton Central High School, shortly after Red had passed away, she wrote about that first meeting.

Dear Mrs. McKenna:

Perhaps your students would like to know how I met their hero . . . (my dear husband). Way back in 1940 I was a stewardess for United Airlines, flying from Chicago to Cheyanne to Denver. We flew DC-3s at that time. Perhaps you have seen pictures of them. Guess who was a passenger on one of my flights? None other than Harold "Red" Grange!

"Red" was on his way to Lincoln, Nebraska, to cover a football game on radio (this was before TV). There were two gentlemen with him, and they were seated in what was called the sky room. This space was re-served for passengers going only a short distance, in this case to Omaha. As this was a DC-3 sleeper, the other passengers had upper and lower berths. (Many were going all the way to Los Angeles).

After I had made up the berths, and gotten the passengers into them, I had a chance to serve "Red" and his friends a cup of coffee, and to sit down and chat a bit. "Red" always kidded me later and said it was the worst service he ever had!

Anyway, I knew who he was (my father and brother were big sports fans). I confessed that I had never seen a college or pro football game, but would love to. "Red," who was always generous, offered to send me a ticket to see a Chicago Bears game. To make a long story short, I gave him my address and telephone number, and about 11 months later we were married! And in the fall of 1941, I saw my first pro game!

Hope I haven't bored you with this—

Margaret Grange[14]

The two shared a brief but memorable conversation on the short flight from Chicago to Omaha. As she wrote in her letter, Margaret knew who Red was, growing up in a family of sports fans. Red had enough time to get Margaret's phone number. After the plane landed, Red traveled the 60 miles to Lincoln.

Red couldn't stop thinking about Margaret. "When Red met Margaret on that plane it was love at first sight," said Dorothy Flora.[15] But he had a job to do. That Friday night, he did his radio show from the University of Nebraska campus. It was broadcast nationally, as well as locally on KFOR. The following afternoon, he arrived at the stadium amid raindrops as the Cornhuskers hosted the Iowa Hawkeyes. He took his seat in box 41 on the east side of the stadium. "Red, during the impromptu halftime fill-in stuff, stepped to the microphone and talked to the stands for a bit," wrote the *Nebraska State Journal*. The hometown Cornhuskers pulled out a close 14–6 victory against the Hawkeyes. After the game, for his Saturday night show, Red interviewed Nebraska head coach Biff Jones and his good friend, Link Lyman, line coach for Nebraska. The *Lincoln Star-Journal* ran a photo of Red at the game trying to stay dry.[16]

All Red wanted to do was get back to Chicago. He wanted to call Margaret. It didn't take long for the two to start dating, and there was an instant attraction on both parts. Red quickly gave her the nickname "Muggs." "I only knew her as Aunt Muggs," said Flora. Margaret called Red "honey," her only name for her future husband for the next 50 years.[17] The only obstacles were their busy schedules and slight age difference. Fourteen years separated the two, but this wasn't uncommon in this era. Most gentlemen married younger women.

Red finished up the football season on the radio and Margaret was balancing being out of town on flights, but they made it work. After a year of dating, Red was confident in popping the question. Margaret said yes. They didn't wait to get married. They eloped. On October 13, 1941, Red drove Margaret 50 miles south of Chicago to the small town of Crown Point, Indiana. On a Monday afternoon, in the town of roughly 4,500 citizens, the couple walked into the Lake County Courthouse to tie the knot. The courthouse, known as the "Grand Old Lady," was a popular place to get married by a justice of the peace. From 1915 to 1940, an estimated 175,000 couples get hitched at the courthouse, with marriage ceremonies performed seven days a week, 24 hours a day. Tom Mix and Rudolph Valentino got married in Crown Point. On this Monday in 1941, it would be Margret and Red's turn.

Red wore a light-colored suit with a striped tie, while holding his fedora. Margaret wore a black polka-dotted coat, fur shawl, and black hat. In front of officiator Harvey T. Minas, the couple said "I do." They put wedding rings on one another's fingers. Minas, who officiated more than 30,000 weddings at the courthouse during his career, always cherished the fact that he was there for the Grange's wedding. Throughout his career he collected the wedding ring boxes from the ceremonies, totaling almost 30,000. "His most treasured box is the one that carried the wedding ring for the bride of Red Grange, the Galloping Ghost of Illinois," wrote the *Marion Star* in 1956, when Minas retired.[18]

While at the courthouse a photographer snapped a photo of the newlyweds. They posed with big smiles, happy to have the moment preserved. The next day, the photo appeared in newspapers nationwide. Most of the headlines read, "Red Grange Weds Air Stewardess." The *Chicago Tribune* wrote, "Wedding Bells for Red Grange; an Air Romance."[19] This was the start of a marriage that would last the next five decades. "They had a great marriage, they were best friends," remembered Dorothy Flora. "They loved each other dearly, and they kidded around all the time." Flora continued,

> Her and Red laughed all the time. Outgoing, laughed a lot, and Red made sure of that, he would give one-liners when we were visiting them. He would tease her in a fun way, and we would all laugh, so he had a good sense of humor and she could dish it back. It was all fun, very much fun being with them and visiting them.[20]

That fall, Red was hired by the NEA to write a weekly column for the season. Under the byline "Red Grange: The Original Man-in-Motion," his weekly articles contained information on coaches, players, matchups, and, of course, his predictions. Even Margaret got in on her husband's work, once posing for a photo of her pointing to his prediction sheets. This photo also appeared in newspapers throughout the country.[21]

After the 1941 season, Bob Zuppke resigned as head coach at the University of Illinois. He was 62 years old. Rumors quickly came out that Red would be offered the job. "I don't want the coaching job at the University of Illinois. I have made no application for the job, and as far as I know there have been no representations made on my behalf," he said to the press. In the end, Ray Eliot was hired to replace Zuppke. Red would continue to support the Illinois program, serving as a trustee for a while, but he had no desire to get back into coaching.[22]

Throughout the years Red would make an effort to see his old coach, visiting him often when he made it back to Champaign. The animosity about him turning pro to play football had faded. The two men would be close friends for their rest of their lives. Even Margaret got in on the act, communicating often with Red's old college coach by mail, writing him numerous letters and notes. Because of this habit, Zuppke gave Red's wife the nickname "Inky."

After getting married, Red put coaching behind him. He wanted to spend time with his new bride. His future was in broadcasting. A new medium was about to explode, and the sport Red loved was going to be at the forefront of its popularity.

㉛

TELEVISION STAR

As Red began his life with Margaret, the rest of the world was plunged into chaos, as the United States entered World War II. Red, at 38 years of age, was appointed a reemployment committeeman for the Selective Service Board, No. 144, in Chicago. His "ceremonial" duties included handling questionnaires and determining the occupational status of prospective selectees who might have been eligible for deferment.

At the start of his marriage, Red purchased a nice, big apartment, located at 6129 North Claremont Avenue, on the city's North Side—five miles from Wrigley Field. It might have been an apartment, but the young couple presented a very warm and loving home. Dorothy Flora, niece of Margaret and Red Grange, recalled her visit to Chicago:

> When I was about nine years old my dad put me on a train and I went to Chicago and they lived in a condo near Lake Michigan, upper level, and they even rented a garden spot and go a few blocks to raise vegetables. She took me to Marshall Field's, and she bought me so much beautiful clothes for school because it was like August, before school started, and wow that was something.
>
> Upstairs, it was like an apartment. It was small. We didn't have a TV, so they had this huge console with this tiny screen. I remember watching TV for the first time in my life. I can remember this wrestler. Gorgeous George, hairpin in his long hair. After he win a match he was take hair pin out of his hair and throw them into the audience. I remember on TV was old Blatz commercial of Milwaukee's finest beer. . . . Also when I got to Red's house, they bought me a big bottle of bubble bath—this was my first time in a tub—and pour the whole thing in and the suds were like deep and I almost drowned (laughing) and so that, it was amazing.

. . . I couldn't believe all the stuff I was experiencing. It was fabulous. I remember like it was yesterday.[1]

Football coach, company spokesperson, and journalist were respectable occupations that Red worked hard at to make a nice living, but he still craved being around the game he loved. As the NFL approaches its 100th season in 2019, today's players have many options to make a "second living." Most ex-players and coaches jump right into the radio or television booth, but in the 1930s and early 1940s, that was not common. Such an opportunity was virtually nonexistent for former players. Red would blaze that trail as the first.

Red continued to write for NEA, and his column, "Red Grange: The Original Man-in-Motion," gave insights into college football and its coaches and players. In 1943, Red severed his connection with Hinckley & Schmitt to go into the insurance business. Encouraged by his good friend, Jim Peterson, who was losing his best promotional star, Red wanted to be on his own, to control his schedule. Red set up his own office, located at 175 West Jackson Blvd., which was a 20-minute drive from his home, in the Insurance Exchange Building. Red Grange Insurance advertisements could be seen throughout town, including small ads that appeared in Bears programs for years. Red eventually became a successful insurance man, something he took pride in his entire life. "I think I was as good an insurance man as there was in Chicago," said Grange in an interview with *True* magazine in 1958. "On the football field I had 10 other men blocking for me, but I'm more proud of what I did in the insurance business, because I did it alone."[2]

At this time—1946—Red was enjoying his life with Margaret in Chicago. That fall, World War II ended, and Red took on a bigger role in broadcasting. He started doing college football games on radio. He joined play-by-play man Bob Elson to do Big Ten and Notre Dame games for WJJD radio in Chicago. He finished that season broadcasting the 1946 NFL Championship Game—between the Chicago Bears and New York Giants—on ABC radio with partner Harry Wismer, ABC's sports director. Red would go on to broadcast the NFL's premier game for the next decade.

In 1947, Red added the *Chicago Tribune's* College All-Star Game to his résumé. He once again joined Wismer in the booth. Just like the NFL Championship Game, Red would cover the College All-Star Game for the next decade-plus. Two years later, Red would add two more broadcasting assignments to his busy schedule. This time the medium would be television.

Red made his initial appearance on television in 1949. First he was hired by ABC-TV to partner with Joe Hasel to broadcast the NFL nationally—broadcasting mostly Bears and Cardinals games. Second, Red was hired for a newly developed show titled *The Chicago Bears Quarterback Club*. Red would host this show for nine years, from 1949 to 1957. The half-hour program usually aired on Mondays after the previous Sunday's game (in 1949 and 1956 it aired on Tuesdays, and in 1950 on Wednesdays), between 7:00 and 9:30 p.m. The first two years it aired on WENR and WBKB in Chicago, and from 1952 to 1957 it aired on WGN-TV, channel 9.

When Red was hired to host the show, producers wanted George Halas to be the other weekly cohost, but Papa Bear suggested another name—his assistant, Luke Johnsos. "They originally asked George Halas if he would do the show with Red, but Halas knew that my dad, having four kids, needed the money, so he switched over to my father doing it. The seasonal package was $15,000 for the season. My dad was more than happy to accept that," said Luke Johnsos Jr., son of Luke Johnsos.[3]

On several occasions, Johnsos would take his son to the taping of *The Chicago Bears Quarterback Club*. "Back then it was on live TV, which was kind of cool," said Luke Johnsos Jr.

> I can recall one time my dad took me down to the show, now the Tribune Tower in Chicago. The format would go, Red Grange would come on and they do the first half with my father going over the Bears highlights, then my father would draw up a play at halftime and then show that play on television and how it worked. Then after the game was over they both would visit with a guest who would come on to talk about the game or some experience in college or whatever. It was so much fun to watch.[4]

The studio had no crowd and just one camera, which was the size of a Buick. The entire show was shot live. "On camera Red and my dad were very compatible," recalled Johnsos Jr. "Red would say to my dad, 'Luke draw up a play that we are going to show you on film in a minute,' and my dad would walk to the board and put the Xs and Os down, the arrows, and now we're going to show you what it looks like on film. It was cool."[5]

The *Chicago Bears QB Club* was a big hit, lasting more than a decade on the air. Sometimes the two hosts—Red and Johnsos—would get criticized for being a "homer." Once, Anton Remenih of the *Chicago Tribune* wrote,

> One of the best film football shows on television is *Bears Quarterback Club* (WGN-TV, 9:30 p.m., Mondays). But it would be a better program if Red Grange and Luke Johnsos, cohosts, eased up on their gosh-awful habit of referring to every Bears player as "wonderful," "great," and "terrific."[6]

Red's busy football schedule would consist of doing his *Red Grange Football Show* on radio every Thursday; he then would travel to college games on Friday, broadcast on Saturday, travel to his NFL game that night, broadcast pro football on Sunday, go back to Chicago late Sunday night, and then head to the studio to do *The Chicago Bears QB Club* on Monday evening. This routine would continue for almost a decade.

Red was given positive reviews for his work on the air. George Alderton, sports editor of the *Lansing State Journal* (who is given credit for giving Michigan State the nickname the Spartans), praised the young broadcaster after the 1949 NFL Championship Game, saying,

> Wonder if some of you won't agree with us that Red Grange contributed considerably to that football broadcast in Los Angeles last Sunday? To our way of thinking, the ol' redhead came in there with some stuff that a football fan should be interested in hearing. He explained considerable of the technical phases of the game that to us, at least, was informative.[7]

At the end of the 1949 season Red received a tremendous honor from his former boss. On November 30, Halas held a special ceremony at the Bears office announcing the retirement of three Chicago Bears jerseys: Bronko Nagurski's number 3, Bill Hewitt's number 56, and Red's famous number 77. "Never again will a Bear player wear one of those numbers on his jersey," announced Halas.[8]

In 1950, the NFL had 13 teams, and more than 7 million Americans now had television sets. That year the Los Angeles Rams would become the first team to have all their games televised. The Washington Redskins soon followed suit. Red was in the midst of the game's biggest growth spurt since he turned pro in 1925. Also in 1950, the NFL adopted the rule of unlimited free substitutions, opening the way for the era of two platoons and specialization in pro football. "Many old-timers argue that it's not fair for some of the large schools to use separate offensive and defensive elevens; however, I believe football's modern specialization has helped the game considerably," said Red to the *United Press*.[9]

After Bears quarterback Sid Luckman retired following the 1950 season, Red gave the press a glimpse into what the future Hall of Famer was experiencing. "I know how Sid feels today," said Red. "When you quit football, something goes out of your life." Red thought about his own retirement, his life, and what he wanted to do. He also got the urge to visit his sister. For more than a decade he had wanted to visit Mildred in New York, but something always came up, whether it was his busy schedule or taking care of his father, who had started to show signs of failing health. Red missed his sister. Red encouraged

Garland to help look after their father, and the younger Grange invited Lyle to live with him in Florida, finding a home in Miami. Garland was now married to his wife, Virginia, while working as a credit manager at Richards Department Store. Soon all three Grange men would call Florida home.[10]

Thinking of family more and more, it was time for Red to see his sister. "Harold has always been very close to our father and always has consulted him on any matter of importance," said Mildred to the *Binghamton Press and Sun-Bulletin* when the paper heard that Red might be visiting. "Harold remained just as common as anyone, and his natural friendliness brought him a host of friends." Mildred was excited to see her younger brother and have Red spend time with her children. "He is fond of my boys," said Mildred. Red decided to go see his sister. "He says nothing is going to interfere with his plans this time," continued Mildred.[11]

In June 1951, Red and Margaret packed their bags to head east. They would stay at Mildred's house for the big trip. While he was visiting his sister, the local newspaper came out to cover the long-awaited reunion. They took a photo of the two Grange siblings sitting on the couch, both smiling, while flipping through the scrapbook that Mildred kept of Red's football accomplishments. "Mildred was friendly, outgoing, and loved having her family around all the time," said Donna Edwards, granddaughter of Mildred. "When Red and Margaret came they stayed with Mildred. Naturally, all family members came to grandma's house. She did all the cooking and baking. Always fun at grandma's house."[12]

Red and his wife spent an entire week catching up with family, visiting with cousins, and attending a family reunion in Forksville, approximately 70 miles from Binghamton. "I was kind of young at that time, but Red Grange went to a couple of the family reunions," said Richard Rinebold, grandson of Cora (Sherman) Rinebold, the sister of Red's mother, Sadie (Sherman) Grange. "He would come up to my grandmother's house to visit; he was a pretty good size man. I was about 10 years old when he visited. He would take the time to mess around with us kids. It was good to visit with him. He would also send Christmas cards and stuff like that." Margaret was also noticed by the Grange family. "I can remember seeing her too when they came to my grandmother's," said Rinebold. "She was a very pretty lady." During the trip to see his sister, Red made memories to last a lifetime.[13]

In 1952, the NFL had two divisions, Eastern and Western, with 12 teams. The league topped 2,000,000 paid fans for the first time ever, with 2,052,126 spectators passing through the turnstiles. It had been 27 years since Red had left college to play professional football, and he was witnessing the game thriving like it had never done before. During the 1950s, the "golden decade," with television being the main driving force for the sport, football would challenge baseball as the country's favorite pastime.

By December of that year, Red's hectic schedule had finally caught up with him. He would suffer his first big health setback at the age of 48. "It was a killing pace, but I didn't realize it because I so enjoyed what I was doing," wrote Red in his autobiography.

> After nearly three months of this, I began to show the effects of overwork. I was looking haggard and felt a fatigue I never knew before. My wife became concerned about my health and asked me to slow down. I promised her I would take a good rest immediately after the season, which was only a few weeks away.[14]

Red didn't make it to the end of the season. On December 14, he was traveling to Kirksville, Missouri, for a speaking engagement at the town's annual football banquet. While in his hotel room, he fell ill. He was able to make it through the banquet, but as soon as he arrived back in Chicago, he went straight to bed. Margaret, as a former nurse, knew something was wrong; his temperature was 103. His condition was grave, and his doctor ordered him to the West Suburban Hospital in Oak Park to undergo some tests. A cardiogram revealed that Red had suffered a heart attack. The redhead spent the next five weeks in bed at the hospital, Margaret never left his side. "Staying with me day and night, she slept on a cot in my room at the hospital," recalled Red.[15]

After being released from the hospital, Red spent the next three months resting in his own bed. "Red is fine, he's up and around," said Dr. Leonard Ceaser, Red's physician. "I imagine he will be going back to work one of these days." Red slowly regained his health, losing 30 pounds, reducing his weight from a heavy 208 pounds to a more manageable 178. As his doctor had said, Red got right back to work.[16] "The last four cardiograms were perfect," said Red to Arch Ward of the *Chicago Tribune*. "I dropped into the Bears' office the other day, and George Halas wanted to sign me as a defensive back."[17]

Red did scale back his schedule, doing fewer speaking engagements, eating healthier, and eliminating some college football games on Saturdays. He started up a new daily newspaper column for NEA titled "The Referee," answering questions from football fans nationwide, as well as working with a young writer on his life story. By chance, Red was introduced to Ira Morton.

A Chicago native, Ira Morton grew up the son of a doctor. After serving in the U.S. Army during World War II, Morton returned to school, attending the University of Illinois, where he received a degree in journalism in 1944. While at Illinois, Morton was a staff announcer at WILL radio (a university radio station), served as sports editor of the *Illio* (the school yearbook), and was a columnist and editorial writer for the *Daily Illini* (the school newspaper). After graduation Morton found his way into the advertising field. In Chicago, he sold advertising space for Time, Inc. and *Esquire* and *McCall's* magazines, as well as television time for WBKB-TV, and Morton was an executive with the Jones-Frankel Advertising Agency. While working in advertising, however, Morton never gave up his love for writing. In 1950 and 1951, he wrote a nationally syndicated television column titled "Watching All Channels," which appeared in the major newspapers, one of which was the *Chicago Herald-American*.

Being an Illinois graduate, Red was Morton's hero, so doing a book on Grange came natural to the writer. "I got the idea from the *Babe Ruth Story* that Bob Considine (sportswriter) did," said Morton in a 1953 Chicago television interview. "I talked to Considine about it when I was in New York. I asked him if he thought a book on Grange would make sense, and he thought it did. He encouraged me. So, when I got back to Chicago I got in touch with Red."[18]

When Morton returned to Chicago with the idea of writing a book on Red, he contacted a mutual friend, Joe Wilson, to get him in touch with Red. Wilson was one of the most popular sports announcers in Chicago, having done play-by-play for the Chicago Cubs, the Chicago Blackhawks, and University of Illinois football. "I was introduced to Red by Joe Wilson, so I went over to speak to him and told him what I had in mind," Morton recalled. "He tried to discourage me; he said it was a difficult job getting a book like this out. He told me he wrote a book on Zuppke (1937). I insisted we go ahead with it, and we did."[19]

Being an Illinois graduate gave Morton an easy connection to Red, as the Galloping Ghost always loved meeting fellow Illini. After the short meeting, Red agreed to let Morton write his story. Morton had gotten the assignment of a lifetime. Even the great Grantland Rice was impressed, sending a short letter on his personal stationery to the novice author.

Dear Mr. Morton:
I want to congratulate you on getting the Grange story. That ought to be a knock-out. Best luck. Sincerely, Grantland Rice (signed)[20]

During the next few months, Red and Morton would get together to write the book. These meetings took place at Red's apartment. Said Morton,

> We get together regularly, once every week or every two weeks. We sit down and talk. We first outlined the thing, then we sit down and go through chapter by chapter at Red's home. Matter of fact we sit down in the kitchen. I'd ask him a lot of questions, then I would check all the facts out at the library, all the old newspapers clippings that they have on microfilm over there, to make sure it was 100 percent authentic.[21]

The book, entitled *The Red Grange Story: The Autobiography of the Galloping Ghost*, as told to Ira Morton, was published in the fall of 1953, by G. P. Putnam's Sons in New York. Printed in hardback, the book is 180 pages long, with 20 chapters, 14 photos, and a foreword by Bob Zuppke. It sold for $3.00 in bookstores.

Reviews were positive. Whitney Martin of the *Associated Press* called it an "entertaining autobiography."[22] The *Salt Lake Tribune* wrote, "It's a book for sports fans young and old—a truly inspiring American success story."[23] The hometown *Chicago Tribune* wrote,

> This autobiography of the Galloping Ghost, one of the greatest ballcarriers ever to step on a football field, is a pleasant departure from the run-of-the-mill "quickie" jobs usually turned out on sports figures. The Grange–Morton combination has scored a literary equivalent of a perfectly planned and executed touchdown march.[24]

But the positivity surrounding the end of the football season and the success of the book quickly spoiled for Red by the loss of his best friend. On January 9, 1954, Lyle Grange passed away at a Miami hospital at the age of 86. After several years of bad health, Lyle succumbed, leaving gaping holes in the hearts of Red and Garland. The family held a private ceremony in Miami at the Lithgow 54th Street Center. Lyle's passing made front-page news in Wheaton, as the *Daily Journal* ran the headline, "Lyle Grange, Retired Wheaton Police Chief, Dies: Father of Grid Hero—Red Grange." But the accompanying article wasn't a celebration of the man who had served almost 20 years as policeman, marshal, deputy sheriff, and chief of police. The article talked about Lyle's battle with the city of Wheaton to get his pension. When the city of Wheaton joined the state pension program, Lyle, who had retired from the force in 1937, was not afforded a pension, although the three patrolmen under his command were.

A controversial ruling went against Lyle, denying him his pension. Because of this decision Red promised to never step foot back in Wheaton.[25]

Shortly after his father passed away, Red and Margaret made the decision to move to Miami to be closer to Garland and Virginia. They bought a large duplex three doors down from Garland, which became their home for most of the year. Garland had lived in Florida for years, but now both Grange men would enjoy the sun of the South. "It looks like I'll spend about eight months a year in Miami and the other four around Chicago and other places," said Red to the *Miami News*. "I've visited here with my brother a lot and like South Florida for living. So well, I'll try some of it."[26]

On January 1, 1954, Red would be paired with a new partner. The duo was about to change the landscape of college football. Hired by NBC to televise the Cotton Bowl in Dallas for the Rice–Alabama matchup, Red was paired with Lindsey Nelson. After graduating from the University of Tennessee, Nelson broke into broadcasting in 1948, following a short career as a reporter in Columbia, Tennessee, for the *Columbia Daily Herald*, as well as the first play-by-play announcer for Tennessee football games. "My father had a deliberate delivery in the booth," said Nancy Wyszynski, daughter of Lindsey Nelson. "He always thought his job on television was just to give it to the viewers. Here is the play, here's the down and distance, just give the information." He was an ideal fit to do college football games. After repeating their coverage of the Cotton Bowl the next year, NBC took the plunge full-time in the fall in 1955, hiring Nelson and Grange to do the network's *College Football Game of the Week*.[27]

"My dad never had an objection with getting help in the booth. My father never saw Red play, but he was awestruck of him. I think they made a great pair," said Wyszynski. "He told me that Red was extremely humble. A man of that stature who was extremely humble. We could use a little Red Grange today to tell you the truth. But they had chemistry in the booth. It was a good thing."[28]

A typical Nelson–Grange broadcast featured Nelson doing most of the talking as play-by-play man with a sprinkling of Red's explanation of strategy. Once during a 1957 game between Syracuse and Penn State, after a Penn State touchdown, Nelson said, "Here's Red Grange," and Red described the scoring play, going over the T formation, the pass route, and then telling the television viewers to "watch the quarterback" as he tossed a perfect spiral for the touchdown. After giving his explanation, Red would always say, "Here's Lindsey . . ." Throughout the NBC broadcast, Nelson would update scores from other games. There was no crawl at the bottom of the screen or any graphics. Red would get very technical with his descriptions of plays and formations, while explaining why a play was called on a certain down.[29]

Nelson was in awe of Red's popularity, particularly the response he received when they traveled by train, plane, or bus. "Everywhere we went, fans formed long lines to meet or just to see Red Grange, perhaps the greatest star the game of football has ever known. His magnitude was immense," wrote Nelson in his 1985 autobiography, *Hello Everybody, I'm Lindsey Nelson*. "For his generation, Red Grange was a lot like Pearl Harbor day was for a later one. Everyone could remember exactly where he was and what his detailed circumstances were when he heard or read about the exploits of Red Grange."[30]

For the next couple of years, Red and Lindsey were the most popular football announcers in the country, and their *College Football Game of the Week*, which aired throughout the fall on Saturdays, became must-see TV for sports fans. NBC was pleased with the popular broadcasting duo.

In 1955, Red engaged in another publishing project. *My Favorite Football Stories*, edited by Grange himself, is a compilation of football stories handpicked by Red. The book was published in hardback by A. S. Barnes and Company. Consisting of 192 pages, it contains 20 football stories written by the likes of Walter Eckersall, Allison Danzig, Pudge Heffelfinger, Knute Rockne, John Kieran, and Grantland Rice. It sold for $3.00. The volume was also released in paperback by Dell in New York that same year and sold for $0.25.[31]

Red composed one chapter for the book, titled "The Greatest Game," a four-page explanation of his love affair with the sport. He wrote,

> Until I got acquainted with this new world presented by the printed word, there wasn't much I thought I didn't know. But I found out pretty quickly that a fellow can learn a lot this way—and man, I smartened up in a hurry after I decided to read about football besides talking about it! There are incidents in some of the following stories which in one way or another carry messages far clever and more memorable than any I can deliver. It was for this reason that I selected them for inclusion in the book, and I hope you'll see my point of view.[32]

During the 1950s, the NFL was a hit on television, first on the DuMont Network (1951–1955) and then on CBS. By the end of the decade, there were almost 50 million television sets in use. Red was one of the few announcers doing NFL games on a regular basis, joining Chris Schenkel, Van Patrick, Harry Wismer, and Chuck Thompson. For the most part, he received positive reviews. "Red Grange's analysis of plays continues to be helpful," wrote Jack Gould of the *New York Times* in 1956.[33]

In 1952, Paul Cotton of the *Des Moines Register* wrote,

> Grange is one of the few football announcers who can get away with the consider-
> able explaining of the game's technicalities. Ordinarily this is supposed to deaden
> a broadcast. Grange succeeds because his listeners don't doubt that he knows
> what he is talking about and because he usually does it in a clear, concise way.
>
> Red keeps football jargon to a minimum, although he has one favorite phrase,
> "He racked him up." That means, "He stopped the ballcarrier with a hard
> tackle." When Red further says, "He really racked him up good," it means the
> ballcarrier was tackled so hard the thud could be heard all over the place.[34]

Red's broadcasting style was one of a kind. His voice was high and his grammar sometimes bad, but he rarely overtalked, giving viewers straight football
dope about what he saw. His football expertise was second to none, and he
could spin a great football yarn if the game became slow or boring. He spent
many hours honing his craft. During Red's final year in the booth in 1963,
Francis Coughlin of the *Chicago Tribune* wrote,

> (Grange) puts in hours of homework before taking over the microphone. He
> studies statistics, items of interest, club releases, information on players, and
> hundreds of personal items. He keeps his own file of 1,000 (index) cards.
>
> For the booth, his spotter prepares four spotting boards—devices indicat-
> ing numbers and players in the offensive formations of both teams on the field.
> Grange calls the offensive play. His spotter keeps track of substitutions and points
> out the defensive moves.[35]

Red's broadcasting spotting boards were preserved and are now part of the Pro
Football Hall of Fame archives.

The only big knock on Red as an announcer was his loyalty to the Chicago
Bears. On one occasion the *Cincinnati Enquirer* called him out, writing,

> Unfortunately, during the course of his topflight coverage, Red commits what to
> many people is the cardinal sin of sports commentators—favoritism. Even though
> an announcer is a former football star—as is Mr. Grange—and his team is going
> down to defeat, he should strive for complete impartiality. This seemed to be
> Red's trouble last Sunday during the Chicago Bears–Detroit Lions game.[36]

On December 22, 1957, Bob Zuppke died at his home in Champaign. He
was 78 years old. Despite the short falling out when Red turned pro, the two
men had become very close during their time together. Zuppke always said that
Red was the greatest player he ever coached, while Red praised the guidance

Zup gave him throughout the years. Zuppke even gave his prized pupil, as well as his brother Garland, original paintings of his. One of them was of Red in full Illinois football uniform, football under his arm—just as he had carried the ball against Michigan in 1924. Red loved this painting so much that he always prominently displayed it wherever he lived. "Zup was in pretty bad shape when I saw him last fall before the (Illinois) Minnesota game," said Red after hearing the news of his friend's passing. "But once we started talking football, he perked right up. Before we talked long, however, he told me he wouldn't be around for another season. He was a great guy and a great coach, and the thing he could do best was handle men."[37]

In the fall of 1958, Red joined *Sports Illustrated*, at the time an up-and-coming weekly sports magazine, as its college football forecaster. During the season Red compiled an impressive record of 70–29–6 (including bowl games) predicting games—a 70 percent winning clip. That same fall, the NFL topped 3,000,000 in paid attendance (3,006,124) for its 72 league games, and ratings were going up with each passing year on television. While doing a Bears–Browns preseason game in Akron, Ohio, Red spoke to John Flynn of the *Akron Beacon-Journal* about the popularity of the pro game. "It's the greatest game in the world," he declared. "The owners and coaches have geared their game to suit the fans. When I played, we would score seven points and attempt to make it hold up, but you don't see that in today's pro ball." Pro football was about to explode and expand even more.[38]

At the end of the 1958 season, the Baltimore Colts traveled to the Big Apple to face the New York Giants in the NFL Championship Game. The game featured a former sandlot quarterback, the Colts' Johnny Unitas, who guided his team to a 23–17 victory in the first overtime game in NFL history. An estimated 45 million people watched the game on television in the United States. A year later, Texas billionaire Lamar Hunt—who watched the 1958 title game—formed the American Football League (AFL), which began play with eight teams in the 1960 season. The growth of the sport—through franchise expansion, the eventual merger with the AFL, and popularity on television—is commonly credited to this game, a turning point in the history of pro football. "There's no doubt that pro football has grown into a tremendously popular game since the introduction of television," said Red in 1959.[39]

Red was traveling about 60,000 miles a year doing his broadcasting work. Heading into 1960, Grange, who was now 57 years old, reduced his workload by giving up college football on Saturdays. NBC decided not to pick up *College Football Game of the Week*, so Red just walked away. After five full seasons, his partnership with Lindsey Nelson was over. "I tried to learn all I could from him about how one charts a steady course, without controversy and furor, when cast into the glare of the public spotlight. No one ever did it more becomingly," wrote Nelson in his autobiography. In addition to continuing to do college football, Nelson would go on to broadcast baseball for 20 years with the New York Mets and San Francisco Giants.[40]

Red would still work Bears games, which were now being seen nationally on CBS, as he would partner with George Connor, former Bears All-Pro tackle, who would be inducted into the Pro Football Hall of Fame in 1975. After the 1963 season, Red retired from the broadcast booth. He had just finished his 45th year in football since his freshman year in high school, missing only the 1928 football season with his knee injury. "It isn't easy to leave Florida sunshine for those icy Sundays in the north," said Red to the *Decatur Daily Review*.[41]

One Chicago newspaper reported that Red called 312 football games in his career, with his final broadcast being the Bears' 24–14 win against the Detroit Lions on December 15, 1963. "I think he enjoyed broadcasting games," said Pat McCaskey, grandson of George Halas. "He was grateful for the game of football, and he wanted to show that to other people. He was enthusiastic and knowledgeable. He was always worth listening too." It doesn't appear that he broadcasted the Bears' win against the New York Giants in the 1963 NFL Championship Game, giving his old coach, George Halas, his sixth and final world championship at the age of 68.[42]

The radio and television star was officially retired. It was time to relax and enjoy the Florida sun.

PART VII

FOOTBALL ROYALTY
(1963–1991)

32

PRO FOOTBALL HALL
OF FAME

On December 6, 1959, Clayton Horn, editor of the *Canton Repository*, instructed one of his sportswriters, Chuck Such, to issue a Hall of Fame challenge to the city of Canton, Ohio. The headline read, "Pro Football Needs a Hall of Fame and Logical Site Is Here." This declaration raised a lot of eyebrows throughout the city, but none were raised higher than those of H. H. Timken Jr., chairman of the board at Canton's largest industry, the Timken Roller Bearing Company. He called Such to offer his support and assigned the company's recreation director, Earl Schreiber, to the project. Other cities that applied for the potential site were Detroit and Pittsburgh. But it was too late. Canton was heavily favored as the future home of the Hall, and, on January 25, 1961, at the NFL's owners meeting in New York, the city of Canton made a formal bid to house the facility.

William Umstattd, chairman of the executive committee at Timken, accompanied Schreiber to New York for the meeting, to be held at the Warwick Hotel. They showed the NFL owners a scale model of the proposed building—not one owner looked at it—and gave a short three-minute presentation, during which Umstattd estimated the cost of construction to be $350,000. He also said the city of Canton would donate $250,000, while Mr. Timken himself would donate $100,000. At this point, the owners began to listen. Three months later, at an NFL meeting in San Francisco, Canton was selected as the Hall of Fame city.

A fund-raising campaign started on December 7, 1961, and in less than three months, the city raised $378,026 through community pledges. Pro football had found a home for its Hall of Fame, where the greats of the sport would live on forever. The Hall became a reality with a groundbreaking ceremony on August

11, 1962, when NFL commissioner Pete Rozelle, who had replaced the recently deceased Bert Bell as commissioner in 1960, shoveled the first dirt.

At the end of the 1962 season, the Hall of Fame selected 14 men to help vote for the charter class of enshrinees. The selection committee would choose 17 charter members from a list of the game's great players and contributors. The committee consisted of 12 sportswriters—one from each NFL city—and two former NFL stars. They were as follows:

Lewis Atchison (*Washington Star*)
Jimmy Conzelman (former NFL player-coach)
Arthur Daley (*New York Times*)
Art Daley (*Green Bay Press-Gazette*)
Herb Good (*Philadelphia Inquirer*)
Sam Greene (*Detroit News*)
Chuck Heaton (*Cleveland Plain-Dealer*)
Charles Johnson (*Minneapolis Star*)
Jack McDonald (*San Francisco News-Call Bulletin*)
Paul Menton (*Baltimore Evening-Sun*)
Bob Oates (*Los Angeles Herald-Examiner*)
Davey O'Brien (former NFL quarterback)
Jack Sell (*Pittsburgh Post-Gazette*)
George Strickler (*Chicago Tribune*)

The committee poured over 80 potential candidates for election and, after reviewing the names, finally made their choices. On January 29, 1963, the Hall of Fame held a press conference to reveal the 17 nominees. The names of the first Hall of Fame class read like the names on the Declaration of Independence. These were the founding fathers of professional football.

Sammy Baugh
Bert Bell (deceased)
Joe F. Carr (deceased)
Dutch Clark
Red Grange
George Halas
Mel Hein
Pete Henry (deceased)

Cal Hubbard
Don Hutson
Curly Lambeau
Tim Mara (deceased)
George Preston Marshall
Johnny "Blood" McNally
Bronko Nagurski
Ernie Nevers
Jim Thorpe (deceased)

When Red heard the news that he was one of the first members of the Pro Football Hall of Fame he was humbled by the prestigious honor. "It really takes me off my feet. I'm flattered to be chosen in that kind of company," he said to the *Associated Press*.[1]

Red traveled to Canton, Ohio, for the first time to attend the Hall of Fame inductions. On September 7, he participated in the annual Hall of Fame parade, which passed through Canton and ended at the steps of the Hall of Fame Museum. The first-ever induction ceremony was held in Fawcett Stadium. At 12:30 p.m., the proceedings began, with sportswriter Bob Considine serving as master of ceremonies.

As the ceremony started, pro football's first class of inductees was honored. First up was George Halas. Then it was Red's turn. Each inductee was assigned a presenter by the Hall. For Red, they selected Jimmy Conzleman, a former NFL player who played against Red during his famous barnstorming tour. Conzleman said,

> Friends, Red Grange was the first professional football explosion. The Galloping Ghost of the Illini captured the nation's attention like no player ever did, and he brought the spotlight with him when he stepped directly from the Big Ten gridirons into the Bears lineup. His pro debut on Thanksgiving Day 1925 sold out Wrigley Field for the first time and then the Polo Grounds, and around the country went Red and pro football went with him. The Galloping Ghost's college reputation got a horse-whipping in the headlines on the exhausting coast-to-coast grind, not to mention Red's aching back. Careless historians fail to recall Red Grange came back to become one of the best of all the Bears. Always dangerous on offense, he distinguished himself on defense with two world championship teams. For almost three decades he's still a Bear but now on television. Thank you.[2]

Red was up next. Those in attendance rose and gave the Galloping Ghost a standing ovation. As he approached the microphone, Grange gathered his thoughts. In his cheery Midwestern voice, he said,

> Bob, Jimmy, thank you very much. Yes, my back did ache, but the first two years with Mr. Halas was on percentage and that took a lot of aches out of it. It's difficult at a time like this to find words to express your thanks. I am certainly deeply honored. I'm flattered very, very much, and of course I'm pleased. I hope a little bit of my plaque will be owned by every teammate that I ever had the privilege of playing with. I think it's wonderful to be involved with all these gentlemen here at my rear, fellas that I have played with, fellas that I have played against. It's certainly a deserving honor. I feel that I am extremely flattered to be in their company. I'm sure as our shrine goes on and on and gets bigger I'll have the opportunity, Jim, someday that you and I can reverse positions, that I will present you a plaque to the Hall of Fame, and I hope it's very, very soon. Just let me say again thanks to the people of Canton. Thanks for having me here, and I'm going to be a worthy member and certainly do everything I can to make this the greatest shrine in the world. Thank you very much.[3]

In just one short minute, Red was done. Deep down he appreciated the honor, but he never wanted to take all the credit for things other people helped him achieve. He thanked his teammates before leaving the platform to pose for photos next to his bronze bust, to be displayed inside the Pro Football Hall of Fame. Future generations of football fans would now get to see the bronze likeness of the Galloping Ghost.

33

50TH ANNIVERSARY OF IMMORTALITY

Near the end of his broadcasting career Red and Margaret decided to make a change with regard to where they wanted to live. Miami was a fine location, but the city was becoming too busy for the quiet couple. Almost 1 million residents called Dade County home. Since the couple decided not to have any children, it would be just the two of them for the rest of their lives. They felt more peace and quiet was better. Through his Florida connections Red had heard about a new piece of property situated in the central part of the state. Indian Lake Estates was located in Polk County, on the eastern shore of Lake Weohyakapka, 14 miles southeast of Lake Wales and 80 miles east of Tampa. Red was one of the first investors in Indian Lake Estates, which was advertised as a "country club community." He and Margaret would be neighbors to other retirees—retired colonels and assorted former vice presidents of businesses and industries.

Amid a sprawling golf course, the homes were laid out in clusters but decently separated with backyards that sloped down to a channel that funneled into the lake. Red's newly built home was located on a half-acre of land at 12 North Amaryllis Drive. Designed by Red himself, the one-level family home was painted white with green trim, with a tile roof and two-car garage. The home was surrounded by a small white picket fence with a wooden welcome sign that read, "The Granges." Spacious inside, Red designed the home with no hallways, and it had three bedrooms with a bathroom in each one, a bar area, a living room, a dining room, and a kitchen. Red also added several comfortable touches to the house. He made sure the home had a screened-in swimming pool (eight feet deep); planters with flowers and tropical plants; and a patio leading out to the backyard, which led to a small boat house that ran right up to the lake. He usually kept two small rowboats on hand to travel up and down the lake. Red took pride in keeping the lawn carefully trimmed, and Margaret made sure the home had plenty of flowers and several bushes decorating the yard.

Family and guests were always impressed with the modest living arrangements. "It had an indoor pool. You could enter from the outside or inside. They had screens on the side," said Dorothy Flora, niece of Margaret and Red Grange.

It was very modest. Small but nice. Red was so crazy, the home had a canal running behind the house. This alligator was always bathing at the end of the property, so Red started to feed it. That thing never wanted to stop being fed, kept getting bigger and bigger. Finally, he was scared not to feed it. I don't think it died. They had to take it away. Margaret had this big white crane that she called Snow Ball outside the screen of the pool. Every night Red would throw feed out there, but this big bird would come once or twice a day, Margaret thought that it was her bird.[1]

Red could relax at anytime, anywhere at the house. His favorite spot was on his lounge chair cuddled up with his dogs—usually dachshunds—on the patio. Here he was 3 feet from the swimming pool, 50 feet from his fishing boat, and a half-mile from the golf course. "I play for fun and exercise, but the game lacks something," said Red in 1968, about his golf game. "It would be better if once in a while someone came up from behind and tackled you just as you were hitting the ball." Red played but couldn't get into the competitive aspect of the sport. Some of his playing partners took the game too serious. It was Margaret who was the competitive golfer of the family, winning several tournaments as the club's top female golfer.[2]

"The two of them got along famously well, always joking and laughing with each other," said Linda Thomas, niece of Margaret and Red. "I remember once staying with them in Florida after I graduated high school, and she called uncle Red 'honey.' She never stopped calling him that. Even neighbors at the country club called him honey."[3]

Finally settled in at Indian Lake, Red still scheduled speaking engagements and attended a few games during his free time. He always praised the current game. "There's simply no comparison," said Red to *United Press International* in 1971. "Today's players are so much bigger and so much faster than the men of my day."[4]

In 1974, the University of Illinois decided to hold a 50th anniversary celebration of Red's historic performance against Michigan in 1924. The celebration would be held on October 19, the same day the Illini would play Michigan State. Red felt humbled by the honor and agreed to come back to Champaign for the celebration.

Red's adopted hometown of Wheaton also joined in. D. Ray Wilson, the publisher of the *Wheaton Daily Journal,* and two of his top writers, Mike Hawkins (sports editor) and Richard Crabb, made sure of that. The *Daily Journal* ran a series of articles titled "Wheaton Remembers Red Grange." Throughout that summer and early fall, Wheaton residents were interviewed or could submit short stories of their memories of the town's greatest athlete. More than 35 submissions were published, some of which included articles submitted by Charles Cruther, Elmer Hoffman, Bim Frazer, and Charles Gates, former classmates and teammates at Wheaton High School. Red's former high school coach, "Dink" Welden, also submitted one. Wilson made sure these articles were sent to Red in Florida.[5]

Wilson and the city of Wheaton also made plans for the townspeople to be able to attend some of the festivities that weekend, including a special luncheon on the day of the game. "The most surprising development has been the remarkable interest shown in honoring Red Grange by the young people of Wheaton and Central DuPage County," declared Wilson. "There have been instances of parents reserving for the big weekend in Champaign and then calling back to increase their reservation because their teenagers wanted to attend." The town was officially going nuts about its hero.[6]

Leaving Margaret behind to watch their two dachshunds, Red landed at Willard Airport in Champaign on the Thursday before the events. He was excited about the game more so than anything else, saying to the local media, "I didn't travel 1,000 miles from sunny Florida to see my Fighting Illini lose." Visiting with old classmates and teammates that weekend couldn't have gone any better for Red. He enjoyed shaking hands and signing autographs, wearing a smile for four days.[7]

On Friday, he was able to speak to the Illinois football team courtesy of head coach Bob Blackman. The Illini were currently 4–1, with an upset win against number 19 ranked Stanford. Although he was almost 50 years older than most of the young players, he had their undivided attention. Coach Blackman introduced Red to the team as the players sat in the stands at Memorial Stadium. Red spoke to the squad for about 20 minutes, spending most of his time talking about his experiences at Illinois and with the Chicago Bears. "I want to congratulate you fellows. There's a guy who lives next door to me who has been belittling me for 10 years because of all the great teams Notre Dame has. But since you guys beat Purdue and they beat Notre Dame, my friend hasn't come out of the house in a week." Red finished by saying, "I've come a thousand miles, and I'm proud Illinois is back where it should be—winning football games."[8]

That night the "Red Grange Testimonial Dinner" was held at the Champaign Ramada Inn Convention Center. A jam-packed convention hall with more than 600 guests paid $20 a plate to attend, with proceeds going to the Red Grange Scholarship Fund. Former Illinois football coach Ray Eliot was the master of ceremonies with special guests that included sports announcer Jack Brickhouse; Big Ten commissioner Wayne Duke; and Red's old pro coach, George Halas, who came from Chicago to see his good friend.

Halas called Red the "greatest player of this century." He added, "I'm positive, too, that no one in the next 26 years of this century will surpass Red, either. . . . Red had more impact on both college and pro football than any man this century. Red brought magic to the fledgling NFL."[9] Eliot then read a congratulatory letter from U.S. president Gerald Ford, who had been an All-American center at the University of Michigan. Written on White House stationery, Ford said,

Dear Red:

When I assumed my present office, I knew there were many difficult tasks ahead. I never dreamed, though, that I would be called upon to congratulate someone for kicking the daylights out of a University of Michigan football team.

Seriously, I wish I could have been in Memorial Stadium 50 years ago today. I wouldn't have liked the score. But I would have savored every minute of your great performance. It was one of those events that helped make college football the great spectator attraction it is today.

Congratulations on your contribution to the sport and best wishes for a memorable evening,

Sincerely, Gerry Ford[10]

The following day found Red very busy from morning to night. At 10:00 a.m., Red's first stop was at his old fraternity house—at a new location—spending time with current and former Zeta Psi brothers. Then it was back to the Ramada Inn for a big luncheon with his friends from Wheaton. More than 250 people from his old hometown spoke of their memories of the redhead, as he greeted friends and new acquaintances from his old stomping grounds. While there Red was presented several gifts, one of which was the game ball from the recent Wheaton Central High School homecoming win, given to him by head coach Andy Hauptman. The short meet and greet was the beginning of healing the wounds that the Grange family felt they had endured when Lyle Grange was not given his pension. Later that night, both Red and the city of Wheaton would finalize an agreement that would have Red returning home.

Red was then off to an Illinois alumni tailgate party, then another "luncheon" at the Varsity Room inside Memorial Stadium. At 1:30 p.m., it was time for the kickoff of the game between Illinois and Michigan State. On a clear, crisp October day on campus, Red entered the stadium at the south end, a loud roar erupting as the entire facility, filled with more than 55,000 fans, gave him a standing ovation. Red had goosebumps as he waved several times to the fans before sitting down in the first row on the east side of the stadium, right behind the Illinois bench. It had been 50 years since he last played there.

Illinois played well in the first half. Even Red got into the game, standing and cheering as Illinois running back Chubby Phillips took a dive into the end zone on the game's first touchdown. The rest of the first half featured more offensive explosions as the two teams traded scores, with a 21-21 score going into halftime.

At halftime, Red was honored for his heroics of 50 years prior. The Galloping Ghost was escorted to midfield. Submerged in a sea of university officials, cameramen, and reporters, he was awarded the school's Distinguished Service Award, the highest honor bestowed on an individual by the university. Tim Swain, a member of the Illinois Board of Trustees, put a medallion around Red's neck. Then Red spoke to the sold-out crowd for a few minutes, thanking them. "I don't know how to thank all of the wonderful people who have taken part in this great weekend," he said. "I have enjoyed it so much."[11]

As he finished his speech, which lasted about four minutes, a small biplane flew over the stadium pulling a banner reading, "We Believe in Ghosts—Hi Red." While walking back to his seat, Red signed numerous autographs, mostly for young fans, before watching the second half from his front-row perch. He didn't see another touchdown. He also didn't see Illinois lose, as the game ended in a 21-21 tie. Later that night, he returned to the Ramada Inn for the 50th anniversary reunion of the class of 1924. Former classmates and teammates gathered to see and talk to their hero and friend.

It was at the Ramada Inn in Champaign that Red ended a feud. He was about to come back home. A young newspaper employee of the *Wheaton Daily Journal*, David Stamps, was in Champaign with his boss, D. Ray Wilson, sports editor Mike Hawkins, and writer Richard Crabb to make a pitch to Red. Stamps remembered how Wilson got Red to agree to come back to Wheaton.

> At one point in the evening he (Red) came over to us and said, "I know you guys want to talk to me so let's go to my room where it is quieter." So, there was myself, D. Ray Wilson, Richard Crabb, and our sports editor, Mike Hawkins. The Jim Beam company made a souvenir decanter of Memorial Stadium, and he asked if we wanted some, so we said yes, and he said, "We don't have any ice so will have to drink it neat."
>
> There wasn't too many chairs so we just sat on the bed, knee-to-knee, so Red started by saying, "Thank you for what you did (writing the articles). I really appreciated that. . . . I was surprised that there was a lot of people who still remember me, but I also know you want me to return to Wheaton for some deal that you got going on there." He said, "Basically no way in hell I'm going to do that, and so let's just finish off our drinks and say farewell and part friends."
>
> And it was at that point Ray Wilson gave one of the greatest sales jobs ever. He leaned back a little bit and said, "Red, we don't give a damn about you." And Grange literally recoiled after hearing that. He took notice because people just didn't talk to Red Grange liked that. And he said, "What do you mean?"
>
> So, you have to harken back. This was 1974, the Vietnam War was still going on, didn't end until 1975, so this was draft dodging, draft card burning, demonstration in the streets, Kent State (shooting), riots, so the country was in a turmoil, so there was precious little to applaud or look up to. . . . Ray said, "Like it or not you're a hero in the eyes of many people, including children. Your success on the field and all you stand for is very positive, and we need that kind of stuff. You are to the youth of Wheaton to help provide a positive influence."
>
> The rest of us were sitting there quiet and didn't say a word. Red then leaned back and said, "I never thought of it that way. But I get your point, so I tell you what, I will come back to do this thing for you but on one condition, that you run the whole show. I don't want to worry about any of that." He wanted no hangers-on, just wanted it to focus on youth and that nature.
>
> So, we shook hands with him, and he said you call me and say when and I'll come.[12]

The conversation took less than an hour. Wilson had done the impossible. He convinced Red to return to Wheaton.

34

SUPER BOWL COIN TOSS

In a Gallup poll taken in October 1972, for the first time football overtook baseball as America's favorite sport. From 1937 to 1960, Gallup polls consistently showed that baseball was far and away the country's national pastime. After 1972, professional football became the country's number-one sport, and it has been number one for the past four and half decades.

Red still enjoyed the game, watching college and pro football every weekend from his home in Florida. As the NFL reached new heights, topping 11,000,000 fans in 1976 (11,070,543), the sport was being seen everywhere. It was being broadcast on television. There was the debut of *Monday Night Football* in 1970, the Pro Bowl, the Pro Football Hall of Fame, and the draft, and many more events allowed the league's players to benefit from this popularity. Movies, commercials, advertising, autograph signings, and many other business avenues also popped up. Such NFL stars as Jim Brown, Johnny Unitas, Vince Lombardi, Paul Hornung, Joe Namath, and Terry Bradshaw became some of the most well-known athletes in the world, while other former NFL stars made an easier transition into the broadcast booth for a "second" career. The likes of Pat Summerall, Frank Gifford, Don Meredith, Johnny Lujack, Tony Canadeo, Kyle Rote, Paul Christman, and Tom Brookshier flourished on the air.

In 1975, CBS debuted *The NFL Today*, a studio show with host Brent Musburger. Cohosts included former NFL player Irv Cross, former Miss America Phyliss George as news reporter, and Jimmy "The Greek" Snyder as football insider to help with the betting side of the sport. Super Bowl XI was contested on January 9, 1977, between the Minnesota Vikings and the Oakland Raiders, setting television records for an NFL game. The NBC telecast had a rating of

44.4 (73 share), with more than 62 million viewers. Ads were sold for $125,000 for a 30-second spot. Inside the Rose Bowl, a Super Bowl–record 103,438 fans paid to see the Raiders thump the Vikings, 32–14. This was a far cry from the small crowds of the early days of professional football. The Galloping Ghost was about to be invited to the NFL and the sporting world's most popular event.

For the first 11 Super Bowls, the NFL had the referee flip the coin at midfield with the team captains present to see who won the toss and would kick off to start the game. For Super Bowl XII, in New Orleans, the NFL decided to add a twist to the coin toss to change this time-honored tradition. Red was chosen to "officiate" the exchange with game referee Jim Tunney.

Red, accompanied by Margaret, was set to see his first live Super Bowl from inside the Superdome. It was the first Super Bowl played indoors. The NFL gave Red a host to show him around town and make sure he was present for all the league activities throughout the weekend. His host was the current Miss America, Susan Perkins. When he arrived in the Big Easy, Red visited the Super Bowl press room. He reminisced about playing in the first couple NFL Championship Games, notably the famous "Sneakers Game." He talked about his time with manager C. C. Pyle and the Bears' barnstorming tour, as well as what he was doing in retirement. "I love it," Red said to the media. "But I have been footballing all my life. It's like going to work. I don't have a routine anymore. I wake up at 8 o'clock in the morning, and if there is something I want to do, I do it. If not, I roll over and go back to sleep." And of course he talked about others. "People ask me sometimes who was the best football player I ever saw. I'll tell you," said Red as he sat up. "It was Bronko Nagurski. Take Larry Csonka (fullback) when he was at his best at Miami (Dolphins). Take Dick Butkus (linebacker) in his heyday with the Bears. Put them together and you have the Bronk."[1]

On Super Sunday, Red strolled onto the Astroturf at the Superdome shaking his head. He had only played on grass, or sandlot dirt. This was a far cry from the Orchard in Wheaton. In the stands Red saw a sold-out crowd of 75,583. He probably thought about the NFL's first-ever playoff game, also played indoors, in front of 11,000 fans at Chicago Stadium in 1932. The NFL had come a long way. Red was happy to be alive to see professional football's biggest event become so popular, even if he didn't see himself as being a contributing factor to that success.

On the sidelines, with Red still accompanied by his host, Susan Perkins, cameramen gathered around the aging football star—sporting gray hair instead of his trademark auburn locks—to get photos. Wearing a dark red sports jacket, white dress shirt, and dark blue tie, Red looked trim and tan, and he gave the media a big smile. He shook hands with NFL commissioner Pete Rozelle. Dangling from his lapel was his sideline pass, given to him by the NFL. The league knew its football history, and in a unique twist the pass number given to Red was number 77. Red appreciated this gesture by the NFL and kept the sideline pass, as well as his two game tickets from section 421, for his personal collection.[2]

It was now time for the coin toss. Over the Superdome's public address system came the voice of CBS announcer Pat Summerall, who would call the game with his partner, Tom Brookshier. Said Summerall, "We are proud to extend a Super Bowl welcome to one of professional football's immortals. Red Grange of the Chicago Bears, will toss the coin for captains to call." The crowd gave a big cheer. With Perkins by his side, Red walked briskly to midfield, greeting the captains of each team. The Cowboys captains were quarterback Roger Staubach; wide receiver Drew Pearson; linebackers D. D. Lewis and Mike Hegman; and defensive end Harvey Martin. On the Broncos side was quarterback Craig Morton; wide receivers Haven Moses and John Schultz; and safety Bill Thompson. Also present at midfield were NFL Films cameraman Steve Sabol, with assistant Hank McElwee and soundman Jack Newman, and a CBS cameraman.

Red shook hands with the captains, saying to the Broncos leaders, "Congratulations, I've seen you guys play the last couple of weeks. Good luck to you." As Grange watched, referee Jim Tunney flipped the coin. Drew Pearson of the Cowboys called "tails." The coin turned over serval times before coming up tails. Dallas had won the privilege of receiving the kickoff for Super Bowl XII. As the captains for both teams jogged to their respective sidelines, Perkins and Red sprinted off the field toward the Broncos sideline.[3]

As for the game, the Cowboys forced eight turnovers in crushing the Broncos, 27–10. The game had a 47.2 share, with more than 78 million people tuning in on CBS—a new Super Bowl record. Pro football had never been more popular than at that moment. Red was the first former NFL player to participate in the pregame coin toss. The following year, George Halas continued the tradition of having a former NFL legend present at the coin toss, and the practice has been a Super Bowl pregame staple for the past 40 years.

After returning home to Florida, Red and Margaret prepared for their trip to Wheaton.

35

WHEATON HOMECOMING

Decades after declaring that he would never step foot back in Wheaton, Red had mellowed out. D. Ray Wilson, publisher of the *Wheaton Daily Journal*, had convinced Red to return home. Because they had Red's word on coming back to town, the townspeople took their time organizing the event. After talking to Red in Champaign in 1974, the town put together an organization called the All-American Seventy-Seven, Inc., a not-for-profit corporation. This organization eventually came up with an idea to establish the DuPage County Heritage Gallery. The gallery would honor several former county residents who had a lasting impact on the community. Red would be joined in the gallery by Elbert H. Gary, founder of the U.S. Steel Corporation; John W. Gates, whose barbed-wire invention revolutionized American agriculture; Robert McCormick, owner and publisher of the *Chicago Tribune*; and Billy Graham, the country's foremost evangelist.

It took the town of Wheaton roughly four years to get their ducks in a row to establish the gallery. Several times, Wilson and *Daily Journal* writer Richard Crabb made trips to Florida to visit with Red and Margaret to update them on the progress of the permanent gallery. The two men also went over Red's proposed itinerary for his visit. The two biggest events would be the dedication of the Heritage Gallery and a special program titled "An Evening with Red Grange," with Red as the guest of honor. It would be a full schedule for the Galloping Ghost.

Wheaton was preparing for the arrival of its most famous son, although the small town was much different in 1978 than the one in which Red had grown up. At this time, the population was roughly 40,000 residents, topping 3,400 citizens in 1910, when Lyle brought his family to town. "We are delighted to have Red Grange return to Wheaton for this special event," said William Carlson, president of All-American Seventy-Seven, Inc. "Red Grange is one of America's living heroes, and we are pleased we can honor him as one of Wheaton's greats."[1]

As the date got closer, Red and Margret faced a crisis—what to do with their two puppies. A few weeks before they were to leave for Wheaton, the Granges' puppy sitter moved to Arkansas, leaving the two without someone to take care of their young pups. Margaret decided not to attend, staying behind to watch their two dachshunds.

In the fall of 1978, Red would stay in Wheaton for four days, from October 26 to October 29. After a travel day, Red would have three full days of activities in his hometown. After a weather delay in getting to Chicago, he arrived at O'Hare Airport for the big celebration. Instead of a hotel, as Red didn't want any big hoopla, he would stay at the home of D. Ray Wilson, who lived in nearby Dundee. "He proved to be a very easy guest, and his time with us was a delight," said Bea Wilson, wife of the late D. Ray Wilson. "He was a very humble person, and I noticed that anytime football and his successes were mentioned, he brushed it off with, 'I didn't deserve the credit, I just carried the ball. The credit belonged to my teammates who cleared the path.'"[2]

Upon arriving at the Wilson residence, Red immediately felt at home. "Red was a very easy and appreciative guest. To accommodate him on the main floor I moved out our 11-year-old daughter Muffy out of her ruffles and roses bedroom for him. I found it amusing to watch this big football hero seem comfortable as he settled into this fluffy little girl's room," recalled Bea Wilson.

> Years later, when Muffy was in high school, one of her teachers referred to Red Grange, then chuckled and added, "Of course none of you would know who he was." With that Muffy's arm shot into the air with her replying, "I do, I do! He slept in my bed!" She enjoyed her moment of fame.[3]

Wilson and one of the newspaper's young executives, managing editor David Stamps, would escort Red around town. "I was the advance man," said David Stamps. "I was 34 years old at the time, so I was just happy to make sure that the schedule was kept and tapped him on the wrist when it was time to go to the next thing." Stamps was impressed with the way Red handled himself the entire weekend with all the people he would meet.[4] He added,

> Red was really surprised by the response of the young people . . . young people can be really blasé—"Who's this old guy?" But there seemed to me there was

this genuine warmth and excitement that this was a famous person from their hometown. . . . I really thought there was a lot of love and emotion in the air, really heartwarming from both sides. Red felt it and responded to it, and the kids felt it too.

Stamps continued,

Red was not there to say how great I am. His message was work hard, be true to yourself, that sort of thing, it wasn't about him, it was about how to live. He was a super hero back in the days when there weren't many, and he wore that manta, humble, and tried to make an impact with no ego that I could sense. . . . He was a great storyteller. He had everybody in stitches over everything that had happened to him. A storyteller has a way of taking facts and putting them together in an entertaining way, and he could do that.

Stamps concluded, "We saw him off camera. He was the same the whole time I was with him. He was the same Red Grange on camera that you saw when the lights go off and the cameras were put away."[5]

THURSDAY, OCTOBER 26

Red started his first full day in Wheaton at 9:00 a.m. by greeting Wheaton College president Hudson Armerding. Then it was off to Longfellow School, his old grade school, where he gave a short speech in the gym to the students. Some students in the back held up signs that read, "Welcome Back to Grange's Range." Shortly after leaving his old school, Red paid a short visit to city hall with Wheaton mayor Ralph Barger. It was here that Red had his "official welcome." On the front steps of city hall, Red was greeted by several hundred citizens, town dignitaries, students, and cheerleading squads from Wheaton North, Wheaton Central, and Franklin Junior high schools, who performed a routine that featured "Hi, Red" yells and a pyramid.

A huge sign, "Wheaton Welcomes Red Grange," hung high on city hall. Red gave a short speech and waved to the rather large crowd that had come out to greet him. "It used to be someone would say, 'I remember seeing you play football.' Then it was, 'My father remembers you,' and then, 'My grandfather remembers you.' Now as I get into my 70s it's, 'My great grandfather remembers you,'" said Red with a chuckle. "A lot of doors have opened for me because of football," he told the gathering of young students. "But it takes a lot of hard work. I really think you are as good as you think you are or want to be."[6]

After the "official welcome" the large crowd walked two blocks to Memorial Park for a special ceremony. In tribute to Red, a red maple tree had recently been planted by the Wheaton Park District, which operated Memorial Park. Red was given the honor of shoveling dirt onto the base of the tree. "When you walk by this tree and say, 'Hi!' you are saying hi to me," said Red to the crowd.[7] The tree is identified by a large brick dug into the ground, about four feet in front of the tree, with a short description that reads, "RED GRANGE TREE October 26, 1978." More than 40 years later, the tree still stands in Memorial Park, standing approximately four stories tall.[8]

At the end of each day, Red, Wilson, and Stamps would return to Wilson's home to wind down. The three would relax and talk for the duration of the evening. "It was neat to me. We would go back after these very long days. Red was in his early 70s then. We would go back to Wilson's (home), and we would sit in his rec room and watch the evening news," said Stamps. "And there on television Red would be at the school speaking or doing an interview, and he would just sit there and he would relax, just taking it in. That's what he wanted, just being at the events."[9]

Despite the busy schedule, Red thoroughly enjoyed his visit to Wheaton. It had been 30 years since he had been back, and he was soaking up the experience, regardless of what was thrown his way. "He was never mobbed, and it never got uncomfortable for him. He always appeared to be comfortable with everything that weekend," Stamps added.[10]

FRIDAY, OCTOBER 27

The following day featured another full schedule of events. On this day Red and his hosts were joined by a film crew to document the rest of the weekend. NBC Sports sent producer Les Dennis and broadcaster Donna de Varona, a former Olympic gold medalist in swimming, to Wheaton to cover the events and interview Red for a five-minute piece that would air on the network's *NFL Today* pregame show that Sunday.

At 10:15 a.m., Red spoke to the student body at Wheaton College during their chapel service at Edman Chapel. His speech lasted 20 minutes, during which time he told stories about living in Wheaton, his coaches at Wheaton, and taking his makeup class on campus at Wheaton College. After finishing, the students gave him a big round of applause.[11]

After a short lunch, Grange attended pep rallies and spoke at Wheaton-Warrenville High School (1:15 p.m.) and Wheaton Central High School (2:00

p.m.). "Never think that because you come from a small town you can't go on to great things," Red said to the high school students. "Just set your objective and go to work."[12]

The day ended with Red attending the Central versus Wheaton-Warrenville football game, where the field was rededicated in his honor as Red Grange Field. On a cool but clear Friday night, Red was greeted by a capacity crowd. After the Wheaton Central band played their pregame routine, Red was escorted by David Stamps onto the field to greet the game's referee, Bob Hern, who gave Red the coin to toss and presented the captains from both teams. "Mr. Red Grange will you flip the coin please," yelled Hern. Unlike the Super Bowl, this time Red tossed the coin into the air. It was tails. Wheaton-Warrenville had won the toss and elected to receive. "Good luck to you fellas," said Red to the two teams. After the coin toss, the band started playing the theme song to the popular television series *Chips*.[13]

Red then said a few words of encouragement to the crowd, but a loud cheer from the stands interrupted his speech. The cheerleaders began to chant again as the PA announcer said, "Thank you Red Grange for coming." Stamps escorted Red down the track. Because of the long day, with another one on tap for Saturday, Red left the game shortly after it started. Wheaton-Warrenville won the game, 25–18.[14]

SATURDAY, OCTOBER 28

The big day had arrived—the dedication of the DuPage County Heritage Gallery and the special "An Evening with Red Grange" event. Red started the day by meeting an old friend. George Halas was going to attend the dedication of the gallery, but he also wanted to spend time with his good friend—helping him with a project. Halas had agreed to write his autobiography, to be published by McGraw-Hill. Papa Bear hired husband-and-wife team Gwen Morgan and Arthur Veysey—former foreign correspondents with the *Chicago Tribune*—to help him. Red, D. Ray Wilson, Richard Crabb, and David Stamps met Halas and his writers at the Cantigny Mansion at Cantigny Park, sitting in the former study of Robert McCormick. The two old friends talked about the old days of professional football, how Red signed to play for the Bears, and the famous barnstorming tour that followed. David Stamps rememberd this once-in-a-lifetime meeting:

The most fascinating thing that happened though was with George Halas's people. . . . George is having his autobiography written, and he would love an opportunity to sit down with Red when he's here. . . . Red was all for that. So that was great. And this was one of the highlights of my life.

Colonel Robert McCormick lived at an estate called Cantigny (named after a French town); it was a big old mansion. The museum was curated by a husband-and-wife team, Gwen and Arthur Veysey. They were the London correspondents for the *Chicago Tribune* during their active days but were now retired. Those were the two people he hired to help him write his autobiography, *Halas by Halas.* So as things evolved, we had Ray Wilson, Richard Crabb, and myself, we were allowed to come with Red and sit in McCormick's study (which is not open to the public), all of us with the Veyseys. George Halas and Red Grange sat down on a couch and just had a gab fest of the early days of pro football, as we just sat in the corner like mice and listened to this.[15]

After a short break, Red again met up with Halas to attend the dedication of the DuPage County Heritage Gallery.

It was inside the DuPage Historical Museum at 4:30 p.m. that the dedication ceremony was to take place. Red and Halas arrived together at the museum, escorted by Wilson and Stamps. The two football legends went inside, heading upstairs to the second level, to the gallery room, where the Red Grange display was housed.

More than 125 people filled the room. At the podium a smiling Red greeted the appreciative audience of friends, former classmates, and ice customers. He related, "I'm really not that important. I am in a couple of Halls of Fame, but none hits me the way this one does. It's been great spending the last three days in my hometown, seeing old friends and making new ones. I love you all."[16]

After Red, Ray Wilson introduced the next speaker, George Halas.

Halas spoke to the crowd.

Fifty-three years ago, Red captured the hearts of the American people and stirred their imagination more than any other pro athlete. His name was magic then, and it is magic now. Probably it isn't proper for one man to love another man. But I certainly love Red in more ways than one. To me, Red is the eternal flame of professional football. Thank you very much.[17]

After 50 years of being Red's boss, coach, father-figure, advisor, and friend, the 83-year-old Halas, one of the founding fathers of the NFL, expressed his true feelings for the man who had help make his Chicago Bears one of the premiere franchises in professional sports. Halas loved Red. And Red loved Halas.

Then the ceremony was over.

The group headed to the South Party Room dining hall at Wheaton College for a special meal at 5:30 p.m. After a short welcome by William Carlson of All-American Seventy-Seven, Halas and Red made short remarks about the weekend. Dinner was served as both Halas and Red sat at the head table. After eating, Halas said good-bye to his friend to head back to Chicago. The Bears were slated to play the Detroit Lions the next day at Soldier Field.

The big event of the weekend was the "An Evening with Red Grange" program at Edman Chapel on the campus of Wheaton College. Admission was free, as 1,500 Wheaton citizens showed up to get a glimpse of their famous son. Former Channel 7 executive Red Quinlan served as master of ceremonies. Quinlan lead off the program by saying, "Usually you can't go home again, but there's always an exception to every rule. Indeed a hometown boy can go home again." "It's been great coming back here for these three days. I just wish I could come back and play for you again," said Red to the large crowd.[18]

Red talked to the enthusiastic crowd about his career—Wheaton, Illinois, Zuppke, the Bears, barnstorming, Nagurski, and so forth. Not one subject was left out. The crowd enjoyed every minute of it. The night was a success. The following day, Red said good-bye to his hosts, his friends, and the city of Wheaton. It was a trip he would never forget. After he returned to Florida, he sent D. Ray Wilson a letter of appreciation.

Dear Ray:

No one in my position has ever received such a homecoming, I am sure. I loved every minute of it.

The NBC report wasn't shown in our area, and I am sorry about that because for one who was not there, it is impossible to explain what happened and how great it was. I even have trouble telling Muggs what took place. I am grateful for the copy of the papers you sent so she could get a better impression of what happened.

May I say again, quite apart from the attention given to me, what a remarkable program you have beginning for DuPage County at the historical museum. If there is any way that I can help with the honoring of the others, I should like to know of it.

I know that these things don't just happen. There had been done a lot of hard work over a very long period of time by William Carlson and all the Seventy-Seven people. The folks at Wheaton College were so gracious . . . as were the people at the other schools, Mayor Barger, the park district, Chicago Golf Club, and so many others.

No one needs to tell me about your role, Ray. It was you, along with Dave Stamps, who spent much of the night when we were in Champaign in the fall of 1974 convincing me that there were people in Wheaton who would remember me, not to mention your visits and else since.

I just want to thank everyone who worked to make it possible for me to have this opportunity to be with so many wonderful people and especially the youngsters. They made me younger.

Wish there was some way that I could thank each of you individually. When you can, stop in and see Muggs and me and give me an opportunity to do just that.

Harold "Red" Grange[19]

Wilson published the heartfelt letter in the *Wheaton Daily Journal* in the "Letters to the Editor" section. After hearing from Red how well the visit to Wheaton had gone, Margaret was moved to write Wilson a letter.

Dear Ray:

First of all, and belatedly, thank you so much for the beautiful roses. My luncheon guests were most impressed! It was so thoughtful of you, especially since I know how busy you were. Red returned home, tired but happy. He really was overwhelmed by the reception he received in Wheaton.

Now a few personal comments: As a nozy [sic] wife, I asked him what your wife was like. He said, "She was so nice—you would like her very much!" And he thought your daughters were lovely. I add my thanks to his for your warm hospitality.

From what he has told me, among his most pleasant memories are the "chats" he had with you. When did you find time! He likes the way you think. In fact, I think he is your greatest fan.

Ray, I realize the time and effort you put in to make the "gallery opening" the success it was—but may I add one thing—you really recharged Red's battery! And I love you for it.

I do hope I will be able to meet your "All-American Family'" someday.
In the meantime—God bless.
Sincerely,
"Muggs"[20]

On June 13, 1980, Red celebrated a milestone birthday. He turned 77 years old—matching his famous jersey number. "I planned to stay home and have a bottle of champagne with my wife," said Red to the *Associated Press*. "But all I've been doing is answering the telephone—and trying to smile," he said laughing. "I've finally arrived at my football number. And I don't know whether that's good or bad. I do know it means. I'm one year older. I've had a good life and an enjoyable one. I can't think of anything I would do differently."[21]

The following year wasn't so happy for Red. At 1:00 a.m. on May 28, 1981, Garland Grange passed away of a sudden heart attack at his home in Miami. He

Dear Mildred:
We are so sorry to send you this sad news. Gardy passed away very suddenly this morning (May 27), apparently a heart attack.
Virginia asked if we would let you know. She is still pretty much in shock. (I'm sure you understand what she is going through.)
In accordance with Gardy's wishes, his remains are being cremated.
Virginia's niece (who is more like a daughter to her) lives only a few miles away. She and her husband are planning to stay with Va. until she gets squared away.
We had talked on the phone to both Virginia and Gardy about three weeks ago. At that time they were both feeling fine. We understand now that Gardy had been ill the past two weeks but was improving. Wish we could give you more details, but this is all we know. It was really a shock to all of us. Virginia said that later on she will take his "urn" up to Illinois for interment (where her family is buried).
We feel so sad, but we are happy that he didn't have to suffer.
I'd write more later. All is okay with us.
Love,
Margaret & Red"[22]

was 74 years old. He left behind his wife Virginia. The couple had never had children. Red was stunned by the news. He was too distraught to tell his sister. Margaret wrote a letter.

It was now only Mildred and Red left.

36

MEETING THE FIGHTING ILLINI

After losing his brother, Red started to withdraw from the public eye. He traveled less, making just two exceptions. On February 6, 1982, Grange attended the Walter Camp Foundation annual dinner in New Haven, Connecticut. His fellow award winners that night were former Cleveland Browns Hall of Fame quarterback Otto Graham (Camp Man of the Year), University of Pittsburgh head coach Jackie Sherrill (College Football Coach of the Year), and University of Southern California running back Marcus Allen (College Football Player of the Year).

Red was honored with the Walter Camp Distinguished American Award, given to an individual who has used his or her talents to attain great success in business, private life, or public service and who may have accomplished that which no other has done.

Red visited the campus where football started and walked the grounds where the great Walter Camp developed the sport he loved so much. To accept an award named after the "Father of American Football" was worth the 1,200-mile trip. "This is one of the most important awards I've ever received because I had a chance to meet Walter Camp in 1924," said Red to Mark Lewis, sports editor of the *New Haven Register*. "In those days, Camp was the number-one name in football. If you weren't on the Camp team, it didn't mean anything."[1] The award was one of the proudest moments of Red's life. Shortly after he returned to Florida, Grange received a letter from his old coach.

Dear "Red":

This will be a bit hurried because tomorrow is our annual meeting, and I have a mound of papers to go through.

I did so want to be with you and Muggs at Yale this past weekend but just couldn't make it. I know it was a wonderful weekend—they have a way of doing everything just right. Great people and so very hospitable. It's an evening you will long remember.

Please send me a bill for yours and Muggs' expenses for the weekend. You know, I told you I would pay your expenses.

I was not at all pleased with the way our 1980 season ended, and I was *very* unhappy with our 6–10 record for 1981. I said I was going to do something about it, and I've been keeping my word. I will continue to do something about it until the Chicago Bears have regained their respectability and their rightful place in professional football. Hope you are pleased with my appointing Mike Ditka as head coach.

Sending you a clipping from the *New York Times*, dated January 19, 1982, which I received. Thought you and Muggs would enjoy it.

Warmest regards, and give my love to Muggs.

Sincerely yours,

George (signed)

Geo. S. Halas[2]

Halas was always looking after his former player, agreeing to pay his travel expenses to Yale. The two men, historically linked together in NFL history, were the best of friends, a friendship spanning almost 60 years. Red made one last trip out of Florida, and of course it was a favor to Halas. He returned to the Chicago area in April 1982, to accept the George Halas Sportsmanship Award, presented by the Marine Corp. This would be the last time he would see his good friend.

On October 31, 1983, George Stanley Halas passed away at the age of 88. The man who had been present at the birth of the National Football League in 1920, and helped guide the league through its first six decades was gone. For Red, he had lost his best friend in football. Halas's death hit Red even harder than he thought it would. He couldn't talk. "He is very distraught—he really doesn't want to talk to anybody for a while," said Margaret on the phone to Will Grimsley of the *Associated Press*. "The phone has been ringing constantly. Later on, I'm sure, he will feel up to it. But not now. It was a great shock to him. And he is taking it badly."[3]

Forty-eight hours later, Red was able to talk to Grimsley on the phone. "I admired George tremendously. He would sell tickets and then go to the locker room to tape the players' ankles," said Red. "After the game, he personally would go around to the Chicago papers to get a little story on the sports pages. He was always very detailed. He worked on little things that most coaches presume the players knew."[4]

Red continued,

> I'd go to see him every spring to renegotiate my contract. He'd say, "How much do you want?" I'd write a figure on a piece of paper. He would look at it, hand it over to his secretary, and say, "Draw up a contract." I never thought I took advantage of him. If I needed $100 million—and he had it—I think he'd lend it to me. . . . Without men like George Halas, we probably would never have had pro football.[5]

Red was 80 years old at the time of Halas's passing. He still gave interviews to those who called or stopped by the house on North Amaryllis Drive. Newspapers, magazines, and radio and television shows still requested that Red tell his story or give them a banquet quote. The Galloping Ghost always said yes. Throughout the years full-scale articles appeared nationally in such periodicals as *Sports Illustrated, American Heritage,* and *Pro! Official Magazine of the National Football League,* as well as chapters in books like *The Game That Was* (1970), by Myron Cope, and *What a Game They Played* (1984), by Richard Whittingham. Even though Red had been retired for more than 50 years, he was never out of the spotlight. For every generation of football fans, his name would always be brought up as the man who "made the NFL."

When Super Bowl XVIII came to Tampa, Red was invited but did not attend. Two years later, Red watched the Bears, led by head coach Mike Ditka, who was hired by Halas, finally win the Super Bowl. Red couldn't help but think of his old coach as the Bears performed the "Super Bowl Shuffle" all the way to the world title.[6]

Aside from still being a media darling, Red helped out his former NFL brothers. He was outspoken about the NFL's pension plan, which didn't include former players who played before 1959. Although he didn't need the money, he supported the need for the additional pension for former players who were the pioneers of the league. "It bothered me that so many players who made the game what it is have been forgotten," said Red to the press in 1985. "They played for little or no money in those days, but without them there wouldn't be a league today."[7]

In November 1985, the NFL alumni awarded pension checks to more than 700 former NFL players who played before 1959. Red was awarded a check for $500, joining such NFL greats as Sammy Baugh, Red Badgro, Don Hutson, Sid Luckman, Marion Motley, and Bronko Nagurski in benefiting from the new NFL policy.

On September 29, 1986, Red suffered his last family heartbreak. His sister, Mildred (Grange) Eston, passed away in New York at the age of 88. She would be buried at Vestal Hills (New York) Memorial Park next to her husband. Red would be the last of Lyle Grange's children to survive.

Now in his early 80s, Red was starting to have some pesky health issues, suffering from back pain and arthritis. Margaret looked after him the best she could. Her nurse instincts always shined through in helping her husband adapt to his failing body. "My husband is in good health for his age," said Margaret to the *Chicago Tribune* during a 1988 telephone interview. "Most all of the letter-writers tell him what an inspiration he has been because of his modesty and gentlemanly behavior." Red did continue mowing the grass and taking walks with the dog—this time Frito, a sausage-shaped chihuahua.[8]

He still watched games on Saturdays (college football) and Sundays (NFL), and an occasional Monday night game, although staying up late wasn't usually on the agenda. "I love football. I like to watch football, whatever it is," said Red to the *Associated Press* in 1987. "I like to watch the pro game on television. I like the game just the way it is today."[9]

Even when Red was asked about his accomplishments, he never took the credit. "Anybody could have done what I did if they had the opportunity. It was really nothing. Everything I did was blown out of proportion," he once said to the *Orlando Sentinel*. "The blockers did all the work."[10]

Red also kept tabs on his Fighting Illini, who were about to make a house visit to the Grange home in Indian Lake. In 1989, the Illinois football team had gone 9-2 under second-year head coach John Mackovic, including an impressive 7-1 mark in the Big Ten. "Everybody knew Red Grange if you were a football fan at all," said John Mackovic, former Illinois head coach. "Although today, take a walk on a college campus, ask the football team, ask 50 of them tell me what you know about Red Grange, 48 or 49 would have no idea. But everywhere we went Red Grange was a hero, a legend."[11]

That season their only loss in the Big Ten was to rival Michigan (8-0), which cost them a shot at winning the conference title and a berth in the Rose Bowl. But they did earn a berth in the Citrus Bowl in Orlando to play against the

University of Virginia on January 1. With the Illinois football team so close to Indian Lake, just a little more than 60 miles, the Citrus Bowl made a formal invitation to Red to be an honorary guest of the game. Because of his health Red didn't think he was up for traveling, so he declined.

But in Champaign, Illinois, the sports information director, Mike Pearson, got a better idea. Knowing it might be a long shot, he asked Margaret if he and head coach John Mackovic could visit the Galloping Ghost. "During that time I was a sports geek, got to know the history of the university, and knew about the impact that Red Grange had made on the school and the nation for that matter," said Pearson. "When I found out Orlando was our bowl game destination I talked to coach about arranging a visit with the Granges at Indian Lake Estates." Pearson got the go-ahead from Margaret to make a visit.[12]

"I was very interested to meet him. I've met some big names before, been in the NFL, players and coaches, had the opportunity to know a lot of famous people in football, both pros and college ranks. But there weren't many people like Red Grange," said Mackovic. "I told the team, 'You'll never believe where I'm going tomorrow morning. I'm going to go and meet with Red Grange.' Of course everybody on that team knew who Red Grange was. Mainly, I was just there as their ambassador. I was going for the team."[13]

Three days before their bowl game—on December 29—Pearson and Mackovic took a chauffeur-driven limousine ride from Orlando to Indian Lake. Arriving at 12 North Amaryllis Drive, the two men were met out front by Margaret. "She was so kind. She had coffee, she had rolls, and we sat with them and just started talking," said Mackovic.[14] She led the men inside into the living room, where Red was sitting in his large recliner with a blanket covering him up. Pearson took out a small tape recorder to preserve the meeting. "He (Red) sat in his chair. I don't believe he ever got up," recalled Mike Pearson. "We just gathered around him and started chatting. It was just a casual conversation."[15]

The two Illinois representatives gave Red some gifts, presenting him with a hat, a T-shirt, a jacket, and an autographed football from the team. "You could just see his hands go over the ball," said Mackovic. "It was almost like he was going to tuck it under his arm and go. It really was an amazing moment."[16] Red spoke deliberately, in a raspy voice, as he gave short answers about living at the fraternity house, working on the ice wagon, playing the University of Chicago, and, of course, playing the game against Michigan in 1924. He also opened up more on his old college coach, reflecting,

Zuppke was a genius around a team. I've heard a lot of coaches from the United States give talks, but I never hear them talk to you liked Zuppke did. I don't know how he did it.

He could look at you and say, "Now I want you to do this, and so-and-so is going to block you and you're going to do this." Zuppke was all coach, and I think I learned more football by going to Zuppke's house than I could any place else.[17]

Red and Margaret told their guests they would try and watch the entire game. After about an hour the two men prepared to leave. "We appreciate the opportunity to visit with you," they said in unison. Red responded, "I appreciate the fact you fellows give the time and effort to come over here. I appreciate it, it's nice of you."[18] Before departing, Margaret gave Pearson and Mackovic some gifts of her own. She made some homemade orange marmalade, because of the Citrus Bowl, to give to her special guests. "She was so nice," recalled Mackovic. "She was just the nicest, warmest, generous women."[19]

Some 30 years later, both men looked back and cherished their short time with the Galloping Ghost. "He was so humble," said Mackovic. "I think he took great pride in being an Illinois football player. I really believe he was genuinely pleased to meet us, and we were, of course, overwhelmed in meeting him. But I think he was genuinely pleased that someone from Illinois took the time to meet him."[20]

"He amazed me with his modesty," said Pearson. "He was always so modest of himself and always giving credit to his teammates, never wanted to step in the spotlight. John and I knew we were in the presence of greatness, a legend." On New Year's Day, the Fighting Illini channeled their best Galloping Ghost energy, defeating 16th ranked Virginia, 31–21, and putting Red's old school back on the college football map.[21]

In June 1990, Red was admitted to Lake Wales Hospital for a checkup. While there he was diagnosed with Parkinson's disease. Margaret had him admitted to the 24-hour extended care section of the facility. She would visit him every day. Talking to Richard Crabb of the *Wheaton Daily Journal*, Margaret noted that Red was eating "like a truck driver." She further commented, "We have a lot for which to be thankful."[22] Red received physical therapy to help with his mobility and speech. "He won't be going dancing, but he's going to outlive all of us," said Margaret to the press.[23] Despite some of his physical limitations, Red always enjoyed meeting with the nurses and visitors. Margaret told Crabb, "He looks forward to them (visitors) if he knows in advance when they are coming."[24]

In 1990, the Fighting Illini continued their winning ways, going 8–4 overall and 6–2 in the Big Ten, once again just missing out on winning the conference title. They were rewarded with another January 1 bowl game—this time the Hall of Fame Bowl in Tampa against the Clemson Tigers.

During that season, running back Howard Griffith did something that not even Red Grange had done. In a game against Southern Illinois, the senior from Chicago scored a NCAA-record eight touchdowns in a 56–21 victory, which also broke Red's single-game scoring record, set against Michigan in 1924. Once again, being so close to Red in Florida, Mike Pearson got the idea of visiting the Granges.

"At the end of the season here we are going back down to Florida for the bowl game in Tampa, not that far away. So, I took the idea to take Howard and introduce him to Red Grange. Howard was totally excited about it," recalled Pearson.

> We called Mrs. Grange, but she was hesitant. Red was in the hospital at this point. She politely declined this visit. She really didn't want anybody to see Red in this condition. Of course we understood, no problem. We thought it would be a great opportunity to connect two guys, especially for Howard, to meet this legend that everybody talked about that year as he was breaking all of his records.[25]

After thinking about the meeting, Margaret decided that it would do Red some good to meet someone from his alma mater, so dear to his heart. Said Pearson, "About two days before we left for Florida, I get another call by Mrs. Grange, and she says, 'I changed my mind. I think it would be good for you to visit. I've asked Red about this and he said sure I would like to meet him.'"[26]

On December 31, the day before the game, Mike Pearson and Howard Griffith drove to Lake Wales Hospital to visit Red. Margaret met the men outside the building. She gave Griffith some homemade caramel corn and an Illinois doll that she had made. She told Griffith that she and Red were proud of him and his accomplishments. She also mentioned that she had been reading Red the recent press clippings about him and the team. It was time to meet the Galloping Ghost.

"We finally arrive at the hospital. At this point he's in intensive care, he's not very good, basically just lying there in his bed," Pearson remembered.

> We walk in, and we don't know if this is going to turn out well. So I went up to Red and said softly, "Mr. Grange this is Howard Griffith, this is the man who's been breaking all of your records." And it felt like 15 minutes of silence but was probably more like 15 seconds, but there was no response, but finally, in a very

soft voice he said, "Oh, I know who Howard is . . ." and Howard's smile just lit up the room. They shook hands. Talked in a very basic way for a few minutes. We didn't stay very long because it wasn't the circumstance to stay long. The primary reason was just to get these two men of history to meet each other.[27]

The three men and Margaret spent roughly 15 minutes together. "He had very little strength at that junction and we didn't want to impose that much, and our mission was accomplished, getting the two of them together, and we were on our way very quickly," recalled Pearson.[28] "You may meet a great person in your life. But to meet a gentleman who knows you are coming and who is as overjoyed to meet you as you are to meet him, that's tough to describe," Griffith stated to the press.[29]

Pearson and Griffith then left Red's room. "We rode back in the car for about an hour back to Tampa, and he couldn't stop talking about it," said Pearson. "He now understood, meeting the legend, he would tell you one of the thrills of his life was to meet Red Grange and to talk to him. . . . So, even though it was in somewhat difficult circumstances, it was a trip that was well deserved for Howard."[30]

For Red, it was a small moment that kept his spirits up for a little while longer. It would be the last visitors Red would have from the football world. "That's a very good chance we were the last ones, so we felt privileged that we put that together," Pearson concluded.[31]

Soon the football world would say good-bye to the Galloping Ghost.

37

GOODBYE TO THE GALLOPING GHOST

After the Illinois bowl game, Red's health started to deteriorate. During this time, Margaret spent days and nights next to her husband. Throughout his retirement and even while he was in the hospital, fans from throughout the country still wrote to the famous football star. Handwritten and typed letters wishing him good health or asking for an autograph still flowed in. In late 1990, the great sports broadcaster Red Barber, speaking on his NPR radio show, talked briefly about Red and his health. After hearing Barber's request to send well-wishes, the Lake Wales Hospital was swamped by letters and handwritten notes of encouragement. "I think if a few cards came in it would make the red-head very happy that he's not forgotten," said Barber on air.[1]

In less than three weeks, almost 500 cards and letters came in. Margaret started to keep tabs on how many states she had received letters from. Margaret wrote Barber, updating him that she had received letters from 49 of 50 states. "Mrs. Grange wrote me a very gracious letter," commented Barber a month later on NPR. "She asked me if I would thank the hundreds of people around the country, all the states in the Union, who sent get-well, good luck, remembering cards to Red Grange, all the states but Maine." As soon as Barber made that announcement, one quickly came in from the Pine Tree State. Red had not been forgotten.[2]

The 1990 NFL season ended with a clash between the Buffalo Bills and the New York Giants in Super Bowl XXV. The game was played at Tampa Stadium in Tampa, just 70 miles from Lake Wales Hospital, where Red was resting. In a close game that wasn't decided until Bills kicker Scott Norwood missed a 47-yard field goal "wide right," the Giants pulled out a 20–19 victory. The

ABC broadcast that night registered a rating of 41.8, with more than 79 million viewers watching one of the NFL's most memorable Super Bowls.

At 3:00 a.m. on January 28, 1991, just hours after the Giants defeated the Bills, Red Grange passed away from complications of pneumonia at Lake Wales Hospital. He was 87 years old. The Galloping Ghost was gone. Margaret was by his side the entire night.

Shortly after Red's passing, she spoke briefly to Tom McEwen of the *Tampa Tribune*, saying, "He left us peacefully and in no pain. He left us after a full life." Red's wishes were that his body be cremated. "We ask that any tribute be given to a church or charity of choice. That was Red's wish," said Margaret to McEwen. The Marion Nelson Funeral Home of Lake Wales handled the cremation.[3]

"I was sad because I loved him very much," said Dorothy Flora, niece of Margaret and Red Grange. "Although I knew it was coming it was a shock. I wanted to go to the funeral, but it was very small. He was private, that was Red."[4]

Margaret held a small, private ceremony for Red, with only her sister, Beverly, her husband, Bucky DeBaker, and Monsignor Walter Grill in attendance. Grill, a retired pastor who achieved the title reverend monsignor, was a volunteer assistant at Holy Spirit Catholic Church in Lake Wales, helping with visitations, baptisms, funerals, and religious education at the church. Despite Red being brought up Methodist, he and Grill became friends and conversationalists during their time together.

During the ceremony, Grill said about Red,

> I loved sports and saw Red when he was running wild. We had some times when he was in the hospital. He was not just a great athlete but a great and humble man. While death does disrupt the family, one thing it does not do is make the grave a final resting place, for were that so there would be no comfort, no consolation for anyone, but in our hearts, there is the feeling will see them again, for as St. Paul told us, our dead will rise again because our Christ did and as he rose, so shall we.

Grill ended the service by saying, "When time was running out for Red, he was handed the ball to carry for one last time and was told to head for the goal line of eternity, and I am sure he made it, and when he crossed it, his spiritual coach, Christ, had dusted off a chair for him in His Hall of Fame."[5]

When it came out that Red had passed away, newspapers throughout the country reported the news that the Galloping Ghost had died. Next to the articles recapping the New York Giants' big Super Bowl victory were tributes to the player who had "made the NFL." Sportswriters and columnists wrote about Red's achievements and impact on the game of football. Several noted that Red was the last of the athletes of the Roaring Twenties to pass away—Babe Ruth (1948), Bill Tilden (1953), Bobby Jones (1971), and Jack Dempsey (1983) were all gone. "Red Grange was one of the NFL's first superstars who gave pro football credibility and recognition. He will be remembered not only for his on-the-field skills, but for his ability to attract capacity crowds for a league in its infancy," said NFL commissioner Paul Tagliabue.[6]

But it was in the cities where Red was most known that people mourned his loss the hardest. "It's very sad to hear. He brought a lot of honor to the city," said Wheaton mayor Gwen Henry.[7] "He was a very humble guy, he never admitted he was a hero," said Wheaton newspaper publisher D. Ray Wilson after hearing the news.[8]

Illinois football head coach John Mackovic spoke at a press conference on campus, saying the following:

> Grange and his wife (Margaret) were extremely gracious in permitting the visit. I tried to make the point that even though he was no longer able to get back to the campus, we never forgot him. He is a living legend.
>
> It's hard to put into words what he means to the university and to all of football. As long as the game of football is played, he will be a legend. He and George Halas (Chicago Bears founder) were such pioneers. There are no easy comparisons. . . . Grange made football into something special and started people believing that pro football could be a worthy endeavor. His name gave our university something that no other individual was able to give it, and he was a lot more than just the favorite son of Illinois.[9]

In Chicago, the city with broad shoulders slumped a little after Red was gone. George Connor, one of his former broadcasting partners, said, "The surprising thing about him was that for all the publicity he retained his simplicity. On airplanes, he traveled coach. He was never too busy to sign an autograph. . . . He was the most down-to-earth person and the greatest friend I ever met in my life." The *Chicago Tribune* ran a small photo of Red in his Illinois football uniform on the front page with several articles in the sports section.[10]

In their own ways, Forksville, Wheaton, Champaign, Chicago, Miami, and Indian Lake Estates, the places where Red had called home, said their final good-byes.

"He was a very humble person," said Margaret to the *Chicago Tribune*. "He didn't have a big head. Truthfully, he was one of the most moral men I've ever met in my life. Right was right and wrong was wrong."[11]

Margaret tried to say good-bye. She would eventually give Red his final resting place.

38

THE LEGACY OF RED GRANGE

After 49 years of marriage Margaret was alone. She handled herself with grace and dignity following the passing of Red. Her friends and sister Beverly, who moved to Florida when Red was sick, kept her company during this difficult time. Although Red was gone, his legacy lived on.

The city of Wheaton quickly readopted its most famous native son. Wheaton Central High School sent a bouquet of flowers to Margaret. She responded with a short note and a small color photo of the flower arrangement: "I thank all of you so much for the beautiful basket of flowers. Enclosed is a picture I took of them in front of the painting of 'Red' by coach (Bob) Zuppke. The statuette on the left is from the University of Illinois All-Century Team. Thank you again, Mrs. Grange."[1]

One of the keepers of Red's legacy in Wheaton was Chuck Baker, principal at Wheaton Central High School. Baker had been working in the Wheaton school district since 1972, and had a great sense of what Red had meant to the young students of Wheaton. "My first connection was the kids I taught at middle school, and that went over to Central, as many of the students played football on Friday nights," said Baker. "When I became principal at Wheaton Central one of the things I thought we needed to do was reach back into our history. Red Grange was an obvious choice."[2]

At about the same time Baker was thinking that the students needed a hero, the school hired a head football coach who also wanted to bring Red Grange back to life. John Thorne was a three-sport star at Milford (Illinois) Township High School, excelling in football. He continued his gridiron career as a running back at Illinois Wesleyan University, making All-Conference one year.

After graduating from college Thorne got into coaching, arriving at Wheaton Central as an assistant coach under Andy Hauptman. Thorne was in Wheaton in 1978 when Red had his homecoming weekend. "It was so awesome to be in his presence and shake his hand and have a little bit of conversation and so forth. He was a wonderful guy," Thorne related.[3]

In 1980, Thorne replaced Hauptman as head coach. Thorne brought new energy and focus to the football team, but it didn't translate into winning success, as he compiled a record of just 38–34 in his first eight seasons at the helm. "In those early years we didn't match up well," recalled Thorne in a 2015 interview. "We were small and couldn't block people very well. We just couldn't quite get enough players out for football. I always felt that you need a lot of players to really make a program work. It took us a long while."[4]

Soon Thorne and his coaching staff started to build a winning program. The roster would eventually hit 80 players, most of them dedicated year-round to being the best football players and students they could be. This success came about because coach Thorne saw the need for his players to follow a philosophy every Wheaton kid could relate to. He agreed that his players needed to know who Red Grange was.

"We have a lot of good athletes, but the program wasn't winning," said Thorne.

> So, we decided that when I took the job we would have a philosophy statement, a role model that the players could look up to, proven over time, a man of honesty and integrity. So, we wrote the Red Grange Philosophy. We showed videos of Red Grange playing, told Red Grange stories, we took a lot of time trying to mentor the players, help them be a good person, and that turns into them being a good teammate, which in turn makes good team success. We did well, won state titles, won a lot of games, showed good sportsmanship, so it was a wonderful experience, and we thought that Red Grange was a big part of it.[5]

The school soon adopted the nickname the "Red Grange Tigers," and Thorne implemented the Red Grange Philosophy. Throughout the years it has morphed into a list of commandments adopted by coaches and players as their personal mantra to live by while being a member of the football team. The 16 commandments include the following areas: academics, confidence, diversity, faith, adversity, character, respect, goals, work ethic, safety, class, technique, training, humility, family, and champions.

Thorne explained the keys to the Red Grange Philosophy:

Well, we always felt unselfishness, no prejudice in your life, how to be humble, how to be a teammate, and how to play with class. Words like honor, dignity, integrity really mean something. So, we spent time every week talking about those things. So, that became what was fun and exciting, and when we were watching practice, we always had the defense at one end against the scout team, and I had the offense at the other end and had the scout team working against us. But I looked up and saw how hard our defensive guys were hitting the scout team players, and all of sudden we started talking about it, what keeps those kids coming back every day. So, we instigated a thing every time you knocked a scout team player down, you had to pick him back up or pat him on the back and say, "Good job that's exactly what we need to see." So pretty soon everything in the program kept getting better and better because everybody realized how important each and every player was. Well the next thing you know even when we would play a game, when they knocked somebody down at the end of the game, or at the end of play, they would pick them back up, so now teams that we played against they enjoyed playing against us, even if we won or not because it was a game that showed sportsmanship. So, I think those were things that Red Grange showed in his career.

During the 1991 season, Wheaton Central High School, coached by Thorne, dedicated its season to Red. "Teaching and coaching in Wheaton always brought with it a sense of pride because it was where Red Grange made his reputation," Thorne reflected in a 2015 interview. "He was a hero to people in all areas of life, including how he handled himself off the field, as well as on. He never tarnished his image. That's difficult in the public eye like he was." That season Thorne and his staff ingrained who Red Grange was as a person into the minds of their players. "The kids ate it up. The more we told them about Red Grange, the more they wanted to be like him," said Thorne. That season the Tigers went on a run to the Class 5A state championship game against Chicago's Mt. Carmel. The magical season ended in heartbreak with a tough 21–14 loss.[6]

In 1992, Wheaton Central High School became a middle school, leaving Wheaton Warrenville-South the only high school in town. The football field was rededicated the Red Grange Field. That fall, the Red Grange Tigers put it all together, winning the state championship by defeating Joliet Catholic Academy in double overtime, 40–34. "I know Red Grange was smiling down at us in that moment," said Chuck Baker in the winning locker room.[7]

The school's biggest fan was Margaret Grange—even if she was 1,200 miles away in Florida. Each year Red's widow would write several letters to Baker to ask about "her boys" and wish them good luck for the season. "I would get these very short letters, each handwritten, and it was always, 'Dear Mr. Baker,

the season has started, I've heard good things, I'm wishing the team well,'"
recalled Chuck.

> I would give those letters to John, and John would read them to the team. He
> knew that we're playing under this moniker the Red Grange Tigers, and there
> really is a Mrs. Grange out there. In 1991, the conclusion of the season was a
> heartbreaker against Illinois powerhouse Mt. Carmel, and we had them on the
> rope. Tough loss for us, and she wrote to us about the quality of the season and
> Red would've been proud of them. So, she would generally write at the beginning
> of each season and generally at the end of each season.[8]

In November 1993, Margaret sent Principal Baker a big gift box. It contained
a note that read as follows:

> Dear Mr. Baker
> Here are the 30 frames I promised (plus six more for you as a bonus).
> Richard Crabb suggested I put magnets on some, so I have put them on
> 12. Hope this meets with your approval.
> So sorry to hear about the last game. I know it must have been a
> disappointment. However, the Tigers have so much to be proud of. I
> wondered how many teams have won 25 consecutive games. This must
> be some kind of record. I am so proud of them.
> The Holidays are almost here. Happy Thanksgiving to all of you.
> Mrs. Grange (Muggs)[9]

Margaret eventually sent the entire team hand-stitched black-and-white
Christmas ornaments that had a small square frame, inside of which was a photo
of Red in his football uniform. Said Baker,

> I wrote to her saying we were doing really well, and when she responded with a
> letter, in came a department store box with some tissue paper in it jammed full of
> little rectangular orange and white picture frames. There was a note she wrote, to
> give these to the football players as a gift from her and Mr. Grange as a reminder
> of their success for the season. I think there were 100 of them. There was one
> picture of him that she attached.

Baker continued,

So I had that picture copied, and we slid that photo into all the frames and coach Thorne presented those to the team that year as a gift directly from Mrs. Grange. Aren't many high school kids in America who received a Christmas ornament from Muggsy Grange. About 100 kids have this hand-stitched plastic ornament with a picture of Red Grange in it. We still have one or two of them on display with the letter she sent.[10]

Today, in Wheaton, every Christmas, you can find former Wheaton High football players and coaches hanging their Red Grange Christmas ornaments—with Red's picture—on their Christmas trees. His legacy and the Red Grange Philosophy continues at Wheaton Warrenville-South High School under coach Ron Muhitch, who was an assistant under Thorne. The school's field is named Red Grange Field, and there is a mural painting inside the school and two full glass displays containing Red's awards and trophies.

In 1974, the Red Grange Award was organized by the All-American Seventy-Seven committee, headed by Wheaton native Howard Gaede. It is given to the most valuable football player in Wheaton, who "best demonstrates a combination of athletic skill, sportsmanship, and scholastic ability." Some of the past winners of the award have been former NFL players Chuck Long, Jim Juriga, Kent Graham, Danny Vitale, and Clayton Thorson. Today the award is sponsored by the *DuPage Daily Herald*.

In 2016, the College of DuPage, located in Glen Ellyn, organized the first annual Red Grange Bowl in honor of Red. Matt Foster, head football coach at the College of DuPage, encouraged the idea of creating an end-of-season bowl game to help preserve the legacy of Wheaton's most famous hero. For the city of Wheaton and DuPage County, the legacy of Red Grange lives on in a strong way.

In 1994, Margaret celebrated her 77th birthday—matching her husband's famous jersey number. Her thoughts continued to drift to her husband's legacy. She mainly thought about what to do with Red's ashes. Since his death the ashes were stored at the Marion Nelson Funeral Home. She now knew what to do.

That fall the University of Illinois would celebrate the 70th anniversary of its big win—as well as Red's monumental five-touchdown performance—against Michigan in 1924. Patrick Hayes, a member of Illinois Alumni Association, came up with the idea of inviting Margaret to the celebration, which would be held the weekend of the Illinois–Michigan game. Moreover, the university would be dedicating a Red Grange Rock at the stadium, using the same rock material that helped build the stadium's columns in 1924.

Margaret was reluctant to leave Florida, but Hayes was relentless. "I have to get dressed up, and we live so casually down here," said Margaret to the *Chicago Tribune*. "Patrick Hayes conned me into it. He wouldn't take 'no' for an answer."[11] "She had never seen the campus or Memorial Stadium," said Hayes. He continued,

> She was reluctant to come, she wasn't seeking a trip, but I sold her on the idea that it didn't seem right that she had never seen our campus or the stadium where Red had his signature moment, and with the timing of the 70th anniversary of the dedication game against Michigan I wasn't going to take no for an answer. I told her I would take care of everything, all she had to do was show up.[12]

As much as Margaret didn't want to leave Florida, she knew she needed to make the trip. Deep down she wanted to make the trip. She was about to take the journey of a lifetime. It would be her first-ever visit to the campus where her husband became a legend. It also would be a trip that would include more than seeing a football game. It would be a trip to find Red's final resting place.

In late October, Margaret arrived in Champaign-Urbana to visit a campus that housed more than 26,000 undergraduate students. She would spend the weekend at the home of Patrick Hayes's mother in Champaign. Several Illinois staff members would take care of their special guest. Mike Pearson (sports information director), Dana Brenner (associate athletic director), Patrick Hayes (of the Alumni Association), and Ron Guenther (athletic director) would be Margaret's hosts for the weekend. "Margaret was just a delightful lady," said Ron Guenther, former Illinois football player and the school's athletic director in 1994.[13]

"She was a very strong woman. One who cared deeply for Red and wanted to foster his remembrance in the most positive light," said Dana Brenner, Illinois associate athletic director in 1994. "You could tell that they loved each other and that she cared deeply for him. She wanted to see the best for him, and whatever we could do to assist, she was all in."[14]

Mike Pearson, former Illinois sports information director, also remembered Margaret's visit, saying, "Red had always traveled up here by himself in previous visits, so we made Margaret feel at home."[15] Lou Tepper was the current head coach, taking over for John Mackovic after being Mackovic's defensive coordinator for four years (1988–1991). After practice on Thursday, Margaret addressed the team. The former Illinois head coach recalled Margaret's visit to practice:

> After our Thursday practice, we traditionally ended practice with 20 minutes of two-minute drills. But the unique thing about Illinois is that the band practiced

on Thursdays. We had a 350-piece band that played the loudest it could play in that 20-minute period. And they really made it realistic, and anytime you put music to kids it becomes more intense and more exciting. So, when she came to speak she saw that, and I think it was something that she was taken aback by a little bit. I'm pretty sure those types of things didn't happen in 1924.

She not only spoke to the team, about 100-plus, she spoke to the band, so there was quite a crowd there, and our players were aware that she was going to be there, but I remember she was very much like what I heard about Red. Just being very humble, meek. She spoke about values, education, those two things, and he was the same way.[16]

Margaret stood in the center of Memorial Stadium, speaking to the entire football team and the Illini marching band members. "Red always stressed the team aspect of football, that no individual can do it without his teammates," said Margaret. "He also reminded that education is important because there is life after football. And Saturday he'd want you to play your best and win the game. He was always proud of the University of Illinois."[17]

"You could hear a pin drop. They were on their knees and she had their full attention," recalled Lou Tepper.[18] "Everybody was pretty respectful of Mrs. Grange," Brenner recollected. "I think she was excited to talk to the team for a little bit. What I remember is, she's in the middle of the team, she didn't have a really loud voice and it was quiet. It was a cool moment."[19]

That weekend Illinois unveiled a permanent monument, the Red Grange Rock, to honor Red. According to Pearson,

The rock had just been put into place, the driveway in between the stadium. The rock was made from limestone from an Indiana quarry, the same quarry that provided the limestone for the stadium when it was built. It was lifted over the wall by a huge crane. It wasn't in place more than three hours or so before the ceremony.[20]

Weighing almost 24 tons, the rock sits at the north end of the stadium, near the locker room entrance, as a tribute to the Galloping Ghost. Illinois players touch the rock as they come out onto the playing field for good luck.

Margaret had something else on her mind to honor her late husband. It was time to let go of him. "When Mrs. Grange came up, she brought Red's remains, and she wanted to sprinkle them on the field at Memorial Stadium," said Pearson. "We had artificial turf surface, so that really wasn't going to work. So, we mentioned the rock."[21]

On the morning of Friday, October 21, as the sun was rising above Memorial Stadium, Margaret was escorted by her hosts to see the new Red Grange Rock. "She had a nice moment to see it," said Brenner about Margaret's time at the Rock. "We took her over there to see it, unveiled it for her. She was pretty excited about it." "Just no fuss, very private viewing for her," Hayes commented. Then Margaret said good-bye to Red. "Yes, the ashes were spread at the base of the stone. It was a very private moment for Mrs. Grange," said Brenner.[22]

Margaret had given Red his final resting place—at the stadium where he had achieved his greatest triumphs. Memorial Stadium was as close to home for Red as it could get—the place where he had been the happiest, doing what he loved more than anything in his life—playing football. During the short, private ceremony, Margaret accomplished wanted she wanted to achieve on her first and only trip to the University of Illinois—giving Red his final resting place.

As for the game, both Illinois and Michigan were 4–2 overall, and 2–1 in the Big Ten, setting up a big matchup in the conference standings. On October 22, a sold-out crowd of more than 72,000 fans jammed into Memorial Stadium on a clear and sunny day in Champaign, as Margaret attended her first-ever Illinois game. Arriving at the stadium as the guest of honor, everyone treated her like football royalty. Wearing a black long-sleeve sweater with a colorful pattern of blue, pink, and purple patches; black dress pants; and white sneakers the tan Florida retiree looked happy to be representing her late husband. She wore glasses, with a rather large orange Illinois flower pinned to her left shoulder. Around her neck was her all-access press pass with "Mrs. Grange" written in blue sharpie to identify her.

During pregame, Margaret was escorted to midfield for the coin toss by Patrick Hayes and the athletic director, Ron Guenther. When she was introduced to the sold-out crowd, Margaret gave a big smile while waving to the Illinois fans. "She was a bit overwhelmed. Over 70,000 fans were roaring. The captains for both teams were there, who were twice her size. Her eyes were huge taking this all in," said Hayes. "But she was thrilled to be there and she did a great job with the coin toss."[23] Big Ten referee Jim Kimmerling handed the coin to her. Margaret flipped the coin high into the air, and it landed softly on the Astroturf. Michigan won the toss. They elected to receive. On the official play-by-play sheet released by Illinois, it reads, "Mrs. Harold 'Red' Grange conducted the pregame coin toss."[24]

Margaret was taken to the President's Box to watch the game. She enjoyed the game, even if she didn't get to see the Illini win, as Michigan got the best of their rival, winning 19–14. Back home on North Amaryllis Drive, Margaret felt relieved that she had visited the school that was so dear to Red. She also was happy that she was able to give him his final resting place. She would soon join him.

During the next few years Margaret kept busy playing golf; doing needle-work; and painting, winning several awards for her original artwork. She also attended a few reunions of the Clipped Wings United Airlines Stewardesses Alumni, but mostly she spent many hours thinking about Red.

"Mrs. Grange was Red's soulmate. That's an overused word, but she was his conscience in so many ways and was his voice when he got older and faced those health issues. She continued to represent him and the legacy that was important to him," said Chuck Baker.

> He was never, in those conversations and letters and so forth, Red Grange was never about his reputation as a superstar. It was him being one guy on a team. It was constant, and Mrs. Grange lived that as his spokesperson. For Red it wasn't about his fame, his glory, about us living down here as important figures. He was anonymous basically. People say, "Who's Red Grange?"[25]

After battling cancer for a year, Margaret Grange passed away on August 21, 1997, at Lake Wales Medical Center. She was 80 years old. "This is part of our past dying. She was sort of the patron saint of Tigers football," said Baker in 1997 to the *Daily Herald*.[26] "It was very sad when it happens to someone that you were very close to. It was sad. She meant a lot to me," said Dorothy Flora, niece of Margaret Grange.[27]

A small service was held at the First United Methodist Church in Indian Lake. "I went to Margaret's funeral. It was a small ceremony," said Flora. "It wasn't large, about 20 people. Her sister Beverly had moved down from Milwaukee, near Lake Wales, a number of years before he got sick. She was there at the funeral. It was very nice."[28] Reverend Harold A. Clarke performed the ceremony in front of the small crowd.

> Let us pray: O God our heavenly Father, from whom we come unto whom we return, and in whom we live and more and have being. . . . We give Thee thanks as we pause to celebrate the life of Muggs Grange. Her life and memory—recall-ing—each one of us—all in her that caused a graciousness, a gentleness, a good-ness that radiated the rich qualities within her. So, we thank Thee for all of the goodness that has passed for her life into the lives of others.
>
> And now bless her sister, Beverly, who stood by daily during time of illness with loving care. Hear us now as we pray.[29]

Back in Wheaton, the news of Margaret's passing spread quickly. Wheaton Warrenville-South High School honored the wife of its most famous son. "I did not get the letter before the season and thought something was up. When we got word that she had passed, I couldn't believe it," said Chuck Baker.

> I can't say I was close friends of Mrs. Grange. I was the principal of the high school. But she appeared to me, if you see these little ornaments, you kind of get an insight into what the woman was all about. She had to sit by herself in her Florida home, stitching these for boys she would never see. What does that say about the character of the woman. I thought this woman had supported this school. She's the last legacy of a key part of our history, and I'm putting the flags half-staff in her honor.[30]

After putting the flags at half-staff for Red in 1991, Principal Baker did the same for Margaret in 1997. It was a small token of the town's respect and admiration for the woman who had supported them for so many years. The Marion Nelson Funeral Home handled Margaret's cremation, just like they did for Red. By her request, Margaret's ashes were sent to the University of Illinois. She would join her husband.

Once again Patrick Hayes handled the arrangements. One late September evening in Champaign, as the sun was setting, Hayes and Brenner reunited the two lovebirds, who had been married for 49 years. "I was there for that," recalled Brenner. "It was Pat and I. It was somber. We said a few words and spread her ashes around. We made sure we used a shovel and dug down a bit, cleared an area. It was a nice moment, and we felt kind of special to be able to reunite them in that way."[31] Margaret and Red had been permanently reunited at the base of the Red Grange Rock in Memorial Stadium.

In 1999, Forksville got into the act of celebrating Red's legacy. On August 25, the town held a small ceremony to erect a historical marker to honor their most famous hometown hero. A small gathering of Forksville natives unveiled the marker at the junction of Route 154 and Route 87, marking the birthplace of Red Grange. The marker is just a few feet from the home where Red was born, a fitting tribute to the Galloping Ghost. A decade later, Red would be memorialized again. This time in bronze.

While he was living, Red was once asked about the potential for Illinois erecting a statue of him. Speaking to the *Chicago Tribune* in 1994, Margaret Grange recalled Red's reaction, saying, "He told that to Red and Red said, 'No way—not unless you have the rest of the team there, too.' He wouldn't stand for that sort of thing." After Red passed away, the movement for a

Red Grange statue continued to gain momentum. Illinois soon committed to putting up a permanent tribute to Red outside Memorial Stadium. George Lundeen, a 1973 Illinois graduate, was commissioned to sculpt the statue. He created 12-foot-tall likeness of Red in the form of a one-ton bronze statue that sits on a 14 × 18-foot base, located outside the west wall of the facility. Forty-five to 50 pieces were welded together in making the piece. "It was like fitting a jigsaw puzzle," said Lundeen. The estimated cost of the statue was $350,000.[32]

The bronze likeness of the Galloping Ghost shows Red carrying the ball in his right hand, left arm slightly extended, with his right leg in a running motion—a perfect image of Red carrying the ball against Michigan in 1924. Red's jersey is blue. Otherwise, the statue has a bronze appearance. "They wanted him running down the field," Lundeen revealed. "We were really fortunate. There were a lot of photos of Grange, unlike any other sports figures of that era."[33]

In 2009, the statue of Red Grange was unveiled at the west end of the stadium. The Galloping Ghost never looked better. "It wasn't hard to make Red Grange look good," said Lundeen in 2009. "He was a Hollywood star after he ran for all those yards on the football field." Every day students and teachers who pass by the stadium can see Red towering over them. The area in front of the statue is called Grange Grove, and on game days it serves as a special tailgating area where fans can mingle. Illini fans usually stop in mass to take pictures or selfies with Red, giving them good luck before they head inside Memorial Stadium. Just like in Forksville and Wheaton, the campus at Illinois continues the legacy of its greatest student-athlete.[34]

NFL LEGACY

As for the NFL and Grange's legacy in helping professional football become the country's greatest rags-to-riches story, Red never wanted to take any credit for establishing the sport. Roger Simon, a columnist for the *Baltimore Sun* (as well as a 1970 Illinois graduate), interviewed Red and couldn't get him to take credit for helping make the NFL a viable league. "Not me, it wasn't me," Red told him. "You write about Halas, George Halas. One of the greatest men ever. He had a vision."[35]

Every time George Halas was asked to comment on the subject, he gave his most prized pupil all the credit. "No other person in this century had a greater impact on the game of football, college or professional, than Red Grange," said George Halas. No player in the first century of the NFL had as much respect and admiration as Red Grange.[36]

"For my dough Red was the greatest team player in pro football history," said Bronco Nagurski in an interview with the *Los Angeles Times*.

> He always went out of his way to make plays go when he himself was not supposed to figure in them prominently. He had a wonderful spirit. His work on pass defense was particularly brilliant. And even when he was far past his prime we were able to recognize his great ability when he turned on the steam for occasional spurts. Red Grange was one of the great football players of all time. He'll always be tops in my book.[37]

Jim McMillen, a former teammate of Red's with Illinois and the Bears, echoed Nagurski's thoughts, saying,

> He is the greatest football player I ever saw, or ever expect to see. He had beautiful coordination. He didn't run powerfully, nor did he seem extremely fast, although he was. He didn't hop, skip, or squirm. He had a fluid, rhythmic sort of motion and a pair of phantom hips that were never there when you grabbed.[38]

In 1925, Red Grange made the blueprint of what a NFL player could become: he left school early, signed with an agent, was paid the biggest salary in the sport, made movies in Hollywood, did endorsements, won two NFL championships, and was elected to the Pro Football Hall of Fame. In 2019, this could be the football résumé of players like Brett Favre, Peyton Manning, and Tom Brady.

After his playing days were over, Red continued to show what a retired NFL player could achieve in his "second" career. He became a coach and radio-television announcer; worked hard to help retired players get their pensions; and attended events and banquets, becoming an ambassador for the sport. Football was good to Red Grange, so much so that he gave back as much as could to the sport he loved so dearly.

Even as far back as 1928, Red praised the sport he loved. In an interview with the *Springfield* (Missouri) *Leader*, he said,

> Football is the greatest sport in in the world. And I am honest in my convictions. There is something about the grip on a football, the shouts of the fans, and the fighting spirit that cannot be compared with other sports. I like baseball and

golf—I played both. I like pool or billiards or bowl. But football for mine as long as I'm able to play.[39]

After seven decades of involvement in the sport of football, he still enjoyed the people in the sport the most. "The score of the game is all-important at the time and for a while afterwards, but in retrospect it doesn't mean much," said Grange. "The best part of the (game) football is its contacts, the friends one makes, the things the players go through together. And I think a little bit of a player's coach rubs off on him and influences him in later years. As I see it, football is a common dominator."[40]

Red couldn't get enough of the game of football. It was his lifeblood. He enjoyed every minute of his involvement with the sport. As the NFL celebrates its 100th season in the fall of 2019, Red can take pride in knowing that he helped professional football become the most successful sport in the United States. He gave the sport hope and media attention like no other player up to that point. He also gave the NFL respectability and, in turn, popularity until football took off on television.

Probably his greatest contribution was giving NFL players something to strive for, a vision of what they could be become, and he did so without getting lost in the uproar of being the most publicized football player of the time. "I never bought that celebrity bunk. I was a poor kid who was lucky to have a good opportunity. I could run, and that was the basis of any success I ever had," said Red in a 1983 interview.[41]

Red's success went much deeper than that. He was more than just a football player who could run. For almost a century, he was a hero for young people in the United States. Whether it was sprinting for touchdowns at the Orchard in Wheaton, running for five touchdowns against Michigan, barnstorming the nation while playing pro football with the Chicago Bears, helping the Bears win two NFL championships, broadcasting football games on the new medium of television, or speaking to the youth of America during his homecoming visit to Wheaton in 1978, Red was and to this day remains a hero for many young people and fans. He showed young football players how to play the game, as well as how to act both on and off the field. He showed them that one can compete hard, helping the team defeat their opponent, while being a gentleman away from the sport. He was the perfect football superstar.

"It was an honor to spend any time with him," said Pat McCaskey, grandson of George Halas. "Because he did so much for football, at all levels. Without Red Grange the NFL might not have succeeded."[42]

Throughout his life, Red never wanted to take credit for his success, giving it to his coaches and teammates. "Football is like life," said Red in a 1927 interview. "One fellow carries the ball and gets most of the credit. Yet 10 men have helped him push through, and without them he would not have gained an inch."[43] Despite his ever-present modesty, one thing can't be rebuffed. He was the NFL's first superstar. He helped show the rest of the football world what the sport could become—the country's most popular sport.

NOTES

INTRODUCTION

1. *Pantagraph*, June 9, 1925.
2. *Orlando Sentinel*, February 12, 1978.
3. George Halas original letter to Red Grange, November 9, 1978, Wheaton College Special Collections, Red Grange Papers.

CHAPTER 1

1. Roger Grange Jr., author interview, March 2, 2017.
2. Michael Tepper, ed., *Passenger Arrivals at the Port of Philadelphia, 1800–1819* (Baltimore, MD: Genealogical Publishing, 1986), 271.
3. Tepper, ed., *Passenger Arrivals at the Port of Philadelphia*.
4. John Wesley obituary, undated newspaper clipping from the Grange family.
5. Grange family photo, 1870–1871, courtesy of Roger Grange Jr.
6. Red Grange, as told to Ira Morton, *The Red Grange Story: The Autobiography of the Galloping Ghost* (New York: G. P. Putnam's Sons, 1953), 3.
7. Dated newspaper clipping, January 22, 1978, Sullivan Historical Society, Red Grange file.
8. *Sullivan County Industries: Then and Now* (Endicott, NY: Endicott Printing, 1954), 55.
9. *Chicago American*, December 10, 1925.
10. *Chicago American*, December 10, 1925.
11. Grange, *The Red Grange Story*, 5.

CHAPTER 2

1. John W. Grange obituary, undated newspaper clipping from the Grange family.
2. Robert Richie letter, October 21, 2016.
3. *Binghampton Press and Sun Bulletin*, November 12, 1950.
4. Red Grange, archival interview, NFL Films, 1973.
5. *Chicago American*, December 10, 1925.
6. Red Grange, as told to Ira Morton, *The Red Grange Story: The Autobiography of the Galloping Ghost* (New York: G. P. Putnam's Sons, 1953), 4.
7. Grange, *The Red Grange Story*, 4.
8. Muncy Historical Society, "My Boyhood Days on a Sullivan County Farm," *Now and Then: Quarterly Magazine of History and Biography* X, no. 1, July 1951, 24.
9. Sadie E. Grange, Sullivan (Pennsylvania) County death certificate, 1910.
10. Grange, *The Red Grange Story*, 5.
11. *Republican News-Item*, April 1, 1910.
12. Photos of headstones, taken by author on visit to East Forks Union Cemetery, 2016.

CHAPTER 3

1. Eliza Grange obituary, undated newspaper clipping from the Grange family.
2. Red Grange interview, *NBC Red Grange Program*, tape cassette, side 2, October 29, 1978, Wheaton College Special Collections, Red Grange Papers.
3. *Chicago American*, November 6, 1925.
4. *Minneapolis Tribune*, "Red Grange: His Story," October 30, 1925.
5. *Minneapolis Tribune*, "Red Grange: His Story," November 1–2, 1925.
6. *Minneapolis Tribune*, "Red Grange: His Story," November 1–2, 1925.
7. Red Grange, as told to Ira Morton, *The Red Grange Story: The Autobiography of the Galloping Ghost* (New York: G. P. Putnam's Sons, 1953), 6.
8. *Port Huron* (Michigan) *Times-Herald*, November 26, 1925.
9. Norma Grange, Sullivan (Pennsylvania) County death certificate, 1906–1963; *Wilkes-Barre Times-Leader*, November 2, 1916.
10. Grange, *The Red Grange Story*, 6.
11. Grange, *The Red Grange Story*, 6.
12. Grange, *The Red Grange Story*, 6.

CHAPTER 4

1. *Minneapolis Tribune*, "Red Grange: His Story," November 1, 1925.
2. Red Grange, as told to Ira Morton, *The Red Grange Story: The Autobiography of the Galloping Ghost* (New York: G. P. Putnam's Sons, 1953), 12.

3. *Wheaton Illinoian*, September 6, 1918.
4. Grange, *The Red Grange Story*, 13.
5. *Daily Journal*, August 7, 1974.
6. *Minneapolis Tribune*, "Red Grange: His Story," November 1, 1925.
7. *Wheaton Illinoian*, October 4, 1918.
8. *Wheaton Illinoian*, October 18, 1918.
9. *Wheaton Illinoian*, November 22, 1918.
10. Red Grange's high school grades from Wheaton High School report card, Wheaton Warrenville-South High School archives.
11. Grange, *The Red Grange Story*, 16.

CHAPTER 5

1. John Thompson, author interview, August 20, 2016.
2. Thompson, author interview.
3. *Christian Cynosure*, August 6, 1885.
4. *Wheaton Daily Journal*, September 3, 1958.
5. Janis Franks, author interview, August 27, 2016.
6. Franks, author interview.
7. Thompson, author interview.
8. *Chicago Tribune*, February 12, 1911.
9. Red Grange, as told to Ira Morton, *The Red Grange Story: The Autobiography of the Galloping Ghost* (New York: G. P. Putnam's Sons, 1953), 22.
10. Red Grange interview, January 14, 1977, Wheaton College Special Collections, Red Grange Papers.
11. Grange, *The Red Grange Story*, 21, 29–30.
12. David Castleman, author interview, January 4, 2017.
13. Grange, *The Red Grange Story*, 17.
14. *Wheaton Illinoian*, September 19, 1919.
15. *Wheaton Illinoian*, October 3, 1919.
16. *Minneapolis Tribune*, "Red Grange: His Story," November 2–3, 1925.
17. *Minneapolis Tribune*, "Red Grange: His Story," November 2–3, 1925.
18. *Wheaton Illinoian*, October 10, 1919.
19. *Wheaton Illinoian*, November 7, 1919.
20. *Wheaton Progressive*, November 7, 1919.
21. *Wheaton Illinoian*, December 5, 1919.

CHAPTER 6

1. Red Grange, as told to Ira Morton, *The Red Grange Story: The Autobiography of the Galloping Ghost* (New York: G. P. Putnam's Sons, 1953), 23.

2. Grange, *The Red Grange Story*, 23.

3. Bob Eustice, author interview, July 30, 2016.

4. Turryann Eustice, author interview, July 30, 2016.

5. *Kalamazoo Normal Record*, October 1914.

6. *Kalamazoo Normal Record*, December 1915.

7. *Wheaton Daily Journal*, August 15, 1974.

8. Eustice, author interview.

9. *Minneapolis Tribune*, "Red Grange: His Story," November 4, 1925.

10. *Chicago Daily News*, undated newspaper clipping, Wheaton College Special Collections, Red Grange Papers, 3-1924-26 scrapbook page.

11. *Wheaton Daily Journal*, July 14, 1974.

12. *Wheaton Illinoian*, September 23, 1920.

13. *Wheaton Illinoian*, October 1, 1920.

14. *Wheaton Illinoian*, October 15, 1920.

15. Craig Mauer, author interview, January 27, 2017.

16. Grange, *The Red Grange Story*.

17. Red Grange interview, cassette 3, July 26, 1978, Wheaton College Special Collections, Red Grange Papers.

18. *Wheaton Daily Journal*, July 14, 1974.

19. *Wheaton Illinoian*, November 5, 1920.

20. *Wheaton Illinoian*, November 5, 1920.

21. *Wheaton Daily Journal*, October 13, 1974.

22. *Wheaton Daily Journal*, July 2, 1974.

23. *Wheaton Daily Journal*, October 10, 1974.

24. *Wheaton Daily Journal*, July 31, 1974.

25. Grange, *The Red Grange Story*, 11.

26. Grange, *The Red Grange Story*, 26.

27. Grange, *The Red Grange Story*, 26.

28. *Wheaton Illinoian*, September 2, 1921.

29. *Wheaton Illinoian*, September 16, 1921.

30. *Wheaton Illinoian*, September 23, 1921.

31. *Wheaton Illinoian*, September 23, 1921.

32. *Wheaton Daily Journal*, October 4, 1974.

33. *Wheaton Illinoian*, November 4, 1921.

34. *Wheaton Illinoian*, November 4, 1921; *Toledo Times*, October 30, 1921.

35. Game recap, undated newspaper clippings, Wheaton College Special Collections, Red Grange Papers.

36. Game recap, undated newspaper clippings.

37. Game recap, undated newspaper clippings.

38. Game recap, undated newspaper clippings.

39. Red Grange interview, *The Red Grange Dinner with George Halas*, cassette tape, October 28, 1978, Wheaton College Special Collections, Red Grange Papers.

40. *1922 Wheaton Orange and Black Yearbook*, 17.

CHAPTER 7

1. Maynard Brichford, *Bob Zuppke: The Life and Football Legacy of the Illinois Coach* (Jefferson, NC: McFarland, 2008), 5-7.

2. Harold E. (Red) Grange, *Zuppke of Illinois* (Chicago: A. L. Glaser, 1937), 3.

3. Grange, *Zuppke of Illinois*, 3.

4. Grange, *Zuppke of Illinois*, 24.

5. Robert C. Zuppke, *Coaching Football* (Champaign, IL: Bailey & Himes, 1930), 9-10.

6. Zuppke, *Coaching Football*, 10.

7. Zuppke, *Coaching Football*, 10.

8. Zuppke, *Coaching Football*.

9. Brichford, *Bob Zuppke*, 102.

10. Red Grange, as told to Ira Morton, *The Red Grange Story: The Autobiography of the Galloping Ghost* (New York: G. P. Putnam's Sons, 1953), 20.

CHAPTER 8

1. Red Grange, as told to Ira Morton, *The Red Grange Story: The Autobiography of the Galloping Ghost* (New York: G. P. Putnam's Sons, 1953), 31.

2. Grange, *The Red Grange Story*, 31.

3. Grange, *The Red Grange Story*, 31.

4. *Daily Illini*, October 1, 1922.

5. Harold E. (Red) Grange, *Zuppke of Illinois* (Chicago: A. L. Glaser, 1937), 67.

6. *Daily Illini*, November 21, 1922.

7. *Urbana Daily Courier*, October 20, 1974.

8. Marilyn Coolley-Carley, author interview, February 26, 2017.

9. 1917 U.S. Adjutant General Records, 1631-1976, Roster of the Illinois National Guard and Illinois Naval Militia, Battery A, Danville, Illinois, 317.

10. *1918 The Medley* (Danville High School yearbook).

11. Coolley-Carley, author interview.

12. *Daily Illini*, February 10, 1923.

13. Grange, *The Red Grange Story*, 34.

14. *Minneapolis Tribune*, "Red Grange: His Story," November 2-3, 1925.

15. Warren Brown, *Win, Lose, or Draw* (New York: G. P. Putnam's Sons, 1947), 122.

16. *Chicago American*, October 29, 1925.

17. *Daily Illini*, October 21, 1923.

18. Lyle Grange quote, undated newspaper clipping, Wheaton College Special Collections, Red Grange Papers. A total of 25,774 fans in the *Illinois Athletic Book*.

19. *Chicago Herald-Examiner*, October 29, 1923.

20. H. O. Crisler scouting report, Box 44, Folder 14, University of Chicago Special Collections, A. A. Stagg Papers; Box 45, Folder 1, Illinois Football Scouting Reports.

21. H. A. Mefford scouting report, Box 44, Folder 14, University of Chicago Special Collections, A. A. Stagg Papers; Box 45, Folder 1, Illinois Football Scouting Reports.

22. *Chicago Tribune*, November 1, 1923; *Illinois Alumni News* 2, vol. 3 (November 1924): 58.

23. *Chicago Tribune*, November 7, 1923.

24. *Chicago American*, November 24, 1923.

25. *Chicago Herald-Examiner*, November 5, 1923.

26. *Fort Wayne Sentinel*, November 8, 1923.

27. *Decatur Herald*, November 9, 1923.

28. *Chicago Tribune*, November 25, 1923.

29. *Chicago Tribune*, December 18, 1923.

30. *Michigan Daily*, December 2, 1923.

31. *Daily Illini*, December 3, 1923.

32. *Chicago Evening American*, November 24, 1923.

33. All quotes from undated newspaper clippings about 1923 Wheaton banquet from scrapbooks, Wheaton College Special Collections, Red Grange Papers.

34. Undated newspaper clippings about 1923 Wheaton banquet from scrapbooks.

35. Red Grange scholastic record, University of Illinois Archives.

36. *1924 The Orange and Black Yearbook*, 10.

CHAPTER 9

1. Red Grange interview, "12 Minutes to Immortality," WGN interview, 1974.

2. Red Grange, as told to Ira Morton, *The Red Grange Story: The Autobiography of the Galloping Ghost* (New York: G. P. Putnam's Sons, 1953), 50.

3. Red Grange interview, October 28, 1978, Wheaton College Special Collections, Red Grange Papers.

4. *(Moline) Dispatch*, November 6, 1923.

5. Red Grange physical description, University of Illinois Athletics Archives.

6. *Detroit Free Press*, December 19, 1934.

7. *St. Louis Post-Dispatch*, October 2, 1924.

8. Grange, *The Red Grange Story*, 51.

9. *Daily Illini*, October 14, 1924.

10. Grange interview, "12 Minutes to Immortality."

11. Grange, *The Red Grange Story*, 53.

12. *Urbana Daily-Courier*, October 23, 1949.

13. Grange, *The Red Grange Story*, 54.

14. Red Grange interview, cassette tape, July 26, 1978, Wheaton College Special Collections, Red Grange Papers.

15. Grange, *The Red Grange Story*, 55.

16. *Chicago Tribune*, October 19, 1924.

17. *Chicago Tribune*, October 19, 1924.

18. *Chicago Tribune*, October 19, 1924.

19. *Chicago Tribune*, October 19, 1924.

20. *Urbana Daily-Courier*, October 23, 1949.

21. 1924 Michigan–Illinois play-by-play, stat sheets, University of Illinois Athletics Archives.

22. Grange, *The Red Grange Story*, 58–59.

23. Grange interview, cassette tape.

24. Grange interview, cassette tape.

25. *Chicago Tribune*, October 19, 1924.

26. *Chicago Tribune*, November 2, 1924.

27. Red Grange headlines, undated newspaper clippings, Wheaton College Special Collections, Red Grange Papers.

28. Grantland Rice quotes, *Wilkes-Barre Record*, October 24, 1924.

29. *Daily Illini*, October 25, 1924.

30. *Akron Beacon-Journal*, October 25, 1924.

31. *Chicago Tribune*, October 20, 1924.

32. *Chicago Tribune*, October 20, 1924.

33. *Daily Illini*, November 2, 1924.

34. Red Grange 1924 scouting reports, Box 44–45, Folders 1, 14, University of Chicago Special Collections, A. A. Stagg Papers.

35. *Indianapolis Star*, October 28, 1924.

36. *Chicago American*, November 7, 1924.

37. *Chicago American*, November 7, 1924.

38. Grange, *The Red Grange Story*; Fred Young note, newspaper clipping, Wheaton College Special Collections, Red Grange Papers.

39. *Urbana Daily Courier*, November 8, 1924.

40. Grange, *The Red Grange Story*, 65.

41. *Chicago Daily News*, undated newspaper clipping, Wheaton College Special Collections, Red Grange Papers; *Chicago Tribune*, November 9, 1924.

42. *Chicago Tribune*, November 16, 1924.

43. *Decatur Daily Review*, November 18, 1924.

44. *Decatur Daily Review*, November 18, 1924.

45. *Decatur Daily Review*, November 18, 1924.

46. Walter Camp quote, *1926 Illio Yearbook*, 174.

47. 1924 Red Grange homecoming banquet menu, Wheaton College Special Collections, Red Grange Papers.

48. 1924 Red Grange homecoming banquet menu.

CHAPTER 10

1. C. C. Pyle family background from Jim Reisler, *Cash and Carry: The Spectacular Rise and Hard Fall of C. C. Pyle, America's First Sports Agent* (Jefferson, NC: McFarland, 2009); Geoff Williams, *C. C. Pyle's Amazing Footrace: The True Story of the 1928 Coast-to-Coast Run across America* (New York: Rodale, 2007).

2. Reisler, *Cash and Carry*; Williams, *C. C. Pyle's Amazing Footrace*.

3. Newspaper quote, undated newspaper clipping, Wheaton College Special Collections, Red Grange Papers.

4. *Daily Illini*, October 22, 1924.

5. Red Grange, as told to Ira Morton, *The Red Grange Story: The Autobiography of the Galloping Ghost* (New York: G. P. Putnam's Sons, 1953), 94.

6. *Chicago Herald-Examiner*, December 1, 1924.

7. *Pittsburgh Post-Gazette*, January 19, 1925; *Racine Journal-Times*, January 31, 1925.

8. *Seymour Tribune*, January 21, 1925.

9. *News Palladium*, February 5, 1925.

10. *Port Huron Times-Herald*, February 6, 1925.

11. *Port Huron Times-Herald*, February 19, 1925.

12. *Port Huron Times-Herald*, February 21, 1925; *Chicago Tribune*, February 24, 1925.

13. Scott Moffatt, author interview, March 17, 2017.

14. Moffatt, author interview.

15. Original contract between Red Grange, C. C. Pyle, Marion Coolley, and Byron Moore, March 27, 1925, Marion F. Coolley Family Collection.

16. Red Grange original photo, Marion F. Coolley Family Collection.

17. *Lincoln Evening Journal*, April 9–11, 1925.

18. Movie quote, undated magazine clipping, *Motion Picture Magazine*, Wheaton College Special Collections, Red Grange Papers.

19. *Milwaukee Sentinel*, May 13, 1925.

20. *Milwaukee Sentinel*, May 13, 1925.

21. *Milwaukee Journal*, May 13, 1925.

22. *St. Louis Star and Times*, May 14, 1925.

23. *Kokomo Daily Tribune*, May 23, 1925.

24. *Kokomo Daily Tribune*, May 23, 1925.

25. Car ad, "The Red Grange of Traffic," undated, Wheaton College Special Collections, Red Grange Papers.

26. *Detroit News*, November 21, 1925.

27. *Detroit News*, November 21, 1925.

28. *Detroit News*, November 21, 1925.

29. *Detroit News*, November 21, 1925.

30. Myron Cope, *The Game That Was: The Early Days of Pro Football* (New York: World Publishing, 1970), 45.

CHAPTER 11

1. *Chicago Tribune*, September 30, 1925.

2. *Chicago Tribune*, September 30, 1925.

3. *Lincoln Star*, October 4, 1925.

4. *Louisville Courier-Journal*, October 4, 1925; *Sportlife*, October 1925.

5. *Time*, October 5, 1925.

6. *Chicago American*, November 4, 1925.

7. 1925 Mayor Pittsford quote, undated clipping, Wheaton College Special Collections, Red Grange Papers.

8. *Minneapolis Star-Tribune*, "Red Grange: His Story," October 28, 1925; *Elmira Star-Gazette*, October 27, 1925.

9. *Minneapolis Star-Tribune*, "Red Grange: His Story," November 19, 1925.

10. *Chicago American*, October 18, 1926–November 21, 1925, 18 articles.

11. *Chicago American*, October 18, 1926–November 21, 1925.

12. *Chicago American*, November 3, 1925.

13. *Chicago American*, November 4–5, 1925.

14. *Chicago American*, November 4–5, 1925.

15. *Chicago American*, November 10, 1925.

16. *Chicago American*, November 12, 1925.

17. *Philadelphia Inquirer*, October 28, 1925.

18. 1925 game expenses for Illinois–Penn game, University of Illinois Athletics Archives.

19. Red Grange interview, cassette 2, July 28, 1978, Wheaton College Special Collections, Red Grange Papers.

20. *Chicago Tribune*, October 31, 1925.

21. Grange interview, cassette 2.

22. Grange interview, cassette 2.

23. Charles L. Allen, ed., *Illinois' Greatest Football Game: As Recorded by American Sports Writers*, 1925), 1.

24. *Chicago Tribune*, November 1, 1925.

25. Allen, *Illinois' Greatest Football Game*, 31.

26. *Philadelphia Inquirer*, November 1, 1925.

27. *Philadelphia Inquirer*, November 1, 1925.

28. *Philadelphia Inquirer*, November 1, 1925.

29. *Chicago American*, October 31, 1925.

30. Allen, *Illinois' Greatest Football Game*, 32.

31. Allen, *Illinois' Greatest Football Game*, 32.

32. Allen, *Illinois' Greatest Football Game*, 32.

33. *Chicago Tribune*, November 2, 1925; *Chicago American*, November 2, 1925.

34. *Chicago Evening Post*, November 2, 1925; *Daily Illini*, November 3, 1925; *Chicago Tribune*, November 2, 1925.

35. *Chicago Tribune*, November 2, 1925.

CHAPTER 12

1. *Chicago American*, November 3, 1925.

2. *Chicago American*, November 2, 1925.

3. *Chicago Daily News*, November 7, 1925.

4. *Chicago Tribune*, November 8, 1925.

5. *Chicago Daily News*, November 7, 1925.

6. *Chicago American*, November 9, 1925.

7. *Elmira Star-Gazette*, November 18, 1925; *Chicago Daily News*, November 12, 1925.

8. *Cincinnati Enquirer*, November 12, 1925.

9. *Chicago Tribune*, November 15, 1925.

10. *Chicago American*, November 14, 1925.

11. *Chicago American*, November 17, 1925.

12. *Davenport Daily Times*, November 18, 1925.

13. *Chicago Evening Post*, November 14, 1925.

14. *New York Times*, November 17, 1925.

15. *Decatur Daily Review*, November 17, 1925; *Chicago American*, November 17, 1925.

16. *Chicago Tribune*, November 18, 1925.

17. *Chicago Tribune*, November 18, 1925.

18. *Chicago Tribune*, November 18, 1925.

19. *Chicago American*, November 18, 1925.

20. *Chicago American*, November 18, 1925.

21. *Franklin* (PA) *News-Herald*, November 19, 1925; *Bakersfield Californian*, November 19, 1925.

22. *Berkeley Daily Gazette*, November 19, 1925.

23. *Detroit News*, November 19, 1923.

24. *Chicago Herald-Examiner*, November 19, 1925.

25. *Chicago American*, November 19, 1925.

26. *Chicago American*, November 20, 1925; *Philadelphia Inquirer*, November 21, 1925.

27. *Chicago Evening Post*, November 21, 1925.

28. *Cleveland Plain Dealer*, November 22, 1922.

29. Red Grange, as told to Ira Morton, *The Red Grange Story: The Autobiography of the Galloping Ghost* (New York: G. P. Putnam's Sons, 1953), 96.

30. *Daily Illini*, November 22, 1925.

CHAPTER 13

1. Paul Gallico, *The Golden People* (New York: Doubleday, 1965), 27.

2. David Neft, Richard Cohen, and Rick Korch, *The Football Encyclopedia* (New York: St. Martin's, 1994), 19.

3. Gallico, *The Golden People*, 27–28.

4. Neft, Cohen, and Korch, *The Football Encyclopedia*, 19–20.

5. Arthur Daley, *Pro Football's Hall of Fame* (New York: Tempo Books, 1963), 6.

6. George S. Halas, with Gwen Morgan and Arthur Veysey, *Halas by Halas: An Autobiography* (New York: McGraw-Hill, 1979), 16.

7. Halas, with Morgan and Veysey, *Halas by Halas*, 16.

8. *Chicago Tribune*, January 23, 1967.

9. *Chicago Tribune*, January 23, 1967.

10. Halas, with Morgan and Veysey, *Halas by Halas*, 53.

11. Halas, with Morgan and Veysey, *Halas by Halas*, 53.

12. Halas, with Morgan and Veysey, *Halas by Halas*, 59.

13. Halas, with Morgan and Veysey, *Halas by Halas*, 60.

14. Mike Rathet and Don Smith, *Their Deeds and Dogged Faith* (New York: Routledge/Balsam Press, 1984), 25.

15. George Vass, *George Halas and the Chicago Bears* (Chicago: Henry Regnery Company, 1971), 6–7.

16. Halas, with Morgan and Veysey, *Halas by Halas*, 70–71.

17. Halas, with Morgan and Veysey, *Halas by Halas*, 71.

18. Halas, with Morgan and Veysey, *Halas by Halas*, 71.

19. Halas, with Morgan and Veysey, *Halas by Halas*, 91.

20. Halas, with Morgan and Veysey, *Halas by Halas*, 91.

21. Halas, with Morgan and Veysey, *Halas by Halas*, 91.

22. Heartley W. Anderson, with Emil Klosinski, *Notre Dame, Chicago Bears, and "Hunk"* (Orlando, FL: Daniels Publishing, 1976), 55.

23. Halas, with Morgan and Veysey, *Halas by Halas*, 102.

24. Original letter, C. C. Pyle to Dutch Sternaman, August 9, 1925; Richard Whittingham, *The Chicago Bears: An Illustrated History* (Chicago: Rand McNally, 1982), 41.

25. Halas, with Morgan and Veysey, *Halas by Halas*, 103.

26. Halas, with Morgan and Veysey, *Halas by Halas*, 103.

27. Halas, with Morgan and Veysey, *Halas by Halas*, 103.

28. Original contract between the Chicago Bears (Halas and Sternaman) and C. C. Pyle, November 10, 1925, Marion F. Coolley Family Collection.

29. Original contract between the Chicago Bears and C. C. Pyle, November 10, 1925.

30. Original contract between the Chicago Bears and C. C. Pyle, November 10, 1925. According to the *Chicago Evening Post*, November 23, 1925, $2,000 was guaranteed per game, 10 percent of the first $5,000, 20 percent of the second $5,000, and 40 percent of every dollar beyond that.

31. Original contract between the Chicago Bears and C. C. Pyle, November 10, 1925.

32. Charles C. Pyle, *Life and Football History of Harold E. "Red" Grange* (Chicago: Bentley, Murray & Company), 1926.

33. *Belvidere* (IL) *Daily Republican*, November 19, 1925.

34. *Chicago American*, November 21, 1925.

35. *Ohio State Journal*, November 18, 1925.

36. 1925–1926 C. C. Pyle original expense sheet, Marion F. Coolley Family Collection.

CHAPTER 14

1. Red Grange interview, October 28, 1978, Wheaton College Special Collections, Red Grange Papers.

2. Red Grange, archival interview, NFL Films, 1973.

3. *Chicago American*, November 22–23, 1925.

4. *Chicago American*, November 22–23, 1925.

5. *Chicago American*, November 22–23, 1925.

6. Original contract between Red Grange, C. C. Pyle, Marion Coolley, and Byron Moore, March 27, 1925, Marion F. Coolley Family Collection, gate splits date crossed out, in ink new date November 23, 1925.

7. *Chicago Tribune*, November 23, 1925.

8. *Chicago Herald-Examiner*, November 23, 1925.

9. *Boston Post*, December 17, 1926; Robert S. Gallagher, "The Galloping Ghost: An Interview with Red Grange," *American Heritage* XXVI, no. 1 (December 1974): 94.

10. *Chicago Herald-Examiner*, November 23, 1925.

11. *New York Sun*, December 2, 1925; *Chicago American*, November 23, 1925.

12. *Chicago Daily News*, November 23, 1925; *Chicago American*, November 23, 1925; *Chicago Evening Post*, November 23, 1925.

13. *Daily Illini*, November 24, 1925; *Chicago Herald-Examiner*, November 24, 1925; *Chicago American*, November 24, 1925.

14. 1925 St. Louis original contract, Dutch Sternaman Collection, Pro Football Hall of Fame.

15. *Chicago Evening Post*, November 24, 1925.

16. *Chicago American*, November 24, 1925.

17. *Chicago Herald-Examiner*, November 25, 1925.

18. *Danville Commercial-News*, November 25, 1925.

19. *Chicago Daily Journal*, November 25, 1925.

20. *Chicago Tribune*, November 26, 1925.

21. *Chicago Daily Journal*, November 27, 1925.

22. *Chicago Herald-Examiner*, November 27, 1925.

23. *Chicago American*, November 27, 1925.

24. Red Grange interview, July 26, 1978, Wheaton College Special Collections, Red Grange Papers.

25. *Chicago American*, November 27, 1925; *Chicago Tribune*, November 28, 1925.

26. John Carroll, *Red Grange and the Rise of Modern Football* (Urbana: University of Illinois Press, 1999), 108.

27. Chris Willis, *The Man Who Built the National Football League: Joe F. Carr* (Lanham, MD: Scarecrow, 2010), 267–68.

CHAPTER 15

1. *Chicago American*, December 10, 1925.

2. *Chicago American*, December 10, 1925.

3. *Daily Illini*, December 2, 1925.

4. *Chicago Tribune*, December 2, 1925.

5. *Chicago Herald-Examiner*, December 2, 1925.

6. *St. Louis Star and Times*, November 30, 1925.

7. *Wheaton Daily Journal*, March 11, 1987.

8. *Chicago Tribune*, December 3, 1925; *St. Louis Post-Dispatch*, December 3, 1925.

9. *Chicago American*, December 3, 1925.

10. *St. Louis Post-Dispatch*, December 3, 1925.

11. *Chicago Herald-Examiner*, December 4, 1925.

12. *Philadelphia Evening Bulletin*, December 4, 1925; *Philadelphia Inquirer*, December 5, 1925.

13. *Philadelphia Evening Bulletin*, December 4, 1925.

14. *Philadelphia Inquirer*, December 3–5, 1925.

15. *Chicago American*, December 6, 1925.

16. *Daily Illini*, December 6, 1925.

17. *Philadelphia Inquirer*, December 6, 1925.

18. *Chicago Herald-Examiner*, December 6, 1925.

19. *Philadelphia Inquirer*, December 6, 1925.

20. *Philadelphia Inquirer*, December 6, 1925; John Carroll, *Red Grange and the Rise of Modern Football* (Urbana: University of Illinois Press, 1999), 111.

21. 1925 Frankford–Bears original gate statement, Dutch Sternaman Collection, Pro Football Hall of Fame.

22. *Chicago Tribune*, December 4, 1925.

23. *Chicago Tribune*, December 5, 1925.

24. *New York Evening Post*, December 4, 1925; *New York Daily News*, December 4, 1925.

25. *New York Evening Journal*, December 5, 1925.

26. Carroll, *Red Grange and the Rise of Modern Football*, 108; *New York Giants vs. Bears Game Day Program*, November 26, 1995, 122.

27. *New York Times*, December 7, 1925.

28. Richard Whittingham, *What a Game They Played: Stories of the Early Days of Pro Football by Those Who Were There* (New York: Harper & Row, 1984), 9.

29. *New York Daily News*, December 7, 1925.

30. Red Grange, as told to Ira Morton, *The Red Grange Story: The Autobiography of the Galloping Ghost* (New York: G. P. Putnam's Sons, 1953), 102.

31. *New York Times*, December 7, 1925.

32. *Brooklyn Daily Eagle*, December 7, 1925.

33. *New York Daily News*, December 7, 1925.

34. *New York Evening Journal*, December 7, 1925.

35. *Pittsburgh Daily Post*, December 20, 1925.

36. *Chicago Tribune*, December 7, 1925. Grange told Westbrook Pegler the amount was $36,000, according to the *Chicago Tribune*, December 8, 1925.

37. *Brooklyn Daily Eagle*, December 7, 1925.

38. *New York Sun*, December 7, 1925.

39. *Chicago Tribune*, December 29, 1929.

40. *New York Daily News*, December 7, 1925.

41. *Daily Illini*, December 8, 1925.

42. *Pittsburgh Post-Gazette*, December 9, 1925; *Champaign News-Gazette*, December 7, 1925.

43. Red Grange interview, July 28, 1978, Wheaton College Special Collections, Red Grange Papers. Photo of Red Grange in front of white house, Marion F. Coolley Family Collection.

44. *Washington Post*, November 25, 1925.

45. *Washington Post*, December 6, 1925.

46. *Washington Post*, December 9, 1925.

47. *Washington Times*, December 9, 1925.

48. *Washington Post*, December 9–10, 1925.

49. *Providence Journal*, December 6, 1925; *Boston Post*, December 5, 1925.

50. *Boston Evening Transcript*, December 8, 1925; *Boston Globe*, December 8–9, 1925; *Providence Journal*, December 6, 1925.

51. *Boston Globe*, December 8–9, 1925.

52. *Boston Evening Transcript*, December 7, 1925.

53. Chicago Bears check (#3091) for the hotel, Dutch Sternaman Collection, Pro Football Hall of Fame.

54. *Boston Evening Transcript*, December 9, 1925.

55. *Boston Globe*, December 10, 1925.

56. *Minneapolis Star*, December 10, 1925.

57. *Providence Journal*, December 10, 1925; *Chicago Herald-Examiner*, December 10, 1925; *Boston Globe*, December 10, 1925; *New York Herald-Tribune*, December 10, 1925. The *Boston Evening Transcript* had 10,000 fans.

58. *Providence Journal*, December 9, 1925.

59. *Providence Journal*, December 10, 1925.

60. *Providence Journal*, December 10, 1925; *Boston Post*, December 10, 1925.

61. Grange, *The Red Grange Story*, 103–4.

62. Grange, *The Red Grange Story*. The *St. Louis Post-Dispatch* reported a $40,000 gate with the same breakdown.

63. *Pittsburgh Press*, December 10, 1925.

64. *Chicago Tribune*, December 11, 1925; *Chicago Herald-Examiner*, December 11, 1925; *Pittsburgh Press*, December 11, 1925; *Pittsburgh Daily Post*, December 11, 1925.

65. Grange, *The Red Grange Story*, 105; *Chicago Tribune*, December 11, 1925.

66. *Pittsburgh Daily Post*, December 11, 1925.

67. *Pittsburgh Press*, December 11, 1925.

68. 1925 Pittsburgh–Bears original gate statement, Dutch Sternaman Collection, Pro Football Hall of Fame.

69. *Detroit News*, December 12, 1925.

70. *Decatur Herald*, December 12, 1925.

71. *Detroit Free Press*, December 12, 1925.

72. *Cincinnati Enquirer*, December 12, 1925.

73. *Chicago Tribune*, December 13, 1925.

74. The *Chicago Tribune*, *Chicago Herald-Examiner*, and *Detroit Free Press* reported that 6,000 fans were in attendance.

75. *Detroit News*, December 13, 1925.

76. *Detroit Free Press*, December 13, 1925.

77. *Detroit News*, December 13, 1925.

78. *Chicago American*, December 14, 1925. A crowd of 15,000 was reported by the *Chicago Tribune*, *Chicago American*, and *Chicago Daily News*, while the *Chicago Evening-Post* listed 16,000 and the *Chicago Herald-Examiner* reported 18,000.

79. *Chicago Daily News*, December 14, 1925.

80. *Logansport Pharos-Tribune*, December 11, 1925.

81. *Muncie Star-Press*, December 15, 1925.

82. *Chicago Daily News*, December 16, 1925.

83. *Pittsburgh Daily Post*, December 16, 1925.

84. *Chicago American*, December 16, 1925.

CHAPTER 16

1. *Detroit News*, December 22, 1925.

2. *Chicago Evening Post*, December 21, 1925.

3. Original contract between the Chicago Bears and C. C. Pyle, December 16, 1925, Dutch Sternaman Collection, Pro Football Hall of Fame.

4. *Palm Beach Press*, December 21, 1925.

5. *Chicago Daily News*, December 21, 1925.

6. *Miami Herald*, November 14, 1925.

7. *Miami Herald*, December 14, 1925; *Miami Daily News*, December 14–16, 1925.

8. *Chicago Herald-Examiner*, December 26, 1925.

9. *Miami News*, December 26, 1925.

10. *Miami News*, December 26, 1925. The *Chicago Daily News* reported nine carries for 89 yards, while the *Chicago Evening Post/Chicago Tribune* had nine carries for 98 yards.

11. 1925 Miami–Coral Gables–Bears original gate statement, Dutch Sternaman Collection, Pro Football Hall of Fame.

12. 1925 Tampa–Bears original game contract, Dutch Sternaman Collection, Pro Football Hall of Fame.

13. *Chicago Tribune*, January 1, 1926.

14. *Tampa Tribune*, December 19, 1925.

15. *Tampa Tribune*, December 30, 1925; *Chicago Tribune*, January 2, 1926; *Pittsburgh Post-Gazette*, January 2, 1926.

16. Red Grange, as told to Ira Morton, *The Red Grange Story: The Autobiography of the Galloping Ghost* (New York: G. P. Putnam's Sons, 1953), 110.

17. *Tampa Tribune*, January 2, 1926.

18. "Frenzied Football," *Liberty Magazine*, February 20, 1926.

19. *Florida Times-Union*, December 6, 1925; *Florida Times-Union*, December 19, 1925; *Chicago Tribune*, January 3, 1926; *Tampa Tribune*, January 3, 1926; *St. Louis Post-Dispatch*, January 3, 1926.

20. *Chicago Tribune*, January 3, 1926.

21. *New Orleans Times-Picayune*, January 5, 1926.

22. *New Orleans Times-Picayune*, January 7–8, 1926.

23. *Chicago Tribune,* January 11, 1926; *New York Times,* January 10, 1926; *Shreveport Times,* January 11, 1926. The *Pittsburgh Daily Post* had Red at 16 carries for 72 yards; the *Chicago Tribune* had him with 16 carries for 136 yards.

24. *Chicago American,* January 11, 1926.

25. 1926 New Orleans–Chicago Bears original gate statement, Dutch Sternaman Collection, Pro Football Hall of Fame.

CHAPTER 17

1. *Los Angeles Evening Express,* January 14, 1926.

2. *Los Angeles Evening Herald,* January 14, 1926; *Los Angeles Evening Express,* January 14, 1926.

3. C. C. Pyle original expense sheet, Marion F. Coolley Family Collection.

4. *Los Angeles Times,* December 13, 1926.

5. *Los Angeles Times,* January 15, 1926.

6. *Los Angeles Times,* January 5, 1926.

7. *Los Angeles Times,* January 12, 1926.

8. *Los Angeles Times,* January 24, 1926.

9. *Chicago Herald-Examiner,* January 17, 1926.

10. *Chicago Tribune,* January 17, 1926; *New York Times,* January 17, 1926; *Los Angeles Herald,* January 17, 1926.

11. *Los Angeles Herald,* January 17, 1926.

12. *Oakland Tribune,* January 17, 1926.

13. *Los Angeles Times,* January 16, 1926.

14. All postgame quotes, *Los Angeles Times,* January 17, 1926.

15. *Los Angeles Times,* January 17, 1926.

16. *Los Angeles Herald-Examiner,* January 17, 1926.

17. *Los Angeles Times,* January 17, 1926.

18. *Los Angeles Times,* January 19, 1926.

19. *San Bernardino County Sun,* January 18, 1926.

20. *San Diego Union,* January 18, 1926.

21. *San Diego Union,* January 18, 1926.

22. 1926 San Diego–Chicago Bears original gate statement, Dutch Sternaman Collection, Pro Football Hall of Fame.

23. *San Francisco Call,* January 19, 1926.

24. *Oakland Tribune,* January 20, 1926.

25. *San Francisco Chronicle,* January 9, 1926.

26. *San Francisco Call,* January 21, 1926.

27. Original Western Union telegram, January 21, 1926, Marion F. Coolley Family Collection.

28. *San Francisco Examiner*, January 25, 1926; *San Francisco Call*, January 25, 1926; *San Francisco Chronicle*, January 25, 1926.

29. 1926 San Francisco–Chicago Bears gate announced as $58,000, with about $34,000 going to the Red–Pyle–Bears group and $24,000 to Cowan. *Seattle Post-Intelligencer*, January 26, 1926.

30. *Seattle Daily Times*, January 29, 1926.

31. *Seattle Post-Intelligencer*, January 29, 1926; *Seattle Daily Times*, January 29, 1926.

32. 1926 Seattle–Chicago Bears original game contract, Dutch Sternaman Collection, Pro Football Hall of Fame.

33. *Corvallis Gazette-Times*, January 20, 1926.

34. *Oregonian*, January 27, 1926.

35. Original Western Union telegram, January 29, 1926, Marion F. Coolley Family Collection.

36. *Chicago Tribune*, January 28, 1926.

37. *Oregonian*, January 31, 1926.

38. *Oregonian*, January 29, 1926.

39. *Oregonian*, January 31, 1926.

40. 1926 Seattle–Chicago Bears original game contract, Dutch Sternaman Collection, Pro Football Hall of Fame.

41. *Seattle Post-Intelligencer*, January 24, 1926.

42. *Seattle Times*, February 1, 1926; *Chicago Daily News*, February 1, 1926.

43. *Seattle Post-Intelligencer*, February 1, 1926.

44. 1926 Seattle–Chicago Bears original gate statement, Dutch Sternaman Collection, Pro Football Hall of Fame.

CHAPTER 18

1. *Chicago Herald-Examiner*, February 8, 1926.

2. *Chicago Tribune*, January 6, 1926.

3. Original expense and deposit statement sheets, Marion F. Coolley Family Collection.

4. George S. Halas, with Gwen Morgan and Arthur Veysey, *Halas by Halas: An Autobiography* (New York: McGraw-Hill, 1979), 116.

5. Red Grange, as told to Ira Morton, *The Red Grange Story: The Autobiography of the Galloping Ghost* (New York: G. P. Putnam's Sons, 1953), 112.

6. Heartley W. Anderson, with Emil Klosinski, *Notre Dame, Chicago Bears, and "Hunk"* (Orlando, FL: Daniels Publishing, 1976), 72–73.

7. *Minneapolis Star-Tribune*, March 27, 1926.

8. *Marion Star*, March 6, 1926; *Pittsburgh Press*, April 18, 1926.

9. Red Grange football box, Wilson Sporting Goods, 1926.

10. Photo of Red Grange doll. The Sterling Doll Company also produced a Red Grange doll, circa 1928. Original letter, $3,500 advance royalty, Marion F. Coolley Family Collection.

11. Jeff Payne, "Red Grange and the Candy Man: The Story of the 1926 Shotwells," *Gridiron Greats* (Summer 2015).

12. Chip Shotwell, author interview, July 10, 2018.

13. Shotwell ad, undated Wheaton College Special Collections, Red Grange Papers.

14. Shotwell, author interview.

15. Original expense and deposit statement sheets, Marion F. Coolley Family Collection.

16. Shotwell, author interview.

17. Shotwell, author interview.

18. *Oregonian*, January 31, 1926.

19. Ann Kakacek, author interview, February 1, 2017.

20. Red Grange audio interview, "Evening with Red Grange," October 28, 1978, Wheaton College Special Collections, Red Grange Papers.

21. *New York Evening Journal*, December 14, 1925.

22. Richard Whittingham, *What a Game They Played: Stories of the Early Days of Pro Football by Those Who Were There* (New York: Harper & Row, 1984), 10–11.

CHAPTER 19

1. George S. Halas, with Gwen Morgan and Arthur Veysey, *Halas by Halas: An Autobiography* (New York: McGraw-Hill, 1979), 121.

2. *Chicago Daily News*, February 4, 1926.

3. NFL league minutes, "President's Report," February 6–7, 1926.

4. *Frankford Yellow Jacket News* 3, no. 17 (July 1926): 7.

5. Dave Klein, *The New York Giants: Yesterday, Today, Tomorrow* (Chicago: Henry Regnery, 1973), 34.

6. Halas, with Morgan and Veysey, *Halas by Halas*, 121.

7. *Chicago American*, February 8, 1926.

8. *Chicago American*, February 9, 1926; *Lincoln Star*, February 9, 1926.

9. *Chicago American*, February 10, 1926.

10. *Ohio State Journal*, February 16, 1926.

11. *Chicago Daily News*, February 18, 1926; *Chicago Herald-Examiner*, February 19, 1926.

12. Original Western Union telegram, March 17, 1926, Marion F. Coolley Family Collection.

13. Original contract between C. C. Pyle, Red Grange, Marion F. Coolley, and Byron Moore, March 15, 1926, Marion F. Coolley Family Collection.

14. Marylin Coolley-Carley, author interview, February 26, 2017.
15. *Danville Commercial-News*, April 11, 1955.

CHAPTER 20

1. Red Grange, as told to Ira Morton, *The Red Grange Story: The Autobiography of the Galloping Ghost* (New York: G. P. Putnam's Sons, 1953), 122.
2. Red Grange audiocassette interview, January 23, 1980, Wheaton College Special Collections, Red Grange Papers.
3. *Pittsburgh Press*, May 16, 1926.
4. *Pittsburgh Press*, May 16, 1926.
5. *Pittsburgh Press*, May 16, 1926.
6. Grange, *The Red Grange Story*, 123.
7. *Los Angeles Times*, June 27, 1926; *San Bernardino County Sun*, May 27, 1926.
8. *Los Angeles Times*, February 1, 1937.
9. Grange, *The Red Grange Story*, 126.
10. Grange, *The Red Grange Story*, 126.
11. *San Bernardino County Sun*, June 12, 1926.
12. *Santa Ana Register*, June 17, 1926.
13. *Ogden Standard-Examiner*, May 27, 1926.
14. *Oakland Tribune*, July 17, 1926.
15. *Film Daily*, July 22, 1926.
16. Grange, *The Red Grange Story*, 126.
17. Newspaper clipping, June 28, 1926, Red Grange file, University of Illinois Archives.
18. *Allentown Morning Call*, August 1, 1926; *Wilkes-Barre Evening News*, July 28, 1926.
19. *Williamsport Gazette and Bulletin*, August 5, 1926.
20. 1926 newspaper clipping, undated, Red Grange file, Sullivan County Historical Museum. Newspaper clipping, August 8, 1926, *Sunday Telegram*, Sullivan County Historical Society.
21. Red Grange welcome home banner, author visit and photos, 2016, Sullivan County Historical Museum.

CHAPTER 21

1. Don Wilson, author interview, August 9, 2017.
2. *Chicago Herald-Examiner*, September 2, 1926.

3. *Los Angeles Times*, September 4, 1926; *Film Daily*, September 14, 1926; *New York Times*, September 6, 1926.

4. *Mattoon* (IL) *Journal-Gazette*, September 18, 1926.

5. *Moving Picture World*, September 25, 1926.

6. *New York Times*, September 6, 1926.

7. *Los Angeles Times*, September 10, 1926.

8. *Motion Picture News*, August 28, 1926.

9. *Moving Picture World*, September 25, 1926.

10. According to the *Los Angeles Times*, February 1, 1937, receipts totaled $750,000.

11. *Ironwood Daily Globe*, November 10, 1926.

12. *St. Louis Star-Times*, September 27, 1926.

13. *Moline Dispatch*, October 4, 1926.

14. *Hartford Courant*, October 3, 1926; *Hartford Courant*, October 11, 1926.

15. *Hartford Courant*, October 11, 1926.

16. *New York Times*, November 16, 1926; *New York Times*, November 21, 1926.

17. *New York Daily News*, October 16, 1926; *New York Daily News*, October 23, 1926; *New York Daily News*, November 14, 1926.

18. *Philadelphia Inquirer*, October 25, 1926; *Philadelphia Inquirer*, October 27, 1926.

19. Jim Reisler, *Cash and Carry: The Spectacular Rise and Hard Fall of C. C. Pyle, America's First Sports Agent* (Jefferson, NC: McFarland, 2008), 98.

20. *New York Times*, November 6, 1926.

21. *Universal News* articles, multiple newspapers, November 1–26, 1926.

22. *Chicago American*, December 11, 1926.

23. Richard Whittingham, *What a Game They Played: Stories of the Early Days of Pro Football by Those Who Were There* (New York: Harper & Row, 1984), 11.

24. George S. Halas, with Gwen Morgan and Arthur Veysey, *Halas by Halas: An Autobiography* (New York: McGraw-Hill, 1979), 127.

25. *San Antonio Light*, December 13, 1926.

26. Wellington Mara, archival interview, NFL Films, 1999.

27. *Waco News-Tribune*, December 17, 1926.

28. *Atlanta Constitution*, December 15, 1926.

29. *Arizona Republic*, December 21, 1926.

30. *Los Angeles Times*, January 17, 1927.

CHAPTER 22

1. *Bridgeport* (CT) *Telegram*, December 25, 1926.

2. Red Grange, as told to Ira Morton, *The Red Grange Story: The Autobiography of the Galloping Ghost* (New York: G. P. Putnam's Sons, 1953), 128–29.

3. Grange, *The Red Grange Story*, 129.

4. *Oxnard Press-Courier*, March 26, 1926.

5. *Wilkes-Barre Record*, March 21, 1927.

6. *Ogden Standard-Examiner*, January 1, 1928.

7. *Photoplay Magazine*, January 1928.

8. *Variety*, October 26, 1927.

CHAPTER 23

1. *Philadelphia Inquirer*, November 18, 1925.

2. *Dayton Daily News*, October 1, 1927.

3. *Dayton Daily News*, October 1, 1927.

4. Richard Whittingham, *What a Game They Played: Stories of the Early Days of Pro Football by Those Who Were There* (New York: Harper & Row, 1984), 25.

5. *New York Times*, October 17, 1927.

6. *Brooklyn Daily Eagle*, October 17, 1927.

7. *Ogden Standard-Examiner*, October 18, 1927.

8. *Green Bay Press-Gazette*, October 24, 1927.

9. *Pittsburgh Press*, December 11, 1927.

CHAPTER 24

1. 1928 official program, first annual "C. C. Pyle's International-Transcontinental Foot Race," quote on back cover.

2. Myron Cope, *The Game That Was: The Early Days of Pro Football* (New York: World Publishing, 1970), 47.

3. *Lincoln Star*, May 27, 1928.

4. *Reno Gazette-Journal*, June 20, 1928.

5. *Harrisburg Evening-News*, June 20, 1928.

6. Cope, *The Game That Was*, 48.

7. Red Grange interview, July 28, 1978, Wheaton College Special Collections, Red Grange Papers.

8. *Exhibitors Herald and Moving Picture World*, November 3, 1928.

9. *Variety*, September 26, 1928.

10. *Exhibitors Herald and Moving Picture World*, December 22, 1928.

11. *Variety*, October 24, 1928.

12. *Chicago American*, October 24, 1928.

13. *Variety*, October 31, 1928.

14. *Danville Bee*, October 19, 1928.

15. *San Bernardino County Sun*, November 1, 1928.

16. *San Bernardino County Sun*, November 1, 1928.

17. Linda Thomas, author interview, January 23, 2017.

18. Thomas, author interview.

19. Red Grange, as told to Ira Morton, *The Red Grange Story: The Autobiography of the Galloping Ghost* (New York: G. P. Putnam's Sons, 1953), 143–44.

CHAPTER 25

1. Red Grange, as told to Ira Morton, *The Red Grange Story: The Autobiography of the Galloping Ghost* (New York: G. P. Putnam's Sons, 1953), 146.

2. George S. Halas, with Gwen Morgan and Arthur Veysey, *Halas by Halas: An Autobiography* (New York: McGraw-Hill, 1979), 134.

3. Grange, *The Red Grange Story*, 146.

4. Myron Cope, *The Game That Was: The Early Days of Pro Football* (New York: World Publishing, 1970), 56.

5. *Los Angeles Times*, August 4, 1929.

6. *Los Angeles Times*, August 4, 1929.

7. Grange, *The Red Grange Story*, 149.

8. *Green Bay Press-Gazette*, September 30, 1929.

9. *Chicago Daily News*, October 28, 1929; *Chicago Evening Post*, October 29, 1929.

10. *Chicago American*, November 2, 1929.

11. *Chicago American*, November 4, 1929.

12. *Green Bay Press-Gazette*, December 9, 1929.

13. Garland Grange's salary, 1929 Bears balance sheet, Dutch Sternaman Collection, Pro Football Hall of Fame.

14. *De Kalb Daily Chronicle*, September 23, 1929.

15. *Lincoln Star*, September 30, 1929.

16. *Des Moines Register*, November 17, 1929.

17. *Chicago Tribune*, December 8, 1929; *Chicago Tribune*, December 15, 1929; *Chicago Tribune*, December 22, 1929; *Chicago Tribune*, December 29, 1929.

18. *Chicago Tribune*, December 22, 1929.

19. *Chicago Tribune*, December 29, 1929.

20. *Chicago Tribune*, December 29, 1929.

21. Greg Kukish, "Along Came Jones," *Coffin Corner* 10, no. 1 (1988): 21.

22. Halas, with Morgan and Veysey, *Halas by Halas*, 136.

23. Halas, with Morgan and Veysey, *Halas by Halas*, 136–37.

24. Halas, with Morgan and Veysey, *Halas by Halas*, 136–37; *Chicago Tribune*, January 28, 1967.

25. Halas, with Morgan and Veysey, *Halas by Halas*.

26. *Belvidere Daily Republican*, May 31, 1930.

27. *Chicago American*, September 4, 1930.

28. *Chicago Herald-Examiner*, October 12, 1930.

29. *Chicago Tribune*, October 20, 1930.

30. *Saturday Evening Post*, November 5, 1933.

31. *Chicago Tribune*, November 3, 1930.

32. *Shreveport Times*, November 13, 1930.

33. *Elwood Call-Leader*, October 12, 1938.

34. *Philadelphia Inquirer*, November 23, 1930.

35. *Indiana Gazette*, November 19, 1930.

36. *Chicago American*, December 16, 1930; *Chicago Daily News*, December 16, 1930.

37. *Muscatine Journal and News-Tribune*, April 17, 1931.

38. Grange, *The Red Grange Story*, 145.

39. *Motion Picture Herald*, April 11, 1931.

40. *Lansing State Journal*, April 25, 1931.

41. Halas, with Morgan and Veysey, *Halas by Halas*, 147–48.

42. *Chicago Tribune*, September 24, 1931.

43. *Chicago Evening Post*, September 24, 1931; the *Chicago Tribune* had the score 36–6.

44. *Chicago Herald-Examiner*, October 19, 1931.

45. *Wilkes-Barre Record*, September 25, 1931.

46. *Chicago Herald-Examiner*, October 31, 1931; *Chicago Herald-Examiner*, November 6, 1931.

47. *Chicago Herald-Examiner*, November 16, 1931; *Lincoln Star*, November 16, 1931.

48. *Chicago American*, December 7, 1931.

49. *Chicago American*, December 7, 1931.

CHAPTER 26

1. *Gaffney Ledger*, October 20, 1931; *National Board of Review Magazine*, December 1931, 22; *New Movie Magazine*, December 1931, 78.

2. Red Grange audio interview, June 13, 1978, Wheaton College Special Collections, Red Grange Papers.

3. Virginia McCaskey, archival interview, NFL Films, 2015.

4. Red Grange, as told to Ira Morton, *The Red Grange Story: The Autobiography of the Galloping Ghost* (New York: G. P. Putnam's Sons, 1953), 145–46.

5. George S. Halas, with Gwen Morgan and Arthur Veysey, *Halas by Halas: An Autobiography* (New York: McGraw-Hill, 1979), 148–49.

6. *Burlington Daily-Times*, September 3, 1932.

7. *Burlington Daily-Times*, September 3, 1932.

8. *Chicago American*, October 7, 1932.

9. *Chicago Evening Post*, October 10, 1932.

10. *Chicago American*, October 17, 1932.

11. *Chicago Daily News*, October 20, 1932.

12. *College Humor*, October 1932–January 1933.

13. *Saturday Evening Post*, October 8, 1932.

14. *Saturday Evening Post*, November 5, 1932.

15. *Saturday Evening Post*, November 5, 1932.

16. *Saturday Evening Post*, October 24, 1933.

17. *Chicago Daily News*, November 9, 1932.

18. *Chicago American*, November 10, 1932.

19. *Chicago Herald-Examiner*, November 28, 1932.

20. *Chicago Herald-Examiner*, December 3, 1932.

21. *Chicago American*, December 10, 1932.

22. *Portsmouth Times*, December 15, 1932.

23. *Chicago American*, December 16, 1932.

24. Charles "Ookie" Miller, author interview, 1999.

25. Red Grange interview, Pro Football Hall of Fame, 1978.

26. Virginia McCaskey, author interview, 1999.

27. Glenn Presnell, author interview, 1999.

28. Presnell, author interview.

29. *Chicago Tribune*, December 19, 1932.

30. Halas, with Morgan and Veysey, *Halas by Halas*, 169.

31. Red Grange audio interview, July 26, 1978, Wheaton College Special Collections, Red Grange Papers.

32. Presnell, author interview.

33. Miller, author interview.

34. Halas, with Morgan and Veysey, *Halas by Halas*, 169.

35. *Decatur Herald*, December 19, 1932.

36. *Chicago Tribune*, December 19, 1932.

37. *Portsmouth Times*, December 20, 1932.

38. *Chicago Tribune*, December 20, 1932; *Green Bay Press-Gazette*, December 20, 1932.

39. Grange audio interview, July 26, 1978.

40. *Bridgewater Courier-News*, December 19, 1932; *Wilmington Morning-News*, December 19, 1932.

41. *Cincinnati Post*, December 24, 1932.

CHAPTER 27

1. *Lincoln Star*, November 18, 1932.

2. *San Mateo Times*, January 19, 1933.

3. *St. Louis Post-Dispatch*, January 25, 1933.

4. *Benton Harbor News-Palladium*, February 8, 1933.

5. *San Bernardino County-Sun*, February 17, 1933.

6. *Daily Illini*, April 20, 1933; *Green Bay Press-Gazette*, May 15, 1933.

7. *Green Bay Press-Gazette*, May 15, 1933.

8. *Daily Illini*, April 25, 1933.

9. *Daily Illini*, April 25, 1933.

10. Quoted in Arthur Daley, *Pro Football's Hall of Fame* (New York: Temp Books, 1963), 154.

11. 1933 NFL Owners Meeting Minutes, February 25–26, 1933.

12. *Chicago Daily News*, August 18, 1933.

13. *Green Bay Press-Gazette*, September 25, 1933.

14. *Saturday Evening Post*, November 25, 1933; *Saturday Evening Post*, October 28, 1933.

15. *Chicago Daily News*, November 31, 1933.

16. *Chicago Daily News*, December 5, 1933.

17. *Chicago Tribune*, December 8, 1933.

18. *Mattoon Journal-Gazette*, December 7, 1933.

19. George Musso, author interview, 1999.

20. Wellington Mara, archival interview, NFL Films, 1999.

21. Harry Newman, archival interview, NFL Films, 1999.

22. Musso, author interview.

23. *Chicago Tribune*, December 18, 1933.

24. John Carroll, *Red Grange and the Rise of Modern Football* (Urbana: University of Illinois Press, 1999), 175.

25. Red Grange, as told to Ira Morton, *The Red Grange Story: The Autobiography of the Galloping Ghost* (New York: G. P. Putnam's Sons, 1953).

26. Red Grange, archival interview, NFL Films, 1973.

27. *New York Times*, December 18, 1933.

28. *Chicago Daily News*, December 18, 1933.

29. *Chicago Tribune*, December 18, 1933.

30. *Associated Press*, December 18, 1933.

31. *Chicago Daily News*, December 20, 1933.

32. Red Grange "77 Club" advertisement clipping, Wheaton College Special Collections, Red Grange Papers.

33. *Lincoln Star*, December 27, 1933.

34. Red Grange audio interview, June 11, 1976, Wheaton College Special Collections, Red Grange Papers.

35. *Lincoln Star*, December 27, 1933.

CHAPTER 28

1. *Cincinnati Enquirer*, January 8, 1934.

2. *Detroit Free Press*, January 18, 1934.

3. *Los Angeles Times*, January 11, 1934.

4. *Oakland Tribune*, January 17, 1934.

5. *Greenville News*, January 22, 1934.

6. *1934 Pro Football*, MGM Pete Smith short, DVD, Turner Classic Movies.

7. *Hollywood Reporter*, February 5, 1934.

8. *Saturday Evening Post*, November 9, 1935.

9. *Baltimore Sun*, March 3, 1934.

10. *Chicago Tribune*, July 6, 1934.

11. *Decatur Daily Review*, August 30, 1934.

12. *Chicago Daily News*, September 1, 1934.

13. *Cincinnati Enquirer*, November 12, 1934.

14. *Mattoon Journal-Gazette*, October 19, 1934; *Saturday Evening Post*, October 20, 1934.

15. *Big Springs* (TX) *Daily Herald*, October 4, 1934; *Bismarck Tribune*, November 2, 1934.

16. *Detroit Free Press*, November 29, 1934.

17. *Chicago Daily News*, December 7, 1934; *Lincoln Star*, December 9, 1934.

18. *Decatur Herald*, December 5, 1934.

19. *New York Times*, December 10, 1934.

20. *New York Times*, December 10, 1934.

21. *New York Times*, December 11, 1934.

22. *Chicago Daily News*, December 10, 1934.

23. *Detroit Free Press*, January 22, 1935.

24. Red Grange, as told to Ira Morton, *The Red Grange Story: The Autobiography of the Galloping Ghost* (New York: G. P. Putnam's Sons, 1953), 158.

25. *Mason City Globe-Gazette*, January 28, 1935.

CHAPTER 29

1. *Argus-Leader*, February 2, 1935.

2. *Argus-Leader*, February 2, 1935.

3. *Chicago Tribune*, June 20, 1935.

4. *Cincinnati Enquirer*, January 23, 1934.

5. *Jefferson City Post-Tribune*, December 4, 1934; *Bloomington Pantagraph*, March 22, 1935.

6. *Saturday Evening Post*, November 9, 1935.

7. *Broadcasting*, December 15, 1936.

8. *Pittsburgh Press*, November 27, 1936.

9. Harold E. (Red) Grange, *Zuppke of Illinois* (Chicago: A. L. Glaser, 1937), 50.

10. Grange, *Zuppke of Illinois*, 50.

11. *Chicago Tribune*, October 30, 1937.

12. *Cincinnati Enquirer*, March 27, 1938.

13. *Los Angeles Times*, February 4, 1939; *Chicago Tribune*, February 4, 1939.

14. *Mount Carmel Item*, September 7, 1940.

CHAPTER 30

1. Newton S. Gordon, ed., *History of Barron County, Wisconsin* (Minneapolis, MN: H. C. Cooper Jr. & Co., 1922), 373.

2. Dorothy Flora, author interview, October 4, 2016.

3. Linda Thomas, author interview, January 23, 2017.

4. Flora, author interview.

5. Thomas, author interview; Flora, author interview.

6. *Barron* (WI) *News-Shield*, September 26, 1924.

7. *Mason City-Globe*, February 21, 1933.

8. 1934 New London school yearbook, 20.

9. 1935 Mah-Wah Lincoln County Normal School yearbook, 15.

10. Flora, author interview.

11. *New York Times*, August 10, 1936.

12. Thomas, author interview.

13. Red Grange, as told to Ira Morton, *The Red Grange Story: The Autobiography of the Galloping Ghost* (New York: G. P. Putnam's Sons, 1953), 168.

14. Original letter from Margaret Grange to Kathy McKenna, September 21, 1991, Wheaton Central High School, Wheaton Warrenville-South High School archives.

15. Flora, author interview, September 15, 2016.

16. *Nebraska State Journal*, November 10, 1940; *Lincoln Star-Journal*, November 10, 1940.

17. Flora, author interview, October 4, 2016.

18. *Marion Star*, June 7, 1956.

19. *Chicago Tribune*, October 14, 1941.

20. Flora, author interview, October 4, 2016.

21. *Mount Carmel Item*, November 7, 1941.

22. *Decatur Daily Review*, December 5, 1941.

CHAPTER 31

1. Dorothy Flora, author interview, October 4, 2016.
2. *True*, November 1958.
3. Luke Johnsos Jr., author interview, January 10, 2017.
4. Johnsos Jr., author interview.
5. Johnsos Jr., author interview.
6. *Chicago Tribune*, November 13, 1951.
7. *Lansing State Journal*, December 21, 1949.
8. *Waukesha Daily Freeman*, December 2, 1949; *Chicago Tribune*, December 1, 1949.
9. *St. Louis Post-Dispatch*, June 14, 1949.
10. *Chicago Tribune*, February 14, 1951.
11. *Binghamton Press and Sun-Bulletin*, November 12, 1950.
12. Donna Edwards quote, written letter, April 1, 2017.
13. Richard Rinebold, author interview, March 18, 2017.
14. Red Grange, as told to Ira Morton, *The Red Grange Story: The Autobiography of the Galloping Ghost* (New York: G. P. Putnam's Sons, 1953), 170.
15. Quote from Grange, *The Red Grange Story*, 172.
16. *Decatur Herald*, February 10, 1952.
17. *Chicago Tribune*, April 4, 1952.
18. Ira Morton quote, audio interview, 1953 Chicago-NBC with Norm Barry, from Debra Gelbart, daughter of Ira Morton.
19. Morton quote, audio interview.
20. Original letter, Grantland Rice to Ira Morton, November 19, 1951, from Debra Gelbart, daughter of Ira Morton.
21. Morton quote, audio interview.
22. *Decatur Herald*, October 16, 1953; *St. Louis Post-Dispatch*, October 14, 1953.
23. *Salt Lake Tribune*, December 15, 1953.
24. *Chicago Tribune*, October 18, 1953.
25. *Wheaton Daily Journal*, January 10, 1954.
26. *Miami News*, June 22, 1954.
27. Nancy Wyszynski, author interview, December 13, 2016.
28. Wyszynski, author interview.
29. NBC-TV game broadcast, Syracuse at Penn State, DVD, October 26, 1957.
30. Lindsey Nelson, *Hello Everybody, I'm Lindsey Nelson* (New York: Beach Tree Books/William Morrow, 1985), 220–21.
31. Red Grange, *My Favorite Football Stories* (New York: Dell, 1955).
32. Grange, *My Favorite Football Stories*, 17.
33. *Louisville Courier-Journal*, September 24, 1956.
34. *Des Moines Register*, November 9, 1952.
35. *Corpus Christi Caller-Times*, October 13, 1963.

36. *Cincinnati Enquirer*, November 26, 1952.

37. *Minneapolis Star-Tribune*, December 27, 1957.

38. *Akron Beacon-Journal*, September 10, 1960.

39. *Tennessean*, September 10, 1959.

40. Nelson, *Hello Everybody, I'm Lindsey Nelson*, 202.

41. *Decatur Daily Review*, May 15, 1964.

42. Pat McCaskey, author interview, May 5, 2017.

CHAPTER 32

1. *Baltimore Sun*, January 30, 1963.

2. 1963 Pro Football Hall of Fame transcript.

3. 1963 Pro Football Hall of Fame transcript.

CHAPTER 33

1. Dorothy Flora, author interview, October 4, 2016.

2. *Decatur Herald*, June 13, 1968.

3. Linda Thomas, author interview, January 23, 2017.

4. *Honolulu Star-Advertiser*, January 9, 1971.

5. Red Grange series of articles, *Wheaton Daily Journal*, July 1, 1974–October 14, 1974.

6. *Wheaton Daily Journal*, August 14, 1974.

7. *Champaign Gazette*, October 20, 1974.

8. *Urbana Daily-Courier*, October 19, 1974.

9. *Wheaton Daily Journal*, October 20, 1974.

10. Gerald Ford original letter, October 10, 1974, Wheaton College Special Collections, Red Grange Papers.

11. 1974 Red Grange halftime speech, footage, Chicago local television, NFL Films.

12. David Stamps, author interview, August 8, 2016.

CHAPTER 34

1. Red Grange quotes, newspaper clipping, January 14, 1978, Wheaton College Special Collections, Red Grange Papers.

2. Super Bowl XII sideline pass and game tickets, Wheaton College Special Collections, Red Grange Papers.

3. Super Bowl XII CBS broadcast; Super Bowl XII footage, Broncos versus Cowboys, sound camera, NFL Films.

CHAPTER 35

1. *Wheaton Daily Journal*, October 4, 1978.
2. Bea Wilson quote, original letter, October 15, 2016.
3. Wilson quote, original letter.
4. David Stamps, author interview, August 8, 2016.
5. Stamps, author interview.
6. *Wheaton Daily Journal*, October 27, 1978.
7. *Wheaton Daily Journal*, October 27, 1978.
8. Brick inscription, author visit, Wheaton, Illinois, April 23, 2017.
9. Stamps, author interview.
10. Stamps, author interview.
11. Stamps, author interview.
12. *New Rochelle Standard-Star*, October 28, 1978.
13. 1978 NBC footage, Red Grange Wheaton homecoming, Wheaton College Special Collections, Red Grange Papers.
14. 1978 NBC footage, Red Grange Wheaton homecoming.
15. Stamps, author interview.
16. *Wheaton Daily Journal*, October 29, 1978; *Champaign News-Gazette*, October 29, 1978.
17. George Halas quote, audiocassette, October 28, 1978, Wheaton College Special Collections, Red Grange Papers.
18. *Champaign News-Gazette*, October 29, 1978; *Wheaton Daily Journal*, October 30, 1978.
19. *Wheaton Daily Journal*, December 1, 1978.
20. Margaret Grange original letter, November 6, 1978, from Bea Wilson, wife of D. Ray Wilson.
21. *Philadelphia Inquirer*, June 14, 1980.
22. Margaret Grange original letter, May 27, 1981, courtesy of Rebecca Phillips, granddaughter of Mildred (Grange) Eston.

CHAPTER 36

1. *New Haven Register*, February 7, 1982.
2. George Halas original letter, February 8, 1982, Wheaton College Special Collections, Red Grange Papers.

3. *Mansfield News*, November 2, 1983.

4. *Asbury Park Press*, November 3, 1983.

5. *Asbury Park Press*, November 3, 1983.

6. *Tampa Tribune*, January 20, 1984.

7. *Florida Today*, November 16, 1985.

8. *Chicago Tribune*, June 14, 1988.

9. *Orlando Sentinel*, October 6, 1987.

10. *Orlando Sentinel*, February 12, 1978.

11. John Mackovic, author interview, July 27, 2016.

12. Mike Pearson, author interview, August 9, 2016.

13. Mackovic, author interview.

14. Mackovic, author interview.

15. Pearson, author interview.

16. Mackovic, author interview.

17. Red Grange interview, audiotape from visit, courtesy of Mike Pearson.

18. Red Grange interview, audiotape.

19. Mackovic, author interview.

20. Mackovic, author interview.

21. Pearson, author interview.

22. *Wheaton Daily Journal*, December 5, 1990.

23. *Daily Herald*, July 25, 1990.

24. Richard Crabb original letter, Margaret Grange quote, September 19, 1990, Wheaton College Special Collections, Red Grange Papers.

25. Pearson, author interview.

26. Pearson, author interview.

27. Pearson, author interview.

28. Pearson, author interview.

29. *Decatur Herald and Review*, January 1, 1991.

30. Pearson, author interview.

31. Pearson, author interview.

CHAPTER 37

1. Red Barber radio transcript, Wheaton College Special Collections, Red Grange Papers.

2. Red Barber radio transcript.

3. *Tampa Tribune*, January 29, 1991.

4. Dorothy Flora, author interview, October 4, 2016.

5. *Tampa Tribune*, January 31, 1991.

6. *USA Today*, January 29, 1991.

7. *Rochester Post-Bulletin*, January 29, 1991.

8. *Wheaton Leader,* January 30, 1991.

9. *Champaign News-Gazette,* February 1, 1991.

10. *Chicago Tribune,* January 29, 1991.

11. *Chicago Tribune,* October 20, 1994.

CHAPTER 38

1. Original letter, February 10, 1991, Wheaton Warrenville-South High School archives.

2. Chuck Baker, author interview, January 11, 2017.

3. John Thorne, author interview, February 8, 2017.

4. Thom Wilder, *The Ghosts of Wheaton: How the "Red Grange" Tigers Conquered Illinois High School Football* (Indianapolis, IN: Dog Ear Publishing, 2015), 40.

5. Thorne, author interview.

6. Wilder, *The Ghosts of Wheaton,* 86–87.

7. Wilder, *The Ghosts of Wheaton,* 87.

8. Baker, author interview.

9. Original handwritten letter, November 17, 1993, Wheaton Warrenville-South High School archives.

10. Baker, author interview.

11. *Chicago Tribune,* October 20, 1994.

12. Patrick Hayes, author interview, February 21, 2017.

13. Ron Guenther, author interview, January 19, 2017.

14. Dana Brenner, author interview, September 4, 2018.

15. Mike Pearson, author interview, August 9, 2016.

16. Lou Tepper, author interview, January 19, 2017.

17. *Champaign News-Gazette,* October 21, 1994.

18. Tepper, author interview.

19. Brenner, author interview.

20. Pearson, author interview.

21. Pearson, author interview.

22. Hayes, author interview; Brenner, author interview.

23. Hayes, author interview.

24. 1994 Michigan–Illinois play-by-play sheet, University of Illinois Athletics archives.

25. Baker, author interview.

26. *Daily Herald,* August 23, 1997.

27. Dorothy Flora, author interview, October 8, 2018.

28. Flora, author interview.

29. Margaret Grange funeral, transcript of prayer, Wheaton College Special Collections, Red Grange Papers.

30. Baker, author interview.

31. Brenner, author interview.

32. *Chicago Tribune*, October 20, 1994.

33. www.rrstar.com, August 14, 2009. https://www.rrstar.com/x1886165080/Grange-statue-to-be-unveiled-before-Illinis-home-opener.

34. *Decatur Herald and Review*, September 10, 2009.

35. *Baltimore Sun*, January 30, 1991.

36. *National*, January 29, 1991.

37. *Los Angeles Times*, July 30, 1944.

38. *Tennessean*, February 9, 1939.

39. *Springfield Leader*, April 22, 1928.

40. *Des Moines Register*, November 15, 1956.

41. *Billings Gazette*, October 27, 1983.

42. Pat McCaskey, author interview, May 5, 2017.

43. *Wilmington Evening Journal*, September 10, 1927.

BIBLIOGRAPHY

Carroll, John. *Red Grange and the Rise of Modern Football*. Urbana: University of Illinois Press, 1999.

Cope, Myron. *The Game That Was: The Early Days of Pro Football*. New York: World Publishing, 1970.

Grange, Harold E. (Red). *Zuppke of Illinois*. Chicago: A. L. Glaser, 1937.

Grange, Red. *My Favorite Football Stories*. New York: Dell, 1955.

Grange, Red, as told to Ira Morton. *The Red Grange Story: The Autobiography of the Galloping Ghost*. New York: G. P. Putnam's Sons, 1953.

Griffith, Howard. *Laying It on the Line: Notes of a Team Player*. Champaign, IL: Sports Publishing, 2000.

Halas, George S., with Gwen Morgan and Arthur Veysey. *Halas by Halas: An Autobiography*. New York: McGraw-Hill, 1979.

Moore, Jean. *A History of Wheaton, Illinois: From Tower to Tower*. Mendota, IL: Wayside Press, 1974.

Nelson, Lindsey. *Hello Everybody, I'm Lindsey Nelson*. New York: Beach Tree Books/ William Morrow, 1985.

Whittingham, Richard. *The Chicago Bears: An Illustrated History*. Chicago: Rand McNally, 1982. Forward by Red Grange.

———. *What a Game They Played: Stories of the Early Days of Pro Football by Those Who Were There*. New York: Harper & Row, 1984.

Wilder, Thom. *The Ghosts of Wheaton: How the "Red Grange" Tigers Conquered Illinois High School Football*. Indianapolis, IN: Dog Ear Publishing, 2015.

Williams, Geoff. *C. C. Pyle's Amazing Footrace: The True Story of the 1928 Coast-to-Coast Run across America*. New York: Rodale, 2007.

INDEX

ABOUT THE AUTHOR

Chris Willis has worked at NFL Films as head of the Research Library since 1996. His first book, *Old Leather: An Oral History of Early Pro Football in Ohio, 1920–1935*, was published in 2005, by Scarecrow Press. His second book, *The Columbus Panhandles: A Complete History of Pro Football's Toughest Team, 1900–1922*, was published by Scarecrow Press in 2007. His third book, *The Man Who Built the National Football League: Joe F. Carr*, was published in 2010, also by Scarecrow. Willis's fourth title, *Dutch Clark: The Life of an NFL Legend and the Birth of the Detroit Lions*, was released in 2012. Rowman & Littlefield published Willis's next two books: *A Nearly Perfect Season: The Inside Story of the 1984 San Francisco 49ers* (2014) and *Walter Lingo, Jim Thorpe, and the Oorang Indians: How a Dog Kennel Owner Created the NFL's Most Famous Traveling Team* (2017).

As the resident historian at NFL Films, Willis helps oversees all aspects of research for the company and their producers. In 2002, he was nominated for an Emmy for his work on the HBO documentary *The Game of Their Lives: Pro Football in the 1950s*. Willis won an Emmy in 2016 for his work on HBO's *Hard Knocks: Training Camp with the Houston Texans*.

Before starting at NFL Films, he graduated with a B.S. in physical education from Urbana (Ohio) University—while playing four years on the Urbana football team—and attended one year of graduate school at The Ohio State University, studying sports history. Willis is a native of Columbus, Ohio, and currently resides in Audubon, New Jersey.